JOHN

VOLUME 5

THE
PREACHER'S
OUTLINE & SERMON
BIBLE®

JOHN

VOLUME 5

THE PREACHER'S OUTLINE & SERMON BIBLE®

NEW TESTAMENT

NEW INTERNATIONAL VERSION

Leadership Ministries Worldwide
PO Box 21310
Chattanooga, TN 37424-0310

Please address all requests for information or permission to:
LEADERSHIP MINISTRIES WORLDWIDE
PO Box 21310
Chattanooga TN 37424-0310
Ph.# (423) 855-2181   FAX (423) 855-8616
E-Mail outlinebible@compuserve.com
http://www.outlinebible.org

Library of Congress Catalog Card Number: 98-067967
International Standard Book Number: 1-57407-080-0

Printed in the United States of America

Publisher &
Distributer

DEDICATED:

To all the men and women of the world
who preach and teach the Gospel of our
Lord Jesus Christ
and
To the Mercy and Grace of God.

——————————— *&* ———————————

• Demonstrated to us in Christ Jesus our Lord.

"In him we have redemption through his
blood, the forgiveness of sins, in accordance with
the riches of God's grace." (Eph. 1:7 NIV)

• Out of the mercy and grace of God His Word has
flowed. Let every person know that God will have
mercy upon him, forgiving and using him to fulfill
His glorious plan of salvation.

"For God so loved the world, that he gave his one
and only Son, that whosoever believes in him shall
not perish, but have eternal life. For God did not send
his Son into the world to condemn the world, but to
save the world through him." (Jn 3:16-17 NIV)

"This is good and pleases God our Saviour; who
wants all men to be saved and to come to the knowledge of the truth." (I Tim. 2:3-4 NIV)

——————————— *&* ———————————

The Preacher's Outline and Study Bible®
is written for God's people to use
in their study and teaching of God's Holy Word.

9/98

OUTLINE BIBLE RESOURCES

This material, like similar works, has come from imperfect man and is thus susceptible to human error. We are nevertheless grateful to God for both calling us and empowering us through His Holy Spirit to undertake this task. Because of His goodness and grace **The Preacher's Outline & Sermon Bible®** - New Testament is complete in 14 volumes, and the Old Testament volumes release periodically. **The Minister's Handbook** is available and *OUTLINE* Bible materials are releasing electonically on **POSB-CD** and our **Web site**.

God has given the strength and stamina to bring us this far. Our confidence is that, as we keep our eyes on Him and grounded in the undeniable truths of the Word, we will continue working through the Old Testament volumes and the second series known as **The Teacher's Outline & Study Bible.** The future includes helpful *Outline Bible* books and **Handbook** materials for God's dear servants.

To everyone everywhere who preaches and teaches the Word, we offer this material firstly to Him in whose name we labor and serve, and for whose glory it has been produced.

Our daily prayer is that each volume will lead thousands, millions, yes even billions, into a better understanding of the Holy Scriptures and a fuller knowledge of Jesus Christ the incarnate Word, of whom the Scriptures so faithfully testify.

> As you have purchased this volume, you will be pleased to know that a small portion of the price you have paid has gone to underwrite and provide similar volumes in other languages (Russian, Korean, Spanish and others yet to come) — To a preacher, pastor, lay leader, or Bible student somewhere around the world, who will present God's message with clarity, authority, and understanding beyond their own. *Amen*.

For information and prices, kindly contact your *OUTLINE* Bible bookseller or:

**LEADERSHIP
MINISTRIES
WORLDWIDE**

P.O. Box 21310, 515 Airport Road, Suite 107
Chattanooga, TN 37424-0310
(423) 855-2181 FAX (423) 855-8616
E-Mail - outlinebible@compuserve.com
www.outlinebible.org — *FREE* download materials   9/98

PUBLISHER & DISTRIBUTOR OF OUTLINE BIBLE MATERIALS

Currently Available Materials, with New Volumes Releasing Regularly

- **THE PREACHER'S OUTLINE & SERMON BIBLE® — DELUXE EDITION**

FULL SET — 14 Volumes

- **THE PREACHER'S OUTLINE & SERMON BIBLE® — OLD TESTAMENT**

- **THE PREACHER'S OUTLINE & SERMON BIBLE® — SOFTBOUND EDITION**
  Identical content as Deluxe above. Lightweight, compact, and affordable for overseas & traveling

- **THE PREACHER'S OUTLINE & SERMON BIBLE® — 3 VOL HARDCOVER w/CD**

- **THE PREACHER'S OUTLINE & SERMON BIBLE® — NIV SOFTBOUND EDITION**

- **The Minister's Personal Handbook - What the Bible Says...to the Minister**
  12 Chapters - 127 Subjects - 400 Verses *OUTLINED* - Paperback, Leatherette, 3-ring

- **THE TEACHER'S OUTLINE & STUDY BIBLE™ • New Testament Books •**
  Complete 45 minute lessons - 4 months of studies/book; 200± pages - Student Journal Guides

- **OUTLINE Bible Studies series: 10 Commandments - The Tabernacle**

- **Practical Word Studies: New Testament - 2,000 Key Words Made Easy**

- **CD-ROM: Preacher, Teacher, and Handbook-** (Windows/STEP) - WORD*Search*

- **Translations of Preacher, Teacher, and Minister's Handbook: Limited Quantities**
  Russian — Spanish — Korean *Future: French, Portuguese, Hindi, Chinese*
  — Contact us for Specific Language Availability and Prices —

For quantity orders and information, please contact either:

LEADERSHIP MINISTRIES WORLDWIDE   *Your OUTLINE Bible Bookseller*
PO Box 21310
Chattanooga, TN 37424-0310
(423) 855-2181 (9am - 5pm Eastern) • FAX (423) 855-8616 (24 hours)
E•Mail - outlinebible@compuserve.com.
   ↪ FREE Download Sample Pages — www.outlinebible.org

• *Equipping God's Servants Worldwide with OUTLINE Bible Materials* •
LMW is a nonprofit, international, nondenominational mission agency   9/98

ACKNOWLEDGMENTS

Every child of God is precious to the Lord and deeply loved. And every child as a servant of the Lord touches the lives of those who come in contact with him or his ministry. The writing ministry of the following servants have touched this work, and we are grateful that God brought their writings our way. We hereby acknowledge their ministry to us, being fully aware that there are so many others down through the years whose writings have touched our lives and who deserve mention, but the weaknesses of our minds have caused them to fade from memory. May our wonderful Lord continue to bless the ministry of these dear servants, and the ministry of us all as we diligently labor to reach the world for Christ and to meet the desperate needs of those who suffer so much.

THE GREEK SOURCES

1. Expositor's Greek Testament, Edited by W. Robertson Nicoll. Grand Rapids, MI: Eerdmans Publishing Co., 1970

2. Robertson, A.T. Word Pictures in the New Testament. Nashville, TN: Broadman Press, 1930.

3. Thayer, Joseph Henry. Greek-English Lexicon of the New Testament. New York: American Book Co, No date listed.

4. Vincent, Marvin R. Word Studies in the New Testament. Grand Rapids, MI: Eerdmans Publishing Co., 1969.

5. Vine, W.E. Expository Dictionary of New Testament Words. Old Tappan, NJ: Fleming H. Revell Co. No date listed.

6. Wuest, Kenneth S. Word Studies in the Greek New Testament. Grand Rapids, MI: Eerdmans Publishing Co., 1966.

THE REFERENCE WORKS

7. Cruden's Complete Concordance of the Old & New Testament. Philadelphia, PA: The John C. Winston Co., 1930.

8. Josephus' Complete Works. Grand Rapids, MI: Kregel Publications, 1981.

9. Lockyer, Herbert. Series of Books, including his Books on All the Men, Women, Miracles, and Parables of the Bible. Grand Rapids, MI: Zondervan Publishing House, 1958-1967.

10. -Nave's Topical Bible. Nashville, TN: The Southwestern Co., No date listed.

11. The Amplified New Testament. (Scripture Quotations are from the Amplified New Testament, Copyright 1954, 1958, 1987 by the Lockman Foundation. Used by permission.)

12. The Four Translation New Testament (Including King James, New American Standard, Williams - New Testament In the Language of the People, Beck - New Testament In the Language of Today.) Minneapolis, MN: World Wide Publications.

13. The New Compact Bible Dictionary, Edited by T. Alton Bryant. Grand Rapids, MI: Zondervan Publishing House, 1967.

14. The New Thompson Chain Reference Bible. Indianapolis, IN: B.B. Kirkbride Bible Co., 1964,

THE COMMENTARIES

15. Barclay, William. Daily Study Bible Series. Philadelphia, PA: Westminster Press, Began in 1953.

16. Bruce, F.F. The Epistle to the Ephesians. Westwood, NJ: Fleming H. Revell Co., 1968.

17. Bruce, F.F. Epistle to the Hebrews. Grand Rapids, MI: Eerdmans Publishing Co., 1964.

18. Bruce, F.F. The Epistles of John. Old Tappan, NJ: Fleming H. Revell Co., 1970.

19. Criswell, W.A. Expository Sermons on Revelation. Grand Rapids, MI: Zondervan Publishing House, 1962-66.

20. Greene, Oliver. The Epistles of John. Greenville, SC: The Gospel Hour, Inc., 1966.

21. Greene, Oliver. The Epistles of Paul the Apostle to the Hebrews. Greenville, SC: The Gospel Hour, Inc., 1965.

22. Greene, Oliver. The Epistles of Paul the Apostle to Timothy & Titus. Greenville, SC: The Gospel Hour, Inc., 1964.

23. Greene, Oliver. The Revelation Verse by Verse Study. Greenville, SC: The Gospel Hour, Inc., 1963.

24. Henry, Matthew. Commentary on the Whole Bible. Old Tappan, NJ: Fleming H. Revell Co.

25. Hodge, Charles. Exposition on Romans & on Corinthians. Grand Rapids, MI: Eerdmans Publishing Co., 1972-1973.

26. Ladd, George Eldon. A Commentary On the Revelation of John. Grand Rapids, MI: Eerdmans Publishing Co., 1972-1973.

27. Leupold, H.C. Exposition of Daniel. Grand Rapids, MI: Baker Book House, 1969.

28. Morris, Leon. The Gospel According to John. Grand Rapids, MI: Eerdmans Publishing Co., 1971.

29. Newell, William R. Hebrews, Verse by Verse. Chicago, IL: Moody Press, 1947.

30. Strauss, Lehman. Devotional Studies in Galatians & Ephesians. Neptune, NJ: Loizeaux Brothers, 1957.

31. Strauss, Lehman. Devotional Studies in Philippians. Neptune, NJ: Loizeaux Brothers, 1959.

32. Strauss, Lehman. James, Your Brother. Neptune, NJ: Loizeaux Brothers, 1956.

33. Strauss, Lehman. The Book of the Revelation. Neptune, NJ: Loizeaux Brothers, 1964.

34. The New Testament & Wycliffe Bible Commentary, Edited by Charles F. Pfeiffer & Everett F. Harrison. New York: The Iverson Associates, 1971. Produced for Moody Monthly. Chicago Moody Press, 1962.

35. The Pulpit Commentary, Edited by H.D.M. Spence & Joseph S. Exell. Grand Rapids, MI: Eerdmans Publishing Co., 1950.

36. Thomas, W.H. Griffith. Hebrews, A Devotional Commentary. Grand Rapids, MI: Eerdmans Publishing Co., 1970.

37. Thomas, W.H. Griffith. Outline Studies in the Acts of the Apostles. Grand Rapids, MI: Eerdmans Publishing Co., 1956.

38. Thomas, W.H. Griffith. St. Paul's Epistle to the Romans. Grand Rapids, MI: Eerdmans Publishing Co., 1946.

39. Thomas, W.H. Griffith. Studies in Colossians & Philemon. Grand Rapids, MI: Baker Book House, 1973.

40. Tyndale New Testament Commentaries. Grand Rapids, MI: Eerdmans Publishing Co., Began in 1958.

41. Walker, Thomas. Acts of the Apostles. Chicago, IL: Moody Press, 1965.

42. Walvoord, John. The Thessalonian Epistles. Grand Rapids, MI: Zondervan Publishing House, 1973.

MISCELLANEOUS ABBREVIATIONS

&	=	And
Arg.	=	Argument
Bckgrd.	=	Background
Bc.	=	Because
Circ.	=	Circumstance
Concl.	=	Conclusion
Cp.	=	Compare
Ct.	=	Contrast
Dif.	=	Different
e.g.	=	For example
Et.	=	Eternal
Govt.	=	Government
Id.	=	Identity or Identification
Illust.	=	Illustration
K.	=	Kingdom, K. of God, K. of Heaven, etc.
No.	=	Number
N.T.	=	New Testament
O.T.	=	Old Testament
Pt.	=	Point
Quest.	=	Question
Rel.	=	Religion
Resp.	=	Responsibility
Rev.	=	Revelation
Rgt.	=	Righteousness
Thru	=	Through
V.	=	Verse
Vs.	=	Verses
Vs.	=	Versus

A	Your *Scripture Passage* always printed out
B	Your *Sermon Outline* located next to each verse
C	A Wealth of *Practical Commentary* Material
D	*Illustrations* and *Applications* for every audience
E	*Support Scripture* thoroughly researched & written out

First: Glance at the **Subject Heading**. Think about it for a moment. *Then*: Glance at the **Subject Heading** & the **Major Points** together.

Now: Glance at both the **Major Points & Subpoints** while reading the Scripture. Note how the points are beside the applicable verse—simply stating what the Scripture is saying—in Outline form.

Finally: Read the **Commentary**. KEY: Note that the *major point numbers* in the *outline* match those in the *commentary*.

MATTHEW 6:1-4

CHAPTER 6

K. The Right Motive for Giving, *DS1* **6:1-4**

1 Acts of righteousness—doing good & giving
  a. Warning: Do not seek recognition
  b. The reason: God will not reward

2 The wrong motive
  a. Giving for recognition

"**B**e careful not to do your 'acts of righteousness' before men, to be seen by them. If you **[A]**, you will have no rew**[A]**rom your Father in heaven.
2 "So when you give to the needy, do not announce it with trumpets, as the hy-

pocrites do in the synagogues and on the streets, to be honored by men. I tell you the truth, they have received their reward in full.
3 But when you give to the needy, do not let your left hand know what your right hand is doing,
4 So that your giving may be in secret. Then your Father, who sees what is done in secret, will reward you.

  b. Characteristic of hypocrites
  c. Reward: Recognition by men only

[B]

3 The right motive
  a. Giving unconsciously
  b. Giving quietly—privately—secretly
4 The reasons
  a. Father sees in secret
  b. Father rewards openly

DIVISION IV

THE TEACHINGS OF THE MESSIAH TO HIS DISCIPLES: THE GREAT SERMON ON THE MOUNT, 5:1-7:29

K. The Right Motive for Giving, 6:1-4

(6:1-4) **Introduction—Motive**: what a man does matters greatly to God. God expects men to be kind and to do good in the world: to help others both through personal involvement and through giving generously and sacrificially.

But there is something else that God expects, something of critical importance: God expects a man to have *the right motive*. Just why **[C]** man does good and shows kindness matters greatly to God. It matters so much that a person's eternal fate is determined by his motive. Because of this, Christ warns us about right and wrong motives.

1. Acts of righteousness—doing good and giving (v.1).
2. The wrong motive (v.2).
3. The right motive (v.3-4).
4. The reasons (v.4).

1 (6:1) **Righteous Acts—Service—Giving**: there are acts of righteousness—doing good and giving to others. The phrase "acts of righteousness" means giving in order to meet the needs of the poor. To the Jew, acts of righteousness and righteousness meant the same thing. Doing righteous acts was the greatest thing a Jew could do; it was the first act of religion. It was considered to be the very embodiment of righteousness, so much so that the two words began to be used synonymously. Giving acts of righteousness merited and assured one of righteousness and salvation. (See note 5—Mt.5:6.) Christ warned there is great danger in giving and doing acts of righteousness. Take heed and guard yourself. Do not give for recognition, or you will lose your reward.

Thought 1. There are two important lessons in this verse.
1) Man must guard and be alert to the deception of giving and doing good before men. A person's heart can be deceiv**[D]** The sin creeps up on man; it is insidious and **[D]** tle. It will keep a person from receiving anything from God.
2) A person must do righteous acts, do good. It is a duty of the Christian. In this passage alone Christ says four times, "Do your acts of righteousness."

2 (6:2) **Motive**: there is the wrong motive for doing good. Christ takes for granted that the believer gives and does good. What Christ strikes at is the motive of the human heart for giving and doing good.

1. Giving for recognition is the wrong motive for giving. Recognition is said to be sought by blowing one's own horn in two places: (a) in the synagogue before religious people, and (b) in the streets before the public.

[E]
"**Everything they do is done for men to see: They make their phylacteries wide and the tassels on their garments long; (Mat 23:5)**
"**Beware of the teachers of the law. They like to walk around in flowing robes and love to be greeted in the marketplaces and have the most important seats in the synagogues and the places of honor at banquets. (Luke 20:46)**

The
Preacher's
Outline
&
Sermon
Bible®

❝

Woe to me if I do not
preach the gospel!

❞ *(I Cor. 9:16 NIV)*

JOHN

INTRODUCTION

AUTHOR: John, the Apostle, the son of Zebedee (see note—Mk.3:17. Also see Introductory Notes—1 John; Revelation for more discussion.)

Irenaeus, bishop of Lyons in A.D. 177, summarizes the testimony of the early church: "John the disciple of the Lord who reclined on his breast and himself issued the Gospel at Ephesus." (Quoted by RVG Tasker. *The Gospel According to St. John.* "Tyndale New Testament Commentaries," ed. by RVG Tasker. Grand Rapids, MI: Eerdmans, 1960, p.17.) Tradition says that John spent the latter years in Ephesus preaching, teaching, and writing. At some point he was exiled to the Isle of Patmos during the reign of the Roman emperor, Domitian.

1. John was one of the very first disciples of Jesus (Jn.1:35, 39).
2. John and James were either partners with their father or worked for their father in a large fishing business (Lk.5:10).
3. John and James left everything to follow Christ (Mt.4:21-22).
4. John, along with Peter and James, comprised the inner circle of disciples, a group that was with Christ on very special occasions. (Cp. the Transfiguration, Mt.17:1f; Gethsemane, Mt.26:36f. Cp. Mk.5:37-43.)
5. John is called the "beloved disciple" because he seems to have been especially close to Christ and because he stresses love so much in his writings. He was a close companion of Peter (cp. Lk.5:10; Jn.19:26; 21:20, 23; Acts 4:13).
6. John was the disciple to whom Jesus committed the care of his mother (Jn.19:26-27).
7. John is said by Paul to be one of the three "pillars" of the church (Gal.2:9).

DATE: uncertain. Probably A.D. 80-95.

John lived at least until the reign of the Roman emperor Trajan, according to Irenaeus. Trajan's reign began in A.D. 98. Clement of Alexandria, who died in A.D. 212, said: "Last of all; John, perceiving that the external facts had been made plain in the Gospels, being urged by his friends and inspired by the Spirit, composed a spiritual Gospel." Fragments of the Gospel were discovered in Egypt in 1925. These fragments were dated in the first half of the second century. This would mean John wrote the Gospel in the first century.

This much is known. John was a young man when called by Jesus, and the early church fathers say that John's Gospel was the last Gospel written. All this points to a late date somewhere in the latter years of John's life; however, John's exact age would have had a bearing as to when it was written. He probably would have been unable to write beyond a certain age because of feebleness.

A moving picture is painted of John by Jerome's Commentary on the Epistle to the Galatians. "When he tarried at Ephesus to extreme old age, and could only with difficulty be carried to the church in the arms of his disciples, and was unable to give utterance to many words, he used to say no more at their several meetings than this, 'Little children, love one another.' At length the disciples and fathers who were there, wearied with hearing always the same words, said, 'Master, why dost thou always say this?' 'It is the Lord's command,' was his worthy reply, 'and if this alone be done, it is enough.'"

TO WHOM WRITTEN: John writes to the lost (3:16), the unbelieving (20:31), the new believers (1:50-51; 15:11; 16:33), the philosopher (1:1), and the theologian (1:12-14).

PURPOSE: "These are written that you may believe that Jesus is the Christ, the Son of God, and that by believing, you may have life in His name" (Jn.20:31). This is John's clearly stated purpose for writing. However, there is a secondary purpose. The Gospel refutes almost any heresy that might arise in any generation.

1. To those who deny Christ's deity, John argues: He is the Son of God, the very Word of God Himself (1:1-5; 7:1f; etc.)
2. To those who deny Jesus' humanity, John argues: He is the Word become flesh, the very flesh which must be experienced (1:14f; 6:31f; etc.)
3. To those who continue to look for a human messiah and an earthly utopia, John argues: He is the Messiah, the Savior of the world, the very One who had been promised by God from the beginning of time (1:1-51, etc.)

SPECIAL FEATURES:

1. John is *The Gospel of Simplicity*. John used the simplest language and the most pure Greek possible. The Gospel serves as a first reader for many Greek students.
2. John is *The Gospel of Revelation*. The stress and compulsion of John is to show that Jesus Christ is the very revelation of God Himself. A quick glance at the outline clearly shows this.
3. John is *The Gospel of the Messiah*. John shows time and again that the Old Testament prophecies find their fulfillment in Jesus. However, there is a unique point in this that differs somewhat from the Synoptic Gospels. John shows that the salvation brought by Jesus is the very climax of Jewish religion. Jesus Himself is the fulfillment of the blessings promised Israel, the substance and truth, the symbolic meaning of the great Jewish festivals.

Jesus claims the Messianic right to secure disciples (1:35-51); to cleanse the temple (2:13-22); to associate and converse with Samaritans (4:1f; esp. 25-26); to work on the Sabbath, overriding the religious prohibitions (5:1-47; esp. 17f; 7:1-53); to feed the people even as Moses, and to claim that He Himself is the very Bread of Life (6:1-14, 22-71; esp., 31f); to forgive sins (8:1-11); and many, many other claims. He dramatically pictures His Messianic claim with the triumphal entry (12:12f).

4. John is *The Gospel of Redemption*. This redemption is centered in the cross and death of Jesus Christ. He is "the (sacrificial) Lamb of God, who takes away the sin of the world" (1:29). His passion is the hour toward which His whole life is moving (2:4; 7:7, 8, 30; 12:23; 17:1). His own flesh and blood is to be *eaten*, that is, *partaken of*, if men are to have life (6:33-53). He compares His death to a kernel of wheat that must fall into the ground before it produces many seeds (12:24). He is to lay down His life for His sheep (10:11). He draws all men to Himself—but it is only by being lifted up on the cross (12:32-33). He is to sacrifice Himself that others might be set apart unto God (17:19).

5. John is *The Gospel of Jesus' Humanity*. John shows Jesus weary and thirsty (4:6-8, 31); spitting on the ground (9:6); weeping at the death of a dear friend, Lazarus (11:35); troubled because He is to die (12:27); disgusted

1

with His betrayer (13:21); burning with thirst while dying (19:28); and having normal blood and water flowing through His body (19:34). John stresses this point by proclaiming that Jesus is the Son of Man (1:51; 5:27; 6:53; 12:23; 13:31).

6. John is *The Gospel of the Word*. John shows Jesus to be the very Word of God. By this he means that Jesus is everything God ever wanted to say to man. God has done more than speak what He wanted to say; God has pictured what He wanted to say in the very life of Jesus. Jesus is the expression, the thought, the idea, the picture of what God wanted to say to man. The Word of God has become flesh. (See note—Jn.1:1.)

7. John is *The Gospel of 'I Am,'* of God Himself, of Yahweh, Jehovah. The words "I Am" are extremely important to Jewish history. It is the great name of God revealed to Moses at the burning bush (Ex.3:13-15). And John shows Jesus revealing Himself as the "I Am" at least ten times. (See note—Jn.6:20.)

8. John is *The Gospel of Signs*. John records eight miracles of Jesus, six of which are given only by him. What he does is select representative examples that point and show that Jesus is the Son of God. The miracles, he says, were not done to amaze people. They were performed as signs of His deity and godly powers (see note—Jn.2:23). These signs are: the water turned into wine (2:1-11); the healing of the royal official's son (4:46-54); the healing of the man at the pool (5:1-9); the healing of the man born blind (9:1-7); the raising of Lazarus (11:1f); and the second catch of fish (21:1-6).

9. John is *The Gospel of the Holy Spirit*. John gives the fullest teaching of Jesus on the Holy Spirit among the Gospel writers (14:16, 26; 15:26; 16:7-8, 13-15).

OUTLINE OF JOHN

THE PREACHER'S OUTLINE & SERMON BIBLE® is *unique*. It differs from all other Study Bibles & Sermon Resource Materials in that every Passage and Subject is outlined right beside the Scripture. When you choose any *Subject* below and turn to the reference, you have not only the Scripture, but you discover the Scripture and Subject *already outlined for you—verse by verse.*

For a quick example, choose one of the subjects below and turn to the Scripture, and you will find this marvelous help for faster, easier, and more accurate use.

In addition, every point of the Scripture and Subject is *fully developed in a Commentary with supporting Scripture* at the bottom of the page. Again, this arrangement makes sermon preparation much easier and faster.

Note something else: The Subjects of John's Gospel have titles that are both Biblical and *practical*. The practical titles sometimes have more appeal to people. This *benefit* is clearly seen for use on billboards, bulletins, church newsletters, etc.

A suggestion: For the quickest overview of John, first read *all the major titles* (I, II, III, etc.), then come back and read the subtitles.

OUTLINE OF JOHN

I.   THE WITNESSES TO THE REVELATION OF JESUS CHRIST, 1:1-51

    A. Jesus the Living Word: The First Witness of John the Apostle, 1:1-5

    B. Jesus the Light of the World: The Special Witness of John the Baptist, 1:6-8

    C. Jesus the Light of Men: The Second Witness of John the Apostle, 1:9-13

    D. Jesus the Word Made Flesh: The Third Witness of John the Apostle, 1:14-18

    E. Jesus the Messiah, the Lord: The Second Witness of John the Baptist, 1:19-28

    F. Jesus the Lamb of God, the Son of God: The Third Witness of John the Baptist, 1:29-34

    G. Jesus the Messiah, the Christ: The Witness of Andrew, 1:35-42

    H. Jesus the One Prophesied: The Witness of Philip, 1:43-45

    I. Jesus the Son of God, the King of Israel: The Witness of Nathanael, 1:46-49

    J. Jesus the Son of Man, God's Mediator: The Witness of Jesus Himself, 1:50-51

II.   THE REVELATION OF JESUS, THE SON OF GOD, 2:1-3:21

    A. Revelation 1: Creative Power, 2:1-11

    B. Revelation 2: Jesus is Supreme Over God's House, 2:12-22
       (Matthew 21:12-16; Mark 11:15-19; Luke 19:34-46)

    C. Revelation 3: Jesus Knows All Men, 2:23-25

    D. Revelation 4: The New Birth, 3:1-15

    E. Revelation 5: God's Great Love, 3:16-17

    F. Revelation 6: Man's Condemnation, 3:18-21

III. THE REVELATION OF JESUS, THE NEW MASTER, 3:22-36

IV.   THE REVELATION OF JESUS, THE LIVING WATER, 4:1-42

    A. The Offer of Living Water, 4:1-14

    B. The Subject of Sin, 4:15-18

    C. The Subject of Worship, 4:19-24

    D. The Subject of Messiah, 4:25-30

    E. The Subject of Labor for God, 4:31-42

V.   THE REVELATION OF JESUS, THE OBJECT OF FAITH, 4:43-54

    A. The Evidence of Faith, 4:43-45

    B. The Stages of Faith, 4:46-54

VI.   THE REVELATION OF JESUS, THE AUTHORITY AND POWER OVER LIFE, 5:1-47

    A. The Essential Authority: Power to Meet the World's Desperate Needs, 5:1-16

    B. The Astounding Authority: Equality With God, 5:17-30

    C. The Five Witnesses to Jesus' Authority and Power, 5:31-39

    D. The Rejection of Jesus' Claim, 5:40-47

VII. THE REVELATION OF JESUS, THE BREAD OF LIFE, 6:1-71

    A. Jesus Feeds Five Thousand: The Provision for Human Need, 6:1-15

    B. Jesus Walks on Water: The Deliverance from Fear, 6:16-21
       (Matthew 14:22-33; Mark 6:45-52)

    C. The Answer to Man's Great Hunger, 6:22-29

    D. The Bread of Life: The Source of Spiritual Satisfaction, 6:30-36

    E. The Assurance of the Believer, 6:37-40

    F. The Way A Person Partakes of the Bread of Life, 6:41-51

    G. The Results of Partaking of the Bread of Life, 6:52-58

    H. The Reason Some People are Offended by Christ, the Bread of Life, 6:59-71

VIII. THE RESPONSES TO THE REVELATION OF JESUS, 7:1-53

    A. The Response of Jesus' Brothers: Mockery and Unbelief, 7:1-9

3

4

XVI. THE REVELATION OF JESUS, THE RISEN LORD, 20:1-21:23

A. Event 1: The Great Discovery—The Empty Tomb, 20:1-10
B. Event 2: The Great Recognition—Jesus Appears to Mary, 20:11-18
(Matthew 28:1-15; Mark 16:1-11; Luke 24:1-49)
C. Event 3: The Great Charter of the Church—Jesus Appears to the Disciples, 20:19-23
(Mark 16:14; Luke 24:36-49)
D. Event 4: The Great Conviction—Thomas' Confession, 20:24-29
E. Event 5: The Great Purpose of the Signs (Wonderful Works) of Jesus, 20:30-31
F. Event 6: The Great Reality of Jesus' Resurrection Body, 21:1-14
G. Event 7: The Great Question of a Disciple's Love and Devotion, 21:15-17
H. Event 8: The Great Call to Total Commitment, 21:18-25

	CHAPTER 1 **I. THE WITNESSES TO THE REVELATION OF JESUS CHRIST, 1:1-51** **A. Jesus the Living Word: The First Witness of John the Apostle,**DS1 **1:1-5**	2 The light shines in the darkness, but the darkness has not understood it. 3 There came a man who was sent from God; his name was John. 4 He came as a witness to testify concerning that light, so that through him all men might believe. 5 He himself was not the light; he came only as a witness to the light.

1 Christ is eternal
a. Preexistent
	In him was life, and that life was the light of men.	b. Coexistent
		c. Self-existent
		2 Christ is the Creator
		a. Positive statement
		b. Absolute statement
		3 Christ is lifeDS2
		a. The source of light
		b. The answer to darkness
		  1) Shines in darknessDS3
		  2) Conquers darknessDS4

DIVISION I

THE WITNESSES TO THE REVELATION OF JESUS CHRIST, 1:1-51

A. Jesus the Living Word: The First Witness of John the Apostle, 1:1-5

(1:1-5) **Introduction**: this passage is one of the summits of Scripture. In fact, it probably reaches the highest of human thought. What is the thought that reaches the height of human concepts? It is this: Jesus Christ, the Son of God, is...
* the Word of God
* the Creator of Life
* the Very Being and Essence of Life

These three truths have to be deeply thought about to understand their meaning. A quick reading of this passage leaves a person disinterested, not even close to understanding what is being said. However, the importance of the truths lie at the very foundation of life. They cannot be overstated, for they determine a man's destiny. If Jesus Christ is the Word of God, then men must hear and understand that Word or else be lost forever in ignorance of God Himself.
1. Christ is eternal (v.1-2).
2. Christ is the Creator (v.3).
3. Christ is Life (v.4-5).

DEEPER STUDY # 1

(1:1-5) **The Word—Jesus Christ, Son of God**: the *Word* (logos) is Jesus Christ. John faced a serious problem in writing to the Gentiles, that is, the non-Jewish world. Most Gentiles had never heard of the Messiah or Savior who was expected by the Jews. The idea was foreign to them. However, the Messiah was the very center of Christianity. How was John going to present Christ so that a Gentile could understand?

The answer lay in the idea of the *Word*, for the *Word* was understood by both Gentile and Jew.

1. The Jews saw a word as something more than a mere sound. A word was something active and existing. It was power—it possessed the power to express something, to do something. This is seen in the many Old Testament references where *The Word of God* was seen as the creative power of God, the power that made the world and gave light and life to every man (Gen.1:3, 6, 11; Ps.33:6; 107:20; 147:15; Is.55:11).

2. The Gentiles or Greeks saw the *Word* more philosophically.
  a. When they looked at the world of nature, they saw that things were not chaotic, but orderly. Everything had its place and moved or grew in an orderly fashion, including the stars above and the vegetation below. Therefore, the Greeks said that behind the world was a mind, a reason, a power that made and kept things in their proper place. This creative and sustaining mind, this supreme reason, this unlimited power was said to be the *Word*.
  b. The *Word* was also seen as the power that enabled men to think and reason. It was the power that brought light and understanding to man's mind, enabling him to express his confused thoughts in an orderly fashion.
  c. More importantly, the *Word* was the power by which men came into contact with God and expressed their feelings to God.

3. John utilized this common idea of the Jews and Gentiles to proclaim that Jesus Christ was the *Word*. John saw that a word is the expression of an idea, a thought, an image in the mind of a person. He saw that a word describes what is in the mind of a person. Thus, he proclaimed that in the life of Jesus Christ, God was speaking to the world, speaking and demonstrating just what He wanted to say to man. John said three things.
  a. God has given us much more than mere words in the Holy Scriptures. God has given us Jesus Christ, The Word. As The Word, Jesus Christ was the picture, the expression, the pattern, the very image of what God wished to say to man. The very image within God's mind of the Ideal Man was demonstrated in the life of Jesus Christ. Jesus Christ was the perfect expression of all that God wishes man to be. Jesus Christ was God's utterance, God's speech, God's Word to man. Jesus Christ was the Word of God who came down to earth in human flesh to bring man into a face-to-face relationship with God (cp. v.1-2). Jesus was the *Word of God who came to earth to live out the written Word of God*.
  b. Jesus Christ is the Mind, the Reason, the Power that both made and keeps things in their proper order. He is the creative and sustaining Mind, the Supreme Reason, the unlimited Power (cp. v.3).
  c. Jesus Christ is the Light, the Illumination, the Power that penetrates the darkness of the world. He, the Life and Light of the world, is what makes sense of the world and enables men to understand the world (cp. v.4-5).

1 (1:1-2) **Jesus Christ, Son of God—Eternal—Preexistent—Revelation**: Christ is eternal. Note three profound statements made about Christ, the Word.

1. Christ was preexistent. This means He was there before creation. He has always existed.
   a. "In the beginning [en archei]" does not mean *from* the beginning. Jesus Christ was already there. He did not *become*; He was not created; He never had a beginning. He "was with God in the beginning" (cp. Jn.17:5; 8:58).
   b. The word "was" (en) is the Greek imperfect tense of *eimi* which is the word so often used for deity. It means *to be* or *I am*. *To be* means continuous existence, without beginning or origin. (See Deeper Study # 1—Jn.6:20.)

> Before the mountains were born or you brought forth the earth and the world, from everlasting to everlasting you are God. (Psa 90:2)
> I was appointed from eternity, from the beginning, before the world began. (Prov 8:23)
> And now, Father, glorify me in your presence with the glory I had with you before the world began. (John 17:5)
> Who, being in very nature God, did not consider equality with God something to be grasped, (Phil 2:6)
> But made himself nothing, taking the very nature of a servant, being made in human likeness. (Phil 2:7)
> And being found in appearance as a man, he humbled himself and became obedient to death— even death on a cross! (Phil 2:8)

The testimony of John was that Jesus Christ was the *Word*, the One who has always existed. He is the Son of the living God. (See outline and notes—Ph.2:5-8.)

2. Christ was coexistent. He was and is face-to-face with God forever. The word "with" (pros) has the idea of both *being with* and *acting toward*. Jesus Christ (the Word) was both with God and acting with God. He was "with God": by God's side, acting, living, and moving in the closest of relationships. Christ had the ideal and perfect relationship *with* God the Father. Their life together—their relationship, communion, fellowship, and connection—was a perfect eternal bond. This is exactly what is said: "*He was with God in the beginning*" (v.2).

> That which was from the beginning, which we have heard, which we have seen with our eyes, which we have looked at and our hands have touched—this we proclaim concerning the Word of life. (1 John 1:1)
> The life appeared; we have seen it and testify to it, and we proclaim to you the eternal life, which was with the Father and has appeared to us. (1 John 1:2)

The testimony of John was that Jesus Christ was the *Word*, the One who has always coexisted with God. Jesus Christ is the Son of the living God.

3. John did not say that "the Word" was *the God* (ho Theos). He says "the Word" was *God* (Theos). He omits the definite article. John was saying that "the Word," Jesus Christ...

- is of the very nature and character of God the Father, but He is not the identical person of God the Father.
- is a distinct person from God the Father, but He is of the very being and essence (perfection) of God the Father.

When a man sees Christ, he sees a *distinct person*, but he sees a person who is of the *very substance and character* of God in all of His perfect being.

> The Son is the radiance of God's glory and the exact representation of his being, sustaining all things by his powerful word. After he had provided purification for sins, he sat down at the right hand of the Majesty in heaven. (Heb 1:3)
> Jesus answered: "Don't you know me, Philip, even after I have been among you such a long time? Anyone who has seen me has seen the Father. How can you say, 'Show us the Father'? (John 14:9)
> Theirs are the patriarchs, and from them is traced the human ancestry of Christ, who is God over all, forever praised! Amen. (Rom 9:5)
> He is the image of the invisible God, the firstborn over all creation. (Col 1:15)
> For in Christ all the fullness of the Deity lives in bodily form, (Col 2:9)
> Beyond all question, the mystery of godliness is great: He appeared in a body, was vindicated by the Spirit, was seen by angels, was preached among the nations, was believed on in the world, was taken up in glory. (1 Tim 3:16)
> Which God will bring about in his own time—God, the blessed and only Ruler, the King of kings and Lord of lords, (1 Tim 6:15)
> Who alone is immortal and who lives in unapproachable light, whom no one has seen or can see. To him be honor and might forever. Amen. (1 Tim 6:16)
> On his robe and on his thigh he has this name written: KING OF KINGS AND LORD OF LORDS. (Rev 19:16)

The testimony of John was that Jesus Christ was the *Word*, self-existent and eternal, the Supreme Majesty of the universe who owes His existence to no one. Jesus Christ was the Son of the living God.

Thought 1. Jesus Christ is eternal. This says several critical things about Christ.
1) Christ reveals the most important Person in all the universe: God. He reveals all that God is and wants to say to man. Therefore, Christ must be diligently studied, and all that He is and says must be heeded to the utmost (cp. Jn.5:24).
2) Christ *reveals* God perfectly. He is just like God, identical to God; therefore, when a person looks at Christ he sees God (see Deeper Study # 1,2,3—Jn.14:6. Cp.Jn.14:9.)
3) Christ reveals that God is the most wonderful Person who ever lived. God is far, far beyond

anyone we could have ever dreamed. He is loving and caring, full of goodness and truth; and He will not tolerate injustices: murder and stealing, lying and cheating of husband, wife, child, neighbor, brother, sister or stranger. God loves and is working and moving toward a perfect universe that will be filled with people who choose to love and worship and live and work for Him (cp. Jn.5:24-29).

Thought 2. The very nature of Christ is...
- to exist eternally
- to exist in a perfect state of being, knowing nothing but eternal perfection
- to exist in perfect communion and fellowship eternally (cp. 1 Jn.1:3)

Note: it is the very nature of Christ that shall be imparted to believers; therefore, all three things will become our experience.

> **On that day you will realize that I am in my Father, and you are in me, and I am in you. (John 14:20)**
> **For those God foreknew he also predestined to be conformed to the likeness of his Son, that he might be the firstborn among many brothers. (Rom 8:29)**
> **And we, who with unveiled faces all reflect the Lord's glory, are being transformed into his likeness with ever-increasing glory, which comes from the Lord, who is the Spirit. (2 Cor 3:18)**
> **Who, by the power that enables him to bring everything under his control, will transform our lowly bodies so that they will be like his glorious body. (Phil 3:21)**
> **Through these he has given us his very great and precious promises, so that through them you may participate in the divine nature and escape the corruption in the world caused by evil desires. (2 Pet 1:4)**
> **Dear friends, now we are children of God, and what we will be has not yet been made known. But we know that when he appears, we shall be like him, for we shall see him as he is. (1 John 3:2)**

2 (1:3) **Jesus Christ, Creator**: Christ is the Creator. Note several things.

1. "All things" (panta) mean every detail of creation—not creation as a whole, but every single detail. Each element and thing, each being and person—whether material or spiritual, angelic or human—has come into being by Christ.

> **For by him all things were created: things in heaven and on earth, visible and invisible, whether thrones or powers or rulers or authorities; all things were created by him and for him. (Col 1:16)**

2. The words "were made" (egeneto) mean *came into being or became*. Note what this is saying. Nothing was existing—no substance, no matter whatsoever. Matter is not eternal. God did not take something outside of Himself,

something less than perfect (evil) and create the world. Christ, the Word, took nothing but His will and power; and He spoke *the Word* and created every single thing *out of nothing* (ex nihilo).

3. Christ was the One who created all things—one by one. Among the Godhead, He was the active Agent, the Person who made all things. Creation was His function and work (cp. Col.1:16 above).

> **Yet for us there is but one God, the Father, from whom all things came and for whom we live; and there is but one Lord, Jesus Christ, through whom all things came and through whom we live. (1 Cor 8:6)**
> **But in these last days he has spoken to us by his Son, whom he appointed heir of all things, and through whom he made the universe. (Heb 1:2)**

4. Note that two statements of fact are made.
   ⇒ The positive statement of fact: "*Through Him all things were made.*"
   ⇒ The absolute statement of fact: "*Without Him nothing was made that has been made.*"

   a. Christ was actively involved in the creation of every single thing: "Without Him nothing was made that has been made."
   b. The word "nothing" (oude hen) means not even *one* thing, not a single thing, not even a detail was made apart from Him.

   Thought 1. Note a critical point for man. The world is God's; He made it, every element of it, one by one. This means several things.
   1) God is not off in some distant place far removed from the world, unconcerned and disinterested in what happens to the world. God cares about the world. He cares deeply, even about the most minute detail and smallest person. He cares about everything and every person in the world.
   2) The problems of the world are not due to God and His attitude. The problems of the world are due to sin, to the attitude and evil of man's heart.
   3) The answer to the world's problems is not men and their technical skills. The answer is Christ: for men to turn to Christ, surrendering and giving their lives to know Christ in the most personal and intimate way possible. Then, and only then, can men set their lives and world in order as God intends.

3 (1:4-5) **Jesus Christ, Life—Light**: Christ is life (see DEEPER STUDY # 2—Jn.1:4).

1. Christ is the source of light. Note the statement: "That life [Christ] was the light of men." From the very beginning man was to know *that life*, to know God personally and intimately. The knowledge of the life of Christ was to be the light of men, the beam that was to...
- give real life to man, both abundant and eternal life.
- infuse energy and motivation into man so that he might walk and live as he should.

There is another way to say this. From the very beginning, that life (Christ) was to be the light of man's...

- quality of being
- essence of being
- power of being
- force of being
- energy of being
- principle of being

That life (Christ) was to be the light of man's purpose, meaning and significance upon earth.

> **The thief comes only to steal and kill and destroy; I have come that they may have life, and have it to the full. (John 10:10)**
>
> **Jesus said to her, "I am the resurrection and the life. He who believes in me will live, even though he dies; (John 11:25)**

2. Christ is the answer to darkness.
   a. Christ's life did shine in the darkness (see DEEPER STUDY # 2, Darkness—Jn.8:12). Very simply, since man had brought darkness into the world (by sin), the life of Christ was the light of man, the *beam* that showed man the way, the truth and the life (see DEEPER STUDY # 3,4—Jn.1:5; DEEPER STUDY # 2—8:12; DEEPER STUDY # 1,2,3—14:6).
   ⇒ Christ showed man the *way* God intended him to live.
   ⇒ Christ showed man the *truth* of life, that is, the truth about God and man and the truth about the world of man.
   ⇒ Christ showed man the *life*, that is, how to save his life and avoid the things that can cause him to stumble and lose his life.

> **When Jesus spoke again to the people, he said, "I am the light of the world. Whoever follows me will never walk in darkness, but will have the light of life." (John 8:12)**
>
> **Then Jesus told them, "You are going to have the light just a little while longer. Walk while you have the light, before darkness overtakes you. The man who walks in the dark does not know where he is going. (John 12:35)**
>
> **I have come into the world as a light, so that no one who believes in me should stay in darkness. (John 12:46)**
>
> **For God, who said, "Let light shine out of darkness," made his light shine in our hearts to give us the light of the knowledge of the glory of God in the face of Christ. (2 Cor 4:6)**
>
> **I pray also that the eyes of your heart may be enlightened in order that you may know the hope to which he has called you, the riches of his glorious inheritance in the saints, and his incomparably great power for us who believe. That power is like the working of his mighty strength, (Eph 1:18-19 ;cp.Eph.5:14)**
>
> **But you are a chosen people, a royal priesthood, a holy nation, a people belonging to God, that you may declare the praises of him who called you out of darkness into his wonderful light. (1 Pet 2:9)**
>
> **Once you were not a people, but now you are the people of God; once you had not received mercy, but now you have received mercy. (1 Pet 2:10)**
>
> **Yet I am writing you a new command; its truth is seen in him and you, because the darkness is passing and the true light is already shining. (1 John 2:8)**
>
> **When they arrived, he said to them: "You know how I lived the whole time I was with you, from the first day I came into the province of Asia. (Acts 20:18)**

   b. Christ's life (the Light) cannot be overcome (see DEEPER STUDY # 3—Jn.1:5).

DEEPER STUDY # 2

(1:4) **Life—Jesus Christ, Life**: the simple statement "in Christ was life" means at least three things.

1. Life is the quality and essence, the energy and power, the force and principle of being. Christ is life; He is...
   - the very quality of life
   - the very essence of life
   - the very energy of life
   - the very power of life
   - the very force of life
   - the very principle of life

Without Christ, there would be no life whatsoever. Life is in Him, within His very being. All things exist and have their being (life) in Him.

2. Life is purpose, meaning, and significance of being. Christ is life; He is...
   - the very purpose of life.
   - the very meaning of life.
   - the very significance of life.

3. Life is perfection. Life is all that a man must be and possess in order to live perfectly. This is what is meant by life. Life is completeness of being, absolute satisfaction, the fulness of all good, and the possession of all good things. Life is perfect love, joy, peace, long-suffering, gentleness, goodness, faith, meekness, and self-control (cp. Gal.5:22-23).

Whatever life is and all that life is, it is all in Jesus Christ. Even the legitimate cravings of man that are sometimes entangled with evil—such as power, fame and wealth—are all included in the life given by Jesus Christ. Those who partake of His life shall reign forever as kings and priests (see note, Rewards—Lk.16:10-12). This is the very thing that is distinctive about life—it is eternal. It lasts forever and it is rewarding. It will eventually exalt the believer to the highest life and place and position. (Cp. Rev.21:1f.)

Jesus Christ is the source of life: He is the way to life, and He is the truth of life. He is the very substance of life, its very being and energy (Jn.5:26; 1 Jn.1:2). (See DEEPER STUDY # 1—Jn.10:10; DEEPER STUDY # 1—17:2-3.)

DEEPER STUDY # 3

(1:5) **Light**: light reveals, strips away (Jn.3:19-20), routs the chaos (cp. Gen.1:2-3), and guides (Jn.12:36, 46). It shows the way, the truth, and the life (Jn.14:6).

DEEPER STUDY # 4

(1:5) **Darkness**: darkness does not understand the light, does not overcome the light, does not extinguish the light (see note—Jn.8:12).

	B. Jesus the Light of the World: The Special Witness of John the Baptist, 1:6-8
1 A man sent from God*DS1*	6 There came a man who was sent from God; his name was John.
2 A man with a mission a. To bear witness b. That men might believe	7 He came as a witness to testify concerning that light, so that through him all men might believe.
3 A man who was great, but was not the Light	8 He himself was not the light; he came only as a witness to the light.

DIVISION I

THE WITNESSES TO THE REVELATION OF JESUS CHRIST, 1:1-51

B. Jesus the Light of the World: The Special Witness of John the Baptist, 1:6-8

(1:6-8) **Introduction**: there was one person who was a very special witness to Christ, John the Baptist. John's sole purpose on earth was to witness and to bear testimony to the Light of the world. His purpose stands as a dynamic example for every believer. The purpose of the believer is to bear the same witness as John: Jesus Christ is the Light of the world.

1. A man sent from God (v.6).
2. A man with a mission (v.7).
3. A man who was great, but was not the Light (v.8).

1 (1:6) **John the Baptist—Commission**: a man sent from God. Note three points.

1. "There came a man" and *only* a man. A strong contrast is being made between what had been said about Christ and what is now being said about John.

⇒ Christ "was... in the beginning"; He was "with God" and He "was God" (Jn.1:1-2).
⇒ John was "a man" who had come into existence at birth, just as all men have the beginning of their existence at birth. John was the son of a man, whereas Jesus Christ was the one and only Son of God (Jn.3:16). John was not a divine being, not even an angel. He was a mere man.

> "What is man that you make so much of him, that you give him so much attention, (Job 7:17)
> What is man that you are mindful of him, the son of man that you care for him? (Psa 8:4)
> Do you not know? Have you not heard? Has it not been told you from the beginning? Have you not understood since the earth was founded? (Isa 40:21)
> He sits enthroned above the circle of the earth, and its people are like grasshoppers. He stretches out the heavens like a canopy, and spreads them out like a tent to live in. (Isa 40:22)
> To this John replied, "A man can receive only what is given him from heaven. (John 3:27)

2. The man, however, was *"sent from God"*; and he was sent on a very special mission. Two facts show this.

a. The word "sent" (see DEEPER STUDY # 1, Sent—Jn.1:6 for discussion).

b. The phrase "from God" (para Theou) means from beside God. John was not only sent by God, He was sent from the very side and heart of God. He was only a man, but a man of high calling and mission, of enormous responsibility and accountability. He was a man sent by God, not by man.

Thought 1. Note three significant points. The servant and messenger of God...

• is not sent forth by men, but by God. He is sent forth as the ambassador of God.
• is sent forth from God, from the very side and heart of God.
• is a man of high calling and mission, of enormous responsibility and accountability.

> You did not choose me, but I chose you and appointed you to go and bear fruit—fruit that will last. Then the Father will give you whatever you ask in my name. (John 15:16)
> All this is from God, who reconciled us to himself through Christ and gave us the ministry of reconciliation: (2 Cor 5:18)
> That God was reconciling the world to himself in Christ, not counting men's sins against them. And he has committed to us the message of reconciliation. We are therefore Christ's ambassadors, as though God were making his appeal through us. We implore you on Christ's behalf: Be reconciled to God. (2 Cor 5:19-20)
> Not that we are competent in ourselves to claim anything for ourselves, but our competence comes from God. He has made us competent as ministers of a new covenant—not of the letter but of the Spirit; for the letter kills, but the Spirit gives life. (2 Cor 3:5-6)
> Therefore, since through God's mercy we have this ministry, we do not lose heart. Rather, we have renounced secret and shameful ways; we do not use deception, nor do we distort the word of God. On the contrary, by setting forth the truth plainly we

commend ourselves to every man's conscience in the sight of God. (2 Cor 4:1-2)

I became a servant of this gospel by the gift of God's grace given me through the working of his power. (Eph 3:7)

I thank Christ Jesus our Lord, who has given me strength, that he considered me faithful, appointing me to his service. (1 Tim 1:12)

But God chose the foolish things of the world to shame the wise; God chose the weak things of the world to shame the strong. He chose the lowly things of this world and the despised things—and the things that are not—to nullify the things that are, so that no one may boast before him. (1 Cor 1:27-29)

3. The man was named John. His name means *gracious*. He was a man sent forth with a name to match his message: *God's grace* is now to enter upon the scene of world history. Prepare the way for the Lord, who is the embodiment of God's glorious grace.

DEEPER STUDY # 1

(1:6) **Sent—Apostle—Commission**: the word "sent" (apestalmenos) means to send out; to commission as a representative, an ambassador, an envoy. Three things are true of the person sent from God.

1. He belongs to God, who has sent him out.
2. He is commissioned to be sent out.
3. He possesses all the authority and power of God, who has sent him out.

---

2 (1:7) **Mission—Witnessing**: a man with a mission. Note two points.

1. The man came to bear witness of the Light. He was sent with a very specific message, and that message was to proclaim the Light, Christ Himself. (See note, pt.2—Jn.1:4-5. Also see DEEPER STUDY # 3,4—Jn.1:5; DEEPER STUDY # 1—8:12; DEEPER STUDY # 5—12:35-36. All these are important notes for this point.)

Thought 1. The message is a *given* message. The servant of God is not left on his own to think up a message; he is not dependent upon his own reason, thoughts, and ideas. His message is Christ, the Light of the world.

Unlike so many, we do not peddle the word of God for profit. On the contrary, in Christ we speak before God with sincerity, like men sent from God. (2 Cor 2:17)

Therefore, since through God's mercy we have this ministry, we do not lose heart. Rather, we have renounced secret and shameful ways; we do not use deception, nor do we distort the word of God. On the contrary, by setting forth the truth plainly we commend ourselves to every man's conscience in the sight of God. (2 Cor 4:1-2)

And we also thank God continually because, when you received the word of God, which you heard from us, you accepted it not as the word of men, but as it actually is, the word of God, which is at work in you who believe. (1 Th 2:13)

Do not add to what I command you and do not subtract from it, but keep the commands of the LORD your God that I give you. (Deu 4:2)

See that you do all I command you; do not add to it or take away from it. (Deu 12:32)

Do not add to his words, or he will rebuke you and prove you a liar. (Prov 30:6)

And if anyone takes words away from this book of prophecy, God will take away from him his share in the tree of life and in the holy city, which are described in this book. (Rev 22:19)

2. The purpose of the man's witness is clearly stated: that through Christ all men might believe. His purpose was not...

- to start a movement for God.
- to organize and administer.
- to minister (note that John never healed or performed a miracle nor built a program around the synagogue or temple, Jn.10:41).

His purpose was *not even to preach*. His purpose was *to lead men to believe* in the Light. He witnessed and proclaimed the Light *so that* all men might believe. The man was sent to focus on people and to lead them to believe in Christ Jesus. (See DEEPER STUDY # 2, Believe—Jn.2:24 for discussion of this point.)

Thought 1. The servant of God has *one primary purpose*: to lead men to believe in Christ Jesus, the Light of the world. The servant's *purpose* is not to organize, to administer, to oversee, to manage, to teach, or to preach. His purpose is as stated: to lead men to believe in Christ Jesus. Everything else is method, not purpose. Men have too often confused methods with purpose. The result has been that teeming millions are still unreached and teeming thousands are being deceived by confusing the methods of religion with the purpose of God: the salvation of men through belief in His Son.

"For God so loved the world that he gave his one and only Son, that whoever believes in him shall not perish but have eternal life. (John 3:16)

"I tell you the truth, whoever hears my word and believes him who sent me has eternal life and will not be condemned; he has crossed over from death to life. (John 5:24)

3 (1:8) **Humility—Ministers**: a man who was great, but he was not the Light. John the Baptist was extraordinarily great. Jesus Himself said, "Among those born of women there has not risen anyone greater than John the Baptist" (Mt.11:11). *But*, he was not the Light. The humility of John was striking. (Read Jn.1:19-23, 27 for the impact of his humility and the example he set for every servant of God.) No matter how great the ministry of a man may be in the eyes of men, that man's ministry is eclipsed by the greatness of John. Yet John says, "The thongs of [His] sandals I am not worthy to untie." (Jn.1:27)

For whoever exalts himself will be humbled, and whoever humbles himself will be exalted. (Mat 23:12)

Do nothing out of selfish ambition or vain conceit, but in humility consider others better than yourselves. Each of you should look not only to your own interests, but also to the interests of others. (Phil 2:3-4; cp. Ro.12:3)

Humble yourselves before the Lord, and he will lift you up. (James 4:10)

Young men, in the same way be submissive to those who are older. All of you, clothe yourselves with humility toward one another, because, "God opposes the proud but gives grace to the humble." (1 Pet 5:5)

	C. Jesus the Light of Men: The Second Witness of John the Apostle, 1:9-13	11 He came to that which was his own, but his own did not receive him. 12 Yet to all who received him, to those who believed in his name, he gave the right to become children of God— 13 Children born not of natural descent, nor of human decision or a husband's will, but born of God.	b. He came to His own people, but they rejected Him 3 Christ was wonderfully received by some a. How: By believing b. Result: Became sons of God c. The Source of becoming a child of God: A new birth 1) Was not of man 2) Was of God
1 Christ was the Light a. The true Light^DS1 b. His mission: To give light to people 2 Christ was tragically rejected by the world a. He was in the world, but He was rejected^DS2	9 The true light that gives light to every man was coming into the world. 10 He was in the world, and though the world was made through him, the world did not recognize him.		

DIVISION I

THE WITNESSES TO THE REVELATION OF JESUS CHRIST, 1:1-51

C. Jesus the Light of Men: The Second Witness of John the Apostle, 1:9-13

(1:9-13) **Introduction**: the world is in desperate straits. It is full of darkness—the darkness of sin and despair, of sickness and death, of corruption and hell. The darkness looms over the whole world. This is the problem dealt with in the present passage. There is hope in Jesus Christ, for Christ is the *true light*, and light dispels darkness.

1. Christ was the Light (v.9).
2. Christ was tragically rejected (v.10-11).
3. Christ was wonderfully received by some (v.12-13).

1 (1:9) **Jesus Christ, Light; Mission**: Christ was "the true Light." Other men may claim to be *lights*; they may claim that they can lead men to the truth. Some may claim they can...

- reveal God to men.
- show the nature, meaning, and destiny of the future and other things.
- guide a man out of the darkness of sin, shame, doubt, despair, and the fear of death and hell.
- do away with and eliminate the darkness entirely.

However, such men are *false* lights. Their claims are only ideas in their minds, ficticious ideas, and counterfeit claims. Their thoughts and positions are defective, frail, and uncertain—just as imperfect as any other man-made position dealing with the truth. Note two glorious truths.

1. The true Light is Jesus Christ (see DEEPER STUDY # 1, Truth—Jn.1:9). What does this mean? It means that Jesus Christ was what other men are not. Other men may claim to be the light of men, but their thoughts are only false imaginations. Christ alone was the true Light. Christ is to man what light is to man, and Christ did for man what light does for man.

⇒ Light is clear and pure: it is clean and good. So is Christ (Eph.5:8).
⇒ Light penetrates: it cuts through and eliminates darkness. So does Christ.
⇒ Light enlightens: it enlarges one's vision and knowledge. So does Christ.
⇒ Light reveals: it opens up the truth of an area, a whole new world and life. It clears up the way to the truth and life. So does Christ (Jn.14:6).
⇒ Light guides: it keeps one from groping and grasping about in the dark trying to find one's way. It directs the way to go, leads along the right path. So does Christ (Jn.12:36, 46).
⇒ Light exposes and strips away darkness. So does Christ (Jn.3:19-20).

⇒ Light routs the chaos. So does Christ (cp. Gen.1:2-3).
⇒ Light discriminates between the right way and the wrong way. So does Christ (see note—Eph.5:10. Cp. Eph.5:8-10.)
⇒ Light warns: it warns of dangers that lie ahead in one's path. So does Christ.
⇒ Light protects: it keeps one from tripping, stumbling, falling, and injuring oneself and losing one's life. So does Christ.

2. The mission of Christ is to give light to men. Note that He gives light to every man. How?

⇒ Christ gives light to men through natural revelation, the creation and order of the universe.

For the director of music. A psalm of David. The heavens declare the glory of God; the skies proclaim the work of his hands. (Psa 19:1)

The heavens proclaim his righteousness, and all the peoples see his glory. (Psa 97:6)

For since the creation of the world God's invisible qualities—his eternal power and divine nature—have been clearly seen, being understood from what has been made, so that men are without excuse. (Rom 1:20)

(Indeed, when Gentiles, who do not have the law, do by nature things required by the law, they are a law for themselves, even though they do not have the law, since they show that the requirements of the law are written on their hearts, their consciences also bearing witness, and their thoughts now accusing, now even defending them. (Rom 2:14-15)

Yet he has not left himself without testimony: He has shown kindness by giving you rain from heaven and crops in their seasons; he provides you with plenty of food and fills your hearts with joy." (Acts 14:17)

⇒ Christ gives light to men by giving good gifts to men. Every "good and perfect gift" which man receives is said to come from the Father of lights.

Every good and perfect gift is from above, coming down from the Father of the heavenly lights, who does not change like shifting shadows. (James 1:17)

But there is much more light given to men since Christ has "come into the world."

a. There is the *light of Christ Himself*: He is the Savior who now stands before the world as "the Christ, the Son of God, who was to come into the world" (Jn.11:27). Every man can now see the truth. They may reject it, but they can see it.

I will raise up for them a prophet like you from among their brothers; I will put my words in his mouth, and he will tell them everything I command him. (Deu 18:18)

"I have much to say in judgment of you. But he who sent me is reliable, and what I have heard from him I tell the world." (John 8:26)

For I did not speak of my own accord, but the Father who sent me commanded me what to say and how to say it. (John 12:49)

Jesus answered: "Don't you know me, Philip, even after I have been among you such a long time? Anyone who has seen me has seen the Father. How can you say, 'Show us the Father'? Don't you believe that I am in the Father, and that the Father is in me? The words I say to you are not just my own. Rather, it is the Father, living in me, who is doing his work. (John 14:9-10)

For I gave them the words you gave me and they accepted them. They knew with certainty that I came from you, and they believed that you sent me. (John 17:8)

b. There is the *light of the gospel*: Christ has now "come into the world as a light, so that no one who believes in [Christ] should stay in darkness" (Jn.12:46). The truth is that every man can now be delivered from the darkness of sin, despair, death, and hell.

When Jesus spoke again to the people, he said, "I am the light of the world. Whoever follows me will never walk in darkness, but will have the light of life." (John 8:12)

For it is light that makes everything visible. This is why it is said: "Wake up, O sleeper, rise from the dead, and Christ will shine on you." (Eph 5:14)

c. There is the *light of the Spirit*: both the guiding and the convicting power of the Spirit.

But when he, the Spirit of truth, comes, he will guide you into all truth. He will not speak on his own; he will speak only what he hears, and he will tell you what is yet to come. (John 16:13)

When he comes, he will convict the world of guilt in regard to sin and righteousness and judgment; in regard to sin, because men do not believe in me; in regard to righteousness, because I am going to the Father, where you can see me no longer; and in regard to judgment, because the prince of this world now stands condemned. (John 16:8-11)

This is the verdict: Light has come into the world, but men loved darkness instead of light because their deeds were evil. (John 3:19)

Note that all the light existing in the world is due to Christ, both the light from nature and from heaven, from the physical world and from the spiritual world. Christ is "the true Light [the Life] that gives light to every man...was coming into the world" (v.9).

DEEPER STUDY # 1

(1:9) **Truth**: the words true, truth, and real are taken from two Greek words very much alike. But each has a different shade of meaning. (See DEEPER STUDY # 1—Jn.8:32; DEEPER STUDY # 2—14:6.)

1. "Alethes" means true, the opposite of false.

2. "Alethinos" means the true, the genuine, the real. It is the *opposite* of the unreal, the ficticious, the counterfeit, the imaginary. It is also the opposite of the imperfect, defective, frail, uncertain.

Jesus Christ is seen as the true, the real, the genuine life which has come to give light to every man (see DEEPER STUDY # 1—Jn.8:12).

---

2 (1:10-11) **Jesus Christ—Rejection**: Christ was tragically rejected by the world.

1. Christ (the Word and the Light) was in the world. He had made the world, and He loved and cared deeply for the world; therefore, He was actively working to help the world and its people from the very beginning of creation.

a. Christ gave the *light of order and purpose and beauty* to the universe as a whole. The universe is lovingly supplied to take care of man's needs, and the world shows the glorious power and deity of God (Ro.1:19-20).

b. Christ gave the *glorious light [privilege] of living* in such a beautiful world to man. He gave man a soul, the very *light* of life by which he could learn and reason, love and care, work and serve—all for the purpose of building a better world, both for God and for himself.

c. Christ gave a spirit to man, the *light of knowing and worshipping* God and living forever in the life of God.

d. Christ gave messengers to men, *prophetic lights* to proclaim the truth and to encourage men to follow God and to be diligent in their work and service to the world.

But note what happened and still happens. "The world did not recognize Him" (auton ouk egno). Men rejected Christ; they closed their eyes and failed to see Him. (Cp. Ro.1:19-32 for the tragic indictment against man's rejection of God's activity in the world.)

2. Christ (the Word and the Light) came to His own people, but they too rejected Him. The words "that which was His own" (eis ta idia) mean literally to His own home, to His own people. There are two meanings here.

a. The world is His home, and all the people are His by creation. He came to all the people of the world, but they did not receive Him. They rejected Him.

b. The nation of Israel was His peculiar home, the people whom He had chosen to be the messengers of God to the world. They, of all people, should have known better because of the special privileges, but they too rejected Him. (See DEEPER STUDY # 1—Jn.4:22.)

> **Then the whole town went out to meet Jesus. And when they saw him, they pleaded with him to leave their region.** (Mat 8:34)
> **Isn't this the carpenter? Isn't this Mary's son and the brother of James, Joseph, Judas and Simon? Aren't his sisters here with us?" And they took offense at him.** (Mark 6:3)
> **All the people in the synagogue were furious when they heard this.** (Luke 4:28)
> **They got up, drove him out of the town, and took him to the brow of the hill on which the town was built, in order to throw him down the cliff.** (Luke 4:29)
> **With one voice they cried out, "Away with this man! Release Barabbas to us!"** (Luke 23:18)
> **I have come in my Father's name, and you do not accept me; but if someone else comes in his own name, you will accept him.** (John 5:43)
> **He came to that which was his own, but his own did not receive him.** (John 1:11)
> **There is a judge for the one who rejects me and does not accept my words; that very word which I spoke will condemn him at the last day.** (John 12:48)

DEEPER STUDY # 2

(1:10) **Revelation**: this verse gives the raw outline and supreme tragedy of revelation. (1) The supreme fact of history: "He was in the world." (2) The supreme truth about the world: "The world was made through Him." (3) The supreme tragedy of humanity: "The world did not recognize Him."

---

3 (1:12-13) **Jesus Christ, Accepted—Salvation**: Christ was wonderfully received by some persons. Not everyone rejected Christ—most did, but a few received Him. Note three points.

1. How men receive Christ. They "believe on His name." (See DEEPER STUDY # 2, Believe—Jn.2:24.)

2. The results of receiving Christ. A person is given the power, the right, to become a child of God.

⇒ The word "right" (exousian) means both power and authority.
⇒ The word "children" (tekna Theou) means sons and daughters of God.
⇒ The words "to become" (genesthai) mean to become something a person is not.

When a person receives Christ into his life (as Lord), Christ gives that person the power and right to become something he is not—a child of God.

> **"Therefore come out from them and be separate, says the Lord. Touch no unclean thing, and I will receive you."; "I will be a Father to you, and you will be my sons and daughters, says the Lord Almighty."** (2 Cor 6:17-18)
> **For you did not receive a spirit that makes you a slave again to fear, but you received the Spirit of sonship. And by him we cry, "Abba, Father." The Spirit himself testifies with our spirit that we are God's children.** (Rom 8:15-16)
> **But when the time had fully come, God sent his Son, born of a woman, born under law, to redeem those under law, that we might receive the full rights of sons. Because you are sons, God sent the Spirit of his Son into our hearts, the Spirit who calls out, "Abba, Father."** (Gal 4:4-6)

3. The source of becoming a child of God is a new birth.
   a. The new birth is not of man.
   ⇒ It is not by natural descent. The idea is that heritage—being born of a particular family, race, nation or people—is of no value in becoming a child of God. Natural descent is not what causes the new birth.
   ⇒ It is not of human decision (ek thelematos sarkos): sexual desire. The idea is that a person is not spiritually born again by wanting and willing to become a child of God just like a person wills to have an earthly child.
   ⇒ It is not by a husband's will (ek thelematos andros, husband). The idea is that even man (the husband, the stronger member, the one who is usually the leader) cannot bring about the spiritual birth of others. No man, no matter who he is—husband or world leader—can cause or make a person a child of God.

   b. The new birth is of God (see DEEPER STUDY # 1, <u>New Birth</u>—Jn.3:1-15 for discussion).

	D. Jesus the Word Made Flesh: The Third Witness of John the Apostle, 1:14-18	'He who comes after me has surpassed me because he was before me'"	
1 Christ became flesh[DS1]	14 The Word became flesh and made his dwelling among us. We have seen his glory, the glory of the One and Only, who came from the Father, full of grace and truth.	16 From the fullness of his grace we have all received one blessing after another.	4 Proof 3: Men have received the fullness & grace of Christ a. Not by law b. By Jesus Christ
2 Proof 1: Christ dwelt visibly among us a. His glory was seen b. Full of grace[DS2] & truth		17 For the law was given through Moses; grace and truth came through Jesus Christ.	
3 Proof 2: John the Baptist bore witness of the superiority of Christ	15 John testifies concerning him. He cries out, saying, "This was he of whom I said,	18 No one has ever seen God, but God the One and Only, who is at the Father's side, has made him known.	5 Proof 4: God's Son alone has seen God

DIVISION I

THE WITNESSES TO THE REVELATION OF JESUS CHRIST, 1:1-51

D. Jesus the Word Made Flesh: The Third Witness of John the Apostle, 1:14-18

(1:14-18) **Introduction**: "The Word became flesh"—God's Son, the Lord Jesus Christ, was made flesh and blood; He became a man. No greater message could ever be proclaimed to man.

1. Christ became flesh (v.14).
2. Proof 1: Christ dwelt visibly among us (v.14).
3. Proof 2: John the Baptist bore witness of the superiority of Christ (v.15).
4. Proof 3: men have received the fulness and grace of Christ (v.16-17).
5. Proof 4: God's Son alone has seen God (v.18).

1 (1:14) **Jesus Christ, Incarnation**: Christ became flesh. The Incarnation did take place. The Son of God was actually made flesh. He came to earth in the person of Jesus Christ. There is no doubt about John's meaning here.

The word "flesh" (sarx) is the same word that Paul used to describe man's nature with all of its weakness and tendency to sin. This is a staggering thought. Jesus Christ is God—fully God, yet Jesus Christ is man—fully man. (Cp. 1 Jn.4:2-3.) The word "seen" (theasthai) means actually seeing with the human eye. It is used about twenty times in the New Testament. There is no room whatever for saying that God becoming a man was merely a vision of some man's mind or imagination. John was saying that he and others actually saw the Word became flesh. Jesus Christ was beyond question God Himself who became man, who partook of the very same flesh as all other men. (Cp. 1 Jn.1:1-4.) (See DEEPER STUDY # 1, Flesh—Jn.1:14 for the meaning of "flesh" and why Jesus Christ had to become flesh. Also see DEEPER STUDY # 1, Flesh—1 Cor.3:1-4 for more discussion.)

DEEPER STUDY # 1

(1:14) **Flesh**: What does the Bible mean by "flesh"? And why did Jesus Christ have to become flesh? The best description of the flesh is probably found in 1 Cor.15:42-44. (See outline and notes—Ro.5:12-21; 8:1f; DEEPER STUDY # 1—1 Cor.3:1-4.)

1. The flesh is corruptible and perishable.
   a. The flesh is tainted, debased, ruined and depraved by sin (lust, 2 Pt.1:4). There is a seed of corruption within human flesh; therefore, the flesh sins (lusts) and thereby ages, dies, deteriorates and decays. It does not live beyond a few years on this earth.

> **Through these he has given us his very great and precious promises, so that through them you may participate in the divine nature and escape the corruption in the world caused by evil desires. (2 Pet 1:4)**
> **The one who sows to please his sinful nature, from that nature will reap destruction; the one who sows to please the Spirit, from the Spirit will reap eternal life. (Gal 6:8)**
> **I declare to you, brothers, that flesh and blood cannot inherit the kingdom of God, nor does the perishable inherit the imperishable. (1 Cor 15:50)**

   b. Christ (the Word) became flesh to correct and to counteract the corruption of flesh.

> **Through these he has given us his very great and precious promises, so that through them you may participate in the divine nature and escape the corruption in the world caused by evil desires. (2 Pet 1:4)**
> **For you know that it was not with perishable things such as silver or gold that you were redeemed from the empty way of life handed down to you from your forefathers, but with the precious blood of Christ, a lamb without blemish or defect. For you have been born again, not of perishable seed, but of imperishable, through the living and enduring word of God. For, "All men are like grass, and all their glory is like the flowers of the field; the grass withers and the flowers fall, but the word of the Lord stands forever." And this is the word that was preached to you. (1 Pet 1:18-19, 23-25)**
> **"For God so loved the world that he gave his one and only Son, that whoever believes in him shall not perish but have eternal life. (John 3:16)**

17

2. The flesh is dishonorable.

a. The flesh is not what God created it to be. It does not exist in the image of God that God intended. It does not hold the glory, the honor, nor the prestige it once did when God created it. It is disgraced and shamed, and it is reproached by sin and lust. It is held in the grip of sin and fear, and subject to being held in bondage—even the bondage of death.

> I know that nothing good lives in me, that is, in my sinful nature. For I have the desire to do what is good, but I cannot carry it out. (Rom 7:18)
> Furthermore, since they did not think it worthwhile to retain the knowledge of God, he gave them over to a depraved mind, to do what ought not to be done. They have become filled with every kind of wickedness, evil, greed and depravity. They are full of envy, murder, strife, deceit and malice. They are gossips, slanderers, God-haters, insolent, arrogant and boastful; they invent ways of doing evil; they disobey their parents; they are senseless, faithless, heartless, ruthless. Although they know God's righteous decree that those who do such things deserve death, they not only continue to do these very things but also approve of those who practice them. (Rom 1:28-32; cp.Gal.5:9-21)
> Those who live according to the sinful nature have their minds set on what that nature desires; but those who live in accordance with the Spirit have their minds set on what the Spirit desires. The mind of sinful man is death, but the mind controlled by the Spirit is life and peace; (Rom 8:5-6)

b. Jesus Christ became flesh to correct and counteract the dishonor of the flesh.

> Since the children have flesh and blood, he too shared in their humanity so that by his death he might destroy him who holds the power of death—that is, the devil—and free those who all their lives were held in slavery by their fear of death. (Heb 2:14-15; cp. 2:14-18)
> But God demonstrates his own love for us in this: While we were still sinners, Christ died for us. Since we have now been justified by his blood, how much more shall we be saved from God's wrath through him! For if, when we were God's enemies, we were reconciled to him through the death of his Son, how much more, having been reconciled, shall we be saved through his life! (Rom 5:8-10)

3. The flesh is weak.

a. The flesh is impotent. It is feeble, frail, fragile, infirmed, and decrepit because of lust and sin.

> Those controlled by the sinful nature [flesh] cannot please God. (Rom 8:8)
> Therefore no one will be declared righteous [justified] in his sight. (Rom 3:20; cp. Gal.2:16)

> The Spirit gives life; the flesh counts for nothing. (John 6:63)

b. Jesus Christ became flesh to correct and counteract the weakness of the flesh.

> You see, at just the right time, when we were still powerless, Christ died for the ungodly. (Rom 5:6)
> For what the law was powerless to do in that it was weakened by the sinful nature, God did by sending his own Son in the likeness of sinful man to be a sin offering. And so he condemned sin in sinful man, (Rom 8:3)

4. The flesh is a natural body.

a. The flesh is of the earth and is part of the earth; it is made up of the chemicals and substances of the earth. It is physical, material, animal. It is "the earthly house," the "tabernacle," the "tent," which houses the human soul and spirit (2 Cor.5:1). It is neither spirit nor spiritual; therefore, it cannot live beyond the strength of the chemicals and substances that form its flesh. It cannot live beyond its *natural life*.

> I declare to you, brothers, that flesh and blood cannot inherit the kingdom of God, nor does the perishable inherit the imperishable. (1 Cor 15:50)
> Look at my hands and my feet. It is I myself! Touch me and see; a ghost does not have flesh and bones, as you see I have." (Luke 24:39)
> It is sown a natural body, it is raised a spiritual body. If there is a natural body, there is also a spiritual body. So it is written: "The first man Adam became a living being" ; the last Adam, a life giving spirit. And just as we have borne the likeness of the earthly man, so shall we bear the likeness of the man from heaven. (1 Cor 15:44, 49)

b. Jesus Christ became flesh to counteract the natural body of the flesh. He became flesh in order to become "a life-giving spirit," the Savior who could quicken and make alive all those who would trust Him (1 Cor.15:45).

> For Christ died for sins once for all, the righteous for the unrighteous, to bring you to God. He was put to death in the body but made alive by the Spirit, (1 Pet 3:18)
> And if the Spirit of him who raised Jesus from the dead is living in you, he who raised Christ from the dead will also give life to your mortal bodies through his Spirit, who lives in you. (Rom 8:11)
> But because of his great love for us, God, who is rich in mercy, made us alive with Christ even when we were dead in transgressions—it is by grace you have been saved. (Eph 2:4-5)

2 (1:14) **Jesus Christ, Incarnation**: the first proof of the Incarnation is that Jesus Christ dwelt visibly among us.

1. God's glory was seen (see previous note, Incarnation—Jn.1:14 for meaning of word "seen"). Two things are meant by the word "glory."
   a. Christ was the *Shekinah glory* of God. The word Shekinah means that which dwells or dwelling. It refers to the *bright cloud* that God used to guide Israel out of Egypt and that rested upon the tabernacle and above the mercy seat in the Most Holy Place (Ex.40:34-38). The cloud symbolized God's presence, and that is just what John was saying. "We have seen," the Shekinah glory, God's very presence, "dwelling among us."
   b. Christ was the very embodiment of God, all that God is and does. John said "we have seen," looked at Him, and could tell He was God. All that Jesus was in His person and being, character and behavior, was so enormously different. In person and behavior, work and ministry He was…
      • the very embodiment of "grace and truth."
      • the perfect embodiment of love, joy, peace, patience, kindness, goodness, faithfulness, gentleness, and self-control.
      • the absolute embodiment of all that God could be.

The glory of all that God was stood right before them, right in their very presence. They had seen Him with their very own eyes. Jesus Christ, the Man who dwelt among them, could be no other than the glory of God among men. It was clearly seen that "in Christ all the fullness of the Deity lives in bodily form" (Col.2:9).
The glory of His being…
   • was the very glory God Himself would possess.
   • was the very glory God would give to His one and only Son (just as any father would give the best of his glory and all he is to a son).

A striking fact is that James, who was the Lord's brother, even called Jesus "our glorious Lord Jesus Christ" or "the Lord of glory." Just think: James was reared with Jesus beginning from the earliest years of childhood stretching right on through the years of adulthood. If anyone ever had an opportunity to see and observe Jesus, it was James. He had every chance to see some act of disobedience, some sin, something contrary to the nature of God. However, James' testimony is: "Our glorious Lord Jesus Christ." Jesus Christ is *the Lord of Glory*, the One in whom the very presence of God dwelt among us (Jas.2:1).

The references in John dealing with glory are as follows: Jn.2:11; 5:41; 7:18; 8:50, 54; 11:4; 12:41; 17:5, 22, 24.
2. Jesus Christ was full of grace and truth.
   a. He was the very embodiment of grace (see DEEPER STUDY # 2, Grace—Jn.1:14).
   b. He was the very embodiment of truth (see DEEPER STUDY # 2, Truth—Jn.14:6; DEEPER STUDY # 1—8:32).

Therefore the Lord himself will give you a sign: The virgin will be with child and will give birth to a son, and will call him Immanuel. (Isa 7:14)

For to us a child is born, to us a son is given, and the government will be on his shoulders. And he will be called Wonderful Counselor, Mighty God, Everlasting Fa-ther, Prince of Peace. (Isa 9:6)

You will be with child and give birth to a son, and you are to give him the name Jesus. "How will this be," Mary asked the angel, "since I am a virgin?" The angel answered, "The Holy Spirit will come upon you, and the power of the Most High will overshadow you. So the holy one to be born will be called the Son of God. (Luke 1:31, 34-35)

The Word became flesh and made his dwelling among us. We have seen his glory, the glory of the One and Only, who came from the Father, full of grace and truth. (John 1:14)

Regarding his Son, who as to his human nature was a descendant of David, (Rom 1:3)

For what the law was powerless to do in that it was weakened by the sinful nature, God did by sending his own Son in the likeness of sinful man to be a sin offering. And so he condemned sin in sinful man, (Rom 8:3)

But made himself nothing, taking the very nature of a servant, being made in human likeness. (Phil 2:7)

Beyond all question, the mystery of godliness is great: He appeared in a body, was vindicated by the Spirit, was seen by angels, was preached among the nations, was believed on in the world, was taken up in glory. (1 Tim 3:16)

Since the children have flesh and blood, he too shared in their humanity so that by his death he might destroy him who holds the power of death—that is, the devil— (Heb 2:14)

This is how you can recognize the Spirit of God: Every spirit that acknowledges that Jesus Christ has come in the flesh is from God, (1 John 4:2)

Many deceivers, who do not acknowledge Jesus Christ as coming in the flesh, have gone out into the world. Any such person is the deceiver and the antichrist. (2 John 1:7)

DEEPER STUDY # 2

(1:14) **Grace**: grace is probably the most meaningful word in the language of men. In the Bible the word *grace* means far more than it does when men use it. To men the word grace means three things.

1. Grace is that quality within a thing that is beautiful or joyful. It may be the fragrance of a flower, the rich green of the grass, the beauty of a lovely person.

2. Grace is anything that has loveliness. It may be a thought, an act, a word, a person.

3. Grace is a gift, a favor that someone might extend to a friend. The favor is always freely done, expecting nothing in return. The favor is always done for a friend.

However, when the early Christians looked at what God had done for men, they had to add a deeper, much richer meaning to the word grace. God had saved sinners, those who had acted against Him. Therefore, grace became the favor of God showered upon men—men who did not deserve His favor. Grace became the kindness and love that dwells within the very nature of God, the kindness and love that God freely gives to His *enemies*.

No other word so expresses the depth and richness of the heart and mind of God. This is the distinctive difference between God's grace and man's grace. Whereas man sometimes does favors for his friends and thereby can be said to be gracious, God has done a thing unheard of among men: He has given His very own Son to die for His *enemies* (Ro.5:8-10). In this act He has done something that shows He is the perfect embodiment of grace, full...

- of beauty and joy
- of loveliness and goodness
- of favors freely given
- of kindness and love freely demonstrated

3 (1:15) **Jesus Christ, Incarnation**: the second proof of the Incarnation is John the Baptist. He, too, bore witness of the Incarnation. John said very simply...

- Jesus was born "after me" (6 months after).
- But He has "surpassed me" (mightier; more important in being, rank, and dignity).
- Why? Because "He was before me."

The words "because He was before me" (hoti protos mou en) literally mean *first to me* or *first of me*. It refers both to time and importance. Jesus Christ was first in time, existing before John. He existed "in the beginning"—throughout all eternity. John proclaimed, "He was before me": He always existed; He was the First; He was the very cause for John's existence. John also declared that Jesus was first in importance. He was first in superiority, Being, Person. His very name is the First and the Last, the Alpha and the Omega, the Beginning and the End.

> "This is what the LORD says— Israel's King and Redeemer, the LORD Almighty: I am the first and I am the last; apart from me there is no God. (Isa 44:6)
> I am the Alpha and the Omega, the First and the Last, the Beginning and the End. (Rev 22:13; cp. Rev.1:8; 21:6; Is,44:6)

4 (1:16-17) **Jesus Christ, Incarnation—Jesus Christ, Deity**: the third proof of the Incarnation is the fullness and grace of Christ which was given to us. Genuine believers can testify to this.

The word "fullness" (pleroma) means that which fills, the sum total, the totality. It is the sum total of all that is in God (Col.1:19). In Jesus dwelt all the wisdom, righteousness, sanctification, and redemption—all the abundance of God (1 Cor.1:30). All that Christ is, the very fullness of His being, is given to us who believe—all His "love, joy, peace, patience, kindness, goodness, faithfullness, gentleness, self-control" (Gal.5:22-23). We are complete in Him.

> For in Christ all the fullness of the Deity lives in bodily form, and you have been given fullness in Christ, who is the head over every power and authority. (Col 2:9-10)

The term "one blessing after another" means that He gives grace enough to meet all our needs, no matter the circumstances. It is one blessing leading to another blessing; new wonders dawning upon one's consciousness every day; fresh experiences constantly springing into one's life.

Note that the fullness of God, His grace and truth, does not come by the law, but by Jesus Christ. It does not come...

- by being as good as we can
- by working to please God as much as we can
- by keeping the rules and commandments of the law

It does not come through law, for no man can keep the law to any degree of perfection. The law only points out a man's failure and condemns him for breaking the law. If a man is to be acceptable to God, it is because he comes and keeps on coming to God, begging God to forgive him; and because God loves him so much that he forgives the man.

Such is the grace, the undeserved favor of God. God's grace comes through Jesus Christ, and we would not know the grace of God unless Jesus Christ had come to reveal it to us. The glorious fact that we do experience the fullness of God and His grace is proof of the Incarnation (that God did become flesh in the person of Jesus Christ).

> For the grace of God that brings salvation has appeared to all men. (Titus 2:11)
> But when the kindness and love of God our Savior appeared, he saved us, not because of righteous things we had done, but because of his mercy. He saved us through the washing of rebirth and renewal by the Holy Spirit, whom he poured out on us generously through Jesus Christ our Savior, so that, having been justified by his grace, we might become heirs having the hope of eternal life. (Titus 3:4-7)
> No! We believe it is through the grace of our Lord Jesus that we are saved, just as they are." (Acts 15:11)
> For all have sinned and fall short of the glory of God, and are justified freely by his grace through the redemption that came by Christ Jesus. (Rom 3:23-24)
> For it is by grace you have been saved, through faith—and this not from yourselves, it is the gift of God—not by works, so that no one can boast. (Eph 2:8-9)

5 (1:18) **Incarnation—Jesus Christ, Deity**: the fourth proof of the Incarnation is Christ—God's Son. He alone has seen God. No man has seen God at any time; however, Jesus Christ claimed...

- that He was "the one and only Son of God" (Jn.3:16).
- that He had come from the Father's side" (from the deepest part, the most intimate place, the most honorable fellowship) (Jn.1:18).
- that He had come to reveal and to proclaim the Father (see DEEPER STUDY # 1,2,3—Jn.14:6; see note, Revelation 14:7).

The fact that Jesus Christ is "God the one and only, who is at the Father's side" is proof of the Incarnation (that God became flesh). Jesus Christ declared unequivocally that He had come from God. A man either believes or does not believe the grace and truth of God as revealed in Jesus Christ. (See note—Jn.3:31 for discussion and verses.)

	E. Jesus The Messiah, the Lord: The Second Witness of John the Baptist, 1:19-28	yourself?" 23 John replied in the words of Isaiah the prophet, "I am the voice of one calling in the desert, 'Make straight the way for the Lord.'"	3	He was only a voice—only a forerunner for the Lord
1 John was questioned by religionists who were suspicious of him[DS1]	19 Now this was John's testimony when the Jews of Jerusalem sent priests and Levites to ask him who he was.	24 Now some Pharisees who had been sent 25 Questioned him, "Why then do you baptize if you are not the Christ, nor Elijah, nor the Prophet?"	4	He was a baptizer a. The questioners were the Pharisees[DS3] b. They questioned John's right to baptize
2 He was a man who knew who he was a. He was not the Christ[DS2] b. He was not Elijah c. He was not "the Prophet"	20 He did not fail to confess, but confessed freely, "I am not the Christ." 21 They asked him, "Then who are you? Are you Elijah?" He said, "I am not." "Are you the Prophet?" He answered, "No." 22 Finally they said, "Who are you? Give us an answer to take back to those who sent us. What do you say about	26 "I baptize with water," John replied, "but among you stands one you do not know. 27 He is the one who comes after me, the thongs of whose sandals I am not worthy to untie." 28 This all happened at Bethany on the other side of the Jordan, where John was baptizing.	5 6	He was an unworthy servant He was a man who brought honor to a place

DIVISION I

THE WITNESSES TO THE REVELATION OF JESUS CHRIST, 1:1-51

E. Jesus the Messiah, the Lord: The Second Witness of John the Baptist, 1:19-28

(1:19-28) **Introduction**: the witness of John the Baptist is a dynamic example for every servant of God.
1. John was questioned by religionists who were suspicious of Him (v.19).
2. He was a man who knew who he was (v.20-22).
3. He was only a voice—only a forerunner for the Lord (v.23).
4. He was a baptizer (v.24-26).
5. He was an unworthy servant (v.27).
6. He was a man who brought honor to a place (v.28).

1 (1:19) **John the Baptist**: John was questioned by the religionists who were very suspicious of him. These particular religionists were a fact finding commission sent from Jerusalem, the headquarters of Jewish religion. The questioning of John by the religionists was to be expected, for John's father, Zechariah, was a priest (Lk.1:5); and in the eyes of the authorities, all the sons of priests were automatically priests by descent. However, John was not a priest like other priests. He was most unusual, for the way he lived and preached was radically different (cp. Mt.3:1-12). He was a non-conformist, and the authorities had to find out why.

Thought 1. Too often institutional religion is suspicious and opposed to the unusual.
⇒ If a person is different or does things differently, he is questioned.
⇒ If a person is unusually blessed or if miraculous things are happening in his life and ministry, he is questioned.

DEEPER STUDY # 1
(1:19) **Levites**: these men were servants of the priests. They were descendants of Levi just as the descendants of Aaron were. However, only Aaron's descendants could serve as priests; all other Levites served under them.

2 (1:20-22) **Minister—Humility**: the messenger was a man who knew who he was. Others had questions about John, but not John. He knew exactly who he was. He knew God personally; therefore, he knew God had sent him into the world for a specific ministry. He was from God, called and commissioned by God; therefore, He knew exactly who he was and what he was doing (see DEEPER STUDY # 1—Jn.1:6. Also see outline and notes—Jn.1:6-8 for more discussion.)

1. John was not the Messiah (see DEEPER STUDY # 2, Christ—Jn.1:20).
2. John was not Elijah. Elijah was expected to return from the dead to proclaim the coming of the Messiah (Mal.4:5). He was expected to do several significant things: to warn the people, to anoint the Messiah to His kingly office, to raise the dead, and to help select those who were to have a part in the Messiah's kingdom. John denied that he was Elijah in person. It should be noted that Jesus did later identify John with Elijah (Mk.9:11f); however, what Jesus meant was that John was Elijah in spirit, not in person.
3. John was not "the Prophet." This Prophet was thought to be another forerunner of the Messiah (Jn.7:40). Some persons thought he would be either Jeremiah or Isaiah. This belief was based on Moses' prediction that there would be a prophet like himself (Dt.18:15). However, today most Christians interpret the Prophet predicted by Moses to be Christ Himself (Acts 3:22; 7:37).

Thought 1. The lessons are clear. The servant (minister or layman) of God must not...
• claim to be the Christ nor any other great prophet.
• pretend to be some great man of God.
• seek recognition.
• assume some honor that does not belong to him.

- allow God's power upon his life and ministry to turn his head toward pride, thinking more highly of himself than he should.

Then Abraham spoke up again: "Now that I have been so bold as to speak to the Lord though I am nothing but dust and ashes, (Gen 18:27)

I am unworthy of all the kindness and faithfulness you have shown your servant. I had only my staff when I crossed this Jordan, but now I have become two groups. (Gen 32:10)

But Moses said to God, "Who am I, that I should go to Pharaoh and bring the Israelites out of Egypt?" (Exo 3:11)

Moses said to the LORD, "O Lord, I have never been eloquent, neither in the past nor since you have spoken to your servant. I am slow of speech and tongue." (Exo 4:10)

Then King David went in and sat before the LORD, and he said: "Who am I, O Sovereign LORD, and what is my family, that you have brought me this far? (2 Sam 7:18)

"Now, O LORD my God, you have made your servant king in place of my father David. But I am only a little child and do not know how to carry out my duties. (1 Ki 3:7)

The centurion replied, "Lord, I do not deserve to have you come under my roof. But just say the word, and my servant will be healed. (Mat 8:8)

For I am the least of the apostles and do not even deserve to be called an apostle, because I persecuted the church of God. (1 Cor 15:9)

Here is a trustworthy saying that deserves full acceptance: Christ Jesus came into the world to save sinners—of whom I am the worst. (1 Tim 1:15)

DEEPER STUDY # 2
(1:20) **Christ—Messiah**: the words "Christ" (christos) and "Messiah" are the same word. Messiah is the Hebrew word and Christ is the Greek word. Both words refer to the same person and mean the same thing: *the anointed one*. The Messiah is the anointed one of God. Matthew said Jesus "is called Christ" (Mt.1:16); that is, He is recognized as *the anointed one of God*, the Messiah Himself.

In the day of Jesus Christ, people feverishly panted for the coming of the long-promised Messiah. The weight of life was harsh, hard, and impoverished. Under the Romans, people felt that God could not wait much longer to fulfill His promise. Such longings for deliverance left the people gullible. Many arose who claimed to be the Messiah and led the gullible followers into rebellion against the Roman state. The insurrectionist Barabbas, who was set free in the place of Jesus at Jesus' trial, is an example (Mk.15:6f). (See note—Mt.1:1; DEEPER STUDY # 2—3:11; notes 11:1-6; 11:2-3; DEEPER STUDY # 1—11:5; DEEPER STUDY # 2—11:6; DEEPER STUDY # 1—12:16; notes 22:42; Lk.7:21-23.)

The Messiah was thought to be several things.

1. Nationally, He was to be the leader from David's line who would free the Jewish state and establish it as an inde-pendent nation, leading it to be the greatest nation the world had ever known.

2. Militarily, He was to be a great military leader who would lead Jewish armies victoriously over all the world.

3. Religiously, He was to be a supernatural figure straight from God who would bring righteousness over all the earth.

4. Personally, He was to be the One who would bring peace to the whole world.

Jesus Christ accepted the title of Messiah on three different occasions (Mt.16:17; Mk.14:61; Jn.4:26). The name *Jesus* shows Him to be man. The name *Christ* shows Him to be God's anointed, God's very own Son. *Christ* is Jesus' official title. It identifies Him officially as Prophet (Dt.18:15-19), Priest (Ps.110:4), and King (2 Sam.7:12-13). These officials were always anointed with oil, a symbol of the Holy Spirit who was to perfectly anoint the Christ, the Messiah (Mt.3:16; Mk.1:10-11; Lk.3:21-22; Jn.1:32-33).

The first thing Andrew did was to find his brother Simon and tell him, "We have found the Messiah" (that is, the Christ). (John 1:41)

Philip found Nathanael and told him, "We have found the one Moses wrote about in the Law, and about whom the prophets also wrote—Jesus of Nazareth, the son of Joseph." (John 1:45)

Then Nathanael declared, "Rabbi, you are the Son of God; you are the King of Israel." (John 1:49)

The woman said, "I know that Messiah" (called Christ) "is coming. When he comes, he will explain everything to us." (John 4:25)

Then Jesus declared, "I who speak to you am he." (John 4:26)

We believe and know that you are the Holy One of God." (John 6:69)

Jesus said to her, "I am the resurrection and the life. He who believes in me will live, even though he dies; (John 11:25)

and whoever lives and believes in me will never die. Do you believe this?" (John 11:26)

"Yes, Lord," she told him, "I believe that you are the Christ, the Son of God, who was to come into the world." (John 11:27)

As they traveled along the road, they came to some water and the eunuch said, "Look, here is water. Why shouldn't I be baptized?" (Acts 8:36-37)

3 (1:23) **Jesus Christ, Messiah—John the Baptist, Forerunner**: the messenger was only a voice, only a forerunner for the Lord. Why was it necessary for the Messiah to have a forerunner? Why did John have to run ahead of Christ crying, "Prepare. Make straight the way of the Lord"? What kind of preparation needed to be done?

1. The people needed their concept of the Messiah straightened out. Their concept had deteriorated through the years.

a. First, few had ever seen "the seed" [the descendants] promised to Adam and Abraham as referring to the Messiah (see DEEPER STUDY # 1—Gal.3:8,

16; DEEPER STUDY # 1—Ro.4:1-25). They interpreted "the seed" as the nation Israel, as all circumcised Jews. "We are Abraham's descendants [seed]" they were later to tell Christ (Jn.8:33). They saw Christ as being "the descendant [seed] of Abraham" only in the sense that an ordinary Jew was. He was just an ordinary man born through Abraham's line. Few ever saw the Messiah as "the Seed" or Descendant in whom all the promises made to Abraham were to be fulfilled.

b. Second, the Jews saw the Messiah primarily as the Son of David. David had liberated and led their nation to its highest peak, so they saw the Messiah as following in David's footsteps. (See notes—Jn.1:45; Lk.3:24-31; Mt.1:1; DEEPER STUDY # 1—1:18; DEEPER STUDY # 2—3:11; notes—11:1-6; 11:2-3; DEEPER STUDY # 1—12:16; notes—22:42; Lk.7:21-23). At first, the Jews saw the Messiah as a *liberator*, One who was going to deliver them from all their enemies and restore their nation to its greatest glory. (Keep in mind how awful the Jews had been treated and persecuted throughout history.) However, as centuries rolled on and they suffered brutal violence after violence, their concept of the Messiah deteriorated into *anger*.

The Jews saw themselves as the subjects of the Messiah's salvation (deliverance) and saw all other people (Gentiles) as the subjects of the Messiah's judgment. The Jews were the ones acceptable to God; all others were unacceptable. Therefore, the Messiah was to come and free Israel, elevating the nation to rule over all the nations of the earth. This, of course, led to two tragic faults. First, the Jews became blind to their own sinful condition and personal need for salvation. Second, the Jews saw salvation as a matter of national heritage and personal rites (being circumcised) and ritual (religious observances). They believed that they were safe because they had been circumcised and their forefathers were godly people.

The forefunner, John the Baptist, had to begin cracking through the crust of these errors. Salvation was not a national thing, not an institutional thing, not even a religious thing. It was not a matter of heritage and rites. It was a personal matter, a spiritual matter of the heart and life. A man had to personally want forgiveness of sins and then repent and be baptized if he wished to be saved. This was to be the message of the Messiah. Therefore, because of the hardness of the people in understanding the personal need for salvation, God had to send a forerunner to begin breaking through the crust of self-righteousness which had become so cemented in the mind of man. (Just how deeply rooted the false concept of the Messiah was can be seen in the enormous struggle the disciples had with it. See note—Mt.18:1-2.)

2. The people needed their religion straightened out. They had allowed their religion to become formal and institutionalized, that is, just a *form* of godliness but denying its power (2 Tim.3:5). So many were going through the motions of religion, its services and rites, yet living as they wished. God and personal righteousness were of little concern. The Messiah was to bring a new message, a message of God's love—a love so strong that it would proclaim the truth:

⇒ that man is sinful and perishing (Jn.3:16).
⇒ that man must repent (Mk.2:17).

⇒ that man must prepare, for the Kingdom of God is near (Mt.4:17).

The message was to be so radical that some preparation of the people was needed before the Messiah appeared on the scene. Therefore, God sent the forerunner, John the Baptist.

3. The world needed to know about the Messiah. As the Son of God, the Messiah would be so different—so pure, so holy, so truthful—that men would not tolerate His presence too long. His proclamation of the truth and salvation would be very, very short. Men would destroy Him. Therefore, men needed to be stirred to a high pitch of excitement when the Messiah arrived. Men needed to be buzzing about with great anticipation and with the glorious news that the Messiah had finally come. People would need to sit up and take notice. They may not respond; they might even react violently, but they needed to be aware of the Messiah's *historical coming* and *claims* to be the Son of God. The forerunner was to arouse and stir the people to expect the Messiah immediately.

Thought 1. The same can be said of men today.
1) Many need their concept of the Messiah straightened out.
   a) Some have never seen that the *promised seed* is Christ.
   b) Some still think of themselves as being *special* to God. They are blind to their sin and need for personal salvation.
2) Many need their religion straightened out.
3) Many simply need to hear about the Messiah: they have never heard that He has come.

Thought 2. The messenger of God is only a voice, only a forerunner for the Lord. But he *is* a voice and a forerunner; therefore, He *must* speak up for the Lord.
1) He must be a *clear voice* proclaiming a *clear message*.

> **For it will not be you speaking, but the Spirit of your Father speaking through you. (Mat 10:20)**
> **He said to them, "Go into all the world and preach the good news to all creation. (Mark 16:15)**
> **This is what we speak, not in words taught us by human wisdom but in words taught by the Spirit, expressing spiritual truths in spiritual words. (1 Cor 2:13)**
> **If anyone speaks, he should do it as one speaking the very words of God. If anyone serves, he should do it with the strength God provides, so that in all things God may be praised through Jesus Christ. To him be the glory and the power for ever and ever. Amen. (1 Pet 4:11)**

2) He must be an *earnest voice* proclaiming the desperate need to prepare and repent.

> **And saying, "Repent, for the kingdom of heaven is near." (Mat 3:2)**
> **Repent, then, and turn to God, so that your sins may be wiped out, that times of refreshing may come from the Lord, (Acts 3:19)**

4 (1:24-26) **Baptism—John the Baptist, Baptism of**: the messenger was a baptizer. John was asked why he baptized.

1. His baptism shocked the Jewish nation, for Jews were never baptized. Baptism was only for non-Jewish persons who were converts to the Jewish faith. The Jews considered all Gentiles unclean, so they had to be baptized when they became converts (all males were also circumcised). However, Jews were thought to be clean and acceptable to God no matter how they lived. Why? Because Jews were "a descendant of Abraham," (Ro.11:1) of his heritage. They were his seed, his descendants, the people promised to Abraham.

2. The religionists wanted to know if John were the Christ. They believed that when the Christ came He might institute the practice of baptism.

3. The religionists wanted to know if John were a prophet. In theory a true prophet was said to have the right to institute new practices and to change some laws.

John's baptism was radical, most unusual, a shocking practice. It was a "baptism of repentance *for* the forgiveness of sins" (Lk.3:3). What does this mean? Simply this: when a person wanted God to forgive his sins, the person made the decision to repent, to turn from his sins, and to change his life. Then he was immediately baptized, thereby proclaiming that he was becoming a follower of the Messiah whom John preached (see note—Lk.3:3 for detailed discussion).

The Old Testament prophets had cried for Israel to wash themselves and to be cleansed of their filthiness. John used water baptism to show that a man was turning from his sins and turning to God, seeking forgiveness of sins.

> **Wash and make yourselves clean. Take your evil deeds out of my sight! Stop doing wrong, (Isa 1:16)**
>
> **"On that day a fountain will be opened to the house of David and the inhabitants of Jerusalem, to cleanse them from sin and impurity. (Zec 13:1)**
>
> **I will sprinkle clean water on you, and you will be clean; I will cleanse you from all your impurities and from all your idols. I will give you a new heart and put a new spirit in you; I will remove from you your heart of stone and give you a heart of flesh. (Ezek 36:25-26)**

Thought 1. Baptism is critical. The believer is to be baptized, but he is to be baptized because he is truly repenting and sincerely turning to God.

Thought 2. The servant of God is to be a baptizer, a man who proclaims and practices the baptism of repentance in its full meaning.

DEEPER STUDY # 3
(1:24) **Pharisees**: see DEEPER STUDY # 3—Acts 23:8.

---

5 (1:27) **Servant—Humility**: the messenger of God was an unworthy servant. Two things demonstrated this.

1. John proclaimed and confessed that Jesus was preferred before him (see note—Jn.1:15).

2. John proclaimed that he was not worthy even to untie the thongs of Jesus' sandals. He confessed the *nothingness of self*. Slaves were the ones who untied the sandals of guests and washed their feet. John said that he was *less* than a slave, unworthy to do even what a slave did.

Thought 1. The same confession of unworthiness must be made by every servant of God.

> **But you are not to be like that. Instead, the greatest among you should be like the youngest, and the one who rules like the one who serves. (Luke 22:26)**
>
> **For by the grace given me I say to every one of you: Do not think of yourself more highly than you ought, but rather think of yourself with sober judgment, in accordance with the measure of faith God has given you. (Rom 12:3)**
>
> **Do nothing out of selfish ambition or vain conceit, but in humility consider others better than yourselves. Each of you should look not only to your own interests, but also to the interests of others. (Phil 2:3-4)**
>
> **He has showed you, O man, what is good. And what does the LORD require of you? To act justly and to love mercy and to walk humbly with your God. (Micah 6:8)**

6 (1:28) **John the Baptist—Minister**: the messenger was a man who brought honor to a place. John was ministering in Bethany on the other side of the Jordan, which means it was a great distance from Jerusalem. John brought honor to the place. It would not be known apart from John, for nothing else is known about the city.

Thought 1. A servant of God who is faithful in his witness and ministry (like John) will bring honor to a place. In God's eyes a place is honored because believers are there (cp. Gen.18:16f).

	F. Jesus The Lamb of God—The Son of God: The Third Witness of John the Baptist, 1:29-34	but the reason I came baptizing with water was that he might be revealed to Israel."	only that He was to come
1 Christ is the Lamb of God	29 The next day John saw Jesus coming toward him and said, "Look, the Lamb of God, who takes away the sin of the world!	32 Then John gave this testimony: "I saw the Spirit come down from heaven as a dove and remain on him.	**3 Christ is the Messiah, the One upon whom the Spirit of God remained**
2 Christ is the Preeminent One a. He was before John: Preexistent b. John did not know Him,	30 This is the one I meant when I said, 'A man who comes after me has surpassed me because he was before me.' 31 I myself did not know him,	33 I would not have known him, except that the one who sent me to baptize with water told me, 'The man on whom you see the Spirit come down and remain is he who will baptize with the Holy Spirit.' 34 I have seen and I testify that this is the Son of God."	 **4 Christ is the Son of God**

DIVISION I

THE WITNESSES TO THE REVELATION OF JESUS CHRIST, 1:1-51

F. Jesus the Lamb of God, the Son of God: The Third Witness of John the Baptist, 1:29-34

(1:29-34) Introduction: John's witness about Jesus Christ is one of the greatest witnesses ever given by man. John was unmistakable in His proclamation of the Lord Jesus Christ (Lk.4:18-19).

1. Christ is the Lamb of God (v.29).
2. Christ is the Preeminent One (v.30-31).
3. Christ is the Messiah, the One upon whom the Spirit of God remained (v.32-33).
4. Christ is the Son of God (v.34).

1 (1:29) **Jesus Christ, Lamb of God**: Jesus Christ is the "Lamb of God." Down through the centuries *"the Lamb of God"* has been one of the most cherished symbols of Jesus Christ held by believers. There are four reasons for this.

1. The Lamb is a picture of Christ our Passover who was sacrificed for us.

> **Get rid of the old yeast that you may be a new batch without yeast—as you really are. For Christ, our Passover lamb, has been sacrificed. (1 Cor 5:7)**

Historically, the Passover refers back to the time when God delivered Israel from Egyptian bondage (Ex.11:1f). God had pronounced judgment, the taking of the firstborn, upon the people of Egypt for their injustices. As He prepared to execute the final judgment, the faithful, those who believed God, were instructed to slay a pure lamb and sprinkle its blood over the door posts of their homes. The blood of the innocent lamb would then serve as a sign that the coming judgment had already been carried out. When seeing the blood, God would *pass over* that house. Those who believed God applied the blood to their homes and were saved, but those who did not believe did not apply the blood to their homes and their firstborn were destroyed.

Symbolically, the Passover pictured the coming of Jesus Christ as the Savior. The *lamb without defect* pictured His sinless life (cp. Jn.1:29; Ex.12:5), and the *blood sprinkled on the door posts* pictured His blood shed or poured out for the believer. It was a sign that the life and blood of the innocent lamb had been substituted for the firstborn. The *eating of the lamb* pictured the need for spiritual nourishment gained by feeding on Christ, the Bread of Life. The unleavened bread (bread without yeast) pictured the need for putting evil out of one's life and household. (See DEEPER STUDY # 1, Feast of Unleavened Bread—Mt.26:17.)

The major point to note is this: it was the blood of the lamb that saved the people. The lamb was sacrificed; that is, its blood was shed or poured out as a substitute for the people. The lamb symbolized Christ our Passover who was sacrificed for us. If we believe and apply His blood to our hearts and homes, He saves us. If we do not believe and do not apply the blood to our hearts and homes, we are destroyed. It is the Lamb of God who was sacrificed for us; it is His blood which saves us.

2. The Lamb is a picture of the precious blood of Christ which redeems us.

> **For you know that it was not with perishable things such as silver or gold that you were redeemed from the empty way of life handed down to you from your forefathers, but with the precious blood of Christ, a lamb without blemish or defect. (1 Pet 1:18-19)**

Historically, two lambs were sacrificed "regularly each day....one in the morning and the other at twilight" (Ex.29:38-39). The sacrifice of the two lambs, the shedding of their precious blood, became a substitute for the people. The people knew their sins had separated them from God and that their sins had to be removed before they could be reconciled to God. Thus, symbolically, the sins of the people were removed from the people and placed upon the two animals. The animals, without defect and without spot, had the sins of the people placed upon them; and symbolically, they bore the judgment of sin, which was death. They were sacrificed for sin, and by their death, they symbolically set the people free by redeeming them from their sins. (But note a critical point. It was not the deed that caused God to remove the sins, but the *faith* of the person in God's Word *that He would remove the sins*.)

This, of course, is a picture of Christ. (Cp. Is.53:6-7; Jer.11:19; Acts 8:32; 1 Cor.5:7; Heb.9:28; 1 Pt.2:22-24; Rev.5:6; 6:1; 7:9; 12:11; 13:8; 14:1; 15:3; 17:14; 19:9; 21:22.) Jesus Christ is...

- the perfect Lamb of God, without sin (defect or spot). (See note, Jesus Christ, Sinless—Jn.8:45-47.)

25

- the One upon whom the sins of the people were placed.
- the One who bore the judgment for sin, which was death.
- the One who was sacrificed for sin.
- the One whose death sets people free by redeeming them.
- the One whose blood is counted precious both by God and believers.

It should be noted that Christ *willingly* offered Himself as the sacrificial Lamb, as our substitute and sin-bearer; and God willingly accepted the offering and sacrifice of His Son for us (Jn.10:17-18). God is *satisfied* with the settlement for sin that Christ made. If any person really believes the blood of Christ to be precious—really believes that the blood of Christ covers his sins—God will take that person's belief and count it as righteousness. That person is counted righteous by God (see DEEPER STUDY # 1,2—Ro.4:22; notes—5:1; 1 Jn.2:1-2).

3. The "Lamb of God" is not *of men*, but *of God* (tou Theou). The idea is that the Lamb belonged to God; that is, God gave, supplied, and provided the Lamb for sacrifice. (Cp. Gen.22:8 where God provided the lamb for Abraham as a substitute for Isaac.)

This glorious truth speaks volumes on...

- the unbelievable love of God for man (Jn.3:16; Ro.5:1).
- the great sacrifice and humiliation Christ underwent for man (Ph.2:6-8; 1 Pt.2:24).
- the forgiveness of sins and salvation which came from God's grace and not from man's resources and works (Eph.2:8-9; Tit.2:4-7).
- the deity of Christ, His being *of God* (see Master Subject Index, Jesus Christ, Deity).

4. The "Lamb of God" takes away the sin of the world.

a. The phrase "takes away" (airon) means to lift away, to carry off. It means to bear in behalf of one, as one's substitute. Jesus Christ was the sacrificial Lamb of God who bore our sins. He lifted our sins off of us and bore and carried them away.

> **He himself bore our sins in his body on the tree, so that we might die to sins and live for righteousness; by his wounds you have been healed. (1 Pet 2:24)**
>
> **So Christ was sacrificed once to take away the sins of many people; and he will appear a second time, not to bear sin, but to bring salvation to those who are waiting for him. (Heb 9:28)**

b. The word "sin" (harmartian) is singular, not plural. All the sins of the world are taken and placed into one package. The whole package of sin—all the sin of every man who has ever lived—was laid upon and borne by Christ.

> **But if we walk in the light, as he is in the light, we have fellowship with one another, and the blood of Jesus, his Son, purifies us from all sin. (1 John 1:7)**

c. The world is looked at as a whole. Christ bore the sins of the whole world, not the sins of just some men. No matter the depth and ugliness of a man's sin, Christ bore the sins of the whole world.

> **My dear children, I write this to you so that you will not sin. But if anybody does sin, we have one who speaks to the Father in our defense—Jesus Christ, the Righteous One. He is the atoning sacrifice for our sins, and not only for ours but also for the sins of the whole world. (1 John 2:1-2)**

2 (1:30-31) **Jesus Christ, Preeminent**: Jesus Christ is the Preeminent One, the *One before all*. Note what John said.

1. John said that Christ "was before me"; that is, He existed before me. He was the Preexistent One, the Eternal God (see note—Jn.1:15 for discussion).

2. John did not know who the Messiah would be, only that the Messiah was to come. Note that John knew Jesus personally; they were cousins (Lk.1:36). However, John did not know that his cousin, Jesus, was to be the Messiah. Note another fact: how faithful John was! He was a man of strong faith. He had never seen the Messiah, yet he went about his mission of preaching and baptizing. He acted on God's Word and on God's Word alone, believing that the Messiah would come.

Thought 1. Christ is the Preeminent One, the Eternal God. Believers must follow the example of John and...

- declare that Christ is before all.
- believe God's promise: the Messiah has come.
- act, and get about their mission of proclaiming Christ.

3 (1:32-33) **Holy Spirit**: Jesus Christ is the Messiah, the One upon whom the Holy Spirit of God remained. Note several facts.

1. This is the "testimony," the strong witness of John.

2. The dove was a sacred bird to the Jews. It was a symbol of peace and gentleness, of purity and innocence; but even more significant, the dove was often identified with the Spirit of God. When the dove descended upon Christ, it symbolized the Spirit of God Himself descending upon Christ. The dove identified Jesus as the Messiah and endued Him with the power of God (see outline and notes—Mk.1:9-10).

3. In the Old Testament the Spirit of God came upon men only on special occasions. He never came and remained upon men. John went out of his way to point out that the Spirit's descent upon Christ was unique: He came down (v.32) and He remained upon Christ (v.32). The Holy Spirit entered the life of Christ once-for-all, permanently and powerfully, in His full manifestation and unlimited power.

Thought 1. When a person is baptized by the Holy Spirit into Christ, the Holy Spirit enters the life of the believer and becomes a permanent experience of the believer.

> **You did not choose me, but I chose you and appointed you to go and bear fruit—fruit that will last. Then the Father will give you whatever you ask in my name. This is my command: Love each other. (John 15:16-17)**
>
> **But I tell you the truth: It is for your good that I am going away. Unless I go away, the Counselor will not come to you;**

but if I go, I will send him to you. (John 16:7)

You, however, are controlled not by the sinful nature but by the Spirit, if the Spirit of God lives in you. And if anyone does not have the Spirit of Christ, he does not belong to Christ. But if Christ is in you, your body is dead because of sin, yet your spirit is alive because of righteousness. (Rom 8:9-10)

For we were all baptized by one Spirit into one body—whether Jews or Greeks, slave or free—and we were all given the one Spirit to drink. (1 Cor 12:13)

4. John repeated, he did not know who the Messiah would be. God's sign to John was the Holy Spirit coming upon the Messiah in the form of a dove.

5. Christ is the One who baptizes believers with the Holy Spirit.

Thought 1. It is the person who receives the Spirit of God that has the presence and care of God looking over his life (see notes—Jn.14:15-26; Jn.16:7-15; DEEPER STUDY # 1—Acts 2:1-4; note—Ro.8:1-17).

4 (1:34) **Jesus Christ, Son of God**: Jesus Christ is the Son of God. (See notes—Jn.1:1-2; 10:30-33; Ph.2:6; 2:7 for more discussion.) What did John mean by "the Son of God"? Note the definite article. Christ is *the* Son, not a son of God. He is...

- the *only* Son
- the *one and only* Son
- the one and only Son who came from the very *side* of God, that is from the deepest part, from the most intimate place, from the most honorable fellowship of God

1. The gospel writers say that Jesus Christ is the Son of God.

Matthew	Mark	Luke	John
1:21	1:1	1:31-32	1:18, 34, 45
2:15	3:11	1:35	3:16-18, 35-36
3:17	13:32	3:38	5:19, 21-23, 25-26
4:3	14:61	4:3, 9	6:40, 42
8:29	15:39	4:41	8:35-36
11:27		8:28	9:35 (cp. 19:7)
14:33		10:22	10:36
14:61		22:70	11:4
16:16			14:13
17:5			17:1
26:63			19:17
27:30, 40, 43, 54			20:31

The gospel writers also say that Jesus Christ constantly claimed that God was His Father, that He was the Son of the Father in a unique sense.

Matthew	Mark	Luke	John
7:21	8:38	2:49	3:35
10:32-33	13:32	9:26	5:17, 19-23, 26, 30, 36-37, 43, 45
11:25-27	14:36	10:21-22	6:27, 32, 37, 39, 42, 44-46, 57, 65
12:50		22:29, 42	8:16, 18-19, 27-29, 38, 49, 54
15:13		23:34, 46	10:15, 17-18, 25, 29-30, 32, 36-38
16:17, 27		24:49	11:41
18:10, 19, 35			12:26-28, 49-50
20:23			14:6-13, 16, 20-21, 26, 23-24, 28, 31
24:36			15:1, 8-10, 15-16, 23-24, 26
25:34			16:3, 10, 15-17, 25-28, 32
26:29, 39, 42, 53			17:1, 5, 11, 24-25
28:19			18:11
			20:17, 21

2. The book of **Acts** says that Jesus Christ is the Son of God.
3:13, 26
8:37
9:20

3. Paul says that Jesus Christ is the Son of God.

Romans	Galatians	Hebrews
1:4, 9	1:16	1:2, 5, 8; 3:6
5:10	2:20	4:14; 5:8
8:3, 29, 32	4:4, 6	6:6; 7:3, 28
		10:29; 11:17

1 Corinthians 1:9; 15:58   **Ephesians** 4:13
2 Corinthians 1:19   **Colossians** 1:13
1 Thessalonians 1:10

Paul also says that God is the Father of our Lord Jesus Christ.
> **Romans** 15:6
> **2 Corinthians** 1:3; 11:31
> **Ephesians** 1:3

4. Peter says that God is the Father of our Lord Jesus Christ.
> **1 Peter** 1:3

5. John, in his Epistles and Revelation, says that Jesus Christ is the Son of God and that God is the Father of our Lord Jesus Christ.

1 John	**2 John**	**Revelation**
1:3, 7	3, 9	2:18, 27
2:22-24		3:5
3:8, 23		
4:9-10, 14-15		
5:5, 9-13, 20		

	G. Jesus the Messiah, the Christ: The Witness of Andrew, 1:35-42	you will see." So they went and saw where he was staying, and spent that day with him. It was about the tenth hour.	invitation: Come
1 Andrew's experience			**3 Andrew's great decision: He went & saw Christ & remained with Christ**[DS1]
a. He stood in the midst of John's preaching	35 The next day John was there again with two of his disciples.	40 Andrew, Simon Peter's brother, was one of the two who heard what John had said and who had followed Jesus.	
b. He heard John proclaim that Jesus was the Lamb of God	36 When he saw Jesus passing by, he said, "Look, the Lamb of God!"	41 The first thing Andrew did was to find his brother Simon and tell him, "We have found the Messiah" (that is, the Christ).	**4 Andrew's first concern: His brother**
c. He followed Jesus	37 When the two disciples heard him say this, they followed Jesus.		**5 Andrew's conviction: Jesus was the Messiah**
2 Andrew's critical hour	38 Turning around, Jesus saw them following and asked, "What do you want?" They said, "Rabbi" (which means Teacher), "where are you staying?"	42 And he brought him to Jesus. Jesus looked at him and said, "You are Simon son of John. You will be called Cephas" (which, when translated, is Peter).	**6 Andrew's fruit: Simon was brought to Jesus & was reaped**
a. Jesus turned: Symbol of initiative			
b. Jesus asked the basic question of life: What do you want?			
c. Jesus extended an	39 "Come," he replied, "and		

DIVISION I

THE WITNESSES TO THE REVELATION OF JESUS CHRIST, 1:1-51

G. Jesus the Messiah, the Christ: The Witness of Andrew, 1:35-42

(1:35-42) **Introduction**: this was Andrew's discovery of Jesus. He discovered that Jesus was the Messiah, the Christ. (See note, Andrew—Mk.3:18 for more discussion.)
1. Andrew's experience (v.35-37).
2. Andrew's critical hour (v.38-39).
3. Andrew's great decision: he came and saw Christ and remained (v.39-40).
4. Andrew's first concern: his brother (v.41).
5. Andrew's conviction: Jesus was the Messiah (v.41).
6. Andrew's fruit: Simon was brought to Jesus and was reaped (v.42).

1 (1:35-37) **Andrew**: there was Andrew's experience. His experience was simple, somewhat like the experience of many who come to Christ.
1. Andrew "stood" where preaching was. Note the words "was there" (v.35). John had been holding his campaign around the Jordan. Andrew, who had an ache for the Word of God, had become interested in what was happening and had attended the meetings, and had at some point became a follower of this preacher of righteousness. The point to see is that Andrew hungered for righteousness; therefore, he availed himself of the opportunity to hear preaching. He stood right in the midst of preaching. He was there to hear the Messiah proclaimed.
2. Andrew "heard him [the preacher] say this." He was listening to the message, not allowing his mind to ramble elsewhere. He was alert and awake; therefore, when the announcement of the Messiah came, he was ready. Note also the message: "Look the Lamb of God." It was the message of the Messiah's sacrificial death (see note—Jn.1:29).
3. Andrew "followed Jesus." The word "followed" (ekolouthesan) is in the Greek aorist tense, meaning a once-for-all act. Andrew was turning to Jesus, *ready* to make a commitment to Him. He wanted to become a disciple of Jesus.

Thought 1. The same three steps must be taken by each of us.

1) A person must *stand* where the Word, Christ Himself, is preached. A person must have a hunger that drives him to preaching, a hunger that drives him to stay alert and awake to hear the Word proclaimed.
2) A person must *hear* the Word, the announcement: the Lamb of God has come to take away the sin of the world.
3) A person must follow Jesus.

> **When Jesus spoke again to the people, he said, "I am the light of the world. Whoever follows me will never walk in darkness, but will have the light of life." (John 8:12)**
>
> **My sheep listen to my voice; I know them, and they follow me. (John 10:27)**
>
> **Whoever serves me must follow me; and where I am, my servant also will be. My Father will honor the one who serves me. (John 12:26)**
>
> **Let us acknowledge the LORD; let us press on to acknowledge him. As surely as the sun rises, he will appear; he will come to us like the winter rains, like the spring rains that water the earth." (Hosea 6:3)**

Thought 2. Two things will cause a man to miss Christ.
1) Neither *standing* nor being where Christ is preached: standing elsewhere in the world, in self, in the flesh; standing in the midst of those who do not care for Christ nor for the preaching of the Word.
2) Not *hearing*: allowing the mind to wander, being sleepy-eyed, disinterested, distracted, inattentive.

Thought 3. Note several significant facts about John.
1) His message was Christ, the Lamb of God, who takes away the sin of the world.

2) His purpose was to point people, even his own followers, to Christ. He wanted people *to be* where they could receive and grow the most. (How different from so many ministers!)
3) His spirit was filled with enormous humility. He was completely selfless. He pointed His own followers to Christ and encouraged them to follow Him.

> **For you know that it was not with perishable things such as silver or gold that you were redeemed from the empty way of life handed down to you from your forefathers, but with the precious blood of Christ, a lamb without blemish or defect. (1 Pet 1:18-19)**

2 (1:38-39) **Andrew—Seeking Christ—Invitation**: there was Andrew's critical hour. This is a most graphic picture: it shows the *great eagerness* of Jesus to reach men. Jesus longs for men to come to Him, and He longs to reach out to help them in their coming. Note: Jesus was walking some distance away and Andrew and his friend were following behind Jesus. Jesus did three things that demonstrated His great eagerness.

1. Jesus "turned around" to face them. This was a clear demonstration of His open arms, His willingness, and His eagerness for them to join Him. He knew their hearts had just been stirred to reach out to Him and to follow Him, so He immediately snapped around to face them and help them. (Cp. Lk.15:20.)

2. Jesus asked the basic question of life: "What do you want?" He did not ask, *Whom do you want?* but "What do you want?" What are you after? Are you seeking…

- meaning, purpose, and significance in life?
- a religion of self-improvement and human development?
- rules and regulations and laws of righteousness?
- fellowship and companionship?
- deliverance from trials and trouble and suffering?
- approval and acceptance of God?
- blessings from God, His care and provision and security?

Note what Andrew and his friend asked: "Rabbi…where are you staying [pou meneis]?" They had never met Jesus before, yet they called Him Master or Teacher, acknowledging His position as *their* Teacher. They were not asking for a simple conversation by the side of the road. They were asking to join Him in the quiet of His home, to open and pour out their hearts to Him and for Him to become their teacher. They wanted Him to meet the crying need of their hearts and to do such in the quiet confines of His dwelling.

> **God did this so that men would seek him and perhaps reach out for him and find him, though he is not far from each one of us. (Acts 17:27)**
> **But if from there you seek the LORD your God, you will find him if you look for him with all your heart and with all your soul. (Deu 4:29)**
> **Seek the LORD while he may be found; call on him while he is near. (Isa 55:6)**
> **You will seek me and find me when you seek me with all your heart. (Jer 29:13)**

3. Jesus extended the invitation: "Come… and you will see." The invitation was immediate: it was while Andrew and his friend were attracted to Jesus. They were invited to Jesus while they sensed their need. Jesus did not postpone their request nor leave them hanging.

> **"Come to me, all you who are weary and burdened, and I will give you rest. (Mat 11:28)**
> **"Come now, let us reason together," says the LORD. "Though your sins are like scarlet, they shall be as white as snow; though they are red as crimson, they shall be like wool. (Isa 1:18)**
> **"Come, all you who are thirsty, come to the waters; and you who have no money, come, buy and eat! Come, buy wine and milk without money and without cost. (Isa 55:1)**
> **The Spirit and the bride say, "Come!" And let him who hears say, "Come!" Whoever is thirsty, let him come; and whoever wishes, let him take the free gift of the water of life. (Rev 22:17)**

3 (1:39-40) **Decision**: there was Andrew's great decision. He "went and saw" and "remained" with Jesus. There are three significant facts here.

1. Andrew "went" to Jesus. He accepted the invitation. He walked up to Jesus and walked along with Him *in order to* see just where Jesus did dwell.

Thought 1. Note two critical points.
1) Andrew had to accept the invitation.
2) Andrew had to be willing to "see" where Jesus was staying and to let Jesus lead him to where He was staying.

> **For he says, "In the time of my favor I Heard you, and in the day of salvation I helped you." I tell you, now is the time of God's favor, now is the day of salvation. (2 Cor 6:2)**
> **But I pray to you, O LORD, in the time Of your favor; in your great love, O God, Answer me with your sure salvation. (Psa 69:13)**

2. The word "saw" (opsesthe) was a promise: "you will see." Jesus was talking about much more than just seeing where He lived. He was talking about *seeing* the truth and learning of Him. Andrew was being assured, if he would come, that he would most definitely see and learn the truth of life. The Lord guaranteed it. (See note, See—Jn.20:20.)

> **For God, who said, "Let light shine out of darkness," made his light shine in our hearts to give us the light of the knowledge of the glory of God in the face of Christ. (2 Cor 4:6)**
> **I pray also that the eyes of your heart may be enlightened in order that you may know the hope to which he has called you, the riches of his glorious inheritance in the saints, and his incomparably great power for us who believe. That power is like the working of his mighty strength, (Eph 1:18-19)**

But you are a chosen people, a royal priesthood, a holy nation, a people belonging to God, that you may declare the praises of him who called you out of darkness into his wonderful light. Once you were not a people, but now you are the people of God; once you had not received mercy, but now you have received mercy. (1 Pet 2:9-10)

3. Andrew and his friend "spent that day with him," that is, by Jesus' side, in His presence. They received of Him and He met their needs. Note a significant fact: this confrontation with Jesus changed their lives forever. This is seen in that the very hour is still remembered fifty or more years later (see DEEPER STUDY # 1—Jn.1:39). Andrew and his friend committed their lives to Jesus.

Yet to all who received him, to those who believed in his name, he gave the right to become children of God— (John 1:12)
For, "Everyone who calls on the name of the Lord will be saved." (Rom 10:13)
Then he said to them all: "If anyone would come after me, he must deny himself and take up his cross daily and follow me. (Luke 9:23)

DEEPER STUDY # 1
(1:39) **John the Apostle—Confrontation—Conversion**: Is the hour known by John the Apostle because he was the other unnamed disciple with Andrew? Apparently so. Note how significant the experience with Jesus was. John still remembered the hour some fifty years later (cp. Jn.18:15; 20:3).

---

4 (1:41) **Witnessing—Family**: Andrew's first concern was his brother Peter. The scene was striking. As quickly as he could after discovering Jesus for himself, Andrew rushed to find his own brother, Simon.

1. Andrew had met Jesus personally, and Jesus had met the crying need of his heart. Andrew could not contain the peace and joy; he just had to tell his loved ones immediately. He wanted them also to experience the love and joy and peace of Jesus.

2. Andrew was a great witness, a great personal worker for the Lord. He was always seen bringing someone to Jesus (cp. Jn.6:8; 12:22).

"Come, follow me," Jesus said, "and I will make you fishers of men." (Mat 4:19)
For the Son of Man came to seek and to save what was lost." (Luke 19:10)
Again Jesus said, "Peace be with you! As the Father has sent me, I am sending you." (John 20:21)
Be merciful to those who doubt; snatch others from the fire and save them; to others show mercy, mixed with fear—hating even the clothing stained by corrupted flesh. (Jude 1:22-23)

The fruit of the righteous is a tree of life, and he who wins souls is wise. (Prov 11:30)
Those who are wise will shine like the brightness of the heavens, and those who lead many to righteousness, like the stars for ever and ever. (Dan 12:3)

5 (1:41) **Messiah—Witnessing**: there was Andrew's conviction, "We have found the Messiah." (For the meaning of the word "Messiah," see DEEPER STUDY # 2, Christ—Jn.1:20.)

6 (1:42) **Witnessing**: Andrew's fruit, Simon, was reached for Jesus and reaped. Andrew saw his brother Simon come to Jesus.

1. Note the word "looked" (emblepsas). It means to look upon with an intense, earnest look, to concentrate, to stare and gaze upon. Jesus looked into the innermost being of Peter.

2. Note the words, "You will be called." They refer to the future. Simon's name would be changed to Cephas. This was a prediction that he would be converted and changed from a self-centered, defensive, overbearing, and carnal man into a strong, solid, immovable and unbreakable rock for God.

Thought 1. Note two significant facts.
1) Jesus "looks at" a man: studies and knows him intimately. This is both a comfort and a warning, depending upon man's response.

He did not need man's testimony about man, for he knew what was in a man. (John 2:25)
There is nothing concealed that will not be disclosed, or hidden that will not be made known. (Luke 12:2)
Can anyone hide in secret places so that I cannot see him?" declares the LORD. "Do not I fill heaven and earth?" declares the LORD. (Jer 23:24)

2) Jesus sees the potential within a man and longs to change that man to make him everything he can become.

Therefore, if anyone is in Christ, he is a new creation; the old has gone, the new has come! (2 Cor 5:17; cp. Eph.4:24)
As for you, you were dead in your transgressions and sins, (Eph 2:1)
For you have been born again, not of perishable seed, but of imperishable, through the living and enduring word of God. (1 Pet 1:23)
I will give you a new heart and put a new spirit in you; I will remove from you your heart of stone and give you a heart of flesh. (Ezek 36:26)

1 Philip's experience a. He was sought by Jesus personally b. He was called by Jesus personally[DS1]	H. Jesus the One Prophesied: The Witness of Philip, 1:43-45 43 The next day Jesus decided to leave for Galilee. Finding Philip, he said to him, "Follow me." 44 Philip, like Andrew and	Peter, was from the town of Bethsaida. 45 Philip found Nathanael and told him, "We have found the one Moses wrote about in the Law, and about whom the prophets also wrote—Jesus of Nazareth, the son of Joseph."	c. The reason: Philip knew Andrew & Peter[DS2] 2 Philip's first concern: Nathanael 3 Philip's conviction: Jesus was the One prophesied[DS3]

DIVISION I

THE WITNESSES TO THE REVELATION OF JESUS CHRIST, 1:1-51

H. Jesus the One Prophesied: The Witness of Philip, 1:43-45

(1:43-45) **Introduction**: Philip's discovery and witness of Jesus Christ was unmistakable. Jesus was the One prophesied in Scripture; He was the promised Messiah.

1. Philip's experience (v.43-44).
2. Philip's first concern: Nathanael (v.45).
3. Philip's conviction: Jesus was the One prophesied (v.45).

1 (1:43-44) **Salvation—Discipleship—Jesus Christ, Seeking Man**: Philip's experience involved three significant points.

1. Jesus Himself went forth and sought Philip—Philip was not seeking Jesus. The initiative came from Jesus entirely. Jesus made the move to find and save Philip and to enlist Philip in His mission.

a. Jesus travelled a long distance to find Philip. Galilee was a long distance away, and note: the stated purpose for Jesus' going to Galilee was to find Philip. This is a picture of how far Christ will go to reach a soul. In order to reach a man, Christ will go any distance…

- to any sin, no matter how terrible or awful. He will prick and prick at the mind and heart of a person.
- to any place, no matter how hidden or shameful. He will send a thought or memory or person of righteousness to remind and warn a person.
- to any condition, no matter how hopeless or helpless. He will see that the message of hope and help crosses a person's path.
- to any person, no matter how shameful or guilty. He will see that a person hears the word of salvation if he repents and hears the word of judgment if he does not repent.

Christ will go any distance to reach people. He will go to any place, to any condition, to any person. He will see that every person has some chance of turning to God. The word of deliverance can come from any number of sources: another person, a thought, a stirring of conscience, a memory, a writing, or just through seeing nature (Ro.1:20). Christ seeks every person, and He will go any distance to reach him, no matter the difficulty.

Thought 1. Every person must heed the *seeking* of Christ when His seeking is sensed. A person must respond immediately, for God's Spirit does not always strive or contend with man. When we first feel the pull to make a decision for Christ, if we put the decision off for an hour or two, the pull fades and eventually leaves us completely. God's Spirit does not continue to strive or contend with us.

> **Then the LORD said, "My Spirit will not contend with man forever, for he is mortal; his days will be a hundred and twenty years." (Gen 6:3)**
> **A man who remains stiff-necked after many rebukes will suddenly be destroyed—without remedy. (Prov 29:1)**

Thought 2. Every believer should be willing to go any distance to reach people, no matter how far or how deeply depraved the person may be. Too many in the world are considered and treated as *untouchable*: the alcoholic, immoral, poor, prisoner, lowly, diseased.

> **But you will receive power when the Holy Spirit comes on you; and you will be my witnesses in Jerusalem, and in all Judea and Samaria, and to the ends of the earth." (Acts 1:8)**
> **For I was hungry and you gave me something to eat, I was thirsty and you gave me something to drink, I was a stranger and you invited me in, (Mat 25:35)**
> **I needed clothes and you clothed me, I was sick and you looked after me, I was in prison and you came to visit me.' (Mat 25:36).** (Remember that the person in *prison* is guilty of the most serious offenses and sins.)

b. Jesus is seen fulfilling His mission in seeking and saving Philip. He came into the world for the very purpose of seeking and saving the lost.

> **For the Son of Man came to seek and to save what was lost." (Luke 19:10)**
> **The thief comes only to steal and kill and destroy; I have come that they may have life, and have it to the full. (John 10:10)**
> **"You are a king, then!" said Pilate. Jesus answered, "You are right in saying I am a king. In fact, for this reason I was born, and for this I came into the world, to testify to the truth. Everyone on the side of truth listens to me." (John 18:37)**
> **Here is a trustworthy saying that deserves full acceptance: Christ Jesus came**

into the world to save sinners—of whom I am the worst. (1 Tim 1:15)

2. Jesus Himself called Philip. He called Philip to "follow Him" (see DEEPER STUDY # 1—Jn.1:43; DEEPER STUDY # 1—Lk.9:23).

> Then he said to them all: "If anyone would come after me, he must deny himself and take up his cross daily and follow me. (Luke 9:23)
> My sheep listen to my voice; I know them, and they follow me. (John 10:27)
> Whoever serves me must follow me; and where I am, my servant also will be. My Father will honor the one who serves me. (John 12:26)

3. The reason Philip was called by Jesus is apparently the reason verse 44 is mentioned. He was from the same town as Andrew and Peter. Philip longed for deliverance; he ached for the Messiah (cp. "We have found the one... v.45). Therefore, he had sought the company of those who were like-minded. He wanted the fellowship of those who sought for godly deliverance. In search for such people he had met Andrew and Peter and had apparently become friends of theirs for some time. Therefore, it was only natural for Andrew and Peter to suggest that Jesus seek out Philip to become a disciple. The point is this: Philip was called by Jesus because...

- he had done something about the longing and aching for deliverance within his soul.
- he had sought the fellowship of those who were seeking for God's salvation.
- he had placed himself where the message would reach him when it came.

> Blessed are those who hunger and thirst for righteousness, for they will be filled. (Mat 5:6)
> Blessed are you who hunger now, for you will be satisfied. Blessed are you who weep now, for you will laugh. (Luke 6:21)
> On the last and greatest day of the Feast, Jesus stood and said in a loud voice, "If anyone is thirsty, let him come to me and drink. (John 7:37)
> For he satisfies the thirsty and fills the hungry with good things. (Psa 107:9)
> "Come, all you who are thirsty, come to the waters; and you who have no money, come, buy and eat! Come, buy wine and milk without money and without cost. (Isa 55:1)

DEEPER STUDY # 1

(1:43) **Follow** (akolouthei): to become a close companion, a close follower, a disciple. Two significant ideas are in the word: union and likeness, or cleaving and conformity. To follow Christ means...
- to cleave, to be united to Him, to be in close union with Him.
- to become like Him, to be conformed to Him.

DEEPER STUDY # 2

(1:44) **Bethsaida**: Jesus carried on a large ministry in Bethsaida, but the gospels tell us nothing about the city itself. The city was denounced by Jesus because of its rejec-

tion of Him (Mt.11:21; Lk.10:13). (Cp. Mk.6:45; 8:22; Lk.9:10; Jn.12:21 for other references to the city.)

2 (1:45) **Witnessing**: Philip's first concern was to reach his friend Nathanael. Philip "found" Nathanael. Jesus had challenged Philip to "follow" Him, to become just like Him, and Philip did. He went out and did exactly what Jesus had done to him. Jesus had sought and found Him. Now, following the example of his Lord, He went out and found his friend Nathanael. Philip became a personal soul-winner just like his Lord.

> Again Jesus said, "Peace be with you! As the Father has sent me, I am sending you." (John 20:21)
> And the things you have heard me say in the presence of many witnesses entrust to reliable men who will also be qualified to teach others. (2 Tim 2:2)
> For we cannot help speaking about what we have seen and heard." (Acts 4:20)
> You will be his witness to all men of what you have seen and heard. (Acts 22:15)
> It is written: "I believed; therefore I have spoken." With that same spirit of faith we also believe and therefore speak, (2 Cor 4:13)

3 (1:45) **Conviction—Decision**: Philip's conviction—the One prophesied was Jesus Christ. "We have found the one Moses wrote about in the Law and about whom the Prophets also wrote—Jesus of Nazereth, the son of Joseph." Note four points.

1. Philip was extremely joyful. "We have found the One." There was jubilation, excitement, and rejoicing beating in the chest of Philip. Jesus had met the needs and craving of his heart.

> I have told you this so that my joy may be in you and that your joy may be complete. (John 15:11)
> Until now you have not asked for anything in my name. Ask and you will receive, and your joy will be complete. (John 16:24)
> For the kingdom of God is not a matter of eating and drinking, but of righteousness, peace and joy in the Holy Spirit, (Rom 14:17)
> You have made known to me the path of life; you will fill me with joy in your presence, with eternal pleasures at your right hand. (Psa 16:11)
> With joy you will draw water from the wells of salvation. (Isa 12:3)

2. God's eternal plan for man and his world is recorded in Scripture. It is there for man's direction.

> You diligently study the Scriptures because you think that by them you possess eternal life. These are the Scriptures that testify about me, (John 5:39)
> All Scripture is God-breathed and is useful for teaching, rebuking, correcting and training in righteousness, (2 Tim 3:16)

3. Philip and Nathanael knew the Scripture. They were familiar with the prophecies of the promised Messiah.

**Do your best to present yourself to God as one approved, a workman who does not need to be ashamed and who correctly handles the word of truth. (2 Tim 2:15)
Like newborn babies, crave pure spiri-** tual milk, so that by it you may grow up in your salvation, (1 Pet 2:2)
Now that you have tasted that the Lord is good. (1 Pet 2:3)

4. Jesus of Nazareth was definitely identified as the Messiah. (See DEEPER STUDY # 3—Jn.1:45.)

DEEPER STUDY # 3
(1:45) Scripture, Fulfilled—Prophecy, Fulfilled:

OLD TESTAMENT PROPHECIES OF JESUS AND THEIR FULFILLMENT IN THE NEW TESTAMENT

Prophecies		Fulfillment
Gen.3:15	The Promised Seed of a Woman	Gal.4:4; Lk.2:7; Rev.12:5
Gen.12:3; 18:18; 22:18	The Promised Seed of Abraham	Acts 3:25; Gal.3:8 (Mt.1:1; Lk.3:34)
Gen.17:19; 22:16-17	The Promised Seed of Isaac	Mt.1:2; Lk.1:55, 72-74
Gen.28:14 (Num.24:17)	The Promised Seed of Jacob	Lk.3:34 (Mt.1:2)
Gen.49:10ᵃ	Will Spring From The Royal Tribe of Judah	Lk.3:33; Heb.7:14
Dt.18:15, 18	Will Be a Prophet	John 6:14; Acts 3:22-23
2 Sam.7:13ᵇ (2 Sam.7:13; Is.9:1, 7; 11:1-5)	Will be the Eternal Heir to David's Throne	Mt.1:1 (Mt.1:6; Lk.1:32-33)
2 Sam.7:14ᵃ	Will be God's Son	Mk.1:1
Is.35:6; 61:1-2 (cp.Ps.72:2; 146:8; Zech.11:11)	Will Meet the Desperate Needs of Men	Mt.11:4-6
Job 17:3	Will Ransom, Secure Men	Eph.1:7 (1 Jn.2:1-2)
Ps.2:1-2	Will Be Rejected By the Nations	Lk.23:36ᵃ, 38
Ps.2:7	The Son of God	Acts 13:33; Heb.1:5; 5:5
Ps.8:2	Is to Be Praised	Mt.21:16
Ps.16:8-11	Will Be Resurrected	Acts 13:34-35; 2:25-28, 31 (Mt.28:1-2; Mk.16:6, 12, 14; Lk.24:1-53)
Ps.22:1	Will be Forsaken by God	Mt.27:46; Mk.15:34
Ps.22:7	People Will Shake Their Heads at the Cross	Mt.27:39
Ps.22:18	Clothes Gambled For	Mt.27:35; Mk.15:24; Lk.23:34; Jn.19:24
Ps.22:22	To Secure Many Brothers	Heb.2:12
Ps.31:5	Commends His Spirit to God	Lk.23:46
Ps.40:6-8	Fulfills God's Will	Heb.10:5-7
Ps.41:9	Is Betrayed by Judas	Jn.13:18; Acts 1:16
Ps.45:6, 7	Is Eternal & Preeminent	Heb.1:8, 9
Ps.68:18	Will Lead Captives in His Train	Eph.4:8-10
Ps.69:21	Offered Drugs on the Cross	Mt.27:48; Mk.15:36; Lk.23:36; Jn.19:28, 29
Ps.69:25; 109:8	Judas' Fate	Acts 1:20
Ps.89:26-27	Exaltation	Ph.2:9 (cp. Rev.11:15)
Ps.95:7-11	Hearts Hardened Against	Heb.3:7-11; 4:3, 5-7
Ps.102:25-27	Is Creator & is Eternal	Heb.1:10-12
Ps.110:1	To Be Exalted	Mt.22:44; Mk.12:36; Lk.20:42; Acts 2:34, 35; Heb.1:13
Ps.110:4	The High Priest	Heb.5:6
Ps.118:22, 23	The Stone	Mt.21:42; Mk.12:10; Lk.20:17; Acts 4:11
Ps.118:25, 26	The Triumphal Entry	Mt.21:9; Mk.11:9; Jn.12:13
Ps.132:11, 17	The Son of David	Lk.1:69; Acts 2:30
Is.7:14	The Virgin Birth	Mt.1:23
Is.9:1, 2	A Light to Those in Darkness	Mt.4:15, 16
Is.11:2	The Spirit Rests Upon in a Special Way	Lk.4:18-21 (cp. Mt.12:18; Jn.3:34)
Is.11:10	To Save the Gentiles (Nations)	Ro.15:12
Is.25:8	To Conquer Death	1 Cor.15:54
Is.28:16	The Stone	Ro.9:33; 1 Pt.2:6
Is.40:3-5	To Have a Forerunner	Mt.3:3; Mk.1:3; Lk.3:4-6
Is.42:1-4	To Minister to the Gentiles (Nations)	Mt.12:17-21

Prophecies (continued)		**Fulfillment** (continued)
Is.49:6	A Light to the Gentiles	Lk.2:32; Acts 13:47, 48; 26:23
Is.53:1	Would Not be Believed	Jn.12:38; Ro.10:16
Is.53:3-6	To Die and Arise	Acts 26:22, 23
Is.53:4-6, 11	To Die for Man's Sins	1 Pt.2:24, 25
Is.53:4	To Heal & Bear Man's Sickness	Mt.8:17
Is.53:9	To Be Sinless	1 Pt.2:22
Is.53:12	To Be Counted a Sinner	Mk.15:28; Lk.22:37
Is.54:13	To Teach as God	Jn.6:45
Is.55:3	To Be Raised	Acts 13:34
Is.59:20, 21	To Save Israel	Ro.11:26, 27
Jer.31:31-34	To Make a New Covenant with Man	Heb.8:8-12; 10:16, 17
Hos.1:10-11	To Bring About the Restoration of Israel	Ro.11:1-36
Hos.1:10	The Conversion of the Gentiles	Ro.9:26
Hos.2:23	The Conversion of the Gentiles	Ro.9:25; 1 Pt.2:10
Joel 2:28-32	The Promise of the Spirit	Acts 2:16-21
Amos 9:11, 12	The Lord's Return & David's Kingdom Reestablished	Acts 15:16, 17
Mic.5:2	The Birthplace of Messiah	Mt.2:5, 6; Jn.7:42
Hab.1:5	The Jews' Unbelief	Acts 13:40, 41
Hag.2:6	The Return of Christ	Heb.12:26
Zech.9:9	The Triumphal Entry	Mt.21:4, 5; Jn.12:14, 15
Zech.11:13	Judas' Betrayal	Mt.27:9, 10
Zech.12:10	The Spear Pierced in Side	Jn.19:37
Zech.13:7	The Scattering of the Disciples at the Cross	Mt.26:31, 56; Mk.14:27, 50
Mal.3:1	The Forerunner, John the Baptist	Mt.11:10; Mk.1:2; Lk.7:27
Mal.4:5, 6	The Forerunner, John the Baptist	Mt.11:13, 14; 17:10-13; Mk.9:11-13; Lk.1:16, 17

	I. Jesus the Son of God, The King of Israel: The Witness of Nathanael,[DS1] 1:46-49	of him, "Here is a true Israelite, in whom there is nothing false." 48 "How do you know me?" Nathanael asked. Jesus answered, "I saw you while you were still under the fig tree before Philip called you."	a. Jesus knew him: His beliefs & character b. Jesus knew his innermost being—all things about him[DS3]
1 Nathanael's experience[DS2] a. A man of despair & prejudice b. Invited to follow Jesus despite prejudice 2 Nathanael's confrontation with Jesus	46 "Nazareth! Can anything good come from there?" Nathanael asked. "Come and see," said Philip. 47 When Jesus saw Nathanael approaching, he said	49 Then Nathanael declared, "Rabbi, you are the Son of God; you are the King of Israel."	3 Nathanael's conviction: Jesus was the Son of God[DS4]

DIVISION I

THE WITNESSES TO THE REVELATION OF JESUS CHRIST, 1:1-51

I. Jesus the Son of God, the King of Israel: The Witness of Nathanael, 1:46-49

(1:46-49) Introduction: Nathanael's confrontation with Jesus was dramatic. Nathanael was a man of prejudice and strong feelings, yet he knew despair and hopelessness; therefore, he was difficult to lead to Christ. However, despite all, his friend Philip persisted and refused to give up in witnessing to him. As a result, Nathanael was won to Christ.

1. Nathanael's experience (v.46).
2. Nathanael's confrontation with Jesus (v.47-48).
3. Nathanael's conviction: Jesus was the Son of God (v.49).

DEEPER STUDY # 1

(1:46-49) **Nathanael**: John alone mentions Nathanael. However, the other three gospels mention a disciple that John does not, Bartholomew. These two names probably refer to the same person. It is thought that Nathanael was a man's first name and Bartholomew was a man's second name.

1 (1:46) **Nathanael—Prejudice—Witnessing**: Nathanael's experience. Note three facts.

1. It was Nathanael's close friend Philip who shared the good news with him (cp. Jn.1:45). He had the privilege of hearing the gospel from someone who cared for him very deeply. He was so loved by Philip that he was the first one with whom Philip shared the most important experience of his life.
2. Nathanael was a man gripped by despair and prejudice.

   a. The despair is seen in his response to Philip. He rejected Philip's testimony and did it in a negative, skeptical, reactionary spirit: "Nazareth! Can anything good come from there?" He struck out at what Philip had said. He questioned it; he would not accept it nor believe it. There was a sense of hopelessness, of despair and skepticism in his question. Apparently he was a man who had tried and followed so many voices in the world that he had just lost hope. Many in the world had promised so much, only to leave him still empty and searching. Why should he believe and follow another voice?

   Thought 1. So many voices in the world promise the path to life and fulfillment and joy and satisfaction. However, their claims are soon discovered to be false, and they still leave the human heart empty and

wondering. A person caught up in despair wonders about the real purpose, meaning, and significance of life.

> "I loathe my very life; therefore I will give free rein to my complaint and speak out in the bitterness of my soul. (Job 10:1)
>
> My life is consumed by anguish and my years by groaning; my strength fails because of my affliction, and my bones grow weak. (Psa 31:10)
>
> My God. My soul is downcast within me; therefore I will remember you from the land of the Jordan, the heights of Hermon—from Mount Mizar. (Psa 42:6)
>
> But as for me, my feet had almost slipped; I had nearly lost my foothold. (Psa 73:2)
>
> When I tried to understand all this, it was oppressive to me (Psa 73:16)
>
> By the rivers of Babylon we sat and wept when we remembered Zion. (Psa 137:1)
>
> But Zion said, "The LORD has forsaken me, the Lord has forgotten me." (Isa 49:14)
>
> Do not run until your feet are bare and your throat is dry. But you said, 'It's no use! I love foreign gods, and I must go after them.' (Jer 2:25)
>
> Brothers, we do not want you to be ignorant about those who fall asleep, or to grieve like the rest of men, who have no hope. (1 Th 4:13)
>
> Remember that at that time you were separate from Christ, excluded from citizenship in Israel and foreigners to the covenants of the promise, without hope and without God in the world. (Eph 2:12)

   b. The prejudice of Nathanael is seen in his slur against Jesus because Jesus was from Nazareth (see DEEPER STUDY # 2, Nazareth—Jn.1:46). Nathanael was apparently a crowd follower. He had allowed himself to be influenced by the world's foolish prejudices.

   Thought 1. Prejudice has a great failing; it disregards the wrong within oneself and with one's own place (city, home, business, church); it overlooks personal wrong, shortcomings, weaknesses, and error.

> Then Peter began to speak: "I now realize how true it is that God does not show favoritism but accepts men from every nation who fear him and do what is right. (Acts 10:34-35)
> For God does not show favoritism. (Rom 2:11)
> For there is no difference between Jew and Gentile—the same Lord is Lord of all and richly blesses all who call on him, (Rom 10:12)

3. Nathanael was still invited to follow Jesus. His sin, despair, and prejudice did not discourage nor keep Philip from inviting his friend and neighbor to "come and see" Jesus. Note also that Philip did not argue with Nathanael. He simply confronted him with Jesus.

Thought 1. Note three things.
1) No matter what the sin is, we must still go and invite men to "come and see" Jesus. Because Philip went to his dear friend, Nathanael did come to Jesus, despite his despair and prejudice.
2) Think what Nathanael would have missed if he had...
   • let his prejudice against the people of Nazareth keep him from the One who was called Jesus the Nazarene.
   • let his wallowing around in despair keep him from coming to Jesus.
3) The way to lead a man to Christ is not by argument, but by confronting him with Christ.

> For we cannot help speaking about what we have seen and heard." (Acts 4:20)
> These, then, are the things you should teach. Encourage and rebuke with all authority. Do not let anyone despise you. (Titus 2:15)
> Come and listen, all you who fear God; let me tell you what he has done for me. (Psa 66:16)

DEEPER STUDY # 2
(1:46) **Nazareth**: the town was an obscure village in Galilee. Galilee bordered Gentile or heathen nations; therefore, it was sometimes called *Galilee of the Gentiles*. The Jews were so deeply prejudiced against the Gentiles that they considered anyone or anything touched by a Gentile to be unclean in the sight of God. Nazareth was despised by the Jews because it was on the border of Gentile country and was so commercially touched by Gentiles. It was despised by the Romans because its citizens were a conquered people. (See note, pt.2—Mt.13:53-58 for more discussion.)

2 (1:47-48) **Guilelessness—Nothing False—Jesus Christ, Knowledge—Sin, Exposed**: Nathanael's confrontation. Two very significant things happened in Nathanael's confrontation with Jesus.
1. Jesus knew Nathanael, his beliefs and character.
   a. Jesus knew his beliefs. This is seen in Jesus' calling Nathanael "a true Israelite." He was the epitomy of an Israelite, everything an Israelite should be. He *believed* the promises of God. He tried to live up to the covenant name, the standard

God had set for Israel, and he was looking for that blessed hope and glorious appearing of the Messiah. Jesus Christ knew Nathanael's beliefs.

Thought 1. Christ knows the beliefs of each man, that upon which the man has set his heart. He knows both the good and bad beliefs, both the godly and evil thoughts of the human heart.

> He did not need man's testimony about man, for he knew what was in a man. (John 2:25)
> It is because of him that you are in Christ Jesus, who has become for us wisdom from God—that is, our righteousness, holiness and redemption. (1 Cor 1:30)
> Whenever our hearts condemn us. For God is greater than our hearts, and he knows everything. (1 John 3:20)
> "Do not keep talking so proudly or let your mouth speak such arrogance, for the LORD is a God who knows, and by him deeds are weighed. (1 Sam 2:3)
> You know my folly, O God; my guilt is not hidden from you. (Psa 69:5)
> "I the LORD search the heart and examine the mind, to reward a man according to his conduct, according to what his deeds deserve." (Jer 17:10)

b. Jesus knew his character. Nathanael was a man "in whom there [was] nothing false" (dolos). This means he did not deceive, bait, or mislead people. He did not hide what he thought; he said what he thought and acted what he felt. He was straightforward, open and honest, not deceptive or hypocritical. This trait had just been demonstrated in his response to Philip. He would not hide his true thoughts (v.46).

Thought 1. One of the great tragedies in the legacy of persons is that they are full of guile or false traits. Many deceive, bait, and mislead others. Few are straightforward, open and honest, free of deception and hypocrisy.

> Blessed are the pure in heart, for they will see God. (Mat 5:8)
> So then, dear friends, since you are looking forward to this, make every effort to be found spotless, blameless and at peace with him. (2 Pet 3:14)
> No lie was found in their mouths; they are blameless. (Rev 14:5)
> Blessed is the man whose sin the LORD does not count against him and in whose spirit is no deceit. (Psa 32:2)
> Who may ascend the hill of the LORD? Who may stand in his holy place? He who has clean hands and a pure heart, who does not lift up his soul to an idol or swear by what is false. (Psa 24:3-4)

2. Jesus knew Nathanael's innermost being, all things about him (see DEEPER STUDY # 3—Jn.1:48).

Thought 1. Jesus knows everything about every man. Nothing escapes His watchful eye, not even a single thought.

1) This offers great hope to the man who will cast himself upon Christ. Christ can help him by meeting his need and giving purpose and direction to his life.
2) This is a great warning to the man who goes his merry way, thinking his sin is hid and will not be judged.

> There is nothing concealed that will not be disclosed, or hidden that will not be made known. (Luke 12:2)
>
> Therefore judge nothing before the appointed time; wait till the Lord comes. He will bring to light what is hidden in darkness and will expose the motives of men's hearts. At that time each will receive his praise from God. (1 Cor 4:5)
>
> If I sinned, you would be watching me and would not let my offense go unpunished. (Job 10:14)
>
> Although you wash yourself with soda and use an abundance of soap, the stain of your guilt is still before me," declares the Sovereign LORD. (Jer 2:22)
>
> My eyes are on all their ways; they are not hidden from me, nor is their sin concealed from my eyes. (Jer 16:17)
>
> But they do not realize that I remember all their evil deeds. Their sins engulf them; they are always before me. (Hosea 7:2)
>
> For I know how many are your offenses and how great your sins. You oppress the righteous and take bribes and you deprive the poor of justice in the courts. (Amos 5:12)

DEEPER STUDY # 3
(1:48) **Fig Tree—Worship**: in Palestine the fig tree stood for peace, security, rest, and worship (cp. 1 Ki.4:25; Mic.4:4). Very often a man would seek solitude and worship under his fig tree. No doubt this is what Nathanael had been doing. When Jesus told Nathanael that He had seen him under his fig tree, He was telling Nathanael that He knew everything about him, even the deepest longings of his heart. Jesus knew Nathanael's despair and sense of hopelessness; He knew his longing for peace and release and freedom. That was enough to cause Nathanael to give his life to Jesus forever.

3 (1:49) **Confession—Decision**: Nathanael's conviction. He confessed that Jesus was the Rabbi (Prophet), the Son of God, the King of Israel. Note two things.

1. How readily Nathanael confessed Jesus as His Lord.

> "Whoever acknowledges me before men, I will also acknowledge him before my Father in heaven. (Mat 10:32)
>
> "I tell you, whoever acknowledges me before men, the Son of Man will also acknowledge him before the angels of God. (Luke 12:8)
>
> That if you confess with your mouth, "Jesus is Lord," and believe in your heart that God raised him from the dead, you will be saved. (Rom 10:9)
>
> No one who denies the Son has the Father; whoever acknowledges the Son has the Father also. (1 John 2:23)
>
> If anyone acknowledges that Jesus is the Son of God, God lives in him and he in God. (1 John 4:15)

2. How clearly Nathanael grasped who Jesus was.
   a. He was "Rabbi," the great Teacher or Prophet promised to Israel (see note—Lk.3:38 for discussion).
   b. He was the Son of God (see notes—Jn.1:1-2; 1:34 for discussion).
   c. He was the King of Israel (see DEEPER STUDY # 4—Jn.1:49 for discussion).

DEEPER STUDY # 4
(1:49) **Jesus Christ, King of Israel**: Jesus was declared to be the Messianic King. God had given to David and his seed (the Messiah) the promise of eternal government (2 Sam.7:12; Ps.39:3f; 132:11).

Note how often Jesus was called the son of David. (Cp. Mt.12:23; 15:22; 20:30-31; 21:9, 15; Acts 2:29-36; Ro.1:3; 2 Tim.2:8; Rev.22:16.) It was the common title and popular concept of the Messiah. Generation after generation of Jews had ached and looked for the promised deliverer of Israel. The people expected Him to be a great general who would deliver and restore the nation to its greatness. In fact, they expected Him to make the nation the center of universal rule. He would, under God, conquer the world and center the glory and majesty of God Himself in Jerusalem; and from His throne, the throne of David, He would execute *the Messianic fire of judgment* upon the nations and peoples of the world (see DEEPER STUDY # 2—Mt.1:18; DEEPER STUDY # 2—3:11; notes—11:1-6; 11:2-3; DEEPER STUDY # 1—11:5; DEEPER STUDY # 2—11:6; note—Lk.7:21. Referring to these notes will show what the Jewish concept of the Messiah was.) (See note, Jesus, Davidic Heir—Lk.3:24-31 for more discussion.)

	J. Jesus the Son of Man, God's Mediator: The Witness of Jesus Himself, 1:50-51	under the fig tree. You shall see greater things than that." 51 He then added, "I tell you the truth, you shall see heaven open, and the angels of God ascending and descending on the Son of Man."	2 The revelation of God, the One who reveals greater things
			3 The Mediator
1 Nathanael's experience (v.46-49)	50 Jesus said, "You believe because I told you I saw you		4 The Son of Man

DIVISION I

THE WITNESSES TO THE REVELATION OF JESUS CHRIST, 1:1-51

J. Jesus the Son of Man, God's Mediator: The Witness of Jesus Himself, 1:50-51

(1:50-51) **Introduction**: Jesus bore witness to Himself. He clearly declared who He was.
1. Nathanael's experience (v.46-49).
2. The revelation of God, the One who reveals greater things (v.50).
3. The Mediator (v.51).
4. The Son of Man (v.51).

1 (1:50) **Nathanael**: Nathanael's experience with Jesus is the background for what Jesus said in this passage.

2 (1:50) **Jesus Christ, Revelation of God**: Jesus Christ is the Revelation of God, the One who reveals greater things. Note two points.
1. It was belief in Jesus that brought "greater things" into Nathanael's life. Nathanael believed Jesus; therefore, he could expect to receive greater things, to receive more and more from God.

> He replied, "Because you have so little faith. I tell you the truth, if you have faith as small as a mustard seed, you can say to this mountain, 'Move from here to there' and it will move. Nothing will be impossible for you." (Mat 17:20)
> "'If you can'?" said Jesus. "Everything is possible for him who believes." (Mark 9:23)
> The thief comes only to steal and kill and destroy; I have come that they may have life, and have it to the full. (John 10:10)
> Oh, the depth of the riches of the wisdom and knowledge of God! How unsearchable his judgments, and his paths beyond tracing out! (Rom 11:33)
> However, as it is written: "No eye has seen, no ear has heard, no mind has conceived what God has prepared for those who love him"— (1 Cor 2:9)
> So that Christ may dwell in your hearts through faith. And I pray that you, being rooted and established in love, may have power, together with all the saints, to grasp how wide and long and high and deep is the love of Christ, and to know this love that surpasses knowledge--that you may be filled to the measure of all the fullness of God. (Eph 3:17-19)

2. It is Jesus Himself who is the Revelation of God; therefore, it is Jesus who reveals the "greater things" of life. (See note—Jn.14:6 for more discussion.)
   a. Jesus Christ is the Embodiment of Revelation.

> In the beginning was the Word, and the Word was with God, and the Word was God. He was with God in the beginning. (John 1:1-2)
> Jesus answered, "I am the way and the truth and the life. No one comes to the Father except through me. (John 14:6)
> For in Christ all the fullness of the Deity lives in bodily form, (Col 2:9)

   b. Jesus Christ is the Communicator of Revelation.

> In him was life, and that life was the light of men. (John 1:4;cp. Jn1:1-3)
> The Word became flesh and made his dwelling among us. We have seen his glory, the glory of the One and Only, who came from the Father, full of grace and truth. (John 1:14)
> Jesus answered: "Don't you know me, Philip, even after I have been among you such a long time? Anyone who has seen me has seen the Father. How can you say, 'Show us the Father'? Don't you believe that I am in the Father, and that the Father is in me? The words I say to you are not just my own. Rather, it is the Father, living in me, who is doing his work. (John 14:9-10)

   c. Jesus Christ is the Liberator of Revelation.

> To the Jews who had believed him, Jesus said, "If you hold to my teaching, you are really my disciples. Then you will know the truth, and the truth will set you free." (John 8:31-32)
> The thief comes only to steal and kill and destroy; I have come that they may have life, and have it to the full. (John 10:10)

3 (1:51) **Jesus Christ, Mediator**: Jesus Christ is the Mediator between God and man. This is seen in the picture Jesus painted by the words, "You shall see heaven open, and the angels of God ascending and descending on the Son of Man" (v.51).

This is a picture of Jacob's ladder (Gen.28:10-22). It is a picture of open access into the very presence of God: the door of heaven is open and the angels are *ascending from earth* to heaven. Jesus was saying...

- He is Jacob's ladder; the ladder is a symbol of Him. He is the One who opens heaven.
- He is the One who reaches *from earth* to heaven, the One by whom man has his communication carried up into heaven.

Thought 1. Three critical facts should be noted.

1) A man *can* approach God and enter heaven through Christ (Jn.14:6). The gulf, the loneliness, and the alienation which man knows have been bridged.
2) A man has access to God *only* through Christ (Jn.14:6).
3) A man can have *constant* communication with God. The picture is that of angels' carrying messages from earth to heaven and back to earth again.

4 (1:51) **Jesus Christ, Son of Man**: Jesus Christ is the Son of Man. This does not mean that Jesus was born of a man. It means that He is more than what an ordinary man is, more than a son of some man. Jesus is what every man ought to be, *the Son of Man Himself.*

1. Jesus Christ is the Ideal Man: the *Representative Man*, the *Perfect Man*, the *Pattern*, the *Embodiment* of everything a man ought to be (see DEEPER STUDY # 3—Mt.1:16). Jesus Christ is the *perfect picture* of a man. Everything God wants a man to be is seen perfectly in Jesus Christ (cp. Jn.1:14; Col.2:9-10; Heb.1:3).
2. Jesus Christ is the *Ideal Servant* of man. The term *Ideal Servant* stresses Jesus' sympathy for the poor, the broken hearted, the captives, the blind, the bruised, the outcasts, the bereaved (cp. Lk.4:18). Jesus is the pattern, the model, the perfect example of concern and caring. He served other people just like every man ought to serve other people.

Jesus called Himself "the Son of Man" about eighty times. It was His favorite term. The title *Son of Man* is probably based upon the Son of Man in Daniel 7:13-14. There is also a picture of Jesus as the heavenly Son of Man contrasted with Adam as the earthly Man in 1 Cor.15:45-47. Both references picture Jesus as *the Representative Man, the Ideal Man*, in God's plan for world history.

> Jesus replied, "Foxes have holes and birds of the air have nests, but the Son of Man has no place to lay his head." (Mat 8:20)

> But so that you may know that the Son of Man has authority on earth to forgive sins...." Then he said to the paralytic, "Get up, take your mat and go home." (Mat 9:6)

> Just as the Son of Man did not come to be served, but to serve, and to give his life as a ransom for many." (Mat 20:28)

> For as lightning that comes from the east is visible even in the west, so will be the coming of the Son of Man. (Mat 24:27)

> If anyone is ashamed of me and my words in this adulterous and sinful generation, the Son of Man will be ashamed of him when he comes in his Father's glory with the holy angels." (Mark 8:38)

> I tell you, he will see that they get justice, and quickly. However, when the Son of Man comes, will he find faith on the earth?" (Luke 18:8)

> For the Son of Man came to seek and to save what was lost." (Luke 19:10)

> For as the Father has life in himself, so he has granted the Son to have life in himself. And he has given him authority to judge because he is the Son of Man. (John 5:26-27)

> Jesus said to them, "I tell you the truth, unless you eat the flesh of the Son of Man and drink his blood, you have no life in you. (John 6:53)

> Jesus replied, "The hour has come for the Son of Man to be glorified. (John 12:23)

> When he was gone, Jesus said, "Now is the Son of Man glorified and God is glorified in him. If God is glorified in him, God will glorify the Son in himself, and will glorify him at once. (John 13:31-32)

> When Jesus came to the region of Caesarea Philippi, he asked his disciples, "Who do people say the Son of Man is?"....Simon Peter answered, "You are the Christ, the Son of the living God." (Mat 16:13,16)

> "Look," he said, "I see heaven open and the Son of Man standing at the right hand of God." (Acts 7:56)

> I turned around to see the voice that was speaking to me. And when I turned I saw seven golden lampstands, and among the lampstands was someone "like a son of man," dressed in a robe reaching down to his feet and with a golden sash around his chest. (Rev 1:12-13)

	CHAPTER 2 **II. THE REVELATION OF JESUS, THE SON OF GOD, 2:1-3:21** **A. Revelation 1: Creative Power, 2:1-11**	twenty to thirty gallons 7 Jesus said to the servants, "Fill the jars with water"; so they filled them to the brim. 8 Then he told them, "Now draw some out and take it to the master of the banquet." They did so,	& quenching thirst b. The command: Prepare c. The obedience: They drew water & experienced the creative power of Jesus
1 A wedding in Cana of Galilee[DS1,2] a. Time: The third day b. Mary attended c. Jesus & the disciples attended	On the third day a wedding took place at Cana in Galilee. Jesus' mother was there, 2 and Jesus and his disciples had also been invited to the wedding.	9 And the master of the banquet tasted the water that had been turned into wine. He did not realize where it had come from, though the servants who had drawn the water knew. Then he called the bridegroom aside	**4 The results of Jesus' creative power** a. Man's need was met[DS3]
2 The concern of Jesus' creative power a. Mary's social concern b. Jesus' deeper concern: To meet man's spiritual need c. Mary's confidence in her Son	3 When the wine was gone, Jesus' mother said to him, "They have no more wine." 4 "Dear woman, why do you involve me?" Jesus replied. "My time has not yet come." 5 His mother said to the servants, "Do whatever he tells you."	10 And said, "Everyone brings out the choice wine first and then the cheaper wine after the guests have had too much to drink; but you have saved the best till now."	
3 The revelation of Jesus' creative power a. The materials: Water jars—used for cleaning	6 Nearby stood six stone water jars, the kind used by the Jews for ceremonial washing, each holding from	11 This, the first of his miraculous signs, Jesus performed at Cana in Galilee. He thus revealed his glory, and his disciples put their faith in him.	b. Christ's glory was revealed c. The disciples' faith was strengthened

DIVISION II

THE REVELATION OF JESUS, THE SON OF GOD, 2:1-3:21

A. Revelation 1: Creative Power, 2:1-11

(2:1-11) **Introduction**: this was the first miraculous sign Jesus performed. It demonstrated His very purpose for coming to earth: to reveal the *creative power* of God. He had the power to *create* and *produce* what was needed to meet man's need.

1. A wedding in Cana of Galilee (v.1-2).
2. The concern of Jesus' creative power (v.3-5).
3. The revelation of Jesus' creative power (v.6-8).
4. The results of Jesus' creative power (v.9-11).

1 (2:1-2) **Jesus Christ, Family—Marriage—Wedding**: there was a wedding in Cana of Galilee.

1. The wedding took place on the third day after Jesus came into Galilee, or two days after Nathanael's encounter with Jesus.

2. Mary, the mother of Jesus, was there. Note that Joseph was not mentioned. It is thought by most commentators that he was already dead. In fact, most commentators think he had been dead for years, and that Jesus, being the older child, had stayed home to take care of the family until the other children were old enough to go out on their own.

> **Thought 1.** Note the extreme sufferings of Christ. He had come to bear all the trials of the world for man. He suffered...
> - the death of a parent (see note, pt.3—Mt.13:53-58).
> - being the child of a one parent family.
> - having to go to work at an early age to provide for His mother and half brothers and sisters.

3. Jesus and His disciples attended the wedding. Marriage was a joyful, happy time—a festive occasion; and it was one of the largest social events in a community. This tells us two things about Jesus.

> a. Jesus was a sociable person: He liked people and people liked Him. He enjoyed the company of people; He was not anti-social; He was people centered. His ministry was focused upon people, being with and helping them all He could. (Cp. Mt.11:19; Lk.7:34. See note—Mt.11:16-19.)

Thought 1. Man is a social being. Jesus was teaching us to be sociable and not to become too busy to be sociable. However, He expects us to balance our lives, and the truth about our day and time is this: most persons are not alone enough. Most persons are not working, producing, and making their God called contribution to the world, not as diligently as they should. Most have the problem of socializing too much, whether in recreation, partying, or on the job.

> **They devoted themselves to the apostles' teaching and to the fellowship, to the breaking of bread and to prayer. (Acts 2:42)**
> **Share with God's people who are in need. Practice hospitality. (Rom 12:13)**
> **If some unbeliever invites you to a meal and you want to go, eat whatever is put before you without raising questions of conscience. (1 Cor 10:27)**
> **Rather he must be hospitable, one who loves what is good, who is self-controlled,**

41

upright, holy and disciplined. (Titus 1:8)

Offer hospitality to one another without grumbling. (1 Pet 4:9)

I am a friend to all who fear you, to all who follow your precepts. (Psa 119:63)

Then Jesus said to his host, "When you give a luncheon or dinner, do not invite your friends, your brothers or relatives, or your rich neighbors; if you do, they may invite you back and so you will be repaid. But when you give a banquet, invite the poor, the crippled, the lame, the blind, and you will be blessed. Although they cannot repay you, you will be repaid at the resurrection of the righteous." (Luke 14:12-14)

b. Jesus honored marriage. He demonstrated His approval and honor in two ways: by attending the wedding feast and by meeting the urgent need of the bridegroom.

Thought 1. Jesus graced and blessed the marriage because He was "invited...to the wedding." He has to be genuinely invited into a marriage before He can bless it.

Here I am! I stand at the door and knock. If anyone hears my voice and opens the door, I will come in and eat with him, and he with me. (Rev 3:20)

Yet to all who received him, to those who believed in his name, he gave the right to become children of God— (John 1:12)

For, "Everyone who calls on the name of the Lord will be saved." (Rom 10:13)

DEEPER STUDY # 1

(2:1) **Wedding—Marriage, Jewish Ceremony**: a Jewish wedding ceremony included three major events. (See DEEPER STUDY # 1—Mt.25:1-13 for more discussion.)

1. There was a marriage feast and ceremony, which were held on the same evening.

2. There was the escort of the couple through the streets to their home. The procession usually took place at night. Flaming torches were used and the longest route to the home was taken to attract more attention and to allow the community to share in the joyful event.

3. There was the open house which lasted for a week. A Jewish wedding ceremony involved a large and long celebration. There was a happy, festive spirit that swept through the community and surrounded the couple. All week long the couple wore their wedding garments (gown and robe) and entertained guests. The whole community was expected to participate and celebrate with the couple in their new found happiness.

DEEPER STUDY # 2

(2:1) **Cana**: a small, remote, obscure country village. It is thought to have been in the highlands of Galilee, for a person travelled from Cana *down* to Capernaum. It was close to Nazareth, and according to the early church father Jerome, the city could be seen from Nazareth. Little else is known about the village. Two miraculous signs took place in Cana: this event of creative power where the water was turned into wine (Jn.2:1-11), and the healing of the royal official's son (Jn.4:46-54). Cana is mentioned only one other time in Scripture (Jn.21:2), three times altogether, and only by John in his gospel.

---

2 (2:3-5) **Jesus Christ, Time of—Social Concerns—Needs**: the concern of Jesus' creative power. Note that everything points toward Mary as having a key part in the wedding. There was a steward overseeing the household affairs (v.9), but Mary was apparently helping in some manner. Note three things.

1. Mary's social concern. The need that arose was extremely serious, for the wine was already gone and the celebration had just begun. There was a *whole* week of celebration yet to go. The couple was to have *open house* and to provide the wine and refreshments for the week. What were they to do? The importance of wine in the Middle East must always be remembered. Good, germ free water was scarce, and it was used only when necessary. Wine was used as a drinking substitute. There was a critical need, a predicament that was going to affect everyone involved.

⇒ The joyful spirit of the guests was to be dampened.

⇒ The couple was to be shamed and humiliated, becoming the object of jokes among some.

⇒ Mary, the mother of Jesus, probably one of the hostesses, was to be embarrassed.

Mary, naturally, was concerned about the matter, but note the point. Mary's concern was a *social concern*, a concern for seeing that the needs of a social group were met. She did what any mother would do. She brought the problem to her Son: "They have no more wine."

2. Jesus' deeper concern: to meet man's spiritual need for regeneration. In Mary's concern, Jesus saw a unique opportunity to begin familiarizing His mother with the truth of who He was: the Son of God who had entered the world for a particular *time (the cross)*. Mary nor anyone else understood Jesus' Person, true mission, or Messiahship—not yet (see note—Mk.3:31-32). Therefore, at the very beginning of His ministry, Jesus began to teach everyone, and in particular the person who was so dear to His heart, His mother. He wanted to do all He could to prepare her and the others for the terrible pain that was to come during *His hour (time)*. He was truly the Son of God; He had been born of God. He—His Person and mission—had *to do with God and the things of the Spirit,* not with Mary and her social and carnal needs. He had nothing in common with her and the sinful nature. *He was of God and of the Spirit.* She must begin to understand and see this. The more she could hear the truth, the more she would see and understand, especially after *His hour* [time] had come. Therefore, Jesus used every opportunity possible to familiarize all His loved ones with the phrase "My hour." *His hour* [time] was to become a constant symbol of His death (cp. Jn.7:6, 8, 30; 8:20; 12:23-24, 27, 33; 13:1; 17:1; Mt.26:18, 45; Mk.14:41).

The point Jesus made was that *His hour* [time] had not yet come...

• the time when He could really meet man's needs.

• the time when He must die for man's regeneration.

Thought 1. Jesus was always focused upon His purpose for coming to earth: to face *His hour (time)*, to die for man's salvation.

Jesus replied, "The hour has come for the Son of Man to be glorified. I tell you the truth, unless a kernel of wheat falls to the ground and dies, it remains only a single seed. But if it dies, it produces many seeds. "Now my heart is troubled, and what shall I say? 'Father, save me from this hour'? No, it was for this very reason I came to this hour. But I, when I am lifted up from the earth, will draw all men to myself." He said this to show the kind of death he was going to die. (John 12:23-24, 27, 32-33)

It was just before the Passover Feast. Jesus knew that the time had come for him to leave this world and go to the Father. Having loved his own who were in the world, he now showed them the full extent of his love. (John 13:1)

Thought 2. Mary's concern pictures the social concern of man. Man has many social needs. Society—whether social workers or communities of individuals—is concerned with …

- social health
- social comfort
- social plenty
- social housing
- social peace
- social justice

Note two things.
1) Christ met the social concern, the need, the predicament. He solved the problem.
2) However, Christ does not stop there. Meeting the physical and material needs of society is not enough. Christ met the deeper concern of man:
   - ⇒ life
   - ⇒ assurance
   - ⇒ happiness
   - ⇒ fulfillment
   - ⇒ love
   - ⇒ security
   - ⇒ satisfaction
   - ⇒ completeness

The thief comes only to steal and kill and destroy; I have come that they may have life, and have it to the full. (John 10:10)

I have told you this so that my joy may be in you and that your joy may be complete. (John 15:11)

3. Mary's confidence in her Son. It was night and wine could not be bought. It was unthinkable that Mary was asking Jesus to perform a miracle. So far as we know, He had performed no miraculous signs yet. What she was doing was seeking His help, asking Him to take care of the matter. Of course, He could attempt to get a merchant to reopen his shop and meet the need, or He could try to secure wine from some neighbors. Mary had utter confidence in Him. But, again, that is not the point. Jesus saw the *opportunity* to demonstrate His creative power, the kind of power needed to meet man's need for regeneration.

"My food," said Jesus, "is to do the will of him who sent me and to finish his work. (John 4:34)

As long as it is day, we must do the work of him who sent me. Night is coming, when no one can work. (John 9:4)

And do this, understanding the present time. The hour has come for you to wake up from your slumber, because our salvation is nearer now than when we first believed. (Rom 13:11)

The night is nearly over; the day is almost here. So let us put aside the deeds of darkness and put on the armor of light. (Rom 13:12)

What I mean, brothers, is that the time is short. From now on those who have wives should live as if they had none; (1 Cor 7:29)

Making the most of every opportunity, because the days are evil. (Eph 5:16)

Be wise in the way you act toward outsiders; make the most of every opportunity. (Col 4:5)

3 (2:6-8) **Cleansing—Conversion**: the revelation of Jesus' creative power. Note three things.
1. The six water jars were used both for drinking water and for the purifying and cleansing of the Jews, that is, the *ceremonial and religious cleansing* of the hands and utensils. When a Jew saw the water jars, he knew they were there both for satisfying his thirst and for his religious cleansing. Jesus used the water jars to show that He had the power…
   - to *purify, cleanse, and satisfy* men.
   - to *create and produce* whatever was necessary to cleanse and satisfy men.

And from Jesus Christ, who is the faithful witness, the firstborn from the dead, and the ruler of the kings of the earth. To him who loves us and has freed us from our sins by his blood, (Rev 1:5)

He saved us, not because of righteous things we had done, but because of his mercy. He saved us through the washing of rebirth and renewal by the Holy Spirit, (Titus 3:5)

Come near to God and he will come near to you. Wash your hands, you sinners, and purify your hearts, you double minded. (James 4:8)

Do you not know that the wicked will not inherit the kingdom of God? Do not be deceived: Neither the sexually immoral nor idolaters nor adulterers nor male prostitutes nor homosexual offenders (1 Cor 6:9)

Nor thieves nor the greedy nor drunkards nor slanderers nor swindlers will inherit the kingdom of God. (1 Cor 6:10)

And that is what some of you were. But you were washed, you were sanctified, you were justified in the name of the Lord Jesus Christ and by the Spirit of our God. (1 Cor 6:11)

2. Jesus had a deeper concern than just meeting the social need of the host. He had come to meet man's need for spiritual purification and inner cleansing, and He was to do it through *His hour* (time) (the cross). Therefore, He seized the opportunity to reveal His creative power, His power to create man anew. (See DEEPER STUDY # 1, New Birth—Jn.3:1-15.)

Thought 1. We either believe Christ is the Messiah or not. We either believe He has the power to create anew or not, that He demonstrated such power in this miracle or not.

But these are written that you may believe that Jesus is the Christ, the Son of God, and that by believing you may have life in his name. (John 20:31)

3. Note another significant point: Jesus simply instructed that preparations be made, and when He was obeyed, everyone experienced His creative power and was fully satisfied.

Thought 1. We have to obey Christ's instructions if we wish to be cleansed and created spiritually.

> "Not everyone who says to me, 'Lord, Lord,' will enter the kingdom of heaven, but only he who does the will of my Father who is in heaven. (Mat 7:21)
> "I tell you the truth, whoever hears my word and believes him who sent me has eternal life and will not be condemned; he has crossed over from death to life. (John 5:24)
> Whoever has my commands and obeys them, he is the one who loves me. He who loves me will be loved by my Father, and I too will love him and show myself to him." (John 14:21)
> Through him you believe in God, who raised him from the dead and glorified him, and so your faith and hope are in God. (1 Pet 1:21)
> The world and its desires pass away, but the man who does the will of God lives forever. (1 John 2:17)
> "Therefore everyone who hears these words of mine and puts them into practice is like a wise man who built his house on the rock. The rain came down, the streams rose, and the winds blew and beat against that house; yet it did not fall, because it had its foundation on the rock. (Mat 7:24-25)

4 (2:9-11) **Jesus Christ, Power; Results**: the results were threefold.

1. The bridegroom's need was met. What he needed was provided.

2. Christ's glory was revealed. His power to create anew was demonstrated.

3. The faith of the disciples was strengthened. They "put their faith in Him" even more. He had given evidence that He was the Messiah.

> He came to Jesus at night and said, "Rabbi, we know you are a teacher who has come from God. For no one could perform the miraculous signs you are doing if God were not with him." (John 3:2)
> Still, many in the crowd put their faith in him. They said, "When the Christ comes, will he do more miraculous signs than this man?" (John 7:31)
> Jesus answered, "I did tell you, but you do not believe. The miracles I do in my Father's name speak for me, (John 10:25)
> What about the one whom the Father set apart as his very own and sent into the world? Why then do you accuse me of blasphemy because I said, 'I am God's Son'? (John 10:36)
> Do not believe me unless I do what my Father does. (John 10:37)
> But if I do it, even though you do not believe me, believe the miracles, that you may know and understand that the Father is in me, and I in the Father." (John 10:38)
> Jesus did many other miraculous signs in the presence of his disciples, which are not recorded in this book. But these are written that you may believe that Jesus is the Christ, the Son of God, and that by believing you may have life in his name. (John 20:30-31)

DEEPER STUDY # 3

(2:9-10) **Jesus Christ, Power; Results**: the master of ceremonies evidently nudged the host and jokingly teased him about holding out on the guests; that is, he had kept the best wine until last.

1 **Jesus left Cana** a. He went to Capernaum for a short time b. He then went to Jerusalem to attend the Passover 2 **His discovery of evil in the temple**DS1 a. He entered the temple b. He found the temple desecrated 3 **His right to cleanse the temple** a. The whip: A symbol b. His unique relationship to God: "My Father"	**B. Revelation 2: Jesus is Supreme Over God's House, 2:12-22** (Mt.21:12-16; Mk.11: 15-19; Lk.19:45-46) 12 After this he went down to Capernaum with his mother and brothers and his disciples. There they stayed for a few days. 13 When it was almost time for the Jewish Passover, Jesus went up to Jerusalem. 14 In the temple courts he found men selling cattle, sheep and doves, and others sitting at tables exchanging money. 15 So he made a whip out of cords, and drove all from the temple area, both sheep and cattle; he scattered the coins of the money changers and overturned their tables. 16 To those who sold doves he said, "Get these out of here! How dare you turn my	Father's house into a market!" 17 His disciples remembered that it is written: "Zeal for your house will consume me." 18 Then the Jews demanded of him, "What miraculous sign can you show us to prove your authority to do all this?" 19 Jesus answered them, "Destroy this temple, and I will raise it again in three days." 20 The Jews replied, "It has taken forty-six years to build this temple, and you are going to raise it in three days?" 21 But the temple he had spoken of was his body. 22 After he was raised from the dead, his disciples recalled what he had said. Then they believed the Scripture and the words that Jesus had spoken.	c. His consuming zeal for God's House 4 **His power to erect a new temple** a. His authority questioned b. His sign: A new meeting place for God & man c. His symbolic meaning: His body—His death & resurrectionDS2 5 **His objective achieved: The disciples believed the Scripture and the Word of the Lord**

DIVISION II

THE REVELATION OF JESUS, THE SON OF GOD, 2:1-3:21

B. Revelation 2: Jesus is Supreme Over God's House, 2:12-22

(2:12-22) Introduction: Jesus Christ has supremacy over God's house, that is, over the temple or church. He alone has the right to rule and reign over God's house.
1. Jesus left Cana (v.12-13).
2. His discovery of evil in the temple (v.14).
3. His right to cleanse the temple (v.15-17).
4. His power to erect a new temple (v.18-21).
5. His objective achieved: the disciples believed (v.22).

1 (2:12-13) **Jesus Christ, Worship—Faithfulness**: Jesus left Cana. He went down to Capernaum and stayed there for just a brief time. Capernaum was His headquarters (see note—Mt.4:12). He then left for Jerusalem to attend the Passover Feast (see note, Passover—Mt.26:17-30).

2 (2:14) **Temple—Church, Abused**: Jesus' discovery of evil in the temple. Note two facts.
1. He entered the temple (see DEEPER STUDY # 1, Temple—Jn.2:14).
2. He found the temple being desecrated. It was the Court of the Gentiles where so much commercialism took place. There was a regular commercial market within its walls. How did a commercial market ever get into the temple of God? Very simply, greed. Worshippers needed animals (oxen, sheep, doves), incense, meal, wine, oil, salt, and other items for their sacrifices and offerings. Pilgrims from foreign nations needed money exchanged. At some point in the history of the temple, the priests had decided to take advantage of the market themselves instead of letting retailers on the outside reap all the profits. Therefore, the priests began to set up booths within the Court of

the Gentiles and to lease space to *outside retailers*. These often turned out to be family members. The owner of the booths or space was apparently the High Priest whose name was Annas. The outer courtyard of the temple, the very worship center for the Gentiles, was filled with booth like spaces where worshippers could find any kind of service they needed. The atmosphere was one of commercial traffic and commotion, not of worship and prayer.

Remembering the teeming thousands who attended the great feasts, we can imagine the loudest commercial commotion, and our picture would still come short of the actual scene. Who can picture thousands of animals with their peculiar noises, wastes, and smells within the temple of God? And for what? What would cause men to so abuse the worship center of God? As said above, money—the greed of men. It is no wonder Jesus did what He did. He could not do otherwise, for He was the Son of God, the Messiah sent into the world to bring about a true worship of God; and there was no hope of worship within the Court of the Gentiles. Prayer and worship were impossible.

> **"It is written," he said to them, "'My house will be a house of prayer'; but you have made it 'a den of robbers.'" (Luke 19:46)**
> **Guard your steps when you go to the house of God. Go near to listen rather than to offer the sacrifice of fools, who do not know that they do wrong. (Eccl 5:1)**
> **In the council of the holy ones God is greatly feared; he is more awesome than all who surround him. (Psa 89:7)**

45

DEEPER STUDY # 1

(2:14) **Temple**: a person must understand the layout of the temple in order to see what was happening in this event. The temple sat on the top of Mt. Zion, and it is thought to have covered about thirty acres of land. The temple consisted of two parts, the temple building itself and the temple precincts or courtyards. The Greek language has two different words to distinguish which is meant.

1. *The temple building* (naos) was a small ornate structure which sat in the center of the temple property. It was called the Holy Place or Holy of Holies. Only the High Priest could enter its walls, and he could enter only once during the year, on the Day of Atonement.

2. *The temple precincts* (hieron) were four courtyards that surrounded the temple building, each decreasing in their importance to the Jewish mind. It is important to know that great walls separated the courts from each other.

a. First, there was the Court of the Priests. Only the priests were allowed to enter this court. Within this courtyard stood the great furnishings of worship: the Altar of Burnt Offering, the Bronze Wash Basin, the Seven Branched Lampstand, the Altar of Incense, and the Table of Showbread.

b. Second, there was the Court of the Israelites. This was a huge courtyard where Jewish worshippers met together for joint services on the great feast days. It was also where worshippers handed over their sacrifices to the priests.

c. Third, there was the Court of the Women. Women were usually limited to this area except for joint worship with men. They could, however, enter the Court of the Israelites when they came to make a sacrifice or worship in a joint assembly on a great feast day.

d. Last, there was the Court of the Gentiles. It covered a vast space, surrounding all the other courtyards, and was the place of worship for all Gentile converts to Judaism.

Two facts need to be noted about the Court of the Gentiles.

1. It was the courtyard farthest removed from the center of worship, the Most Holy Place, which represented God's very presence (see note, pt.2—Eph.2:14-15).

2. A high wall separated the Court of the Gentiles from the other courts, disallowing any Gentile a closer approach into God's presence. In fact, there were tablets hanging all around the wall threatening death to any Gentile who went beyond their own courtyard or center of worship.

3 (2:15-17) **Jesus Christ, Duty—Temple—Church**: Jesus' right to cleanse the temple. Three points show His right.

1. The whip of cords. This was a symbol of His righteous anger, of His right to be obeyed, of His right to enforce obedience within the temple. The whip was a symbol of the power and cleansing judgment of God—the kind of power and cleansing judgment that causes men to tremble before God (Ph.2:9-11).

He ran through the temple doing three things: (a) He chased out *all* who were buying and selling; (b) He threw over the tables of the moneychangers; and (c) He threw over the chairs of the dove dealers.

Thought 1. The temple (church) can be abused by...
- forgetting what worship is all about.
- misusing the facilities and buildings of God's house.
- ignoring God's holiness and forgetting one's duty to reverence God.
- allowing questionable, non-worshipful activities.

2. Jesus' unique relationship to God. He called God "My Father" and called the temple "My Father's house."

a. "My Father." Jesus was continually calling God "My Father" (see notes—Jn.1:34; 10:30-33 for discussion).

b. "My Father's house." Jesus was saying the temple was God's; therefore, it was to be a house of worship *for all people*. This included the Gentiles as well as the Jews. All people should be able to worship in quietness and peace within God's temple. No one should be barred, separated, or discouraged from worshipping God in His temple. All should be welcomed.

Note another fact. The temple (church) was called a house of worship, not a house of sacrifice, offerings, teaching, prophecy, or preaching. Everything done within the House of God is to lead to the *worship* of the Father and *communion* with the Father.

Thought 1. The temple is not to be used as a commercial center. It is not to be a place for buying and selling, marketing and retailing, stealing and cheating. It is not to be profaned. The temple is the House of God, God's House of worship. It is to be a place of sanctity, refined and purified by God Himself. It is to be a place of quietness and meditation, a place set aside for worship, not for buying and selling where man gets gain.

Then they worshiped him and returned to Jerusalem with great joy. And they stayed continually at the temple, praising God. (Luke 24:52-53; cp.Jn.4:24)

I love the house where you live, O LORD, the place where your glory dwells. (Psa 26:8;cp.Ps.23:6)

One thing I ask of the LORD, this is what I seek: that I may dwell in the house of the LORD all the days of my life, to gaze upon the beauty of the LORD and to seek him in his temple. (Psa 27:4)

Blessed are those you choose and bring near to live in your courts! We are filled with the good things of your house, of your holy temple. (Psa 65:4)

My soul yearns, even faints, for the courts of the LORD; my heart and my flesh cry out for the living God. (Psa 84:2)

Better is one day in your courts than a thousand elsewhere; I would rather be a doorkeeper in the house of my God than dwell in the tents of the wicked. (Psa 84:10)

A song of ascents. Of David. I rejoiced with those who said to me, "Let us go to the house of the LORD." (Psa 122:1)

Guard your steps when you go to the house of God. Go near to listen rather than to offer the sacrifice of fools, who do not know that they do wrong. (Eccl 5:1)

Thought 2. A man either believes Jesus is the Son of God and over the Temple of God or else he believes neither (Jn.20:31).

3. Jesus' consuming zeal. His zeal fulfilled Scripture and demonstrated that He was the Messiah. The Messiah was bound to be zealous for God's house and to react in anger at such corruption within the temple. Scripture had predicted the Lord's zeal (Ps.69:9); therefore, Jesus had the right to show *zeal and anger* against such desecration of the temple. He was the Messiah, and His act stirred the memory of the disciples.

> "'Each of you must respect his mother and father, and you must observe my Sabbaths. I am the LORD your God. (Lev 19:30)
>
> But the LORD is in his holy temple; let all the earth be silent before him." (Hab 2:20)
>
> In the council of the holy ones God is greatly feared; he is more awesome than all who surround him. (Psa 89:7)

4 (2:18-21) **Temple—Church—Jesus Christ, Death, Predicted**: Jesus' power to erect a new temple. Note four things.

1. His authority was questioned by the religionists. What right did He have to do what He was doing? He claimed that the temple was His *Father's*. They knew that He was claiming to be the Messiah; therefore, they wanted proof that His claim was true. They wanted some spectacular sign.

2. His sign was to be given in the future. He was going to build a *new meeting place* for God. Note His exact words: "[You] destroy this temple, and I will raise it in three days."

3. His puzzling statement was misunderstood. They could not understand how He could possibly build a temple in three days. The present temple had taken forty-six years to build.

4. His puzzling statement had a *symbolic meaning*. Jesus was speaking of His body, of His death and resurrection.
   a. The proof that He was the Son of God with authority over God's house was to be given. The sign was to be His body, His death and resurrection. The resurrection was to be the supreme proof of His Messiahship. They were to destroy (kill) Him, but He would be raised from the dead after three days (see outline and notes—Lk.11:29-36).

> With great power the apostles continued to testify to the resurrection of the Lord Jesus, and much grace was upon them all. (Acts 4:33)
>
> "We are witnesses of everything he did in the country of the Jews and in Jerusalem. They killed him by hanging him on a tree, but God raised him from the dead on the third day and caused him to be seen. He was not seen by all the people, but by witnesses whom God had already chosen—by us who ate and drank with him after he rose from the dead. (Acts 10:39-41)
>
> Aand who through the Spirit of holiness was declared with power to be the Son of God by his resurrection from the dead: Jesus Christ our Lord. (Rom 1:4)

   b. His death and resurrection was to provide a new temple, a new meeting place for God and man. It was to be *in Him* that men would thereafter meet God. The temple of His body was to become the temple of men, the temple whereby men would worship and be reconciled to God (see note, Mediator—Jn.1:51 for discussion. Also see notes—1 Cor.3:16; 6:19. Cp. Jn.14:16-21.)

> Jesus answered, "I am the way and the truth and the life. No one comes to the Father except through me. (John 14:6)
>
> For there is one God and one mediator between God and men, the man Christ Jesus, (1 Tim 2:5)

DEEPER STUDY # 2

(2:19-20) **Jesus—Charges Against**: this is the statement used to charge Jesus with being an insurrectionist at His trial (Mt.26:61; Mk.14:58). It was also used to taunt Jesus as He hung upon the cross (Mt.27:40). The Jews, showing their spiritual blindness and attachment to a materialistic world, understood Jesus to be saying that He would perform an architectural wonder.

---

5 (2:22) **Prophecy, Belief in**: Jesus' objective was achieved. The disciples believed the Scriptures which had predicted the coming and resurrection of the Messiah (see DEEPER STUDY # 3—Jn.1:45; Mt.17:23).

> Because you will not abandon me to the grave, nor will you let your Holy One see decay. (Psa 16:10; cp. Acts2:31; 13:35)
>
> Therefore I will give him a portion among the great, and he will divide the spoils with the strong, because he poured out his life unto death, and was numbered with the transgressors. For he bore the sin of many, and made intercession for the transgressors. (Isa 53:12)

	C. Revelation 3: Jesus Knows All Men, 2:23-25	believed in his name.	the miraculous signs*DS1*
1 Fact 1: Many believed in Jesus a. Believed in His name b. Believed because of	23 Now while he was in Jerusalem at the Passover Feast, many people saw the miraculous signs he was doing and	24 But Jesus would not entrust himself to them, for he knew all men. 25 He did not need man's testimony about man, for he knew what was in a man.	**2 Fact 2: Jesus did not commit nor entrust Himself to men***DS2* a. He knew all men b. He knew what was in a man*DS3*

DIVISION II

THE REVELATION OF JESUS, THE SON OF GOD, 2:1-3:21

C. Revelation 3: Jesus Knows All Men, 2:23-25

(2:23-25) Introduction: this is a brief passage packed full of powerful truths. Jesus revealed that He knew all men.
1. Fact 1: many believed in Jesus (v.23).
2. Fact 2: Jesus did not commit nor entrust Himself to men (v.24-25).

1 (2:23) **Belief—Profession, False**: first, many believed in Jesus. There are two very significant facts here.

1. Many *believed in His name*. The word "believe" (episteusan) is in the Greek aorist tense, which means they believed *once-for-all*. Their belief was genuine, at least the belief of some. However, the belief of others was not genuine. The fact that Jesus knew "all men" (all of those professing belief) and did not commit (entrust) Himself to them shows the inadequacy of their faith (v.24).

2. They believed because of the "miraculous signs" (semeia). (See DEEPER STUDY # 1, Signs—Jn.2:23 for discussion.)

DEEPER STUDY # 1

(2:23) Signs—Miracles—Power—Works—Sensationalism: there are four words used in the Bible for miracles or signs. These words are used to describe the works of God, and they show why people believed in Jesus.

1. *Teras* means the spectacular, staggering, amazing, dazzling. Many believed in Jesus because of the spectacular signs He performed. However, such belief made a person only a spectator, not a participant in His life. The word *teras* also means the sensational; that is, it appeals to the sensations of men. Many believed and followed Jesus because it made them feel good and comfortable and secure. Such belief is weak and often fails. This word is never used by itself to initiate faith in the Lord Jesus. If a person is to have genuine faith in the Lord Jesus, he must have some basis other than the spectacular sign (teras).

> Some fell on rock, and when it came up, the plants withered because they had no moisture. Those on the rock are the ones who receive the word with joy when they hear it, but they have no root. They believe for a while, but in the time of testing they fall away. (Luke 8:6,13. See note, pt.2—Lk.8:11-15 for discussion of this person)
> Jesus replied, "No one who puts his hand to the plow and looks back is fit for service in the kingdom of God." (Luke 9:62)
> But my righteous one will live by faith. And if he shrinks back, I will not be pleased with him." (Heb 10:38)

2. *Dunamis* means power—unusual, extraordinary power; effective, explosive power. There were those who were attracted to Jesus because of the unusual power (dunamis) they witnessed. They believed because of the power. Such is a legitimate belief and leads to salvation for everyone who believes.

> I am not ashamed of the gospel, because it is the power of God for the salvation of everyone who believes: first for the Jew, then for the Gentile. (Rom 1:16)
> But to those whom God has called, both Jews and Greeks, Christ the power of God and the wisdom of God. (1 Cor 1:24)
> He could not do any miracles there, except lay his hands on a few sick people and heal them. And he was amazed at their lack of faith. Then Jesus went around teaching from village to village. (Mark 6:5-6)

3. *Ergon* means distinctive works, deeds, and miracles. Such works come from God (Jn.14:10) and bear witness to Christ. They point men to Christ (Jn.5:36; 10:25). Some men look at the very special works of Christ and believe because of the works (ergon).

> Do not believe me unless I do what my Father does. But if I do it, even though you do not believe me, believe the miracles, that you may know and understand that the Father is in me, and I in the Father." (John 10:37-38)
> Believe me when I say that I am in the Father and the Father is in me; or at least believe on the evidence of the miracles themselves. (John 14:11)

4. *Semeion* means a sign that characterizes the person, his nature and character. A few throughout Jesus' ministry did believe because they saw *in the miracles* exactly who He was, the very Son of God.

> This, the first of his miraculous signs, Jesus performed at Cana in Galilee. He thus revealed his glory, and his disciples put their faith in him. (John 2:11)
> Jesus did many other miraculous signs in the presence of his disciples, which are not recorded in this book. But these are written that you may believe that Jesus is the Christ, the Son of God, and that by believing you may have life in his name. (John 20:30-31)

However, the word *semeion* is also used of those who believed the signs but *did not have* the highest or right kind of faith. Their faith was *not a faith that committed itself* (see DEEPER STUDY # 2—Jn.2:24).

    a. It was a faith that arose only from...
- a mental conviction, a head knowledge, an intellectual belief.
- a surface acceptance of the fact that Jesus was the Savior.

Now while he was in Jerusalem at the Passover Feast, many people saw the miraculous signs he was doing and believed in his name. But Jesus would not entrust himself to them, for he knew all men. (John 2:23-24; believe and commit are the same words)

    b. It was also a faith...
- that only sought Jesus for what a person could get out of Him.
- that never gave any thought to what a person might do for Christ.
- that was unaware of the cost of discipleship, unaware that a person had to sacrifice himself and give all he was and had to Christ in order to become a follower of His (see note—Lk.9:23).

Jesus answered, "I tell you the truth, you are looking for me, not because you saw miraculous signs but because you ate the loaves and had your fill. (John 6:26)

2 (2:24-25) **Belief—Jesus Christ, Knowledge of—Sin, Secret**: second, Jesus did not commit nor entrust Himself to men. The word "entrust" is the very same word as "believe" in v.23. (See DEEPER STUDY # 2, Believe—Jn.2:24.) Jesus did not trust nor believe in the people; He did not commit and entrust Himself into their lives or hands. The verb is continuous action: Jesus kept on refusing to trust men, kept on refusing to entrust Himself into their lives. Two reasons are given for this continuing attitude of Jesus.

1. Jesus knew all men. The idea is that He knew every single man personally. Not a person escaped His knowledge.

2. Jesus knew what was in a man. No one needed to tell Him about man. He knew man's nature: his depravity, evil, deception, and fickleness. He knew the men He could trust and could not trust. He knew every man who professed to believe, yet would...
- betray Him
- deny his faith under pressure
- forsake Him, turning back to the world
- slip and fall back into sin
- be weak and easily influenced, tossed to and fro
- prove untrustworthy
- lack zeal and genuine commitment
- lack courage to stand

Jesus knew all this about every man. Nothing was hid from Him. Therefore, He was not able to commit nor entrust Himself and His blessings to some men despite the fact that they professed to believe.

Thought 1. Some so-called believers (those who make false professions) never receive the *indwelling presence of Christ*. Christ cannot commit nor entrust Himself to them. Tragically, this means that He...
- cannot give the assurance of salvation: the confidence that a person is really saved.
- cannot give the Holy Spirit to live within the heart of a person: the presence and knowledge of Him.
- cannot give the fulness of life: the sense of completeness and the security of God's care and of being looked after.
- cannot give the hope and certainty of eternal life.
- cannot commit nor entrust His mission into their hands.

We are witnesses of these things, and so is the Holy Spirit, whom God has given to those who obey him." (Acts 5:32)

For the wages of sin is death, but the gift of God is eternal life in Christ Jesus our Lord. (Rom 6:23)

Those who live according to the sinful nature have their minds set on what that nature desires; but those who live in accordance with the Spirit have their minds set on what the Spirit desires. (Rom 8:5)

The mind of sinful man is death, but the mind controlled by the Spirit is life and peace; (Rom 8:6)

For if you live according to the sinful nature, you will die; but if by the Spirit you put to death the misdeeds of the body, you will live, (Rom 8:13)

"Therefore come out from them and be separate, says the Lord. Touch no unclean thing, and I will receive you." (2 Cor 6:17)

"I will be a Father to you, and you will be my sons and daughters, says the Lord Almighty." (2 Cor 6:18)

Thought 2. Christ knows everything about everyone. As this Scripture says: He knows *"all men"* and He knows what is *"in man"*: all his thoughts and deeds—good or bad, done in the light or in the dark, in the open or behind closed doors, publicly or secretly.

There is nothing concealed that will not be disclosed, or hidden that will not be made known. (Luke 12:2)

And again, "The Lord knows that the thoughts of the wise are futile." (1 Cor 3:20)

Therefore judge nothing before the appointed time; wait till the Lord comes. He will bring to light what is hidden in darkness and will expose the motives of men's hearts. At that time each will receive his praise from God. (1 Cor 4:5)

For it is shameful even to mention what the disobedient do in secret. (Eph 5:12)

"I the LORD search the heart and examine the mind, to reward a man according to his conduct, according to what his deeds deserve." (Jer 17:10)

Can anyone hide in secret places so that I cannot see him?" declares the LORD.

"Do not I fill heaven and earth?" declares the LORD. (Jer 23:24)

"Do not keep talking so proudly or let your mouth speak such arrogance, for the LORD is a God who knows, and by him deeds are weighed. (1 Sam 2:3)

If I sinned, you would be watching me and would not let my offense go unpunished. (Job 10:14)

"His eyes are on the ways of men; he sees their every step. (Job 34:21)

For the LORD watches over the way of the righteous, but the way of the wicked will perish. (Psa 1:6)

You know my folly, O God; my guilt is not hidden from you. (Psa 69:5)

You have set our iniquities before you, our secret sins in the light of your presence. (Psa 90:8)

You know when I sit and when I rise; you perceive my thoughts from afar. You discern my going out and my lying down; you are familiar with all my ways. (Psa 139:2-3)

For a man's ways are in full view of the LORD, and he examines all his paths. (Prov 5:21)

For God will bring every deed into judgment, including every hidden thing, whether it is good or evil. (Eccl 12:14)

Woe to those who go to great depths to hide their plans from the LORD, who do their work in darkness and think, "Who sees us? Who will know?" (Isa 29:15)

Do you not know? Have you not heard? The LORD is the everlasting God, the Creator of the ends of the earth. He will not grow tired or weary, and his understanding no one can fathom. (Isa 40:28)

Although you wash yourself with soda and use an abundance of soap, the stain of your guilt is still before me," declares the Sovereign LORD. (Jer 2:22)

My eyes are on all their ways; they are not hidden from me, nor is their sin concealed from my eyes. (Jer 16:17)

Great are your purposes and mighty are your deeds. Your eyes are open to all the ways of men; you reward everyone according to his conduct and as his deeds deserve. (Jer 32:19)

He said to me, "Son of man, have you seen what the elders of the house of Israel are doing in the darkness, each at the shrine of his own idol? They say, 'The LORD does not see us; the LORD has forsaken the land.'" (Ezek 8:12; cp.Ezk.11:5)

He reveals deep and hidden things; he knows what lies in darkness, and light dwells with him. (Dan 2:22)

But they do not realize that I remember all their evil deeds. Their sins engulf them; they are always before me. (Hosea 7:2)

DEEPER STUDY # 2
(2:24) **Believe (episteusan)—Commit—Entrust (episteuen)**: the word commit or entrust is the very same word "believe" (cp. Jn.2:23). This gives an excellent picture of *saving faith*, of what *genuine faith* is—of the kind of faith that really saves a person.

1. Saving faith is not head knowledge, not just a mental conviction and intellectual assent. It is not just *believing the fact* that Jesus Christ is the Savior of the world. It is not just believing history, that Jesus Christ lived upon earth as the Savior just as George Washington lived upon earth as the President of America. It is not just believing the words and claims of Jesus in the same way that a person would believe the words of George Washington.

2. Saving faith is believing in Jesus, *who* and *what* He is, that He is the *Savior* and *Lord* of life. It is a man's giving and turning his life over to Jesus. It is a man's casting himself upon Jesus as Savior and Lord.

3. Saving faith is commitment—the commitment of a man's total being and life to Jesus Christ. It is a man's commitment of all he *is and has* to Jesus. It gives Jesus everything; therefore, it involves all of a man's affairs. The man trusts Jesus to take care of his past (sins), his present (welfare), and his future (destiny). He entrusts his whole life, being, and possessions into Jesus' hands. He lays himself upon Jesus' keeping, confiding in Him about his daily necessities and acknowledging Him in all the ways of life. He follows Jesus in every area and in every detail of life, seeking His instructions and leaving his welfare up to Him. It is simply commitment of a man's whole being, all he is and has, to Jesus. (See notes—Jn.4:50; pt.4, Heb.5:5-10.)

There are three steps involved in faith, steps that are clearly seen in this passage. (See note—Ro.10:16-17 for more discussion.)

1. There is the step of *seeing* (Jn.2:23) or *hearing* (Ro.10:16). A man must be willing to listen to the message of Christ, the revelation of truth.

2. There is the step of *mental assent*. A man must agree that the message is true, that the facts of the case are thus and so. But this is not enough. Mere agreement does not lead to action. Many a person knows that something is true, but he does not change his behavior to match his knowledge. For example, a man knows that eating too much harms his body, but he may continue to eat too much. He agrees to the truth and knows the truth, but he does nothing about it. A person may believe and know that Jesus Christ is the Savior of the world and yet do nothing about it, never make a decision to follow Christ. This man still does not have faith, not the kind of faith that the Bible talks about.

3. There is the step of *commitment*. When the New Testament speaks of faith, it speaks of *commitment*, a *personal commitment to the truth*. A man hears the truth and agrees that it is true and does something about it. He commits (entrusts) and yields his life to the truth. The truth becomes a part of his very being, a part of his behavior and life.

DEEPER STUDY # 3
(2:25) **Man**: the human race. Jesus knew man's nature, depravity, evil, deception, fickleness.

CHAPTER 3

D. Revelation 4: The New Birth,[DS1] **3:1-15**

1 Nicodemus approached Jesus
  a. He came in behalf of the religionists: "We"
  b. He acknowledged Jesus only as a teacher from God
  c. He asked,"Who are you?"

2 The new birth: A necessity
  a. A strong assertion
  b. Importance: One can never see God's kingdom unless born again

3 The new birth: A spiritual birth

  a. Its source: Being born of the Spirit[DS2]
  b. Its importance repeated: One will never enter God's kingdom unless born again
  c. Its nature: Spiritual, not physical & material

Now there was a man of the Pharisees named Nicodemus, a member of the Jewish ruling council.
2 He came to Jesus at night and said, "Rabbi, we know you are a teacher who has come from God. For no one could perform the miraculous signs you are doing if God were not with him."
3 In reply Jesus declared, "I tell you the truth, no one can see the kingdom of God unless he is born again."
4 "How can a man be born when he is old?" Nicodemus asked. "Surely he cannot enter a second time into his mother's womb to be born!"
5 Jesus answered "I tell you the truth, no one can enter, the kingdom of God unless he is born of water and the Spirit.
6 Flesh gives birth to flesh, but the Spirit gives birth to spirit.

7 You should not be surprised prised at my saying,'You must be born again.'
8 The wind blows wherever it pleases. You hear its sound, but you cannot tell where it comes from or where it is going. So it is with everyone born of the Spirit."
9 "How can this be?" Nicodemus asked.
10 "You are Israel's teacher," said Jesus, "and do you not understand these things?
11 I tell you the truth, we speak of what we know, and we testify to what we have seen, but still you people do not accept our testimony.
12 I have spoken to you of earthly things and you do not believe; how then will you believe if I speak of heavenly things?
13 No one has ever gone into heaven except the one who came from heaven—the Son of Man.
14 Just as Moses lifted up the snake in the desert,so the Son of Man must be lifted up,
15 That everyone who believes in him may have eternal life.

  d. Its absolute necessity: Reemphasized

  e. Its illustration: The wind

4 The new birth: A true experience
  a. Nicodemus' heart touched

  b. Jesus' strong assertion: We do know; have seen

5 The new birth: Rejected
  a. Some did not accept the witness
  b. The reason: Man's nature of unbelief

6 The new birth: Revealed only by Jesus
  a. His origin: Heaven
  b. His timeless experience: "From heaven"

7 The new birth: Secured by two acts
  a. By Jesus' death
  b. By believing in Jesus

DIVISION II

THE REVELATION OF JESUS, THE SON OF GOD, 2:1-3:21

D. Revelation 4: The New Birth, 3:1-15

(3:1-15) **Introduction**: the new birth, along with God's great love (v.16-17), is the most important revelation ever made in all of human history. Jesus revealed the new birth.
  1. Nicodemus approached Jesus (v.1-2).
  2. The new birth: a necessity, an imperative (v.3).
  3. The new birth: a spiritual birth (v.4-8).
  4. The new birth: a true experience (v.9-11).
  5. The new birth: rejected (v.11-12).
  6. The new birth: revealed only by Jesus (v.13).
  7. The new birth: secured by two acts (v.14-15).

DEEPER STUDY # 1
(3:1-15) **New Birth—Born Again—New Creation—Regeneration**: a spiritual birth, a rebirth of one's spirit, a new life, a renewed soul, a regenerated spirit. It is the regeneration and renewal of one's spirit and behavior (2 Cor.5:17). It is the enduement of a new life, of a godly nature (2 Pt.1:4). The new birth is so radical a change in a person's life that it can be described only as being *born again*. Something so wonderful happens to the soul that it is just like a *new birth*. It is a spiritual birth, a birth beyond the grasp of man's hands and efforts. It is so radical, so life changing, and so wonderful that it can be wrought only by the love and power of God Himself.
    The New Testament teaching on the new birth is rich and full.

1. The new birth is a necessity. A person will never see (Jn.3:3) nor ever enter (Jn.3:5) the Kingdom of God unless he is born again (Jn.3:7).
2. The new birth is a spiritual birth, the birth of a new power and spirit in life. It is not reformation of the old nature (Ro.6:6). It is the actual creation of a new birth within—spiritually (Jn.3:5-6; cp. Jn.1:12-13; 2 Cor.5:17; Eph.2:10; 4:24). (See notes—Eph.1:3; 4:17-19; DEEPER STUDY # 3—4:24.) A person is spiritually born again:
    a. By water, even the Spirit (see DEEPER STUDY # 2—Jn.3:5).
    b. By the choice (will) of God (Jas.1:18).
    c. By imperishable or incorruptible seed, even by the Word of God (1 Pt.1:23).
    d. By God from above (1 Pt.1:3). The word *again* (ana) in the phrase "born again" also means *above*. (Cp. Jn.1:12-13.)
    e. By Christ, who gives both the *power and right* to be born again (Jn.1:12-13).
3. The new birth is a definite experience, a real experience. A person experiences the new birth:
    a. By believing that Jesus is the Christ, the Son of God (1 Jn.5:1; cp. Jn.3:14-15).
    b. By the gospel as it is shared by believers (1 Cor. 4:15; Phile.10).
    c. By the Word of God (1 Pt.1:23) or by the Word of Truth (Jas.1:18).

4. The new birth is a changed life, a totally new life. A person proves that he is born again:
  a. By doing righteous acts (1 Jn.2:29; cp. Eph.2:10; 4:24).
  b. By not practicing sin (1 Jn.3:9; 5:18).
  c. By loving other believers (1 Jn.4:7).
  d. By overcoming the world (1 Jn.5:4).
  e. By keeping himself (1 Jn.5:18).
  f. By possessing the divine seed or nature (1 Jn.3:9; 1 Pt.1:23; 2 Pt.1:4; cp. Col.1:27).

1 (3:1-2) **Nicodemus**: Nicodemus approached Jesus. Note these facts about Nicodemus.

1. He was a member of the Jewish ruling (archon) council. This means he was a senator or a member of the Sanhedrin, the ruling body of the Jews (see DEEPER STUDY # 1—Mt.26:59).
  a. He was a Pharisee (see DEEPER STUDY # 3—Acts 23:8).
  b. He was *Israel's teacher* (v.10, ho didaskalos); that is, he held some official position of the highest rank. He was either the *leading official* or the *leading teacher* of Israel who was either authorized or accepted as such by the public.
  c. He apparently was wealthy. He spent a great deal of money on the burial of Jesus (Jn.19:39).
  d. He was silent at the trial of Jesus, saying nothing to defend Jesus, but he boldly stepped forth after the Lord's death to publicly help in the burial of Jesus (Jn.19:39-42).

2. He came in behalf of the religionists. He said, *"We know."* Some of the religionists wondered if Jesus were the true Messiah, thinking that perhaps He was. Some eventually become believers (cp. Lk.13:31; Acts 6:7; 15:5; 18:8, 17). Jesus was claiming to be the Messiah and performing the spectacular works that were prophesied of the Messiah; therefore, He was the talk of everyone throughout the nation. The rulers were questioning and wondering: Is He really the Messiah? (See notes—Mt.21:8-9; 21:23.) This was the question, the thing that Nicodemus felt compelled to find out. (See DEEPER STUDY # 2—Mt.1:18.) Note that Nicodemus came to Jesus at night. He apparently did this because he *feared* the other leaders who opposed Jesus. John seemed to be saying this at the burial of Jesus (cp. Jn.19:39).

3. He acknowledged Jesus only as a teacher from God. He and others saw the miracles Jesus did, and they knew something: only a man from God could do such miracles.

4. In essence, Nicodemus was asking, "Who are you? The miracles show that God is *with you*, but you are claiming to be the Messiah, the Son of God. Are you—truthfully—in all honesty?"

Note that Jesus did not answer Nicodemus directly. He saw into the empty, searching heart of Nicodemus and saw the honesty of his question. So Jesus went right to the heart of the matter. Miracles and signs were not what was important. What was important was for Nicodemus to be changed: changed spiritually, changed within, and changed completely—to undergo such a spiritual change that it could only be described as being born again.

2 (3:3) **New Birth**: the new birth is a necessity, an imperative. Two facts show this:

1. The strong assertion, "Unless he is born <u>again</u>." The word "again" (anothen) has three different meanings in Greek. It means...

- *From the first*: from the beginning or completely and fully (cp. Lk.1:3).
- *Again*: a second time, a repeated act (v.4) (cp. Gal.4:9).
- *From above*: from the top, which means from God (cp. Jn.19:11).

The point is this. A man must be "born <u>again</u>." He must be...

- born completely and fully, a complete and full change
- born all over *again*, in the sense of a second time
- born *from above*, from God

2. The importance of the words, "no one can see the kingdom of God." One must be "born again" or else he will never "see" (v.3) nor "enter" (v.5) the Kingdom of God. It is an absolute imperative that a person be born again (3:7). (See DEEPER STUDY # 3, <u>Kingdom of God</u>—Mt.19:23-24.)

> **Whoever believes in him is not condemned, but whoever does not believe stands condemned already because he has not believed in the name of God's one and only Son. (John 3:18)**
>
> **Peter replied, "Repent and be baptized, every one of you, in the name of Jesus Christ for the forgiveness of your sins. And you will receive the gift of the Holy Spirit. (Acts 2:38)**
>
> **Repent, then, and turn to God, so that your sins may be wiped out, that times of refreshing may come from the Lord, (Acts 3:19)**
>
> **For the wages of sin is death, but the gift of God is eternal life in Christ Jesus our Lord. (Rom 6:23)**
>
> **This day I call heaven and earth as witnesses against you that I have set before you life and death, blessings and curses. Now choose life, so that you and your children may live (Deu 30:19)**

3 (3:4-8) **New Birth**: the new birth is a spiritual birth. (See note, pt.2—Jn.3:1-15.) Nicodemus was puzzled by the words "born again." He did not know what Jesus meant. He understood Jesus to be saying that a man must be born a "second time." Jesus answered Nicodemus by doing five things.

1. Jesus gave the *source of the new birth*. It was being born of water, even of the Spirit (see DEEPER STUDY # 1, pt.2—Jn.3:1-15. Also see DEEPER STUDY # 2, <u>Water</u>—Jn.3:5 for discussion.)

2. Jesus *repeated the importance* of being born again. Note what v.3 says: a man "no one can see" (grasp, understand, know, experience) the Kingdom of God; v.5 says a man "no one can enter" (gain entrance to) the Kingdom of God.

3. Jesus gave the *nature* of the new birth. It is spiritual, not physical and material (see notes—Eph.1:3; 4:17-19; DEEPER STUDY # 3—4:24). The flesh cannot bridge the gap between flesh and spirit. Flesh is only flesh; it has no power to be born again, to become spirit (see DEEPER STUDY # 1, <u>Flesh</u>—Jn.1:14).

4. Jesus reemphasized the absolute necessity of the new birth. "You <u>must</u> be born again." The word "must" (dei) means absolute necessity, an imperative.

5. Jesus illustrated the point by picturing the wind. The Spirit of God works just like the wind. We may not know how the wind works, but we can see the effects. It is the

same with the Spirit of God: we may not know *how* He works, but we can see the effects of His working.

> Yet to all who received him, to those who believed in his name, he gave the right to become children of God—children born not of natural descent, nor of human decision or a husband's will, but born of God. (John 1:12-13)
>
> He saved us, not because of righteous things we had done, but because of his mercy. He saved us through the washing of rebirth and renewal by the Holy Spirit, (Titus 3:5)
>
> He chose to give us birth through the word of truth, that we might be a kind of firstfruits of all he created. (James 1:18)
>
> Praise be to the God and Father of our Lord Jesus Christ! In his great mercy he has given us new birth into a living hope through the resurrection of Jesus Christ from the dead, (1 Pet 1:3)
>
> For you have been born again, not of perishable seed, but of imperishable, through the living and enduring word of God. (1 Pet 1:23)
>
> If you know that he is righteous, you know that everyone who does what is right has been born of him. (1 John 2:29)
> No one who is born of God will continue to sin, because God's seed remains in him; he cannot go on sinning, because he has been born of God. (1 John 3:9)
>
> Dear friends, let us love one another, for love comes from God. Everyone who loves has been born of God and knows God. (1 John 4:7)
>
> Everyone who believes that Jesus is the Christ is born of God, and everyone who loves the father loves his child as well. (1 John 5:1)

DEEPER STUDY # 2

(3:5) **Water—Spirit**: the word "*and*" (kai) can also be translated "even." The way it is translated here is left up to the translator. In light of the rest of Scripture, it probably should be translated "even." This would mean that water with all of its cleansing power is a symbol of the Holy Spirit: "No one can enter the Kingdom of God unless he is born of water and the Spirit." A strong argument for this is in the very next verse. The new birth is spiritual, apart from any natural phenomenon. It has nothing to do with any physical substance, including water. It is not of the flesh, not of any material thing. It is of the Spirit (cp. Ro.8:11; Eph.2:1).

Is it possible that *water* means "baptism" here? When John was writing the gospel, he and the readers of his gospel would have known what was meant by *Christian baptism*. However, when Jesus was speaking to Nicodemus, there was no such thing as Christian baptism. It is unlikely that Jesus would say something that Nicodemus could not grasp and understand. Jesus was not out to confuse him, but to lead him to be born again. There was no way Nicodemus could be baptized in order to be born again—not then—for Christian baptism had not yet been instituted. (Regardless of our position on baptism, honesty demands that we note this.)

---

4 (3:9-11) **New Birth**: the new birth is a true experience, a definite experience (see DEEPER STUDY # 1, pt.3—Jn.3:1-15). Nicodemus' heart was touched by what Jesus was saying, and he wished to know what was meant by being "born again." Note: he did not know, but he wished to know. (Think how many do not even care to know.)

> The man without the Spirit does not accept the things that come from the Spirit of God, for they are foolishness to him, and he cannot understand them, because they are spiritually discerned. (1 Cor 2:14)

Note the great tragedy of Nicodemus. He was Israel's teacher, yet he did not know about spiritual things (see note, pt.1—Jn.3:1-2). Note the strong assertion of Jesus: "We know...we have seen" (v.11. See note—Jn.3:13 for how Jesus knows about the new birth.)

> The Spirit himself testifies with our spirit that we are God's children. (Rom 8:16)
>
> Because you are sons, God sent the Spirit of his Son into our hearts, the Spirit who calls out, "Abba, Father." (Gal 4:6)
>
> Because our gospel came to you not simply with words, but also with power, with the Holy Spirit and with deep conviction. You know how we lived among you for your sake. (1 Th 1:5)
>
> That is why I am suffering as I am. Yet I am not ashamed, because I know whom I have believed, and am convinced that he is able to guard what I have entrusted to him for that day. (2 Tim 1:12)
> We know that we have come to know him if we obey his commands. (1 John 2:3)
>
> Dear children, let us not love with words or tongue but with actions and in truth. (1 John 3:18)
>
> This then is how we know that we belong to the truth, and how we set our hearts at rest in his presence (1 John 3:19)
>
> Those who obey his commands live in him, and he in them. And this is how we know that he lives in us: We know it by the Spirit he gave us. (1 John 3:24)
>
> We know that we live in him and he in us, because he has given us of his Spirit. (1 John 4:13)
>
> This is the one who came by water and blood—Jesus Christ. He did not come by water only, but by water and blood. And it is the Spirit who testifies, because the Spirit is the truth. (1 John 5:6)

5 (3:11-12) **New Birth**: the new birth is rejected. There are two tragic facts here.

1. There are the statements: "you people do not accept out testimony" and "you do not believe." Apparently, Nicodemus did not believe and receive Jesus at this point in his life. He did what so many do: he rejected Jesus.

2. It is man's nature not to believe (cp. 1 Cor.2:14. See note—Jn.2:24.)

> Anyone who believes in the Son of God has this testimony in his heart. Anyone who

does not believe God has made him out to be a liar, because he has not believed the testimony God has given about his Son. (1 John 5:10)

He came to that which was his own, but his own did not receive him. (John 1:11)

There is a judge for the one who rejects me and does not accept my words; that very word which I spoke will condemn him at the last day. (John 12:48)

6 (3:13) **New Birth—Jesus Christ, Son of Man—Mediator**: the new birth is revealed only by Jesus. Jesus said two things.

1. He came *from* (ek, out of) heaven. No man can go up into heaven; no man can penetrate the spiritual world. Flesh is flesh, that is, born of the earth; therefore, it is earthly (1 Cor.15:47). However, Jesus Christ was different from all other men. His origin was *out of* heaven, out of the spiritual world and dimension of being. (See DEEPER STUDY # 1—Jn.3:31; note—1:18; DEEPER STUDY # 1,2,3—14:6 for discussion.)

2. He is timeless. "the one who came from heaven—the Son of Man" means His existence and experience are timeless. He is eternal (see note, Son of Man—Jn.1:51).

For the bread of God is he who comes down from heaven and gives life to the world." For I have come down from heaven not to do my will but to do the will of him who sent me. (John 6:33, 38)

But here is the bread that comes down from heaven, which a man may eat and not die. I am the living bread that came down from heaven. If anyone eats of this bread, he will live forever. This bread is my flesh, which I will give for the life of the world." (John 6:50-51)

Jesus said to them, "If God were your Father, you would love me, for I came from God and now am here. I have not come on my own; but he sent me. (John 8:42)

Jesus knew that the Father had put all things under his power, and that he had come from God and was returning to God; (John 13:3)

And now, Father, glorify me in your presence with the glory I had with you before the world began. (John 17:5)

7 (3:14-15) **New Birth**: the new birth is secured by two acts.

1. The first act is Jesus' death. Jesus illustrated His point by using the Old Testament story of Moses lifting up the bronze snake in the wilderness (Num.21:4-9). The children of Israel had begun to murmur and grumble about the trials of the wilderness, wishing they had never left Egypt. God disciplined them by sending snakes to plague them. The discipline worked; the people repented and begged for mercy. God met the people's need by telling Moses to make a bronze image of a snake and to hold it up upon a pole in the midst of the people. The person who looked upon the *lifted up* snake was healed.

Jesus said that He must be lifted up just as the snake was lifted up. What did He mean? There are several pictures here.

a. The people of Israel had great need, for they were dying from the poison of the snakes. Men today are dying from the poison of the snake, the deadly poison of sin.

b. The snake is a symbol of the evil one, Satan (Gen.3:1f; Rev.12:9; 20:2). Jesus Christ destroyed the works of the devil by being lifted up (Heb.2:14-15); therefore the snake hanging upon the pole symbolized the defeat of Satan. By looking upon the *defeated evil* (the snake), Israel was healed. Today man is healed by looking upon the Son of Man who has been lifted up upon the cross.

Now is the time for judgment on this world; now the prince of this world will be driven out. But I, when I am lifted up from the earth, will draw all men to myself." (John 12:31-32)

Since the children have flesh and blood, he too shared in their humanity so that by his death he might destroy him who holds the power of death—that is, the devil—and free those who all their lives were held in slavery by their fear of death. (Heb 2:14-15)

c. The snake was a cursed creature from the very beginning (Gen.3:14-15). Jesus became a curse for man (Gal.3:13).

Christ redeemed us from the curse of the law by becoming a curse for us, for it is written: "Cursed is everyone who is hung on a tree." (Gal 3:13)

He himself bore our sins in his body on the tree, so that we might die to sins and live for righteousness; by his wounds you have been healed. (1 Pet 2:24)

2. The second act is man's belief in Jesus. The man who believes in the Son of Man's being lifted up...
- will not perish (see DEEPER STUDY # 2, Perish—Jn.3:16)
- but will have eternal life (see DEEPER STUDY # 2, Life—Jn.1:4; DEEPER STUDY # 1—10:10; DEEPER STUDY # 1—17:2-3)

Note: if an Israelite believed God's message (the good news of healing), he looked upon the lifted up snake, and he was healed. If a man did not believe God's message, he did not look, and he died. Thus it is with us today: every man must believe the message of Christ in order to be healed, that is, be born again.

"For God so loved the world that he gave his one and only Son, that whoever believes in him shall not perish but have eternal life. (John 3:16)

"I tell you the truth, whoever hears my word and believes him who sent me has eternal life and will not be condemned; he has crossed over from death to life. (John 5:24)

But he was pierced for our transgressions, he was crushed for our iniquities; the punishment that brought us peace was upon him, and by his wounds we are healed. (Isa 53:5)

		E. Revelation 5: God's Great Love, 3:16-17	not perish but have eternal life.	b. To eternal life c. By believing
1	The fact: God so loved[DS1]	16 "For God so loved the world that he gave his one and only Son, that whoever believes in him shall	17 For God did not send his Son into the world to condemn the world, but to save the world through him.	4 The proof: God sent His Son (the Incarnation) a. Not to condemn b. But to save
2	The evidence: God gave			
3	The purpose: To save a. From perishing[DS2]			5 The means: Thru Him

DIVISION II

THE REVELATION OF JESUS, THE SON OF GOD, 2:1-3:21

E. Revelation 5: God's Great Love, 3:16-17

(3:16-17) **Introduction**: this is the world's most well-known Scripture. Brief and to the point, Jesus revealed God's great love.

1. The fact: God so loved (v.16).
2. The evidence: God gave (v.16).
3. The purpose: to save (v.16).
4. The proof: God sent His Son (the Incarnation) (v.17).
5. The means: through Him (v.17).

1 (3:16) **God, Love of**: God so loved the world. He loved the whole world. Note several facts.

1. The idea that God loves the whole world is a new idea. The Jews believed God loved the religious (the true Jew) and hated the non-religious (the Gentiles). The same thoughts are held by many in every generation, especially by *religionists*. The fact that God truly loves is shocking to many. Some wonder and others question how God could possibly love the...

- vile person
- murderer
- immoral person
- wife beater
- child abuser
- prostitute
- thief
- alcoholic
- street person
- oppressor
- enslaver
- bitter, vengeful

Thought 1. God loves *every person*, not just the religious and the good. He does not love only the people who love Him. He loves everyone, even the unlovely and the unloving, the unbelieving and the obstinate, the selfish and the greedy, the spiteful and the vengeful.

> I have other sheep that are not of this sheep pen. I must bring them also. They too will listen to my voice, and there shall be one flock and one shepherd. (John 10:16)
> For there is no difference between Jew and Gentile—the same Lord is Lord of all and richly blesses all who call on him, for, "Everyone who calls on the name of the Lord will be saved." (Rom 10:12-13)
> Who wants all men to be saved and to come to a knowledge of the truth. (1 Tim 2:4)
> The Lord is not slow in keeping his promise, as some understand slowness. He is patient with you, not wanting anyone to perish, but everyone to come to repentance. (2 Pet 3:9)

2. The basis of God's love is His nature. God is love (1 Jn.4:8, 16); therefore, He loves. He acts, demonstrates, and shows His love.

> But God demonstrates his own love for us in this: While we were still sinners, Christ died for us. (Rom 5:8)
> Whoever does not love does not know God, because God is love. And so we know and rely on the love God has for us. God is love. Whoever lives in love lives in God, and God in him. (1 John 4:8, 16)

3. Love acts; it expresses itself. Love does not sit still, doing nothing. It is not dormant, complacent, inactive. If love actually exists, it has to act and express itself; it has to do something good. Love is *loving*; that is, love is always demonstrating love to others. Therefore, God's love acts and reveals Him to be love.

> **Thought 1.** God wants man to know His love. He wants to reach everyone in the world with His love.

> This is how we know what love is: Jesus Christ laid down his life for us. And we ought to lay down our lives for our brothers. (1 John 3:16)
> This is how God showed his love among us: He sent his one and only Son into the world that we might live through him. (1 John 4:9)

DEEPER STUDY # 1

(3:16) **God Loved**: past tense. A past, proven fact. An outline of the greatness of God's love is seen in this verse. (1) Height: God loved. (2) Depth: so loved. (3) Length: God gave. (4) Breadth: whoever. (See note—Jn.21:15-17.)

2 (3:16) **God, Love, of**: there is the evidence of God's love—God gave His one and only Son. Note several points.

1. God demonstrated His love in the *most perfect way* possible: He gave His one and only Son to the world. As God, He is perfect, which means His love is perfect. Therefore, God not only loves, but He *so* loves. He loves to perfection, loves to the ultimate degree. Whatever the ultimate degree and the perfect act and expression of love is, God shows it. Without question, the greatest act of love is the sacrifice of a man's own life; therefore, God sacrificed the life of His own Son to save man.

Greater love has no one than this, that he lay down his life for his friends. (John 15:13)

2. The word *gave* (edoken) has a twofold meaning. God gave His Son to the world, and He gave His Son to die. The idea of *sacrifice*, of great cost, is in both acts. It cost God dearly to give His Son *up to the world and up to the cross*.

a. He gave up His Son to be separated from Him, *allowing Jesus to leave His presence*, to leave the majesty and glory, worship and honor of heaven. (See note—Mk.9:2-3.)

b. He gave up His Son to be separated from Him, *allowing Jesus to come to earth...*

Into a world that was...	*Into a world full of...*
• fallen	• darkness
• depraved	• selfishness, greed
• wicked	• hostility, war
• rebellious	• bitterness, barriers
• revolting	• immorality
• apostate	• wrath, anger
	• sin, shame

c. He gave up His Son to be separated from Him, *allowing Jesus to die* for the sins of men (see Deeper Study # 2—Mt.26:37-38).

But he was pierced for our transgressions, he was crushed for our iniquities; the punishment that brought us peace was upon him, and by his wounds we are healed. (Isa 53:5)

We all, like sheep, have gone astray, each of us has turned to his own way; and the LORD has laid on him the iniquity of us all. (Isa 53:6)

You see, at just the right time, when we were still powerless, Christ died for the ungodly. (Rom 5:6)

He who did not spare his own Son, but gave him up for us all—how will he not also, along with him, graciously give us all things? (Rom 8:32)

For what I received I passed on to you as of first importance : that Christ died for our sins according to the Scriptures, (1 Cor 15:3)

God made him who had no sin to be sin for us, so that in him we might become the righteousness of God. (2 Cor 5:21)

Thanks be to God for his indescribable gift! (2 Cor 9:15)

Christ redeemed us from the curse of the law by becoming a curse for us, for it is written: "Cursed is everyone who is hung on a tree." (Gal 3:13)

But we see Jesus, who was made a little lower than the angels, now crowned with glory and honor because he suffered death, so that by the grace of God he might taste death for everyone. (Heb 2:9)

So Christ was sacrificed once to take away the sins of many people; and he will appear a second time, not to bear sin, but to bring salvation to those who are waiting for him. (Heb 9:28)

He himself bore our sins in his body on the tree, so that we might die to sins and live for righteousness; by his wounds you have been healed. (1 Pet 2:24)

For Christ died for sins once for all, the righteous for the unrighteous, to bring you to God. He was put to death in the body but made alive by the Spirit, (1 Pet 3:18)

3. A most glorious evidence of God's love is that God took the *initiative* to save man. Man did not seek to save himself; God sought to save him. God gave His Son so that we might be forgiven and saved. God is the *seeking Savior*.

God is not...	*God does not..*
• angry	• hate men
• unloving	• have to be persuaded to love men
• unforgiving	• have to be convinced to forgive men

The LORD appeared to us in the past, saying: "I have loved you with an everlasting love; I have drawn you with loving kindness. (Jer 31:3)

But because of his great love for us, God, who is rich in mercy, made us alive with Christ even when we were dead in transgressions—it is by grace you have been saved. (Eph 2:4-5)

4. The most glorious truth is that God gave His *one and only Son*. This is the most remarkable proof of God's love. It magnifies and shows how great His love really is. He was willing to give the thing most dear to His heart in order to save the world. Note this: God even planned to give His Son throughout eternity.

This man was handed over to you by God's set purpose and foreknowledge; and you, with the help of wicked men, put him to death by nailing him to the cross. But

God raised him from the dead, freeing him from the agony of death, because it was impossible for death to keep its hold on him. (Acts 2:23-24)

3 (3:16) **Salvation**: there is the purpose of God's love: to save men. God's purpose in giving His Son was threefold.

1. To save men from perishing (see Deeper Study # 2, Perish—Jn.3:16).

2. To save men to eternal life (see Deeper Study # 2—Jn.1:4; Deeper Study # 1—10:10; Deeper Study # 1—17:2-3).

3. To save men through belief (see Deeper Study # 2—Jn.2:24). Note: this fact says that salvation is conditional.

DEEPER STUDY # 2

(3:16) **Perish—Perishing** (apoletai): to be lost, to destroy utterly, to lose utterly, to lose eternal life, to be spiritually destitute, to be cut off.

1. Perishing means to be in a lost state in this world. It means to be...

• aging, deteriorating, decaying, dying. (See Deeper Study # 2—Mt.8:17; notes—1 Cor.15:50; Col. 2:13; Deeper Study # 1—2 Pt.1:4.)

• without life (purpose, meaning, significance). (See Deeper Study # 2—Jn.1:4; Deeper Study # 1—10:10; Deeper Study # 1—17:2-3.)

• without peace (assurance, confidence, security in God's keeping). (See note—Jn.14:27.)

• without hope (of living forever). (See Deeper Study # 1—2 Tim.4:18.)

2. Perishing means to be in a lost state in the world to come. It means...
- having to die
- facing judgment
- being condemned
- suffering separation from God and all loved ones
- experiencing all that hell is

(See DEEPER STUDY # 2—Mt.5:22; DEEPER STUDY # 4—Lk.16:24; DEEPER STUDY # 1—Heb.9:27.)

4 (3:17) **God, Love of**: there is the proof of God's love, the Incarnation. God actually sent His Son into the world (see notes—Jn.1:14).

1. Christ was not sent to condemn or to judge the world. We, the world, deserve to be judged and condemned.
⇒ We are guilty both of breaking God's law and of coming short of God's glory (Ro.3:23).
⇒ We are convicted (Ro.3:9-18; cp. Ro.1:18-32).

However, Christ *was not* sent to condemn or judge us. Judgment and condemnation were not His purpose.

2. Christ was sent to save us. His purpose was to save us from perishing and to save us to eternal life. (See DEEPER STUDY # 1—1 Cor.1:18.)

> Today in the town of David a Savior has been born to you; he is Christ the Lord. (Luke 2:11)
> Just as the Son of Man did not come to be served, but to serve, and to give his life as a ransom for many." (Mat 20:28)
> For the Son of Man came to seek and to save what was lost." (Luke 19:10)

5 (3:17) **Salvation—Jesus Christ, Mediator**: there is the means of salvation. Salvation is *through Him* (Christ Jesus) and through Him alone.

> Here is a trustworthy saying that deserves full acceptance: Christ Jesus came into the world to save sinners—of whom I am the worst. (1 Tim 1:15)
> For there is one God and one mediator between God and men, the man Christ Jesus, (1 Tim 2:5)
> And we have seen and testify that the Father has sent his Son to be the Savior of the world. (1 John 4:14)
> But when the kindness and love of God our Savior appeared, he saved us, not because of righteous things we had done, but because of his mercy. He saved us through the washing of rebirth and renewal by the Holy Spirit, whom he poured out on us generously through Jesus Christ our Savior, so that, having been justified by his grace, we might become heirs having the hope of eternal life. (Titus 3:4-7)
> They said to the woman, "We no longer believe just because of what you said; now we have heard for ourselves, and we know that this man really is the Savior of the world." (John 4:42)
> Jesus answered, "I am the way and the truth and the life. No one comes to the Father except through me. (John 14:6)
> Salvation is found in no one else, for there is no other name under heaven given to men by which we must be saved." (Acts 4:12)
> God exalted him to his own right hand as Prince and Savior that he might give repentance and forgiveness of sins to Israel. (Acts 5:31)
> Therefore he is able to save completely those who come to God through him, because he always lives to intercede for them. (Heb 7:25)

	F. Revelation 6: Man's Condemnation, 3:18-21	men loved darkness instead of light because their deeds were evil.	c. He loves darkness; loves his evil, his sin
1 Who is condemned: Not the believer but the unbeliever	18 Whoever believes in him is not condemned, but whoever does not believe stands	20 Everyone who does evil hates the light, and will not come into the light for fear that his deeds will be exposed.	d. He does not come to the light
2 When is he condemned: Already	condemned already because he has not believed in the name of God's one and only	21 But whoever lives by the truth comes into the light, so	**4 Who escapes condemnation**
3 Why is he condemned	Son.	that it may be seen plainly	a. He who practices truth
a. He has not believed	19 This is the verdict: Light	that what he has done has	b. He who comes to light
b. Light has come into the world	has come into the world, but	been done through God."	c. He whose works are done through God

DIVISION II

THE REVELATION OF JESUS, THE SON OF GOD, 2:1-3:21

F. Revelation 6: Man's Condemnation, 3:18-21

(3:18-21) **Introduction**: God sent His Son into the world to save the world, but this does not mean that everyone is automatically saved. In fact, some are condemned and doomed. Jesus reveals man's condemnation.

1. Who is condemned: not the believer, but the unbeliever (v.18).
2. When is he condemned: already (v.18).
3. Why is he condemned (v.18-20).
4. Who escapes condemnation (v.21).

1 (3:18) **Condemnation—Faith**: Who is condemned? Not the believer, but the unbeliever.

1. The believer is not condemned. Note three facts.
   a. The critical importance of belief cannot be overstressed. Belief stays, prevents, arrests, and stops judgment. The person who *believes on Christ*...
      • is acquitted as though he never sinned
      • is released
      • is not to be captivated again (by guilt, fear, bondage, shame)
      • is not to be condemned (judged)
      • is not to be dealt with in justice
   b. The believer is saved. He is as guilty as the unbeliever, but there is one critical difference: the believer believes on Jesus Christ and has committed his life to Him. The believer is actively and diligently seeking Christ (Heb.11:6). God will save any man who will believe and seek and honor His Son (cp. Jn.12:26. See Deeper Study # 2—Jn.2:24; note—3:17.)
   c. The believer is released from condemnation because he believes on Christ. The believer believes that Christ died for his sins, in his place, as his substitute, paying the penalty for his sins (which was death).

   "I tell you the truth, whoever hears my word and believes him who sent me has eternal life and will not be condemned; he has crossed over from death to life. (John 5:24)
   Therefore, there is now no condemnation for those who are in Christ Jesus, (Rom 8:1)
   Who is he that condemns? Christ Jesus, who died—more than that, who was

raised to life—is at the right hand of God and is also interceding for us. (Rom 8:34 See Deeper Study #1, 2—Ro.4:22; note—5:1.)

2. The unbeliever is condemned. Note two critical points.
   a. Note who the unbeliever is. He is the person who "has not believed in the name of God's one and only Son." God has one and only one Son. The man who *has not already* believed on God's Son is the unbeliever. It does not matter who the man is or where he is; he is an unbeliever if he *has not already* believed in the one and only Son of God.
   b. Note what it means to be condemned or judged. (See Deeper Study # 2, Perish—Jn.3:16 for discussion.)

2 (3:18) **Judgment—Condemnation**: When is the unbeliever condemned? Already, right now. It is not that he is to be condemned; he is already condemned. At least three things are meant by being "condemned already" (ede kekritai).

1. Condemnation is a sure fact. The unbeliever's judgment is sure, so sure it is as though he has already been condemned. Nothing can change or stop the judgment from coming upon the unbeliever. Ignoring, denying, and struggling against the great day of judgment will not change one detail of the day. It is coming, and every single unbeliever will be judged.
2. The unbeliever is *already* under the present curse of sin. He is...
   • separate from Christ
   • excluded from citizenship with the people of God
   • a foreigner to the promises of God
   • without hope
   • without God in the world (Eph.2:12)

(See Deeper Study # 2, pt.1, Perish—Jn.3:16 for a description of what this means.)
3. The unbeliever already stands guilty of all the sins he has ever committed; he is already condemned. The law of God already exists. Every time a man breaks the law of God, he immediately becomes guilty and is condemned. The judgment is already pronounced. The unbeliever must pay the penalty for every transgression of God's law. He is already *under the curse, the full force* of the law.

All who rely on observing the law are under a curse, for it is written: "Cursed is everyone who does not continue to do everything written in the Book of the Law." (Gal 3:10)

The law is not based on faith; on the contrary, "The man who does these things will live by them." (Gal 3:12)

3 (3:18-20) **Condemnation**: Why is the unbeliever condemned? Four reasons are given.

1. The unbeliever has not believed. The great sin of unbelief is that it neglects, ignores, denies, abuses, and rejects God's Son.

⇒ The dignity of God's Son is ignored (see note—Jn.1:1-2).

⇒ The truth of God's Son is not believed (see notes—Jn.1:14).

⇒ The goodness of God's Son is not embraced (see notes—Jn.1:14).

⇒ The dearest thing to God's heart is denied (see notes—Jn.3:16).

⇒ The name that is above every name is abused and cursed (Ph.2:9).

⇒ The one and only Son of God is rejected (Jn.3:16-19).

Christ is the great remedy for man's sins. Therefore, unbelief—rejecting and refusing to believe Him—is the great damning sin.

Whoever believes in the Son has eternal life, but whoever rejects the Son will not see life, for God's wrath remains on him." (John 3:36)

I told you that you would die in your sins; if you do not believe that I am the one I claim to be, you will indeed die in your sins." (John 8:24)

2. The unbeliever is condemned because Light has come into the world. The Light came into the world to give light to men, to enable men to walk out of the darkness of a sinful and perishing world. The Light came to show men the way, the truth, and the life:

⇒ The Light shows man the way God intends for him to live.

⇒ The Light shows man the truth of life, that is, the truth of God and of man and of the world that surrounds man.

⇒ The Light shows man the life, that is, how to save his life and avoid the things that cause him to stumble and lose his life.

The point is this: the life of Jesus Christ now stands in the world to give Light. Any man who does not turn and walk in the Light is naturally in the dark. He is condemned to the darkness and to all that happens to those who walk in the darkness. (See DEEPER STUDY # 1, Light—Jn.1:9; DEEPER STUDY # 1—8:12.)

3. The unbeliever is condemned because he loves darkness. Why would he love darkness? Because his deeds are evil, and to turn and walk in the Light would expose his evil deeds for what they are: immoral, unrighteous, and disobedient to God. There are at least four reasons why man prefers to walk in darkness and prefer to hang on to his sins.

a. The unbeliever loves his sin and does not want to turn and face the conviction of the Light. If he turned to the Light, He would have to give up his sin; and he loves the feeling, the stimulation, the comfort, the ease, the challenge, the recognition, the power, the fame, the possessions, the things which the sin brings. He loves it all too much to give it up.

b. The unbeliever is full of pride. He does not want to confess his sin, the fact that he is in darkness and short of what God demands. He denies he is in darkness, refusing to turn to the Light (Christ).

c. The unbeliever is enslaved, in bondage to sin and gripped by the darkness; he has been in darkness so long that he does not have the strength to break the enslavement.

d. The unbeliever fears the shame, embarrassment, and consequence of his sin. In some cases he would like to confess his evil and correct it, but fear keeps him from coming out and facing the Light (Christ).

But among you there must not be even a hint of sexual immorality, or of any kind of impurity, or of greed, because these are improper for God's holy people. Nor should there be obscenity, foolish talk or coarse joking, which are out of place, but rather thanksgiving. For of this you can be sure: No immoral, impure or greedy person—such a man is an idolater—has any inheritance in the kingdom of Christ and of God. Let no one deceive you with empty words, for because of such things God's wrath comes on those who are disobedient. Have nothing to do with the fruitless deeds of darkness, but rather expose them. (Eph 5:3-6, 11)

But you, brothers, are not in darkness so that this day should surprise you like a thief. So then, let us not be like others, who are asleep, but let us be alert and self-controlled. For those who sleep, sleep at night, and those who get drunk, get drunk at night. (1 Th 5:4, 6-7)

If we claim to have fellowship with him yet walk in the darkness, we lie and do not live by the truth. (1 John 1:6)

"They know nothing, they understand nothing. They walk about in darkness; all the foundations of the earth are shaken. (Psa 82:5)

But the way of the wicked is like deep darkness; they do not know what makes them stumble. (Prov 4:19)

4. The unbeliever is condemned because he does not come to the Light. Whatever his reasons, the unbeliever refuses to come to the Light; therefore, he is condemned.

The night is nearly over; the day is almost here. So let us put aside the deeds of darkness and put on the armor of light. (Rom 13:12)

Leave them; they are blind guides. If a blind man leads a blind man, both will fall into a pit." (Mat 15:14)

"Therefore their path will become slippery; they will be banished to darkness and

there they will fall. I will bring disaster on them in the year they are punished," declares the LORD. (Jer 23:12)
I will bring distress on the people and they will walk like blind men, because they have sinned against the LORD. Their blood will be poured out like dust and their entrails like filth. (Zep 1:17)

Thought 1. The unbeliever is uncomfortable in the Light. Therefore, he shuns everything that presents the Light to him: the church, believers, the Bible, prayer, and spiritual conversation.

Note that unbelievers are said to hate the Light. They ignore, reject, deny, and fight the Light. They speak and write against it, ridicule and curse it, persecute and seek to stamp it out.

In him was life, and that life was the light of men. The light shines in the darkness, but the darkness has not understood it. (John 1:4-5)
When Jesus spoke again to the people, he said, "I am the light of the world. Whoever follows me will never walk in darkness, but will have the light of life." (John 8:12)
Then Jesus told them, "You are going to have the light just a little while longer. Walk while you have the light, before darkness overtakes you. The man who walks in the dark does not know where he is going. (John 12:35)
I have come into the world as a light, so that no one who believes in me should stay in darkness. (John 12:46)
For God, who said, "Let light shine out of darkness," made his light shine in our hearts to give us the light of the knowledge of the glory of God in the face of Christ. (2 Cor 4:6)
For it is light that makes everything visible. This is why it is said: "Wake up, O sleeper, rise from the dead, and Christ will shine on you." (Eph 5:14)
The people walking in darkness have seen a great light; on those living in the land of the shadow of death a light has dawned. (Isa 9:2)

4 (3:21) **Condemnation**: Who escapes condemnation? The man who does three things.

1. The man who practices truth and lives righteously escapes condemnation. He knows what is right and he does it. The verb is continuous action. He practices truth, continually and habitually. Note two things about this man.
   a. This does not mean he lives perfectly, without ever sinning. No man is or can be perfect. It means that the man directs his life toward truth: diligently seeks the truth and seeks to be truthful. He may slip and sin, but he immediately turns back to God, repenting and hanging on to his integrity.
   b. Christ said that the man who does truth hears His voice (Jn.18:37; 1 Jn.1:6). Only the man who de-

sires truth is saved, and every man who comes to the truth is saved. Christ is truth.

Then you will know the truth, and the truth will set you free." (John 8:32)
Jesus answered, "I am the way and the truth and the life. No one comes to the Father except through me. (John 14:6)
If we claim to have fellowship with him yet walk in the darkness, we lie and do not live by the truth. But if we walk in the light, as he is in the light, we have fellowship with one another, and the blood of Jesus, his Son, purifies us from all sin. (1 John 1:6-7)
It has given me great joy to find some of your children walking in the truth, just as the Father commanded us. (2 John 1:4)
It gave me great joy to have some brothers come and tell about your faithfulness to the truth and how you continue to walk in the truth. (3 John 1:3)
For your love is ever before me, and I walk continually in your truth. (Psa 26:3)
Teach me your way, O LORD, and I will walk in your truth; give me an undivided heart, that I may fear your name. (Psa 86:11)

2. The man who comes to the Light escapes condemnation. Only the Light (Christ) can dispel the darkness in a man's life (see DEEPER STUDY # 1—Jn.1:9).
3. The man whose works are done through God escapes condemnation. The words "done through" (eirgasmena) mean to work, produce, perform, originate, manufacture, and fashion from something. The idea is that the man *comes to Christ* (the Light) so that his works will be "done through," originated, and worked in and of God. The man who comes to Christ lives close to God. He walks and talks and listens to God (His Word), and he does what God says (cp. 2 Cor.1:12).

In the same way, let your light shine before men, that they may see your good deeds and praise your Father in heaven. (Mat 5:16)
Whoever has my commands and obeys them, he is the one who loves me. He who loves me will be loved by my Father, and I too will love him and show myself to him." (John 14:21)
Command those who are rich in this present world not to be arrogant nor to put their hope in wealth, which is so uncertain, but to put their hope in God, who richly provides us with everything for our enjoyment. Command them to do good, to be rich in good deeds, and to be generous and willing to share. (1 Tim 6:17-18)
In everything set them an example by doing what is good. In your teaching show integrity, seriousness (Titus 2:7)
And do not forget to do good and to share with others, for with such sacrifices God is pleased. (Heb 13:16)
In the same way, faith by itself, if it is not accompanied by action, is dead. (James 2:17)

	III. THE REVELATION OF JESUS, THE NEW MASTER, 3:22-36	him.' 29 The bride belongs to the bridegroom. The friend who attends the bridegroom waits and listens for him, and is full of joy when he hears the bridegroom's voice. That joy is mine, and it is now complete.	but as the forerunner **Answer 2: Jesus alone was the Bridegroom** a. He is the One by whom the friend stands b. He is the voice that is to be heard c. He is the cause of joy d. He is the only object of loyalty
1 The setting for the revelation a. Jesus & His disciples were baptizing in Judaea b. John & his disciples were baptizing close by	22 After this, Jesus and his disciples went out into the Judean countryside, where he spent some time with them, and baptized. 23 Now John also was baptizing at Aenon near Salim, because there was plenty of water, and people were constantly coming to be baptized.	30 He must become greater; I must become less. 31 "The one who comes from above is above all; the one who is from the earth belongs to the earth, and speaks as one from the earth. The one who comes from heaven is above all.	**4 Answer 3: Jesus alone was from above—from heaven** a. Meaning: "Out of"[DS1] b. Result: Jesus is above all
c. Two basic questions of life 1) Who really purifies man's heart? 2) Who is the supreme Master?	24 (This was before John was put in prison.) 25 An argument developed between some of John's disciples and a certain Jew over the matter of ceremonial washing. 26 They came to John and said to him, "Rabbi, that man who was with you on the other side of the Jordan—the one you testified about—well, he is baptizing, and everyone is going to him."	32 He testifies to what he has seen and heard, but no one accepts his testimony. 33 The man who has accepted it has certified that God is truthful. 34 For the one whom God has sent speaks the words of God, for God gives the Spirit without limit.	**5 Answer 4: Jesus alone was God's Spokesman** a. He testifies b. Some reject c. Some accept & seal His testimony[DS2] d. Proof: Sent from God & speaks God's Word[DS3]
2 Answer 1: Jesus alone was God's appointed Messiah a. God alone appoints men b. God had not appointed John as the Messiah,	27 To this John replied, "A man can receive only what is given him from heaven. 28 You yourselves can testify that I said, 'I am not the Christ but am sent ahead of	35 The Father loves the Son and has placed everything in his hands. 36 Whoever believes in the Son has eternal life, but whoever rejects the Son will not see life, for God's wrath remains on him."	**6 Answer 5: Jesus alone had the Spirit without measure or limit** **7 Answer 6: Jesus alone determines man's destiny** a. To believe Him brings eternal life[DS4] b. Not to obey Him brings wrath[DS5]

DIVISION III

THE REVELATION OF JESUS, THE NEW MASTER, 3:22-36

(3:22-36) **Introduction**: this passage does one thing—it points to Jesus Christ as the New Master, the One whom God has set before man as the only Master worthy of serving.

1. The setting for the revelation (v.22-26).
2. Answer 1: Jesus alone was God's appointed Messiah (v.27-28).
3. Answer 2: Jesus alone was the Bridegroom (v.29-30).
4. Answer 3: Jesus alone was from above, from heaven (v.31).
5. Answer 4: Jesus alone was God's Spokesman (v.32-34).
6. Answer 5: Jesus alone had the Spirit without measure or limit (v.34).
7. Answer 6: Jesus alone determines man's destiny (v.35-36).

1 (3:22-26) **Jesus Christ, Baptized**: the setting for the revelation. After His interview with Nicodemus, Jesus moved out into the country districts of Judaea.

1. Jesus and His disciples were baptizing. The words "spent some time" (dietriben) have the idea of spending *much time* in sharing and ministering. Note the statement: He baptized. This is the only place in Scripture where Jesus is said to baptize, though strictly speaking it was His dis-

ciples who actually did the baptizing (Jn.4:2). It was His baptizing that set the ground for what was now to happen.

2. John and his disciples were also baptizing in Aenon, which was near to Salim. Nothing is known about either place beyond what is mentioned here.

People began to flock from John to Jesus. This decline in John's popularity gave the religionists an opportunity to attack John. They attacked him by asking his disciples a crucial question, and in their questioning, they stirred the two basic questions of life.

3. The religionists questioned the cleansing and purifying value of John's baptism. They thought he must be a sham, a false prophet. If John's baptism were really cleansing the people's hearts and giving them a sense of cleanliness, why were the people now flocking to Jesus? If his baptism were really meeting the people's needs, they would continue to come to him for cleansing. Instead, they were deserting him and flocking to Jesus.

This charge, of course, cut John's disciples to the core, so they asked John why all men were now turning to Jesus instead of remaining with him.

Note how the question of purifying strikes at the two basic questions of life.

1. There is the question of washing and cleansing. Can the human heart really be cleansed? Can the need of men for cleansing really be met?

2. There is the question of supremacy, of a man's Master in life. Who is man to follow? To whom should men turn for cleansing? To other men such as religious leaders, or to Jesus Christ?

Thought 1. Note two tragic facts.

1) Every man seeks the cleansing of his heart from someplace. He seeks release from sensing wrong and failure; He seeks some dissolving of guilt. However, few seek cleansing in Christ. They seem to seek cleansing everywhere except in Christ:

⇒ in religion
⇒ in attending church enough to salve their conscience and give a feeling of acceptance by God
⇒ in giving to charity
⇒ in doing some good deed for others
⇒ in being loyal to some good man's teaching or leadership

2) Every man follows some master and gives his allegiance to something, whether person or thing (cp. Mt.6:24; Lk.16:13; Ro.6:16).

Thought 2. Note a significant point: only Christ can cleanse and purify a man's heart and give him true cleansing from sin.

2 (3:27-28) **Jesus Christ, Messiah—Ministers**: first, Jesus alone was God's appointed Messiah. John answered the questions by pointing to Jesus Christ. He alone was Messiah, God's appointed One.

1. God is the One who appoints men.
⇒ He is God, so He has the right to appoint men.
⇒ He calls men to be His servants.
⇒ He appoints those men to a particular service and equips those men with gifts.

No man can receive a *true* appointment, a *true* service, or a *true* gift unless it is given from heaven, that is, from God Himself. All appointments and gifts that have not come from heaven *are false*.

> Every good and perfect gift is from above, coming down from the Father of the heavenly lights, who does not change like shifting shadows. (James 1:17)
>
> To one he gave five talents of money, to another two talents, and to another one talent, each according to his ability. Then he went on his journey. (Mat 25:15)
>
> We have different gifts, according to the grace given us. If a man's gift is prophesying, let him use it in proportion to his faith. (Rom 12:6)
>
> For who makes you different from anyone else? What do you have that you did not receive? And if you did receive it, why do you boast as though you did not? (1 Cor 4:7)
>
> There are different kinds of gifts, but the same Spirit. (1 Cor 12:4)
>
> But it is the spirit in a man, the breath of the Almighty, that gives him understanding. (Job 32:8)

2. God did not appoint John to be the Messiah, but to be the forerunner. John was clear about this. He was not the Messiah; Jesus Christ was the Messiah. Note several facts.

⇒ John's strong witness to Jesus Christ's being the Messiah
⇒ John's clear understanding of who he himself was and what his specific appointment and ministry were (the forerunner)
⇒ John's humility

Thought 1. Jesus Christ is the Messiah; He *alone* is the One appointed from heaven. This is the strong declaration of John.

> "But what about you?" he asked. "Who do you say I am?" Simon Peter answered, "You are the Christ, the Son of the living God." Jesus replied, "Blessed are you, Simon son of Jonah, for this was not revealed to you by man, but by my Father in heaven. (Mat 16:15-17)
>
> But Jesus remained silent. The high priest said to him, "I charge you under oath by the living God: Tell us if you are the Christ, the Son of God." "Yes, it is as you say," Jesus replied. "But I say to all of you: In the future you will see the Son of Man sitting at the right hand of the Mighty One and coming on the clouds of heaven." (Mat 26:63-64)
>
> He said to them, "How foolish you are, and how slow of heart to believe all that the prophets have spoken! Did not the Christ have to suffer these things and then enter his glory?" (Luke 24:25-26)
>
> The woman said, "I know that Messiah" (called Christ) "is coming. When he comes, he will explain everything to us." Then Jesus declared, "I who speak to you am he." (John 4:25-26)
>
> So Jesus said, "When you have lifted up the Son of Man, then you will know that I am the one I claim to be and that I do nothing on my own but speak just what the Father has taught me. The one who sent me is with me; he has not left me alone, for I always do what pleases him." (John 8:28-29)

Thought 2. The true servants of God are appointed to their service and ministry by God. This says several things.

1) The servant serves God and God alone.
2) The servant can trust God to take care of him and his ministry.
3) The servant should be humble.
⇒ He should not envy others, for every servant's ministry is special to God and necessary to His plan of salvation.
⇒ He should be satisfied in his service and ministry, for he is there by God's appointment.

> You did not choose me, but I chose you and appointed you to go and bear fruit—fruit that will last. Then the Father will give you whatever you ask in my name. (John 15:16)

3 (3:29-30) **Jesus Christ, Bridegroom—Humility—Ministers, Purpose**: John declared that Jesus was the Bridegroom. The bridegroom is the One who has the bride (the church, the followers of God). The friend is important, but he is not the bridegroom. John said four things about Jesus as the Bridegroom.

1. The Bridegroom (Christ) is the One for whom the friend waits. It is true that the friend (God's servant) is important, for he takes care of matters for the bridegroom, and he has the privilege of bringing the bride to the bridegroom. But there is only one Bridegroom, and He is the focus of the friend's attention.

2. The Bridegroom's (Christ's) voice is the voice to be heard. His voice is the important voice. His will is the will to be done: serving Him and doing what He says are what is important.

3. The Bridegroom (Christ) is the cause of joy. It is not the friend who brings joy to the bride or to the guests and community; it is the Bridegroom. Everyone's joy is found in seeing the Bridegroom's will done and in seeing Him pleased.

4. The Bridegroom (Christ) is the only object of loyalty. The words "He" and "I" are an *emphatic contrast* (v.30). That is to say, there is a *compulsion* to lift up the Person and the honor of the Bridegroom. In no sense nor in any place does the servant try to draw attention, praise, or honor toward himself.

⇒ The servant draws back and shrinks from attention, becoming less in the eyes of all. He does nothing for himself but does *all for the Bridegroom*, for His honor and greatness.
⇒ The servant focuses attention upon the Bridegroom: pushes Him out front, increases His presence and stature before everyone.

That all may honor the Son just as they honor the Father. He who does not honor the Son does not honor the Father, who sent him. (John 5:23)

For this very reason, Christ died and returned to life so that he might be the Lord of both the dead and the living. (Rom 14:9)

Your attitude should be the same as that of Christ Jesus: Who, being in very nature God, did not consider equality with God something to be grasped, but made himself nothing, taking the very nature of a servant, being made in human likeness. And being found in appearance as a man, he humbled himself and became obedient to death— even death on a cross! Therefore God exalted him to the highest place and gave him the name that is above every name, (Phil 2:5-9)

And he is the head of the body, the church; he is the beginning and the firstborn from among the dead, so that in everything he might have the supremacy. (Col 1:18)

Jesus has been found worthy of greater honor than Moses, just as the builder of a house has greater honor than the house itself. (Heb 3:3)

Then I heard every creature in heaven and on earth and under the earth and on the sea, and all that is in them, singing: "To him who sits on the throne and to the Lamb be praise and honor and glory and power, for ever and ever!" (Rev 5:13)

Let us rejoice and be glad and give him glory! For the wedding of the Lamb has come, and his bride has made herself ready. (Rev 19:7)

Ascribe to the LORD the glory due his name; worship the LORD in the splendor of his holiness. (Psa 29:2)

Glorify the LORD with me; let us exalt his name together. (Psa 34:3)

Let them exalt him in the assembly of the people and praise him in the council of the elders. (Psa 107:32)

O LORD, you are my God; I will exalt you and praise your name, for in perfect faithfulness you have done marvelous things, things planned long ago. (Isa 25:1)

Though you soar like the eagle and make your nest among the stars, from there I will bring you down," declares the LORD. (Oba 1:4)

4 (3:31) **Revelation—Heaven**: third, Jesus alone was from above, that is, from heaven. Note two things.

1. The meaning of "from above" is significant (see DEEPER STUDY # 1—Jn.3:31).

2. The words "above all" are mentioned twice; they are very important. They mean superior and preeminent. Jesus, who came from heaven (out of the dimension of heaven), was the Superior and preeminent One. He was above all. The reasons He was "above all" are twofold.

a. His origin was "from above." He was not of the earth, not earthly. Men are. Men are born of the flesh, that is, they are born of a man and woman who live on earth. Therefore, men are of the earth and are earthly. But not Jesus. He was "from heaven"—*out of* God Himself. Therefore, He was superior and preeminent. (See DEEPER STUDY # 1, Flesh, pt.4—Jn.1:14.)

b. A man can only speak of the earth and of earthly things. He comes *only* out of the earth; therefore, he can know *only* earthly things. When he speaks of heavenly things, he only shares his *ideas* and *speculations*, for he has never been to heaven. Therefore, the only conceivable way for man to know anything about heaven is for Someone from heaven to come and tell him. (See notes—Jn.1:18; 3:13; DEEPER STUDY # 1,2,3—14:6.)

DEEPER STUDY # 1

(3:31) **"From Above"—Jesus Christ**: Jesus came *out of* (ek) the spiritual world into the physical world, out of the heavenly dimension of being into the earthly dimension of being. Jesus came out of...

• the incorruptible and imperishable world into the corruptible and perishable world.
• the glorious world into the dishonorable world.
• the powerful world into the weak world.
• the spiritual world into the natural world. (Cp. 1 Cor.15:42-44.)

No one has ever gone into heaven except the one who came from heaven—the Son of Man. (John 3:13)

For the bread of God is he who comes down from heaven and gives life to the world." For I have come down from heaven not to do my will but to do the will of him who sent me. (John 6:33, 38)

At this the Jews began to grumble about him because he said, "I am the bread that came down from heaven." They said, "Is this not Jesus, the son of Joseph, whose father and mother we know? How can he now say, 'I came down from heaven'?" (John 6:41-42)

But here is the bread that comes down from heaven, which a man may eat and not die. I am the living bread that came down from heaven. If anyone eats of this bread, he will live forever. This bread is my flesh, which I will give for the life of the world." (John 6:50-51)

This is the bread that came down from heaven. Your forefathers ate manna and died, but he who feeds on this bread will live forever." (John 6:58)

What if you see the Son of Man ascend to where he was before! (John 6:62)

But he continued, "You are from below; I am from above. You are of this world; I am not of this world. (John 8:23)

Jesus said to them, "If God were your Father, you would love me, for I came from God and now am here. I have not come on my own; but he sent me. (John 8:42)

Jesus knew that the Father had put all things under his power, and that he had come from God and was returning to God; (John 13:3)

Now we can see that you know all things and that you do not even need to have anyone ask you questions. This makes us believe that you came from God." (John 16:30)

And now, Father, glorify me in your presence with the glory I had with you before the world began. (John 17:5)

The first man was of the dust of the earth, the second man from heaven. (1 Cor 15:47)

a. He was the Apostle of God.

For I have come down from heaven not to do my will but to do the will of him who sent me. (John 6:38)

But I know him because I am from him and he sent me." (John 7:29)

Jesus said to them, "If God were your Father, you would love me, for I came from God and now am here. I have not come on my own; but he sent me. (John 8:42)

What about the one whom the Father set apart as his very own and sent into the world? Why then do you accuse me of blasphemy because I said, 'I am God's Son'? (John 10:36)

That all of them may be one, Father, just as you are in me and I am in you. May they also be in us so that the world may believe that you have sent me. (John 17:21)

b. He is the Spokesman of God.

For the one whom God has sent speaks the words of God, for God gives the Spirit without limit. (John 3:34)

The Spirit gives life; the flesh counts for nothing. The words I have spoken to you are spirit and they are life. (John 6:63)

Simon Peter answered him, "Lord, to whom shall we go? You have the words of eternal life. (John 6:68)

"No one ever spoke the way this man does," the guards declared. (John 7:46)

I tell you the truth, if anyone keeps my word, he will never see death." (John 8:51)

There is a judge for the one who rejects me and does not accept my words; that very word which I spoke will condemn him at the last day. (John 12:48)

He who does not love me will not obey my teaching. These words you hear are not my own; they belong to the Father who sent me. (John 14:24)

For I gave them the words you gave me and they accepted them. They knew with certainty that I came from you, and they believed that you sent me. (John 17:8)

Heaven and earth will pass away, but my words will never pass away. (Mark 13:31)

All spoke well of him and were amazed at the gracious words that came from his lips. "Isn't this Joseph's son?" they asked. (Luke 4:22)

They were amazed at his teaching, because his message had authority. (Luke 4:32)

5 (3:32-34) **Jesus Christ, Apostle; God's Spokesman:** fourth, Jesus alone was God's Spokesman. Jesus was "from above," *out of the dimension of heaven*; therefore, He had seen and heard the truth of heaven.

1. Jesus testified, revealed, and proclaimed what He had seen and heard. He was the Spokesman of God who revealed heaven and the truth of it. (See DEEPER STUDY # 3, Kingdom of God—Mt.19:23-24.) He is the only One who can share heaven with men.

2. Most men reject His testimony. Note the words "no one"—this simply means the vast, vast majority of men (cp. v.33 where some few do accept His words). So many men reject the Lord's words that it can be said that "no one" accepts His message.

3. Some few men do accept and seal the Lord's testimony (see DEEPER STUDY # 2—Jn.3:33).

4. The proof that Jesus was God's Spokesman is clearly stated without any equivocation.

⇒ Jesus was sent from God. He was the *Apostle of God* (see DEEPER STUDY # 3—Jn.3:34).

⇒ Therefore, He spoke the Words of God. Whatever He said was the Word of God. How can we be sure? Because God sent Him and gave His Spirit *without measure or limit* to Him.

DEEPER STUDY # 2

(3:33) **Seal—Certify:** a man's seal or certificaton was affixed to a document to show he agreed with it. He reckoned it as legal, binding, valid, authentic. A seal guaranteed that the record was true and genuine. When a man receives the testimony of Jesus, he shows that God is true. Conversely, the only way a man can show that God is true is to accept the testimony of Jesus (cp. Jn.6:27).

(3:34) **"God has Sent"—Jesus Christ, Origin**: Jesus is the Apostle of God. He is God's Ambassador, God's perfect Spokesman. It should be noted that God poured out His Spirit *without measure or limit* upon Jesus—the only apostle upon whom this was ever done. (Cp. Jn.4:34; 5:23-24, 30, 36-37; 6:38-40, 44, 57; 7:16, 18; 8:16, 42; 9:4; 10:36; 11:42; 12:44-45, 49; 14:24; 15:21; 16:5; 17:3, 18, 21, 23, 25; 20:21.)

6 (3:34) **Jesus Christ, Fulness of Spirit**: fifth, Jesus alone had the full measure of the Spirit. There was no limit to the Spirit's...

- presence
- call
- equipping
- blessings
- fullness
- appoinment
- work

The Spirit was of the same Being with Jesus, in perfect harmony, communion, and fellowship with Jesus. He was given to Jesus in a way far different than He was given to other men. There was no limit to His presence with Jesus. Jesus had the perfect and full limit of the Spirit. The purpose for the full limit was clearly stated by Jesus.

> **"The Spirit of the Lord is on me, because he has anointed me to preach good news to the poor. He has sent me to proclaim freedom for the prisoners and recovery of sight for the blind, to release the oppressed, to proclaim the year of the Lord's favor." (Luke 4:18-19)**
>
> **How God anointed Jesus of Nazareth with the Holy Spirit and power, and how he went around doing good and healing all who were under the power of the devil, because God was with him. (Acts 10:38)**

7 (3:35-36) **God, Love for Christ—Man, Destiny**: sixth, Jesus alone determines man's destiny.

1. There has never been a more tender statement than "the Father loves the Son." God loves His Son beyond anything that could ever be understood. How much does God love Him? So much that He has given all things into the hands of His Son: all power, all authority, all rule, all reign, all supremacy, all dominion, all honor, all glory, all praise, all worship, all service. As clearly and as simply as can be said, all things have been given to God's only Son. There is nothing existing that has not been given to Him.

> **Who has gone into heaven and is at God's right hand—with angels, authorities and powers in submission to him. (1 Pet 3:22)**

2. There are four primary reasons why God loves His Son so much.
 ⇒ Jesus is God's *only* Son, the Son in His very own side (see note—Jn.1:18).
 ⇒ Jesus is God's one and only Son, the Son who willingly partook of flesh and came into the world to save men, thereby fulfilling the will of God perfectly (see notes—Jn.1:14).
 ⇒ Jesus gave Himself as an *offering* and a *sacrifice to God Himself*. (See note—Eph.5:2.)

⇒ Jesus willingly learned perfect obedience by the things which He suffered (see notes—Jn.13:31-32; Heb.5:5-10).

3. The man who believes in the Son has eternal life (see DEEPER STUDY # 2—Jn.1:4; DEEPER STUDY # 1—10:10; DEEPER STUDY # 1—17:2-3). God will receive and honor anyone who receives and honors His Son whom He loves so much. It does not matter who the person is or what the person has done. If the person believes in God's only Son, God gives eternal life to him.

4. The man who does not believe the Son faces two things.
 a. He will not see life. He perishes (see DEEPER STUDY # 2, Perish—Jn.3:16).
 b. The wrath of God abides on him (see DEEPER STUDY # 5—Jn.3:36).

(3:36) **Rejection—Believe Not** (ho apeithon): to obey not. If a person does not obey, he does not really believe. Conversely, if a person really believes, he obeys. (See note and DEEPER STUDY # 2—Jn.2:24; DEEPER STUDY # 1—Heb.5:9.)

(3:36) **Wrath** (orge): anger, temper, indignation. It is not an uncontrolled, unthinking, violent reaction. It is deep, permanent, settled, thoughtful, controlled anger and temper.

There is another Greek word which also means wrath (thumos), and it is also used of God's wrath. Thumos is anger that arises more quickly, blazes forth, and just as quickly cools down. It is an anger that is more turbulent, more sudden, but the agitation lasts for only a short period of time. This simply means that God does not dodge His responsibility to execute justice and to punish injustice and sin (cp. Ro.1:22). His wrath is His...

- anger against sin.
- reaction against unrighteousness.
- opposition to the injustices of men.
- punishment of evil and wicked men.

The wrath or anger of God is aroused for four reasons.
1. Men do not believe in the Son of God. They allow their hearts to become hardened, stubborn, and unrepentant (Ro.2:5). They spurn and wound God's love—rejecting, abusing, cursing and denying His Son, the dearest thing to His heart (Jn.3:36; 2 Th.1:7-9. See notes—Jn.3:18-20; 3:35-36.)
2. Men reject God's mercy, which is ever attempting to reach out and save them (Ro.2:3-6).
3. Men transgress God's law (Ro.1:18f; Col.3:6).
4. Men sin and come short of God's will, violating His holiness (Eph.5:6).

God's wrath is real and active. God is holy, righteous, and pure as well as loving, gracious, and merciful. He executes justice as well as love. He shows wrath and anger as well as compassion. His wrath is both present and future.
1. God's wrath is present and active in this life. His remains on men now. His wrath is manifested against all ungodliness and unrighteousness of men (Ro.1:18). God punishes sin in this life by giving men up...
- to sexual impuriy
- to shameful lusts
- to depraved minds

2. God's wrath is future and it is to be actively executed in the next life (see DEEPER STUDY # 2—Mt.5:22; DEEPER STUDY # 4—Lk.16:24; DEEPER STUDY # 1—Heb.9:27). God will punish sin by giving men up...
- to eternal fire (Mt.25:41; 25:46)
- to hell (Mt.5:22)
- to the darkness (Mt.8:12)
- to weeping and gnashing of teeth (Mt.8:12)
- to the Lake of Fire (Rev.20:15)

3. God's wrath will be especially manifested and active in the last days (cp. Rev.6:16; 11:8; 14:10; 16:19; 19:15).

CHAPTER 4

IV. THE REVELATION OF JESUS, THE LIV-ING WATER, 4:1-42

A. The Offer of Living Water, 4:1-14

1 **Jesus left Judea**
  a. He left out of necessity
    1) For John's sake

    2) For His destiny: "He had to go
  b. He left to confront a Samaritan woman
    1) He entered Sychar, Samaria[DS1,2]
    2) He was weary, sat by a well

    3) He requested drink from a woman

The Pharisees heard that Jesus was gaining and baptizing more disciples than John,
2 Although in fact it was not Jesus who baptized, but his disciples.
3 When the Lord learned of this, he left Judea and went back once more to Galilee.
4 Now he had to go through Samaria.
5 So he came to a town in Samaria called Sychar, near the plot of ground Jacob had given to his son Joseph.
6 Jacob's well was there, and Jesus, tired as he was from the journey, sat down by the well. It was about the sixth hour.
7 When a Samaritan woman came to draw water, Jesus said to her, "Will you give me a drink?"
8 (His disciples had gone into the town to buy food.)
9 The Samaritan woman said to him, "You are a Jew and I am a Samaritan woman. How can you ask me for a drink?" (For Jews do not associate with Samaritans.)
10 Jesus answered her, "If you knew the gift of God and who it is that asks you for a drink, you would have asked him and he would have given you living water."
11 "Sir," the woman said, "you have nothing to draw with and the well is deep. Where can you get this living water?
12 Are you greater than our father Jacob, who gave us the well and drank from it himself, as did also his sons and his flocks and herds?"
13 Jesus answered, "Every one who drinks this water will be thirsty again,
14 But whoever drinks the water I give him will never thirst. Indeed, the water I give him will become in him a spring of water welling up to eternal life."

    4) The disciples had gone for food
  c. The woman questioned Jesus
    1) She was shocked that Jesus talked with her
    2) She questioned racial prejudice

2 **Living water is alive**
  a. Is "of God"
  b. Is "the gift" of God
  c. Is given by asking for it

3 **Living water is from a Person much greater than a religious father**

4 **Living water is the only water that will quench thirst**

DIVISION IV

THE REVELATION OF JESUS, THE LIVING WATER, 4:1-42

A. The Offer of Living Water, 4:1-14

(4:1-42) **DIVISION OVERVIEW: Salvation**: Jesus offered the Samaritan woman living water, and she showed an intriguing interest. However, there were some matters that she had to straighten out before she could ever have the living water. There was the matter of sin in her life, of worship, of the Messiah, and of laboring for God. Therefore, Jesus began to discuss these subjects with her one by one.

(4:1-14) **Introduction**: this is one of the most profound revelations of Jesus: He is the Living Water, the water which men can drink and thereby never thirst again.

  1. Jesus left Judea (v.1-9).
  2. Living water is alive (v.10).
  3. Living water is from a Person much greater than a religious father (v.11-12).
  4. Living water is the only water that will quench thirst (v.13-14).

1 (4:1-9) **Jesus Christ, Mission**: Jesus left Judea. Note two significant facts.

  1. Jesus left Judaea out of necessity. He left for John's sake. The crowds were leaving John and coming to Jesus, and the religionists were using the fact to downgrade John's ministry (see note—Jn.3:22-26). Jesus did not want to create a competitive scene that would damage John's ministry, so He left the area to return to Galilee.

Note the words, "Now he had to go through Samaria." The word "had" (edei) means necessity, compulsion, destiny. Jesus was driven to go through Samaria for the sake of His mission. Samaria needed the gospel as much as other areas. (The words "had" and "must" are so often used in connection with Jesus' mission that it makes an excellent word study. Cp. Jn.3:14; 9:4; 10:16; 12:34; 20:9.)

  2. Jesus left Judea to confront a Samaritan woman. He entered Sychar, a city of Samaria (see DEEPER STUDY # 2—Jn.4:5). He sat on the wall of a well, for He was both tired and thirsty from His journey. While sitting there, one of the events for which He had come into Samaria happened: He confronted a woman with the claims of the Messiah.

She came to draw water, and He initiated a conversation by asking her for a drink of water. She was shocked, for the Jews did not associate with the Samaritans (see DEEPER STUDY # 1—Jn.4:5). She asked Jesus why He would ask her, a Samaritan, for a drink. It was this question, this subject of water, that Jesus used...

  • to discuss one of the greatest truths of spiritual life, that of living water.
  • to present the claims of God upon a life.

DEEPER STUDY # 1
(4:5) **Samaria—Samaritans**: Samaria was the central part of Palestine. Palestine was a small country, stretching only

120 miles north to south. The country was divided into three sections:

⇒ Judea, the southern section
⇒ Galilee, the northern section
⇒ Samaria, the central section, lying right between the two

There was bitter hatred between the Jews and Samaritans. Two things in particular caused this hatred.

1. The Samaritans were mongrel or half Jews, a mixed breed *by birth*. Centuries before (about 720 B.C.), the King of Assyria had captured the ten tribes of Israel and deported a large number of the people, scattering them all throughout the Media empire (cp. 2 Ki.17:6-41). He then took people from all over the Assyrian empire to transplant them into Samaria to repopulate the land. The result was only natural. Intermarriage took place and the people became a mixed breed, a breed including...

• the transplanted people
• the weak of the land who had been left behind
• the outcast and irreligious who had intermarried with the original Samaritans

The fact of a mixed breed, of course, infuriated the strict Jews who held to a pure race.

2. The Samaritans were mongrel or half Jews, a mixed breed *by religion*. The transplanted heathen, of course, brought their gods with them. Eventually the God of Israel won out, but the Samaritan religion never became pure Judaism. Three things happened to cause this.

a. When Ezra led the Jews back from exile in Babylon, the first thing the Jews did was to start rebuilding their temple. The Samaritans offered to help them, but the Jews rejected their help, declaring that the Samaritans—through intermarriage and worship of false gods—had lost their purity and forfeited their right to worship the only true God. This severe denunciation embittered the Samaritans against the Jews in Jerusalem.

b. The Samaritans built a rival temple on Mount Gerizim to stand in competition with the Jewish temple at Jerusalem.

c. The Samaritans twisted both the Scripture and history to favor their own people and nation.

⇒ They twisted Scripture in that they accepted only five books of the Bible, the Pentateuch. (Just imagine! They missed all the richness and depth of the Psalms and prophets.)

⇒ They twisted history in that they claimed three great events took place on Mt. Gerizim that set it apart as a place of worship. They claimed it was the place where Abraham offered Isaac, where Melchizedek met Abraham, and where Moses built his first altar after leading Israel out from Egyptian bondage.

DEEPER STUDY # 2

(4:5) **Sychar**: little is known about the city; however, three significant Biblical events happened there.

⇒ Jacob bought a piece of land in the area (Gen.33:19).
⇒ Jacob, as he was dying, willed the land to Joseph (Gen.48:22).
⇒ Joseph's bones were buried there (Josh.24:32).

2 (4:10) **Water, Living—Jesus Christ—Salvation**: living water *is* alive. To the Jew, living water was water that was always flowing and moving along, such as a creek fed by springs or a lake with both an inflow and an outflow. Dead water was stagnant water such as ponds or pools that were always sitting still with no inflow or outflow. However, when Jesus spoke of "living water," He meant much more than living streams and lakes.

1. Living water is "of God." It is of Him who is living, always has and always will be living. The water that God gives is the most *alive* water there is. No other water, no matter how alive it may be considered, can compare with the living water that is of God.

> **For with you is the fountain of life; in your light we see light. (Psa 36:9)**

2. Living water is "the gift" of God. The word "gift" means it is freely given, is *not earned* and is *not deserved*.

> **"Come, all you who are thirsty, come to the waters; and you who have no money, come, buy and eat! Come, buy wine and milk without money and without cost. (Isa 55:1)**
>
> **For it is by grace you have been saved, through faith—and this not from yourselves, it is the gift of God—not by works, so that no one can boast. (Eph 2:8-9)**

3. Living water is given by asking for it. Note what Jesus said: "If you knew...you would have asked." The woman had never received living water because she *had never known* about it and *had never asked* for it. It was now available simply by asking for it.

3 (4:11-12) **Water, Living—Jesus Christ**: living water is from a Person much greater than a religious father. The woman saw clearly that Jesus was making an unusual claim. She did not yet understand what the claim was, but she knew He was alluding to something. She noticed He had no leather pouch with which to draw water, so she asked two significant questions.

⇒ From where did He get this living water?
⇒ Was He *greater* than Jacob who was one of the great religious partriarchs of the Samaritans? Jacob had to dig the well in order to secure water for his family. Was Jesus greater, able to do more than Jacob did?

The point is this: the woman recognized something most people do not. Jesus was claiming to be greater than one of the greatest religious fathers, Jacob himself. He was claiming to have access to a much better water for quenching the thirst of men.

Thought 1. Throughout Scripture Jesus claimed to be...

• greater than the temple (Mt.12:6)
• greater than Jonah (Mt.12:41)
• greater than Solomon (Mt.12:42; Lk.11:31).
• greater than Abraham, "before Abraham" (Jn.8:53, 58)
• greater than Jacob (Jn.4:11-12)
• worthy of greater honor than Moses (Heb.3:3; Jn.5:45-47)

> **"The one who comes from above is above all; the one who is from the earth belongs to the earth, and speaks as one**

from the earth. The one who comes from heaven is above all. (John 3:31)

And he is the head of the body, the church; he is the beginning and the first-born from among the dead, so that in everything he might have the supremacy. (Col 1:18)

Jesus has been found worthy of greater honor than Moses, just as the builder of a house has greater honor than the house itself. (Heb 3:3)

4 (4:13-14) **Water, Living—Jesus Christ**: living water is the only water that will quench thirst. Men have two thirsts: a physical thirst and a spiritual thirst.

For the director of music. A maskil of the Sons of Korah. As the deer pants for streams of water, so my soul pants for you, O God. (Psa 42:1)

"On that day a fountain will be opened to the house of David and the inhabitants of Jerusalem, to cleanse them from sin and impurity. (Zec 13:1)

Men know immediately how to quench their physical thirst, but their spiritual thirst is a different matter. Within their hearts men sense a thirst for...

- purpose
- meaning
- significance
- satisfaction
- fulfillment
- something that is missing
- something to fill the void, the emptiness, and the loneliness
- deliverance from a sense of lostness
- freedom from undue anxiety, stress, and pressure

Men have a problem, however. They usually misunderstand the spiritual thirst and try to quench it with the stagnant waters of the flesh and of this world. The result is poison and death.

⇒ The stagnant waters of the flesh and sinful nature are such things as lust, immorality, drunkenness, indulgence, and pride.

⇒ The stagnant waters of the world are such things as the love of money, cars, houses, lands, clothes, extravagant living, position, and power.

The stagnant waters of the flesh and the world never quench a man's thirst. They are like salt water; they only make a man crave for more and more. (See DEEPER STUDY # 1, Lust—Jas.4:1-3.)

"My people have committed two sins: They have forsaken me, the spring of living water, and have dug their own cisterns, broken cisterns that cannot hold water. (Jer 2:13)

Note several facts about the living water.
1. The living water comes from Christ. He and He alone is its source.

On the last and greatest day of the Feast, Jesus stood and said in a loud voice, "If anyone is thirsty, let him come to me and drink. (John 7:37)

He said to me: "It is done. I am the Alpha and the Omega, the Beginning and the End. To him who is thirsty I will give to drink without cost from the spring of the water of life. (Rev 21:6)

2. The living water keeps a man from ever thirsting again. His inner thirst is gone forever. It is quenched and fully satisfied.

"On that day a fountain will be opened to the house of David and the inhabitants of Jerusalem, to cleanse them from sin and impurity. (Zec 13:1)

The LORD will guide you always; he will satisfy your needs in a sun scorched land and will strengthen your frame. You will be like a well-watered garden, like a spring whose waters never fail. (Isa 58:11)

3. The living water is "a spring of water" placed "in" the man. The well is not placed outside the man, not placed anywhere out in the world, not in his home, nor in his business. It is placed "in" him.

Whoever believes in me, as the Scripture has said, streams of living water will flow from within him." By this he meant the Spirit, whom those who believed in him were later to receive. Up to that time the Spirit had not been given, since Jesus had not yet been glorified. (John 7:38-39)

4. The living water springs up and continues to spring up and bubble, flowing on and on. It is ever in motion.

With joy you will draw water from the wells of salvation. (Isa 12:3)

5. The living water springs up into eternal life. It will never end.

For the Lamb at the center of the throne will be their shepherd; he will lead them to springs of living water. And God will wipe away every tear from their eyes." (Rev 7:17. Cp. Ezk.47:1-12, the river of life.)

The Spirit and the bride say, "Come!" And let him who hears say, "Come!" Whoever is thirsty, let him come; and whoever wishes, let him take the free gift of the water of life. (Rev 22:17)

(Note: Jesus interpreted what He was saying in Jn.7:37-39. All five of the above facts are seen fulfilled in the Holy Spirit.)

	B. The Subject of Sin, 4:15-18	husband and come back." 17 "I have no husband," she replied. Jesus said to her, "You are right when you say you have no husband.	Facing the truth, the fact of sin
1 There was the request for living water	15 The woman said to him, "Sir, give me this water so that I won't get thirsty and have to keep coming here to draw water."	18 The fact is, you have had five husbands, and the man you now have is not your husband. What you have just said is quite true."	a. Jesus stirred conviction b. Jesus accepted no evasion c. Jesus knew all d. Jesus reproved sin
2 There was the first essential:	16 He told her, "Go, call your		

DIVISION IV

THE REVELATION OF JESUS, THE LIVING WATER, 4:1-42

B. The Subject of Sin, 4:15-18

(4:15-18) **Introduction**: Jesus promised the living water of spiritual rebirth. However, something had to be discussed before spiritual rebirth could be given: the subject of sin.
1. There was the request for living water (v.15).
2. There was the first essential: facing the truth, the fact of sin (v.16-18).

1 (4:15) **Water, Living—Satisfaction—Fulfillment—Purpose—Emptiness—Dissatisfaction**: there was the request for living water. Jesus had just made a profound claim.

> **But whoever drinks the water I give him will never thirst. Indeed, the water I give him will become in him a spring of water welling up to eternal life." (John 4:14)**

The woman wanted such water. She asked for it, but note the reasons why:
⇒ That I won't get thirsty (physical thirst).
⇒ That I will not have to come and draw water every day.

The woman may have been jesting with Jesus; some commentators think she was. They hold that she certainly knew this man (Jesus) did not have a well of water from which she could drink and never thirst again, water that would cause her to live forever, never having to die. She thought that Jesus was jesting with her, so she played along, humoring Him. Others think she was sincere and just did not understand, but whatever the man's magical waters were, she wanted a drink.

Whatever the case may be, the woman was thinking in terms of the physical world, only of the physical benefits. She had grasped nothing of the spiritual meaning, nothing of the inner satisfaction that Jesus could give which would quench all the thirst of a person's heart.

Thought 1. Note two facts.
1) Man does thirst, but his thirst is much deeper than physical thirst. Man has an inner, spiritual thirst. (See note—Jn.4:13-14 for discussion of man's thirst.)
2) Christ alone can satisfy man's thirst. If a man drinks of the water Christ gives, he is infused with purpose, meaning, significance, energy, and motivation. Once a man drinks of Christ, he does not mind drawing water; that is, he does not mind work and labor. In fact, the water of Christ stirs

him to work and serve, helping mankind in every way possible. He wants to help and to share the wonderful news of a saving God, a God who can save from the thirst of...
• emptiness • despair
• loneliness • hopelessness
• lostness

2 (4:16-18) **Sin, Exposed—Repentance**: there was the first essential of facing the truth, the fact of sin. The woman had requested living water, but before she could be given the living water of spiritual rebirth, she had to be convicted of her sin and renounce it. Note four things.
1. Jesus stirred conviction and the confession of sin. Why was this necessary? Why did the woman have to face the truth of her sin before she could be spiritually reborn? There are two reasons.
   a. She was weary and burdened, and it was caused by sin. She had to know this in order to seek the cure. Sin had to be removed and renounced, forgiven and cleansed before *true rest* and *true relief* could come. Once she was freed from sin, rest and relief would come. She would no longer be weary and burdened under the load of sin and irresponsibility, guilt and shame. She would be set free and given a life of spiritual rest and security. (See notes, Rest—Mt.11:28, 30; Heb.4:1 for more discussion.)
   b. She had the symptoms of disease and did not know what the disease was; therefore, she was unable to cure her disease. She needed deliverance and did not know how to be delivered. The woman's disease was the same as the disease of all men: sin. Sin had to be renounced before the living water of spiritual rebirth could be given.

> **Therefore, get rid of all moral filth and the evil that is so prevalent and humbly accept the word planted in you, which can save you. (James 1:21)**
> **"Blessed are those who wash their robes, that they may have the right to the tree of life and may go through the gates into the city. (Rev 22:14)**
> **Now make confession to the LORD, the God of your fathers, and do his will. Separate yourselves from the peoples around you and from your foreign wives." (Ezra 10:11)**

2. Jesus accepted no evasion. Note how the woman tried to evade the fact of her sin. She told the truth; she did not have a husband, but she was living with a man just as she would live with a husband.

> **Thought 1.** The point is clear: the sinner cannot evade his sin. He has to face it and renounce it if he wishes the living water of spiritual rebirth.

> > He who conceals his sins does not prosper, but whoever confesses and renounces them finds mercy. (Prov 28:13)
> > Only acknowledge your guilt— you have rebelled against the LORD your God, you have scattered your favors to foreign gods under every spreading tree, and have not obeyed me,'" declares the LORD. (Jer 3:13)
> > Can anyone hide in secret places so that I cannot see him?" declares the LORD. "Do not I fill heaven and earth?" declares the LORD. (Jer 23:24)
> > If we confess our sins, he is faithful and just and will forgive us our sins and purify us from all unrighteousness. (1 John 1:9)

3. Jesus knew all about the woman, that she had gone through five husbands. He knew the truth about her, what she had done to fail in so many marriages. He knew whether she was guilty...
- of making ungodly, worldly choices.
- of being argumentative and defensive.
- of being a poor housekeeper, wife, and mother.
- of being cold, distant, withdrawn, and indifferent.
- of being unfaithful and immoral.

Jesus knew the truth about her sin, and He knows the truth about every man's sin.

> > If I sinned, you would be watching me and would not let my offense go unpunished. (Job 10:14;cp. Job 14:16)
> > Although you wash yourself with soda and use an abundance of soap, the stain of your guilt is still before me," declares the Sovereign LORD. (Jer 2:22)
> > My eyes are on all their ways; they are not hidden from me, nor is their sin concealed from my eyes. (Jer 16:17)
> > He reveals deep and hidden things; he knows what lies in darkness, and light dwells with him. (Dan 2:22)

> > And again, "The Lord knows that the thoughts of the wise are futile." (1 Cor 3:20)

4. Jesus reproved her sin. She had not only gone through five different husbands, but she was now living with a man who was not her husband.

> **Thought 1.** Christ not only knows all—He keeps an account. The sinner is guilty of every act of disobedience. He stands guilty of every law he breaks.

> > All who rely on observing the law are under a curse, for it is written: "Cursed is everyone who does not continue to do everything written in the Book of the Law." The law is not based on faith; on the contrary, "The man who does these things will live by them." (Gal 3:10, 12)

Man has to face the truth, the fact of his sin, and renounce it if he wishes to receive the living water of spiritual rebirth. A man has to do what Christ is pointing out to the woman: renounce his sin. Once he has done this, he can then ask for the living water and Christ will give it. But note: drinking the water of Christ is essential.

> > But whoever drinks the water I give him will never thirst. Indeed, the water I give him will become in him a spring of water welling up to eternal life." (John 4:14)
> > Repent, then, and turn to God, so that your sins may be wiped out, that times of refreshing may come from the Lord, (Acts 3:19)
> > "Therefore since we are God's offspring, we should not think that the divine being is like gold or silver or stone—an image made by man's design and skill. In the past God overlooked such ignorance, but now he commands all people everywhere to repent. For he has set a day when he will judge the world with justice by the man he has appointed. He has given proof of this to all men by raising him from the dead." (Acts 17:29-31)
> > For the wages of sin is death, but the gift of God is eternal life in Christ Jesus our Lord. (Rom 6:23)

		C. The Subject of Worship, 4:19-24	tain nor in Jerusalem	3	Fact 2: True worship & salvation are from the Jews[DS1]
1	The woman was troubled a. She sensed Jesus to be a prophet b. She sensed her sin & the need for true worship	19 "Sir," the woman said, "I can see that you are a prophet. 20 Our fathers worshiped on this mountain, but you Jews claim that the place where we must worship is in Jerusalem."	22 You Samaritans worship what you do not know; we worship what we do know, for salvation is from the Jews.		
2	Fact 1: The place of worship is not what is important	21 Jesus declared, "Believe me, woman, a time is coming when you will worship the Father neither on this moun-	23 Yet a time is coming and has now come when the true worshipers will worship the Father in spirit and truth, for they are the kind of worshipers the Father seeks. 24 God is spirit, and his worshipers must worship in spirit and in truth."	4	Fact 3: True worshippers worship God in spirit & in truth[DS2,3]

DIVISION IV

THE REVELATION OF JESUS, THE LIVING WATER, 4:1-42

C. The Subject of Worship, 4:19-24

(4:19-24) **Introduction**: man's whole concept and approach to worship is changed by Jesus in this passage.

1. The woman was troubled (v.19-20).
2. Fact 1: the place of worship is not what is important (v.21).
3. Fact 2: true worship and salvation are from the Jews (v.22).
4. Fact 3: true worshippers worship God in spirit and truth (v.23-24).

1 (4:19-20) **Conviction, Response to**: the woman was troubled. Jesus had confronted her with her sin (v.15-18), and she could either respond or react. She could have reacted by...

- being angry
- ignoring
- neglecting
- arguing
- counting it as foolishness

However, she did not react. Instead, she was stirred and convicted, and she sensed two things.

1. She sensed that Jesus was a prophet, a man who was in touch with God; therefore, Jesus was a man who could help her.
2. She sensed her sin and the need to take care of her sin, to truly worship God. But where was she to worship? There was a dispute about where God's presence really was, a dispute about where a person could truly meet God. The Samaritans said that God's presence was in Mount Gerizim; the Jews said He dwelt in Jerusalem (see note—Jn.4:5).

Standing before her was the prophet who wrought the piercing conviction in her that she was to worship. He was a prophet; therefore, He could help and direct her, so she asked Him where to worship. Where could she find help from God?

Thought 1. The woman was under a powerful conviction. She knew that she had to worship God, to make sacrifice for her sin. When a man is stirred and convicted, he needs to turn to God immediately. If he does not know how to turn to God, he needs to ask a person who is in touch with God.

2 (4:21) **Worship**: first, the place of worship is not what is important. Note three things.

1. Note the phrase "a time is coming." Jesus said that *a time* was coming that would change the whole nature of worship. The way men approached God was going to experience a volcanic eruption. Worship of God was going to be radically and completely changed. There was a time, an historical event, coming that would change it. Jesus was, of course, referring to His death and the coming of the Holy Spirit. The place of worship is no longer the temple or any other particular location on earth. God's presence now dwells in the hearts and lives of His people. His people worship Him wherever they are, and they can worship Him every day all day long.

> **Do you not know that your body is a temple of the Holy Spirit, who is in you, whom you have received from God? You are not your own; you were bought at a price. Therefore honor God with your body. (1 Cor 6:19-20)**
>
> **And I will ask the Father, and he will give you another Counselor to be with you forever—the Spirit of truth. The world cannot accept him, because it neither sees him nor knows him. But you know him, for he lives with you and will be in you. (John 14:16-17)**
>
> **You, however, are controlled not by the sinful nature but by the Spirit, if the Spirit of God lives in you. And if anyone does not have the Spirit of Christ, he does not belong to Christ. But if Christ is in you, your body is dead because of sin, yet your spirit is alive because of righteousness. (Rom 8:9-10)**
>
> **As for you, the anointing you received from him remains in you, and you do not need anyone to teach you. But as his anointing teaches you about all things and as that anointing is real, not counterfeit—just as it has taught you, remain in him. (1 John 2:27)**

And I will put my Spirit in you and move you to follow my decrees and be careful to keep my laws. (Ezek 36:27)

2. The place of worship is not what is important. Some do worship in Mount Gerizim and some worship in Jerusalem, but the place is not what is important.

3. What is important is *the object of worship*, being sure one is truly worshipping *the Father, God Himself*. A person may be in the temple worshipping, and yet not be worshipping the Father: "You worship what you do not know" (v.22). A man's whole being must be focused upon the only true and living God, the Father Himself, to be truly worshipping.

"You are my witnesses," declares the LORD, "and my servant whom I have chosen, so that you may know and believe me and understand that I am he. Before me no god was formed, nor will there be one after me. (Isa 43:10)

So that with one heart and mouth you may glorify the God and Father of our Lord Jesus Christ. (Rom 15:6)

Through Jesus, therefore, let us continually offer to God a sacrifice of praise—the fruit of lips that confess his name. (Heb 13:15)

But you are a chosen people, a royal priesthood, a holy nation, a people belonging to God, that you may declare the praises of him who called you out of darkness into his wonderful light. (1 Pet 2:9)

3 (4:22) Salvation, Source—Jesus Christ, Mediator—God, Ignorance of—Jesus Christ, Ignorance of: second, worship and salvation are from the Jews. Note three things.

1. The word "salvation" in the Greek has the definite article (he soteria), "the salvation." The Messiah, who is the salvation of all men, comes through the Jews, not from any other source.

Jesus answered, "I am the way and the truth and the life. No one comes to the Father except through me. (John 14:6)

Salvation is found in no one else, for there is no other name under heaven given to men by which we must be saved." (Acts 4:12)

For there is one God and one mediator between God and men, the man Christ Jesus, who gave himself as a ransom for all men—the testimony given in its proper time. (1 Tim 2:5-6)

But the ministry Jesus has received is as superior to theirs as the covenant of which he is mediator is superior to the old one, and it is founded on better promises. (Heb 8:6)

For this reason Christ is the mediator of a new covenant, that those who are called may receive the promised eternal inheritance—now that he has died as a ransom to set them free from the sins committed under the first covenant. (Heb 9:15)

To Jesus the mediator of a new covenant, and to the sprinkled blood that speaks a better word than the blood of Abel. (Heb 12:24)

My dear children, I write this to you so that you will not sin. But if anybody does sin, we have one who speaks to the Father in our defense—Jesus Christ, the Righteous One. (1 John 2:1)

2. Jesus said "we." He identified Himself with the Jews. He was a fully born Jew; He was not of another nationality, nor was He a mixture of bloods.

3. Salvation is from the Jews. All other worship is an expression of man's own ideas, no matter how rational and highly esteemed and followed: "You worship what you do not know." (See DEEPER STUDY # 1, Israel—Jn.4:22 for more discussion.)

   a. Men are ignorant of God Himself, of the only living and true God.

For this people's heart has become calloused; they hardly hear with their ears, and they have closed their eyes. Otherwise they might see with their eyes, hear with their ears, understand with their hearts and turn, and I would heal them.' (Mat 13:15)

For as I walked around and looked carefully at your objects of worship, I even found an altar with this inscription: TO AN UNKNOWN GOD. Now what you worship as something unknown I am going to proclaim to you. (Acts 17:23)

For since the creation of the world God's invisible qualities—his eternal power and divine nature—have been clearly seen, being understood from what has been made, so that men are without excuse. For although they knew God, they neither glorified him as God nor gave thanks to him, but their thinking became futile and their foolish hearts were darkened. Although they claimed to be wise, they became fools and exchanged the glory of the immortal God for images made to look like mortal man and birds and animals and reptiles. (Rom 1:20-23)

Furthermore, since they did not think it worthwhile to retain the knowledge of God, he gave them over to a depraved mind, to do what ought not to be done. (Rom 1:28)

Since they did not know the righteousness that comes from God and sought to establish their own, they did not submit to God's righteousness. (Rom 10:3)

They are darkened in their understanding and separated from the life of God because of the ignorance that is in them due to the hardening of their hearts. (Eph 4:18)

But they deliberately forget that long ago by God's word the heavens existed and the earth was formed out of water and by water. (2 Pet 3:5)

Always learning but never able to acknowledge the truth. (2 Tim 3:7)

Yet they say to God, 'Leave us alone! We have no desire to know your ways. (Job 21:14)

"My people are fools; they do not know me. They are senseless children; they have no understanding. They are skilled in doing evil; they know not how to do good." (Jer 4:22)

I thought, "These are only the poor; they are foolish, for they do not know the way of the LORD, the requirements of their God. (Jer 5:4)

Even the stork in the sky knows her appointed seasons, and the dove, the swift and the thrush observe the time of their migration. But my people do not know the requirements of the LORD. (Jer 8:7)

"They make ready their tongue like a bow, to shoot lies; it is not by truth that they triumph in the land. They go from one sin to another; they do not acknowledge me," declares the LORD. (Jer 9:3)

"They do not know how to do right," declares the LORD, "who hoard plunder and loot in their fortresses." (Amos 3:10)

But they do not know the thoughts of the LORD; they do not understand his plan, he who gathers them like sheaves to the threshing floor. (Micah 4:12)

"But they refused to pay attention; stubbornly they turned their backs and stopped up their ears. They made their hearts as hard as flint and would not listen to the law or to the words that the LORD Almighty had sent by his Spirit through the earlier prophets. So the LORD Almighty was very angry. (Zec 7:11-12)

b. Men are ignorant of Christ, the Son of God.

He was in the world, and though the world was made through him, the world did not recognize him. (John 1:10)

Jesus answered her, "If you knew the gift of God and who it is that asks you for a drink, you would have asked him and he would have given you living water." (John 4:10)

Then they asked him, "Where is your father?" "You do not know me or my Father," Jesus replied. "If you knew me, you would know my Father also." (John 8:19)

The man answered, "Now that is remarkable! You don't know where he comes from, yet he opened my eyes. (John 9:30)

Jesus answered: "Don't you know me, Philip, even after I have been among you such a long time? Anyone who has seen me has seen the Father. How can you say, 'Show us the Father'? (John 14:9)

They will do such things because they have not known the Father or me. (John 16:3)

The people of Jerusalem and their rulers did not recognize Jesus, yet in condemning him they fulfilled the words of the prophets that are read every Sabbath. (Acts 13:27)

No one who lives in him keeps on sinning. No one who continues to sin has either seen him or known him. (1 John 3:6)

DEEPER STUDY # 1
(4:22) **Israel—God's Plan—History—Jews**: why did Jesus Christ come to the Jewish nation and come to earth as a Jew? Very simply stated, the Jews were God's special people. They had been born by a special act of God. It all started long, long ago. God had wanted four things.

1. He wanted a people who would love Him supremely and give Him their first loyalty. (Cp. Gen.17:7; Is.43:10.)

2. He wanted a people who would witness to all other nations that He and He alone was the one true and living God. (Cp. Gen. 12:3; 22:18; Acts 13:26, 47.)

3. He wanted a people through whom He could send the promised Seed, the Savior and Messiah, Jesus Christ, to all men everywhere. (Cp. Gen.3:15; 17:7; 22:18; Gal.3:16; Jn.4:22.)

4. He wanted a people through whom He could send His written Word, the Holy Bible, and preserve it for all generations. (Ro.9:4-5; 1 Pt.2:10-12.)

In searching the earth for such a people, God could find none (cp. Ro.1:18-32). God could do only one thing. He had to find one man and through him begin a new people, a new nation.

1. God found and chose Abraham and through him established the Jewish nation. (Gen.12:1-5; 13:14-17; 15:1-7; 17:1-8, 15-19; 22:16-18; 26:2-5, 24; 28:13-15; 31:13; 35:9-12.) God chose one man and challenged him to worship God supremely. If that man would worship God supremely, then God would cause a special people to be born of his seed. That man was Abraham. Abraham was the first Jew (cp. Gen.12:1-4; Gal.3:16). In the Old Testament the Jews and their land (Palestine) were continually pointed to as the very special people and land of God. They were called...

⇒ God's treasured possession (Ex.19:5; Dt.7:6; 14:2; 26:18; Ps.135:4).
⇒ the Lord's portion (Dt.32:9).
⇒ the Lord's land (Lev.25:23; Jer.2:7; 16:18; Hos.9:3).
⇒ the holy land (Zech.2:12). (See DEEPER STUDY # 1—Ro.4:1-25 for more discussion.)

However, the Jewish nation failed to obey God supremely. The whole plot of the Old Testament centers around God's pleading and dealing with the Jews. Again and again, He gave the nation the opportunity to obey Him. He dealt with them in mercy and in judgment, but at every turn they refused to heed His pleading.

2. God chose the family of David. (See DEEPER STUDY # 4—Jn.1:49.) God had no choice but to make another move, so He chose one faithful family within the Jewish nation and gave to that family one great promise. The family was that of King David, and the promise was that of the Messiah, God's great King, God's very own Son. God's Son was to come through the line of David and establish an eternal nation of people who would love God supremely. However, the Jewish nation again failed God. They misinterpreted God's Word—the prophecies of His coming.

a. The Jews misinterpreted God's Word by saying the seed of Abraham included only the Jewish nation. In their minds, God had no children except the children of the Jewish nation. The Bible says explicitly that the seed of Abraham is Christ, and the special people of God are those individuals within all nations who worship God supremely (Gal.3:16).

b. The Jews misinterpreted God's Word by saying that the eternal kingdom promised to David was the Jewish nation and the Jewish nation only. They expected Israel to be established as an earthly nation forever and all other nations to be subservient to Israel. But again, God's promise was not that narrow, nor was it that prejudiced. The Bible says there is not, and never has been, any respect of persons with God (Dt.10:17;2 Chron.19:7; Job 34:19; Acts 10:34; Ro.2:11; Gal.2:6; Eph.6:9; Col.3:25; 1 Pt.1:17). God did say that Christ was to come from the Davidic line, but He also said that He was going to establish an eternal nation made up of people everywhere who would love God supremely (Ro.2:28-29).

By misinterpreting God's promises, the Jews failed to be the missionaries to the world that God had chosen them to be. They became earthly bound and materialistic minded. They twisted the idea of the promised Messiah to fit their own schemes. They conceived of Him as One who was to establish an earthly kingdom for the Jewish nation alone. They failed to see that God was speaking…

- of an eternal kingdom of righteousness.
- of a kingdom that is of another dimension entirely—the dimension of the spiritual.
- of a new heaven and a new earth that would give each person an eternal life beyond just one earthly generation.

3. God had no choice but to make a third move. This He did by sending His own Son into the world through the Jewish nation. God sent Him so that the world through Him might be saved (Jn.3:16-19). However, man rejected God's Son and crucified Him. This act—the killing of God's Son—was the final blow. When man slew the only Son of God, the whole world *was* involved. Both Jew and Gentile were represented symbolically in the Jewish religionists and the Roman authorities. They both actually did the plotting, sentencing, and execution. If the world were ever to be saved, it was now perfectly clear that God had to make every move Himself.

This He did once-for-all. In His eternal purpose and plan for man's salvation, God took the sins of all men and laid them upon His Son while He was being slain upon the cross. He allowed His Son to bear the sins of the world (1 Pt.2:24). Then He took His Son and raised Him from the dead—never to die again. He did what man had always failed to do: in His Son's resurrection God began to build a lasting kingdom of righteousness, a new nation that is presently being made up of men from all earthly nations who desire and are willing to follow Jesus Christ supremely. He is calling out and forming a new people who have genuinely been born again—spiritually. These new born people shall live eternally—beyond just one earthly generation. These people are identified as His church, as a body of people who genuinely believe and follow Him. They are destined to be the inhabitants of the new heavens and earth. (See notes—pt.5, Lk.8:21; Eph.2:11-18; 4:17-19.)

God, acting solely upon His own through the death and resurrection of His Son, has fulfilled His promises to both Abraham and David. All the people of the nations of the world now have the opportunity to become children of God, the special people of God.

4 (4:23-24) **Worship**: third, true worshippers worship God in spirit and in truth. Note four points.

1. Note the change in worship: "A time is coming and has now come." Christ changed worship. Before Christ, men worshipped God in special places, for example, in temples and before altars. Since Christ, place and locality mean nothing. Christ has opened the door into God's presence from anyplace in the universe (see note—Jn.4:21 for more discussion).

2. Note the nature of worship. Man is to worship God in spirit and in truth. (See DEEPER STUDY # 2—Jn.4:23.)

a. To worship God in spirit means to worship God…

- with the *spiritual drive and ability* of one's soul, seeking the most intimate communion and fellowship with God.
- with the *spiritual core* of one's life and being, trusting and resting in God's acceptance and love and care.

b. To worship God in truth means…

- to approach God in the right or true way. There is only one way, through His Son Jesus Christ (see note—Jn.4:21; 14:6).
- to worship God sincerely and truthfully, not coming half-heartedly with wandering mind and sleepy eyes.

3. Note the reason for worship. The Father seeks men to worship Him. God desires worship, for He created man to worship and fellowship with Him. Therefore, God seeks men who will worship Him in spirit and truth.

> **The LORD works out everything for his own ends— even the wicked for a day of disaster. (Prov 16:4)**
>
> **Everyone who is called by my name, whom I created for my glory, whom I formed and made." "You are my witnesses," declares the LORD, "and my servant whom I have chosen, so that you may know and believe me and understand that I am he. Before me no god was formed, nor will there be one after me. (Isa 43:7-10)**
>
> **For those God foreknew he also predestined to be conformed to the likeness of his Son, that he might be the firstborn among many brothers. (Rom 8:29)**
>
> **For he chose us in him before the creation of the world to be holy and blameless in his sight. In love he predestined us to be adopted as his sons through Jesus Christ, in accordance with his pleasure and will—to the praise of his glorious grace, which he has freely given us in the One he loves. (Eph 1:4-6)**
>
> **But you are a chosen people, a royal priesthood, a holy nation, a people belonging to God, that you may declare the praises of him who called you out of darkness into his wonderful light. (1 Pet 2:9; cp.Ro.15:6; 1 Cor.6:20)**

4. Note the one essential in worship. It is not the place that is important in worship but how a person worships God. A person must worship God in spirit and in truth. There is no other way. "God is Spirit, and His worshippers must worship in spirit and in truth."

To worship in spirit means…

- *from* the spiritual drive and depth of the soul
- *from* the spiritual core of the life and being

To worship in truth means…
- as God dictates, that is, worship must be in the name of God's Son, Jesus Christ
- in sincerity

Jesus said to him, "Away from me, Satan! For it is written: 'Worship the Lord your God, and serve him only.'" (Mat 4:10)

Then they worshiped him and returned to Jerusalem with great joy. (Luke 24:52)

Let us not give up meeting together, as some are in the habit of doing, but let us encourage one another—and all the more as you see the Day approaching. (Heb 10:25)

He said in a loud voice, "Fear God and give him glory, because the hour of his judgment has come. Worship him who made the heavens, the earth, the sea and the springs of water." (Rev 14:7)

Ascribe to the LORD the glory due his name. Bring an offering and come before him; worship the LORD in the splendor of his holiness. (1 Chr 16:29)

Ascribe to the LORD the glory due his name; worship the LORD in the splendor of his holiness. (Psa 29:2)

Come, let us bow down in worship, let us kneel before the LORD our Maker; (Psa 95:6)

Worship the LORD in the splendor of his holiness; tremble before him, all the earth. (Psa 96:9)

Exalt the LORD our God and worship at his footstool; he is holy. (Psa 99:5)

DEEPER STUDY # 2

(4:23) **Man, Creation—Spirit—Worship**: man is to worship God in Spirit. Three points need to be looked at to fully understand what this means.

1. There is the creation of man.

The LORD God formed the man from the dust of the ground and breathed into his nostrils the breath of life, and the man became a living being. (Gen 2:7)

The material used to form man was *dust*; or as Isaiah said, "clay" (Is.64:8); or as Luther translated, a lump of earth (erdenkloss). Man's physical material or substance is of the earth; the forming of his body is like that of earthly pottery (Job 10:8-9; Ro.9:21); the food he eats is of the earth (Job 28:5); and the end of his body is to return to the earth (Eccl.3:20).

There is a sense in which man is a paradox. He was created with all the dignity and honor possible—created by the hand of God and given the very breath of God. Yet, he was also created out of the most base and lowly stuff of all—dirt. So in one sense man has every reason to glory; in another sense he has every reason to be humble. What is to be man's attitude, his air? There is nothing wrong with glorying; there is nothing wrong with being humble. It is the reason or object for glorying and being humble that makes one right or wrong. Man is to worship and glory in God—that God gave him life and the dignity and honor (privilege) of life. Man is to walk humbly toward God and toward other men because all men come from the same material, the earth. (Jer.9:24; cp. 1 Cor.1:31; 2 Cor.10:17; Ro.11:36; Gal.1:5; 2 Tim.4:18; Heb.13:21; 1 Pt.5:11.) Therefore, man is exhorted to present his body to

God as "a living sacrifice" and as "the temple of the Holy Spirit" (Ro.12:1; 1 Cor.6:19-20).

But note: man is not only body and soul; he is also spirit (see DEEPER STUDY # 3—Jn.4:23-24). This is man's distinctive difference from all other creatures. As the Psalmist says, "I am fearfully and wonderfully made….my frame was not hidden from you" (Ps.139:14-15). Two distinctive facts need to be noted here.

a. It is not just the breath of life that is given to man. It is the very breath of God Himself. God's breath is life, eternal life; therefore, man was given the eternal life, the very Spirit of God Himself. Just think! God's very own breath, His Spirit, is within every person who is "renewed" (recreated) after the image of Him that created him.

And to put on the new self, created to be like God in true righteousness and holiness. (Eph 4:24)

And have put on the new self, which is being renewed in knowledge in the image of its Creator. (Col 3:10)

b. God breathes His own breath or spirit into the nostrils of man. Just imagine the picture. The body of Adam was lying before God; it had just been formed by God's hands from the dust of the earth. Adam was lifeless—just a body—never having breathed. God then breathed into Adam's nostrils His own breath or Spirit, the life of His very own being (which is the life that goes on and on, never ending, that is eternal).

Now, here is the point. God made no other creature like this. God gave no other creature His own breath, nor did He use this method of creation with any other creature. These two facts make man's creation distinctive.

What a shame that man cleaves to this earth and its worldliness! "He who ignores discipline despises himself" (Prov.15:32). How often the spirit of man should breath after God (Mt.5:6)!

2. The creation of man is in *the image and likeness of God*.

Then God said, "Let us make man in our image, in our likeness, and let them rule over the fish of the sea and the birds of the air, over the livestock, over all the earth, and over all the creatures that move along the ground." So God created man in his own image, in the image of God he created him; male and female he created them. (Gen 1:26-27)

Whatever *the image and likeness of God* means, it is that which distinguishes man from all other life which God created. No where else does God say He created a being in *His own image* and *after His own likeness*. Only man is in the image and likeness of God. What is the *image and likeness* of God in man?

a. It is unlikely that it means the *soul* of man. The Bible says all living creatures are souls. They were created as *living souls*. This is clearly pointed out in the Hebrew language of Gen. 1:20 which says, "Let the water teem with living creatures [souls, nephesh]." All living creatures possess the breath of life. (See DEEPER STUDY # 5, Soul—Mt.22:37 for more discussion.)

b. It is unlikely that it means the ability to reason. Apparently animals have the ability to reason and learn to varying degrees. Animals show ability to think when facing an enemy or difficulties in the innumerable experiences of life.

c. It is unlikely that it means the ability to be moral and just. Some animals (both individually and within family groups) have rules, practices, deeds, or acts that lead to moral and virtuous behavior among themselves and even toward others. There seems to be an exercise of right and wrong among some animals. However, it needs to be pointed out that just as man is far superior to animals mentally, they are also far superior to animals morally. Man is far superior to animals both as a rational being (a being that reasons) and a moral being (a being that is just, relating to others as he should). (Note that being *spiritually* and *mentally renewed* in Christ affects the rational and moral powers of man. Man can be *created* in righteousness and *true* holiness. Man can be delivered from the legalistic bondage and rules of a man-conceived righteousness and holiness. Cp. Eph.4:24; Col.3:10.)

d. It means that God gave man His spirit: His immortal breath, His life that lives forever just like God. God went beyond what He had made when He created the animals of the earth (a soul, an earthly life, a temporal breath); God made man a spirit (an eternal life, an immortal breath) that is just like Himself, just like His own life. To be in the image and likeness of God means "God is spirit, and his worshipers must worship *in spirit* and in truth" (Jn.4:24). Apparently, no animal is a spirit; animals are only souls. As living souls, they are enabled by varying degrees to breathe, to reason and to relate; but none of them have the inherent power to breathe eternally, nor the drive and ability to reason after God and to relate to God. Man does have that power, that drive, and that ability. *Man is spirit, even as God is Spirit.* Man is not only body and soul as the animals of creation. Man is not only a *living, breathing soul made for this earth*; *man is a spirit, an immortal being made to live with God eternally.*

3. In light of the above fact, there are at least two distinguishing marks of God's image in man, two distinguishing marks of man as a spirit.

a. God's image in man is the *spirit or power of immortality*. Man lives beyond this earth, lives eternally just like God. As mentioned above, according to the Bible, no animal is a spirit. Animals are only souls. As souls they are enabled to breathe and to live on this earth, but they do not have the inherent power to breathe eternally. However, man does have that power. Man is spirit, even as God is Spirit. *Man is not only a living, breathing soul and body like the animals made for this earth; man is a spirit, an immortal being made both for this earth and for eternity.*

b. God's image in man is the *spirit or the drive and ability (choice) to worship*. Man has not only the soulish ability to reason and to relate, but an unquenchable spiritual drive and ability to reason after God and to relate to God. Again, as mentioned above, no earthly animal has that spiritual drive and ability (freedom of choice). The Bible does ascribe to souls varying abilities, but no ani-

mal soul has the ability to reason *after God* or to *relate to God*. Worship is a spiritual drive and ability, an ability of spirit (of man) only. Just like animals, *man knows and understands the things* of this earth; but man is to know, believe, and understand God first and foremost (Is.43:10). Man is to worship God. God is Spirit and He has created man as spirit; therefore, man is to worship God in spirit and in truth (Jn.4:24).

There are two very significant facts to be noted about the image of God in man or of man as a spirit.

1. The rebellion of man against God (man's fall) affected God's image within man. God had created man as an immortal being. Man was to live on this earth and to live with God forever. When man exercised his ability or choice and turned against God, he lost both rights. He could no longer live on the earth forever, nor could he live with God forever. In his rebellion against God, man was saying that he preferred a different world other than God's world and he preferred a different god (his own will) other than God Himself. Man thereby condemned himself to leave this earth (to die, Gen.2:17; 31f; 3:19) and to be separated from God eternally (Jn.3:18). Note that man was already created as an immortal being.

Therefore, man would continue on, he would exist forever—but he was (a) to be placed somewhere else other than this earth (he had chosen such); and (b) he was to be separated from God forever. It was his choice. The image of God—the power of immortality and the drive and ability to worship and live with God—was marred eternally.

2. The image of God within man can be renewed.

a. Man can now put on the new self or the new man.

> **And to put on the new self, created to be like God in true righteousness and holiness. (Eph 4:24)**
> **And have put on the new self, which is being renewed in knowledge in the image of its Creator. (Col 3:10)**

b. Man can be "born again" spiritually; he can be made alive to God just as he was in the beginning—never to perish. (Jn.3:3f; 1 Pt.1:23).

c. Man can live and worship God forever (Jn.3:16; 2 Pt.1:4). He can now partake of God's divine nature and be assured of living forever in the new heavens and new earth (2 Pt.3:3-4, 8-18; Rev.21:1-7).

d. Man is renewed, reborn, recreated in Christ Jesus. "He himself bore our sins in his body on the tree, so that we might die to sins and live for righteousness; by his wounds you have been healed" (1 Pt. 2:24; cp. 3:18. See notes—Ro.5:1; 2 Cor.5:1; cp. 5:17.)

> **Then God said, "Let us make man in our image, in our likeness, and let them rule over the fish of the sea and the birds of the air, over the livestock, over all the earth, and over all the creatures that move along the ground." So God created man in his own image, in the image of God he created him; male and female he created them. (Gen 1:26-27)**
> **And just as we have borne the likeness of the earthly man, so shall we bear the likeness of the man from heaven. (1 Cor 15:49)**

DEEPER STUDY # 3

(4:23-24) **Spirit—God, Spirit**: what is meant by "spirit"? At least three things are gleaned from Scripture.

1. Spirit is not flesh and bone. Spirit is not physical and material. Spirit is immaterial, non-physical, incorporeal. Spirit is of another dimension of being, another dimension entirely different from the physical and material dimension of being.

2. Spirit is the innermost part of being, the very core and heart of life. Spirit is the very *breath of God's life*, the very *breath of God's existence*, the very *being of God's life*. That is, spirit is *eternal existence and being*. It is permanent, unending existence. A spirit has the breath of life, of existence, of *being forever*.

> **The LORD God formed the man from the dust of the ground and breathed into his nostrils the breath of life, and the man became a living being (Gen 2:7).**

3. God is Spirit. This means He is the very embodiment of life eternal, of permanent, unending existence. His nature is not flesh and bone; for the physical ages, deteriorates, dies, and decays—it ends. But not Spirit, not God. God exists forever and ever. He is life, the very embodiment of life eternal. Whatever life is—in all of its perfection—*God is*. God is the perfect Person, Life, Intelligence, Being. The basic nature of God is Spirit: eternal being, eternal life, the Perfect Being, the Perfect Life.

> **Now this is eternal life: that they may know you, the only true God, and Jesus Christ, whom you have sent. (John 17:3)**

	D. The Subject of Messiah, 4:25-30	woman. But no one asked, "What do you want?" or "Why are you talking with her?"	& pride
1 There was the sense that Jesus was the Messiah	25 The woman said, "I know that Messiah" (called Christ) "is coming. When he comes, he will explain everything to us."	28 Then, leaving her water jar, the woman went back to the town and said to the people,	4 There was the proclamation that Jesus is the Messiah
2 There was the great claim of Jesus: He is the Messiah	26 Then Jesus declared, "I who speak to you am he." Just then his disciples returned and were surprised to find him talking with a	29 "Come, see a man who told me everything I ever did. Could this be the Christ?"	
3 There was the spirit contrary to the Messiah: A spirit of evil thought		30 They came out of the town and made their way toward him.	5 There was the response of searching for the Messiah

DIVISION IV

THE REVELATION OF JESUS, THE LIVING WATER, 4:1-42

D. The Subject of Messiah, 4:25-30

(4:25-30) **Introduction**: this is a dramatic picture of conversion and witnessing. The Messiah was discovered, and the discovery was excitedly shared.

1. There was the sense that Jesus was the Messiah (v.25).
2. There was the great claim of Jesus: He is the Messiah (v.26).
3. There was the spirit contrary to the Messiah: a spirit of evil thought and pride (v.27).
4. There was the proclamation that Jesus is the Messiah (v.28-29).
5. There was the response of searching for the Messiah (v.30).

1 (4:25) **Jesus Christ, Messiah—Gospel, Open to—Truth, Open to**: there was the sense that Jesus was the Messiah. The woman's heart was burning within her. There was an intense, flaming sense of God's presence. The subject of her sin and of true worship was causing her heart to reach out for God. She sensed something very, very special about Jesus...

* that no man could speak as He had spoken unless He had a very special relationship with God.
* that perhaps He was the Messiah Himself.

She brought up the subject. Note the two things *she believed*.

1. That the Messiah was coming (erchetai). The idea is that the Messiah was *coming soon*. His coming was at hand, imminent. Her belief was based upon such Scriptures as Gen.3:15; 49:10; Num.24:17; Dt.18:15.
2. That the Messiah would be the Supreme Authority: "He will explain everything to us."

The point is this: the woman did not deny the Messiah; she believed in the coming and authority of the Messiah. Her belief was not a saving belief, not a belief of commitment (see DEEPER STUDY # 2—Jn.2:24). It was only a mental or an intellectual belief, a belief of knowledge; but the fact that she believed in the Messiah made her *open* to personal belief. She did not reject the witness of Jesus: she was not rude; she listened to Him. Therefore, God was able to give her a sense of His presence.

Thought 1. The person who constantly rejects Jesus Christ or claims to be agnostic or atheistic is seldom reached for Christ. However, a person who listens to the Scripture and believes intellectually, mentally accepting the facts of God's promises, stands a much better chance of being reached by God. Mental or intellectual belief is more open; it is exposed to God's Word. Thereby it is more likely to become a saving belief, the belief of commitment.

However, a warning does need to be issued. A person with only a mental belief can hear and reject so much that he becomes gospel hardened, that is, so hardened against the gospel that he never trusts Jesus Christ as his Savior. (See DEEPER STUDY # 1—Mt.13:4, 19 for more discussion.)

> "Well said, teacher," the man replied. "You are right in saying that God is one and there is no other but him. To love him with all your heart, with all your understanding and with all your strength, and to love your neighbor as yourself is more important than all burnt offerings and sacrifices." When Jesus saw that he had answered wisely, he said to him, "You are not far from the kingdom of God." And from then on no one dared ask him any more questions. (Mark 12:32-34)
>
> His God instructs him and teaches him the right way. (Isa 28:26)
>
> Who is wise? He will realize these things. Who is discerning? He will understand them. The ways of the LORD are right; the righteous walk in them, but the rebellious stumble in them. (Hosea 14:9)
>
> A simple man believes anything, but a prudent man gives thought to his steps. A wise man fears the LORD and shuns evil, but a fool is hotheaded and reckless. (Prov 14:15-16)
>
> The heart of the discerning acquires knowledge; the ears of the wise seek it out. (Prov 18:15)
>
> A prudent man sees danger and takes refuge, but the simple keep going and suffer for it. (Prov 22:3)

2 (4:26) **Jesus Christ, Messiah**: there was the great claim of Jesus, that He was the Messiah. Note three phenomenal claims.

1. He claimed to be "the Messiah" (see DEEPER STUDY # 2—Jn.1:20 for discussion).

2. He claimed to be the great "I Am," which is the basic name for God. (See DEEPER STUDY # 1—Jn.6:20 for discussion.)

3. He claimed to be the Supreme One, the Supreme Authority who would tell her all things. He claimed...
   • that what He told her about her sin was true
   • that she must take care of her sin
   • that the only way to take care of her sin was to worship God in spirit and in truth (see DEEPER STUDY # 2—Jn.4:23 for more discussion)

3 (4:27) **Prejudice—Evil Thoughts—Tongue:** there was the spirit contrary to the Messiah, the spirit of evil thought and pride. Just as Jesus made His phenomenal claims, the disciples arrived. They were suprised (ethaumazon): were astonished, amazed, bewildered because He was talking with the woman. There were two reasons for this.

1. She was a woman. The Rabbis of that day would not be *alone* or *talk* with women in public. They feared what people might think and say.

Thought 1. Very honestly, there is some merit to this idea. A person, especially a leader, must guard himself and his thoughts around the opposite sex. Of course, one can carry the practice too far. Wisdom and self-control are both needed.

> **But I tell you that anyone who looks at a woman lustfully has already committed adultery with her in his heart. (Mat 5:28)**
> **We demolish arguments and every pretension that sets itself up against the knowledge of God, and we take captive every thought to make it obedient to Christ. (2 Cor 10:5)**
> **Finally, brothers, whatever is true, whatever is noble, whatever is right, whatever is pure, whatever is lovely, whatever is admirable—if anything is excellent or praiseworthy—think about such things. (Phil 4:8)**
> **The LORD saw how great man's wickedness on the earth had become, and that every inclination of the thoughts of his heart was only evil all the time. (Gen 6:5)**
> **A heart that devises wicked schemes, feet that are quick to rush into evil, (Prov 6:18)**
> **He said to me, "Son of man, have you seen what the elders of the house of Israel are doing in the darkness, each at the shrine of his own idol? They say, 'The LORD does not see us; the LORD has forsaken the land.'" (Ezek 8:12)**

2. She was a Samaritan, a person considered despicable, below their social standing, unfit to be seen with in public.

Note how Christ tore down the barriers of both problems and how the disciples controlled their tongue from questioning and gossiping.

> **Then Peter began to speak: "I now realize how true it is that God does not show favoritism but accepts men from every nation who fear him and do what is right. (Acts 10:34-35)**

> **For there is no difference between Jew and Gentile—the same Lord is Lord of all and richly blesses all who call on him, (Rom 10:12)**
> **There is neither Jew nor Greek, slave nor free, male nor female, for you are all one in Christ Jesus. (Gal 3:28)**
> **"If you have played the fool and exalted yourself, or if you have planned evil, clap your hand over your mouth! (Prov 30:32)**
> **For the director of music. For Jeduthun. A psalm of David. I said, "I will watch my ways and keep my tongue from sin; I will put a muzzle on my mouth as long as the wicked are in my presence." But when I was silent and still, not even saying anything good, my anguish increased. My heart grew hot within me, and as I meditated, the fire burned; then I spoke with my tongue: "Show me, O LORD, my life's end and the number of my days; let me know how fleeting is my life. (Psa 39:1-4)**

4 (4:28-29) **Witnessing:** there was the proclamation that Jesus was the Messiah. Note the tender, yet meaningful statement: "Then, leaving her water jar." She was very excited. The Messiah had confronted her; she had actually met Him, and He had met the need of her heart and life. She had to tell everyone about Him.

Note also the strength of the woman's witness. She was an outcast from society, had no friends because of the immoral life she had lived. However, meeting the Messiah changed all that. He dealt with her sin and shame. She could now face everyone. They, too, must have the opportunity to meet the Messiah.

Thought 1. What a lesson for every believer!

> **Jesus did not let him, but said, "Go home to your family and tell them how much the Lord has done for you, and how he has had mercy on you." (Mark 5:19)**
> **For we cannot help speaking about what we have seen and heard." (Acts 4:20)**
> **You will be his witness to all men of what you have seen and heard. (Acts 22:15)**
> **These, then, are the things you should teach. Encourage and rebuke with all authority. Do not let anyone despise you. (Titus 2:15)**
> **But in your hearts set apart Christ as Lord. Always be prepared to give an answer to everyone who asks you to give the reason for the hope that you have. But do this with gentleness and respect, (1 Pet 3:15)**
> **Come and listen, all you who fear God; let me tell you what he has done for me. (Psa 66:16)**
> **I will tell of the kindnesses of the LORD, the deeds for which he is to be praised, according to all the LORD has done for us— yes, the many good things he has done for the house of Israel, according to his compassion and many kindnesses. (Isa 63:7)**

It is my pleasure to tell you about the miraculous signs and wonders that the Most High God has performed for me. (Dan 4:2)

5 (4:30) **Jesus Christ, Response—Seeking, Jesus:** there was the response of searching for the Messiah. Note two facts.

1. The woman was of no social importance, not to the men of the city. In fact, she had often been misused, and she was often the very subject of gossip and jokes. But now something had happened to her: she had met the Messiah. The event had so changed her appearance, behavior, and attitude that people listened eagerly to what she said.

Therefore, if anyone is in Christ, he is a new creation; the old has gone, the new has come! (2 Cor 5:17)

But when the kindness and love of God our Savior appeared, he saved us, not because of righteous things we had done, but because of his mercy. He saved us through the washing of rebirth and renewal by the Holy Spirit, whom he poured out on us generously through Jesus Christ our Savior, so that, having been justified by his grace, we might become heirs having the hope of eternal life. (Titus 3:4-7)

He chose to give us birth through the word of truth, that we might be a kind of firstfruits of all he created. (James 1:18)

Praise be to the God and Father of our Lord Jesus Christ! In his great mercy he has given us new birth into a living hope through the resurrection of Jesus Christ from the dead, and into an inheritance that can never perish, spoil or fade—kept in heaven for you, (1 Pet 1:3-4)

I will give you a new heart and put a new spirit in you; I will remove from you your heart of stone and give you a heart of flesh. (Ezek 36:26)

2. The people responded—at least a good number did. The idea of the words "made their way toward him" is that of a long streaming procession. The people kept on "making their way toward him." It was her dynamic witness, the striking change seen in her life, that caused this enormous response. Because of her witness, many set out to find the Messiah for themselves.

I led them with cords of human kindness, with ties of love; I lifted the yoke from their neck and bent down to feed them. (Hosea 11:4)

But I, when I am lifted up from the earth, will draw all men to myself." (John 12:32)

	E. The Subject of Labor for God, 4:31-42		
1 Physical vs. spiritual concerns a. The disciples' concern: Physical nourishment b. Jesus' concern: Spiritual food—to do the will & work of God c. Jesus' challenge: Work & labor for God *right now* **2 Labor—for the harvest is ripe, the task is urgent** **3 Labor—for there are rewards & great benefits** a. Wages b. Eternal life c. Joy & rejoicing	31 Meanwhile his disciples urged him, "Rabbi, eat something." 32 But he said to them, "I have food to eat that you know nothing about." 33 Then his disciples said to each other, "Could someone have brought him food?" 34 "My food," said Jesus, "is to do the will of him who sent me and to finish his work. 35 Do you not say, 'Four months more and then the harvest'? I tell you, open your eyes and look at the fields! They are ripe for harvest. 36 Even now the reaper draws his wages, even now he harvests the crop for eternal life, so that the sower and the reaper may be glad	together. 37 Thus the saying 'One sows and another reaps' is true. 38 I sent you to reap what you have not worked for. Others have done the hard work, and you have reaped the benefits of their labor." 39 Many of the Samaritans from that town believed in him because of the woman's testimony, "He told me everything I ever did." 40 So when the Samaritans came to him, they urged him to stay with them, and he stayed two days. 41 And because of his words many more became believers. 42 They said to the woman, "We no longer believe just because of what you said; now we have heard for ourselves, and we know that this man really is the Savior of the world."	d. The privilege of having a specific part in God's great work e. The privilege of being being sent by Christ f. The privilege of serving with other great servants of God **4 Labor—for results follow** a. Many believed the woman's testimony b. Other opportunities were given c. Many more believed: "This man really is the Savior of the world"^DS1

DIVISION IV

THE REVELATION OF JESUS, THE LIVING WATER, 4:1-42

E. The Subject of Labor for God, 4:31-42

(4:31-42) **Introduction**: the believer is to labor for God. His life is to be focused upon the will and work of God. His purpose for being on earth is to serve God, to obey and work for Him.

1. Physical vs. spiritual concerns (v.31-35).
2. Labor—for the harvest is ripe, the task is urgent (v.35).
3. Labor—for there are rewards and great benefits (v.36-38).
4. Labor—for results follow (v.39-42).

1 (4:31-35) **Concern, Physical vs. Spiritual—God, Work—Diligence—Faithfulness—Commitment**: physical vs. spiritual concerns. The disciples returned from town. They had gone to buy food (v.8). Earlier, when they had arrived at the well on the outskirts of the city, Jesus had been tired and hungry. But now, as the disciples sat eating, they noticed Jesus made no effort to eat. He had been famished and exhausted. They were concerned, so they suggested He eat. Note two significant points.

1. The concern of the disciples was for physical nourishment. Their minds were not on the woman to whom Jesus had just witnessed, not on her spiritual needs. They had no spiritual depth yet. Their minds were not...
   - focused on Christ and His mission of salvation.
   - concentrating upon a world lost in sin and shame.
   - looking for every opportunity possible to reach and help people for God.

They had not yet learned the great warfare being waged between the physical and spiritual concerns of life. Their minds were on the physical: on food, on not missing a meal, on satisfying a temporary craving of the body.

2. The concern of Christ was for spiritual food and nourishment, to do the will and work of God. Three points are seen in this verse.
   a. The will that must concern men is *God's will*, and the work that must concern men is *God's work*, the will and work of...
      - leading people to the Living Water (Jn.4:10).
      - helping people quench their inner thirst (Jn.4:14).
      - bringing people to God.
      - seeking and saving the lost, even *Samaritans*: those who are looked upon with prejudice, thought to be of a lower caste, treated as the most despicable *outcasts* (Lk.19:10).

   No greater will or work exists or can be done. God alone is God. His will and work is supreme.
   ⇒ Note the *esteem* with which Christ holds God: it is *God's will and work* that is to be done.
   ⇒ Note the *devotion* of Christ to God: God's will and work *must* be done.
   b. God sent Christ. The words "sent me" are significant (see DEEPER STUDY # 3—Jn.3:34). Christ was not sent to do the will of men, but of God. His work was not the work of men, but of God.

   Thought 1. Note two lessons.
   1) Note the warning to all believers. *Believers* are sent by God. They are to be single-minded. They are not to allow their *goals* and *energy* to

become entangled with the business and affairs of the world.

> **No one serving as a soldier gets involved in civilian affairs—he wants to please his commanding officer. (2 Tim 2:4)**

2) Note the mission to all believers. Believers are *sent* by God. They are on earth primarily to do the will and work of God, even in their *secular* labor in the world.

> **Again Jesus said, "Peace be with you! As the Father has sent me, I am sending you." (John 20:21)**
> **He who has been stealing must steal no longer, but must work, doing something useful with his own hands, that he may have something to share with those in need. (Eph 4:28)**

c. Christ had to finish the will and work of God. God expected it to be completed. God expected obedience, faithfulness and perseverance until His will and work was done. Note: Christ did complete God's mission (Jn.17:4; 19:30). He now challenges His followers: "Labor for God—finish your task—complete your purpose for being on earth."

Thought 1. Note two warnings.
1) Note the responsibility and duty of believers. Believers are expected to finish the work that God sent them to do. Believers are not to become entangled and distracted by worldly affairs. They are to conquer wandering thoughts and desires, cravings for food, complacency, sleepiness. They are not to be given over to the world and the flesh, indulgence and license, money and material possessions.
2) Note the accountability of believers: God *expects* believers to be faithful, so there has to be a day of accounting, a day when wages are paid out.

2 (4:35) **Vision—Evangelism**: labor, for the harvest is ripe, the task is urgent. Note three points.

1. The heart of Jesus was upon the harvest of souls. Men focus their hearts upon the world's harvest, the planting of seed and the reaping of grain, the investment of energy and money, and the receiving of wages and gain. But the heart of Jesus was, and still is, upon people, upon the planting of the gospel seed and the reaping of souls for God.

2. The challenge of Jesus was, "Open your eyes, and look at the fields." The challenge was to quit looking down upon the earth and upon the affairs of the world, but instead to open your eyes and observe the fields of people streaming across the world. The scene was probably dramatic. The Samaritans in their long flowing white robes were probably streaming across the fields by the hundreds, if not the thousands. Jesus' heart and arms reached out in a burst of compassion and intense feeling; He cried, "Look, open your eyes and look at the fields of lost souls streaming toward you. Let the things of earth grow strangely dim."

3. The fields of souls are white *already*: they are ready for harvesting *right now*. Since Christ has come to earth,

God has put His Spirit into the world and supernaturally activated...
- a thirst for God.
- a sense of sin, a conviction of coming short.
- a deep loneliness and emptiness.
- a sense of purposelessness.
- the knowledge that Jesus Christ has come to earth claiming to be the Savior of the world, the very Son of God.

It is absolutely necessary that believers open their eyes and look *now*. If not, the ripe harvest of souls and bodies will...
- remain in the fields of the earth.
- ripen *beyond* being tasteful and useful (be too old, too far gone).
- rot and be lost forever.
- fall to the ground and decay.

Thought 1. Two significant points for the believer.
1) We must open our eyes in order to look. We cannot see ahead or around us if we do not open our eyes to look. The things of the earth have to grow *strangely* dim *before* we can look and see.

> **Do not conform any longer to the pattern of this world, but be transformed by the renewing of your mind. Then you will be able to test and approve what God's will is—his good, pleasing and perfect will. (Rom 12:2)**
> **Those who use the things of the world, as if not engrossed in them. For this world in its present form is passing away. (1 Cor 7:31)**
> **May I never boast except in the cross of our Lord Jesus Christ, through which the world has been crucified to me, and I to the world. (Gal 6:14)**
> **Do not love the world or anything in the world. If anyone loves the world, the love of the Father is not in him. (1 John 2:15)**

2) We must look where we are so that our eyes will see the reality of what is around us. It is the harvest of souls around us that we are to look upon and focus our attention upon.

Note: we can look upon foreign fields through the challenge of others. Note another fact: the world is becoming more and more *one neighborhood*. Distance is becoming more and more insignificant. Every believer is becoming more and more responsible for the individual in the foreign land. In fact, a man's country is foreign to everyone else in the world, no matter who he is.

> **The one who sows to please his sinful nature, from that nature will reap destruction; the one who sows to please the Spirit, from the Spirit will reap eternal life. Let us not become weary in doing good, for at the proper time we will reap a harvest if we do not give up. (Gal 6:8-9)**
> **As soon as the grain is ripe, he puts the sickle to it, because the harvest has come." (Mark 4:29)**
> **He told them, "The harvest is plentiful, but the workers are few. Ask the Lord of**

the harvest, therefore, to send out workers into his harvest field. (Luke 10:2)

You did not choose me, but I chose you and appointed you to go and bear fruit—fruit that will last. Then the Father will give you whatever you ask in my name. (John 15:16)

For I could wish that I myself were cursed and cut off from Christ for the sake of my brothers, those of my own race, (Rom 9:3)

Brothers, my heart's desire and prayer to God for the Israelites is that they may be saved. (Rom 10:1)

Though I am free and belong to no man, I make myself a slave to everyone, to win as many as possible. To the Jews I became like a Jew, to win the Jews. To those under the law I became like one under the law (though I myself am not under the law), so as to win those under the law. To the weak I became weak, to win the weak. I have become all things to all men so that by all possible means I might save some. (1 Cor 9:19-20, 22)

Remember this: Whoever turns a sinner from the error of his way will save him from death and cover over a multitude of sins. (James 5:20)

Snatch others from the fire and save them; to others show mercy, mixed with fear—hating even the clothing stained by corrupted flesh. (Jude 1:23)

Those who sow in tears will reap with songs of joy. He who goes out weeping, carrying seed to sow, will return with songs of joy, carrying sheaves with him. (Psa 126:5-6)

Sow for yourselves righteousness, reap the fruit of unfailing love, and break up your unplowed ground; for it is time to seek the LORD, until he comes and showers righteousness on you. (Hosea 10:12)

3 (4:36-38) **Rewards**: labor, for there are rewards and great benefits. Christ mentioned six particular rewards and benefits.

1. The laborer will receive wages. God is going to pay the believer and pay him well. Note that the wages are already there, ready to be paid (see note, Rewards—Lk.16:10-12; Mt.20:8-16. Cp. Lk.10:7; 2 Tim.2:6.)

And everyone who has left houses or brothers or sisters or father or mother or children or fields for my sake will receive a hundred times as much and will inherit eternal life. (Mat 19:29)

"His master replied, 'Well done, good and faithful servant! You have been faithful with a few things; I will put you in charge of many things. Come and share your master's happiness!' (Mat 25:23)

Those who are wise will shine like the brightness of the heavens, and those who lead many to righteousness, like the stars for ever and ever. (Dan 12:3)

2. The laborer gathers fruit *for eternal life*. What he does is of supreme value. It is the greatest work imaginable. His work is lasting; it endures forever. His work actually delivers people from *ever* perishing, and it causes God to give them abundant and eternal life.

"For God so loved the world that he gave his one and only Son, that whoever believes in him shall not perish but have eternal life. (John 3:16)

Whoever believes in the Son has eternal life, but whoever rejects the Son will not see life, for God's wrath remains on him." (John 3:36)

3. The laborer experiences the overflowing joy of serving God with other laborers. (See note, Joy—Ph.1:4.) Note: there is no envy or conflict between the two laborers. Both laborers work and rejoice together. (How different from so many!)

And goes home. Then he calls his friends and neighbors together and says, 'Rejoice with me; I have found my lost sheep.' I tell you that in the same way there will be more rejoicing in heaven over one sinner who repents than over ninety-nine righteous persons who do not need to repent. (Luke 15:6-7)

For what is our hope, our joy, or the crown in which we will glory in the presence of our Lord Jesus when he comes? Is it not you? Indeed, you are our glory and joy. (1 Th 2:19-20)

He who goes out weeping, carrying seed to sow, will return with songs of joy, carrying sheaves with him. (Psa 126:6)

4. The laborer is given the privilege of having a *specific part* in God's great work. It may be sowing; it may be reaping. It does not matter. It is God's work, and it is a *privilege for any man to have a part in it*.

Note something else. Each man has only a part. No man does it all. One man sows, and another man reaps. The task is too great for one man. All men are needed.

⇒ If the sower fails to sow, the reaper cannot reap. Some soul is not fed enough to ripen for the picking.

⇒ If the reaper does not reap, the soul ripened by the sower passes its usefulness: it rots and falls to the ground and decays.

I planted the seed, Apollos watered it, but God made it grow. So neither he who plants nor he who waters is anything, but only God, who makes things grow. The man who plants and the man who waters have one purpose, and each will be rewarded according to his own labor. (1 Cor 3:6-8)

5. The laborer has the privilege of being chosen and sent by Christ, the Son of God Himself.

You did not choose me, but I chose you and appointed you to go and bear fruit—fruit that will last. Then the Father will give you whatever you ask in my name. (John 15:16)

6. The laborer is given the privilege of serving with other great servants. Other great believers are laboring, and each servant enters into the labors of all others. (What a challenge to pray for all of God's servants and to get to the task of either sowing or reaping, whichever God has called us to do!)

> For we are God's fellow workers; you are God's field, God's building. By the grace God has given me, I laid a foundation as an expert builder, and someone else is building on it. But each one should be careful how he builds. For no one can lay any foundation other than the one already laid, which is Jesus Christ. (1 Cor 3:9-11)

4 (4:39-42) **Witnessing, Results—Ministry**: labor, for results do follow. What follows gives a picture of exactly what Christ had been saying about laboring for God.

1. Many "believed in Him [Christ]" because of the woman's testimony. The seed had been sown in the woman's heart by the prophets of old and through the first five books of Scripture (cp. v.12, 19-20). Jesus reaped her soul. She in turn went and bore her testimony within the city. And "many...from that town believed in Him because of the woman's testimony."

2. Other opportunities were given. The new believers begged Christ to stay with them. They wanted to learn more, and they had friends who needed to hear Him as well.

> It is written: "I believed; therefore I have spoken." With that same spirit of faith we also believe and therefore speak, (2 Cor 4:13)
> Then those who feared the LORD talked with each other, and the LORD listened and heard. A scroll of remembrance was written in his presence concerning those who feared the LORD and honored his name. (Mal 3:16)

3. Many more believed that Jesus was the Christ, the "Savior of the world."
   a. The Christ (see DEEPER STUDY # 2—Jn.1:20).
   b. The Savior of the world (see DEEPER STUDY # 1—Jn.4:42).

DEEPER STUDY # 1

(4:42) **Jesus Christ, Savior**: the word "Savior" (soter) means a Deliverer, a Preserver. It has the idea of a Deliverer, a Savior who snatches a person from some terrible disaster that leads to perishing (cp. Jn.3:16). (See DEEPER STUDY # 6, Salvation—Mt.1:21 for more discussion.)

1. Jesus Christ is said to be the Savior (Lk.2:11; Jn.4:42; Acts 5:31; 13:23; Eph.5:23; Ph.3:20; 2 Tim.1:10; Tit.1:4; 2:13; 3:6; 2 Pt.1:1, 11; 2:20; 3:2, 18; 1 Jn.4:14).

2. God is said to be the Savior (Lk.1:47; 1 Tim.1:1; 2:3; 4:10; Tit.1:3; 2:10; 3:4; Jude 25).

	V. THE REVELATION OF JESUS, THE OBJECT OF FAITH, 4:43-54 A. The Evidence of Faith, 4:43-45	44 (Now Jesus himself had pointed out that a prophet has no honor in his own country.) 45 When he arrived in Galilee, the Galileans welcomed him. They had seen all that he had done in Jerusalem at the Passover Feast, for they also had been there.	2 Evidence 1: Honoring Jesus 3 Evidence 2: Welcoming & receiving Jesus
1 Jesus entered Galilee[DS1]	43 After the two days he left for Galilee.		

DIVISION V

THE REVELATION OF JESUS, THE OBJECT OF FAITH, 4:43-54

A. The Evidence of Faith, 4:43-45

(4:43-45) **Introduction**: this passage is very simple, yet it pictures one of the great lessons of the gospel—the evidence of faith.

1. Jesus entered Galilee (v.43).
2. Evidence 1: honoring Jesus (v.44).
3. Evidence 2: welcoming and receiving Jesus (v.45).

1 (4:43) **Jesus, Ministry**: Jesus entered Galilee. He had spent two days with the Samaritans and had experienced great success. However, Galilee was the area especially prepared by God for the Lord's ministry, so Jesus returned to the area where most of His ministry was to be conducted. (See DEEPER STUDY # 1, Galilee—Jn.4:43.)

DEEPER STUDY # 1

(4:43) **Galilee**: the district of Galilee was the northernmost part of Palestine. Palestine was divided into three districts: Judaea in the far south, Samaria in the middle, and Galilee in the north. God had prepared Galilee down through history for the coming of His Son's ministry. Several facts show this (cp. Gal.4:4).

1. Throughout history Galilee had been invaded and re-populated again and again with different people and cultures from all over the world. Over the years such an influx of differing people had created an atmosphere susceptible to new personalities and ideas.
2. Galilee was strategically located. The world's leading roads passed right through its borders. Merchants from all over the world passed through and boarded in the inns of the cities.
3. Galilee was heavily populated. It was also surrounded by the Samaritans, Phoenicians, and Syrians, making it an open door for world evangelization. It was one of the most fertile lands in that part of the world. This fact, plus the travelling trade, led numbers of people to settle within its borders. There were within the district over two hundred cities with a population of fifteen thousand people or more (Josephus. Quoted by William Barclay. *The Gospel of Matthew*, Vol.1. "The Daily Study Bible." Philadelphia, PA: The Westminister Press, 1956, p.66). There were multitudes for Jesus to reach.
4. Galilee was open to new and fresh ideas. Its people, having come from all over the world, were liberal minded, always looking for new and fresh ideas to stimulate and challenge their thinking.

It was for these reasons that Jesus chose Galilee to begin His ministry. The area was an open door for people to spread the news that the Messiah had come and that the Kingdom of Heaven was being ushered in.

---

2 (4:44) **Honor—Jesus Christ, Honored—Belief**: the first evidence of faith is honoring Jesus. When Jesus went into Galilee, He stayed away from His hometown of Nazareth. His neighbors and fellow citizens had rejected Him and had attempted to kill Him (Lk.4:29). As a result Jesus had declared, "No prophet is accepted in his hometown" (Lk.4:24).

⇒ Joseph was not honored by his brothers (Gen.37:23-36).
⇒ David was not honored by his brother (1 Sam. 17:28).
⇒ Jeremiah was not honored by his hometown, Anathoth (Jer.11:21; cp. Jer.1:1).
⇒ Paul was not honored by his countrymen (Acts 9:23-24; see note—2 Cor.1:12-22).
⇒ Jesus was not honored by His hometown (Mk.6:1-6).

Now as Jesus returned to Galilee, bypassing the city of Nazareth, He again referred to the fact that a prophet has no honor in His own country.

A question needs to be asked. Why did Jesus make the declaration about dishonor here? It seems out of place. Glance at the three verses again (v.43-45). There are at least two reasons.

1. Jesus' heart was broken over His hometown. They were a special people to Him: He had played with some of them as a child, grown up with them, lived as a friend with them; and had fellowshipped, worked, eaten, and moved among them day in and day out. The thought of their rejection and hostility toward Him often preyed upon His mind. (See outline and notes—Mk.6:1-6 for discussion of their rejection.)
2. Jesus had to prepare the disciples for persecution. They were to be severely persecuted by their fellow countrymen. He repeated the fact time and again to drive it into their minds. He wanted them prepared and not caught off guard when persecution came.

Now, note the point: the first evidence that a person has faith is that he honors Jesus. A sharp contrast is being drawn between the refusal of Nazareth to honor Jesus and the receiving of Him by other Galilaeans. Several things need to be considered.

1. Jesus is due honor. He is due all the honor and glory in the universe.
   a. He is the Son of God who brought God's presence among men.

"The virgin will be with child and will give birth to a son, and they will call him Immanuel" —which means, "God with us." (Mat 1:23)

The Word became flesh and made his dwelling among us. We have seen his glory, the glory of the One and Only, who came from the Father, full of grace and truth. (John 1:14)

b. He is the Savior of the world who came to save men from perishing and made it possible for them to live forever (see DEEPER STUDY # 1—Jn.4:42).

"For God so loved the world that he gave his one and only Son, that whoever believes in him shall not perish but have eternal life. (John 3:16)

The God of our fathers raised Jesus from the dead—whom you had killed by hanging him on a tree. God exalted him to his own right hand as Prince and Savior that he might give repentance and forgiveness of sins to Israel. (Acts 5:30-31)

c. He is the Son of Man who came to earth to experience all the trials of life that He might feel and be touched by man's infirmities and his weaknesses, and thereby become qualified to help man in all his suffering.

Just as the Son of Man did not come to be served, but to serve, and to give his life as a ransom for many." (Mat 20:28)

For we do not have a high priest who is unable to sympathize with our weaknesses, but we have one who has been tempted in every way, just as we are—yet was without sin. Let us then approach the throne of grace with confidence, so that we may receive mercy and find grace to help us in our time of need. (Heb 4:15-16)

2. People who believe in Jesus honor Him. Honoring Jesus is a clear evidence of faith. The word "honor" (timen) means to value, esteem, respect. It has three ideas that are significant.
   a. The idea of superior standing, exaltation, distinction, homage, reverence, and, of course, worship when referring to the Son of God.

Therefore God exalted him to the highest place and gave him the name that is above every name, that at the name of Jesus every knee should bow, in heaven and on earth and under the earth, and every tongue confess that Jesus Christ is Lord, to the glory of God the Father. (Phil 2:9-11)

   b. The idea of a price paid or received, of credit due, of counting something of extreme value. Jesus is due the payment of man's life. True honor pays the price due to the Lord: the man who honors the Lord gives his life to the Lord (see note, Self-denial—Lk.9:23).

Do you not know that your body is a temple of the Holy Spirit, who is in you, whom you have received from God? You

are not your own; you were bought at a price. Therefore honor God with your body. (1 Cor 6:19-20)

When he found one of great value, he went away and sold everything he had and bought it. (Mat 13:46)

With this in mind, we constantly pray for you, that our God may count you worthy of his calling, and that by his power he may fulfill every good purpose of yours and every act prompted by your faith. We pray this so that the name of our Lord Jesus may be glorified in you, and you in him, according to the grace of our God and the Lord Jesus Christ. (2 Th 1:11-12)

   c. The idea of preciousness. The Greek word for precious (time) means to be due honor, to be of precious value.

Now to you who believe, this stone is precious. But to those who do not believe, "The stone the builders rejected has become the capstone," (1 Pet 2:7)

What is more, I consider everything a loss compared to the surpassing greatness of knowing Christ Jesus my Lord, for whose sake I have lost all things. I consider them rubbish, that I may gain Christ (Phil 3:8)

3. People who do not believe in Jesus do not honor Him. This is particularly seen in the dishonor of Jesus by His fellow citizens and the religionists (see outline and notes—Mk.6:1-6; Lk.4:16-30; DEEPER STUDY # 2—Jn.5:15-16). An unbeliever…
   • does not give Christ the worship, exaltation, or reverence due His name.
   • does not pay the price of surrendering his life to Christ as Lord.
   • does not count Christ as precious (due honor). Jesus' fellow citizens demonstrated this fact. He, the very Prophet of God Himself, had no honor in His own country.

For this people's heart has become calloused; they hardly hear with their ears, and they have closed their eyes. Otherwise they might see with their eyes, hear with their ears, understand with their hearts and turn, and I would heal them.' (Mat 13:15)

I have come in my Father's name, and you do not accept me; but if someone else comes in his own name, you will accept him. How can you believe if you accept praise from one another, yet make no effort to obtain the praise that comes from the only God? (John 5:43-44)

There is a judge for the one who rejects me and does not accept my words; that very word which I spoke will condemn him at the last day. (John 12:48)

They will turn their ears away from the truth and turn aside to myths. (2 Tim 4:4)

It claps its hands in derision and hisses him out of his place. (Job 27:23)

To whom can I speak and give warning? Who will listen to me? Their ears are closed so they cannot hear. The word of the

LORD is offensive to them; they find no pleasure in it. (Jer 6:10)

"Son of man, you are living among a rebellious people. They have eyes to see but do not see and ears to hear but do not hear, for they are a rebellious people. (Ezek 12:2)

"But they refused to pay attention; stubbornly they turned their backs and stopped up their ears. (Zec 7:11)

3 (4:45) **Faith, Evidence—Receiving, Jesus Christ**: the second evidence of faith is welcoming and receiving Jesus. The only way to be saved and to receive the benefits of Jesus' presence is to welcome and receive Him. Common sense tells us that a person who does not have the presence of Jesus Christ does not have the blessings of Jesus' presence. Jesus is just not there to bless and care for the person. However, this was not the case with the Galilaeans. They were receiving the benefits of Jesus' life and ministry, and they were receiving His blessings for three very specific reasons.

1. They had heard the Lord preach and seen His marvellous works in Jerusalem at the Passover Feast. They had not been the target of Jesus' ministry there; the citizens of Jerusalem had been the people upon whom Jesus had focused in Jerusalem. However, the Galilaeans had not felt slighted, not to the point that they shut Him out and refused to listen. They were attracted to Him, for their souls were reaching out for God. Therefore, they attended His preaching and observed His ministry. They opened their hearts to what He was saying about repentance and receiving the Kingdom of God. (See note—Mk.1:14-15.)

Thought 1. A man can never be led to believe in Christ *until* he is receptive to Christ. He *must be willing* to listen to the message of Christ.

But blessed are your eyes because they see, and your ears because they hear. (Mat 13:16)

Now the Bereans were of more noble character than the Thessalonians, for they received the message with great eagerness and examined the Scriptures every day to see if what Paul said was true. (Acts 17:11)

And we also thank God continually because, when you received the word of God, which you heard from us, you accepted it not as the word of men, but as it actually is, the word of God, which is at work in you who believe. (1 Th 2:13)

My dear brothers, take note of this: Everyone should be quick to listen, slow to speak and slow to become angry, (James 1:19)

Blessed is the man who listens to me, watching daily at my doors, waiting at my doorway. (Prov 8:34)

He who listens to a life giving rebuke will be at home among the wise. (Prov 15:31)

Guard your steps when you go to the house of God. Go near to listen rather than to offer the sacrifice of fools, who do not know that they do wrong. (Eccl 5:1)

2. They were a people seeking and worshipping God. Note why they had been to Jerusalem. They had gone to seek and worship God at the Passover, and it had cost them. The journey was long and difficult, for they were in the northernmost part of Palestine, whereas the temple was in Jerusalem which was in the south. Also, they had to take a circular route because Samaria lay between Galilee and Jerusalem, and the Samaritans considered them enemies, posing a threat to their safety.

The point is this: these Galilaeans had a hunger for God; therefore, their hearts were better prepared and willing to receive Christ.

Thought 1. A man who *sincerely* seeks God is better prepared to receive Christ. For this reason, men should be constantly seeking after God. Seeking God and receiving Christ are evidences of true faith (Heb.11:6).

Blessed are those who hunger and thirst for righteousness, for they will be filled. (Mat 5:6)

But if from there you seek the LORD your God, you will find him if you look for him with all your heart and with all your soul. (Deu 4:29)

Seek the LORD while he may be found; call on him while he is near. (Isa 55:6)

And without faith it is impossible to please God, because anyone who comes to him must believe that he exists and that he rewards those who earnestly seek him. (Heb 11:6)

3. The idea being conveyed is that the Galilaeans welcomed and received Christ. They wanted to experience Christ for themselves. They had seen Him preach and minister in Jerusalem, and they wanted the same experience for themselves and for the rest of their people. Of course, some Galilaeans did not receive Him into their lives and hearts. They deserted Him (cp. Jn.6:66). But to all who received him, to those who believed in his name, he gave the right to become children of God." (See note—Jn.1:12-13.)

Thought 1. Welcoming, receiving, and experiencing Christ for oneself is the greatest evidence of genuine faith.

But the seed on good soil stands for those with a noble and good heart, who hear the word, retain it, and by persevering produce a crop. (Luke 8:15)

Here I am! I stand at the door and knock. If anyone hears my voice and opens the door, I will come in and eat with him, and he with me. (Rev 3:20)

	B. The Stages of Faith, 4:46-54		working faith
1 A beginning faith		may go. Your son will live." The man took Jesus at his word and departed.	a. The promise: Your need is met
a. There was a desperate need	46 Once more he visited Cana in Galilee, where he had turned the water into wine. And there was a certain royal official whose son lay sick at Capernaum.		b. He believed & obeyed Jesus' Word
b. There was hearing about Jesus	47 When this man heard that Jesus had arrived in Galilee from Judea, he went to him and begged him to come and heal his son, who was close to death.	51 While he was still on the way, his servants met him with the news that his boy was living.	**4 A confirmed faith** a. He "was on the way"
c. There was coming to Jesus		52 When he inquired as to the time when his son got better, they said to him, "The fever left him yesterday at the seventh hour."	b. He received glorious news: His prayer was answered
d. There was begging Jesus to help			c. He confimed the supernatural vs. the natural
2 A persistent faith a. A lesson in faith	48 "Unless you people see miraculous signs and wonders," Jesus told him, "you will never believe."	53 Then the father realized that this was the exact time at which Jesus had said to him, "Your son will live." So he and all his household believed.	d. He believed & knew that Jesus had healed his son
b. A desperate insistence	49 The royal official said, "Sir, come down before my child dies.	54 This was the second miraculous sign that Jesus performed, having come from Judea to Galilee.	**5 A witnessing faith**
3 A trusting, obedient, &	50 Jesus replied, "You		

DIVISION V

THE REVELATION OF JESUS, THE OBJECT OF FAITH, 4:43-54

B. The Stages of Faith, 4:46-54

(4:46-54) **Introduction**: this nobleman was a government official, probably holding some high position in Herod's court. His experience reveals the various stages of faith, the kind of growing faith that every man should experience.

1. A beginning faith (v.46-47).
2. A persistent faith (v.48-49).
3. A trusting, obedient, and working faith (v.50).
4. A confirmed faith (v.51-53).
5. A witnessing faith (v.53-54).

1 (4:46-47) **Faith—Seeking Jesus—Contrition**: the first stage is a beginning faith. When Jesus entered the city of Cana, a certain royal official (basilixos), a nobleman of the King's court, approached Jesus. The actions of the man demonstrated exactly what is involved in a beginning faith.

1. There was a desperate need. The man's son was at the point of death.

Thought 1. Needs confront every human being. Eventually the severe needs arising from accident, illness, disease, suffering, and death strike everyone. No one is exempt. One may be an official in government or even the king himself—it does not matter. The day eventually comes when every man needs help. The severe disasters of life are beyond any man's control.

2. There was hearing about Jesus. The man heard about Jesus, and he listened attentively to what he heard. He did not...

• turn a deaf ear to the message.
• think himself too important.
• consider the message to be foolish.
• mock the person sharing about Jesus.

3. There was coming to Jesus. Facing one of the severe disasters of life, the man came to Jesus. Jesus was the only person he had ever heard about that might be able to help. Note what the man had to sacrifice in order to go to Jesus.

a. The man had to leave the side of his dying son knowing he would be gone for many hours. Imagine the anxiety and fear that his son might die while he was away. The man would literally have to tear himself away from his son. Such an act shows how strongly he believed that Jesus could help him.

b. The man had to travel almost a day's journey to reach Jesus. Capernaum was about twenty miles from Cana. Imagine the concern and apprehension gripping the father's heart every foot of the way, wonderingif he should have left his son's side. The fact that he *persevered* and kept his eyes on the hope of Jesus shows the faith of his heart.

Be strong and take heart, all you who hope in the LORD. (Psa 31:24)

But the eyes of the LORD are on those who fear him, on those whose hope is in his unfailing love, (Psa 33:18)

"But now, Lord, what do I look for? My hope is in you. (Psa 39:7)

Why are you downcast, O my soul? Why so disturbed within me? Put your hope in God, for I will yet praise him, my Savior and my God. (Psa 42:11)

For you have been my hope, O Sovereign LORD, my confidence since my youth. (Psa 71:5)

Blessed is he whose help is the God of Jacob, whose hope is in the LORD his God, (Psa 146:5; cp.v.6-9)

"But blessed is the man who trusts in the LORD, whose confidence is in him. (Jer 17:7)

c. The man did not let his high position keep him from Jesus. He did not wrap himself in pride nor did he allow what others might say keep him from Jesus. Swallowing his pride, he confessed his need in the face of all who ridiculed, and he went to Jesus.

> He will call upon me, and I will answer him; I will be with him in trouble, I will deliver him and honor him. (Psa 91:15)
>
> Then you will call, and the LORD will answer; you will cry for help, and he will say: Here am I. "If you do away with the yoke of oppression, with the pointing finger and malicious talk, (Isa 58:9)
>
> 'Call to me and I will answer you and tell you great and unsearchable things you do not know.' (Jer 33:3)

4. There was begging Jesus to help. The man literally begged (erota) and kept on begging for Jesus to meet his need.

2 (4:48-49) **Faith—Belief—Signs**: the second stage was a persistent faith. Note two crucial lessons.

1. A lesson in faith. The man said, "Come down, and heal my son." Jesus was saying, "Unless I come and you see signs and miracles you will not believe. Is that what you are saying?" Jesus had to teach the man that *His Word alone* was enough. *Belief in His Word* was what was going to assure the request. His power was at the royal official's disposal if he would just believe Him. Belief is to precede signs and wonders. Note that "you" is plural. Jesus was addressing both the man and the crowd. He wanted the crowd to get the message as well. (See DEEPER STUDY # 1—Jn.2:23; DEEPER STUDY # 2—2:24.)

2. A desperate insistence. The man was in no position to argue, not even to think through what Jesus had just said. He was desperate. A severe disaster had stricken his life. He believed Jesus was the only One who could help him, and he was determined to secure Jesus' help. He cried out, "Lord [Kurie] come before my child dies."

Note two significant points. (1) The man did not allow Jesus' rebuke to deter him, and (2) he kept after Jesus.

Thought 1. Note the crucial lessons.
1) Signs and wonders (the boy's healing) were not as important as *believing Jesus*. A man's eternal salvation was at stake, and the man had to believe to be saved.
2) The man was helped because he persisted. Persistence was absolutely necessary in securing the Lord's help. Persistence shows that one really recognizes and acknowledges his need and really believes God can and will help. Note: if a man ceases to ask, he shows that he does not believe God will answer. He gives up on God, disbelieving Him. This man did not allow the Lord's hesitation to stop him.

> "Ask and it will be given to you; seek and you will find; knock and the door will be opened to you. For everyone who asks receives; he who seeks finds; and to him who knocks, the door will be opened. (Mat 7:7-8; cp. v.9-11)
>
> And without faith it is impossible to please God, because anyone who comes to him must believe that he exists and that he rewards those who earnestly seek him. (Heb 11:6)
>
> The LORD redeems his servants; no one will be condemned who takes refuge in him. (Psa 34:22)
>
> Trust in the LORD forever, for the LORD, the LORD, is the Rock eternal. (Isa 26:4)
>
> You will seek me and find me when you seek me with all your heart. (Jer 29:13)

3 (4:50) **Faith—Obedience**: the third stage was a trusting, obedient, working faith. Note three things.
1. The charge and the promise of Jesus was forceful.
⇒ The charge: "You may go."
⇒ The promise: "Your son will live."
2. The man's belief in Jesus' Word and his obedience. He "took Jesus at his word " and "departed." The idea is that of *instantaneous faith and action*: he believed immediately and he turned immediately, heading home to his son. He *acted* on his faith. Note what he believed.
⇒ The Lord's love, compassion, and concern: that Jesus cared for those who had desperate need.
⇒ The Lord's knowledge (omniscience): that Jesus knew his son was healed, although he was twenty miles away.
⇒ The Lord's power (omnipotence): that Jesus had the power to heal his son, even from a great distance.

3. Both faith and obedience were necessary to receive the promise and help of Jesus. The man would not have received the help of Jesus if he had not *accepted and believed* the Word of Jesus or if he had rebelled and acted childishly. The man could have easily acted like so many when they bring their needs to God: "Your word is not good enough. My son is not healed. He is there in Capernaum and you are far away, *no place close* to him. How could he be helped with you so far away? Come, visit, *show yourself, stand before us*: help us." Such, of course, is pleading to God for help; but it is not crying to God in faith, not basing one's request upon the Word and promise of Christ. It is asking God to help, but it is also dictating how God is to help. It is telling God how He is to act instead of *accepting and acting* upon His Word.

Thought 1. There is no real faith apart from obedience and work. (See DEEPER STUDY # 2—Jn.2:24; DEEPER STUDY # 1—Heb.5:9.)

> Jesus looked at them and said, "With man this is impossible, but with God all things are possible." (Mat 19:26)
>
> For nothing is impossible with God." (Luke 1:37)
>
> That is why I did not even consider myself worthy to come to you. But say the word, and my servant will be healed. (Luke 7:7)
>
> When he saw them, he said, "Go, show yourselves to the priests." And as they went, they were cleansed. (Luke 17:14)
>
> And, once made perfect, he became the source of eternal salvation for all who obey him (Heb 5:9)
>
> In the same way, faith by itself, if it is not accompanied by action, is dead. (James 2:17)

"I know that you can do all things; no plan of yours can be thwarted. (Job 42:2)

The LORD redeems his servants; no one will be condemned who takes refuge in him. (Psa 34:22)

Commit your way to the LORD; trust in him and he will do this: (Psa 37:5)
A song of ascents. Those who trust in the LORD are like Mount Zion, which cannot be shaken but endures forever. (Psa 125:1)

Trust in the LORD with all your heart and lean not on your own understanding; (Prov 3:5)

You will keep in perfect peace him whose mind is steadfast, because he trusts in you. Trust in the LORD forever, for the LORD, the LORD, is the Rock eternal. (Isa 26:3-4)

4 (4:51-53) **Faith**: the fourth stage was a confirmed faith. Note the words "still on the way." He was in the act of *obeying Christ* when he received the glorious news that his prayer was answered. Again, it was believing the promise of Jesus and obeying Him that brought the blessing. Both belief and obedience were essential.

Note also that the man confirmed the supernatural versus. the natural. He asked the exact hour the boy recovered. He wanted to be certain; he wanted absolute confirmation. He was reaching out for stronger faith in Jesus. He was so full of joy and thankfulness to Jesus that he wanted to believe on Him more and more.

"Have faith in God," Jesus answered. "I tell you the truth, if anyone says to this mountain, 'Go, throw yourself into the sea,' and does not doubt in his heart but believes that what he says will happen, it will be done for him. Therefore I tell you, whatever you ask for in prayer, believe that you have received it, and it will be yours. (Mark 11:22-24)

But I know that even now God will give you whatever you ask." (John 11:22)

Therefore he is able to save completely those who come to God through him, be-

cause he always lives to intercede for them. (Heb 7:25)

Now faith is being sure of what we hope for and certain of what we do not see. (Heb 11:1)

But I the LORD will speak what I will, and it shall be fulfilled without delay. For in your days, you rebellious house, I will fulfill whatever I say, declares the Sovereign LORD.'" (Ezek 12:25)

5 (4:53-54) **Witnessing**: the fifth stage was a witnessing faith. Note two things.
1. The man witnessed to "all his household." He told them about the experience, the Word of promise and instructions Jesus had given, and they all believed. They committed themselves fully to Jesus as the Messiah.
2. Witnessing for Jesus was not easy for this man. He was a high official, moving about in the halls of a corrupt government and among immoral officials. He would definitely be facing ridicule and persecution, and perhaps loss of position and even loss of life. But note: his faith was a witnessing faith. He loved Jesus for what Jesus had done for him, and he wanted others to know Jesus' glorious salvation.

In the same way, let your light shine before men, that they may see your good deeds and praise your Father in heaven. (Mat 5:16)

"Return home and tell how much God has done for you." So the man went away and told all over town how much Jesus had done for him. (Luke 8:39)

He then brought them out and asked, "Sirs, what must I do to be saved?" They replied, "Believe in the Lord Jesus, and you will be saved—you and your household." (Acts 16:30-31)

But in your hearts set apart Christ as Lord. Always be prepared to give an answer to everyone who asks you to give the reason for the hope that you have. But do this with gentleness and respect, (1 Pet 3:15)

CHAPTER 5

VI. THE REVELATION OF JESUS, THE AUTHORITY & POWER OVER LIFE, 5:1-47

A. The Essential Authority: Power to Meet the World's Desperate Needs, 5:1-16

1 Jesus attended a Jewish feast in Jerusalem

2 Scene 1: The diseased & the ill—a picture of the world's desperate need
  a. Man's desperate hope: Lying in a pool of water
  b. Man's desperate faith: Seeking for healing power in a worldly source, in a pool of water

3 Scene 2: Jesus & the man—a picture of Jesus' power to meet the world's need
  a. The man's plight
  b. The Lord's compassion
    1) Saw his state
    2) Initiated a relationship
  c. The man's helplessness: He had no family & no friends to help him

Some time later, Jesus went up to Jerusalem for a feast of the Jews.
2 Now there is in Jerusalem near the Sheep Gate a pool, which in Aramaic is called Bethesda and which is surrounded by five covered colonnades.
3 Here a great number of disabled people used to lie—the blind, the lame, the paralyzed.
5 One who was there had been an invalid for thirty-eight years.
6 When Jesus saw him lying there and learned that he had been in this condition for a long time, he asked him, "Do you want to get well?"
7 "Sir," the invalid replied, "I have no one to help me into the pool when the water is stirred. While I am trying to

get in, someone else goes down ahead of me."
8 Then Jesus said to him, "Get up! Pick up your mat and walk."
9 At once the man was cured; he picked up his mat and walked. The day on which this took place was a Sabbath,
10 And so the Jews said to the man who had been healed, "It is the Sabbath; the law forbids you to carry your mat."
11 But he replied, "The man who made me well said to me, 'Pick up your mat and walk.'"
12 So they asked him, "Who is this fellow who told you to pick it up and walk?"
13 The man who was healed had no idea who it was, for Jesus had slipped away into the crowd that was there.
14 Later Jesus found him at the temple and said to him, "See, you are well again. Stop sinning or something worse may happen to you."
15 The man went away and told the Jews that it was Jesus who had made him well.
16 So, because Jesus was doing these things on the Sabbath, the Jews persecuted him.

  d. The Lord's power

  e. The sinister problem: Jesus healed the man *on* the Sabbath

4 Scene 3: The religionists & the man—a picture of dead religion trying to meet the world's need[DS1]
  a. A religion of legalism
  b. A religion ignorant of true authority

  c. A religion blind to love & good

5 Scene 4: Jesus & the man after his healing—a picture of the believer's responsibility
  a. To worship in the temple
  b. To remember his healing
  c. To stop sinning
  d. To fear the judgment

6 Scene 5: The religionists & Jesus: A picture of the world rejecting God's Savior[DS2]

DIVISION VI

THE REVELATION OF JESUS, THE AUTHORITY AND POWER OVER LIFE, 5:1-47

A. The Essential Authority: Power to Meet the World's Desperate Needs, 5:1-16

(5:1-47) **DIVISION OVERVIEW: Jesus, Authority**: Chapter 5 reveals Jesus to be the Authority over all of life. He is due the same worship, obedience, and service as God; for He is equal with God (Jn.5:17-18). As God possesses life within Himself, so Jesus possesses life within Himself (Jn.5:26). As God has authority over all of life, so Jesus has authority over all of life.

In revealing His authority, Jesus first demonstrated the truth of His authority. He healed a man who had been ill for thirty-eight years—and He healed him on the Sabbath. Both acts pictured the truth of His authority. The healing of the man showed His authority over the physical world, and the breaking of the Jewish Sabbath law showed His authority to determine the rules of worship. After demonstrating the truth of His equality with God, He then began to teach the truth. This procedure, first demonstrating some truth

and then teaching it, was to be followed time and again as Jesus revealed who He was throughout the Gospel of John. (See Chapters 6, 8.)

(5:1-16) **Introduction—Sabbath**: through this healing miracle, Jesus was claiming to have supreme authority over the Sabbath (see DEEPER STUDY # 1, Sabbath—Mt.12:1; cp. Jn.5:9-10, 16, 18). However, there are also other striking lessons: the Lord's compassion (v. 6-9), the problem of formal religion (v. 10-12), and the charge to a converted man (v. 13-14).

  1. Jesus attended a Jewish feast in Jerusalem (v.1).
  2. Scene 1: the diseased and the ill—a picture of the world's desperate need (v.2-3).
  3. Scene 2: Jesus and the man—a picture of Jesus' power to meet the world's need (v.5-9).

---

4 *From time to time an angel of the Lord would come down and stir up the waters. The first one into the pool after each such disturbance would be cured of whatever disease he had.*

4. Scene 3: the religionists and the man—a picture of dead religion trying to meet the world's need (v.10-12).
5. Scene 4: Jesus and the man after healing—a picture of the believer's responsibility (v.13-14).
6. Scene 5: the religionists against Jesus—a picture of the world rejecting God's Savior (v.15-16).

1 (5:1) **Feasts—Jesus Christ, Worship of God**: Jesus attended a Jewish feast in Jerusalem. The feast is not named, but it was probably one of the three Feasts of Obligation: the Passover, the Feast of Tabernacles, or Pentecost. These were called Feasts of Obligations because every male Jew who lived within twenty miles of Jerusalem was required by law to attend them. It is significant that Jesus was seen attending the feast.

1. It gave Him an opportunity to reach a large number of people. Most of the people who attended the feast would be God-fearing people and have their minds upon God; therefore, they would be more prepared for the gospel.

2. It gave Him an opportunity to teach people to be faithful to the worship of God. He, the Son of God Himself, was faithful.

Thought 1. All persons should be faithful in their worship of God.

2 (5:2-3) **Needy, The**: the first scene was that of the diseased and the ill. These—the diseased and the ill—picture those in the world who are gripped by desperate need. The setting is a pool by a sheep gate. The words *sheep gate* is supplied by the translator; it is not in the Greek text. It may have been a sheep market or sheep gate or sheep stall where the animals were kept. Whatever it was, there was a pool to provide water for the animals to drink and five porches to provide a resting area for the comfort of the people. The pool and a "great number of disabled people" lying around the pool were the focus of attention. Note two points.

Their need—which is a picture of all in the world who live in desperate need.
⇒ There were the blind who could not see.
⇒ There were the lame who could not walk.
⇒ There were the paralyzed who were deformed.
⇒ There were so many who were poor and beggarly.

Thought 1. So many in the world are blind, lame and withered spiritually.

"I loathe my very life; therefore I will give free rein to my complaint and speak out in the bitterness of my soul. (Job 10:1)
My life is consumed by anguish and my years by groaning; my strength fails because of my affliction, and my bones grow weak. (Psa 31:10)
My God. My soul is downcast within me; therefore I will remember you from the land of the Jordan, the heights of Hermon—from Mount Mizar. (Psa 42:6)
I sink in the miry depths, where there is no foothold. I have come into the deep waters; the floods engulf me. (Psa 69:2)
But as for me, my feet had almost slipped; I had nearly lost my foothold. (Psa 73:2)

When I tried to understand all this, it was oppressive to me (Psa 73:16)
By the rivers of Babylon we sat and wept when we remembered Zion. (Psa 137:1)
But Zion said, "The LORD has forsaken me, the Lord has forgotten me." (Isa 49:14)
Do not run until your feet are bare and your throat is dry. But you said, 'It's no use! I love foreign gods, and I must go after them.' (Jer 2:25)
Brothers, we do not want you to be ignorant about those who fall asleep, or to grieve like the rest of men, who have no hope. (1 Th 4:13)
Remember that at that time you were separate from Christ, excluded from citizenship in Israel and foreigners to the covenants of the promise, without hope and without God in the world. (Eph 2:12)

Thought 2. Men are always grasping for something to help them in their daily lives. It may be some *supernatural or destined power* in a pool of water or in the astrology of stars above or in some magical person on earth. Men never change, regardless of the generation. In their grasp for help in life, they continue to seek everywhere except in Christ, the Son of God Himself. They hope and put their faith in everything except Him.

There is a way that seems right to a man, but in the end it leads to death. (Prov 14:12)

3 (5:5-9) **Jesus Christ, Compassion—Power—Healing—Faith—Obedience**: the second scene was that of Jesus and the man. This is a picture of Jesus, who has the power to meet the needs of the desperate in the world. The outline of this point is adequate to see what happened.

1. The man's plight. He was either paralyzed or lame; he had been that way for thirty-eight *long* years.

2. Jesus' *compassion*: it was heart warming, touching, and revealing—demonstrating how He wants to reach out to every person. He *saw* the man lying there and *knew* all about his desperate condition. Note the striking point: it was Jesus who initiated the relationship, approaching the man and reaching out to help Him.

Thought 1. Jesus *sees* and *knows* every man's condition. He reaches out to every man in compassion, offering help. He reaches out through…
• the message of the Word.
• the witness of family or friend.
• the beauty of nature.
• the thoughts about God that penetrate every man's mind.

Who shall separate us from the love of Christ? Shall trouble or hardship or persecution or famine or nakedness or danger or sword? (Rom 8:35)
For we do not have a high priest who is unable to sympathize with our weaknesses, but we have one who has been tempted in every way, just as we are—yet was without sin. (Heb 4:15)

Cast all your anxiety on him because he cares for you. (1 Pet 5:7)

He remembered that they were but flesh, a passing breeze that does not return. (Psa 78:39)

As a father has compassion on his children, so the LORD has compassion on those who fear him; (Psa 103:13)

But from everlasting to everlasting the Lord's love is with those who fear him, and his righteousness with their children's children— (Psa 103:17)

In all their distress he too was distressed, and the angel of his presence saved them. In his love and mercy he redeemed them; he lifted them up and carried them all the days of old. (Isa 63:9)

Because of the Lord's great love we are not consumed, for his compassions never fail. (Lam 3:22)

3. The man's helplessness. He was all alone in this world, having no family or friend who could help him.

4. The Lord's power. This is a significant point: the man did not know he was healed *until he obeyed* the command of the Lord. Jesus did not pronounce a "word of healing"; He merely commanded the man to act. In the act the man was to show his faith. *If he believed*, he would arise and walk; *if he did not believe*, he would simply lie there, continuing on just as he had always done. (See DEEPER STUDY # 2—Jn.2:24.)

Thought 1. No man has to continue on and on through life just as he has always been, enslaved to the sin and corruption and desperate needs of the world. He can experience the healing power of Jesus Christ, the power to change his life and make him into a new man. All he has to do is one simple thing: believe the Word of Jesus Christ enough to obey, doing exactly what Jesus says. It is a clear fact: if we believe Him, we obey Him; if we do not believe Him, we do not obey Him. To be made whole and changed into a new man—a new man who is freed from the sin and desperate needs of this corruptible world—we have to believe Him enough to obey Him. (See note—Jn.4:50 for more verses of Scripture.)

For nothing is impossible with God." (Luke 1:37)

When he saw them, he said, "Go, show yourselves to the priests." And as they went, they were cleansed. (Luke 17:14)

And, once made perfect, he became the source of eternal salvation for all who obey him (Heb 5:9)

In the same way, faith by itself, if it is not accompanied by action, is dead. (James 2:17)

5. The sinister problem: Jesus had healed the man on the Sabbath. By healing the man on the Sabbath, Jesus was breaking the Jewish ceremonial law; He was committing a serious sin, violating a ritual and rule of religion. The rest of the man's story centers upon this fact.

4 (5:10-12) **Religion:** the third scene was that of the religionists and the man. This is a picture of dead religion trying to meet the world's desperate need. Note three things.

1. Dead religion is a religion of legalism. The religionists were trying to meet the needs of people through rules and regulations, ceremony and rituals. (See DEEPER STUDY # 1—Lk.6:2; DEEPER STUDY # 2—Jn.5:15-16.) They were more concerned with the man who was violating the ritual of the Sabbath than with the man who was suffering in a pitiful condition.

2. Dead religion is a religion ignorant of true authority. They should have known that the power of God had healed the man and should have been eager to share with the man Jesus, the man upon whom such power rested. But note: they cared little about the power of God and His messenger. They cared only that the status quo be maintained, that their religious practices continue as they were and not be violated. Their thoughts were upon their own religious position and security. (See DEEPER STUDY # 2—Jn.5:15-16 for discussion.)

3. Dead religion is a religion blind to love and good. Note the question of the religionists. It was not, "Who is the man who has healed and helped you so much?" but, "Who is the man that broke the religious law?" They did not see the good that had been done. They saw only that their position and security were threatened, that someone had more power and influence, doing more good than they were.

Thought 1. How many true messengers of God are criticized by powerless religionists, criticized because they do things differently or do more good than others? Men fear the loss of their position and security, fear that people may begin to wonder about their lack of true power—power that honestly helps men.

If you had known what these words mean, 'I desire mercy, not sacrifice,' you would not have condemned the innocent. For the Son of Man is Lord of the Sabbath." (Mat 12:7-8)

And the second is like it: 'Love your neighbor as yourself.' (Mat 22:39)

And he said to them: "You have a fine way of setting aside the commands of God in order to observe your own traditions! (Mark 7:9)

Love does no harm to its neighbor. Therefore love is the fulfillment of the law. (Rom 13:10)

They claim to know God, but by their actions they deny him. They are detestable, disobedient and unfit for doing anything good. (Titus 1:16)

This is how we know what love is: Jesus Christ laid down his life for us. And we ought to lay down our lives for our brothers. If anyone has material possessions and sees his brother in need but has no pity on him, how can the love of God be in him? (1 John 3:16-17)

DEEPER STUDY # 1

(5:10) **Jews:** the Jews (Ioudaio) are spoken of some seventy times in the Gospels. They are always spoken of as the opposition to Jesus Christ—as those who set themselves against Him. They include some Pharisees, Sadducees, Teachers of the law (Scribes), priests, and secular leaders. They were the religionists and leaders who personally refused to believe Jesus Christ. They rejected both His claim to be the Son of God and His offer of salvation and eternal life (cp. Jn.1:10-11, 19. See Subject Index.)

5 (5:13-14) **Follow-up—Maturity—Growth**: the fourth scene was that of Jesus and the man after healing. This is a picture of the believer's responsibility. Note that Jesus had left the man right after healing him because of the large crowd on the porches. For some unstated reason, Jesus did not want to attract a crowd at this time. The point is striking: Jesus sought the man out again! Remember, Jesus had reached out to save the man; now He was reaching out for another purpose. When He found the man, a picture of the believer's responsibility was painted.

1. There was the duty to worship. Jesus found the man in the temple worshipping and giving thanks to God.

> **Let us not give up meeting together, as some are in the habit of doing, but let us encourage one another—and all the more as you see the Day approaching. (Heb 10:25)**
>
> **Ascribe to the LORD the glory due his name. Bring an offering and come before him; worship the LORD in the splendor of his holiness. (1 Chr 16:29)**
>
> **Surely goodness and love will follow me all the days of my life, and I will dwell in the house of the LORD forever. (Psa 23:6)**
>
> **Blessed are those you choose and bring near to live in your courts! We are filled with the good things of your house, of your holy temple. (Psa 65:4)**
>
> **My soul yearns, even faints, for the courts of the LORD; my heart and my flesh cry out for the living God. (Psa 84:2)**
>
> **Enter his gates with thanksgiving and his courts with praise; give thanks to him and praise his name. (Psa 100:4)**

2. There was the duty to remember his healing, his salvation. The moment should never be forgotten or lost (cp. 2 Pt.1:9).

> **Giving thanks to the Father, who has qualified you to share in the inheritance of the saints in the kingdom of light. (Col 1:12)**
>
> **Always giving thanks to God the Father for everything, in the name of our Lord Jesus Christ. (Eph 5:20)**
>
> **Give thanks in all circumstances, for this is God's will for you in Christ Jesus. (1 Th 5:18)**
>
> **Only be careful, and watch yourselves closely so that you do not forget the things your eyes have seen or let them slip from your heart as long as you live. Teach them to your children and to their children after them. (Deu 4:9)**

3. There was the duty to stop sinning. Apparently the man had been lame or paralyzed because of some accident caused by sin. Jesus cautioned the man: "Stop sinning."

Thought 1. How many are physically crippled or diseased because of some sin? Many suffer *crippling accidents and diseases* because of sin such as drunkenness, immorality, or driving over the speed limit.

> **"No one, sir," she said. "Then neither do I condemn you," Jesus declared. "Go now and leave your life of sin." (John 8:11)**
>
> **Therefore do not let sin reign in your mortal body so that you obey its evil desires. (Rom 6:12)**
>
> **Come back to your senses as you ought, and stop sinning; for there are some who are ignorant of God—I say this to your shame. (1 Cor 15:34)**
>
> **Wash and make yourselves clean. Take your evil deeds out of my sight! Stop doing wrong, (Isa 1:16)**

4. There was the duty to fear the judgment. Jesus warned the man that if he did not repent and turn from his sin, he would face a more terrible judgment than his crippling paralysis.

6 (5:15-16) **Jesus Christ, Rejection**: the fifth scene was that of the religionists and Jesus. This is a picture of the world rejecting God's Savior. Note two things.

1. The man told the religionists who had healed him. He did not do this to bring harm to Jesus. He thought the religionists should know and would want to benefit from knowing Jesus personally.

2. The reason the religionists opposed Jesus needs to be studied closely (see note—Jn.5:17-18 for discussion).

DEEPER STUDY # 2

(5:15-16) **Religionists—Rules and Regulations—Jesus Christ, Opposed**: breaking the Sabbath law was a serious matter to the Jew. Just how serious can be seen in the strict demands governing the Sabbath. Law after law was written to govern all activity on the Sabbath. A person could not travel, fast, cook, buy, sell, draw water, walk beyond a certain distance, lift anything, fight in a war, or heal on the Sabbath unless life was at stake. A person was not to contemplate any kind of work or activity. A good example of the legal restriction and the people's loyalty to it is seen in the women who witnessed Jesus' crucifixion. They would not even walk to His tomb to prepare the body for burial until the Sabbath was over (Mk.16:1f; Mt.28:1f).

It was a serious matter to break the Sabbath law. A person was condemned, and if the offense were serious enough, the person was to die.

The leaders' conflict with Jesus over religious beliefs and rules is sometimes thought by modern man to be petty and harsh, or else such conflicts are just not understood. Three facts will help in understanding why the conflicts happened and were life threatening, ending in the murder of Jesus Christ.

1. The Jewish nation had been held together by their religious beliefs. Through the centuries the Jewish people had been conquered by army after army, and by the millions they had been deported and scattered over the world. Even in the day of Jesus, they were enslaved by Rome. Their religion was the *binding force* that kept Jews together, in particular...

- their belief that God had called them to be a distinctive people (who worshipped the only true and living God).
- their rules governing the Sabbath and the temple.
- their laws governing intermarriage, worship, and cleansing.
- their rules governing what foods they could and could not eat.

Their religious beliefs and rules protected them from alien beliefs and from being swallowed up by other nationalities through intermarriage. Their religion was what maintained their distinctiveness as a people and as a nation. Jewish leaders knew this. They knew that *their religion was the binding force* that held their nation together. They therefore opposed anyone or anything that threatened or attempted to break the laws of their religion and nation.

2. Many of the religionists were men of deep, deep conviction, strong in their beliefs. Therefore, they became steeped in religious belief and practice, law and custom, tradition and ritual, ceremony and liturgy, rules and regulations. To break any law or rule governing any belief or practice was a serious offense, for it taught loose behavior. And loose behavior, once it had spread enough, would weaken their religion. Therefore, in their minds Jesus was committing a terrible offense by breaking their law. He was weakening their religion and threatening their nation.

3. The religionists were men who had profession, position, recognition, esteem, livelihood, and security. Anyone who went contrary to what they believed and taught was a threat to all they had. Some religionists undoubtedly felt that Jesus was a threat to them. Every time Jesus broke their law, they felt He was undermining their very position and security. (See notes—Mt.12:1-8; 16:1-12; 21:23; 22:15-22; 22:23-33; 22:34-40; 23:1-12.)

The error of the religionists was fourfold.

1. They misinterpreted and corrupted God's Word (see notes—Mt.12:1-3; DEEPER STUDY # 1—Jn.4:22; cp. Ro.9:4).

2. They committed serious sin after sin in God's eyes (see notes—1 Th.2:15-16; cp. Ro.2:17-29).

3. They rejected God's way of righteousness, God's Messiah, who is Jesus Christ (see notes—Ro.11:28-29; 1 Th.2:15-16; cp. Ro.10:1-21, esp. 1-4, 19-21).

4. They allowed religion in its tradition and ritual, ceremony and rules to become more important than meeting the basic needs of human life: the need for God and the need for spiritual, mental, and physical health. Being the true Messiah, Jesus was bound to expose such error. Therefore, the battle lines were drawn.

The Messiah had to liberate people from such enslaving behavior. He had to liberate them so they could be saved and worship God in freedom of spirit.

The religionists had to oppose anyone who broke their law. They had to oppose Jesus because He was a threat to their nation and to their own personal position and security.

The religionists' attack took two forms.

1. First, they tried to discredit Jesus so the crowds would stop following Him (cp. Mt.21:46).

> **And a man with a shriveled hand was there. Looking for a reason to accuse Jesus, they asked him, "Is it lawful to heal on the Sabbath?" (Mat 12:10)**
>
> **The Pharisees and the teachers of the law were looking for a reason to accuse Jesus, so they watched him closely to see if he would heal on the Sabbath. (Luke 6:7)**
>
> **Then the Pharisees went out and laid plans to trap him in his words. They sent their disciples to him along with the Herodians. "Teacher," they said, "we know you are a man of integrity and that you teach the way of God in accordance with the truth. You aren't swayed by men, because you pay no attention to who they are. Tell us then, what is your opinion? Is it right to pay taxes to Caesar or not?" (Mat 22:15-17)**

2. Second, failing to discredit Jesus, they looked for some way to kill Him.

> **But the Pharisees went out and plotted how they might kill Jesus. (Mat 12:14; cp. Mt.26:3-4)**
>
> **And the chief priests and the teachers of the law were looking for some way to get rid of Jesus, for they were afraid of the people. (Luke 22:2)**
>
> **For this reason the Jews tried all the harder to kill him; not only was he breaking the Sabbath, but he was even calling God his own Father, making himself equal with God. (John 5:18; cp. Jn.7:1; 7:19-20, 25)**

| 1 Jesus claimed equality with God
  a. His claim: My Father
  b. His claim clearly understood

2 Proof 1: His obedience
  a. He did not act alone
  b. He did exactly what He saw the Father do

3 Proof 2: His great works
  a. God loves His Son
  b. God shows Him what to do

4 Proof 3: His power to quicken, to give life, to raise up the dead
5 Proof 4: His control over the whole judicial process

  a. Purpose: That all may honor the Son
  b. Fact: If Christ is not | B. The Astounding Authority: Equality With God, 5:17-30

17 Jesus said to them, "My Father is always at his work to this very day, and I, too, am working."
18 For this reason the Jews tried all the harder to kill him; not only was he breaking the Sabbath, but he was even calling God his own Father, making himself equal with God.
19 Jesus gave them this answer: "I tell you the truth, the Son can do nothing by himself; he can do only what he sees his Father doing, because whatever the Father does the Son also does.
20 For the Father loves the Son and shows him all he does. Yes, to your amazement he will show him even greater things than these.
21 For just as the Father raises the dead and gives them life, even so the Son gives life to whom he is pleased to give it.
22 Moreover, the Father judges no one, but has entrusted all judgment to the Son,
23 That all may honor the Son just as they honor the Father. He who does not | honor the Son does not honor the Father, who, sent him.
24 "I tell you the truth, whoever hears my word and believes him who sent me has eternal life and will not be condemned; he has crossed over from death to life.
25 I tell you the truth, a time is coming and has now come when the dead will hear the voice of the Son of God and those who hear will live.
26 For as the Father has life in himself, so he has granted the Son to have life in himself.
27 And he has given him authority to judge because he is the Son of Man.
28 "Do not be amazed at this, for a time is coming when all who are in their graves will hear his voice
29 And come out—those who have done good will rise to live, and those who have done evil will rise to be condemned.
30 By myself I can do nothing; I judge only as I hear, and my judgment is just, for I seek not to please myself but him who sent me. | honored, God is not honored

6 Proof 5: His power over man's destiny, to save men from death to life
  a. How men are saved
    1) Hearing His Word
    2) Believing that God sent His Son, Jesus
  b. Result: Eternal life
  c. Facts
    1) The spiritually dead can hear the voice of God's Son[DS1]—now
    2) The spiritually dead can live—now
7 Proof 6: His energy of life, His self-existence

8 Proof 7: His authority to execute judgment
9 Proof 8: His claim to be the Son of Man
10 Proof 9: His power to resurrect all men from the grave

  a. Men who have done good: Resurrected to life
  b. Men who have done evil: Resurrected to condemnation
  c. The judgment: Will be a just judgment |

DIVISION VI

THE REVELATION OF JESUS, THE AUTHORITY AND POWER OVER LIFE, 5:1-47

B. The Astounding Authority: Equality With God, 5:17-30

(5:17-30) **Jesus Christ, Claims—Deity**: all men have to face this earth shaking, shattering claim of Christ. He made the astounding claim that all authority belonged to Him. How could He make such an astounding claim? Because He proclaimed that He possessed equality with God and then He proceeded to give proof after proof which unequivocally verified His claim.

1. Jesus claimed equality with God (v.17-18).
2. Proof 1: His obedience (v.19).
3. Proof 2: His great works (v.20).
4. Proof 3: His power to quicken, to give life, to raise up the dead (v.21).
5. Proof 4: His control over the whole judicial process (v.22-23).
6. Proof 5: His authority over man's destiny, to save men from death to life (v.24-25).
7. Proof 6: His energy of life, His self-existence (v.26).
8. Proof 7: His power to execute judgment (v.27).
9. Proof 8: His claim to be the Son of Man (v.27).
10. Proof 9: His power to resurrect all men from the grave (v.28-30).

1 (5:17-18) **Jesus Christ, Claims—Deity—Religionists, Opposed Christ**: Jesus claimed equality with God. Note the astounding claim: He called God "My Father" not "our Father." Jesus was claiming a unique relationship, a Father-Son union with God; and note: the shattering fact was *clearly understood* by the religionists. They understood clearly...

- that He had said God was *His Father*. (Cp. "His own Son" Ro.8:32.)
- that He was making Himself equal with God. (Cp. "Equality with God," Ph.2:6.)

His claim was unquestionable. They knew exactly what He was claiming. (See note—Jn.1:34 for more discussion.)

A second claim was this: Jesus said, "My Father is always at his work" (heos arti ergazetai), which means "My Father keeps on working even until now." That is, God never ceases to work, even on the Sabbath (Sunday). It is true that when God created the world, Scripture says He rested on the Sabbath day; but this means He rested from His creative work, not from His other work. His work of love and mercy, helping and caring (compassion), looking after and overseeing (sovereignty) continued. Note: Jesus said, "And I too am working," meaning that He did good on the Sabbath as well as God. Again, He was claiming to be equal with God, claiming to have the same right to work even as God works: that is, to erase the wrong laws of men and to establish the just and compassionate laws of God.

It was for these two reasons that the religionists tried to kill Jesus.

1. He clearly said, "My Father," claiming that God was His Father and making Himself *equal* with God. He was clearly claiming that He was "the Son of God," "the one and only Son of God" (cp. Jn.3:16).

2. He broke the law against working on the Sabbath (Sunday), claiming that He had the same authority as God, the authority to do good on the Sabbath: to be compassionate by teaching and helping and caring for men.

Thought 1. A person either accepts the claim of Jesus to be equal with God or else he rejects the claim. The claim was clearly made. There is no longer a middle ground upon which men can stand. Man is now forced to make a decision.

Thought 2. Some take the words and behavior of Jesus on the Sabbath as the approval for working on Sunday. This is false reasoning. Jesus was not violating nor erasing the Lord's day as the day for man's rest and worship. Just the opposite is true. He was saying that the day was to be used for compassion and mercy and good, helping men in their needs.

2 (5:19) **Obedience—Jesus Christ, Nature—Deity**: the first proof that Jesus was equal with God was His obedience. Jesus stated two astounding facts.

1. He did not act alone. He did not act independently of God (cp. Jn.5:30; 7:28; 8:28; 14:10). He was not disobedient to God. He did not...
  • take His life into His own hands
  • do His own thing
  • act selfishly
  • walk separately from God

Note the stress, the crucial importance of this point. Jesus said, "I tell you the truth"; that is, listen, listen. Pay close attention to what is said.

2. He did exactly what He saw the Father do. There was no divergence whatsoever between the Father and Jesus. There are three claims here.
  ⇒ Jesus was in *perfect, unbroken communion* with God.
  ⇒ Jesus was of the very *same nature and person* as God.
  ⇒ Jesus *acted as God because He was God*: He did exactly what God did. He did "the very same things" (tauta) in "the very same manner" (homoios). He acted and behaved exactly as God acted and behaved.

Jesus Christ was perfectly obedient; He acted exactly in the nature of God. (What a lesson *on* obedience! A challenge *for* obedience!)

"All things have been committed to me by my Father. No one knows the Son except the Father, and no one knows the Father except the Son and those to whom the Son chooses to reveal him. (Mat 11:27)

But I know him because I am from him and he sent me." (John 7:29)

Though you do not know him, I know him. If I said I did not, I would be a liar like you, but I do know him and keep his word. (John 8:55)

Just as the Father knows me and I know the Father—and I lay down my life for the sheep. (John 10:15)

I and the Father are one." (John 10:30)

Do not believe me unless I do what my Father does. But if I do it, even though you do not believe me, believe the miracles, that you may know and understand that the Father is in me, and I in the Father." (John 10:37-38)

Don't you believe that I am in the Father, and that the Father is in me? The words I say to you are not just my own. Rather, it is the Father, living in me, who is doing his work. (John 14:10)

I will remain in the world no longer, but they are still in the world, and I am coming to you. Holy Father, protect them by the power of your name—the name you gave me—so that they may be one as we are one. (John 17:11)

That all of them may be one, Father, just as you are in me and I am in you. May they also be in us so that the world may believe that you have sent me. I have given them the glory that you gave me, that they may be one as we are one: (John 17:21-22)

"Righteous Father, though the world does not know you, I know you, and they know that you have sent me. (John 17:25)

3 (5:20) **Jesus Christ, Deity—Works**: the second proof that Jesus was equal with God was His great works. Two astounding statements were made. (See note—Jn.5:36 for more discussion.)

1. The Father loves the Son. The idea is that the Father continues to love and never stops loving the Son. There is never a moment when the love diminishes. It is a perfect love that never ceases to give.

The reason my Father loves me is that I lay down my life—only to take it up again. (John 10:17)

No, the Father himself loves you because you have loved me and have believed that I came from God. (John 16:27)

I in them and you in me. May they be brought to complete unity to let the world know that you sent me and have loved them even as you have loved me. (John 17:23)

I have made you known to them, and will continue to make you known in order that the love you have for me may be in them and that I myself may be in them." (John 17:26)

While he was still speaking, a bright cloud enveloped them, and a voice from the cloud said, "This is my Son, whom I love; with him I am well pleased. Listen to him!" (Mat 17:5)

As Jesus was coming up out of the water, he saw heaven being torn open and the Spirit descending on him like a dove. And a voice came from heaven: "You are my Son, whom I love; with you I am well pleased." (Mark 1:10-11)

For he has rescued us from the dominion of darkness and brought us into the kingdom of the Son he loves, (Col 1:13)

So Christ also did not take upon himself the glory of becoming a high priest. But God said to him, "You are my Son; today I have become your Father." (Heb 5:5)

Whoever has my commands and obeys them, he is the one who loves me. He who loves me will be loved by my Father, and I too will love him and show myself to him." (John 14:21; cp. Jn14:23)

"As the Father has loved me, so have I loved you. Now remain in my love. (John 15:9)

2. Therefore, the Father showed the Son all things which He did.

a. All things which Jesus did were the very things which the Father did.

b. Jesus said that the Father was going to show Him greater things to do, greater things than the healing of the paralyzed man (v.8-9). Jesus would be…
- controlling the forces of nature (storms on the Sea of Galilee).
- multiplying food.
- raising the dead and healing crowds of people.
- instituting a greater law, the law of the Son of Man. (See note—Mt.5:17-18.)
- instituting new ordinances.
- creating people anew.

"I have testimony weightier than that of John. For the very work that the Father has given me to finish, and which I am doing, testifies that the Father has sent me. (John 5:36)

As long as it is day, we must do the work of him who sent me. Night is coming, when no one can work. (John 9:4)

Jesus answered, "I did tell you, but you do not believe. The miracles I do in my Father's name speak for me, (John 10:25)

Do not believe me unless I do what my Father does. But if I do it, even though you do not believe me, believe the miracles, that you may know and understand that the Father is in me, and I in the Father." (John 10:37-38)

Don't you believe that I am in the Father, and that the Father is in me? The words I say to you are not just my own. Rather, it is the Father, living in me, who is doing his work. Believe me when I say that I am in the Father and the Father is in me; or at least believe on the evidence of the miracles themselves. (John 14:10-11)

If I had not done among them what no one else did, they would not be guilty of sin. But now they have seen these miracles, and yet they have hated both me and my Father. (John 15:24)

4 (5:21) **Jesus Christ, Deity—Life—Salvation—Resurrection**: the third proof that Jesus was equal with God was His power to give life.

1. God gives life, and only God *can* give life. Therefore if He wishes to give life to a dead body, He can. In giving life and raising the dead, God…
- is sovereign, acting fully as He alone wills.
- is not constrained nor restrained.
- has the power and authority.
- exercises perfect love, justice, and wisdom. He knows exactly what He is doing, and He does it perfectly.

2. The Son, Jesus Christ, gives life to whom *He wills*. Just as God does, so Christ does. Christ is equal with God in giving life and raising the dead. Note…
- there is a state of death (see DEEPER STUDY # 1—Heb.9:27).
- there is a state of life, of being quickened, of being made alive from the dead. (Cp. Eph.2:1f.)

Christ quickens, gives life to a person when that person believes on Him, and the life which He gives is both abundant and eternal (see note—Jn.3:16).

But so that you may know that the Son of Man has authority on earth to forgive sins…." Then he said to the paralytic, "Get up, take your mat and go home." (Mat 9:6)

Then Jesus came to them and said, "All authority in heaven and on earth has been given to me. (Mat 28:18)

For you granted him authority over all people that he might give eternal life to all those you have given him. (John 17:2)

And if the Spirit of him who raised Jesus from the dead is living in you, he who raised Christ from the dead will also give life to your mortal bodies through his Spirit, who lives in you. (Rom 8:11)

As for you, you were dead in your transgressions and sins, (Eph 2:1; cp.v.2-3)

But because of his great love for us, God, who is rich in mercy, made us alive with Christ even when we were dead in transgressions—it is by grace you have been saved. And God raised us up with Christ and seated us with him in the heavenly realms in Christ Jesus, in order that in the coming ages he might show the incomparable riches of his grace, expressed in his kindness to us in Christ Jesus. For it is by grace you have been saved, through faith—and this not from yourselves, it is the gift of God—not by works, so that no one can boast. (Eph 2:4-9)

When you were dead in your sins and in the uncircumcision of your sinful nature, God made you alive with Christ. He forgave us all our sins, (Col 2:13)

5 (5:22-23) **Jesus Christ, Deity—Judgment—Honor, of Jesus Christ—Relationship, To God**: the fourth proof that

Jesus was equal with God was His control over the whole judicial process. Most men think that God (the Father) will judge the world and that they will have to stand before God in the day of judgment. But not so, Jesus says. He claims that God will judge "no one, but [He] has entrusted <u>all judgment to the Son</u>." The scene is the picture of a supreme court—not just the supreme court of a nation, but the supreme court of the universe presided over by Jesus Christ.

> For he has set a day when he will judge the world with justice by the man he has appointed. He has given proof of this to all men by raising him from the dead." (Acts 17:31)

> All the nations will be gathered before him, and he will separate the people one from another as a shepherd separates the sheep from the goats. (Mat 25:32)

> He commanded us to preach to the people and to testify that he is the one whom God appointed as judge of the living and the dead. (Acts 10:42)

> For he has set a day when he will judge the world with justice by the man he has appointed. He has given proof of this to all men by raising him from the dead." (Acts 17:31)

> This will take place on the day when God will judge men's secrets through Jesus Christ, as my gospel declares. (Rom 2:16)

> You, then, why do you judge your brother? Or why do you look down on your brother? For we will all stand before God's judgment seat. (Rom 14:10)

> Therefore judge nothing before the appointed time; wait till the Lord comes. He will bring to light what is hidden in darkness and will expose the motives of men's hearts. At that time each will receive his praise from God. (1 Cor 4:5)

> In the presence of God and of Christ Jesus, who will judge the living and the dead, and in view of his appearing and his kingdom, I give you this charge: (2 Tim 4:1)

> But they will have to give account to him who is ready to judge the living and the dead. (1 Pet 4:5)

1. The purpose for all judgment being given to Christ is onefold: God has willed that all men honor the Son just as they honor Him. The idea is that God has determined that everyone will *keep on honoring the Son* with the very same honor and worship they give Him. (This is seen in the Greek tense which is *present active* subjective.)

2. This is a truth that shatters people, for it means that if a person does not honor Christ, he does not honor God; and if he does not worship Christ, he does not worship God.

> He who hates me hates my Father as well. (John 15:23)

> No one who denies the Son has the Father; whoever acknowledges the Son has the Father also. (1 John 2:23)

> He who listens to you listens to me; he who rejects you rejects me; but he who rejects me rejects him who sent me. (Luke 10:16)

> If anyone is ashamed of me and my words in this adulterous and sinful generation, the Son of Man will be ashamed of him when he comes in his Father's glory with the holy angels." (Mark 8:38)

> Who is the liar? It is the man who denies that Jesus is the Christ. Such a man is the antichrist—he denies the Father and the Son. (1 John 2:22)

6 (5:24-25) **Jesus Christ, Deity—Salvation—Sin—Death:** the fifth proof that Jesus was equal with God was His power over man's destiny, the power to save men from death to life. Note three significant points.

1. How men are saved.
   a. They are saved by hearing Jesus' Word. The idea is *commitment and obedience* to it. In order to be saved, men must hear and follow Jesus' Word, doing exactly as He says.
   b. They are saved by believing God, that is, by believing that God has sent His Son Jesus Christ to save them.

> "For God so loved the world that he gave his one and only Son, that whoever believes in him shall not perish but have eternal life. (John 3:16)

> But God demonstrates his own love for us in this: While we were still sinners, Christ died for us. (Rom 5:8)

2. The result of being saved: eternal life. A man passes from the state of death into the state of life, from the state of condemnation into the state of justification. When a man is truly saved, he is never condemned to die; he is declared righteous and given eternal life. Note the descriptive way of expressing it: "has crossed over from death to life." Note also that man is presently in a *state of death*; that is, man is in the process of dying. Man *must die and will die.* He cannot stop the process. (See DEEPER STUDY # 1—Heb.9:27. Cp. Eph.2:1, 5; 5:14.)

3. The facts are twofold. A time has come and now is…
   • when the spiritually dead *can hear* the voice of the Son of God.
   • when the spiritually dead, who hear, *can live.*

> For he says, "In the time of my favor I heard you, and in the day of salvation I helped you." I tell you, now is the time of God's favor, now is the day of salvation. (2 Cor 6:2)

> Whoever believes in the Son has eternal life, but whoever rejects the Son will not see life, for God's wrath remains on him." (John 3:36)

DEEPER STUDY # 1

(5:25) **Jesus Christ, Son of God:** there are three places in the Gospel of John where Jesus calls Himself the Son of God (Jn.5:25; 10:36; 11:4; cp. Jn.19:7). Note also the claim to be the Son (Jn.5:19-23, 26; 6:40; 8:35-36; 14:13; 19:1). John's stated purpose should also be noted at this point.

> But these are written that you may believe that Jesus is the Christ, the Son of God, and that by believing you may have life in his name. (John 20:31)

100

7 (5:26) **Jesus Christ, Deity—Life, Source**: the sixth proof that Jesus was equal with God was His energy of life, His self-existence. God is the...

- Energy of life
- Power of life
- Being of life
- Possessor of life
- Source of life
- Essence of life
- Sovereign of life
- Self-existent life

God has life within Himself. And note: God has given the very same energy of life to the Son. Jesus Christ possesses "the very being" of life, the power and energy of self-existence within Himself.

The implication is clear: Jesus Christ has the *power* to give eternal life to those who hear Him and believe in God.

> **The LORD God formed the man from the dust of the ground and breathed into his nostrils the breath of life, and the man became a living being. (Gen 2:7)**
>
> **And that you may love the LORD your God, listen to his voice, and hold fast to him. For the LORD is your life, and he will give you many years in the land he swore to give to your fathers, Abraham, Isaac and Jacob. (Deu 30:20)**
>
> **The Spirit of God has made me; the breath of the Almighty gives me life. (Job 33:4)**
>
> **Of David. The LORD is my light and my salvation— whom shall I fear? The LORD is the stronghold of my life— of whom shall I be afraid? (Psa 27:1)**
>
> **For with you is the fountain of life; in your light we see light. (Psa 36:9)**
>
> **By day the LORD directs his love, at night his song is with me— a prayer to the God of my life. (Psa 42:8)**
>
> **He has preserved our lives and kept our feet from slipping. (Psa 66:9)**
>
> **In him was life, and that life was the light of men. (John 1:4)**
>
> **The thief comes only to steal and kill and destroy; I have come that they may have life, and have it to the full. (John 10:10)**
>
> **Jesus said to her, "I am the resurrection and the life. He who believes in me will live, even though he dies; (John 11:25)**
>
> **Jesus answered, "I am the way and the truth and the life. No one comes to the Father except through me. (John 14:6)**
>
> **So that, just as sin reigned in death, so also grace might reign through righteousness to bring eternal life through Jesus Christ our Lord. (Rom 5:21)**
>
> **But it has now been revealed through the appearing of our Savior, Christ Jesus, who has destroyed death and has brought life and immortality to light through the gospel. (2 Tim 1:10)**
>
> **He who has the Son has life; he who does not have the Son of God does not have life. (1 John 5:12)**

8 (5:27) **Jesus Christ, Deity—Judgment—Sympathy**: the seventh proof that Jesus was equal with God was His power to execute judgment. Jesus Christ is the Son of Man, having lived just as all sons of men live. He walked through life as Man, bearing all the weight and pressure, trials and temptations, sufferings and death, joys and victories that men experience. He knows every facet and fiber of human life; therefore, He is able to execute perfect judgment. For this reason, God has given Him the right and the authority to judge men. (See note, Son of Man—Jn.1:51.)

9 (5:27) **Jesus Christ, Deity—Son of Man**: the eighth proof that Jesus was equal with God was His claim to be the Son of Man. This was Jesus' favorite description of Himself (see notes, Son of Man—Jn.1:51 for discussion. Cp. 3:13-14; 5:27; 6:27, 53, 62; 8:28; 9:35; 12:3-34; 13:31.)

10 (5:28-30) **Resurrection, the—Judgment**: the ninth proof that Jesus was equal with God was His power to resurrect all men from the grave. Note several facts.

1. It is the voice—the Word, the power of Jesus—that shall resurrect "all who are in their graves."

2. "All who are in their graves" shall be resurrected. Not a single one will be left in the earth. Everyone will "come out."

3. "A time is coming" when all shall be resurrected. The time is set, fixed, already determined.

4. Men must "not be amazed at this." It is not incredible or ridiculous, for *God is*; He does exist, and He has a plan for the world. The world has not just happened. Life has not happened by chance, without purpose and meaning beyond a few brief years. Life is not doomed, without hope, destined to despair and dirt. There is meaning, purpose, and significance, both to life and to the world.

5. Men who have done good "will rise to live" How one lives matters. The man who professes and lives for God will take part in the resurrection of life, but they who have done evil will "rise to be condemned (the resurrection of damnation)" (judgment, condemnation, cp. Jn.3:17). What a person has professed will not matter. All that will matter will be how a person has lived. Has he lived righteously and godly in this present world—believing on Christ and serving Him? Believing on Christ means that a person has committed His life to follow Christ, to obey and serve Him (see note—Jn.2:2).

Thought 1. Note two critical facts about the resurrection.

1) There is to be a resurrection of all who have believed and obeyed the Lord Jesus Christ.

> **I tell you the truth, a time is coming and has now come when the dead will hear the voice of the Son of God and those who hear will live. (John 5:25)**
>
> **For my Father's will is that everyone who looks to the Son and believes in him shall have eternal life, and I will raise him up at the last day. (John 6:40)**
>
> **Jesus said to her, "I am the resurrection and the life. He who believes in me will live, even though he dies; (John 11:25)**
>
> **For as in Adam all die, so in Christ all will be made alive. (1 Cor 15:22)**
>
> **Because we know that the one who raised the Lord Jesus from the dead will also raise us with Jesus and present us with you in his presence. (2 Cor 4:14)**

For the Lord himself will come down from heaven, with a loud command, with the voice of the archangel and with the trumpet call of God, and the dead in Christ will rise first. After that, we who are still alive and are left will be caught up together with them in the clouds to meet the Lord in the air. And so we will be with the Lord forever. (1 Th 4:16-17)

But God will redeem my life from the grave; he will surely take me to himself. Selah (Psa 49:15)

Though you have made me see troubles, many and bitter, you will restore my life again; from the depths of the earth you will again bring me up. (Psa 71:20)

"I will ransom them from the power of the grave ; I will redeem them from death. Where, O death, are your plagues? Where, O grave, is your destruction? "I will have no compassion, (Hosea 13:14)

2) There is to be not only a resurrection of believers but also a resurrection of all those who have rejected and disobeyed the Lord Jesus Christ.

"Do not be amazed at this, for a time is coming when all who are in their graves will hear his voice and come out—those who have done good will rise to live, and those who have done evil will rise to be condemned. (John 5:28-29)

And I have the same hope in God as these men, that there will be a resurrection of both the righteous and the wicked. (Acts 24:15)

Multitudes who sleep in the dust of the earth will awake: some to everlasting life, others to shame and everlasting contempt. (Dan 12:2)

6. The judgment of Christ will be a *just* judgment. He will judge precisely as He "hears," exactly as *God wills*. He hears and does the will of God perfectly; therefore, He will hear God and execute God's judgment exactly as He wills. Only men who have lived godly lives will rise to live. All others will rise to be condemned.

For the Son of Man is going to come in his Father's glory with his angels, and then he will reward each person according to what he has done. (Mat 16:27)

God "will give to each person according to what he has done." (Rom 2:6)

For we must all appear before the judgment seat of Christ, that each one may receive what is due him for the things done while in the body, whether good or bad. (2 Cor 5:10)

Since you call on a Father who judges each man's work impartially, live your lives as strangers here in reverent fear. (1 Pet 1:17)

And I saw the dead, great and small, standing before the throne, and books were opened. Another book was opened, which is the book of life. The dead were judged according to what they had done as recorded in the books. The sea gave up the dead that were in it, and death and Hades gave up the dead that were in them, and each person was judged according to what he had done. Then death and Hades were thrown into the lake of fire. The lake of fire is the second death. If anyone's name was not found written in the book of life, he was thrown into the lake of fire. (Rev 20:12-15)

"Behold, I am coming soon! My reward is with me, and I will give to everyone according to what he has done. (Rev 22:12) and that you, O Lord, are loving. Surely you will reward each person according to what he has done. (Psa 62:12)

"I the LORD search the heart and examine the mind, to reward a man according to his conduct, according to what his deeds deserve." (Jer 17:10)

	C. The Five Witnesses to Jesus' Authority & Power, 5:31-39	36 "I have testimony weightier than that of John. For the very work that the Father has given me tofinish, and which I am doing, testifies that the Father has sent me.	4 The witness of miraculous works
1 One's own testimony is unacceptable	31 "If I testify about myself, my testimony is not valid.		
2 The witness within: The Spirit	32 There is another who testifies in my favor, and I know that his testimony about me is valid.	37 And the Father who sent me has himself testified concerning me. You have never heard his voice nor seen his form,	5 The witness of God Himself[DS1]
3 The witness of John the Baptist	33 "You have sent to John and he has testified to the truth.	38 nor does his word dwell in you, for you do not believe the one he sent.	
	34 Not that I accept human testimony; but I mention it that you may be saved.	39 You diligently study the Scriptures because you think that by them you possess eternal life. These are the Scriptures that testify about me,	6 The witness of the Scriptures
	35 John was a lamp that burned and gave light, and you chose for a time to enjoy his light.		

DIVISION VI

THE REVELATION OF JESUS, THE AUTHORITY AND POWER OVER LIFE, 5:1-47

C. The Five Witnesses to Jesus' Authority and Power, 5:31-39

(5:31-39) **Introduction**: there are five witnesses to Jesus' authority.

1. One's own testimony is unacceptable (v.31).
2. The witness within: the Spirit (v.32).
3. The witness of John the Baptist (v.33-35).
4. The witness of miraculous works (v.36).
5. The witness of God Himself (v.37-38).
6. The witness of the Scriptures (v.39).

1 (5:31) **Jesus Christ, Deity—Witness—Judicial System**: a man's own testimony is unacceptable and suspicious. The witness of a man has to be supported by other witnesses, and at least two witnesses are required. This is one of the most fundamental laws of society throughout the world. (Cp. Dt.17:6; 19:15; Mt.18:16; 2 Cor.13:1; 1 Tim.5:19.) This is the point that Jesus was making. Note how He was stooping down to the level of man. What He had said was true. He was the Son of God; He could not lie. He was precisely who He claimed to be, and the fact should have been known. Men should have been searching and seeking after God so diligently that they could not miss the fact that He was the Son of God. He was so different and so Godly. However to meet their need, He would prove the fact by meeting the demands of justice. He would call forth five witnesses to prove His claim.

Thought 1. The fact that a man's word is untrustworthy reflects the poor stuff of which men are made. Man's word, his honesty and integrity, cannot be trusted—not even in a court of law. Note his nature of self-centeredness: he loves himself much more than truth, even when the life of society and its laws are threatened.

Thought 2. Note the love of Christ for man—His seeking after man, using every method He can to convince men so that they might be saved.

2 (5:32) **Holy Spirit—Jesus Christ, Witnesses to**: there is the witness within, the Holy Spirit. Christ did not iden-

tify who He meant by "another" (allos). (Cp. Jn.14:16.) Most commentators believe He was referring to God Himself. There are three reasons why the Holy Spirit is thought to be the One to whom Christ was referring.

1. The Holy Spirit had already been given to Christ "without limit" (see note—Jn.3:34). He was, of course, very conscious of the witness of the Spirit both within and without Him. The Spirit was empowering Him and doing the works of God through Him.

2. The Holy Spirit is One of the witnesses that bears witness of Christ (cp. 1 Jn.5:6-12). When John the apostle discusses the testimony to Christ in his epistle, he mentions the Spirit. If the present verse is not referring to the Spirit, then the Spirit is not listed as one of the witnesses in the present passage. This would be most unlikely, especially since the testimony of the Father is covered in v.37-38, and the ministry and testimony of the Spirit is covered so thoroughly in this Gospel. (See outline and notes—Jn.14:15-26; 16:7-15.)

3. Note how the verse reads. Christ seems to be talking more about an inner witness, the testimony of a Presence which He senses within His innermost Being, a Power that works in and through Him. This of course could be God, but again it could also be the Spirit which would fit more naturally in the context.

Note the Lord's words, "I <u>know</u> that this testimony about me is <u>valid</u>." The Lord meant at least two things.

1. He knew the truth of the testimony within His own heart and life. He had the consciousness, the sense, the awareness, the personal knowledge of the Spirit's witness within His own inner Being. The Spirit bore witness with Jesus' own Spirit that He was the Son of God.

2. He knew that the testimony and the work of the Holy Spirit, in and through Him, was true. The Spirit was convicting men, working in their hearts and lives, convincing them of the claims of Christ. (See outline and notes—Jn.16:7-15 for the Lord's discussion of the Spirit's work.)

For the one whom God has sent speaks the words of God, for God gives the Spirit without limit. (John 3:34)

The Spirit gives life; the flesh counts for nothing. The words I have spoken to you are spirit and they are life. (John 6:63)

How God anointed Jesus of Nazareth with the Holy Spirit and power, and how he went around doing good and healing all who were under the power of the devil, because God was with him. (Acts 10:38)

3 (5:33-35) **John the Baptist**: there was the witness of John the Baptist. The religionists had sent some men to ask John about his witness, and John bore witness to *the truth*. Note several points.

1. The words "has testified" (memartureken) mean a permanent and continuing testimony or witness. His message was not a fly-by-night testimony that appeared on the scene and suddenly disappeared. His witness continued and still continues and will always continue. It was a trustworthy message, a testimony to the truth. (Cp. Jn.1:19-27, 29-36.)

In those days John the Baptist came, preaching in the Desert of Judea and saying, "Repent, for the kingdom of heaven is near." Produce fruit in keeping with repentance. (Mat 3:1-2, 8)

The ax is already at the root of the trees, and every tree that does not produce good fruit will be cut down and thrown into the fire. "I baptize you with water for repentance. But after me will come one who is more powerful than I, whose sandals I am not fit to carry. He will baptize you with the Holy Spirit and with fire. (Mat 3:10-11)

2. The words "the truth" are a reference not only to the truth of John's message but also to Christ Himself, who is *the Truth*, the very embodiment of Truth. (See DEEPER STUDY # 2—Jn.14:6.)

Jesus answered, "I am the way and the truth and the life. No one comes to the Father except through me. (John 14:6)

3. Jesus did not need or plead the testimony of a mere man. The implication for man is clear: men should not plead the testimony of a mere man when dealing with eternal issues that determine their destiny. The testimony of God's Son should be counted the strongest of witnesses, yet tragically men want the testimony of other men just like themselves.

Note: Jesus did not receive the testimony of men, for He knew what was in man (cp. Jn.2:24-25). He also rebuked Nicodemus for not receiving His testimony and letting it be enough (Jn.3:11).

4. Jesus reached out to men, giving them what they required, hoping to save some. He gave them the most dynamic human testimony He could—John the Baptist. John's testimony was as clear and pointed as it could be: "Look the Lamb of God, who takes away the sin of the world" (Jn.1:29).

5. The testimony of John was that of a burning and shining light. His light was clearly seen to be of God, lit by God as the light of God. That John's message (witness) was of God could not be questioned by any reasonable and honest person. John definitely showed men the way to God, just as a light shows men the way out of darkness.

6. The people rejoiced in John's light, but *only for a season*. They looked upon John as a sensation, a moment of excitement, listening and accepting only what they wished. Very simply, if John said anything that did not allow them to do as they desired, they rejected it.

4 (5:36) **Jesus Christ, Deity—Works—Testimony to—Witness to**: there was the witness of miraculous works. Four significant things were said by Jesus. (See notes—Jn.5:19; 5:20; DEEPER STUDY # 2—10:25 for more discussion.)

1. Jesus' works were a weighter testimony than the testimony of John the Baptist.

2. Jesus' works were given to Him by the Father. He was on a mission for God; therefore, what He did—all the works—were of God (cp. Jn.3:35).
   ⇒ He was the One appointed by God to carry out the works of God.
   ⇒ He was the One empowered by God to do the works of God.

3. Jesus' works were the Father's works. The Father was the Originator, the Planner, the Overseer of the works. He was the One who had given the works to be done and completed. Note that Jesus claimed to have completed the works perfectly (cp. Jn.17:4; 19:30).

4. Jesus' works proved that the Father had sent Him. They were works which had never been, or ever would be, done by others (Jn.15:24). They were so unusual—so full of power and wisdom, love and care, glory and honor to God—that all men who failed to see and believe were without excuse. Remember, He had just performed one of the Godly works, healing the paralyzed man.

As long as it is day, we must do the work of him who sent me. Night is coming, when no one can work. (John 9:4)

Jesus answered, "I did tell you, but you do not believe. The miracles I do in my Father's name speak for me, (John 10:25)

Do not believe me unless I do what my Father does. (John 10:37)

But if I do it, even though you do not believe me, believe the miracles, that you may know and understand that the Father is in me, and I in the Father." (John 10:38)

Believe me when I say that I am in the Father and the Father is in me; or at least believe on the evidence of the miracles themselves. (John 14:11)

If I had not done among them what no one else did, they would not be guilty of sin. But now they have seen these miracles, and yet they have hated both me and my Father. (John 15:24)

Coming to his hometown, he began teaching the people in their synagogue, and they were amazed. "Where did this man get this wisdom and these miraculous powers?" they asked. (Mat 13:54; cp. Mk.6:2, 14)

5 (5:37-38) **Jesus Christ, Deity—Testimony to — Witnesses to—Word of God**: there was the testimony of God Himself. God sent Christ into the world, so Christ naturally testified about God. The testimony included all that God had ever revealed to man down through the centuries. Everything God did was to prepare the way for His

Son, and every single act bore testimony that God was sending His Son. (See DEEPER STUDY # 1—Jn.4:22.)

> **But when the time had fully come, God sent his Son, born of a woman, born under law, to redeem those under law, that we might receive the full rights of sons. Because you are sons, God sent the Spirit of his Son into our hearts, the Spirit who calls out, "Abba, Father." (Gal 4:4-6)**

The point is striking: the way was being prepared for the coming of God's Son...
- every time God spoke.
- every time God appeared (theophany, in whatever form or manner).
- every time God acted.

Christ made two charges against the religionists. (The same charges can be made against the world.)

1. "You have never heard his voice nor seen his form [what he is like] (v.37)." Some people may think they have seen God, but they have not. However, it is not because God has not spoken or shown what He is like. He has revealed the truth about Himself and the coming of His Son.
⇒ Some in the *Old Testament* did hear and see what God was like (Gen.32:30; Ex.24:10; 33:11; Num.12:8; Dt.4:12; 5:4, 24).
⇒ Some in the *New Testament* did hear and see what God was like: Simeon (Lk.1:25f), Anna (Lk.1:36f), and others (Jn.1:40f; 12:28-30).

However, most down through the centuries have not heard and seen God, and most still do not.

> **No one has ever seen God, but God the One and Only, who is at the Father's side, has made him known. (John 1:18)**
> **He is the image of the invisible God, the firstborn over all creation. (Col 1:15)**
> **Now to the King eternal, immortal, invisible, the only God, be honor and glory for ever and ever. Amen. (1 Tim 1:17)**
> **Who alone is immortal and who lives in unapproachable light, whom no one has seen or can see. To him be honor and might forever. Amen. (1 Tim 6:16)**
> **No one has ever seen God; but if we love one another, God lives in us and his love is made complete in us. (1 John 4:12)**
> **But," he said, "you cannot see my face, for no one may see me and live." (Exo 33:20)**
> **When he passes me, I cannot see him; when he goes by, I cannot perceive him. (Job 9:11)**
> **"But if I go to the east, he is not there; if I go to the west, I do not find him. (Job 23:8)**

2. "You do not have his word dwelling in you." They had the Old Testament Scriptures, but they did not have the Word of God *dwelling* in their hearts and lives (see DEEPER STUDY # 1—Jn.5:38 for discussion).

DEEPER STUDY # 1
(5:38) Word of God—Dwelling: the Word of God must dwell in a person for a person to know God in a personal way. Two things are necessary for the Word of God to dwell in a person.

1. The Word of God must be accepted as *God's* Word. The Word must be accepted as coming from God; it must be accepted as truth, as fact, as gospel. Where the religionists failed is seen in the next point. (Also see note—Jn.5:39.)

2. The Word of God *must be dwelling* in a person. This means two things.
a. The Word of God must be "in you" not just *among* you (v.38). The religionist had the Word of God all around him: on his desk and table, in his home and church, on his tongue, and sounding upon his ears. However, he did not have the Word *in* his heart, and *unless something is within, it is not dwelling* in a person.
b. The Word of God must be "dwelling." It must not only be allowed to come into a person's mind and heart, it must be grasped and clung to. It must stay within and remain and not be allowed to depart. *Dwelling* means the Word of God is...
- living, moving, ruling, and reigning in a person's life and heart.
- stirring, convicting, and challenging a person.
- leading to confession, repentance, growth, and maturity.
- teaching love, compassion, forgiveness, goodness, and just behavior.
- causing one to believe and trust God's Son, Jesus Christ, as his Savior and Lord.

Thought 1. When God's word *truly dwells* in a person, that person naturally *accepts what God says and lives as God says*, and that person believes God's Son. It would be impossible to accept what God says and not accept what He says about His Son. To reject what God says about His Son is to reject God's Word. If a person does not believe God's Son, to whom God testifies, then God's Word does not dwell in that person.

> **There is a judge for the one who rejects me and does not accept my words; that very word which I spoke will condemn him at the last day. (John 12:48)**
> **For the word of God is living and active. Sharper than any double-edged sword, it penetrates even to dividing soul and spirit, joints and marrow; it judges the thoughts and attitudes of the heart. (Heb 4:12)**

6 (5:39) **Scripture—Jesus Christ, Deity—Eternal Life**: there is the witness of Scripture. Note three things.

1. The word "study" (eraunate, "you study") can be either a fact, that " you diligently study the scriptures," or a command, "diligently study the scriptures." It seems that the words "because you think that by them" point toward the meaning's being a statement of fact. The religionists do "diligently study the scriptures," for they think they have eternal life "in their studying."

2. The Scriptures *proclaim* the message of eternal life and show us how to secure eternal life, but the Scriptures do not impart or give eternal life. Only Christ can give eternal life. A person does not secure eternal life...
- by reading the Scripture, no matter how much he reads.
- by knowing the Scripture, no matter how much he knows.

- by being religious, no matter how religious he is.
- by doing religious works, no matter how much good he does.

A person receives eternal life only by believing and giving his heart and life to Jesus Christ. (See DEEPER STUDY # 2—Jn.2:24.)

> "For God so loved the world that he gave his one and only Son, that whoever believes in him shall not perish but have eternal life. (John 3:16)
> And this is the testimony: God has given us eternal life, and this life is in his Son. He who has the Son has life; he who does not have the Son of God does not have life. (1 John 5:11-12)

3. The Scriptures testify of Christ.

> And beginning with Moses and all the Prophets, he explained to them what was said in all the Scriptures concerning himself. Then he opened their minds so they could understand the Scriptures. (Luke 24:27, 45)
> Concerning this salvation, the prophets, who spoke of the grace that was to come to you, searched intently and with the greatest care, trying to find out the time and circumstances to which the Spirit of Christ in them was pointing when he predicted the sufferings of Christ and the glories that would follow. (1 Pet 1:10-11)

	D. The Rejection of Jesus' Claim, 5:40-47	44 How can you believe if you accept praise from one another, yet make no effort to obtain the praise that comes from the only God?	4 Men seek the approval & honor of mere men
1 Men refuse to come to Christ	40 yet you refuse to come to me to have life. 41 "I do not accept praise from men,	45 "But do not think I will accuse you before the Father. Your accuser is Moses, on whom your hopes are set.	5 Men do not believe prophecy—do not believe Moses' writings
2 Men do not love God	42 but I know you. I know that you do not have the love of God in your hearts.	46 If you believed Moses, you would believe me, for he wrote about me.	
3 Men accept false messiahs	43 I have come in my Father's name, and you do not accept me; but if someone else comes in his own name, you will accept him.	47 But since you do not believe what he wrote, how are you going to believe what I say?"	6 Men do not believe the words of the true Messiah

DIVISION VI

THE REVELATION OF JESUS, THE AUTHORITY AND POWER OVER LIFE, 5:1-47

D. The Rejection of Jesus' Claim, 5:40-47

(5:40-47) **Introduction**: men reject Jesus' claim to be "equal with God" (Jn.5:18). Jesus gave six reasons for their rejection.

1. Men refuse to Christ (v.40-41).
2. Men do not love God (v.42).
3. Men accept false messiahs (v.43).
4. Men seek the approval and honor of *mere* men (v.44).
5. Men do not believe prophecy—do not believe Moses' writings (v.45-46).
6. Men do not believe the words of the true Messiah (v.47).

1 (5:40-41) **Will**: men refuse to come to Christ. The *will* of man is stressed. Men deliberately choose to reject Jesus Christ. They actually exercise the will not to come to Him for salvation. There is an obstinacy and a hardness within man, a rebellion against God (cp. Jn.1:11; Mt.23:37).

> "You stiff-necked people, with uncircumcised hearts and ears! You are just like your fathers: You always resist the Holy Spirit! (Acts 7:51)
> Although the LORD sent prophets to the people to bring them back to him, and though they testified against them, they would not listen. (2 Chr 24:19)
> They turned their backs to me and not their faces; though I taught them again and again, they would not listen or respond to discipline. (Jer 32:33)
> "We will not listen to the message you have spoken to us in the name of the LORD! (Jer 44:16)

1. Jesus claimed that life was in Him (see DEEPER STUDY # 2—Jn.1:4; DEEPER STUDY # 1—10:10; DEEPER STUDY # 1—17:2-3).

> In him was life, and that life was the light of men. (John 1:4)
> For as the Father has life in himself, so he has granted the Son to have life in himself. (John 5:26)
> The thief comes only to steal and kill

and destroy; I have come that they may have life, and have it to the full. (John 10:10)
> Jesus said to her, "I am the resurrection and the life. He who believes in me will live, even though he dies; (John 11:25)
> Jesus answered, "I am the way and the truth and the life. No one comes to the Father except through me. (John 14:6)

2. Men receive life by coming to Jesus Christ. They keep from dying by coming to Jesus Christ (see notes—Jn.5:21; 5:24-25; DEEPER STUDY # 1—Heb.9:27).

> For just as the Father raises the dead and gives them life, even so the Son gives life to whom he is pleased to give it. (John 5:21)
> "I tell you the truth, whoever hears my word and believes him who sent me has eternal life and will not be condemned; he has crossed over from death to life. I tell you the truth, a time is coming and has now come when the dead will hear the voice of the Son of God and those who hear will live. (John 5:24-25)

3. Jesus was not claiming to be the Son of God in order to receive the praise and glory of men (v.41). He was proclaiming the truth because He loved them, and the fact of His deity is the truth. Men must face up to the truth if they wish to be saved. Man's rejection cuts the heart of Christ, and the hurt is seen in the tenderness and appeal of this verse. There is a pleading in His words: "You refuse to come to me to have life."

> For this people's heart has become calloused; they hardly hear with their ears, and they have closed their eyes. Otherwise they might see with their eyes, hear with their ears, understand with their hearts and turn, and I would heal them.' (Acts 28:27)
> How shall we escape if we ignore such a great salvation? This salvation, which was first announced by the Lord, was confirmed to us by those who heard him. (Heb 2:3)

See to it that you do not refuse him who speaks. If they did not escape when they refused him who warned them on earth, how much less will we, if we turn away from him who warns us from heaven? (Heb 12:25)

2 (5:42) **Rejection—Profession, False:** men will to reject Christ, to reject the claim of Christ because they do not love God. The love of God is not in their hearts.

1. The people to whom Jesus was speaking professed to love God deeply. They...
- worshipped faithfully
- knew the Scriptures
- were always praying
- were unashamed to talk about Him

However, the love of God was not *in* them, not really. It was not poured out in their hearts, not the kind of love that honors and praises God, giving all that one is and has to love and help people.

And hope does not disappoint us, because God has poured out his love into our hearts by the Holy Spirit, whom he has given us. (Rom 5:5)

Dear friends, let us love one another, for love comes from God. Everyone who loves has been born of God and knows God. Whoever does not love does not know God, because God is love. (1 John 4:7-8)

"'These people honor me with their lips, but their hearts are far from me. (Mat 15:8)

Thought 1. If men loved God, they would receive Christ.

This is how God showed his love among us: He sent his one and only Son into the world that we might live through him. This is love: not that we loved God, but that he loved us and sent his Son as an atoning sacrifice for our sins. And so we know and rely on the love God has for us. God is love. Whoever lives in love lives in God, and God in him. (We love because he first loved us. (1 John 4:9-10, 16, 19)

2. Jesus said, "I know you." He knows a man's heart, if a man's profession is true and genuine or false and counterfeit. Jesus sees right through a man's words, down deep into his heart.

For there is nothing hidden that will not be disclosed, and nothing concealed that will not be known or brought out into the open. (Luke 8:17)

"His eyes are on the ways of men; he sees their every step. (Job 34:21)

For a man's ways are in full view of the LORD, and he examines all his paths. (Prov 5:21)

Although you wash yourself with soda and use an abundance of soap, the stain of your guilt is still before me," declares the Sovereign LORD. (Jer 2:22)

My eyes are on all their ways; they are not hidden from me, nor is their sin concealed from my eyes. (Jer 16:17)

Great are your purposes and mighty are your deeds. Your eyes are open to all the ways of men; you reward everyone according to his conduct and as his deeds deserve. (Jer 32:19)

Then the Spirit of the LORD came upon me, and he told me to say: "This is what the LORD says: That is what you are saying, O house of Israel, but I know what is going through your mind. (Ezek 11:5)

For I know how many are your offenses and how great your sins. You oppress the righteous and take bribes and you deprive the poor of justice in the courts. (Amos 5:12)

3 (5:43) **Messiah—Messiahship:** men receive false messiahs. There is a contrast here.

1. Jesus said, "I have come in my Father's name," but "someone else comes in his own name." Jesus came in the name, that is, in the authority and truthfulness, of God. "Someone else," the false messiah, comes in the authority and word of himself.

2. Jesus said, "You do not accept me," but "you will accept him." Men reject God's Son, the true Messiah, but they receive the false messiah. Why?

Men want either to escape from the world or to get all they can from the world.
⇒ Some want to escape the pressure, tension, immorality, selfishness, hatred, and injustices of the world.
⇒ Others want either a reasonable amount of prosperity, pleasure, power, recognition, or fame of the world.

Jesus, being the Son of God, cannot lie to man. He has to tell the truth. The way to life is not by escaping the world nor by getting plenty of the world. The way to life is to do exactly as Jesus said:

Then he said to them all: "If anyone would come after me, he must deny himself and take up his cross daily and follow me. For whoever wants to save his life will lose it, but whoever loses his life for me will save it. What good is it for a man to gain the whole world, and yet lose or forfeit his very self? (Luke 9:23-25)

The false messiah or human deliverer is not truthful. He is a mere man, full of all the weaknesses and infirmities of men. A false messiah is a person born of mere man and woman; he is a person who will die as a mere man just as all other men die. The false messiah is a deceiving person with leadership qualities and charisma who has learned to promise what men crave: escapism and possessions. Therefore, he sets himself up claiming that belief in his "name," that is, in what he says, will meet man's needs. Jesus says that most men "will accept" such a false messiah or deliverer. (Cp. Mt.24:23-26. Cp. DEEPER STUDY # 2—Mt.1:18.)

Anyone who breaks one of the least of these commandments and teaches others to do the same will be called least in the kingdom of heaven, but whoever practices and teaches these commands will be called great in the kingdom of heaven. (Mat 5:19)

For such men are false apostles, deceitful workmen, masquerading as apostles of Christ. And no wonder, for Satan himself masquerades as an angel of light. It is not surprising, then, if his servants masquerade as servants of righteousness. Their end will be what their actions deserve. (2 Cor 11:13-15)

They want to be teachers of the law, but they do not know what they are talking about or what they so confidently affirm. (1 Tim 1:7)

For the time will come when men will not put up with sound doctrine. Instead, to suit their own desires, they will gather around them a great number of teachers to say what their itching ears want to hear. They will turn their ears away from the truth and turn aside to myths. (2 Tim 4:3-4)

But there were also false prophets among the people, just as there will be false teachers among you. They will secretly introduce destructive heresies, even denying the sovereign Lord who bought them—bringing swift destruction on themselves. (2 Pet 2:1)

Who is the liar? It is the man who denies that Jesus is the Christ. Such a man is the antichrist—he denies the Father and the Son. No one who denies the Son has the Father; whoever acknowledges the Son has the Father also. (1 John 2:22-23)

4 (5:44) **Seeking Approval—Pride—Self-Suffering**: men seek the approval and honor of *mere* men. Men make two gross mistakes.

1. They seek the acceptance and approval, the recognition and honor, of other men, and such becomes the driving force of their lives. People seek...

- the right position in which to be seen
- the right place to live and work
- the right car to drive
- the right clothes to wear
- the right looks to attract
- the right gifts to secure honor
- the power and wealth to possess
- the recognition and fame to be known

They do not seek the acceptance and approval, nor the recognition and honor of God.

2. They measure themselves against other men, not against God. When a man measures himself by other men, he is seen to be good and acceptable. He does not come short often, if at all. But note something: when a person is being praised and honored by others, he feels acceptable, complete, fulfilled. Therefore, he often senses no need for God. Only when men measure themselves against God do they see themselves for what they are: "short of the glory of God" (Ro.3:23). Only then do they bow in humility and beg forgiveness and cast themselves upon the mercy of God. Note the question of Christ: "[In light of this,] How can you believe?"

If anyone thinks he is something when he is nothing, he deceives himself. (Gal 6:3)

If anyone considers himself religious and yet does not keep a tight rein on his tongue, he deceives himself and his religion is worthless. (James 1:26)

If we claim to be without sin, we deceive ourselves and the truth is not in us. (1 John 1:8)

You say, 'I am rich; I have acquired wealth and do not need a thing.' But you do not realize that you are wretched, pitiful, poor, blind and naked. (Rev 3:17)

Many a man claims to have unfailing love, but a faithful man who can find? (Prov 20:6)

It is not good to eat too much honey, nor is it honorable to seek one's own honor. (Prov 25:27)

Woe to those who are wise in their own eyes and clever in their own sight. (Isa 5:21)

But you have planted wickedness, you have reaped evil, you have eaten the fruit of deception. Because you have depended on your own strength and on your many warriors, (Hosea 10:13)

The pride of your heart has deceived you, you who live in the clefts of the rocks and make your home on the heights, you who say to yourself, 'Who can bring me down to the ground?' Though you soar like the eagle and make your nest among the stars, from there I will bring you down," declares the LORD. (Oba 1:3-4)

5 (5:45-46) **Man, Unbelief—Prophecy**: men do not believe prophecy, do not believe Moses' writings. Note two things.

1. Jesus said, "Moses wrote about me." All the prophecies in Genesis through Deuteronomy are the prophecies to which Jesus was referring (see DEEPER STUDY # 3—Jn.1:45 for the prophecies by Moses).

2. Jesus said that Moses was the one who condemned man's unbelief, not Him. The men standing before Jesus professed to believe Moses, but they did not—not really.

⇒ They did not believe what Moses said about the promised Messiah.
⇒ They did not live as Moses said to live.
⇒ Their profession would be condemned by the very one whom they said they trusted, by Moses himself.

And he said to them: "You have a fine way of setting aside the commands of God in order to observe your own traditions! (Mark 7:9)

Thus you nullify the word of God by your tradition that you have handed down. And you do many things like that." (Mark 7:13)

He said to them, "How foolish you are, and how slow of heart to believe all that the prophets have spoken! (Luke 24:25)

Whoever believes in the Son has eternal life, but whoever rejects the Son will not see life, for God's wrath remains on him." (John 3:36)

I told you that you would die in your sins; if you do not believe that I am the one I claim to be, you will indeed die in your sins." (John 8:24)

You hate my instruction and cast my words behind you. (Psa 50:17)

Therefore, as tongues of fire lick up straw and as dry grass sinks down in the flames, so their roots will decay and their flowers blow away like dust; for they have rejected the law of the LORD Almighty and spurned the word of the Holy One of Israel. (Isa 5:24)

These are rebellious people, deceitful children, children unwilling to listen to the Lord's instruction. (Isa 30:9)

Therefore, this is what the Holy One of Israel says: "Because you have rejected this message, relied on oppression and depended on deceit, this sin will become for you like a high wall, cracked and bulging, that collapses suddenly, in an instant. (Isa 30:12-13)

To whom can I speak and give warning? Who will listen to me? Their ears are closed so they cannot hear. The word of the LORD is offensive to them; they find no pleasure in it. (Jer 6:10)

Hear, O earth: I am bringing disaster on this people, the fruit of their schemes, because they have not listened to my words and have rejected my law. (Jer 6:19)

The wise will be put to shame; they will be dismayed and trapped. Since they have rejected the word of the LORD, what kind of wisdom do they have? (Jer 8:9; cp. Jer.9:13-16; Hos 4.6; Amos2:4)

They made their hearts as hard as flint and would not listen to the law or to the words that the LORD Almighty had sent by his Spirit through the earlier prophets. So the LORD Almighty was very angry. (Zec7:12)

6 (5:47) **Unbelief—Jesus Christ, Words—Word of God**: men do not believe the words of the true Messiah. Jesus gave two reasons why men do not believe Him.

1. They did not believe Moses' writings, the words of Scripture. How then could men believe the promises of the Messiah?

2. They did not believe the testimony of a man whom they professed was a great and honorable man. They honored Moses, calling him great and honorable; yet they treated him as a liar, a man whose testimony was unreliable. How then could men believe the words of Christ?

> **Thought 1.** How many acknowledge Christ as a great and honorable man yet treat Him as a liar, a man whose testimony and claims are totally untrustworthy?

> There is a judge for the one who rejects me and does not accept my words; that very word which I spoke will condemn him at the last day. (John 12:48)
> He who does not love me will not obey my teaching. These words you hear are not my own; they belong to the Father who sent me. (John 14:24)
> If anyone teaches false doctrines and does not agree to the sound instruction of our Lord Jesus Christ and to godly teaching, he is conceited and understands nothing. He has an unhealthy interest in controversies and quarrels about words that result in envy, strife, malicious talk, evil suspicions (1 Tim 6:3-4)
> I tell you the truth, if anyone keeps my word, he will never see death." (John 8:51)
> "If you love me, you will obey what I command. (John 14:15)
> We know that we have come to know him if we obey his commands. (1 John 2:3)

CHAPTER 6

VII. THE REVELATION OF JESUS, THE BREAD OF LIFE, 6:1-71

A. Jesus Feeds Five Thousand: The Provision for Human Need, 6:1-15

1 The setting
a. After this sometime Jesus crossed the Lake of Galilee[DS1]
b. Feverish, surging crowds followed Him

c. Jesus sought rest & relief
d. The pilgrims were gathering for the Feast
e. The two concerns of Jesus[DS2]
  1) The missing of a meal—Jesus wants to meet every need
  2) The testing & strengthening of His disciples: Teaching the kinds of faith

2 Lesson 1: There is a pessimistic faith[DS3]

Some time after this, Jesus crossed to the far shore of the Sea of Galilee (that is, the Sea of Tiberias),
2 And a great crowd of people followed him because they saw the miraculous signs he had performed on the sick.
3 Then Jesus went up on a mountainside and sat down with his disciples.
4 The Jewish Passover Feast was near.
5 When Jesus looked up and saw a great crowd coming toward him, he said to Philip, "Where shall we buy bread for these people to eat?"
6 He asked this only to test him, for he already had in mind what he was going to do.
7 Philip answered him, "Eight months' wages would not buy enough bread for each one to have a bite!"

8 Another of his disciples, Andrew, Simon Peter's brother, spoke up,
9 "Here is a boy with five small barley loaves and two small fish, but how far will they go among so many?"
10 Jesus said, "Have the people sit down." There was plenty of grass in that place, and the men sat down, about five thousand of them.
11 Jesus then took the loaves, gave thanks, and distributed to those who were seated as much as they wanted. He did the same with the fish.
12 When they had all had enough to eat, he said to his disciples, "Gather the pieces that are left over. Let nothing be wasted."
13 So they gathered them and filled twelve baskets with the pieces of the five barley loaves left over by those who had eaten.
14 After the people saw the miraculous sign that Jesus did, they began to say, "Surely this is the Prophet who is to come into the world."
15 Jesus, knowing that they intended to come and make him king by force, withdrew again to a mountain by himself.

3 Lesson 2: There is an optimistic but questioning faith[DS4]
a. Andrew searched for & brought food
b. He questioned the supply

4 Lesson 3: There is a positive, unswerving faith

a. Jesus' faith
  1) He took & gave thanks for what He had
  2) He gave what He had
  3) He used others to help Him
b. God's answer & provision
  1) He met the people's need: He fed & filled them
  2) He gave an overabundance
  3) He allowed no waste

5 Lesson 4: There is a materialistic profession of Jesus
a. The people's profession: Jesus was the Messiah
b. The people's concept: Jesus was an earthly, materialistic king

DIVISION VII

THE REVELATION OF JESUS, THE BREAD OF LIFE, 6:1-71

A. Jesus Feeds Five Thousand: The Provision for Human Need, 6:1-15

(6:1-71) **DIVISION OVERVIEW: Man, Needs of—Christ, Bread of Life**: Chapter 6 reveals Jesus to be the Provision for every human and material need. Jesus first demonstrated the truth, then He began to preach and teach it. He showed that He was...
- concerned with every need in life (even a missed meal, Jn.6:1-15).
- concerned with every overpowering need (the calming of a storm, Jn.6:16-21).

No matter how small the need or how stormy the problem, Jesus is the Provision, the Bread of Life, and the power to meet man's every need. He can provide a single meal, and He can calm the most stormy problem.

(6:1-15) **Introduction**: Jesus Christ is the Bread of Life, the Provision for human and material needs. (See outline and notes—Mt.6:25-34.) Note two significant facts.

First, trying to meet human needs by any other source than Christ is doomed to failure and will not satisfy.

Second, believing and trusting are essential for God to meet human need. However, there are several levels of faith and trust. This is the lesson man must learn in order

to see that Christ is the Bread of Life, the Provision for human need.

1. The setting (v.1-6).
2. Lesson 1: there is a pessimistic faith (v.7).
3. Lesson 2: there is an optimistic but questioning faith (v.8-9).
4. Lesson 3: there is a positive, unswerving faith (v.10-13).
5. Lesson 4: there is a materialistic profession (v.14-15).

1 (6:1-6) **Jesus Christ, Concerns—Ministering**: the setting is descriptive. Jesus crossed over the sea or lake of Galilee (see DEEPER STUDY # 1—Mk.1:16; note—Lk.8:22). The lake was about thirteen miles long and eight miles wide. The feverish, surging crowds saw where He was heading, so they rushed around the lake by foot. The journey was about nine miles.

Note the words "followed" (eklouthei) and "saw" (etheoroun). The two words mean that the people *had been following* Jesus for a long time and *kept on following Him, seeing the ministry* of His miracles upon people (the Greek imperfect active tense).

Jesus was tired and weary from the pressure of facing the crowd day after day. He sought refuge across the lake on the top of some unknown mountain. He needed time to be alone with God and with His disciples. It was the Passover season, a time when thousands of pilgrims flooded Jerusalem and the surrounding suburbs.

The picture is that of Jesus sitting on the mountainside, lifting up His eyes from resting upon His knees and seeing "a great crowd" of thousands streaming across the fields and up the mountain toward Him. The "great crowd" included both those who had followed Him around the lake and pilgrims who were caught up in the excitement of hearing about Jesus, the proclaimed Messiah.

Jesus used the occasion to demonstrate two concerns.

1. His concern for meeting the needs of man, even the most minute need of missing a meal. There is no need that Jesus does not want to meet. The crowd that had been following Him for days had just made a nine mile journey, having rushed ("followed," eklouthei) to keep from losing Him. They were not only hungry and apparently out of food, but they were in mountainous country, an area without any possibility of purchasing food. The point is this: the people were so desperate to find and keep up with Him that they just forgot about eating. As usual, Jesus was filled with compassion for those who so desperately sought Him out. He used the occasion to teach the great lesson: He will meet even the most minute need of men. He asked His disciples, "Where shall we buy bread, for those people to eat?"

2. His concern to strengthen the disciples. He knew what He was going to do, but He used the occasion to test and strengthen the disciples, teaching them a tremendous lesson on faith. They were as we are, full of needs; and their greatest need was the same as ours, to grow in faith.

DEEPER STUDY # 1

(6:1) **"Sometime after this"**: this is a reference to the closing days of the Galilaean ministry, the events covered between Mt.4:12-14:12. These events are not covered by John. His concentration is the Judaean ministry of Jesus; therefore, He simply moves over the Galilaean events by using the words "sometime after this."

DEEPER STUDY # 2

(6:5-15) **Faith**: Jesus was showing that He was concerned with every little need in life (even a missed meal), and that He was able to provide for every need—if man would just believe Him. Therefore, He taught a necessary lesson: there are four ways to respond to needs. (See note—Mk.11:22-23.)

---

2 (6:7) **Faith—Pessimism**: there is a pessimistic faith. This is seen in Philip. Philip needed to see his faith for what it was—pessimistic. Philip was from Bethsaida, so he was the natural disciple to question Jesus (Jn.1:44). The disciples either had eight months' wages [two hundred denarii] in their treasury or else Philip was just pulling a figure out of the air stressing that even such a large amount would not feed the crowd (see DEEPER STUDY # 3, Denarii—Jn.6:7).

1. A pessimistic faith sees money and human resources, and that is all. A pessimistic faith...

- sees only the available resources. It stresses the hopelessness.
- stresses the impossibility of the situation.
- despairs of such meager resources.

- is swamped by the hopelessness of an answer. (Note the tone of Philip's answer, v.7).

2. A pessimistic faith does not see God nor the power of God. A pessimistic faith *professes* God and *professes* Christ to be the Son of God. It professes the belief that Christ has the power to meet the needs of man. It even witnesses the miraculous working of Christ in other instances. But when a problem arises, the immediate response of a pessimistic faith is to see the problem, not the power of God. It does not see the opportunity for the power of God to be demonstrated in conquering the problem and bearing a strong testimony to His name. In the crises of the problem, the power of God seems forgotten.

a. A pessimistic faith forgets God's glorious power in the past.

> **Jesus was in the stern, sleeping on a cushion. The disciples woke him and said to him, "Teacher, don't you care if we drown?" He got up, rebuked the wind and said to the waves, "Quiet! Be still!" Then the wind died down and it was completely calm. He said to his disciples, "Why are you so afraid? Do you still have no faith?" (Mark 4:38-40)**
>
> **Aware of their discussion, Jesus asked, "You of little faith, why are you talking among yourselves about having no bread? Do you still not understand? Don't you remember the five loaves for the five thousand, and how many basketfuls you gathered? (Mat 16:8-9)**

b. A pessimistic faith fails to think of God's power. It's mind is on earthly things, not on spiritual things. It is carnal, not spiritual.

> **Those who live according to the sinful nature have their minds set on what that nature desires; but those who live in accordance with the Spirit have their minds set on what the Spirit desires. The mind of sinful man is death, but the mind controlled by the Spirit is life and peace; (Rom 8:5-6)**

c. A pessimistic faith feels that the problem is too big for God's power or either too little for God to be interested in.

> **Again I tell you, it is easier for a camel to go through the eye of a needle than for a rich man to enter the kingdom of God." When the disciples heard this, they were greatly astonished and asked, "Who then can be saved?" Jesus looked at them and said, "With man this is impossible, but with God all things are possible." (Mat 19:24-26)**

d. A pessimistic faith fears that God's power will fail and the person's faith will be weakened. Therefore, the person is safer to pray weakly, "Lord, if you will, handle this problem."

> **But when he asks, he must believe and not doubt, because he who doubts is like a wave of the sea, blown and tossed by the wind. That man should not think he will receive anything from the Lord; he is a**

double minded man, unstable in all he does. (James 1:6-8)

e. A pessimistic faith fails to see God's care and love, interest and concern, over every little thing that happens to a person.

Look at the birds of the air; they do not sow or reap or store away in barns, and yet your heavenly Father feeds them. Are you not much more valuable than they? (Mat 6:26)

And even the very hairs of your head are all numbered. (Mat 10:30)

f. A pessimistic faith gives thanks and praise to God for what one has (health, money, things) but fails to trust God for the miraculous (healing and multiplication of resources so that one can better serve and help others).

Then the disciples came to Jesus in private and asked, "Why couldn't we drive it out?" He replied, "Because you have so little faith. I tell you the truth, if you have faith as small as a mustard seed, you can say to this mountain, 'Move from here to there' and it will move. Nothing will be impossible for you." (Mat 17:19-20)

g. A pessimistic faith looks to others for help instead of looking to God and depending upon Him alone.

Do not be anxious about anything, but in everything, by prayer and petition, with thanksgiving, present your requests to God. And the peace of God, which transcends all understanding, will guard your hearts and your minds in Christ Jesus. (Phil 4:6-7)

I know, O LORD, that a man's life is not his own; it is not for man to direct his steps. (Jer 10:23)

A song of ascents. Of Solomon. Unless the LORD builds the house, its builders labor in vain. Unless the LORD watches over the city, the watchmen stand guard in vain. (Psa 127:1)

Stop trusting in man, who has but a breath in his nostrils. Of what account is he? (Isa 2:22)

h. A pessimistic faith fails to see that God is glorified when He provides and meets the need.

I rejoice greatly in the Lord that at last you have renewed your concern for me. Indeed, you have been concerned, but you had no opportunity to show it. (Phil 4:10)

I have received full payment and even more; I am amply supplied, now that I have received from Epaphroditus the gifts you sent. They are a fragrant offering, an acceptable sacrifice, pleasing to God. And my God will meet all your needs according to his glorious riches in Christ Jesus. To our God and Father be glory for ever and ever. Amen. (Phil 4:18-20)

DEEPER STUDY # 3
(6:7) **Denarii—Eight months' wages**: one denarii was the average pay for a day's work. The amount in any generation's coinage would be equal to that generation's average daily wage. Two hundred denarii would equal about eight months' wages.

---

3 (6:8-9) **Faith—Optimism**: there is an optimistic, but questioning faith. This is seen in Andrew. Note three things.

1. An optimistic, questioning faith loves the Lord and is committed to the Lord. Andrew saw Christ's concern, so he went among the crowd to search for food. He found and gathered all the resources he could.

2. An optimistic, questioning faith lays what it can find before the Lord. No matter how little the resources or how poor the quality, it is all laid before the Lord. The barley bread was the bread of the poor, the very cheapest bread that could be made or bought. It was anything but a delicacy. The two fish were even "small." Note the simple, optimistic faith of Andrew. He had searched and could find nothing but five small barley cakes and two small fish, but he offered what he had found—the *boy* and his *food*—to the Lord.

3. An optimistic, questioning faith does question: "How far will they go among so many?" The questioning faith often deteriorates into…

- complaining about the problem
- being anxious about meager resources
- grumbling over the small provision
- griping over the poor quality

A questioning faith looks at the need and then looks at the *meager resources*, both how little and how poor the quality of the resources are, and it questions God. It questions instead of believing God to take care of the problem. The need may be what it is in this event, the need for food; or it may be the need for health, money, deliverance, or a myriad of other human needs. Whatever the need may be, the fundamental need is for one to learn to trust Christ and not to question and doubt His love and care, wisdom and power.

"Therefore I tell you, do not worry about your life, what you will eat or drink; or about your body, what you will wear. Is not life more important than food, and the body more important than clothes? (Mat 6:25)

So do not worry, saying, 'What shall we eat?' or 'What shall we drink?' or 'What shall we wear?' For the pagans run after all these things, and your heavenly Father knows that you need them. (Mat 6:31-32)

But Martha was distracted by all the preparations that had to be made. She came to him and asked, "Lord, don't you care that my sister has left me to do the work by myself? Tell her to help me!" "Martha, Martha," the Lord answered, "you are worried and upset about many things, (Luke 10:40-41)

And do not set your heart on what you will eat or drink; do not worry about it. (Luke 12:29)

Do not be anxious about anything, but in everything, by prayer and petition, with thanksgiving, present your requests to God. (Phil 4:6)

If any of you lacks wisdom, he should ask God, who gives generously to all without finding fault, and it will be given to him. But when he asks, he must believe and not doubt, because he who doubts is like a wave of the sea, blown and tossed by the wind. (James 1:5-6)

DEEPER STUDY # 4

(6:8-9) **Andrew**: little is said about Andrew in the New Testament, but what is said shows a faithful and humble follower of the Lord. (Also see DEEPER STUDY # 7—Mk.3:18.)

1. Andrew was a follower of John the Baptist (Jn.1:35-40).

2. Andrew willingly took the second place. He was one of the very first to follow Christ, and he was also one of the very first to bring another person to Christ (his own brother, Peter). However, Andrew was called to take a back seat. He was to live under the shadow of Peter. Throughout the New Testament Peter is always mentioned first, but from all indications Andrew never resented his place. To be with Jesus and to do what Jesus wanted was enough for Andrew.

3. Andrew was the man who was always bringing others to Jesus. He was the focus of attention only three times in the New Testament, and in all three cases he was seen bringing someone to Jesus: Peter (Jn.1:41), the small boy with the loaves and fish (Jn.6:8-9), and the Greeks (Jn.12:22).

4. Andrew was an approachable person. He was able to approach his brother Peter without difficulty, and the small boy with the loaves and fish felt comfortable enough with him to follow him to Jesus. The Greeks also felt comfortable enough to approach Andrew first in seeking an interview with Jesus.

---

4 (6:10-13) **Faith—Positive—Provision—Supply—Necessities**: there is a positive, unswerving faith. This is seen in Christ. Christ Himself demonstrated for His disciples the kind of strong faith they were to have in God.

1. Note Jesus' faith.
   a. Jesus took what He had and gave thanks to God for what He had. He had only a meager supply of bread. In fact, He could hold all He had in the palm of His hand. But note...
   - He did not stand there looking at the meagerness of what He had, questioning, being gripped with despair and hopelessness, wondering how the need was going to be met.
   - He looked up and gave thanks to God. The small supply and poor quality did not matter. What mattered was that He had something; there was some provision. A gift, a sacrifice, a resource—small though it was—had been given and laid at His feet for Him to use as He willed. So He took it, being ever so appreciative, and lifted it up to God, giving thanks to God and trusting God to meet the need of the hour. Note how positive and unswerving the act of Christ was. He knew beyond any question that God would meet the need and multiply the resources.
   b. Jesus gave what He had, and note: all He could do was distribute what was in His hands and trust God. This He did. He simply gave what He had and God did the rest.

Thought 1. All any man can do is give what he has, what he holds in his hands. But he can do that, and he is expected to do that. If a man so gives, God does the rest. The need will be met. (Note: the needs of the whole world can be met only if we will give what we hold.) Because many are holding and grasping after more and more, the world is reeling in the desperation of hunger and disease, war and death, sin and evil, doomed to live apart from God eternally.

For where your treasure is, there your heart will be also. (Mat 6:21)

Jesus answered, "If you want to be perfect, go, sell your possessions and give to the poor, and you will have treasure in heaven. Then come, follow me." (Mat 19:21)

And the second is like it: 'Love your neighbor as yourself.' (Mat 22:39)

John answered, "The man with two tunics should share with him who has none, and the one who has food should do the same." (Luke 3:11)

In everything I did, I showed you that by this kind of hard work we must help the weak, remembering the words the Lord Jesus himself said: 'It is more blessed to give than to receive.'" (Acts 20:35)

Share with God's people who are in need. Practice hospitality. (Rom 12:13)

Therefore, as we have opportunity, let us do good to all people, especially to those who belong to the family of believers. (Gal 6:10)

He who has been stealing must steal no longer, but must work, doing something useful with his own hands, that he may have something to share with those in need. (Eph 4:28)

Command them to do good, to be rich in good deeds, and to be generous and willing to share. (1 Tim 6:18)

And do not forget to do good and to share with others, for with such sacrifices God is pleased. (Heb 13:16)

   c. Jesus used others to help Him in meeting the need. Note that He gave to the disciples and the disciples gave to the people. His *disciples were essential* to the task. They were the ones made responsible for feeding the people.
   ⇒ Christ received the offering of the resources, meager as they were.
   ⇒ Christ trusted God to multiply the resources.
   ⇒ Christ then gave the supply to the disciples, not to consume but for the purpose of distributing. This is critical to note.
   ⇒ The disciples distributed the food and fed the people. They were a vital part of the Lord's plan.

2. Note that God met the need *because* of the positive, unswerving faith of Jesus. God met the people's need and filled them. In fact, and this is extremely important, He *more* than met their need. There was provision *left over*. How much? Twelve baskets full. Why twelve baskets?

There were twelve disciples, twelve servants who had so obediently and trustingly helped Christ. Each servant had a supply that would last him for days. God always provides abundantly for His true servants (Ph.4:19). Note: not a morsel was to be wasted. Every ounce of provision was to be used at some future date.

> **Thought 1.** While a man is giving what he has, he must trust the power and provision of God.
>
> > **But seek first his kingdom and his righteousness, and all these things will be given to you as well. (Mat 6:33)**
> > **For nothing is impossible with God." (Luke 1:37)**
> > **And my God will meet all your needs according to his glorious riches in Christ Jesus. (Phil 4:19)**
> > **Now faith is being sure of what we hope for and certain of what we do not see. (Heb 11:1)**
> > **And without faith it is impossible to please God, because anyone who comes to him must believe that he exists and that he rewards those who earnestly seek him. (Heb 11:6)**
> > **In the same way, faith by itself, if it is not accompanied by action, is dead. (James 2:17)**
> > **Wealth and honor come from you; you are the ruler of all things. In your hands are strength and power to exalt and give strength to all. (1 Chr 29:12)**
> > **"I know that you can do all things; no plan of yours can be thwarted. (Job 42:2)**
> > **Of David. A psalm. The earth is the Lord's, and everything in it, the world, and all who live in it; (Psa 24:1)**
> > **How great is your goodness, which you have stored up for those who fear you, which you bestow in the sight of men on those who take refuge in you. (Psa 31:19)**
> > **Commit your way to the LORD; trust in him and he will do this: (Psa 37:5)**
> > **Trust in the LORD with all your heart and lean not on your own understanding; (Prov 3:5)**
> > **Bring the whole tithe into the storehouse, that there may be food in my house. Test me in this," says the LORD Almighty, "and see if I will not throw open the floodgates of heaven and pour out so much blessing that you will not have room enough for it. (Mal 3:10)**

5 (6:14-15) **Messiah—Profession:** there is a materialistic profession of Jesus. The people professed Jesus to be the Messiah, but they were thinking of an earthly, materialistic king, a Messiah who could meet both their personal and community or national needs (see DEEPER STUDY # 2—Jn.1:20; note—1:23).

Jesus had fed and healed them. He had done what every man wanted, met their need for health and food. Therefore, hey wanted to set Him up as the King of their lives. They did not want to ever hunger or be sick again, not as long as they lived. They saw in Jesus the possibility of an earthly, human Messiah, One who could provide...

- food for their hunger
- healing for their sicknesses
- deliverance from their trials
- comfort for their sorrows
- plenty for their wants
- peace through their disturbances
- victory over their enemies

Jesus, of course, can help any person through anything. But the problem with the crowd was their desire for earthly and worldly satisfaction. They thought in terms of the physical and material, not the spiritual. Even when Christ meets physical and material needs, the physical and material are only temporary. They pass away. The Lord's concern is primarily spiritual—spiritual strength and spiritual blessings, the strength and blessings that last forever (see note—Eph.1:3). This is the reason most men forsake Christ. He demands the...

- denial of self

> **Then he said to them all: "If anyone would come after me, he must deny himself and take up his cross daily and follow me. (Luke 9:23)**

- separation from the world

> **Jesus answered, "I tell you the truth, you are looking for me, not because you saw miraculous signs but because you ate the loaves and had your fill. Do not work for food that spoils, but for food that endures to eternal life, which the Son of Man will give you. On him God the Father has placed his seal of approval." (John 6:26-27)**
> **Therefore, I urge you, brothers, in view of God's mercy, to offer your bodies as living sacrifices, holy and pleasing to God—this is your spiritual act of worship. Do not conform any longer to the pattern of this world, but be transformed by the renewing of your mind. Then you will be able to test and approve what God's will is—his good, pleasing and perfect will. (Rom 12:1-2)**
> **"Therefore come out from them and be separate, says the Lord. Touch no unclean thing, and I will receive you." "I will be a Father to you, and you will be my sons and daughters, says the Lord Almighty." (2 Cor 6:17-18)**
> **Do not love the world or anything in the world. If anyone loves the world, the love of the Father is not in him. For everything in the world—the cravings of sinful man, the lust of his eyes and the boasting of what he has and does—comes not from the Father but from the world. (1 John 2:15-16)**

	B. Jesus Walks on Water: The Deliverance From Fear, 6:16-21 (Mt.14:22-33; Mk.6: 45-52)	ing and the waters grew rough.		
		19 When they had rowed three or three and a half miles, they saw Jesus approaching the boat, walking on the water; and they were terrified.	d.	Being tired & gripped with a sense of horror, of impending death
1 The disciples set sail to cross the lake	16 When evening came, his disciples went down to the lake,			
2 The causes of fear a. Being in the dark b. Being without Jesus	17 Where they got into a boat and set off across the lake for Capernaum. By now it was dark, and Jesus had not yet joined them.	20 But he said to them, "It is I; don't be afraid." 21 Then they were willing to take him into the boat, and immediately the boat reached the shore where they were heading.	3	The answer to fear a. The presence & Word of Jesus: "I Am"DS1 b. Receiving the presence of Jesus c. The result: Deliverance thru the storms of life
c. Being caught in a storm	18 A strong wind was blow-			

DIVISION VII

THE REVELATION OF JESUS, THE BREAD OF LIFE, 6:1-71

B. Jesus Walks on Water: The Deliverance from Fear, 6:16-21

(6:16-21) **Introduction**: Jesus Christ is the great Deliverer from fear. He is definitely revealed as the great Deliverer in this experience.
1. The disciples set sail to cross the lake (v.16).
2. The causes of fear (v.17-19).
3. The answer to fear (v.20-21).

1 (6:16) **Temptation, Fleeing**: the disciples set sail to cross the sea. The crowd was about to take Jesus by force and make Him a king (see outline and note—Jn.6:14-15). There was danger in that the disciples might be swept up in the *excitement of the temptation*, so Jesus instructed them to set sail. They obeyed Jesus, did exactly what He said: they fled and escaped the temptation.

Note the words: "Jesus had not yet joined them." Apparently, Jesus had told them to row out some distance and then to turn and pick Him up at some other point on the shore. However, they were not to wait for Him beyond a certain time. He was going to send the crowd away and withdraw to pray (cp. Mk.6:45-46). The "strong," violent storm caught the disciples by surprise and, apparently, pulled them out into the lake (v.18).

2 (6:17-19) **Fear—Trials—Storms—Frailty, of Man**: the causes of fear. This experience of the disciples clearly illustrates the causes of fear.
1. Being in the dark will cause fear. It was now dark, so the disciples could not see. The threat and danger and the emotional strain of the storm was to be much more intense because of the dark.

> **Thought 1.** A person in spiritual darkness cannot see. His blindness is a strong threat and emotional strain upon him.
> 1) It is a strong threat in that he does not know what lies ahead (trouble, sorrow, difficulty, loss, death).
>
> **But if your eyes are bad, your whole body will be full of darkness. If then the light within you is darkness, how great is that darkness! (Mat 6:23)**
> **Leave them; they are blind guides. If a blind man leads a blind man, both will fall into a pit." (Mat 15:14)**

> **The god of this age has blinded the minds of unbelievers, so that they cannot see the light of the gospel of the glory of Christ, who is the image of God. (2 Cor 4:4)**
> **But whoever hates his brother is in the darkness and walks around in the darkness; he does not know where he is going, because the darkness has blinded him. (1 John 2:11)**

> 2) It is a strong danger in that he will definitely face some difficult times ahead. Being in darkness, he will be caught unprepared. He will be *in the dark* about God, about how to call upon Him and to receive strength and help from Him.
>
> **They are darkened in their understanding and separated from the life of God because of the ignorance that is in them due to the hardening of their hearts. (Eph 4:18)**
> **"They know nothing, they understand nothing. They walk about in darkness; all the foundations of the earth are shaken. (Psa 82:5)**
> **But the way of the wicked is like deep darkness; they do not know what makes them stumble. (Prov 4:19)**
> **I thought, "These are only the poor; they are foolish, for they do not know the way of the LORD, the requirements of their God. (Jer 5:4)**
> **But they do not know the thoughts of the LORD; they do not understand his plan, he who gathers them like sheaves to the threshing floor. (Micah 4:12)**

> 3) It is a strong emotional strain in that fear will swarm over his being, covering him with a sense of helplessness and hopelessness.
>
> **At midday you will grope about like a blind man in the dark. You will be unsuccessful in everything you do; day after day you will be oppressed and robbed, with no one to rescue you. (Deu 28:29)**

May their path be dark and slippery, with the angel of the LORD pursuing them. (Psa 35:6)

The way of peace they do not know; there is no justice in their paths. They have turned them into crooked roads; no one who walks in them will know peace. So justice is far from us, and righteousness does not reach us. We look for light, but all is darkness; for brightness, but we walk in deep shadows. (Isa 59:8-9)

"Therefore their path will become slippery; they will be banished to darkness and there they will fall. I will bring disaster on them in the year they are punished," declares the LORD. (Jer 23:12)

2. Being without Jesus will cause fear. Jesus had not yet joined the disciples; therefore, they did not have His presence and help. They were left alone to fend for themselves, having only the help of each other. The strength of each other's mind and arm had to save them or else they were lost; they were going to die. They had every reason to fear, for they were honest men, and each one knew down deep within his heart that their strength was limited and would eventually fail.

So I also will choose harsh treatment for them and will bring upon them what they dread. For when I called, no one answered, when I spoke, no one listened. They did evil in my sight and chose what displeases me." (Isa 66:4)

Remember that at that time you were separate from Christ, excluded from citizenship in Israel and foreigners to the covenants of the promise, without hope and without God in the world. (Eph 2:12)

3. Being caught in one of the strong, *violent storms of life* will cause fear. "A strong [gale like] wind" and a violent storm arose. Note: when they had launched out, it was calm and peaceful; they thought their journey would be successful, confronting no trouble whatsoever. They never expected a violent storm, but the winds and clouds *did come*. The terrible storm *did strike and threaten* their lives.

So it is with the "strong," violent storms of life. Trouble, trial, sickness, death, financial difficulties, and a host of other storms strike everyone. They strike unexpectedly, too often when we are least prepared. The result is great fear and the emotional upheaval of our lives.

4. Being tired and gripped with a sense of horror, of impending death, will cause fear. The disciples had been struggling against the storm for six to nine hours, and they had progressed only three or four miles.

And free those who all their lives were held in slavery by their fear of death. (Heb 2:15)

Therefore, just as sin entered the world through one man, and death through sin, and in this way death came to all men, because all sinned— (Rom 5:12)

Like water spilled on the ground, which cannot be recovered, so we must die. But God does not take away life; instead, he devises ways so that a banished person may not remain estranged from him. (2 Sam 14:14)

I know you will bring me down to death, to the place appointed for all the living. (Job 30:23)

For all can see that wise men die; the foolish and the senseless alike perish and leave their wealth to others. (Psa 49:10)

What man can live and not see death, or save himself from the power of the grave? Selah (Psa 89:48)

Man's fate is like that of the animals; the same fate awaits them both: As one dies, so dies the other. All have the same breath ; man has no advantage over the animal. Everything is meaningless. (Eccl 3:19)

For there is a proper time and procedure for every matter, though a man's misery weighs heavily upon him. Since no man knows the future, who can tell him what is to come? No man has power over the wind to contain it ; so no one has power over the day of his death. As no one is discharged in time of war, so wickedness will not release those who practice it. (Eccl 8:6-8)

In the evening, sudden terror! Before the morning, they are gone! This is the portion of those who loot us, the lot of those who plunder us. (Isa 17:14)

Note what happened (cp. Mk.6:47-49 for full explanation). The disciples saw Jesus "approaching the boat, walking on the water." They were stricken with a horrifying fear. Remember, they were physically exhausted and mentally drained from using all the seaman skills at their disposal. Their lives were at stake; they were struggling for survival. All of a sudden out of nowhere they saw a figure, an apparition (ghost) walking on the water. And it was not just one of them who saw it; all of them saw the figure. They were frightened, perhaps bordering on going into shock—perhaps thinking that the death angel or a premonition of their death was at hand.

The point is forceful: the storms of life can cause a sense of horror, of impending death, and can strike an awful fear in our hearts.

In fact, when we were with you, we kept telling you that we would be persecuted. And it turned out that way, as you well know. (1 Th 3:4)

We are hard pressed on every side, but not crushed; perplexed, but not in despair; persecuted, but not abandoned; struck down, but not destroyed. (2 Cor 4:8-9)

Yet man is born to trouble as surely as sparks fly upward. (Job 5:7)

"Man born of woman is of few days and full of trouble. (Job 14:1)

He feels but the pain of his own body and mourns only for himself." (Job 14:22)

The cords of death entangled me, the anguish of the grave came upon me; I was overcome by trouble and sorrow. (Psa 116:3)

We hoped for peace but no good has come, for a time of healing but there was only terror. (Jer 8:15)

Do not be far from me, for trouble is near and there is no one to help. (Psa 22:11)

Deep calls to deep in the roar of your waterfalls; all your waves and breakers have swept over me. (Psa 42:7)

The flood would have engulfed us, the torrent would have swept over us, (Psa 124:4)

The engulfing waters threatened me, the deep surrounded me; seaweed was wrapped around my head. (Jonah 2:5)

3 (6:20-21) **Fear—Receiving Jesus**: the answer to fear is Jesus Himself. Note three points.

1. The Word of Christ delivers from fear. He proclaimed, "It is I; don't be afraid" (see DEEPER STUDY # 1, "It is I"—Jn.6:20).

Then Jesus came to them and said, "All authority in heaven and on earth has been given to me. (Mat 28:18)

"I have told you these things, so that in me you may have peace. In this world you will have trouble. But take heart! I have overcome the world." (John 16:33)

'Call to me and I will answer you and tell you great and unsearchable things you do not know.' (Jer 33:3)

2. Receiving the presence of Christ delivers from fear. This is critical to note, for having Christ present and hearing His Word s"don't be afraid" are not enough. A person must "be willing to take" Christ into his life. Deliverance came to the disciples only after they had taken Jesus into the ship.

Here I am! I stand at the door and knock. If anyone hears my voice and opens the door, I will come in and eat with him, and he with me. (Rev 3:20)

Yet to all who received him, to those who believed in his name, he gave the right to become children of God— (John 1:12)

Peace I leave with you; my peace I give you. I do not give to you as the world gives. Do not let your hearts be troubled and do not be afraid. (John 14:27)

Strengthening the disciples and encouraging them to remain true to the faith. "We must go through many hardships to enter the kingdom of God," they said. (Acts 14:22)

So do not fear, for I am with you; do not be dismayed, for I am your God. I will strengthen you and help you; I will uphold you with my righteous right hand. (Isa 41:10)

Even to your old age and gray hairs I am he, I am he who will sustain you. I have made you and I will carry you; I will sustain you and I will rescue you. (Isa 46:4)

3. The results of receiving Christ were twofold: deliverance from fear and the calming of the storm. Jesus Christ gives the strength to row through all the storms of life. He has the power to erase fear and calm any storm.

Therefore we do not lose heart. Though outwardly we are wasting away, yet inwardly we are being renewed day by day. For our light and momentary troubles are achieving for us an eternal glory that far outweighs them all. So we fix our eyes not on what is seen, but on what is unseen. For what is seen is temporary, but what is unseen is eternal. (2 Cor 4:16-18)

And free those who all their lives were held in slavery by their fear of death. (Heb 2:15)

But Christ is faithful as a son over God's house. And we are his house, if we hold on to our courage and the hope of which we boast. (Heb 3:6)

If this is so, then the Lord knows how to rescue godly men from trials and to hold the unrighteous for the day of judgment, while continuing their punishment. (2 Pet 2:9)

Surely he will save you from the fowler's snare and from the deadly pestilence. (Psa 91:3)

For you, O LORD, have delivered my soul from death, my eyes from tears, my feet from stumbling, (Psa 116:8)

He saw that there was no one, he was appalled that there was no one to intervene; so his own arm worked salvation for him, and his own righteousness sustained him. (Isa 59:16; cp.Is63:5)

DEEPER STUDY # 1

(6:20) **"It is I"** (eimi): this is one word in the Greek, *eimi*, which is simply "I AM" (Jn.18:6). Jesus was saying, "I AM" has come—fear not. He was reminding the disciples who He was, the Son of God Himself. He possessed all power; therefore, there was no need to fear. This was the same message that God gave to Moses at the burning bush, "I AM WHO I AM" (Ex.3:13-15, esp. 14). It was the same message that Jesus used as a defense against the religionists, "Before Abraham was born, I am" (Jn.8:58). It is the same message that Col.1:15-17 claims for Him; and it is the same message that is proclaimed by the book of Revelation, He"who is and was and is to come" (Rev.1:4, 8; 11:17; 16:5). (See note—Jn.1:1-2.)

There are several "I Am's" claimed by Christ.
⇒ I Am the Messiah (Jn.4:26).
⇒ I Am (It is I); don't afraid (Jn.6:20).
⇒ I Am the Bread of Life (Jn.6:35).
⇒ I Am from Above (Jn.8:23).
⇒ I Am the Light of the World (Jn.8:12; 9:5; 12:46).
⇒ I Am before Abraham was born, I am (eternal) (Jn.8:58).
⇒ I Am the Door (Jn.10:7).
⇒ I Am the Good Shepherd (Jn.10:14).
⇒ I Am the God's Son (Jn.10:36).
⇒ I Am the Resurrection and Life (Jn.11:25).
⇒ I Am the Lord and Teacher (Jn.13:13).
⇒ I Am the Way, the Truth, and the Life (Jn.14:6).
⇒ I Am the True Vine (Jn.15:1).
⇒ I Am the Alpha and the Omega (Rev.1:8).
⇒ I Am the First and the Last (Rev.1:17).

	C. The Answer to Man's Great Hunger, 6:22-29	25 When they found him on the other side of the lake, they asked him, "Rabbi, when did you get here?"	e. The people questioned Jesus' absence
1 Answer 1: Know that man has a great hunger, a great need a. The people were miraculously fed, v.1-15 b. The people acknowledged their need c. The people noted Jesus' absence d. The people sought Jesus	22 The next day the crowd that had stayed on the opposite shore of the lake realized that only one boat had been there, and that Jesus had not entered it with his disciples, but that they had gone away alone. 23 Then some boats from Tiberias landed near the place where the people had eaten the bread after the Lord had given thanks. 24 Once the crowd realized that neither Jesus nor his disciples were there, they got into the boats and went to Capernaum in search of Jesus.	26 Jesus answered, "I tell you the truth, you are looking for me, not because you saw miraculous signs but because you ate the loaves and had your fill. 27 Do not work for food that spoils, but for food that endures to eternal life, which the Son of Man will give you. On him God the Father has placed his seal of approval." 28 Then they asked him, "What must we do to do the works God requires?" 29 Jesus answered, "The work of God is this: to believe in the one he has sent."	**2 Answer 2: Acknowledge that man's motive is corrupt** a. Sought the Messiah for what they could get out of Him b. Sought food that spoiled—misplaced labor **3 Answer 3: Work for food that endures—that gives eternal life** a. Source: Son of Man*DS1* b. God guaranteed*DS2* **4 Answer 4: Do the work of God—believe**

DIVISION VII

THE REVELATION OF JESUS, THE BREAD OF LIFE, 6:1-71

C. The Answer to Man's Great Hunger, 6:22-29

(6:22-29) **Introduction**: man has a gnawing hunger within for both the physical and the spiritual. He hungers for both food and material things and for God and spiritual things, things such as love and joy and peace. Therefore, most of man's time and energy are spent in seeking to satisfy his hunger. This passage deals with the answer to man's great hunger.

1. Answer 1: know that man has a great hunger, a great need (v.22-25).
2. Answer 2: acknowledge that man's motive is corrupt (v.26-27).
3. Answer 3: work for food that endures—that gives eternal life (v.27).
4. Answer 4: do the work of God—believe (v.28-29).

1 (6:22-25) **Hunger, Spiritual—Seeking Jesus**: the first answer to man's great hunger is to *recognize* the hunger. The people had been miraculously fed. It was a common belief that the Messiah would give manna from heaven even as Moses had done; in fact, it was thought that the Messiah would give more than Moses had given. The people were convinced that Jesus was the Messiah, so they wanted to lay hold of Him and make Him king (v.1-15). Note four things.

1. The people acknowledged their need for the Messiah. They had need and they knew it. Confessing their need was not a problem for them (see DEEPER STUDY # 2, Messiah—Jn.1:20).

2. The people noted Jesus' absence. There had been only one boat docked at shore, and the disciples had taken it to cross the lake. However, Jesus had not accompanied them; He had stayed behind. The people thought He was over in another section of the crowd or else off somewhere by Himself. The fact that He was not close by did not dawn upon them until the next day. The point is filled with lessons: the people, knowing they had need, wanted their need met. Jesus had proclaimed that He could meet their

need, but He was gone; therefore, their need was going to go unmet unless they could find Him.

> **Thought 1.** Man does have a great need for God's Messiah.
> 1) Man must acknowledge his need.
> 2) Man must observe to see if Christ is present. If Christ is absent, then man's need goes wanting.

3. The people sought Jesus. Believing that Jesus was the answer to their need, they did what they should have done: they sought Him. Other boats had drawn up to shore during the night, probably seeking refuge from the storm. Therefore, the people immediately took passage on these boats to cross over to Capernaum, hoping to find Jesus. Note how diligent they were in seeking Him.

> **Thought 1.** Man should search diligently to find Christ. He should seek and seek until the Lord is found.
>
> **"So I say to you: Ask and it will be given to you; seek and you will find; knock and the door will be opened to you. For everyone who asks receives; he who seeks finds; and to him who knocks, the door will be opened. (Luke 11:9-10)**
> **And without faith it is impossible to please God, because anyone who comes to him must believe that he exists and that he rewards those who earnestly seek him. (Heb 11:6)**
> **Seek the LORD while he may be found; call on him while he is near. (Isa 55:6)**

4. The people questioned Jesus' absence. In their minds the Messiah was to give manna from heaven to meet the needs of the people just as Moses had done, only more so.

They could not understand why Jesus would leave them, especially if He were the true Messiah.

Thought 1. This point is crucial, for men of every generation do wonder and question the fact: If Jesus is really the Messiah, why does He so often seem absent and far away, especially in times of trouble? Another way to word the same thought is: If there is a God and if Christ really is the Son of God, why is the world in so much trouble and why are so many people suffering? Why would Christ not place Himself right in the midst of the world and its problems? Why would He not go ahead and solve the problems, meeting man's needs immediately? The answer, of course, is what this passage is all about.

2 (6:26-27) **Motive—Messiah—Seeking Jesus—Utopia**: the answer to man's great hunger is acknowledging that man's motive is corrupt. This point is critical to see. Jesus stressed it with a solemn *attention getter*, "I tell you the truth" (listen). Man's motive in seeking the Messiah—in seeking the answer to his problems—is often corrupt. In the case of these people it was, and tragically, it is with so many in every generation.

1. Man seeks a Messiah (Savior), but not to worship and serve Him. He seeks a Messiah for what he can get out of Him.

   a. *Man is interested* in getting his needs met, whether by someone human or divine. Man is interested in himself, not in acknowledging and honoring Jesus to be Lord and not in serving Him and making Him known to a lost world. The thoughts of the crowd were focused on how wonderful it was to be *saved from hunger* and to have their *needs met*. Here was a Savior (Messiah) who could meet all their needs, who could satisfy and give them a complete and full life. He could provide all things for them and deliver them from all their enslavements and enemies. He could bring utopia (the Kingdom of God) to earth. Every need could be filled and satisfied. Note that man's thoughts are focused...
      * on the earth
      * on material things and personal possessions
      * on the flesh (sinful nature) and its satisfaction
      * on the human and the carnal only

   b. *Man should be interested* in the Messiah for who He is and not for what he can get out of Him. Very simply, as with any person, the Lord wants to be sought and loved for who He is and not for what He can do for a person. The Lord (Messiah) is not a tool to be used; He is a Person to be sought and loved. The crowd should have seen that such a miracle could have been done *only by the Son of God* Himself. Therefore, seeing and standing before the Son of God, they should have fallen down before Him in all humility. They should have humbled themselves...
      * to recognize and acknowledge Him to be the Son of God.
      * to worship and praise Him for who He is.
      * to offer their lives to Him, all they were and had.
      * to see that all things belonged to Him and were due Him.

* to see that He was not the One who should be giving to them, but they were the ones who should be giving to Him. He was the One who should be receiving, not them.

2. Man seeks food that spoils. He simply misplaces his work. He centers and focuses his thoughts, energies, and efforts upon the moment, that is, upon his years on earth. Man seeks to *feed his soul* on...
   * feelings and pleasures
   * comfort and ease
   * plenty and more
   * recognition and honor
   * position and power
   * fame and self

Such self-seeking is foolish, for all things pass away, even man himself. A day is not guaranteed, much less a year. Even if a man has years left to live, they pass ever so rapidly, as any middle age or older adult knows. Man desperately needs to heed two eternal truths.

   a. The things of the earth with all their pleasures and feelings do not satisfy (Is.55:2). They still leave a man empty, incomplete, unfulfilled, hungry, dissatisfied, seeking more and more.

   You want something but don't get it. You kill and covet, but you cannot have what you want. You quarrel and fight. You do not have, because you do not ask God. When you ask, you do not receive, because you ask with wrong motives, that you may spend what you get on your pleasures. You adulterous people, don't you know that friendship with the world is hatred toward God? Anyone who chooses to be a friend of the world becomes an enemy of God. (James 4:2-4)

   "They will say, 'The fruit you longed for is gone from you. All your riches and splendor have vanished, never to be recovered.' (Rev 18:14)

   "Food for the stomach and the stomach for food"—but God will destroy them both. The body is not meant for sexual immorality, but for the Lord, and the Lord for the body. (1 Cor 6:13)

   He wanders about—food for vultures ; he knows the day of darkness is at hand. (Job 15:23)

   All man's efforts are for his mouth, yet his appetite is never satisfied. (Eccl 6:7)

   As when a hungry man dreams that he is eating, but he awakens, and his hunger remains; as when a thirsty man dreams that he is drinking, but he awakens faint, with his thirst unquenched. So will it be with the hordes of all the nations that fight against Mount Zion. (Isa 29:8)

   He feeds on ashes, a deluded heart misleads him; he cannot save himself, or say, "Is not this thing in my right hand a lie?" (Isa 44:20)

   Why spend money on what is not bread, and your labor on what does not satisfy? Listen, listen to me, and eat what is good, and your soul will delight in the richest of fare. (Isa 55:2)

   b. The earth and its things with all their pleasures and feelings pass away. They age, deteriorate, die, and decay. (See notes—Mt.8:17; 1 Cor.15:50; Col. 2:13; 2 Pt.1:4; Heb.9:27.)

Those who live according to the sinful nature have their minds set on what that nature desires; but those who live in accordance with the Spirit have their minds set on what the Spirit desires. The mind of sinful man is death, but the mind controlled by the Spirit is life and peace; (Rom 8:5-6)
I declare to you, brothers, that flesh and blood cannot inherit the kingdom of God, nor does the perishable inherit the imperishable. (1 Cor 15:50)
For everything in the world—the cravings of sinful man, the lust of his eyes and the boasting of what he has and does—comes not from the Father but from the world. The world and its desires pass away, but the man who does the will of God lives forever. (1 John 2:16-17)

3

(6:27) **Seeking Jesus—Jesus Christ, Son of Man—Provision**: the third answer to man's great hunger is to work for food that endures, that gives or lasts "to eternal life" (eis zoen aionion). The basic hunger within man is for...

- an abundant life, a life that is complete and fulfilled, full of love, joy, peace and all the good things of life (see DEEPER STUDY # 1—Jn.10:10).
- an eternal life, a life that survives, that is not snatched away, but goes on forever and ever. (See DEEPER STUDY # 1—Jn.17:2-3.)

1. Jesus said that the Son of Man is the One who can give food that lasts forever, the One who can give life that is both abundant and eternal. (See note, Son of Man—Jn.1:51.)
2. Jesus said that the Son of Man is sealed, that is, guaranteed by God (see DEEPER STUDY # 2—Jn.3:33). God guarantees...

- that Christ is the Messiah
- that Christ is the One who can give food that is abundant and lasts forever

But whoever drinks the water I give him will never thirst. Indeed, the water I give him will become in him a spring of water welling up to eternal life." (John 4:14 cp. Jn.7:37)
For the bread of God is he who comes down from heaven and gives life to the world." "Sir," they said, "from now on give us this bread." Then Jesus declared, "I am the bread of life. He who comes to me will never go hungry, and he who believes in me will never be thirsty. (John 6:33-35)

4

(6:28-29) **Works vs. Grace**: the fourth answer to man's great hunger is to do *the work* of God—believe. Note two crucial facts.

1. The people thought in terms of works (plural). They thought that by *doing good works* they could win the approval and acceptance of God. If they did enough good and lived a life that was moral and just, God would save them and give them the food that satisfied, the food and life that was both abundant and eternal.

Thought 1. There are those who see people in three categories.
1) There are *good people*, people who do plenty of good works. They live good, moral, and just lives; therefore, they are acceptable to God.
2) There are *bad people*, people who do mostly bad works. They live immoral and unjust lives; therefore, they are not acceptable to God. They are not saved.
3) There are *compromising people*, people who do both good and bad. They live both moral and immoral, just and unjust lives. They are close to securing God's approval, not quite, but close. By doing just a few more *good works* and living just a little more morally, God will accept them.

2. Jesus corrected the people's thoughts, their concept of salvation by works. They did not secure the favor of God and were not acceptable to God because of works (plural). They received God's favor and acceptance because of a work, one work (singular). The work of God is only one: believe—"in the One he has sent" (see DEEPER STUDY # 2—Jn.2:24).

Now while he was in Jerusalem at the Passover Feast, many people saw the miraculous signs he was doing and believed in his name. (John 2:23)
Know that a man is not justified by observing the law, but by faith in Jesus Christ. So we, too, have put our faith in Christ Jesus that we may be justified by faith in Christ and not by observing the law, because by observing the law no one will be justified. (Gal 2:16)
For it is by grace you have been saved, through faith—and this not from yourselves, it is the gift of God—not by works, so that no one can boast. (Eph 2:8-9)

	D. The Bread of Life: The Source of Spiritual Satisfaction, 6:30-36	Father who gives you the true bread from heaven.	true bread: true satisfaction
1 The people demanded proof a. Jesus' great claim, v.27-29 b. The specific proof demanded **2 Christ is the true bread** a. Man cannot provide true bread: satisfaction b. God alone provides	30 So they asked him, "What miraculous sign then will you give that we may see it and believe you? What will you do? 31 Our forefathers ate the manna in the desert; as it is written: 'He gave them bread from heaven to eat.'" 32 Jesus said to them,"I tell you the truth, it is not Moses who has given you the bread from heaven, but it is my	33 For the bread of God is he who comes down from heaven and gives life to the world." 34 "Sir," they said, "from now on give us this bread." 35 Then Jesus declared, "I am the bread of life. He who comes to me will never go hungry, and he who believes in me will never be thirsty. 36 But as I told you, you have seen me and still you do not believe.	**3 Christ is the Bread of God** a. He came from heaven b. He gives life **4 Christ is the Bread of Life**^DSI^ a. The request for the Bread of God b. The phenomenal claim c. If man comes to Jesus, he will never hunger b. If man believes, he will never thirst **5 Christ was seen, but rejected**

DIVISION VII

THE REVELATION OF JESUS, THE BREAD OF LIFE, 6:1-71

D. The Bread of Life: The Source of Spiritual Satisfaction, 6:30-36

(6:30-36) **Introduction—Jesus Christ, Bread of Life—Satisfaction**: Jesus Christ is the Source of spiritual satisfaction, of man's spiritual nourishment. He is the only Bread that can feed man's great hunger, the hunger that gnaws and gnaws within his inner being. There is no other source upon which man can feed and be nourished.
 1. The people demanded proof (v.30-31).
 2. Christ is the true bread (v.32).
 3. Christ is the Bread of God (v.33).
 4. Christ is the Bread of Life (v.34-35).
 5. Christ was seen, but rejected (v.36).

1 (6:30-31) **Jesus Christ, Claims**: the people demanded proof. Jesus had just made some phenomenal claims. He claimed to be...
 • the Son of Man (v.27).
 • the One who feeds man, who gives man bread which issues forth eternal life (v.27).
 • the One whom God had sealed (v.27).
 • the One whom God had sent into the world (v.29).
 • the One upon whom men were to believe (v.29).

The people demanded proof. Note two revealing things about the nature of man.
 1. Man focuses upon the physical and material. (See notes—Jn.6:26-27.) He ignores all the signs, even the miracles of God which surround him. Christ had just miraculously fed the crowd, yet the crowd ignored the witness of that particular sign (Jn.6:1f). It was not enough. They were so attached to the earth, to its physical pleasures and material goods, that they wanted more and more. To them...
 • Moses had fed Israel for forty years in the wilderness. Christ had fed them only once.
 • Moses had fed Israel with manna falling out of the sky from heaven. Christ had merely multiplied bread from a few loaves in His hands.
 2. Man demands that he first see, *then he will believe.* This is contrary to *true* faith. It is not the way faith works. A man must first believe God, then he sees. (See DEEPER STUDY # 1—Heb.11:6.) However, note this fact: faith is not fate; it is a matter of the heart, a matter of how the heart must relate to others. God relates with us just as we relate to others. If a person does not believe in us, they do not see; that is, they may ask all they want, but it is unlikely that we will do what they ask. But if they believe and trust us, we usually do whatever they ask, and they see their desires and requests fulfilled by our hands. Repeating the above, a man must first believe God, then he sees. Faith must precede sight. Believe God and He will fulfill the desires of your heart (Ps.37:4-5)

The people's complaint was twofold.
 1. Christ had not fed them enough—not enough to prove that He was who He claimed to be.
 2. Christ had not fed them in the right way, not given "them bread from heaven to eat."

> **Thought 1.** Man never has enough. He craves and craves, never being fully satisfied. He experiences a gnawing hunger, a restlessness, emptiness, loneliness, vacuum, and a lack of purpose, meaning, and significance. Even in dealing with God, he never has enough evidence or proof to believe—not within his human nature.
> Note another fact: man always wants to tell God how to act and deal with him and his life. Man wants his needs met in certain ways. It is not enough for God to meet his needs; man wants his needs met as he wills and desires. He tries to dictate how God is to act and behave toward him. So much human religion is nothing more than this, nothing more than man trying to spell out how God is to act and behave toward him.

2 (6:32) **Jesus Christ, Bread of Life—Satisfaction—Hunger**: Christ is the true bread. Note two strong points.
 1. Man cannot provide true bread, that is, true satisfaction. Only God can. Moses was not the one who gave Israel the manna from heaven; God was the One who gave the manna. A man has to do something if he wishes...
 • to have his hunger met
 • to be truly filled
 • to be completely satisfied
 • to be content
 • to be comfortable
 • to be at peace

A man must look both beyond other men and beyond the things of this world. Men and things cannot meet the gnawing hunger of man; they cannot provide true satisfaction, for they do not possess the *true* bread.

2. God alone provides true bread, that is, provides true satisfaction. Note three things.

 a. Christ called God "My Father" (see note—Jn.1:34; 10:30-33).
 b. The bread God gives is "true" bread (see DEEPER STUDY # 1, True—Jn.1:9).
 c. The "bread" or "manna" of God is not physical and material bread: it is spiritual. God may provide and actually does promise to provide for the physical necessities of *His followers* (Mt.6:24-33), but physical and material bread is not what Christ was talking about in this passage. Physical and material bread lasts only for a short while. Once consumed, it is gone. Its satisfaction passes and man's gnawing hunger arises again. But the bread God gives is spiritual bread, that is, spiritual food for the soul (see note—Eph.1:3). It is the bread that man really needs more than anything else on earth. It is the only bread that can feed and meet the need of man's...

 • gnawing hunger
 • restlessness
 • emptiness
 • vacuum
 • loneliness
 • lack of purpose, meaning, and significance

But here is the bread that comes down from heaven, which a man may eat and not die. I am the living bread that came down from heaven. If anyone eats of this bread, he will live forever. This bread is my flesh, which I will give for the life of the world." (John 6:50-51)

Jesus said to them, "I tell you the truth, unless you eat the flesh of the Son of Man and drink his blood, you have no life in you. Whoever eats my flesh and drinks my blood has eternal life, and I will raise him up at the last day. (John 6:53-54)

Just as the living Father sent me and I live because of the Father, so the one who feeds on me will live because of me. This is the bread that came down from heaven.

Your forefathers ate manna and died, but he who feeds on this bread will live forever." (John 6:57-58)

3 (6:33) **Jesus Christ, Origin:** Christ is the Bread of God. Christ made at least two points.

1. The origin of the true Bread is God Himself. It is bread which came down from or "out of" (ek) heaven itself. This means several things.

 a. The bread of God is not bread which comes out of the clouds above earth. Rather, it is bread which comes "out of" (ek) heaven itself, out of the spiritual dimension of being, from the very presence of God Himself. It is bread which comes from the very household of God.
 b. The bread of God is not physical bread. It is of the nature of God Himself, spiritual and eternal bread (cp. v.50-51).
 c. The bread of God is possessed by God; therefore, only He can give it, and man cannot have the Bread of God unless God gives it to man.

 d. The Bread of God was a person. Note the personal pronoun "He" and the word "bread" (ho artos) which is masculine. Note that "He," the Bread of God who feeds and nourishes man, came down or "out of" heaven. He was not born of the earth. He came from the very presence of God Himself.

"The one who comes from above is above all; the one who is from the earth belongs to the earth, and speaks as one from the earth. The one who comes from heaven is above all. (John 3:31)

For I have come down from heaven not to do my will but to do the will of him who sent me. (John 6:38)

But he continued, "You are from below; I am from above. You are of this world; I am not of this world. (John 8:23)

Jesus said to them, "If God were your Father, you would love me, for I came from God and now am here. I have not come on my own; but he sent me. (John 8:42)

Now we can see that you know all things and that you do not even need to have anyone ask you questions. This makes us believe that you came from God." (John 16:30)

The first man was of the dust of the earth, the second man from heaven. (1 Cor 15:47)

2. The Bread of God gives *life* to the world. The purpose of bread is to give life. (See DEEPER STUDY # 2—Jn.1:4; DEEPER STUDY # 1—10:10; DEEPER STUDY # 1—17:2-3.)

 a. Bread gives life by...
 • nourishing and sustaining
 • satisfying
 • energizing
 • creating desire (the need) for more (See note—Lk.4:3-4. Cp. Neh.9:15.)
 • being partaken on a regular basis

Thought 1. Christ (and the Word of God) gives life to the believer by doing the same five things as bread.

In him was life, and that life was the light of men. (John 1:4)

The thief comes only to steal and kill and destroy; I have come that they may have life, and have it to the full. (John 10:10)

For you granted him authority over all people that he might give eternal life to all those you have given him. Now this is eternal life: that they may know you, the only true God, and Jesus Christ, whom you have sent. (John 17:2-3)

 b. The Bread of God came from heaven to give life to the *whole* world. It was not just to one person or to one nation that He came. He came to the whole world (cp. 1 Jn.2:1-2). He came to sacrifice Himself, to feed and save a starving world.

 Note that His coming as the sacrificial Bread of God had been foreshadowed by the sacrifices of the Old Testament. They are said to be the Bread of God or "food of his God" (Lev.21:21-22. Cp. Jn.6:50-51.)

123

On the last and greatest day of the Feast, Jesus stood and said in a loud voice, "If anyone is thirsty, let him come to me and drink. (John 7:37)

For there is no difference between Jew and Gentile—the same Lord is Lord of all and richly blesses all who call on him, (Rom 10:12)

Who wants all men to be saved and to come to a knowledge of the truth. For there is one God and one mediator between God and men, the man Christ Jesus, who gave himself as a ransom for all men—the testimony given in its proper time. (1 Tim 2:4-6)

"Come, all you who are thirsty, come to the waters; and you who have no money, come, buy and eat! Come, buy wine and milk without money and without cost. (Isa 55:1)

4 (6:34-35) **Jesus Christ, Bread of Life:** Christ is the Bread of Life. There are four significant points here.

1. The people requested the Bread of God. The people called Jesus "Lord" (Kurios), but how much they understood of His deity is not known. Apparently it was just an address of respect. However, the point is clear in the Bible. When a person asks for the Bread of God, he must call Jesus "Lord" and be ready to submit to Him as Lord, serving Jesus day by day (cp. Lk.9:23; Ro.10:13).

Note that the people requested: "from now on give us this bread" (pantote dos herim ton arton touton). This was a *once-for-all* request (the Greek aorist tense). The people wanted this Bread of God once-for-all, so that they might have a *permanent provision*. The Bible is again clear on this point. Salvation, that is, partaking of the Bread of Life, is to be a permanent experience. It is to be a once-for-all experience.

2. The phenomenal claim of Jesus: "I am the Bread of life" (see DEEPER STUDY # 1, "I Am"—Jn.6:20. Also see DEEPER STUDY # 2—Jn.1:4; DEEPER STUDY # 1—10:10; DEEPER STUDY # 1—17:2-3.) Jesus Christ made the phenomenal claim: He was...

- the true Bread
- the Bread of God
- the Bread of Life

3. If a man comes to Christ, the Bread of Life, he will never hunger. Man has a starving, craving need for life. Man craves a life that...

- is full and satisfying.
- is nourishing and sustaining.
- is energizing and has its desires fulfilled.

If a man comes to Christ, He will never hunger. The gnawing of starvation, the craving for life will be fully satisfied.

4. If a man believes, he will never thirst. The picture (symbolism) is switched from hunger to thirst. Man's need is more than met; not only is his hunger satisfied, but his thirst is quenched. Every need of life, of nourishment, and of growth is met. Nothing is left out or lacking. When a person comes to Christ and believes (continuous action, meaning continuing to believe), every need of his life and growth is met. Of course, this does not mean he will never hunger after righteousness. He will, but his hunger and thirst will never go unsatisfied. He "will be filled" (cp.

Mt.5:6). Note the word "never." It is a strong, emphatic word: "[He] will never be thirsty."

Note how a person is *saved* from hungering and thirsting after life. One is saved...

- by "coming to Christ" (v.35, 37, 44-45, 65).
- by "believing in Christ" (see DEEPER STUDY # 2—Jn.2:24).

Blessed are those who hunger and thirst for righteousness, for they will be filled. (Mat 5:6)

But whoever drinks the water I give him will never thirst. Indeed, the water I give him will become in him a spring of water welling up to eternal life." (John 4:14)

Then Jesus declared, "I am the bread of life. He who comes to me will never go hungry, and he who believes in me will never be thirsty. (John 6:35)

I tell you the truth, he who believes has everlasting life. I am the bread of life. (John 6:47-48)

On the last and greatest day of the Feast, Jesus stood and said in a loud voice, "If anyone is thirsty, let him come to me and drink. (John 7:37)

The Spirit and the bride say, "Come!" And let him who hears say, "Come!" Whoever is thirsty, let him come; and whoever wishes, let him take the free gift of the water of life. (Rev 22:17)

DEEPER STUDY # 1

(6:34-35) **Jesus—the Living Bread:** bread does at least four things. It nourishes or sustains life; it satisfies; it energizes; and it creates a desire (the need) for more and more. (See note—Lk.4:3-4. Cp. Neh.9:15.)

5 (6:36) **Jesus Christ, Rejected:** Christ was seen, but rejected. The point is that the people were without excuse. They had every opportunity in the world.

⇒ The Bread of God had "come down from heaven."
⇒ The Bread of God had come to give life to the world.
⇒ The Bread of God had been seen (cp. 1 Jn.1:1-3).
⇒ The Bread of God was being seen and proclaimed that very moment.

Any of the people could have easily come to Christ, yet sitting there and hearing the glorious news, they still did not believe.

He came to that which was his own, but his own did not receive him. (John 1:11)

Whoever believes in the Son has eternal life, but whoever rejects the Son will not see life, for God's wrath remains on him." (John 3:36)

I told you that you would die in your sins; if you do not believe that I am the one I claim to be, you will indeed die in your sins." (John 8:24)

There is a judge for the one who rejects me and does not accept my words; that very word which I spoke will condemn him at the last day. (John 12:48)

	E. The Assurance of the Believer, 6:37-40	39 And this is the will of him who sent me, that I shall lose none of all that he has given me, but raise them up at the last day.	4	Assurance 4: God's will for those whom He gives to Christ a. That Jesus should not lose a single one b. That Jesus should resurrect every one
1 Assurance 1: God's predestination 2 Assurance 2: Jesus' Word	37 All that the Father gives me will come to me, and whoever comes to me I will never drive away.	40 For my Father's will is that everyone who looks to the Son and believes in him shall have eternal life, and I will raise him up at the last day."	5	Assurance 5: God's will for the believer a. Is eternal life b. Result: Jesus "will raise him up"
3 Assurance 3: Jesus' purpose—to do God's will	38 For I have come down from heaven not to do my will but to do the will of him who sent me.			

DIVISION VII

THE REVELATION OF JESUS, THE BREAD OF LIFE, 6:1-71

E. The Assurance of the Believer, 6:37-40

(6:37-40) **Introduction**: the believer has great assurance and security.

1. Assurance 1: God's predestination (v.37).
2. Assurance 2: Jesus' Word (v.37).
3. Assurance 3: Jesus' purpose—to do God's will (v.38).
4. Assurance 4: God's will for *those whom He gives* to Christ (v.39).
5. Assurance 5: God's will for *the believer* (v.40).

1 (6:37) **Assurance—Predestination**: the first assurance for the believer is God's predestination. The meaning of the verse is clear. It is those whom "the Father gives" that come to Christ. However, note a critical fact. The stress is not predestination; it is assurance to the believer. Christ wants believers to take heart and to be assured of their salvation. It is God Himself who has drawn believers, who has moved upon and stirred them to *come to Christ*. (See note, Draw—Jn.6:44-46 for explanation and more discussion.) Something should be noted at this point. There is a predestination thread that runs throughout John's gospel. Things are controlled and happen as God means them to happen. The purpose of God is being done. He is God; therefore, He rules and controls all things (cp. Jn.1:12-13; 6:37; 6:44-46; 10:26; 16:8).

> My sheep listen to my voice; I know them, and they follow me. I give them eternal life, and they shall never perish; no one can snatch them out of my hand. My Father, who has given them to me, is greater than all ; no one can snatch them out of my Father's hand. (John 10:27-29)
> And we know that in all things God works for the good of those who love him, who have been called according to his purpose. For those God foreknew he also predestined to be conformed to the likeness of his Son, that he might be the firstborn among many brothers. And those he predestined, he also called; those he called, he also justified; those he justified, he also glorified. (Rom 8:28-30)
> Praise be to the God and Father of our Lord Jesus Christ! In his great mercy he has given us new birth into a living hope through the resurrection of Jesus Christ from the dead, and into an inheritance that can never perish, spoil or fade—kept in

heaven for you, who through faith are shielded by God's power until the coming of the salvation that is ready to be revealed in the last time. (1 Pet 1:3-5)

2 (6:37) **Assurance—Security**: the second assurance for the believer is Jesus' Word. Note the enormous security given to the believer.

1. Jesus clearly said that any man who comes to Him will never "be driven away". This is a double negative, a strong, forceful promise: "Never, no never be driven away."

2. Jesus was claiming the authority to accept and reject men (cp. Mt.8:12; 22:13). He accepts the person who comes to Him, the person who turns from the world and the flesh (sinful nature) to Him.

The point is simply this. Jesus gives His Word: "Whoever comes to me I will never, no never drive away." The believer's assurance and security are as good as Jesus' Word. If Jesus is who He claimed to be, "the Bread of Life," then the person who comes to Him for spiritual nourishment can rest assured that...

- Jesus will receive him into God's household.
- Jesus will feed, nourish, satisfy, and fill him.
- Jesus will not cast him away.
- Jesus will keep His Word with every generation of people.

> I tell you the truth, until heaven and earth disappear, not the smallest letter, not the least stroke of a pen, will by any means disappear from the Law until everything is accomplished. (Mat 5:18)
> Heaven and earth will pass away, but my words will never pass away. (Luke 21:33)
> The works of his hands are faithful and just; all his precepts are trustworthy. (Psa 111:7)
> But I the LORD will speak what I will, and it shall be fulfilled without delay. For in your days, you rebellious house, I will fulfill whatever I say, declares the Sovereign LORD.'" (Ezek 12:25)

3 (6:38) **Assurance—God, Will of**: the third assurance for the believer is Jesus' purpose. He came to do God's will. Note two points.

1. Jesus declared His origin: He came down out of heaven (see DEEPER STUDY # 1—Jn.3:31).

2. Jesus came *not* to do His own will, but the will of God.

    a. Jesus had a mind and a will distinct and separate from the Father's. He could will and act separately from God. In Gethsemane He prayed, "Yet not as I will, but as you will" (Mt.26:39). He actually willed something different from God. He willed the cup to be removed, for some way other than the cross to be chosen for man's salvation. Jesus had a distinct, separate will from God.

    b. Christ subjected His will to God's will. He fought and struggled to control His mind and will, to do exactly as God willed, and He conquered His will. He always succeeded. In every instance He subjected Himself totally to God. He always did what God willed—perfectly.

> But the world must learn that I love the Father and that I do exactly what my Father has commanded me. "Come now; let us leave. (John 14:31)
>
> If you obey my commands, you will remain in my love, just as I have obeyed my Father's commands and remain in his love. (John 15:10)
>
> For just as through the disobedience of the one man the many were made sinners, so also through the obedience of the one man the many will be made righteous. (Rom 5:19)
>
> Then he said, "Here I am, I have come to do your will." He sets aside the first to establish the second. (Heb 10:9)
>
> God made him who had no sin to be sin for us, so that in him we might become the righteousness of God. (2 Cor 5:21)
>
> For we do not have a high priest who is unable to sympathize with our weaknesses, but we have one who has been tempted in every way, just as we are—yet was without sin. (Heb 4:15)
>
> For you know that it was not with perishable things such as silver or gold that you were redeemed from the empty way of life handed down to you from your forefathers, but with the precious blood of Christ, a lamb without blemish or defect. (1 Pet 1:18-19)

The believer's assurance is Jesus' purpose. He set out to do God's will and He did it perfectly. The believer can rest assured—Jesus is the full revelation of God. Jesus revealed God perfectly. What Jesus did—everything He did—is a picture of the perfect will of God. Man can come to Jesus for spiritual food and nourishment and *know* that He is coming to God.

> For I did not speak of my own accord, but the Father who sent me commanded me what to say and how to say it. (John 12:49)
>
> Jesus answered: "Don't you know me, Philip, even after I have been among you such a long time? Anyone who has seen me has seen the Father. How can you say, 'Show us the Father'? Don't you believe that I am in the Father, and that the Father is in me? The words I say to you are not just my own. Rather, it is the Father, living in me, who is doing his work. (John 14:9-10)
>
> For I gave them the words you gave me and they accepted them. They knew with certainty that I came from you, and they believed that you sent me. (John 17:8)

4 (6:39) **Assurance—Predestination**: the fourth assurance is God's will for *those whom He* gives to Christ. Note: the fact that God sent Christ is stressed again (v.38). Note also that Jesus calls God His "Father." This stresses the love and care of God. God's will is like the will of a father for His children. He wills only good and loving things.

1. God wills to give some followers to His Son: "All that he has given me." This has to do with predestination, but in the sense covered before (v.37). God wills that His Son Jesus be the first, that is, the most preeminent Person, among many brothers. Jesus is to have many brothers and sisters (see note—Ro.8:29). The follower of Jesus can rest assured that he is chosen by God to follow Jesus; therefore, he will not be lost, not ever.

2. God wills that Jesus should *lose nothing*. The words "I shall lose none" (me apoleso ex autou) mean that He will not lose anything, not even a fragment, not any part of what God has given to Him. No person, not a single one, will be lost.

It was true while He was on earth: He lost none (Jn.17:12). It will also be true of every believer throughout history.

> I will remain in the world no longer, but they are still in the world, and I am coming to you. Holy Father, protect them by the power of your name—the name you gave me—so that they may be one as we are one. (John 17:11)
>
> Being confident of this, that he who began a good work in you will carry it on to completion until the day of Christ Jesus. (Phil 1:6)
>
> Do not be anxious about anything, but in everything, by prayer and petition, with thanksgiving, present your requests to God. And the peace of God, which transcends all understanding, will guard your hearts and your minds in Christ Jesus. (Phil 4:6-7)
>
> But the Lord is faithful, and he will strengthen and protect you from the evil one. (2 Th 3:3)
>
> That is why I am suffering as I am. Yet I am not ashamed, because I know whom I have believed, and am convinced that he is able to guard what I have entrusted to him for that day. (2 Tim 1:12)
>
> The Lord will rescue me from every evil attack and will bring me safely to his heavenly kingdom. To him be glory for ever and ever. Amen. (2 Tim 4:18)
>
> To him who is able to keep you from falling and to present you before his glorious presence without fault and with great joy— (Jude 1:24)
>
> Since you have kept my command to endure patiently, I will also keep you from the hour of trial that is going to come upon the whole world to test those who live on the earth. (Rev 3:10)

Love the LORD, all his saints! The LORD preserves the faithful, but the proud he pays back in full. (Psa 31:23)

For the LORD loves the just and will not forsake his faithful ones. They will be protected forever, but the offspring of the wicked will be cut off; (Psa 37:28)

For he guards the course of the just and protects the way of his faithful ones. (Prov 2:8)

This is what the LORD says: "In the time of my favor I will answer you, and in the day of salvation I will help you; I will keep you and will make you to be a covenant for the people, to restore the land and to reassign its desolate inheritances, (Isa 49:8)

3. God wills a most wonderful thing: Jesus shall save every true believer through all, even up until the final hour of the very last day—the day of the resurrection. The Lord's salvation is complete, ultimate, and final. No matter the trials, the heartaches, the hurts, the attacks of the enemy and the evil persecutors, Christ will save His dear follower through all; and He will raise him up at the last day. The *genuine believer* is assured and secure in the will of God. God wills that His Son lose no one—that each one will be saved through all circumstances—saved right up to the point of being raised up at the last day.

5 (6:40) **Assurance—God, Will of:** the fifth assurance is God's will for *the believer*. This verse also concerns God's will, but it differs from the former point in that it centers upon those who *look to Jesus and believe* in Jesus. In the former verse the stress is upon *God choosing* those who come to Christ, whereas in this verse, the stress is upon *man choosing* Christ. Both are necessary steps in salvation as already discussed (v.37. See note—Jn.6:44-46.)

A person must "look to" (behold, grasp) and believe Jesus...

- that God "sent" Him to spiritually feed and nourish man (to save and to give life).
- that He is "the Son," the Savior of the world.

1. God wills that a person who *looks to Jesus and believes* Jesus should have eternal life (see DEEPER STUDY # 2—Jn.2:24; DEEPER STUDY # 1—10:10; DEEPER STUDY # 1—17:2-3).

2. The result of looking to Jesus and believing Jesus is being *raised up from the dead.* Jesus said very emphatically, "I will raise him up at the last day." "I" is emphatic. Jesus and no one else can raise the dead, and He will take the person who looks to and believes and raise him up. The believer is assured of three very significant things.

a. The believer is assured of eternal life.

"For God so loved the world that he gave his one and only Son, that whoever believes in him shall not perish but have eternal life. (John 3:16)

"I tell you the truth, whoever hears my word and believes him who sent me has eternal life and will not be condemned; he has crossed over from death to life. (John 5:24)

b. The believer is assured of victory over death.

In a flash, in the twinkling of an eye, at the last trumpet. For the trumpet will sound, the dead will be raised imperishable, and we will be changed. For the perishable must clothe itself with the imperishable, and the mortal with immortality. When the perishable has been clothed with the imperishable, and the mortal with immortality, then the saying that is written will come true: "Death has been swallowed up in victory." "Where, O death, is your victory? Where, O death, is your sting?" The sting of death is sin, and the power of sin is the law. But thanks be to God! He gives us the victory through our Lord Jesus Christ. (1 Cor 15:52-57)

Since the children have flesh and blood, he too shared in their humanity so that by his death he might destroy him who holds the power of death—that is, the devil—and free those who all their lives were held in slavery by their fear of death. (Heb 2:14-15)

c. The believer is assured of the resurrection.

I tell you the truth, a time is coming and has now come when the dead will hear the voice of the Son of God and those who hear will live. For as the Father has life in himself, so he has granted the Son to have life in himself. And he has given him authority to judge because he is the Son of Man. "Do not be amazed at this, for a time is coming when all who are in their graves will hear his voice and come out—those who have done good will rise to live, and those who have done evil will rise to be condemned. (John 5:25-29; cp. Jn.11:25)

And I have the same hope in God as these men, that there will be a resurrection of both the righteous and the wicked. (Acts 24:15)

Because we know that the one who raised the Lord Jesus from the dead will also raise us with Jesus and present us with you in his presence. (2 Cor 4:14)

For the Lord himself will come down from heaven, with a loud command, with the voice of the archangel and with the trumpet call of God, and the dead in Christ will rise first. (1 Th 4:16)

	F. The Way a Person Partakes of the Bread of Life, 6:41-51	tens to the Father and learns from him comes to me. 46 No one has seen the Father except the one who is from God; only he has seen the Father.	c. He must hear & learn *through Christ* (man's part) 1) Because no man has seen God 2) Because Christ is from God & has seen God
1 The religionists rebelled against the claims of Jesus	41 At this the Jews began to grumble about him because he said, "I am the bread that came down from heaven."	47 I tell you the truth, he who believes has everlasting life.	**3 A person must believe on Christ**
a. They questioned Jesus' origin b. They misunderstood the incarnation	42 They said, "Is this not Jesus, the son of Joseph, whose father and mother we know? How can he now say, 'I came down from heaven'?"	48 I am the bread of life. 49 Your forefathers ate the manna in the desert, yet they died.	a. Believe He is the Bread of Life
c. Jesus appealed: Stop grumbling	43 "Stop grumbling among yourselves," Jesus answered.	50 But here is the bread that comes down from heaven, which a man may eat and not die.	b. Believe He is "out of" heaven—has come to deliver man from death
2 A person must be drawn by God a. The result: He will be raised up at the last day b. He must be taught by God (God's part)ᴰˢ¹	44 "No one can come to me unless the Father who sent me draws him, and I will raise him up at the last day. 45 It is written in the Prophets: 'They will all be taught by God.' Everyone who lis-	51 I am the living bread that Came down from heaven. If anyone eats of this bread, he will live forever. This bread is my flesh, which I will give for the life of the world."	c. Believe He is the living bread—the One who gives life to man forever d. Believe He gave His flesh for the life of the worldᴰˢ²

DIVISION VII

THE REVELATION OF JESUS, THE BREAD OF LIFE, 6:1-71

F. The Way A Person Partakes of the Bread of Life, 6:41-51

(6:41-51) Introduction: how one partakes of the Bread of Life, that is, how one comes to know Jesus personally, is the focus of this passage.

1. The religionists rebelled against the claims of Jesus (v.41-43).
2. A person must be drawn by God (v.44-46).
3. A person must believe on Christ. (v.47-51).

1 (6:41-43) **Religionists, Opposed Jesus**: the religionists rebelled against the claims of Jesus. They grumbled (gogguzete) against Him. The word refers to the grumbling, the buzzing, the discontent that arises from a crowd that is upset and confused; that is, misunderstanding, rejecting, and opposing a speaker. They radically disagreed with Jesus' claim that He had come "down from heaven."

They questioned His origin. They knew Him personally; and they knew His father, Joseph, and His mother, Mary. They knew He was a mere man just as they were, having been reared by human parents. How could He possibly claim to be "from heaven"? Note: their problem was twofold.

⇒ They were ignorant of the incarnation (see DEEPER STUDY # 3—Mt.1:16; DEEPER STUDY # 8—1:23; DEEPER STUDY # 2—Jn.1:10; 1:14-18).
⇒ They were so fixed on His origin, on where He had come from, that they lost sight of His mission, which was to feed and nourish men spiritually (to save and to give life).

Jesus appealed to the crowd, "stop grumbling." He loved and cared for them and longed for them to listen to the truth. As long as they grumbled, they would never be willing to listen to the truth. (What a lesson for us all: "Be still, and know that I am God" [Ps.46:10].)

2 (6:44-46) **Draw (helkuein)—Salvation—Predestination**: a person must be drawn by God. These three verses have to do with predestination (cp. v.37). The truth of predesti-

nation in the Bible is not so much a statement of theology or philosophy as it is a message that speaks to the spiritual experience of the believer. If the pure logic of philosophy and theology is applied, then predestination says that God chooses some for heaven and others for a terrible hell. But this is simply not what God means in the passages dealing with predestination, and this fact needs to be given close attention by all who so interpret the Scriptures. What God wants believers to do is to take heart, for He has assured their salvation. This is what He means by predestination. (See note—Ro.8:29.)

The person who comes to Christ is a person who has been *drawn by God*, a person who has experienced the *divine initiative*. A man does not act alone, coming to Christ by his own effort and energy, not by his own works, whether mental (thought or will, Jn.1:13) or physical labor (good deeds, Eph.2:8-9). A man is a dead spirit; therefore, he can do nothing spiritually just as a dead body can do nothing physically. The natural man prefers self and sin; therefore, if a man with a dead spirit is to come to Christ, he has to be acted upon and drawn by God. Both God and man have a part in salvation.

1. God's part in salvation is to draw man. God has to draw because man resists the gospel. Man's resistance is seen in the word *draw*. The word "draw" has the idea of both initiative and rebellion, of constraint and resistance. For example, the pulling in of a net loaded with fish involves both actions of pulling and resistance (cp. Jn.21:6); a person being dragged to court encounters both actions of pulling and resistance (Acts 16:19).

How God draws a man is clearly stated. He draws by teaching (v.45). The teaching may come from the voice of a preacher, the observation of nature, the reading of Scripture, or a myriad of other sources. But one thing is always common: the movement of God's Spirit upon the human heart, teaching the need for God and drawing the heart toward God for salvation. The Spirit of God teaches a man and moves upon the heart of a man.

a. The Holy Spirit quickens, makes the gospel alive to a man's mind so that he *sees it as never before.* He sees, understands, grasps as never before that "the Father...who has sent" Christ to feed and nourish man (to save and to give him life).

> In reply Jesus declared, "I tell you the truth, no one can see the kingdom of God unless he is born again." (John 3:3)
> For just as the Father raises the dead and gives them life, even so the Son gives life to whom he is pleased to give it. (John 5:21)
> The Spirit gives life; the flesh counts for nothing. The words I have spoken to you are spirit and they are life. (John 6:63)
> And if the Spirit of him who raised Jesus from the dead is living in you, he who raised Christ from the dead will also give life to your mortal bodies through his Spirit, who lives in you. (Rom 8:11)
> As for you, you were dead in your transgressions and sins, (Eph 2:1)
> But because of his great love for us, God, who is rich in mercy, made us alive with Christ even when we were dead in transgressions—it is by grace you have been saved. (Eph 2:4-5)
> You were taught, with regard to your former way of life, to put off your old self, which is being corrupted by its deceitful desires; to be made new in the attitude of your minds; (Eph 4:22-23)
> And have put on the new self, which is being renewed in knowledge in the image of its Creator. (Col 3:10)
> So I prophesied as he commanded me, and breath entered them; they came to life and stood up on their feet—a vast army. (Ezek 37:10)

b. The Holy Spirit convicts a man of sin, of righteousness and of judgment, that is, of his need to be fed and nourished (saved and given life).

> When he comes, he will convict the world of guilt in regard to sin and righteousness and judgment: (John 16:8)

c. The Holy Spirit attracts men to the cross of Christ through its glorious provisions.

> "But a time is coming, and has come, when you will be scattered, each to his own home. You will leave me all alone. Yet I am not alone, for my Father is with me. (John 16:32)
> For the message of the cross is foolishness to those who are perishing, but to us who are being saved it is the power of God. (1 Cor 1:18)
> May I never boast except in the cross of our Lord Jesus Christ, through which the world has been crucified to me, and I to the world. (Gal 6:14)
> And in this one body to reconcile both of them to God through the cross, by which he put to death their hostility. (Eph 2:16)
> And through him to reconcile to himself all things, whether things on earth or things in heaven, by making peace through his blood, shed on the cross. (Col 1:20)

d. The Holy Spirit stirs a man to respond by coming to Christ.

> "Come to me, all you who are weary and burdened, and I will give you rest. (Mat 11:28)
> On the last and greatest day of the Feast, Jesus stood and said in a loud voice, "If anyone is thirsty, let him come to me and drink. (John 7:37)
> The Spirit and the bride say, "Come!" And let him who hears say, "Come!" Whoever is thirsty, let him come; and whoever wishes, let him take the free gift of the water of life. (Rev 22:17)
> Whether you turn to the right or to the left, your ears will hear a voice behind you, saying, "This is the way; walk in it." (Isa 30:21)
> "Come, all you who are thirsty, come to the waters; and you who have no money, come, buy and eat! Come, buy wine and milk without money and without cost. Why spend money on what is not bread, and your labor on what does not satisfy? Listen, listen to me, and eat what is good, and your soul will delight in the richest of fare. Give ear and come to me; hear me, that your soul may live. I will make an everlasting covenant with you, my faithful love promised to David. (Isa 55:1-3)

2. Man's part in salvation is threefold.
   a. Man must hear the voice of God when God draws. When the pull, tug, or movement of God's Spirit is felt, man must listen to the conviction of the Spirit.
   b. Man must learn of God. However, he can learn of God only through Christ. If a man wishes to learn of God, He has to come to Christ. The reasons are clearly stated by Christ (v.46):
      ⇒ No man has seen God.
      ⇒ Christ alone is of God.
      ⇒ Christ alone has seen God.

> Jesus answered, "My teaching is not my own. It comes from him who sent me. If anyone chooses to do God's will, he will find out whether my teaching comes from God or whether I speak on my own. (John 7:16-17)
> To the Jews who had believed him, Jesus said, "If you hold to my teaching, you are really my disciples. Then you will know the truth, and the truth will set you free." (John 8:31-32)
> Now this is eternal life: that they may know you, the only true God, and Jesus Christ, whom you have sent. (John 17:3)
> But let him who boasts boast about this: that he understands and knows me, that I am the LORD, who exercises kindness, justice and righteousness on earth, for in these I delight," declares the LORD. (Jer 9:24)

Let us acknowledge the LORD; let us press on to acknowledge him. As surely as the sun rises, he will appear; he will come to us like the winter rains, like the spring rains that water the earth." (Hosea 6:3)

c. Man must come to Christ: he must yield to the drawing power of God. God reveals, pulls, and tugs at the heart of a man to come to Christ. Why? Because the only way a man can *learn of God* is to come to Christ, and God wants every man to learn of Him, to know Him personally.

Being self-centered and rebellious, man likes to feel independent; consequently, man resists the quickening pull and drawing power of God. However, those who give in to the godly constraint (Jn.6:44) and who partake of Christ (Jn.6:47-51) learn of God and are accepted into His household to partake and feast at His table. (See this note, pt.1c for verses of Scripture.)

DEEPER STUDY # 1
(6:45) **Prophetic Reference**: cp. Is.54:13.

3 (6:47-51) **Salvation—Believe**: a person must believe on Christ. (See Deeper Study # 2, Believe—Jn.2:24.) The person who believes has eternal life (see Deeper Study # 2—Jn.1:4; Deeper Study # 1—10:10; Deeper Study # 1—17:2-3). Christ calls for man to pay close attention, "I tell you the truth," that is, "listen" (cp. v.26, 32). What He now says is critical: a person must believe four things.

1. A person must believe that Christ is *the* Bread of Life: the Bread that feeds and nourishes man spiritually, that saves and gives man life (see notes—Jn.6:32; 6:33; 6:34-35). Note the Lord's claim: "I am the Bread of Life."
   ⇒ Note how straightforward the claim is.
   ⇒ Note how brief, clear cut, straight to the point, and unmistakable the claim is.
   ⇒ Note His claim to deity: "I Am." There is no hesitation—no reservation—no holding back. He pulls no punches: "I Am" (see Deeper Study # 1—Jn.6:20).
   ⇒ Note how Christ refers to the manna again (cp. v.32). Eating physical food will only sustain man temporarily; man still dies. The point is clear: man's concern should not be physical food. If it is, man has only death to anticipate.

Then Jesus declared, "I am the bread of life. He who comes to me will never go hungry, and he who believes in me will never be thirsty. (John 6:35)

2. A man must believe that Christ is "out of" heaven, that He has come to deliver man from death. Christ claims two things.
   a. He has come "out of heaven," from God Himself (see note—Jn.3:31).
   b. If a man eats and partakes of Him, that man will not die (see Deeper Study # 1, Death—Heb.9:27). Note: the word "eat" (phagei) is in the Greek aorist tense. This means that a man eats and partakes (receives) of Christ *once-for-all*. It is a one-time experience.

For I have come down from heaven not to do my will but to do the will of him who sent me. And this is the will of him who sent me, that I shall lose none of all that he has given me, but raise them up at the last day. For my Father's will is that everyone who looks to the Son and believes in him shall have eternal life, and I will raise him up at the last day." (John 6:38-40)

This is the bread that came down from heaven. Your forefathers ate manna and died, but he who feeds on this bread will live forever." (John 6:58)

3. A man must believe that Christ is the living Bread, the One who gives life to man forever.
   a. The Bread is living; it is a life (Jn.1:4; 5:26). The words are literally, "the Bread, the Living" (ho artos ho zon). (Cp. v.35, 41, 48.)
   b. The Bread "came down from heaven." The phrase "came down" (katabas) is again in the aorist tense which means Christ *came once*. The incarnation had never taken place before, nor will it ever take place again. The miraculous entrance of the living Bread into the world is a *one-time-only event*.
   c. The Bread, the Lord Jesus Christ, came to provide spiritual food for man: spiritual and eternal life.
   d. The offer of eternal life is conditional, "If anyone eats of this Bread, he will live forever."

Jesus said to them, "I tell you the truth, unless you eat the flesh of the Son of Man and drink his blood, you have no life in you. Whoever eats my flesh and drinks my blood has eternal life, and I will raise him up at the last day. For my flesh is real food and my blood is real drink. (John 6:53-55)

I tell you the truth, if anyone keeps my word, he will never see death." (John 8:51)

And whoever lives and believes in me will never die. Do you believe this?" (John 11:26)

4. A man must believe that Christ gave His flesh for the life of the world. Note that Christ identifies the Bread: it is His flesh which He gives for the life of the world (see Deeper Study # 2—Jn.6:51).

DEEPER STUDY # 2
(6:51) **Jesus Christ, Humanity; Death**: the phrase "my flesh, which I will give for the life of the world" says two things.
   1. Jesus Christ came in the flesh.

Beyond all question, the mystery of godliness is great: He appeared in a body, was vindicated by the Spirit, was seen by angels, was preached among the nations, was believed on in the world, was taken up in glory. (1 Tim 3:16)

This is how you can recognize the Spirit of God: Every spirit that acknowledges that Jesus Christ has come in the flesh is from God, but every spirit that does not acknowledge Jesus is not from God. This is the spirit of the antichrist, which you have heard is coming and even now is already in the world. (1 John 4:2-3)

2. Jesus Christ gave His flesh (life) for the life of the world.

> Since the children have flesh and blood, he too shared in their humanity so that by his death he might destroy him who holds the power of death—that is, the devil—and free those who all their lives were held in slavery by their fear of death. (Heb 2:14-15)

> For what the law was powerless to do in that it was weakened by the sinful nature, God did by sending his own Son in the likeness of sinful man to be a sin offering. And so he condemned sin in sinful man, (Rom 8:3)

> He himself bore our sins in his body on the tree, so that we might die to sins and live for righteousness; by his wounds you have been healed. (1 Pet 2:24)

> For Christ died for sins once for all, the righteous for the unrighteous, to bring you to God. He was put to death in the body but made alive by the Spirit, (1 Pet 3:18)

	G. The Results of Partaking of the Bread of Life, 6:52-58	him up at the last day.	
1 The religionists were perplexed a. They questioned partaking of His flesh b. Jesus proclaimed a much more shocking thing: Unless one partakes of Him, he does not have life*DS1* **2 Result 1: Eternal life—conquering death & being resurrected**	52 Then the Jews began to argue sharply among themselves, "How can this man give us his flesh to eat?" 53 Jesus said to them, "I tell you the truth, unless you eat the flesh of the Son of Man and drink his blood, you have no life in you. 54 Whoever eats my flesh and drinks my blood has eternal life, and I will raise	55 For my flesh is real food and my blood is real drink. 56 Whoever eats my flesh and drinks my blood remains in me, and I in him. 57 Just as the living Father sent me and I live because of the Father, so the one who feeds on me will live because of me. 58 This is the bread that came down from heaven. Your forefathers ate manna and died, but he who feeds on this bread will live forever."	**3 Result 2: True, not false satisfaction** **4 Result 3: Supernatural companionship & fellowship** **5 Result 4: A life that is full of purpose & meaning** **6 Result 5: Incorruptible food received within the heart—energizing life forever**

DIVISION VII

THE REVELATION OF JESUS, THE BREAD OF LIFE, 6:1-71

G. The Results of Partaking of the Bread of Life, 6:52-58

(6:52-58) Introduction: a man must receive and partake of the Bread of Life. When he does, he receives five wonderful things.

1. The religionists were perplexed over Jesus' words (v.52-53).
2. Result 1: eternal life—conquering death and being resurrected (v.54).
3. Result 2: true, not false satisfaction (v.55).
4. Result 3: supernatural companionship and fellowship (v.56).
5. Result 4: a life that is full of purpose and meaning (v.57).
6. Result 5: incorruptible food received within the heart—energizing life forever (v.58).

1 (6:52-53) **Man, State of—Sin, Dead in**: the religionists were perplexed and argued among themselves. The word "argue" (*emachonto*) means to fuss, debate. They were debating what Jesus meant. He had just said:

> **I am the living bread that came down from heaven. If anyone eats of this bread, he will live forever. This bread is my flesh, which I will give for the life of the world." (John 6:51)**

1. The Jews (religionists) began to argue over the meaning of the words. "How can this man give us His flesh to eat?"

⇒ Some interpreted His words as a parable, in a figurative and symbolic way. They knew He often spoke in parables.
⇒ Others had no idea what He meant, but they did see that He was claiming to be the most important person in the world, the very Savior of men. This, of course, bothered them beyond reason. How could any man claim to be so important to the world? As materialists and humanists they asked, "How can this be? He is but a man. How can He give His flesh for the world and the world receive eternal life?"
⇒ A few disciples, genuine followers of the Lord, perhaps understood.

The point is that the religionists were disturbed. The message had been going on for a long time, and Jesus had made claim after claim—all most unusual. Moreover, what He was saying was not clear, and some of it was offensive. Therefore, they were angry and perplexed and began to argue among themselves about what He meant and how they should respond to Him.

2. Jesus responded by proclaiming a much more shocking thing: unless a man partake, that is, receive Him, that man has no life dwelling within him.

The words "eat" and "drink" are in the Greek aorist tense which means a once-for-all act. Jesus was not speaking of partaking time and again. He was not speaking of feasting upon Him day by day through prayer and Bible study. He was speaking of a one-time event. A person is to eat and drink of Christ, that is, receive Him once for all. (See DEEPER STUDY # 1—Jn.6:53.)

Thought 1. Unless a man receives (eats and drinks) Christ, he has no life within him. He is a dead man spiritually and eternally. He is walking around as a dead man.

⇒ Physically he is in the process of aging and dying, of living in the realm of death and being doomed to die.
⇒ Spiritually he is already dead, having no life with God. He has no life, no real and true relationship with the *true and living God*. He is doomed to eternal death and separation from God.

Partaking, eating and drinking, of Christ is absolutely essential in order to truly live—in order to possess real life that lasts now and forever.

> **As for you, you were dead in your transgressions and sins, (Eph 2:1)**
> **For it is light that makes everything visible. This is why it is said: "Wake up, O sleeper, rise from the dead, and Christ will shine on you." (Eph 5:14)**
> **When you were dead in your sins and in the uncircumcision of your sinful nature, God made you alive with Christ. He forgave us all our sins, (Col 2:13)**
> **But the widow who lives for pleasure is dead even while she lives. (1 Tim 5:6)**
> **"To the angel of the church in Sardis write: These are the words of him who holds the seven spirits of God and the seven stars. I know your deeds; you have a repu-**

tation of being alive, but you are dead. (Rev 3:1)

DEEPER STUDY # 1

(6:53) **Eat—Drink—Salvation**: to receive, accept, partake, appropriate, assimilate, absorb, and to make part of oneself. A person can actually receive and partake of Christ in the most intimate and nourishing sense of his being (flesh and blood). The receiving and partaking can be just as intimate and nourishing as eating and drinking.

The point is this: a man must receive Christ into his heart, into his innermost being if he wishes to live. In fact, he is dead spiritually and eternally unless he so receives Christ.

---

2 (6:54) **Salvation, Results—Growth**: the first result of receiving Christ, the Bread of Life, is eternal life. Note three things.

1. The word for "eat" (trogon) is different. It means to eat eagerly, to grasp at chunks, to eat with pleasure. It is the picture of hungering after Christ and eagerly wanting to feed and feast on Him.

2. The tense is also different. It is present tense, which means continuous action. A person must continue to eat and to develop and grow into the habit of feasting upon Christ. Christian growth day by day is the picture.

Now note the point. A genuine believer, a man who really receives Christ, is a man who partakes of Him continually. Day by day the man will feast upon Christ. It is this man who has the promise of eternal life, and eternal life includes three great things.

    a. Abundant and eternal life. (See DEEPER STUDY # 2—Jn.1:4; DEEPER STUDY # 1—10:10; DEEPER STUDY # 1—17:2-3.)

    b. The conquest of death. (See note—Jn.3:14-15.)

    c. The resurrection. (See note—Jn.5:28-30.)

> I am the living bread that came down from heaven. If anyone eats of this bread, he will live forever. This bread is my flesh, which I will give for the life of the world." (John 6:51)
>
> "For God so loved the world that he gave his one and only Son, that whoever believes in him shall not perish but have eternal life. (John 3:16)
>
> "I tell you the truth, whoever hears my word and believes him who sent me has eternal life and will not be condemned; he has crossed over from death to life. (John 5:24)
>
> Now this is eternal life: that they may know you, the only true God, and Jesus Christ, whom you have sent. (John 17:3)

3 (6:55) **Satisfaction—Life, Abundant**: the second result of receiving Christ is true satisfaction, not false satisfaction.

1. The word "real" (alethes) means true as opposed to false (see DEEPER STUDY # 1—Jn.1:9). The things of the world do not feed and fill men, not with a true satisfaction. Worldly pleasures and satisfactions are false; and false satisfaction does not last, not permanently, not with full assurance and confidence and security. Worldly pleasures and satisfactions always leave men somewhat empty, dissatisfied, craving, void, unassured and wondering if this

world is all there is—wondering if there is not more to life than what this world and its possessions have to offer.

2. True satisfaction comes from receiving Christ into one's life, and it comes only through Christ. This is the Lord's point in this verse. Just as real life on the earth comes from eating and drinking food, so real and abundant life comes from eating and drinking Christ. One must receive Christ in the closest and most intimate and nourishing sense in order to have true life, life that is abundant and full of...

- assurance
- strength
- meekness
- goodness
- love
- security
- decisiveness
- temperance
- patience
- joy
- confidence
- courage
- faith
- gentleness
- peace

> Blessed are those who hunger and thirst for righteousness, for they will be filled. (Mat 5:6)
>
> But whoever drinks the water I give him will never thirst. Indeed, the water I give him will become in him a spring of water welling up to eternal life." (John 4:14)
>
> On the last and greatest day of the Feast, Jesus stood and said in a loud voice, "If anyone is thirsty, let him come to me and drink. (John 7:37)
>
> But the fruit of the Spirit is love, joy, peace, patience, kindness, goodness, faithfulness, gentleness and self-control. Against such things there is no law. (Gal 5:22-23)
>
> Never again will they hunger; never again will they thirst. The sun will not beat upon them, nor any scorching heat. (Rev 7:16)
>
> And I—in righteousness I will see your face; when I awake, I will be satisfied with seeing your likeness. (Psa 17:15)
>
> They feast on the abundance of your house; you give them drink from your river of delights. (Psa 36:8)
>
> for he satisfies the thirsty and fills the hungry with good things. (Psa 107:9)
>
> With joy you will draw water from the wells of salvation. (Isa 12:3)
>
> For I will pour water on the thirsty land, and streams on the dry ground; I will pour out my Spirit on your offspring, and my blessing on your descendants. (Isa 44:3)
>
> "Come, all you who are thirsty, come to the waters; and you who have no money, come, buy and eat! Come, buy wine and milk without money and without cost. (Isa 55:1)
>
> The LORD will guide you always; he will satisfy your needs in a sun scorched land and will strengthen your frame. You will be like a well watered garden, like a spring whose waters never fail. (Isa 58:11)

4 (6:56) **Abiding—Companionship—Fellowship—Care—Providence**: the third result is supernatural companionship and fellowship, care and being looked after. This is seen in the word "remains" (menei). It means to abide, continue, dwell, rest in or upon. It is being fixed and set and remaining there, continuing on and on. Such is the state and condition and being of the person who receives Christ. The person receives Christ into his being, and Christ enters the person's life, remaining within him. The person is also placed into Christ, that is, placed with all other believers into the spiritual body of Christ. (See notes—1 Cor.12:12-31; Eph.1:22-23; 2:11-22. Also see DEEPER STUDY # 1—Acts 2:1-4, the section on baptism for more discussion.) The person "remains" or dwells in Christ even as Christ remains in him. This, of course, means fellowship and companionship with Christ and the presence of His care and watchful eye in looking after us. (See DEEPER STUDY # 1—Jn.15:1-8; DEEPER STUDY # 3—Acts 2:42 for more discussion.)

> **On that day you will realize that I am in my Father, and you are in me, and I am in you. (John 14:20)**
> **Remain in me, and I will remain in you. No branch can bear fruit by itself; it must remain in the vine. Neither can you bear fruit unless you remain in me. "I am the vine; you are the branches. If a man remains in me and I in him, he will bear much fruit; apart from me you can do nothing. (John 15:4-5)**
> **I have been crucified with Christ and I no longer live, but Christ lives in me. The life I live in the body, I live by faith in the Son of God, who loved me and gave himself for me. (Gal 2:20)**
> **To them God has chosen to make known among the Gentiles the glorious riches of this mystery, which is Christ in you, the hope of glory. (Col 1:27)**
> **Those who obey his commands live in him, and he in them. And this is how we know that he lives in us: We know it by the Spirit he gave us. (1 John 3:24)**
> **Here I am! I stand at the door and knock. If anyone hears my voice and opens the door, I will come in and eat with him, and he with me. (Rev 3:20)**

5 (6:57) **Purpose—Life, Spiritual:** the fourth result of receiving Christ is a life that is full of purpose, meaning, and significance.

1. Jesus said, "I live because of the Father." This means at least two things.
   a. He lived *because of* the Father, that is, of the Father, on account of the Father. His life was due to the Father.
   b. He lived *for* the Father; that is, He lived to do the Father's will. The Father "sent" Him to live on earth for a specific purpose: to fulfill the Father's will and task.

2. The man who receives Christ ("feeds on me") *lives because of Christ.* He begins to live in all the purpose, meaning, and significance of life, for apart from Christ

there is no life. Note: the tense is present, continuous action. A person must *continue* to partake, eat, and feast upon Christ to keep his sense of purpose and meaning, to really live and live abundantly.

> **I have been crucified with Christ and I no longer live, but Christ lives in me. The life I live in the body, I live by faith in the Son of God, who loved me and gave himself for me. (Gal 2:20)**
> **For to me, to live is Christ and to die is gain. (Phil 1:21)**
> **For we who are alive are always being given over to death for Jesus' sake, so that his life may be revealed in our mortal body. (2 Cor 4:11)**

3. Jesus called God "the living Father."

> **For as the Father has life in himself, so he has granted the Son to have life in himself. (John 5:26)**
> **Simon Peter answered, "You are the Christ, the Son of the living God." (Mat 16:16)**
> **What agreement is there between the temple of God and idols? For we are the temple of the living God. As God has said: "I will live with them and walk among them, and I will be their God, and they will be my people." (2 Cor 6:16)**

6 (6:58) **Life—Jesus Christ, Only Savior:** the fifth result of receiving Christ is incorruptible food within our hearts—energizing our lives forever. Christ made a strong, descriptive contrast.

⇒ The manna eaten by Israel in the Old Testament *did come* from the clouds above, but it did not give life to the people. They were *all dead.*

⇒ "This [the Lord Himself] is the Bread that came down from heaven...he who feeds on this bread will live forever."

The idea is striking: it is the Living Bread, Christ Himself, who energizes and quickens a man to live forever. Christ has the quality, the power, the substance to energize a man and give him eternal life. However, He and He alone has such energizing power.

> **In him was life, and that life was the light of men. (John 1:4)**
> **For as the Father has life in himself, so he has granted the Son to have life in himself. (John 5:26)**
> **But it has now been revealed through the appearing of our Savior, Christ Jesus, who has destroyed death and has brought life and immortality to light through the gospel. (2 Tim 1:10)**

	H. The Reason Some People Are Offended by Christ, the Bread of Life, 6:59-71	beginning which of them did not believe and who would betray him.	
1 Jesus' message was to the synagogue crowd in Capernaum a. Many disciples were present b. They had difficulty accepting His message	59 He said this while teaching in the synagogue in Capernaum. 60 On hearing it, many of his disciples said, "This is a hard teaching. Who can accept it?"	65 He went on to say, "This is why I told you that no one can come to me unless the Father has enabled him." 66 From this time many of his disciples turned back and no longer followed him.	**5 There is the fact that God saves man, man does not save himself** **6 The conclusion: There were three responses**
2 There is the idea of eating Jesus' flesh & drinking His blood v.51-56	61 Aware that his disciples were grumbling about this, Jesus said to them, "Does this offend you?	67 "You do not want to leave too, do you?" Jesus asked the Twelve.	a. The disciples who turned back b. The disciple who believed Jesus was the Christ
3 There is the ascension & exaltation of Christ	62 What if you see the Son of Man ascend to where he was before!	68 Simon Peter answered him, "Lord, to whom shall we go? You have the words of eternal life.	
4 There is the teaching that the spirit quickens, gives life & the flesh counts for nothing	63 The Spirit gives life; the flesh counts for nothing. The words I have spoken to you are spirit and they are life. 64 Yet there are some of you who do not believe." For Jesus had known from the	69 We believe and know that you are the Holy One of God." 70 Then Jesus replied, "Have I not chosen you, the Twelve? Yet one of you is a devil!" 71 (He meant Judas, the son of Simon Iscariot, who, though one of the Twelve, was later to betray him.)	c. The disciple who betrayed Christ

DIVISION VII

THE REVELATION OF JESUS, THE BREAD OF LIFE, 6:1-71

H. The Reason Some People are Offended by Christ, the Bread of Life, 6:59-71

(6:59-71) **Introduction**: men are often offended by Christ. Four things in particular offend them.

1. Jesus' message was to the synagogue crowd in Capernaum (v.59-60).
2. There is the idea of eating Jesus' flesh and drinking His blood (v.61).
3. There is the ascension and exaltation of Christ. (v.62).
4. There is the teaching that the spirit quickens, gives life and the flesh counts for nothing (v.63-64).
5. There is the fact that God saves man; man does not save himself (v.65).
6. The conclusion: there were three responses (v.66-71).

1 (6:59-60) **Jesus Christ, Preaching**: Jesus' message was to the synagogue crowd in Capernaum. Many disciples and followers of His were present, but they had difficulty accepting what He had said. The words "a hard teaching" (skleros) mean rough and harsh. What Jesus had said was *hard* and *difficult to accept*, but His words were clearly understood. The people's problem was not in their understanding, but in their hearts. Jesus knew this, so He covered some reasons why men are offended by Him.

2 (6:61) **Blood, Repulsive—Cross, Offense**: men are offended by the claims of Christ and the idea of eating His flesh and drinking His blood (cp. v.51-56). Men, including counterfeit disciples, are offended and repulsed by what is sometimes called...

- a *grotesque god,* a god who came to earth to impregnate a young girl, becoming incarnated into human flesh, being born half-man and half-god.
- a *bloody religion* or a religion of cannibalism.

Note two things.

1. Jesus claimed to be God *incarnated* in human flesh, but not in a grotesque sense—not half-man, half-god. In very simple terms, He was man, fully man; that is, He had the nature of man, being made of the very same substance as all men. However, there was one difference: He was not born of a human father; He was born of God. God very simply *spoke the Word* and a miracle took place, just as He spoke the Word and created the world. There is nothing grotesque about God's speech nor about His willing something to be done and doing it. God did what He always does when He wills something. He simply spoke and the event was set in motion. Very simply stated, Jesus Christ was born *by the Word of God and by human flesh.* He was fully Man, fully God. He came *from God's* Word; He became a Man *by God's* Word. Therefore, all men owe their obedience to Christ. (See note—Jn.6:62 for more discussion.)

2. The cross or the blood of Christ *is offensive and repulsive* just as some people feel it is. It represents the awful shame of sin and the death of Jesus Christ, God's very own Son; therefore, it is bound to be repulsive. But it also represents salvation and deliverance from sin and its awful guilt. Therefore, the cross is also the most attractive symbol in all the world (see note, Cross—Mt.16:21-23).

He himself bore our sins in his body on the tree, so that we might die to sins and live for righteousness; by his wounds you have been healed. (1 Pet 2:24)

For Christ died for sins once for all, the righteous for the unrighteous, to bring you to God. He was put to death in the body but made alive by the Spirit, (1 Pet 3:18)

135

The words "take...eat" of Christ are not cannibalism. The words simply mean that a man is to spiritually receive Christ into his life, into his whole being. A man's deliverance from the bondage of sin and death is by *spiritually taking and eating* of Christ's body; that is, the man must spiritually receive, partake, consume, absorb, and assimilate Christ into his life. He must allow Christ to become the very nourishment, the innermost part and energy, the very consumption, of his being.

> **Yet to all who received him, to those who believed in his name, he gave the right to become children of God— (John 1:12)**
> **Here I am! I stand at the door and knock. If anyone hears my voice and opens the door, I will come in and eat with him, and he with me. (Rev 3:20)**

3 (6:62) **Ascension—Exaltation**: men are offended by the ascension and exaltation of Christ. (See note, Ascension—Mk.16:19-20.) Why? If a man accepts the ascension and exaltation of Christ, he has to surrender the control of his life to Christ. He can no longer control his own life and do the things he wishes. Note three things.

1. Christ referred to himself as the Son of Man (see note—Jn.1:51). The counterfeit disciple is unwilling to look at Jesus as the "Son of Man," that is, as the Ideal and Perfect Man, as the Pattern for all men to copy (see DEEPER STUDY # 3—Mt.8:20). If a man accepted Christ as the Son of Man, he would have to pattern his life after Christ by doing his very best to live as Christ lived. The man would have to diligently seek to be like Christ (cp. Heb.11:6).

2. God exalted Jesus as Lord and Master. The counterfeit disciple is unwilling to submit himself under the control and dominion of Jesus. He is adamantly opposed to patterning his life after Jesus.

3. The words "where He was before" point to the fact that Jesus is eternal. He was preexistent: God of very God. Therefore, a man is to believe and surrender to Him as Lord.

> **Therefore God exalted him to the highest place and gave him the name that is above every name, that at the name of Jesus every knee should bow, in heaven and on earth and under the earth, and every tongue confess that Jesus Christ is Lord, to the glory of God the Father. (Phil 2:9-11)**
> **Who has gone into heaven and is at God's right hand—with angels, authorities and powers in submission to him. (1 Pet 3:22)**

4 (6:63-64) **Holy Spirit—Life**: men are offended by the teaching that the Spirit quickens, gives life and the flesh counts for nothing. Note three significant points.

1. The flesh cannot quicken and make a man alive. The flesh can neither profit nor count for a man. Men do not like to accept or think about the *zero value* of the flesh. They do everything they can to keep its youth, attractiveness, and stamina. They use cosmetics, clothing, and activities to appear young, attractive, and physically capable. But before too long, before they ever imagine, the flesh proves unprofitable; it ages, deteriorates, and surrenders to the process of decay. The *seed of corruption* within wins, and man dies. The flesh proves its *zero value*; it profits nothing, not eternally. Once a man dies, his flesh is gone forever, never to return, and there has never been an exception to the fact.

Such a thought, such a teaching—despite its truthfulness—offends men. They love the world and the flesh (sinful nature), its pleasures and feelings; therefore, they want the right to feed it. They want more and more good feelings, getting and keeping all the physical and material pleasures they can. They want the...

- worldly ego
- fleshy image
- human recognition
- institutional praise
- self-centered fame
- benevolent honor
- stimulating pleasures
- earthly wealth

2. Only the Spirit can quicken a man and make him alive, giving him abundant and eternal life. How? By receiving the Word of Christ. The words that Christ spoke were Spirit and life. When a man receives the words of Christ into his heart and life, he begins to live: he actually experiences the Spirit of God entering his life and begins to experience real life.

> **The thief comes only to steal and kill and destroy; I have come that they may have life, and have it to the full. (John 10:10)**
> **And if the Spirit of him who raised Jesus from the dead is living in you, he who raised Christ from the dead will also give life to your mortal bodies through his Spirit, who lives in you. (Rom 8:11)**
> **As for you, you were dead in your transgressions and sins, (Eph 2:1)**
> **But because of his great love for us, God, who is rich in mercy, made us alive with Christ even when we were dead in transgressions—it is by grace you have been saved. (Eph 2:4-5)**

3. But note what Jesus said. "Yet there are some of you who do not believe." They did not accept His Words; therefore, they did not have the Spirit of God remaning in them nor did they have life. They were only existing, not living abundantly and eternally. They did not have the knowledge and *unswerving assurance* of living forever. They doubted and wondered, ever hoping, but they were not quite sure.

5 (6:65) **Salvation—Draw**: men are offended by the fact that God draws and saves man, that man does not save himself. Christ said : "No one can come to me, unless the father has enabled him." Christ was saying:

⇒ No man can come to Him unless God draws and stirs him to come.
⇒ No man really belongs to God who has not come to Him.
⇒ No man is saved unless they have come to Him.
⇒ All men are lost unless they come to Him.

This fact disturbs people greatly, for most people feel they are good enough and have done enough good to be acceptable to God. Few people think they are lost and doomed to be separated from God; therefore, hearing the fact preached offends them. But note the critical point. The only saved person is a person who has been drawn to Christ by God and who has surrendered to God's pull and movement within his heart.

"No one can come to me unless the Father who sent me draws him, and I will raise him up at the last day. (John 6:44)

The one who sent me is with me; he has not left me alone, for I always do what pleases him." (John 8:29)

who has saved us and called us to a holy life—not because of anything we have done but because of his own purpose and grace. This grace was given us in Christ Jesus before the beginning of time, (2 Tim 1:9)

Who have been chosen according to the foreknowledge of God the Father, through the sanctifying work of the Spirit, for obedience to Jesus Christ and sprinkling by his blood: Grace and peace be yours in abundance. (1 Pet 1:2)

6 (6:66-71) **Jesus Christ, Response to**: there were three responses to the Lord's message.

1. There were disciples or followers who turned back. Note that "many...turned back, and no longer followed Him." They forsook and deserted the Lord. Why? Very simply, following Christ cost too much. It involved the cross, which meant complete denial of oneself.
    a. Jesus was claiming to be Lord. This meant that a man had to give all he was and had to Christ.
    b. Jesus was claiming to be the very Son of God, to have come down *out of* heaven. Some just could not receive and accept the fact.

    c. Jesus was demanding total allegiance and complete self-denial, and following Him would just cost too much (see DEEPER STUDY # 1—Lk.9:23).
2. There was the disciple who believed that Jesus was the Lord. Note four facts.
    a. Peter spoke for all the apostles. He was their leader and spokesman.
    b. Peter called Jesus "Lord," and he used the title in its fullest meaning (cp. v.68-69). Jesus was recognized to be the sovereign Lord of the universe, the One to whom all men owe their allegiance.
    c. Peter declared that Jesus' words *were* the words of eternal life. He declared that what Jesus had just proclaimed was true (v.63). (See DEEPER STUDY # 2—Jn.1:4; DEEPER STUDY # 1—10:10; DEEPER STUDY # 1—17:2-3.)
    d. Peter proclaimed that he and the apostles both *believed* and *knew* something: Jesus was...
        • "the Christ, the Son of the living God" (the latest manuscripts read this).
        • "the Holy One of God" (the oldest manuscripts read this).
3. There was the disciple who betrayed Jesus. Note these facts.
    a. Judas was a "chosen" man, chosen not only to be saved, but to be a minister of Christ.
    b. Judas was called "a devil," slanderous, a false accuser (2 Tim.3:3), an adversary, an enemy of Christ.
    c. Judas was a betrayer, a professed follower, but a hypocrite.

CHAPTER 7

VIII. THE RESPONSES TO
THE REVELATION
OF JESUS, 7:1-53

A. The Response of Jesus'
Brothers: Mockery &
Unbelief, 7:1-9

1 Jesus was forced to withdraw & minister in Galilee a. The reason: The religionists sought His life b. The Feast of Tabernacles was at hand **2 The brothers' response: Mockery & unbelief** a. Their mockery: Show your works (miracles)	After this, Jesus went around in Galilee, purposely staying away from Judea because the Jews there were waiting to take his life. 2 But when the Jewish Feast of Tabernacles was near, 3 Jesus' brothers said to him, "You ought to leave here and go to Judea, so that your disciples may see the mira-cles you do. 4 No one who wants to become a public figure acts in secret. Since you are doing these things, show yourself to the world." 5 For even his own brothers did not believe in him. 6 Therefore Jesus told them, "The right time for me has not yet come; for you any time is right. 7 The world cannot hate you, but it hates me because I testify that what it does is evil. 8 You go to the Feast. I am not yet going up to this Feast, because for me the right time has not yet come." 9 Having said this, he stayed in Galilee.	b. Their unbelief **3 Jesus' reply** a. It is not time (the day) for His acclaim; but for man's acclaim b. It is time for the world's works to be proclaimed evil c. It is not time for His full revelation, that is, the revelation of His death

DIVISION VIII

THE RESPONSES TO THE REVELATION OF JESUS, 7:1-53

A. The Response of Jesus' Brothers: Mockery and Unbelief, 7:1-9

(7:1-53) **DIVISION OVERVIEW: Jesus Christ, Response to**: Chapter 7 is a brief pause in the revelation of who Jesus is. Chapter 7 shows the reactions of various groups to the revelations and claims of Jesus.

(7:1-9) **Introduction**: the first reaction or response to Jesus came from his half-brothers. The incident teaches us how to answer mockery, ridicule, sarcasm, and unbelief. We answer such reactions by proclaiming the same three facts that Jesus proclaimed (point 3, v.6-9).

1. Jesus was forced to withdraw and minister in Galilee (v.1-2).
2. The brother's response: mockery and unbelief (v.3-5).
3. Jesus' reply (v.6-9).
   a. It is not time (the day) for His acclaim, but for man's acclaim.
   b. It is time for the world's works to be proclaimed evil.
   c. It is not time for His full revelation, that is, the revelation of His death.

1 (7:1-2) **Ministry—Ministering—Jesus Christ, Opposition**: Jesus was forced to withdraw and minister in Galilee. The reason was tragic: the religionists throughout Judaea and Jerusalem had reacted so violently against Him that they were waiting to take His life. The word "waiting" is continuous action. They kept on seeking to kill Him.

Just how long Jesus was away from Judaea and Jerusalem is not known. Ideas range from six months to one and a half years. On His last journey into Jerusalem, He was seen attending the Passover (Jn.6:4). In this chapter, Chapter 7, He is seen attending the Feast of Tabernacles (v.10).

Thought 1. Note two instructive lessons.
1) Jesus withdrew from conflict and danger so that He might continue to minister.
2) Galilee was not as prominent as Judaea. In fact, it was an obscure place, considered both insignificant and unimportant. But note: God chose for His Son to minister there. This should speak to the hearts of believers. A believer should not feel embarrassed or less important to be placed in an obscure ministry by the Lord.

Note another fact: when Jesus was forced to withdraw, He did not withdraw from ministry. He did not become idle, sitting still and doing nothing. He ministered wherever He was. Ministering to people and meeting their needs and teaching and preaching the gospel were His life. To live was to minister.

2 (7:3-5) **Jesus Christ, Family of**: the brothers' response was mockery and unbelief. Note several things.

Jesus had four half-brothers whose names were James, Joses, Simon, and Judas. He also had some half-sisters who were not named (Mt.13:55-56). Their attitude toward Jesus was one of extreme concern and embarrassment. His claim to be *the Son of God* embarrassed them immensely and led them to think He was *beside Himself*, that is mad or insane. On one occasion the rumor of madness caused so much pressure from neighbors and friends that they actually travelled a great distance to find Him and bring Him home (see note—Mk.3:31-32 for more discussion. This is an important note in grasping the background of the brothers' attitude of mockery toward Jesus.)

Jesus, of course, did not heed the urgings of His family to cease making such phenomenal claims. He had to proclaim the truth: He was the Son of God, the very Bread of Life, the only One who could fill and satisfy men, giving them abundant and eternal life.

The embarrassment felt by the family was bound to be a heavy load, making the family extremely self-conscious and stirring some sense of responsibility for Jesus' abnormal behavior. The brothers compensated for their embarrassment by mocking Jesus. Note their mockery: they challenged Him to go up to Jerusalem to the Feast and do His marvelous miracles there. They suggested that He was failing to help and to strengthen the disciples He left there when He withdrew and that if He really wanted to be ac-

138

claimed the Messiah, the Son of God, He had to prove Himself in the center of the nation, Jerusalem itself.

The brothers, of course, knew the rumors about the leaders seeking to kill Jesus. It was not likely they really wanted Jesus to go and jeopardize His life, nor did they think He would. The whole scene was one of mockery (v.3-4) and unbelief (v.5). They were tolerating Him through sarcasm, through a half-amused teasing. They entertained themselves by goading Him on and by treating Him with an amused disrespect; and, unfortunately, their disrespect and teasing were open for all to see. Note three points.

1. There was the hurt and ache of Jesus over the family. His heart was bound to be cut to the core by the family's mockery, embarrassment, and unbelief. He was deeply hurt by their rejection.

2. *Jesus' suffering upon earth* included the rejection of His earthly family. He is thereby able to help everyone, no matter his trial, even the person who stands alone in the world, having been rejected by his own family.

3. The response of Jesus' family, in particular His brothers, was embarrassment, mockery, and unbelief. The unbelief of the brothers was a persistent, continuing attitude (the Greek imperfect tense). To some degree this is understandable in light of...

- Jesus' phenomenal claims.
- Jesus' rejection by His hometown, Nazareth, which the family witnessed. He was probably rejected twice by His former neighbors and city, once with so much hostility that they tried to kill Him (Lk.4:16-30; Mk.6:1-6. Cp. Mt.13:53-58.)
- Jesus' rejection by His neighbors and the leaders of the nation, both religious and civil. The neighbors thought Him insane, and the leaders thought Him demon-possessed (Mk.3:20-21; 3:22-30; 3:31-35. Cp. Mt.12:46-50; Lk.8:19-21.)

Thought 1. Jesus Christ bore every imaginable suffering for men, even the rejection of His own family. It is through His suffering—the very fact that He has borne all our sufferings—that He is able to help us through any and all trials.

> **Because he himself suffered when he was tempted, he is able to help those who are being tempted. (Heb 2:18; cp. Heb. 4:15-16)**

3 (7:6-9) **Man, Acclaim—Jesus Christ, Response to**: Jesus' reply to mockery, ridicule, sarcasm, and unbelief was threefold.

1. It was not time (the day) for His acclaim, not time for the world to accept and acknowledge His claims and works, not yet.
   a. The day of the Lord's acclaim had not yet come. It was not time for the day...
      - when many would proclaim Him the Savior, the King of kings and Lord of lords.
      - when many would bow, acknowledging that His claim to be the Messiah, the Son of God, was true.

   The day was coming. There was a time appointed by God, a destined time. (See note, My Hour—Jn.2:3-5.) But it was not yet.

   Note that Jesus had turned the mockery into a teaching situation. He used the very point of the mockery against His claims and works and made

the claim again. There would be a time, a day, when He would be acclaimed, but not then.

> **Jesus replied, "The hour has come for the Son of Man to be glorified. I tell you the truth, unless a kernel of wheat falls to the ground and dies, it remains only a single seed. But if it dies, it produces many seeds. (John 12:23-24)**
>
> **"Now my heart is troubled, and what shall I say? 'Father, save me from this hour'? No, it was for this very reason I came to this hour. But I, when I am lifted up from the earth, will draw all men to myself." He said this to show the kind of death he was going to die. (John 12:27, 32-33)**
>
> **It was just before the Passover Feast. Jesus knew that the time had come for him to leave this world and go to the Father. Having loved his own who were in the world, he now showed them the full extent of his love. (John 13:1)**

   b. The time for man's acclaim is now. Jesus said to his brothers, "Your time—man's time, the world's time—is now." It was and still is man's day, the day...
      - for acceptance and acclaim.
      - for reception and recognition.
      - for honoring and receiving honor.

   It should be noted that some interpret "time" to mean "the opportune time." In this interpretation Jesus was simply saying it was not the best time for Him to attend the feast. His brothers could go anytime, but He could not. This interpretation is based on the word "time" (kairos, which stresses opportune time). It differs from the word usually used for Jesus' "time" (hora, Jn.2:4). However, *kairos* is a frequently used word in the New Testament, and its meaning cannot be held to opportune time. Three things support the interpretation that kairos means "Jesus' time" in this passage.
   ⇒ The contrast Jesus makes between His time and His brothers' time.
   ⇒ The context of verses 7-8.
   ⇒ The emphasis given to Jesus' answer. If the reply means only that He was waiting for the opportune time to go to Jerusalem, then the reply seems trivial, almost meaningless; so does the contrast between His time and His brothers' time and the points of verses 7-8.

2. It is time for the world's works to be proclaimed evil. Christ said "It is time for the world's reaction against me, not time for its acceptance." It is time for Christ...
   - to point out the sin of the world not to receive its acclaim.
   - to point out the false religion of the world not to proclaim its hypocritical goodness.
   - to point out the depravity of the world not to camouflage the truth.
   - to point out the corruption within the world not to paint a rosy picture.
   - to point out the need of the world not to praise it.
   - to point out the destiny of the world not to hide its fate.

Because of this, the fact that He proclaimed the truth, the world hated Him and would not acknowledge and acclaim Him. It was time for the world's reaction against Him, not time for its acceptance.

It is time for man's acceptance, time for the men of the world to accept each other. His brothers were part of the world, and the world does not hate its own. The world does not reject and hate, but receives those...

- who love it
- who serve it
- who participate in it
- who approve of its behavior
- who go along with it

Therefore, the world receives those who look at Christ and mock, ridicule, criticize, reject, and treat Him sarcastically. The world does not hate, but welcomes, opposition to Jesus Christ.

Thought 1. This is the time and the day when the works of the world must be proclaimed evil. The truth must be preached and proclaimed by the ministers of God. The world cannot be saved unless the evil of the world is acknowledged and corrected. It is the task of God's people to proclaim the truth; however, it must be proclaimed as Jesus proclaimed it: in love, appealing to the desperate needs of man.

> **If I had not come and spoken to them, they would not be guilty of sin. Now, however, they have no excuse for their sin. (John 15:22)**
>
> **for all have sinned and fall short of the glory of God, (Rom 3:23; cp. Is53:6; 64:6)**
>
> **For the wages of sin is death, but the gift of God is eternal life in Christ Jesus our Lord. (Rom 6:23)**
>
> **If we claim to be without sin, we deceive ourselves and the truth is not in us. (1 John 1:8)**
>
> **The LORD saw how great man's wickedness on the earth had become, and that every inclination of the thoughts of his heart was only evil all the time. (Gen 6:5)**
>
> **The truly righteous man attains life, but he who pursues evil goes to his death. (Prov 11:19)**
>
> **Who can say, "I have kept my heart pure; I am clean and without sin"? (Prov 20:9)**

3. It is not time for Jesus' full revelation. Note the words "has not yet come" or "fully come" (peplerotai). His predestined *time to die* for the world was not to be, not yet. It was to come, but in God's time. And when it came, His claims and works would be validated and proven beyond question. Many would proclaim Him to be both Lord and Savior, the Bread of Life who alone can fill and satisfy the desperate and starving needs of men.

Thought 1. The believer's answer to mockery, ridicule, sarcasm, and unbelief is the same as the answer proclaimed by Jesus.

1) This is not the day for His acclaim, but for man's acclaim.
2) It is time for the world's works to be proclaimed evil.
3) It is not time for His full revelation, that is, for the climax of human history, the day when He shall return in glory and majesty, dominion and power.

> **It is written: "'As surely as I live,' says the Lord, 'every knee will bow before me; every tongue will confess to God.'" (Rom 14:11)**
>
> **Therefore God exalted him to the highest place and gave him the name that is above every name, that at the name of Jesus every knee should bow, in heaven and on earth and under the earth, and every tongue confess that Jesus Christ is Lord, to the glory of God the Father. (Phil 2:9-11)**
>
> **Who will not fear you, O Lord, and bring glory to your name? For you alone are holy. All nations will come and worship before you, for your righteous acts have been revealed." (Rev 15:4)**
>
> **All the ends of the earth will remember and turn to the LORD, and all the families of the nations will bow down before him, for dominion belongs to the LORD and he rules over the nations. (Psa 22:27-28)**
>
> **"Turn to me and be saved, all you ends of the earth; for I am God, and there is no other. By myself I have sworn, my mouth has uttered in all integrity a word that will not be revoked: Before me every knee will bow; by me every tongue will swear. (Isa 45:22-23; cp. Is.66:23)**

	B. The Response of the Jews: Seeking, Yet Questioning, 7:10-19	15 The Jews were amazed and asked, "How did this man get such learning without having studied?"	1) Jesus went to the temple & taught 2) People questioned His credentials
1 Jesus went to the Feast a. After his brothers had already gone b. Quietly, in secret **2 The Jews' response: Sought & questioned & whispered about Him** a. A good man b. A deceiver	10 However, after his brothers had left for the Feast, he went also, not publicly, but in secret. 11 Now at the Feast the Jews were watching for him and asking, "Where is that man?" 12 Among the crowds there was widespread whispering about him. Some said, "He is a good man." Others replied,	16 Jesus answered, "My teaching is not my own. It comes from him who sent me. 17 If anyone chooses to do God's will, he will find out whether my teaching comes from God or whether I speak on my own. 18 He who speaks on his	**3 Jesus' reply: My teaching is God's teaching** a. Proven by the subjective test (the inward or moral test): Man knows the truth by doing it b. Proven by the objec-
c. A man not significant enough to defend d. A man unaccredited— so capable, yet uneducated	"No, he deceives the people." 13 But no one would say anything publicly about him for fear of the Jews. 14 Not until halfway through the Feast did Jesus go up to the temple courts and begin to teach.	own does so to gain honor for himself, but he who works for the honor of the one who sent him is a man of truth; there is nothing false about him. 19 Has not Moses given you the law? Yet not one of you keeps the law. Why are you trying to kill me?"	tive test (the outward or observation test): Does man speak for his own glory or for God's glory? c. Proven by the personal test: Are you keeping the law?

DIVISION VIII

THE RESPONSES TO THE REVELATION OF JESUS, 7:1-53

B. The Response of the Jews: Seeking, Yet Questioning, 7:10-19

(7:10-19) **Introduction**: the second reaction or response to Jesus came from the Jewish crowds, including both religionists and pilgrims. This passage gives the answer to four false beliefs about Jesus, the belief that He was…
- only a *good man*
- a deceiver
- a man not important enough to defend
- a man unaccredited

1. Jesus went to the Feast (v.10).
2. The Jews' response: sought and questioned and whispered about Him (v.11-15).
3. Jesus' reply: My teaching is God's teaching (v.16-19).
   a. Proven by the subjective test (the inward or moral test): Man knows the truth by doing it.
   b. Proven by the objective test (the outward or observation test): Does man speak for his own glory or for God's glory?
   c. Proven by the personal test: Are you keeping the law?

1 (7:10) **Jesus Christ, Faithfulness to Jewish Feast**: Jesus finally went up to Jerusalem to attend the Feast, but He did not go up with His brothers. They had left sometime before, probably in a large caravan. The caravans of the day were huge expeditions (cp. Lk.2:43-44); therefore, He went quietly, almost in secret, so as not to attract too much attention. He was going to step forward to teach publicly, but He needed to be inconspicuous until that moment came (v.14). If He had travelled to Jerusalem publicly, the people might have escorted Him into the city, proclaiming Him King and causing His arrest before His "time" (Jn.7:6). The Triumphal Entry would have taken place too soon.

2 (7:11-15) **Jesus Christ, Response to**: the Jews' response was that of seeking Him and of questioning and murmuring about Him. The term "Jews" in this instance probably refers to all Jews, religionists and pilgrims. Everyone wanted to find Him: the Jewish authorities wanted to entrap and discredit Him before the people, for they wished to have Him arrested and sentenced to death. The common people wanted to find Him so they could hear His teaching and see His miracles for themselves.

The Jewish crowds are to be commended for having sought Christ, for He is to be sought. Every man should seek Christ until He is found.
⇒ But the motives of the religionists were evil. They were not seeking Jesus to worship and learn of Him, but to harm Him. They wanted to discredit Him, lest they lose the loyalty of the people and their own security and position.
⇒ But the motives of the common people were corrupt. They were not seeking Jesus as Savior and Lord, the One to whom they owed their allegiance. They were seeking Him out of curiosity, to see Him perform spectacular miracles (see DEEPER STUDY # 1—Jn.2:23).

The response of the Jewish crowds was that of whispering and questioning. It was not a discontented whispering, but that of buzzing about, excitedly so. People were quietly asking and discussing their opinions about Him; but in soft voices and off to the side, in the corners and away from strangers, lest they arouse the suspicion that they were followers of Jesus and endanger their own lives.

1. Some thought He was a good man: a man to be supported, listened to, and heeded. By *good* they meant at least

the following: a man who was…

- loving and caring
- giving and unselfish
- true and honest
- just and moral
- believing and worshipful

But note the inadequacy and weakness of this belief. It sees Jesus only as a man, a good man, yes; but still only as a man. It does not believe Jesus is the *Son of Man.* (See note—Jn.1:51.)

2. Some thought Jesus was the exact opposite: a deceiver, a man who was deliberately deceiving and leading the people away from the true religion. By *deceiving* they meant that He was…

- misleading, deluding, beguiling, actually leading the people away from God.
- boasting of Himself, His own ideas and position.
- revelling in the admiration, adulation, and flattery of the people.
- trying to be novel and creative, to be recognized as a man of new ideas.
- trying to attract attention and secure a following.

In reality, they said He was…

- not of God, but of Beelzebub (the devil) (Mt.12:24; Mk.3:22; Lk.11:15).
- a drunkard and a glutton (Mt.11:19; Lk.7:34).
- an associate of sinners (Mt.9:11; Mk.2:16; Lk.5:30; 15:2).
- a criminal and a law breaker (Mt.12:1-8; 12:10; 15:1-20; 16:1-12).

Now note: if all this were true, if Jesus were a deceiver, then He was the most evil and deceptive man the world has ever seen.

3. Some thought Jesus was a man not significant enough to defend. Even those who felt Jesus was a good man cowered in fear rather than speak up for Jesus. They feared the religious authorities. They felt Jesus was not worth the bother, the cost, the risk of jeopardizing their own safety.

4. Some thought Jesus was a man unaccredited and without proper credentials. About the middle of the Feast, Jesus ended His seclusion and hiding. He went into the temple and began teaching. The people were astonished; they were amazed at His knowledge. He had never been a student of their school or of a Rabbi, yet He knew the Scriptures well. Their question was asked in contempt: "How does this man know so much? Who is He claiming to be? What right does He have to teach? He has never learned or studied in our schools, under our teachers. He is a *mere carpenter*, uneducated, and unlearned. What right does He have to set Himself up as a great teacher, a person to be heard? He is not accredited nor ordained by our schools and leaders."

> **Thought 1.** How often people are rejected, despite their call and gifts, simply because they are not accredited by the right schools or leaders or do not have the *proper* education.

3 (7:16-19) **Jesus Christ, Claims—Knowledge, of God:** Jesus' reply was threefold. He answered all four charges, the charges that He was…

- only a good man
- a deceiver
- a man not significant enough to defend
- a man unaccredited

Jesus made the phenomenal claim: "My teaching is not my own, but God's." Note…

- He did not claim to be the Source of His message.
- He claimed to be "sent" by God, to be the Representative, the Ambassador of God. He claimed to have been in the most intimate relationship with God: in His presence, communion, and fellowship. (See note—Jn.3:34.)

> **For I have come down from heaven not to do my will but to do the will of him who sent me. (John 6:38)**
> **But I know him because I am from him and he sent me." (John 7:29)**
> **Jesus said to them, "If God were your Father, you would love me, for I came from God and now am here. I have not come on my own; but he sent me. (John 8:42)**
> **As long as it is day, we must do the work of him who sent me. Night is coming, when no one can work. (John 9:4)**
> **What about the one whom the Father set apart as his very own and sent into the world? Why then do you accuse me of blasphemy because I said, 'I am God's Son'? (John 10:36)**
> **That all of them may be one, Father, just as you are in me and I am in you. May they also be in us so that the world may believe that you have sent me. (John 17:21)**

- He claimed that His message and teaching were God's. He was only the Messenger of God.

> **So Jesus said, "When you have lifted up the Son of Man, then you will know that I am the one I claim to be and that I do nothing on my own but speak just what the Father has taught me. (John 8:28)**
> **For I gave them the words you gave me and they accepted them. They knew with certainty that I came from you, and they believed that you sent me. (John 17:8)**
> **Anyone who runs ahead and does not continue in the teaching of Christ does not have God; whoever continues in the teaching has both the Father and the Son. (2 John 1:9)**

Jesus said a person can actually test His claim. There are three tests that prove His claim.

1. There is the subjective test, the inward or moral test. How can a person know if Jesus' claim is true? He can know by doing God's will. If a person will do what God says, that person *will know* the truth. Jesus was saying…

- that God's teaching, God's Word, is not for storing up head knowledge, but for experiencing real life.
- that the person who really knows God is not the person who has some thoughts about God, but the person who does and lives as God wills, the person who is holy even as God is holy.
- that the only person who can know God is the person who thinks and lives as God lives. A person who does not live as God lives does not *know* God; he only knows *about* God.
- that the only way to know God is to "<u>believe</u> that He exists, and that He rewards those who earnestly seek Him" (Heb.11:6).

In summary, there is a way to know if Jesus' claim is true. A person can know by...

- believing and seeking to know God, believing that He is a rewarder of those who seek Him.
- living and doing God's will, by being holy even as He is holy (1 Pt.1:15-16).

> **Whoever has my commands and obeys them, he is the one who loves me. He who loves me will be loved by my Father, and I too will love him and show myself to him."** (John 14:21)
>
> **Do not conform any longer to the pattern of this world, but be transformed by the renewing of your mind. Then you will be able to test and approve what God's will is—his good, pleasing and perfect will.** (Rom 12:2)
>
> **But just as he who called you is holy, so be holy in all you do; for it is written: "Be holy, because I am holy."** (1 Pet 1:15-16)

2. There is the objective test, the outward or observation test. Does Christ speak for His own glory or for God's glory? A person can look at Christ and observe and see the truth.

⇒ A man who is *sent by another person* and ends up speaking for himself is not a true representative. He is seeking his own glory.

⇒ A man who is *sent by another person* and speaks the message of that person *is* true, for he is doing what he should do: representing the person who sent him.

Note three very significant things.

a. Jesus did not seek to glorify Himself, but God. Jesus sought to stir men to glorify God in their lives. Such an effort is the constant subject of Jesus' preaching and teaching. He claimed to be empty of personal ambition and glory.

> **And I will do whatever you ask in my name, so that the Son may bring glory to the Father.** (John 14:13)
>
> **I have brought you glory on earth by completing the work you gave me to do.** (John 17:4)

b. Jesus was not just claiming to tell the truth; He was claiming to be *the truth*.

> **Jesus answered, "I am the way and the truth and the life. No one comes to the Father except through me.** (John 14:6)
>
> **"You are a king, then!" said Pilate. Jesus answered, "You are right in saying I am a king. In fact, for this reason I was born, and for this I came into the world, to testify to the truth. Everyone on the side of truth listens to me."** (John 18:37)

c. Jesus claimed that there was no unrighteousness in Him.

> **Can any of you prove me guilty of sin? If I am telling the truth, why don't you believe me?** (John 8:46)
>
> **God made him who had no sin to be sin for us, so that in him we might become the righteousness of God.** (2 Cor 5:21)
>
> **For we do not have a high priest who is unable to sympathize with our weaknesses, but we have one who has been tempted in every way, just as we are—yet was without sin.** (Heb 4:15)
>
> **Such a high priest meets our need—one who is holy, blameless, pure, set apart from sinners, exalted above the heavens.** (Heb 7:26)
>
> **How much more, then, will the blood of Christ, who through the eternal Spirit offered himself unblemished to God, cleanse our consciences from acts that lead to death, so that we may serve the living God!** (Heb 9:14)
>
> **But with the precious blood of Christ, a lamb without blemish or defect.** (1 Pet 1:19)
>
> **"He committed no sin, and no deceit was found in his mouth."** (1 Pet 2:22)

3. There is the personal test. A person can use the law to tell if Christ is true. A man can measure himself by the law and clearly see that he does not keep it. He breaks the law; therefore, he stands in need of God's forgiveness. This was exactly what Christ was preaching and teaching. He cried out that God loved the world and had sent His Son to save the world.

Note what Jesus said: "You are the recipients of the law. God has been very gracious to you in giving the law. But being a recipient is not enough—you must keep the law. However, you do not keep the law. You go about opposing and standing against me, not surrendering to God's Son. You oppose me, even seek to kill me, God's Son."

> **All who rely on observing the law are under a curse, for it is written: "Cursed is everyone who does not continue to do everything written in the Book of the Law."** (Gal 3:10)
>
> **The law is not based on faith; on the contrary, "The man who does these things will live by them."** (Gal 3:12)
>
> **Since they did not know the righteousness that comes from God and sought to establish their own, they did not submit to God's righteousness.** (Rom 10:3)

	C. The Response of the People: A Charge of Insanity, Yet Still Questioning, 7:20-31	to ask, "Isn't this the man they are trying to kill? 26 Here he is, speaking publicly, and they are not saying a word to him. Have the authorities really concluded that he is the Christ ?	a. Their response was questioning: Is this not He? 1) Their reasoning: Could He be the Messiah?
1 The pilgrims' response a. Their response: Jesus was possessed by a demon, that is, insane b. Jesus' reply: Doing good proves a man	20 "You are demon-possessed," the crowd answered. "Who is trying to kill you?" 21 Jesus said to them, "I did one miracle, and you are all astonished.	27 But we know where this man is from; when the Christ comes, no one will know where he is from."	2) Their conclusion: Unbelief—they knew His earthly origin b. Jesus' reply: A pivotal claim
1) Circumcision is doing good: Meets a religious & a ceremonial need of man	22 Yet, because Moses gave you circumcision (though actually it did not come from Moses, but from the patriarchs), you circumcise a child on the Sabbath.	28 Then Jesus, still teaching in the temple courts, cried out, "Yes, you know me, and you know where I am from. I am not here on my own, but he who sent me is true. You do not know him,	1) He is a man 2) He also came from God
2) Healing is doing good: Meets a personal & a bodily need of man	23 Now if a child can be circumcised on the Sabbath so that the law of Moses may not be broken, why are you angry with me for healing the whole man on the Sabbath?	29 but I know him because I am from him and he sent me."	3) He knows God: Is from God—God sent Him c. The local people's reaction[DS1]
3) A principle: Judge not superficially, think & consider	24 Stop judging by mere appearances, and make a right judgment."	30 At this they tried to seize him, but no one laid a hand on him, because his time had not yet come.	1) Some disbelieve & reject 2) Some believe
2 The local residents' response	25 At that point some of the people of Jerusalem began	31 Still, many in the crowd put their faith in him. They said, "When the Christ comes, will he do more miraculous signs than this man?"	

DIVISION VIII

THE RESPONSES TO THE REVELATION OF JESUS, 7:1-53

C. The Response of the People: A Charge of Insanity, Yet Still Questioning, 7:20-31

(7:20-31) **Introduction**: the third reaction or response to Jesus came from all the people—the pilgrims and the local residents of Jerusalem. The charges against Jesus ranged all the way from being demon-possessed to being a mere man. Jesus' answer to all charges against Him was incisive.

1. The pilgrims' response (v.20-24).
2. The local residents' response (v.25-31).

1 (7:20-24) **Jesus Christ, Response to**: the pilgrims' response was a charge that Jesus was demon-possessed and insane.

1. The charge was made primarily by the pilgrims, not by the local residents of Jerusalem. The local residents are covered in the next passage (v.25-31). The pilgrims were the people who did not know Jesus very well. They had come from all over the world; therefore, they did not know as much about Jesus, which made it easier to charge Him with being demon-possessed and mad or insane. He was opposing...

- the religious establishment
- the religious leaders
- the religion that had proven itself for generations
- the religion that contributed so much to society and the nation
- the religion that was founded by the forefathers, the most godly leaders of history

Only an evil man or a man filled with an evil spirit would have opposed such a religion; therefore, Jesus must have been crazed. His mind must have been deranged, running wild with the imagination that people were out to get Him. He must have been controlled by an evil spirit. The pilgrims thought their religious leaders could do little if any evil. They thought their religious leaders would never...

- harm anyone
- be so unjust and immoral
- be so undisciplined and out of control
- react against anyone
- be so corruptible
- do such an unholy thing

Thought 1. Some people think religious leaders can do no wrong. However, religion and religious leaders can be wrong just as any establishment or anyone else can be wrong. Everyone can fail and fall, come short and sin, be misled and become corruptible. Christ came...

- to point out this misconception
- to correct this misconception
- to forgive this misconception
- to pass judgment upon those who would not repent or receive God's forgiveness and be corrected

Thought 2. A man's choice, his decision, must be made for Jesus Christ and not for religion and religious leaders. Christ is the Truth, not religion and its leaders. Religion and religious leaders are to follow

Christ just as all other men are to follow Christ. Christ is the Lord and Master, not religion and its leaders.

2. Jesus answered the pilgrims by appealing to the great work He had just done. He had healed the crippled man by the pool of Bethsaida. The man had been bedridden for thirty-eight years, and the people had marvelled at the power of Jesus (Jn.5:1f). But there was a problem. Jesus had healed the man on the Sabbath, which was considered work, and working on the Sabbath was strictly forbidden. It was a serious offense in the minds of the Jews, for it taught the people to break the law. And this the civil and religious leaders could not allow, for it was their religion that had held the nation together (see DEEPER STUDY # 2—Jn.5:15-16 for more discussion).

The point is this. Jesus said that He was not evil; He was not demon-possessed and mad. Doing good proves whether a man is full of evil or full of good. His work, healing the crippled man, was a good work not an evil work. His healing did as much good as the religious leaders who circumcised on the Sabbath day. Note three points.

a. The religious leaders criticized Jesus for healing the crippled man on the Sabbath, and it was for this work and other so called law-breaking deeds that they were opposing Him, some even plotting to kill Him. But the pilgrims did not know this, not yet.

b. Jesus wanted all men, even the religionists, to see the truth. He was not a law-breaker, not an evil man. He was not out to destroy men and nations. He was the Son of God who had come to save men and nations and to correct and set religion straight.

c. Jesus appealed to the people to judge rightly, that is, by facts, not by appearance.

⇒ When they circumcised a man on the Sabbath, they were not doing evil, but good. They were meeting a man's religious and ceremonial need. Therefore, they were correct in circumcising on the Sabbath, for God commands circumcision on the eighth day, and sometimes the eighth day after a child's birth was bound to fall on the Sabbath (Lev.12:3).

⇒ When He healed a man on the Sabbath, He was not doing evil, but good. He was meeting a personal and bodily need of a man, a need much more desperate than a religious and ceremonial need.

Jesus told the people to judge not according to appearance, but to look at what He did; and to look realistically, honestly, and objectively. If a person did, he would see that Jesus was not full of evil but full of good and righteousness. He would see that Jesus was the Son of God.

But the LORD said to Samuel, "Do not consider his appearance or his height, for I have rejected him. The LORD does not look at the things man looks at. Man looks at the outward appearance, but the LORD looks at the heart." (1 Sam 16:7)

"Woe to you, teachers of the law and Pharisees, you hypocrites! You are like whitewashed tombs, which look beautiful on the outside but on the inside are full of dead men's bones and everything unclean. (Mat 23:27)

"I have testimony weightier than that of John. For the very work that the Father has given me to finish, and which I am doing, testifies that the Father has sent me. (John 5:36)

The Jews gathered around him, saying, "How long will you keep us in suspense? If you are the Christ, tell us plainly." Jesus answered, "I did tell you, but you do not believe. The miracles I do in my Father's name speak for me, (John 10:24-25)

Do not believe me unless I do what my Father does. But if I do it, even though you do not believe me, believe the miracles, that you may know and understand that the Father is in me, and I in the Father." (John 10:37-38)

Follow justice and justice alone, so that you may live and possess the land the LORD your God is giving you. (Deu 16:20)

2 (7:25-31) **Jesus Christ, Deity—Origin—Response—God, Ignorance of**: the local people's response was that of reasoning and drawing a tragic conclusion.

They questioned among themselves: is this the One who is so opposed and feared? Is He the One whom they seek to kill? They also reasoned: He speaks so openly and boldly, and He is not stopped. Is He indeed the Messiah? But the local residents came to a tragic conclusion: Jesus is not the Messiah. Why? Because they knew His origin. They knew all about His family and rearing; therefore, they concluded that He was a mere man, a carpenter from Nazareth. In their minds there was absolutely nothing unusual about His origin; therefore, He could not possibly be of God. He could not be the promised Messiah.

Thought 1. Some men always have and always will question, reason, and draw the wrong conclusion.

⇒ Some will question: is this He, the One promised by God, the One so needed by the world?

⇒ Some will reason: this is the very Christ, the Messiah. He is bound to be, for He continues on. He is still proclaimed, forcibly so, despite being so threatened and persecuted with the intention of being wiped out.

⇒ Some will conclude: this could not be the Son of God. It is impossible for a man to be born of God, to literally come from God. A man is a man, just flesh and blood like all other men. His origin has to be that of a man and a woman. Note: unbelief prevails when the mind is set only upon the earth and its physical law. If God is God, He must be allowed to act supernaturally, above natural law. This was the problem with the people in Jesus' day, and it is the problem with so many of every generation.

Jesus' reply to those who questioned and disbelieved Him is a critical point. His answer centered around His origin. Note that He was gripped with great emotion in answering this point. He cried (ekrazen) and shouted three things.

1. He *is* a man, and men do know where He came from. He was born of Mary and did come from Nazareth, but that is not all. There is much, much more.

145

2. He has come *from God*. God sent Him. Note exactly what Jesus claimed.
   a. "I am not here on my own": His mission and message were not His own. He did not dream it up, plan it or plot it. He was not out for self glory or to build a movement and a following. What He did was not of Himself.
   b. "He who sent me is true." A real Person sent Jesus, and note: the Person is not only real, He is true. He is a Person who is the very embodiment of truth. (See Deeper Study # 1—Jn.1:9; Deeper Study # 2—14:6.) What Jesus was claiming and doing was exactly what He had been sent and commissioned to claim and to do.
   c. "You do not know Him." They did not know that Person who is truth. Jesus was saying, of course, that they did not know God. If they knew God, really knew Him, they would recognize and know that Jesus' mission and works were of God. They would know that only God's perfect love and power could speak and do as Jesus did.

They will treat you this way because of my name, for they do not know the One who sent me. (John 15:21)

They will do such things because they have not known the Father or me. (John 16:3)

"My people are fools; they do not know me. They are senseless children; they have no understanding. They are skilled in doing evil; they know not how to do good." (Jer 4:22)

Even the stork in the sky knows her appointed seasons, and the dove, the swift and the thrush observe the time of their migration. But my people do not know the requirements of the LORD. (Jer 8:7)

"They make ready their tongue like a bow, to shoot lies; it is not by truth that they triumph in the land. They go from one sin to another; they do not acknowledge me," declares the LORD. (Jer 9:3)

3. "I know Him [God]." Jesus told how He knew God.
   a. He knew God because He was from God (see Deeper Study # 1—Jn.3:31 for verses of Scripture).

He actually came from God's presence, from being face to face with Him.
   b. He knew God because He was sent by God (see Deeper Study # 3—Jn.3:34). While face to face with God, God commissioned Him and sent Him forth to *proclaim* and *live* the truth before men. (See Deeper Study # 2—Jn.14:6.)

For I have come down from heaven not to do my will but to do the will of him who sent me. (John 6:38)

But I know him because I am from him and he sent me." (John 7:29)

Jesus said to them, "If God were your Father, you would love me, for I came from God and now am here. I have not come on my own; but he sent me. (John 8:42)

What about the one whom the Father set apart as his very own and sent into the world? Why then do you accuse me of blasphemy because I said, 'I am God's Son'? (John 10:36)

That all of them may be one, Father, just as you are in me and I am in you. May they also be in us so that the world may believe that you have sent me. (John 17:21)

DEEPER STUDY # 1

(7:30-31) **Jesus Christ, Response to**: the reaction of the local residents was twofold.

1. Some still did not believe and some even became sworn enemies. They tried to stop Jesus, but they failed, for God stopped them. He overrode their opposition and plots. Jesus' "time" had not yet come, so they were not allowed to stop Him (see note, "My Time"—Jn.2:3-5).
2. Some believed in Him (see Deeper Study # 2—Jn.2:24).

Whoever believes in him is not condemned, but whoever does not believe stands condemned already because he has not believed in the name of God's one and only Son. (John 3:18)

Whoever believes in the Son has eternal life, but whoever rejects the Son will not see life, for God's wrath remains on him." (John 3:36)

	D. The Response of the Rulers & Authorities: A Charge of Being a Rabble-Rouser, 7:32-36	34 You will look for me, but you will not find me; and where I am, you cannot come."	& ascension b. He foretold man's destiny: Men will seek to find Him—but cannot come where He is
1 The rulers' response a. They considered Him a threat, a rabble-rouser b. They sought to arrest Him	32 The Pharisees heard the crowd whispering such things about him. Then the chief priests and the Pharisees sent temple guards to arrest him.	35 The Jews said to one another, "Where does this man intend to go that we cannot find him? Will he go where our people live scattered among the Greeks, and teach the Greeks?	3 The reaction of the rulers & authorities: They questioned His reply
2 Jesus' reply a. He foretold His destiny: His death, resurrection,	33 Jesus said, "I am with you for only a short time, and then I go to the one who sent me.	36 What did he mean when he said, 'You will look for me, but you will not find me,' and' Where I am, you cannot come'?"	

DIVISION VIII

THE RESPONSES TO THE REVELATION OF JESUS, 7:1-53

D. The Response of the Rulers and Authorities: A Charge of Being a Rabble-Rouser, 7:32-36

(7:32-36) **Introduction**: the fourth reaction or response to Jesus is that of the authorities, both religious and civil. They paint a clear picture of men in every generation who reject and oppose Jesus. What Jesus says is both striking and tragic for all unbelievers.

1. The rulers' response (v.32).
2. Jesus' reply (v.33-34).
   a. He foretold His destiny: His death, resurrection, and ascension.
   b. He foretold man's destiny: men shall seek to find Him—but cannot come where He is.
3. The reaction of the rulers and authorities: they questioned His reply (v.35-36).

1 (7:32) **Jesus Christ, Response—Religionists**: the response of the rulers, both religious and civil. Note several facts.

1. The religionists or the Pharisees took the lead in opposing Jesus (see DEEPER STUDY # 3, Pharisees—Acts 23:8; DEEPER STUDY # 2, Religionists—Jn.5:16. This last note discusses why the religionists opposed Jesus so vehemently.) They apparently approached the chief priests and persuaded them that Jesus was a threat.

2. The chief priests were primarily leaders among the Sadducees who held most of the high offices of Jewish government under Roman rule (see DEEPER STUDY # 2, Sadducees—Acts 23:8). When Rome became dissatisfied with a chief priest, he was removed and another one was placed in authority. The removal from office was a common occurence, so there were quite a few chief priests surviving. In the eyes of the people, they were still honored despite being removed. The people blamed Rome for their removal, not the chief priests.

3. In the four gospels, when the Pharisees, chief priests, and Scribes are mentioned as standing together against Jesus, it means that the ruling body of the Jewish nation has taken action. (See DEEPER STUDY # 1, Sanhedrin—Mt.26:59.) In the present situation, the Sanhedrin had apparently met and dispatched the palace or temple police to arrest Jesus. From what follows it seems that they were told to watch for an appropriate moment lest they cause a riot among His supporters.

4. Note what disturbed the religionists so much. It was the whispering of the people, in particular the fact that so many were "putting their faith in Him" (v.31). He was a threat to their security and position, esteem and authority, profession and livelihood. (See DEEPER STUDY # 2—Jn.5:15-16 for more discussion.) They wanted nothing to do with Him; they wanted things to be left alone. They wanted to get rid of Him as soon as possible.

Thought 1. A man (leader) often murmurs against and opposes Jesus because Jesus is a threat to his way of life. Because the man is unwilling to change his life, Jesus is a threat to him and his security. Wanting absolutely nothing to do with Jesus, he tries to dispose of Him and His influence the best way he can.

> **What good will it be for a man if he gains the whole world, yet forfeits his soul? Or what can a man give in exchange for his soul? (Mat 16:26)**
> **"Be careful, or your hearts will be weighed down with dissipation, drunkenness and the anxieties of life, and that day will close on you unexpectedly like a trap. (Luke 21:34)**
> **It teaches us to say "No" to ungodliness and worldly passions, and to live self-controlled, upright and godly lives in this present age, (Titus 2:12)**
> **You adulterous people, don't you know that friendship with the world is hatred toward God? Anyone who chooses to be a friend of the world becomes an enemy of God. (James 4:4)**
> **But thanks be to God that, though you used to be slaves to sin, you wholeheartedly obeyed the form of teaching to which you were entrusted. You have been set free from sin and have become slaves to righteousness. (Rom 6:17-18)**
> **So he made a whip out of cords, and drove all from the temple area, both sheep and cattle; he scattered the coins of the money changers and overturned their tables. To those who sold doves he said, "Get these out of here! How dare you turn my Father's house into a market!" (John 2:15-16)**

You say, 'I am rich; I have acquired wealth and do not need a thing.' But you do not realize that you are wretched, pitiful, poor, blind and naked. (Rev 3:17)

They close up their callous hearts, and their mouths speak with arrogance. (Psa 17:10)

"'Now this was the sin of your sister Sodom: She and her daughters were arrogant, overfed and unconcerned; they did not help the poor and needy. (Ezek 16:49)

2 (7:33-34) **Jesus Christ,** Death; **Ascension; Exaltation:** Jesus' reply was puzzling and tragic both to the unbeliever of His day and to the unbeliever of today.

1. Jesus foretold His destiny.
   a. He foretold His death: "I am with you for only a short time."

> **"My children, I will be with you only a little longer. You will look for me, and just as I told the Jews, so I tell you now: Where I am going, you cannot come. (John 13:33)**
>
> **"You heard me say, 'I am going away and I am coming back to you.' If you loved me, you would be glad that I am going to the Father, for the Father is greater than I. (John 14:28)**
>
> **"Now I am going to him who sent me, yet none of you asks me, 'Where are you going?' (John 16:5)**
>
> **I will remain in the world no longer, but they are still in the world, and I am coming to you. Holy Father, protect them by the power of your name—the name you gave me—so that they may be one as we are one. (John 17:11)**

   b. He foretold His resurrection and ascension: "Then I go to the one who sent me" (cp. Jn.8:14; 13:3; 14:2-3; 16:5, 10, 17).

> **Jesus answered, "Even if I testify on my own behalf, my testimony is valid, for I know where I came from and where I am going. But you have no idea where I come from or where I am going. (John 8:14)**
>
> **Jesus knew that the Father had put all things under his power, and that he had come from God and was returning to God; (John 13:3)**
>
> **In my Father's house are many rooms; if it were not so, I would have told you. I am going there to prepare a place for you.**
>
> **And if I go and prepare a place for you, I will come back and take you to be with me that you also may be where I am. (John 14:2-3)**
>
> **in regard to righteousness, because I am going to the Father, where you can see me no longer; (John 16:10)**
>
> **Some of his disciples said to one another, "What does he mean by saying, 'In a little while you will see me no more, and then after a little while you will see me,' and' Because I am going to the Father'?" (John 16:17)**

What did the death and resurrection have to do with those who opposed Jesus? Why did Jesus predict His destiny in answering those who wanted nothing to do with Him?

   a. He was saying that those who opposed Him could get rid of Him. They could reject and have nothing to do with Him. They did not have to worry about getting rid of Him; they would be allowed to do that. He would go away.
   b. He was saying, however, that He would not cease to be; He would not be annihilated and cease to exist. His life would not be extinguished. He would be killed because men would try to stop Him from living as a man on earth. But He would arise and return to His Father who sent Him. He would experience glory and give great hope to all those who have believed and do believe in Him (see note—Mk.16:19-20).

2. Jesus foretold man's destiny. Jesus predicted a tragic future for those who opposed Him and wanted nothing to do with Him. He said that the day is coming when…
   • they will look for Him,
   • but they will not find Him;
   • where He is they will not be allowed to come.

What Jesus meant is *just what He said*.

   a. The man who rejects Christ will face the day when he will seek Christ.
   ⇒ In this life, God's Spirit does not always strive or contend with man (Gen.6:3; cp. Pr.29:1). When a man is in church or anywhere else and feels pulled to make a decision and puts the decision off for an hour or two (a half day or a day at most), the pull fades and eventually dies completely. God's Spirit does not continue to strive or contend with him. Most of us have experienced such movements and killed the Spirit's contending within us.

> **Then the LORD said, "My Spirit will not contend with man forever, for he is mortal; his days will be a hundred and twenty years." (Gen 6:3)**
>
> **A man who remains stiff-necked after many rebukes will suddenly be destroyed—without remedy. (Prov 29:1)**
>
> **Do not cast me from your presence or take your Holy Spirit from me. (Psa 51:11)**

   ⇒ In the next life, at the day of judgment, the unbeliever will seek Christ.

> **"Not everyone who says to me, 'Lord, Lord,' will enter the kingdom of heaven, but only he who does the will of my Father who is in heaven. Many will say to me on that day, 'Lord, Lord, did we not prophesy in your name, and in your name drive out demons and perform many miracles?' (Mat 7:21-22)**
>
> **"But while they were on their way to buy the oil, the bridegroom arrived. The virgins who were ready went in with him to the wedding banquet. And the door was shut. "Later the others also came. 'Sir! Sir!' they said. 'Open the door for us!' (Mat 25:10-11)**

JOHN 7:32-36

b. However, the great tragedy is that the unbeliever will not find Christ. It will be too late (cp. Mt.25:31-46). The unbeliever has never known Christ nor what it is to walk in the Lord's kingdom on earth; therefore, he will not know Christ or His kingdom in that day. As Christ and heaven are alien and unknown to the unbeliever today, so will Christ and heaven be alien and unknown to the unbeliever in that day. Unbelievers will not be allowed to come where He is, that is, live in God's presence, not eternally.

Note: "I" and "you" are a climactic contrast. Jesus said "Where I am, you cannot come" (v.36). "Where I am" means two things.

⇒ It means the rest and life of Christ, which is love, joy, and peace. (See note, Rest—Jn.4:16-18.)
⇒ It means the state of eternal life (see DEEPER STUDY # 2—Jn.1:4; DEEPER STUDY # 1—10:10; DEEPER STUDY # 1—17:2-3. Cp. DEEPER STUDY # 3, Kingdom of God—Mt.19:23-24.)

For I tell you that unless your righteousness surpasses that of the Pharisees and the teachers of the law, you will certainly not enter the kingdom of heaven. (Mat 5:20)

Once the owner of the house gets up and closes the door, you will stand outside knocking and pleading, 'Sir, open the door for us.' "But he will answer, 'I don't know you or where you come from.' "Then you will say, 'We ate and drank with you, and you taught in our streets.' "But he will reply, 'I don't know you or where you come from. Away from me, all you evildoers!' "There will be weeping there, and gnashing of teeth, when you see Abraham, Isaac and Jacob and all the prophets in the kingdom of God, but you yourselves thrown out. (Luke 13:25-28)

Do you not know that the wicked will not inherit the kingdom of God? Do not be deceived: Neither the sexu-ally immoral nor idolaters nor adulterers nor male prostitutes nor homosexual offenders (1 Cor 6:9)

I declare to you, brothers, that flesh and blood cannot inherit the kingdom of God, nor does the perishable inherit the imperishable. (1 Cor 15:50)

Nothing impure will ever enter it, nor will anyone who does what is shameful or deceitful, but only those whose names are written in the Lamb's book of life. (Rev 21:27)

3 (7:35-36) **Jesus Christ, Response to**: the reaction of the rulers and authorities. Very simply, they were *puzzled*, questioning what Jesus meant.

1. The scattered or dispersed (diasporan) refers to the Jews who were scattered all over the world. It seems that the rulers thought Jesus was going to leave Israel and go to some foreign nation, preaching to the Jews there.

2. Those who opposed Jesus were puzzled by His death and resurrection and ascension. It was difficult for them to grasp its meaning and to believe in Him. In fact, it was offensive to them. This was exactly what Jesus had said (see note—Jn.6:62).

But if your eyes are bad, your whole body will be full of darkness. If then the light within you is darkness, how great is that darkness! (Mat 6:23)

The god of this age has blinded the minds of unbelievers, so that they cannot see the light of the gospel of the glory of Christ, who is the image of God. (2 Cor 4:4)

They are darkened in their understanding and separated from the life of God because of the ignorance that is in them due to the hardening of their hearts. (Eph 4:18)

But whoever hates his brother is in the darkness and walks around in the darkness; he does not know where he is going, because the darkness has blinded him. (1 John 2:11)

149

	E. The Great Claim of Jesus and Divided Opinions About Him, 7:37-53	vided because of Jesus.	d. Some: Would take & do away with Him
1 The Feast day	37 On the last and greatest	44 Some wanted to seize him, but no one laid a hand on him.	**4 The rulers' response**
2 The claims of Jesus	day of the Feast, Jesus stood	45 Finally the temple guards went back to the chief priests	a. Wished to remove Him
a. He is the source of life^DS1	and said in a loud voice, "If anyone is thirsty, let him come to me and drink.	and Pharisees, who asked them, "Why didn't you bring him in?"	1) The officers were sent to arrest Jesus, v.32
b. He is the source of abundant life	38 Whoever believes in me, as the Scripture has said, streams of living water will flow from within him."	46 "No one ever spoke the way this man does," the guards declared.	2) The officers' response: He is a great Teacher
c. He is the source of the Holy Spirit^DS2	39 By this he meant the Spirit, whom those who believed in him were later to receive. Up to that time the Spirit had not been given, since Jesus had not yet been glorified.	47 "You mean he has deceived you also?" the Pharisees retorted. 48 "Has any of the rulers or of the Pharisees believed in him? 49 No! But this mob that knows nothing of the law—there is a curse on them."	b. Claimed He was a deceiver: Charged the people with being mistaken & accursed
3 The people's divided response	40 On hearing his words, some of the people said, "Surely this man is the Prophet."	50 Nicodemus, who had gone to Jesus earlier and who was one of their own number, asked,	c. Rejected Him
a. Many: The prophet^DS3			1) Nicodemus spoke up for Him^DS5
b. Others: The Christ	41 Others said, "He is the Christ." Still others asked, "How can the Christ come from Galilee?	51 "Does our law condemn anyone without first hearing him to find out what he is doing?"	
c. Some: Questioned His birthplace & misinterpreted Scripture^DS4	42 Does not the Scripture say that the Christ will come from David's family and from Bethlehem, the town where David lived?" 43 Thus the people were di-	52 They replied, "Are you from Galilee, too? Look into it, and you will find that a prophet does not come out of Galilee." 53 Then each went to his own home.	2) They rejected Nicodemus' questions, misinterpreting Scripture d. Went to their own homes: Lived as always

DIVISION VIII

THE RESPONSES TO THE REVELATION OF JESUS, 7:1-53

E. The Great Claim of Jesus and Divided Opinions About Him, 7:37-53

(7:37-53) **Introduction**: this is a picture of the great claim of Jesus and the divided opinions about Him. It is a picture that should cause every man to search his own response to Jesus.

1. The Feast day (v.37).
2. The claims of Jesus (v.37-39).
3. The people's divided response (v.40-44).
4. The rulers' response (v.45-53).

1 (7:37) **Feast of Tabernacles**: the Feast of Tabernacles was the most popular feast among the Jews. For that reason it was simply known as *The Feast* (1 Ki.8:20). It was also called *The Feast of Ingathering* (Ex.23:16) and *The Festival to the Lord* (Lev.23:39). The Feast of Tabernacles was celebrated for seven days. Each Jewish family built a small stucco or tent-like structure in their yard or upon some other property they owned or secured for the occasion. Then they moved out of their home into the structure for the seven-day period. The Feast celebrated two significant events. Historically, it celebrated the day when Israel wandered about in the wilderness as strangers and pilgrims without a homeland. The purpose for moving into the stucco or tent-like structure was to keep before their minds the wilderness wanderings of their forefathers (Lev.23:40-

43). Secondly, the Feast was to be a period of thanksgiving for the completion of the harvest season and for the goodness of God in all of life (Ex.23:16; Dt.16:13, 16). The people were to give thanks for all that God had given them: all the fruit of the land that enriched life and made life possible.

The ceremony of the festival was most impressive and gives a dramatic picture of Christ's claims (Jn.7:37-39). On each of the seven days, the people came to the temple and brought some fruit as an offering and a few palm and willow branches. The branches were used to form a roof over the altar. Then the priest took a golden pitcher and led the people in a processional down to the pool of Siloam where he filled the pitcher with water. During this march the people played the flute and sang the Hillel, which was Psalms 113-118.

It was on the return march that the significant drama took place.

⇒ As the pitcher of water passed through the Water Gate, the people repeated in unison: "With joy you will draw water from the wells of salvation" (Is.12:3).

⇒ When the pitcher reached the altar, the water was poured out over the altar as an offering to God. While this was being done, the people

150

waved palm branches and recited the words "O Lord, save us; O Lord, grant us success" (Ps.118:25).

The idea of the processional was a dramatic way to thank God for rain, to offer prayer to God for more rain, and for a fruitful season in the coming year. It was a dramatic way for the people to acknowledge their need and dependence upon God for the rains, the water that gave them the fruit of the ground and the bounty of life. The last day of the Feast was dramatic in particular, for the people repeated the processional seven times. Note a significant point: Scripture says the Feast of Tabernacles will be celebrated and fulfilled in the end time when our Lord returns. The Feast will apparently symbolize our joy, liberty, and victory through the wilderness experience of life and the glorious provision of God: the glorious provision of living eternally and worshipping and serving God throughout the universe (Zech.14:16).

2 (7:37-39) **Jesus Christ, Claims**: the claims of Jesus. It was on "the last and greatest day of the Feast," the day when the people marched in the processional seven times, that Jesus made His phenomenal claim. Some imagine Jesus shouting His claim just as the people finished saying, "Grant us success" (Ps.118:25).

Imagine the scene: Jesus did two unusual things. He "stood" (a teacher always sat in that day), and He "cried out" (ekrazen) shouting loudly. Both actions would startle and shock the people to attention. Picture thousands of voices praying to God for the living rains in the coming season, reciting: "grant us success," and then piercing the air comes the thundering cry:

> **On the last and greatest day of the Feast, Jesus stood and said in a loud voice, "If anyone is thirsty, let him come to me and drink. Whoever believes in me, as the Scripture has said, streams of living water will flow from within him." (John 7:37-38)**

Jesus made three phenomenal claims.

1. Jesus Christ is the source of life: He is the One who can quench the real thirst of man's being, who can meet the desperate need of man for prosperity, the real fruit and bounty of life.
   a. Men do thirst. They thirst for physical water and they thirst for spiritual life (see note—Jn.4:13-14 for a discussion of this point).
   b. Jesus Christ claims to be the source, that is, the Water that can quench man's thirst and give the fruit and bounty man so desperately needs in his life. He claims that He can do what water does (see DEEPER STUDY # 1—Jn.7:37).
   ⇒ He can cleanse and purify.

> **In him we have redemption through his blood, the forgiveness of sins, in accordance with the riches of God's grace (Eph 1:7; cp. 1 Jn.1:9)**

⇒ He can refresh.

> **To whom he said, "This is the resting place, let the weary rest"; and, "This is the place of repose"— but they would not listen. (Isa 28:12)**

> **Repent, then, and turn to God, so that your sins may be wiped out, that times of refreshing may come from the Lord, (Acts 3:19)**

⇒ He can revitalize and energize.

> **"Come to me, all you who are weary and burdened, and I will give you rest. (Mat 11:28)**

2. Jesus Christ is the source of abundant life. Rivers of *living water* can flow out from a person. An abundance of life can be experienced (see DEEPER STUDY # 1—Jn.1:4; DEEPER STUDY # 1—10:10).

> **Blessed are those who hunger and thirst for righteousness, for they will be filled. (Mat 5:6)**
> **But whoever drinks the water I give him will never thirst. Indeed, the water I give him will become in him a spring of water welling up to eternal life." (John 4:14)**
> **Never again will they hunger; never again will they thirst. The sun will not beat upon them, nor any scorching heat. (Rev 7:16)**
> **The Spirit and the bride say, "Come!" And let him who hears say, "Come!" Whoever is thirsty, let him come; and whoever wishes, let him take the free gift of the water of life. (Rev 22:17)**
> **The thief comes only to steal and kill and destroy; I have come that they may have life, and have it to the full. (John 10:10)**

a. The death of Jesus Christ (His having been struck for the sins of the world) is the source of the living water. Out of His death (because He died) He was able to arise, and by arising He was able to conquer sin and death and to bring forth eternal life in all of its abundance. Note: the Word of God to Moses was a picture of the living water that was to come from Christ after He was struck.

> **I will stand there before you by the rock at Horeb. Strike the rock, and water will come out of it for the people to drink." So Moses did this in the sight of the elders of Israel. (Exo 17:6; cp. Num.20:11)**

b. Living water comes only through "believing in Christ." (See DEEPER STUDY # 2—Jn.2:24.)

> **Then Jesus declared, "I am the bread of life. He who comes to me will never go hungry, and he who believes in me will never be thirsty. (John 6:35)**

3. Jesus Christ is the source of the Holy Spirit. Rivers of living water refer to the Holy Spirit. This is a crucial verse, for it is the only place "living waters" is defined. When Jesus spoke of giving "living water," He meant He would give the Holy Spirit to a person. The presence of the Holy Spirit, of course, meant the experience of abundant and eternal life.

Note: it is only the person who believes in Christ who receives the Holy Spirit. Belief in Him is essential. Christ is the Giver of the Spirit. (See note—Jn.4:13-14 for more discussion.)

> But the fruit of the Spirit is love, joy, peace, patience, kindness, goodness, faithfulness, gentleness and self-control. Against such things there is no law. (Gal 5:22-23)
> (For the fruit of the light consists in all goodness, righteousness and truth) (Eph 5:9)

DEEPER STUDY # 1

(7:37) **Jesus Christ—Living Water**: water does at least three things. It cleanses or purifies; it refreshes; and it revitalizes or energizes.

DEEPER STUDY # 2

(7:39) **Holy Spirit**: what does the statement mean, "the [Holy] Spirit had not been given"? It does not mean the Spirit was not active in the Old Testament. He was very active (Gen.1:2; 6:3; Job 26:13; 33:4; Ps.51:11; 139:7; Ezk.3:24, 27; Hag.2:5). It seems to mean that the Holy Spirit was not *fully present* until after the death and glorification of Christ. He was not present...

- in all His fulness
- in the lives of believers all the time
- in equipping believers with permanent spiritual gifts

These three things certainly happened after the glorification of Christ.

⇒ He entered the world in all His fulness at Pentecost. (See DEEPER STUDY # 1—Acts 2:1-4 for more discussion.)
⇒ He entered the lives of believers at conversion, and their bodies became "the temple of the Holy Spirit" (1 Cor.6:19).
⇒ He equips believers with spiritual gifts that are permanent (1 Cor.12:7f).

---

3 (7:40-44) **Jesus Christ, Response to; Opinions of**: the people's response was very divided.

1. Some said He was the Prophet (see DEEPER STUDY # 2—Jn.1:20).
2. Some said He was the Christ (see DEEPER STUDY # 2—Jn.1:20).
3. Some questioned if He could be the Messiah. They knew that He was from Galilee, and they knew the true Messiah was to come out of Bethlehem, the city of David. Therefore, they saw no possible way He could be the Messiah.

Thought 1. Note what happened immediately upon the heels of the Lord's dramatic claim. People began to argue over Him, arguing if He were the real Messiah. What men need is to accept the fact: He is the Messiah, the Christ. There is too much evidence to deny it, too much evidence...

- within the human soul that senses the truth of God
- within the lives of so many who bear clear testimony to His love and forgiveness, presence and assurance

> I tell you the truth, we speak of what we know, and we testify to what we have seen, but still you people do not accept our testimony. (John 3:11)

> The Jews gathered around him, saying, "How long will you keep us in suspense? If you are the Christ, tell us plainly." Jesus answered, "I did tell you, but you do not believe. The miracles I do in my Father's name speak for me, (John 10:24-25)
> Even after Jesus had done all these miraculous signs in their presence, they still would not believe in him. (John 12:37)

Thought 2. Many do question the *Lord's origin* and continue in unbelief because of it. When they look at Jesus, they see a great man, but only a man. They see and believe that He was flesh and blood, but not God incarnate in human flesh. They do not believe Jesus is the Son of God—a great prophet, yes; but the Messiah, the very Son of God, no.

> He was in the world, and though the world was made through him, the world did not recognize him. He came to that which was his own, but his own did not receive him. (John 1:10-11)
> But he replied, "The man who made me well said to me, 'Pick up your mat and walk.'" So they asked him, "Who is this fellow who told you to pick it up and walk?" (John 5:11-12)

4. Some would take and do away with Him. They wanted nothing to do with Him. He was a threat to their peace and security and to their desire to live as they wished. (See note, pt.4—Jn.7:32 for more discussion and thought.)

> "Be careful, or your hearts will be weighed down with dissipation, drunkenness and the anxieties of life, and that day will close on you unexpectedly like a trap. (Luke 21:34)
> You adulterous people, don't you know that friendship with the world is hatred toward God? Anyone who chooses to be a friend of the world becomes an enemy of God. (James 4:4)
> Do not love the world or anything in the world. If anyone loves the world, the love of the Father is not in him. (1 John 2:15)

DEEPER STUDY # 3

(7:40) **Prophetic Reference**: cp. Dt.18:15.

DEEPER STUDY # 4

(7:42) **Prophetic Reference**: cp. Mic.5:2.

---

4 (7:45-53) **Jesus Christ, Response**: the rulers' response was fourfold. Their response should be carefully noted, for it speaks volumes to rulers and leaders of every generation.

1. The leaders wished to be rid of Jesus. They opposed Him and wanted nothing to do with Him (see note, pts. 3, 4—Jn.7:32 for more discussion and thought).

Note the temple police were greatly impressed with the Lord's teaching. To them He was a great teacher.

2. The leaders claimed that He was a deceiver and that the people were mistaken and cursed because they followed Him. (See note, pt.2—Jn.7:11-15.)

3. The leaders rejected Him, strongly so. Nicodemus spoke up for Christ, charging the leaders with breaking the law themselves and suggesting that they all hear Christ and observe His works closely (cp. Nicodemus, Jn.3:1f). The leaders used Scripture as the basis for rejecting Christ. They said that no Scripture pointed to a prophet coming out of Galilee. They were wrong of course, wrong on two counts.

⇒ Jonah came from Galilee.
⇒ God is able to raise up prophets from anywhere He chooses.

4. The leaders went to their own houses and lived just as they had always chosen. God does not force any man to subject himself to His Son. Every man has the freedom to live as He wishes, either for God or for self. The leaders chose to live for self.

> Whoever believes in the Son has eternal life, but whoever rejects the Son will not see life, for God's wrath remains on him." (John 3:36)
> I told you that you would die in your sins; if you do not believe that I am the one I claim to be, you will indeed die in your sins." (John 8:24)

DEEPER STUDY # 5
(7:50) **Nicodemus**: see Jn.3:1-15.

	CHAPTER 8 IX. THE REVELATION OF JESUS, THE LIGHT OF LIFE, 8:1-9:41 A. Man's Dark Sinfulness & God's Great Forgivenss, 8:1-11	6 They were using this question as a trap, in order to have a basis for accusing him. But Jesus bent down and started to write on the ground with his finger.	2) A hypocritical attitude d. Jesus ignored them as long as possible
1 A picture of Jesus' life a. His life of devotion b. His life of worship c. His life of mission & teaching	**B**ut Jesus went to the Mount of Olives. 2 At dawn he appeared again in the temple courts, where all the people gathered around him, and he sat down to teach them.	7 When they kept on questioning him, he straightened up and said to them, "If any one of you is without sin, let him be the first to throw a stone at her." 8 Again he stooped down and wrote on the ground.	**3 Man's dark nature: All men are sinful—guilty of serious sin** a. The counter question by Jesus: Think—if without sin, then condemn b. The result: All men are convicted
2 Man's dark guilt a. A woman (& some man) were guilty of adultery b. Some witnesses who were offended were guilty of being vindictive & seeking revenge c. The religionists & the public were guilty 1) A self-righteous, critical spirit	3 The teachers of the law and the Pharisees brought in a woman caught in adultery. They made her stand before the group 4 And said to Jesus, "Teacher, this woman was caught in the act of adultery. 5 In the Law Moses commanded us to stone such women. Now what do you say?"	9 At this, those who heard began to go away one at a time, the older ones first, until only Jesus was left, with the woman still standing there. 10 Jesus straightened up and asked her, "Woman, where are they? Has no one condemned you?" 11 "No one, sir," she said. "Then neither do I condemn you," Jesus declared. "Go now and leave your life of sin."	1) The oldest accuser 2) The last accuser **4 Conclusion: The great revelation—Jesus alone has the right to condemn & forgive** a. He gives a second chance b. He wishes to forgive c. He challenges d. He warns

DIVISION IX

THE REVELATION OF JESUS, THE LIGHT OF LIFE, 8:1-9:41

A. Man's Dark Sinfulness and God's Great Forgiveness, 8:1-11

(8:1-9:41) DIVISION OVERVIEW: Jesus Christ, Revelation of—Man, Enslaved by Sin: in Chapter 8 Christ reveals Himself to be the Light of life. Man is seen gripped by sin (illustrated by the woman taken in adultery and by hypocritical religionists). Man is pictured as being critical, condemnatory, self-righteous, and adulterous—every single person is sinful. In the woman, man is seen as adulterous and guilty—living a life of darkness, without purpose and meaning and significance. In the religionists, man is seen as deceitful, critical, condemnatory, selfish, self-righteous, and loaded with guilt. Not a single religionist is seen to be free from the darkness of serious sin. Jesus reveals Himself to be the Light of the World, the One who brings liberty, forgiveness, purpose, meaning, and significance to the life of man.

(8:1-11) Introduction: this event is a most striking picture of "Man's Dark Sinfulness and God's Great Forgiveness."
1. A picture of Jesus' life (v.1-2).
2. Man's dark guilt (v.3-6).
3. Man's dark nature: all men are sinful—guilty of serious sin (v.7-9).
4. Conclusion: the great revelation—Jesus alone has the right to condemn and forgive (v.10-11).

1 (8:1-2) **Christian Believer—World—Jesus Christ, Devotional Life**: a picture of Jesus' life. There is a real contrast of lives here. The contrast is that of Jesus' quiet and worshipful life contrasted with the turbulent and judgmental lives of the religionists. Jesus is drawn within the turbulence to calm, settle, and leaven it. A picture can be drawn of the Christian life as quiet and worshipful contrasted with a turbulent world.

Note the secret to Jesus' calm and peace: He got alone with God. He often went off into the mount of Olives to be alone with God. (See note—Lk.21:37.) It was a favorite spot of His, a place where He could be alone with God and His disciples, a place of quietness where God could meet with Him face to face, strengthening and encouraging Him (Mt.26:30, 36f). (See outline and notes—Lk.21:37-38 for more discussion of this point.)

Note also that Jesus began His teaching early in the morning. The words "gathered" and "teach" are continuous action in the Greek. The people *kept gathering* to Him, and He *kept teaching* them. His very mission in life was that of worshipping God and teaching and ministering to people. By this He demonstrated how all men should walk through life: worshipping God, teaching and ministering to people. Every man needs to be taught, and every man needs the ministry of others during the trials of life.

2 (8:3-6) **Guilty—Sin—Man, Depravity**: man's dark guilt. Man's guilt and sin are pictured in all the parties involved.

1. There was the guilt of the woman and some unknown man. They were both guilty of the serious sin of adultery, a sin that affects so many lives. Under Jewish law it was considered so serious that the parties were to be stoned to death (Lev.20:10; Dt.22:13-24). Note how the sin speaks to the sin of every person.

⇒ The sin was a work of darkness. All sin is, and most sin is actually done under the cover of darkness. An attempt is made to hide it from wife, husband, mother, father, employer, classmate.

⇒ The man and woman thought what we all often think—that their sin would never be discovered, that no one would ever find out. But they overlooked two things that we all ignore: in the vast majority of cases, sin has been discovered; and sin, the very act of it, is always seen by God.

⇒ The sin took place at the time of the feast, where the atmosphere was party-like and where men and women were brought together by drinking and dancing and the indulgence of the crowd (cp. Jn.7:37f). Such an atmosphere corrupts even those with the best intentions and the highest morals.

2. There was the guilt of some witnesses, some people who were offended by the woman in particular. Jewish law required two witnesses to convict a person. It is most unlikely that the woman and her male companion were seen by the religionists. They would not have been in such a *defiled atmosphere*. The Pharisees and Scribes were too strict in their rules and regulations. Some commentators do think, however, that the religionists had some scoundrels set a trap for the woman in order to drag her before Jesus to entrap Him. This seems most unlikely. Plotting a sin of the flesh does not fit in with the nature of the Pharisees and Scribes. Their sins were more of the spirit, much deeper, but less visible and less condemnatory to the public.

The point is this: the witnesses who caught the woman in the act of adultery were *great sinners*.

a. They were vindictive and revengeful. They wanted to strike out, to get back at her. She was *publicly exposed*. She should have been held in custody in some private place until judgment was passed, but she was unmercifully dragged before the public to expose her sin and to shame and punish her. Why? Apparently, she had hurt her husband or some loved one so much that he struck out at her. Public exposure was his way to strike back at her.

b. The man who committed adultery with her was not exposed. Why?

⇒ He could have escaped, fled before they grabbed him.

⇒ He could have been feared or bought off his accusers.

⇒ He could have been released because, as is the case in so many societies, misbehavior (sin) by men was more acceptable than by women.

3. There was the guilt of the religionists and the public. When the accusers dragged the woman to the religionists, people all along the way joined in, as is the case so often is. The religionists saw a chance to test Jesus, so they took the woman before Him, hoping to discredit Him.

⇒ If Jesus said the woman was not guilty, He would be breaking Jewish law and be leaving Himself open to the charge of being too lenient with sin.

⇒ If Jesus said the woman was guilty and should be killed, He would be breaking Roman law which did not consider adultery a sin worthy of death. He would also be criticized as lacking mercy and love, compassion and forgiveness.

Note several things about the dark nature of man seen in these religionists and in the crowd who joined in the public exposure.

a. There was a sinful spirit among all these involved, a spirit...

• of self-righteousness that lacked forgiveness
• of criticism that lacked love
• of judging that lacked compassion
• of censoring that lacked understanding
• of condemning that lacked sympathy
• of punishing that lacked restoration
• of savagery that lacked curing
• of destroying that lacked the second chance

b. There was hypocrisy. They felt and claimed that they were religious, better than the woman, free from any sin serious enough to be exposed. They even used Scripture to condemn *her* sin and *to support* their right to condemn her.

c. There was complete failure to "love your neighbor as yourself" (Mt.5:43; 19:19; 22:39; Mk.12:31; Lk.10:27; Ro.13:9; Gal.5:14; Jas.2:8):

⇒ a complete failure to do what we all need sometime, to be embraced and pulled out of the sin and hurt gripping us.

⇒ a complete failure to hush—be quiet, and say nothing, except to the one caught in sin—and to set about a ministry of restoration and reconciliation to God and man.

4. There was Jesus' ignoring sinful man as long as He could. "He bent down, and started to write on the ground with his fingers," saying nothing. He was silent for a long time. We are not told why Jesus stooped in silence or what He wrote on the ground. Various commentators say it was...

• to allow Him to think through the situation.
• to force the accusers to repeat the charges (v.7). By so doing, they and the public would begin to see and sense their lack of compassion.
• to write Scripture or some of the sins of those standing around, hoping to convict them (cp. Job 13:26).

Note this: Jesus did ignore them in all their sinful, critical, self-righteous, hypocritical spirit; but He ignored them only for a time. Jesus will not ignore nor allow sin to go on forever. He will arise, face it, and judge it.

3 (8:7-9) **Man, Depravity—Judging Others**: man's dark nature. All men are sinful and guilty of serious sin.

1. The woman was guilty of a very serious sin. The law said she was to be condemned to death. Her accusers and the people were right, legally justified in their charge. If they were to be stopped from killing her, and even more, if they were to be corrected and rebuked, something phenomenal would have to happen. It did, and note what it was:

⇒ "If any one of you is without sin, let him be the first to throw a stone at her" (v.7).

No man is without sin. Every one of the men standing there knew it, and every one of them was convicted within his conscience. They all left, leaving Jesus and the woman alone.

This is the verdict: Light has come into the world, but men loved darkness instead of light because their deeds were evil. (John 3:19)

As it is written: "There is no one righteous, not even one; (Rom 3:10; cp.v.9-18; 3:23)

2. Jesus said that stones could be thrown at the sinner. But He placed a limitation on throwing or casting stones. "If any one of you is without sin, let him be the first to throw a stone at her." (Note: this means that only Christ can judge, for no person is without sin.)

Throwing or casting stones is not based on how much Scripture a person knows, nor on how great a person's calling and gifts are, nor on the position a person has. It is based upon moral goodness and perfection, and *no man* has achieved that.

> "Why do you look at the speck of sawdust in your brother's eye and pay no attention to the plank in your own eye? How can you say to your brother, 'Let me take the speck out of your eye,' when all the time there is a plank in your own eye? You hypocrite, first take the plank out of your own eye, and then you will see clearly to remove the speck from your brother's eye. (Mat 7:3-5; cp. Ro14.4, 13; 1 Cor.4:5; Jas.4:12)

> What shall we conclude then? Are we any better ? Not at all! We have already made the charge that Jews and Gentiles alike are all under sin. As it is written: "There is no one righteous, not even one; there is no one who understands, no one who seeks God. All have turned away, they have together become worthless; there is no one who does good, not even one." (Rom 3:9-12)

4 (8:10-11) **Salvation—Jesus Christ, Savior—Forgiveness**: the great revelation. Jesus alone has the right to condemn and forgive. The picture of the woman is the picture of every person. When it comes to sin and judgment, every person stands alone before Christ—stands naked and stripped of all righteousness, for no person possesses righteousness. There are no accusers, not among men. No man can condemn the woman nor anyone else. The only righteousness and the only perfection, the only One who is not guilty of sin, is Christ and Christ alone. He alone is worthy to stand in judgment. However, note the most glorious news in all of human history.

1. Jesus did not condemn but gave a *second chance*.

> If he sins against you seven times in a day, and seven times comes back to you and says, 'I repent,' forgive him." (Luke 17:4)

> Then Peter came to Jesus and asked, "Lord, how many times shall I forgive my brother when he sins against me? Up to seven times?" Jesus answered, "I tell you, not seven times, but seventy-seven times. (Mat 18:21-22)

> My dear children, I write this to you so that you will not sin. But if anybody does sin, we have one who speaks to the Father in our defense—Jesus Christ, the Righteous One. He is the atoning sacrifice for our sins, and not only for ours but also for the sins of the whole world. (1 John 2:1-2)

2. Jesus wished to forgive and did forgive: "Neither do I condemn you."

> Who is he that condemns? Christ Jesus, who died—more than that, who was raised to life—is at the right hand of God and is also interceding for us. (Rom 8:34)

> In him we have redemption through his blood, the forgiveness of sins, in accordance with the riches of God's grace (Eph 1:7)

> If we confess our sins, he is faithful and just and will forgive us our sins and purify us from all unrighteousness. (1 John 1:9)

3. Jesus challenged, but warned: "Go now and leave your life of sin" Stop your sinning—make a clean break—do it no more. The warning is clear: repentance is essential for forgiveness.

> Later Jesus found him at the temple and said to him, "See, you are well again. Stop sinning or something worse may happen to you." (John 5:14)

> And repentance and forgiveness of sins will be preached in his name to all nations, beginning at Jerusalem. (Luke 24:47)

> Peter replied, "Repent and be baptized, every one of you, in the name of Jesus Christ for the forgiveness of your sins. And you will receive the gift of the Holy Spirit. (Acts 2:38)

> Therefore do not let sin reign in your mortal body so that you obey its evil desires. (Rom 6:12)

> Come back to your senses as you ought, and stop sinning; for there are some who are ignorant of God—I say this to your shame. (1 Cor 15:34)

	B. Man's Need: The Light of the World, 8:12-20	no one.	
1 Jesus made a great claim & promise a. The claim: The Light of the world[DS1] b. The promise: "Follow me &...."[DS2] c. The objection: By the Pharisees	12 When Jesus spoke again to the people, he said, "I am the light of the world. Whoever follows me will never walk in darkness, but will have the light of life."	16 But if I do judge, my decisions are right, because I am not alone. I stand with the Father, who sent me.	a. Man judges by appearance b. Jesus judges not by appearance but by God's standards
2 Proof 1: Jesus' great sense & knowledge of His origin & destiny a. He knew His origin & destiny b. Men could not know **3 Proof 2: Man's incompetence to judge**	13 The Pharisees challenged him, "Here you are, appearing as your own witness; your testimony is not valid." 14 Jesus answered, "Even if I testify on my own behalf, my testimony is valid, for I know where I came from and where I am going. But you have no idea where I come from or where I am going. 15 You judge by human standards; I pass judgment on	17 In your own Law it is written that the testimony of two men is valid. 18 I am one who testifies for myself; my other witness is the Father, who sent me." 19 Then they asked him, "Where is your father?" "You do not know me or my Father," Jesus replied. "If you knew me, you would know my Father also." 20 He spoke these words while teaching in the temple area near the place where the offerings were put. Yet no one seized him, because his time had not yet come.	**4 Proof 3: The law's testimony** a. Jesus met the legal requirements b. Jesus had two witnesses: Himself & God **5 Proof 4: The Father's presence within** a. Jesus was mocked b. The Father was in Him **6 Conclusion: The tragedy—He was rejected in the temple**

DIVISION IX

THE REVELATION OF JESUS, THE LIGHT OF LIFE, 8:1-9:41

B. Man's Need: The Light of the World, 8:12-20

(8:12-20) **Introduction**: man has great need. He is not always aware of it, but the need is still there. Man is in darkness.

⇒ He cannot see into the future nor into the next world.

⇒ He cannot see God, who He is and what He is like.

⇒ He cannot see the real meaning, significance, and purpose in life.

⇒ He cannot grasp perfect knowledge nor assurance of eternal life.

Therefore, man's great need is to see "the Light of the world."

1. Jesus made a great claim and promise (v.12-13).
2. Proof 1: Jesus' great sense and knowledge of His origin and destiny (v.14).
3. Proof 2: man's incompetence to judge (v.15-16).
4. Proof 3: the law's testimony (v.17-18).
5. Proof 4: the Father's presence within (v.19).
6. Conclusion: the tragedy—Jesus was rejected in the temple (v.20).

1 (8:12-13) **Jesus Christ, Claims**: Jesus made a great claim and promise.

1. The great claim was, "I am the Light of the world" (see DEEPER STUDY # 1—Jn.8:12 for discussion. Also see note—Mt.5:14.) Note that He made the great claim of deity: "I Am." The Lord's claim to deity was emphatic. The claim was the very first thing He said in this passage (see DEEPER STUDY # 1—Jn.6:20).

2. The great promise was twofold: "Whoever follows me...

• will never walk in darkness." (See DEEPER STUDY # 2—Jn.8:12 for discussion.)

• will have the light of life."

Note two critical points.

a. A man does not possess light, not within himself, not by nature. Men are in darkness by nature.

b. A man is delivered "out of darkness" by following Jesus Christ. Note the word "follows" is continuous action. A man must continue to follow in order to receive light.

> **In whom we have redemption, the forgiveness of sins. He is the image of the invisible God, the firstborn over all creation. (Col 1:14-15)**

3. Jesus used the term "light of life." A man exists in darkness until He follows Christ. The meaning, purpose, and significance of life cannot be seen and known apart from following Christ. It is Christ who throws light upon life, revealing what life really is.

4. The religionists (Pharisees) objected to the claim of Jesus. They knew exactly what He was claiming: that He was the Messsiah and that He alone could give light to the world. In their minds, only God could give light to the world. Note their charge against Him: He alone was bearing witness to His claim. He had no other witnesses; therefore, His claim was false. (See note—Jn.5:31 for more discussion of the witnesses required to prove a man's testimony. Jesus gave five witnesses in Jn.5:31-39.)

DEEPER STUDY # 1

(8:12) **Light**: Jesus is said to be the *Light of men* (Jn.1:4) and the *Light of the world* (Jn.8:12; 9:5; 12:46). It is possible for the Light, Jesus Himself, to be *in men* (Jn.11:10; cp. Col.1:27) and for men to become children of Light (see notes—Jn.12:34-36).

Apparently, Jesus used the word *light* often. John uses the word twenty-four times. What is meant by calling Jesus the Light?

1. Jesus, the Light, is light by nature. Light is what He is within Himself, within His being, His nature, His essence, His character. Scripture says...

- that "God is Light" (1 Jn.1:5);
- that Jesus is "the image of the invisible God" (Col.1:15);
- therefore, "Jesus is Light." He is "the Light of the world."

2. Jesus, the Light, tells us that He is holy, righteous, and pure. Light is the symbol of purity and holiness. Light means the absence of darkness and blindness; it has no spots of darkness or blackness, nor of sin and shame.

3. Jesus, the Light, reveals. His light shows clearly the nature, the meaning, and the destiny of all things. His light shines in, spots, opens up, identifies, illuminates, and shows things as they really are. The light of Jesus Christ shows the truth about the world and man and God. The light of Jesus Christ reveals that He loves and cares for man and wants man to love and care for Him.

4. Jesus, the Light, guides. His light allows a man to walk out of darkness. Man no longer has to grope, grasp, and stumble about trying to find his way through life. The path of life can now be clearly seen.

5. Jesus, the Light, does away with darkness and with chaos. His light routs, wipes out, strips away, and erases the darkness. The empty chaos of creation was routed by the light given by God (Gen.1:3). Jesus Christ is the Light that can save man from chaos (Jn.14:1, 17; 12:46; 16:33).

Jesus proclaimed Himself to be the Light of the world at the great Feast of Tabernacles (Jn.7:2). The very first ceremony of the Feast holds great significance for Jesus' claim. It was called "The Illumination of the Temple" and was held in the Court of the Women. The center of the Court was surrounded by large sections of stadium-like seats. In the open space of the Court sat four huge candelabra. When darkness fell the candelabra were lit, and the elders danced and led the people in singing psalms before the Lord all night. The brilliance and glow from the burning flames of the huge candelabra were said to be so bright that the light could be seen throughout the whole city. It was against this background that Jesus cried out, "I am the Light of the world."

DEEPER STUDY # 2

(8:12) **Darkness** (skotos, skotia): the word is used in Scripture to describe both the state and the works of man. Darkness is very real in Scripture.

1. The darkness refers to the world of the natural man who does not know Jesus Christ (Jn.8:12). The natural man walks in ignorance...

- of Jesus Christ
- of God as revealed by Jesus Christ
- of the real purpose and destiny of life as shown by Jesus Christ

The natural man stumbles and gropes about in this world. He knows nothing other than the things of this world as he sees them. His only hope is the hope of living a long life before death overtakes him. He walks in darkness, ignorant of real life now and hereafter (cp. Jn.12:35, 46).

2. The darkness symbolizes unpreparedness and unwatchfulness. It symbolizes the time when evil occurs (1 Th.5:4-8).

3. The darkness is loved by men. Sinful men do their evil deeds under the cover of darkness. Men therefore hate the light because the light uncovers their evil behavior (Jn.3:19-20).

4. The darkness is hostile to light (see DEEPER STUDY # 4—Jn.1:5).

---

2 (8:14) **Jesus Christ, Deity; Witness of God—Spiritual World**: the first proof of Jesus' claim is His great knowledge. He knew His origin and destiny. He declared, "I am the Light of the world," and He declared that His witness was enough. He said, "My testimony is valid [true]" (alethes).

⇒ It is not false
⇒ It is not a lie
⇒ It is not a deceptive claim
⇒ It is not the claim of an ego-maniac setting Himself up as a *god*
⇒ It is not the claim of a man who is out to shatter men's dreams
⇒ It is not the claim of a man who is set on destroying other men

The witness of Jesus Christ was valid; it was true, and His witness was sufficient evidence for a very strong reason. Jesus knew His origin and destiny, where He had come from and where He was going. He was "*out of*" heaven, "*out of*" the spiritual dimension of being, and He was to return to heaven.

Man could not tell where Jesus had come from nor where He was going. Why? For a very simple reason: man cannot penetrate nor see the spiritual world. Physical eyes are blind to the world of the Spirit (cp. Jn.1:18). If there is to be communication with the spiritual dimension, the spiritual world must come into this world, into the physical dimension. This is exactly what has happened; this is just what Jesus was saying. He had come from heaven, from the spiritual dimension of being. He had been an eyewitness of heaven. He had been in the very presence of God Himself, and God had sent Him from heaven into this world to declare the glorious message of salvation:

> **When Jesus spoke again to the people, he said, "I am the light of the world. Whoever follows me will never walk in darkness, but will have the light of life." (John 8:12)**
>
> **I tell you the truth, we speak of what we know, and we testify to what we have seen, but still you people do not accept our testimony. (John 3:11; cp.Jn3:32)**
>
> **Jesus answered, "Even if I testify on my own behalf, my testimony is valid, for I know where I came from and where I am going. But you have no idea where I come from or where I am going. (John 8:14)**
>
> **"You are a king, then!" said Pilate. Jesus answered, "You are right in saying I am a king. In fact, for this reason I was born, and for this I came into the world, to testify to the truth. Everyone on the side of truth listens to me." (John 18:37)**
>
> **And from Jesus Christ, who is the faithful witness, the firstborn from the dead, and the ruler of the kings of the earth. To him who loves us and has freed us from our sins by his blood, (Rev 1:5)**

3 (8:15-16) **Jesus Christ, Deity—Origin, From God—Oneness with the Father—Spiritual Dimension**: the second proof of Jesus' claim is man's incompetence. Again, this is because of the difference between the two worlds, the difference between the physical and spiritual worlds or dimensions of being.

1. Men judge by human standards, that is, by appearance. Men judge by what they see and know. The only evidence they have is what they see in their world, the world of the physical. However, if men are to judge Jesus' claim, they cannot do it on the basis of physical evidence. Why? Because Jesus is not of this world. Men have to judge Him by faith. They either accept His testimony or reject it.

Stop judging by mere appearances, and make a right judgment." (John 7:24)

2. But note: Jesus' judgment was true. He did not judge—not by appearance—but by God's presence.

This was a phenomenal claim. Jesus was saying that He was not alone. He did not speak nor act alone. The Father was *with Him* and the Father *sent Him*; therefore, what He claimed and did was of the Father. Note two points.

a. Jesus said that what He claimed was "right," "true" (alethes)...
- it was not false
- it was not a lie
- it was not a deceptive claim

b. Jesus called God "Father" and referred to His mission: "the Father that sent me." He had a Father-Son relationship with God. He knew God in a very personal and intimate way as "Father." He *had come* from the presence and the household of His Father, that is, from heaven or from the spiritual world and dimension of being. Therefore, He *alone* could know all the facts. He had come, being *sent* of the Father to proclaim the glorious message of salvation: "I am the Light of the world: whoever follows me will never walk in darkness, but will have the light of life" (Jn.8:12).

I and the Father are one." (John 10:30)

Do not believe me unless I do what my Father does. But if I do it, even though you do not believe me, believe the miracles, that you may know and understand that the Father is in me, and I in the Father." (John 10:37-38)

Don't you believe that I am in the Father, and that the Father is in me? The words I say to you are not just my own. Rather, it is the Father, living in me, who is doing his work. (John 14:10)

I will remain in the world no longer, but they are still in the world, and I am coming to you. Holy Father, protect them by the power of your name—the name you gave me—so that they may be one as we are one. (John 17:11; cp. Jn.17:22)

4 (8:17-18) **Jesus Christ, Deity—Law, Witnesses to Christ**: the third proof of Jesus' claim is the law's testimony. Jesus appealed to the law of man. The law required two witnesses to validate a claim (Dt.19:15). Jesus met the demand of the law, for He was one witness, and "the Father who sent" Him was the second witness.

Now note two clear facts that man should see.

1. Jesus' testimony was valid, true. It is perfectly clear that He spoke and acted only for God. Everything He said and did was to glorify God and to lead men to God: to worship and praise and to honor and serve God. It is also clear

that He spoke and acted only for men. Everything He said and did was to save men, to awaken them and to show them compassion and mercy, meeting their desperate needs.

Very simply, everything Jesus said and did bore witness that His claim was true, that He was *of God* and *sent from God* to be "the Light of the world."

For the one whom God has sent speaks the words of God, for God gives the Spirit without limit. (John 3:34; cp. Jn 7.29)

Jesus said to them, "If God were your Father, you would love me, for I came from God and now am here. I have not come on my own; but he sent me. (John 8:42)

He who does not love me will not obey my teaching. These words you hear are not my own; they belong to the Father who sent me. (John 14:24)

For I gave them the words you gave me and they accepted them. They knew with certainty that I came from you, and they believed that you sent me. (John 17:8)

2. God's testimony was valid, true. It is perfectly clear that God acted in and through Jesus. The life, the words, and the works of Jesus demonstrated God's presence and power. The presence and power of God was in and upon Christ "without limit" (Jn.3:34). There is no other sensible explanation. "The Father who sent Him" bore clear, indisputable testimony that He is "the Light of the world."

And a voice from heaven said, "This is my Son, whom I love; with him I am well pleased." (Mat 3:17)

While he was still speaking, a bright cloud enveloped them, and a voice from the cloud said, "This is my Son, whom I love; with him I am well pleased. Listen to him!" (Mat 17:5)

There is another who testifies in my favor, and I know that his testimony about me is valid. (John 5:32)

And the Father who sent me has himself testified concerning me. You have never heard his voice nor seen his form, (John 5:37)

We accept man's testimony, but God's testimony is greater because it is the testimony of God, which he has given about his Son. Anyone who believes in the Son of God has this testimony in his heart. Anyone who does not believe God has made him out to be a liar, because he has not believed the testimony God has given about his Son. (1 John 5:9-10)

5 (8:19) **Jesus Christ, Deity—Spiritual World**: the fourth proof of Jesus' claim was the Father's presence *within Him*. The religionists mocked Jesus. They told Him to present His Father: "Go get Him and bring Him, so He can testify of your claims." Note how they proved Jesus' words: they judged by the human standards, by sight and appearance. They wanted physical evidence. (Of course they had physical evidence in Christ Himself and in the working God's power through Him, but obstinate unbelief blinded them.)

Jesus answered three things to *mocking unbelief*.

1. The unbeliever *does not know Him*. He was Man standing before them, and they could see and know Him as Man, but He was also the Son of God. If they rejected His claim and refused to accept Him as Lord, they naturally did not know Him. The only way to know Jesus is to follow Him as Lord, as "the Light of the world." (Note: no person knows any other person until he spends time with that individual—getting to know him, associating with him, and learning all about him.)

> Jesus answered her, "If you knew the gift of God and who it is that asks you for a drink, you would have asked him and he would have given you living water." (John 4:10)

> Then they asked him, "Where is your father?" "You do not know me or my Father," Jesus replied. "If you knew me, you would know my Father also." (John 8:19)

> The man answered, "Now that is remarkable! You don't know where he comes from, yet he opened my eyes. (John 9:30)

> Jesus answered: "Don't you know me, Philip, even after I have been among you such a long time? Anyone who has seen me has seen the Father. How can you say, 'Show us the Father'? (John 14:9)

> The people of Jerusalem and their rulers did not recognize Jesus, yet in condemning him they fulfilled the words of the prophets that are read every Sabbath. (Acts 13:27)

2. The unbeliever *does not know God*. "No one has ever seen God" (Jn.1:18). The only conceivable way a man can ever know God is for God to *reveal* Himself: God must come from the heavenly world, the spiritual dimension of being, and enter this world, revealing the truth about Himself to man. But note: *if God does come* and a man does not accept and believe Him, then that man will never get to know God.

> No one has ever seen God, but God the One and Only, who is at the Father's side, has made him known. (John 1:18)

> And the Father who sent me has himself testified concerning me. You have never heard his voice nor seen his form, (John 5:37)

> He is the image of the invisible God, the firstborn over all creation. (Col 1:15)

> Now to the King eternal, immortal, invisible, the only God, be honor and glory for ever and ever. Amen. (1 Tim 1:17)

> Who alone is immortal and who lives in unapproachable light, whom no one has seen or can see. To him be honor and might forever. Amen. (1 Tim 6:16)

> They will treat you this way because of my name, for they do not know the One who sent me. (John 15:21)

> They will do such things because they have not known the Father or me. (John 16:3)

> "My people are fools; they do not know me. They are senseless children; they have no understanding. They are skilled in doing evil; they know not how to do good." (Jer 4:22)

> Even the stork in the sky knows her appointed seasons, and the dove, the swift and the thrush observe the time of their migration. But my people do not know the requirements of the LORD. (Jer 8:7)

> "They make ready their tongue like a bow, to shoot lies; it is not by truth that they triumph in the land. They go from one sin to another; they do not acknowledge me," declares the LORD. (Jer 9:3)

> "No man hath seen God at any time; the only begotten Son, which is in the bosom of the Father, he hath declared him" (Jn.1:18).

3. God is in Christ. If a man knows Christ, He knows the Father *also*. This is a phenomenal claim. Christ said that He was the revelation of God; He was "God incarnate" in human flesh.

a. He was the express "image of the invisible God" (Col.1:15) (cp.Heb.1:3). Therefore, the only way to know God is to know Christ. (See note—Jn.14:6.)

> That has come to you. All over the world this gospel is bearing fruit and growing, just as it has been doing among you since the day you heard it and understood God's grace in all its truth. (Col 1:6)

> For in Christ all the fullness of the Deity lives in bodily form, (Col 2:9)

> Jesus answered, "I am the way and the truth and the life. No one comes to the Father except through me. (John 14:6)

b. He is the One who instructs men in the truth of God. (See note—Jn.3:32-34 for verses of Scripture.)

6 (8:20) **Jesus Christ, Response to**: the great tragedy was that Jesus was rejected in the temple. The religionists wanted nothing to do with Him. They rejected and opposed Him, desiring to get rid of Him. And note: it was in the temple where He was rejected, yet they could not destroy Him. "His time" had not come. God protected Him.

Thought 1. How often this scene of unbelief among religionists is repeated in the church. Down through the centuries many religionists have wanted nothing to do with Christ, choosing self over Him.

> "Not everyone who says to me, 'Lord, Lord,' will enter the kingdom of heaven, but only he who does the will of my Father who is in heaven. (Mat 7:21)

> He replied, "Isaiah was right when he prophesied about you hypocrites; as it is written: "'These people honor me with their lips, but their hearts are far from me. (Mark 7:6)

> They claim to know God, but by their actions they deny him. They are detestable, disobedient and unfit for doing anything good. (Titus 1:16)

> Having a form of godliness but denying its power. Have nothing to do with them. (2 Tim 3:5)

1 Man's search[DS1]	C. Man's Futile Search for Messiah: Search for Utopia & Light, 8:21-24	why he says, 'Where I go, you cannot come'?"	Jesus' Messiahship
a. Man seeks Messiah		23 But he continued, "You are from below; I am from above. You are of this world; I am not of this world.	2 Man's futility & failure
b. Man fails & dies in sin	21 Once more Jesus said to them, "I am going away, and you will look for me, and you will die in your sin. Where I go, you cannot come."		a. Reason 1: Man has a different origin & being than Christ[DS2]
c. Man's end: Separated from the Messiah		24 I told you that you would die in your sins; if you do not believe that I am the one I claim to be, you will indeed die in your sins."	b. Reason 2: Man sins & dies
d. Man mocks the idea of	22 This made the Jews ask" Will he kill himself? Is that		c. Reason 3: Man does not believe

DIVISION IX

THE REVELATION OF JESUS, THE LIGHT OF LIFE, 8:1-9:41

C. Man's Futile Search for Messiah: Search for Utopia and Light, 8:21-24

(8:21-24) **Introduction**: this discussion of Christ is brief, but it is earthshaking. It is the message that desperately needs to be proclaimed to the world. Man's search for an earthly deliverer (Messiah), that is, for utopia and for light is futile.

1. There is man's search (v.21-22).
2. There is man's futility and failure (v.23-24).

1 (8:21-22) **Messiah—Seek—Utopia—Heaven—Deliverer Sin—Death—Judgment**: there is man's search. Jesus announced, "I am going away." He meant He was leaving the world, dying and returning to the Father. *Then* He announced the terrible fate of man, a fate so terrible it is *the tragedy of tragedies*. Man's fate is fourfold.

1. Man seeks for a great Deliverer upon earth. He seeks for the Messiah, that is, for someone who can lead him to utopia and light and heaven. And man's search is tragic, because the great Deliverer (Messiah) has already come and brought the presence of utopia to man (see DEEPER STUDY # 1—Jn.8:21 for discussion).

2. Man fails to find the Messiah: he dies in his sin. In the Greek the word "sin" (hamartiai) is singular, "sin." Note two things.

   a. Man's sin is singular; that is, his great and terrible sin is the sin of unbelief. So long as he continues to disbelieve, he is in a *state of unbelief* or a *position of unbelief*.
   b. Man dies because of unbelief; he dies because he is in a *state of unbelief*. When he dies, he dies "in his sin"; that is, he goes right on into the next world still "in sin," in the *state*, and *position,* and *condition* of an unbeliever. (See note—Ro.5:12-21.)

> **Don't you know that when you offer yourselves to someone to obey him as slaves, you are slaves to the one whom you obey—whether you are slaves to sin, which leads to death, or to obedience, which leads to righteousness? (Rom 6:16)**
> **What benefit did you reap at that time from the things you are now ashamed of? Those things result in death! (Rom 6:21)**
> **For the wages of sin is death, but the gift of God is eternal life in Christ Jesus our Lord. (Rom 6:23)**
> **The mind of sinful man is death, but the mind controlled by the Spirit is life and peace; (Rom 8:6)**

> **For if you live according to the sinful nature, you will die; but if by the Spirit you put to death the misdeeds of the body, you will live, (Rom 8:13)**
> **Christ redeemed us from the curse of the law by becoming a curse for us, for it is written: "Cursed is everyone who is hung on a tree." (Gal 3:13)**
> **Just as man is destined to die once, and after that to face judgment, (Heb 9:27)**
> **The wall was made of jasper, and the city of pure gold, as pure as glass. (Rev 21:18)**

3. Man's tragic end is separation from where Christ is. Note exactly what Christ says, "Where I go, you cannot come." Wherever Christ is, the unbeliever cannot go. Since Christ is...

- the Light of the world, the unbeliever cannot enter the Light
- the Son of God, the unbeliever cannot enter the presence of God
- the Lord of heaven, the unbeliever cannot enter heaven

Unbelieving man is separated forever from the presence of God and Christ (see DEEPER STUDY # 1—Heb.9:27).

> **For I tell you that unless your righteousness surpasses that of the Pharisees and the teachers of the law, you will certainly not enter the kingdom of heaven. (Mat 5:20)**
> **"But while they were on their way to buy the oil, the bridegroom arrived. The virgins who were ready went in with him to the wedding banquet. And the door was shut. "Later the others also came. 'Sir! Sir!' they said. 'Open the door for us!' "But he replied, 'I tell you the truth, I don't know you.' (Mat 25:10-12)**
> **I tell you the truth, anyone who will not receive the kingdom of God like a little child will never enter it." (Mark 10:15)**
> **"Then you will say, 'We ate and drank with you, and you taught in our streets.' "But he will reply, 'I don't know you or where you come from. Away from me, all you evildoers!' "There will be weeping there, and gnashing of teeth, when you see**

Abraham, Isaac and Jacob and all the prophets in the kingdom of God, but you yourselves thrown out. (Luke 13:26-28)

Do you not know that the wicked will not inherit the kingdom of God? Do not be deceived: Neither the sexually immoral nor idolaters nor adulterers nor male prostitutes nor homosexual offenders (1 Cor 6:9)

I declare to you, brothers, that flesh and blood cannot inherit the kingdom of God, nor does the perishable inherit the imperishable. (1 Cor 15:50)

The acts of the sinful nature are obvious: sexual immorality, impurity and debauchery; idolatry and witchcraft; hatred, discord, jealousy, fits of rage, selfish ambition, dissensions, factions and envy; drunkenness, orgies, and the like. I warn you, as I did before, that those who live like this will not inherit the kingdom of God. (Gal 5:19-21)

For of this you can be sure: No immoral, impure or greedy person—such a man is an idolater—has any inheritance in the kingdom of Christ and of God. (Eph 5:5)

Nothing impure will ever enter it, nor will anyone who does what is shameful or deceitful, but only those whose names are written in the Lamb's book of life. (Rev 21:27)

Outside are the dogs, those who practice magic arts, the sexually immoral, the murderers, the idolaters and everyone who loves and practices falsehood. (Rev 22:15)

4. Man mocks the idea of Jesus' Messiahship. He still thinks in terms of the physical world and the dimension of sight only. The Jews understood prefectly that Jesus was referring to death. They mocked Him: "You say you are going to kill yourself. We do not care to follow you."

Thought 1. Men do not care to follow Christ in His death. They are unwilling to take up the cross and follow Him (see DEEPER STUDY # 1—Lk.9:23). They want the world and the things it has to offer, so they continue to seek for an earthly deliverer (Messiah) and his utopia and heaven.

DEEPER STUDY # 1

(8:21) **Utopia—Messiah—Heaven**: utopia would be the ideal world, a world of perfection, provision, possessions, comfort, protection, peace, and security. Utopia would be four things: freedom from all negative circumstances, freedom from sin and its bondages, freedom from death, and freedom from hell. (See note—Ro.10:6-7.) Man uses all the scientific technology and human wisdom available to relieve and escape the reality of all these and their results. He looks everywhere for an escape except the one place where it is found: in Jesus Christ, God's Son.

---

2 (8:23-24) **Man, Failure**: there is man's futility and failure. There are three reasons why man fails to find the true Messiah and utopia.

1. Man fails because he has a different origin and being than Christ. (See DEEPER STUDY # 2—Jn.8:23 for discussion.)

Since the children have flesh and blood, he too shared in their humanity so that by his death he might destroy him who holds the power of death—that is, the devil—and free those who all their lives were held in slavery by their fear of death. (Heb 2:14-15)

Therefore, just as sin entered the world through one man, and death through sin, and in this way death came to all men, because all sinned— (Rom 5:12)

It is sown a natural body, it is raised a spiritual body. If there is a natural body, there is also a spiritual body. (1 Cor 15:44)

The first man was of the dust of the earth, the second man from heaven. As was the earthly man, so are those who are of the earth; and as is the man from heaven, so also are those who are of heaven. (1 Cor 15:47-48)

For, "All men are like grass, and all their glory is like the flowers of the field; the grass withers and the flowers fall, (1 Pet 1:24)

But man, despite his riches, does not endure; he is like the beasts that perish. (Psa 49:12)

He remembered that they were but flesh, a passing breeze that does not return. (Psa 78:39)

What man can live and not see death, or save himself from the power of the grave? Selah (Psa 89:48)

For he knows how we are formed, he remembers that we are dust. (Psa 103:14)

All go to the same place; all come from dust, and to dust all return. (Eccl 3:20)

Stop trusting in man, who has but a breath in his nostrils. Of what account is he? (Isa 2:22)

A voice says, "Cry out." And I said, "What shall I cry?" "All men are like grass, and all their glory is like the flowers of the field. (Isa 40:6)

All of us have become like one who is unclean, and all our righteous acts are like filthy rags; we all shrivel up like a leaf, and like the wind our sins sweep us away. (Isa 64:6)

2. Man fails because he sins and dies. The word "sins" here is plural (hamartiais); that is, it refers to the *acts of sin*. Man dies because he sin*s* (Rev.21:8).

Do you not know that the wicked will not inherit the kingdom of God? Do not be deceived: Neither the sexually immoral nor idolaters nor adulterers nor male prostitutes nor homosexual offenders nor thieves nor the greedy nor drunkards nor slanderers nor swindlers will inherit the kingdom of God. (1 Cor 6:9-10)

3. Man fails because he does not believe *that Jesus is God*, the great "*I Am*" (see DEEPER STUDY # 1, I Am—Jn.6:20; DEEPER STUDY # 2, Believe—Jn.2:24).

Whoever believes in him is not condemned, but whoever does not believe stands condemned already because he has not believed in the name of God's one and only Son. (John 3:18)

Whoever believes in the Son has eternal life, but whoever rejects the Son will not see life, for God's wrath remains on him." (John 3:36)

I told you that you would die in your sins; if you do not believe that I am the one I claim to be, you will indeed die in your sins." (John 8:24)

DEEPER STUDY # 2
(8:23) **Jesus—Incarnation**: Jesus was born from above or from heaven; that is, He was born of God, as well as of Mary. Therefore, Jesus is not only Man, but He is also God. He is the God-Man. Think of it this way. A man is born of the earth, from beneath: he is born of his father

and his mother. Both are of this earth, of human flesh only. Therefore, a man is only a man; he is only human flesh and blood just like his mother and father.

However, this is not true with Jesus. Jesus is Man, but He is also God. He is Man through the flesh of His mother, and He is the eternal Son of God by the miraculous act of the Holy Spirit through Mary. God incarnated His Son in human flesh and sent Him into the world through Mary (cp. Jn.8:12-59, esp. 14, 23, 42, 57-58. See DEEPER STUDY # 3—Mt.1:16.)

This means something critical. The only messiah and utopia that man can find is of this world, of the physical dimension. Therefore, man's messiah and utopia fail; they waste away, deteriorate, decay, and die. But not Christ and His utopia. He is "from heaven," from the spiritual world and eternal dimension. Therefore, He and His utopia last forever. (See notes, Corruption—Mt.6:19-20; DEEPER STUDY # 2—8:17; DEEPER STUDY # 1—2 Pt.1:4.)

| 1 Man's asks a very basic question
  a. Who is Jesus?
  b. Jesus' reply: He is just who He claims to be

2 Man does not grasp that Jesus is God's Spokesman & Judge—the One who brought the message of the true God | D. Man's Tragic Failure to Understand the Light, 8:25-30

25 "Who are you?" they asked. "Just what I have been claiming all along," Jesus replied.
26 "I have much to say in judgment of you. But he who sent me is reliable, and what I have heard from him I tell the world."
27 They did not understand that he was telling them | about his Father.
28 So Jesus said, "When you have lifted up the Son of Man, then you will know that I am the one I claim to be and that I do nothing on my own but speak just what the Father has taught me.
29 The one who sent me is with me; he has not left me alone, for I always do what pleases him."
30 Even as he spoke, many put their faith in him. | 3 Man does not grasp that Jesus is the Son of Man—the One who was to be lifted up
4 Man does not grasp that Jesus is the great "I Am"—the Son of God Himself
5 Man does not grasp that Jesus was the One who God never left alone
  a. God sent—was with
  b. Jesus pleased God always
6 Conclusion: Many believed |

DIVISION IX

THE REVELATION OF JESUS, THE LIGHT OF LIFE, 8:1-9:41

D. Man's Tragic Failure to Understand the Light, 8:25-30

(8:25-30) **Introduction**: man misunderstands Jesus and His claim to be the Light of the world.

1. Man asks a very basic question (v.25).
2. Man does not grasp that Jesus is God's Spokesman and Judge—the One who brought the message of the true God (v.26-27).
3. Man does not grasp that Jesus is the Son of Man—the One who was to be lifted up (v.28).
4. Man does not grasp that Jesus is the great "I Am"—the Son of God Himself (v.28).
5. Man does not grasp that Jesus is the One whom God has never left alone (v.29-30).
6. Conclusion: many believed (v.30).

1 (8:25) **Man, Question of**: man asks a very basic question. Jesus had just made a phenomenal claim: "I am the Light of the world" (v.12). His claim and His explanation of the claim shocked man. The reason is clear, for Jesus had declared...

- "Whoever follows me will never walk in darkness" (v.12).
- "I am not alone, I stand with the father who sent me" (v.16).
- "You do not know me or my father" (v.19).
- "I am from above you are of this world" (v.23).
- "If you do not believe that I am the one I claim to be, then you will indeed die in your sins" (v.24).

Men of every generation blurt out, just as the men of His generation did: "Who are you?" Jesus proclaimed the wonderful truth...

- "I am just who I claim to be."
- "I am who I have claimed to be from the very beginning."
- "I am all that I have claimed to be."

Note: the Greek text of Jesus' words in this verse is most difficult. His words are translated various ways. A glance at various translations and commentaries will give other possible meanings.

2 (8:26-27) **Jesus Christ, Deity—Spokesman for God**: man does not grasp that Jesus is God's Spokesman and

Judge. Jesus was the One who brought the message of God to the world. Note two significant points.

1. Jesus claimed to be God's Spokesman to the world: "What I have heard from him I will tell the world."

  a. What Jesus spoke of was *what He had heard from God*. His message, His words, were given Him by God.

> **The Spirit gives life; the flesh counts for nothing. The words I have spoken to you are spirit and they are life. (John 6:63)**
>
> **Jesus answered, "My teaching is not my own. It comes from him who sent me. If anyone chooses to do God's will, he will find out whether my teaching comes from God or whether I speak on my own. (John 7:16-17)**
>
> **"I have much to say in judgment of you. But he who sent me is reliable, and what I have heard from him I tell the world." (John 8:26)**
>
> **So Jesus said, "When you have lifted up the Son of Man, then you will know that I am the one I claim to be and that I do nothing on my own but speak just what the Father has taught me. (John 8:28)**
>
> **I am telling you what I have seen in the Father's presence, and you do what you have heard from your father." (John 8:38)**
>
> **For I did not speak of my own accord, but the Father who sent me commanded me what to say and how to say it. I know that his command leads to eternal life. So whatever I say is just what the Father has told me to say." (John 12:49-50)**
>
> **Don't you believe that I am in the Father, and that the Father is in me? The words I say to you are not just my own. Rather, it is the Father, living in me, who is doing his work. (John 14:10)**

  b. Jesus was "sent" by God to speak the words of God. He was on earth for the very special mission of proclaiming the message of God. Jesus came from the very presence of God, from an intimate relationship with Him. It was God Himself who appointed and sent Jesus into the world. Note that God's message is "reliable." It is not false or evil, not a lie or a deception. Men can trust and depend upon it.

Note also that Jesus was sent to the *whole world*. This means at least two things: His message was for the whole world, and His message was the only message for the world.

> **For the one whom God has sent speaks the words of God, for God gives the Spirit without limit. (John 3:34)**
> **Simon Peter answered him, "Lord, to whom shall we go? You have the words of eternal life. (John 6:68)**
> **He who does not love me will not obey my teaching. These words you hear are not my own; they belong to the Father who sent me. (John 14:24)**
> **For I gave them the words you gave me and they accepted them. They knew with certainty that I came from you, and they believed that you sent me. (John 17:8)**

2. Jesus claimed to be the Judge of the world. As the Spokesman of God, He had the duty not only "to say much things" but "to judge much things." His function as Spokesman included judgment.

   a. His first mission to earth was to proclaim the message of salvation.

   > **For he has set a day when he will judge the world with justice by the man he has appointed. He has given proof of this to all men by raising him from the dead." (Acts 17:31)**
   > **This will take place on the day when God will judge men's secrets through Jesus Christ, as my gospel declares. (Rom 2:16)**

   b. His second mission to earth will be to judge men.

   > **Moreover, the Father judges no one, but has entrusted all judgment to the Son, (John 5:22)**
   > **He commanded us to preach to the people and to testify that he is the one whom God appointed as judge of the living and the dead. (Acts 10:42)**

Note: man did not understand, and he still does not understand that Jesus is God's Spokesman and Judge.

3 (8:28) **Jesus Christ, Deity**: man does not grasp that Jesus is the Son of Man. He is the One who was to be lifted up. Note that Jesus claimed to be the Son of Man. (See note—Jn.1:51.) The point of His claim is that the Son of Man will be lifted up. This is a definite reference to the cross and exaltation of Jesus. It is as the Son of Man, as the Perfect and Ideal Man, that Jesus was able to die for all men (see notes—Jn.1:51; Jn.12:31-33 for discussion of this point).

4 (8:28) **Jesus Christ, Deity—I Am**: man does not grasp that Jesus is the great "I Am," the Son of God Himself (see DEEPER STUDY # 1 —Jn.6:20). Note that it was His being lifted

up—the cross and the resurrection and the ascension—that was to convince men that He is the great "I Am."

1. The cross awakens men to the glorious love and salvation of God.

> **"For God so loved the world that he gave his one and only Son, that whoever believes in him shall not perish but have eternal life. (John 3:16)**
> **But God demonstrates his own love for us in this: While we were still sinners, Christ died for us. (Rom 5:8)**
> **For Christ's love compels us, because we are convinced that one died for all, and therefore all died. And he died for all, that those who live should no longer live for themselves but for him who died for them and was raised again. (2 Cor 5:14-15)**

2. The resurrection declares Jesus to be the Son of God with power.

> **And who through the Spirit of holiness was declared with power to be the Son of God by his resurrection from the dead: Jesus Christ our Lord. (Rom 1:4)**

3. The ascension allowed the Holy Spirit to replace Christ on earth. It brought about the *pouring out* of the Spirit and His convicting power.

> **But I tell you the truth: It is for your good that I am going away. Unless I go away, the Counselor will not come to you; but if I go, I will send him to you. When he comes, he will convict the world of guilt in regard to sin and righteousness and judgment: in regard to sin, because men do not believe in me; in regard to righteousness, because I am going to the Father, where you can see me no longer; and in regard to judgment, because the prince of this world now stands condemned. (John 16:7-11)**
> **On the last and greatest day of the Feast, Jesus stood and said in a loud voice, "If anyone is thirsty, let him come to me and drink. Whoever believes in me, as the Scripture has said, streams of living water will flow from within him." By this he meant the Spirit, whom those who believed in him were later to receive. Up to that time the Spirit had not been given, since Jesus had not yet been glorified. (John 7:37-39)**

4. The cross proves that Jesus ...
   - is the great "*I Am*": deity, God Himself incarnate in human flesh. (See DEEPER STUDY # 1—Jn.6:20; notes—8:12-13; 8:54-59.)
   - is *One with God*: does not act alone—does nothing of Himself. (See note—Jn.8:15-16 for discussion and verses of Scripture.)
   - is *the Spokesman of God*: speaks only as His Father taught Him. (See note—Jn.3:32-34 for discussion and verses of Scripture.)

5 (8:29) **Jesus Christ, Deity**: man does not grasp that Jesus was the One who God never left alone. This is critical. Jesus claimed three things.

165

1. He claimed that His Father had sent Him. (See DEEPER STUDY # 3—Jn.3:34 for discussion and verses of Scripture.)

2. He claimed that His Father was with Him and had never left Him alone. The idea and claim was that His Father had never abandoned Him; therefore, what Jesus said and did was always the message of God to men.

> Do not believe me unless I do what my Father does. But if I do it, even though you do not believe me, believe the miracles, that you may know and understand that the Father is in me, and I in the Father." (John 10:37-38)

> Jesus answered: "Don't you know me, Philip, even after I have been among you such a long time? Anyone who has seen me has seen the Father. How can you say, 'Show us the Father'? Don't you believe that I am in the Father, and that the Father is in me? The words I say to you are not just my own. Rather, it is the Father, living in me, who is doing his work. Believe me when I say that I am in the Father and the Father is in me; or at least believe on the evidence of the miracles themselves. (John 14:9-11)

3. He claimed that He had not failed. He always did the things God said, He obeyed God perfectly and completely, never sinning. Men could trust and depend upon Him.

> God made him who had no sin to be sin for us, so that in him we might become the righteousness of God. (2 Cor 5:21)

> In bringing many sons to glory, it was fitting that God, for whom and through whom everything exists, should make the author of their salvation perfect through suffering. (Heb 2:10)

> Although he was a son, he learned obedience from what he suffered and, once made perfect, he became the source of eternal salvation for all who obey him (Heb 5:8-9)

> For the law appoints as high priests men who are weak; but the oath, which came after the law, appointed the Son, who has been made perfect forever. (Heb 7:28)

> For you know that it was not with perishable things such as silver or gold that you were redeemed from the empty way of life handed down to you from your forefathers, But with the precious blood of Christ, a lamb without blemish or defect. (1 Pet 1:18-19)

6 (8:30) **Jesus Christ, Deity**: the result of Jesus' words was that many believed, many put their faith in Him (see DEEPER STUDY # 2—Jn.2:24). They became convinced that Jesus was all He claimed to be:
⇒ the Light of the world
⇒ the Spokesman and Judge of God
⇒ the Son of Man
⇒ the "I Am," the Son of God Himself
⇒ the One who God never left alone

> "For God so loved the world that he gave his one and only Son, that whoever believes in him shall not perish but have eternal life. (John 3:16)

> "I tell you the truth, whoever hears my word and believes him who sent me has eternal life and will not be condemned; he has crossed over from death to life. (John 5:24)

> But these are written that you may believe that Jesus is the Christ, the Son of God, and that by believing you may have life in his name. (John 20:31)

> That if you confess with your mouth, "Jesus is Lord," and believe in your heart that God raised him from the dead, you will be saved. For it is with your heart that you believe and are justified, and it is with your mouth that you confess and are saved. (Rom 10:9-10)

	E. Man's Freedom from Sin Is Conditional, 8:31-32
1 The conditions: Believing & abiding	31 To the Jews who had believed him, Jesus said, "If you hold to my teaching, you are really my disciples.
2 The results a. Will know the truth^{DS1} b. Will be made free	32 Then you will know the truth, and the truth will set you free."

DIVISION IX

THE REVELATION OF JESUS, THE LIGHT OF LIFE, 8:1-9:41

E. Man's Freedom from Sin Is Conditional, 8:31-32

(8:31-32) **Introduction**: man is enslaved by sin and all the consequences of it. He cannot keep from sinning; therefore, he bears the consequences of sin: guilt, shame, hurt, pain, sorrow, suffering, destruction, devastation, brokenness, death, and judgment. Man needs to be freed from sin, set loose and delivered from its enslaving tentacles. He can be freed, but his freedom from sin is conditional.

1. The conditions: belief and abiding (v.31).
2. The results (v.32).
   a. He will know the truth.
   b. He will be made free.

1 (8:31) **Salvation—Discipleship—Belief—Faith—Remaining—Abiding—The Word**: there are two conditions for being delivered from sin, two conditions for salvation and discipleship.

1. The first condition is belief: "Many put their faith in Christ" (v.30). As the gospel was proclaimed, they listened. They did not slumber or sleep, nor allow their minds to wander. They allowed no distraction whatsoever. They heard and "put their faith in Christ"; therefore, their hearts were stirred. As a result they sensed...

- a need, a lack, an emptiness
- a hunger, a thirst, a desire
- a darkness, a sin, a pollution
- a guilt, a shame, an ugliness
- an hope, a tug, a pull

Their hearts reached out for Jesus. They experienced the *beginning* and the *infancy* of faith. They were like lambs or like "newborn babies" (cp. Jn.3:3; 1 Pt.2:2-3).

The point is this: the *very first* condition of deliverance and salvation is belief, faith in Christ. (See DEEPER STUDY # 2, Belief—Jn.2:24.)

> That everyone who believes in him may have eternal life. "For God so loved the world that he gave his one and only Son, that whoever believes in him shall not perish but have eternal life. (John 3:15-16)
> "I tell you the truth, whoever hears my word and believes him who sent me has eternal life and will not be condemned; he has crossed over from death to life. (John 5:24)
> Martha answered, "I know he will rise again in the resurrection at the last day." (John 11:24)
> I have come into the world as a light, so that no one who believes in me should stay in darkness. (John 12:46)
> But these are written that you may believe that Jesus is the Christ, the Son of God, and that by believing you may have life in his name. (John 20:31)
> All the prophets testify about him that everyone who believes in him receives forgiveness of sins through his name." (Acts 10:43)
> Through him everyone who believes is justified from everything you could not be justified from by the law of Moses. (Acts 13:39)
> They replied, "Believe in the Lord Jesus, and you will be saved—you and your household." (Acts 16:31)
> Everyone who believes that Jesus is the Christ is born of God, and everyone who loves the father loves his child as well. (1 John 5:1)

2. However, there is a second condition—a condition that completes the experience of deliverance and salvation. It is that of *continuing* or *abiding* (meinete) in the Lord's Word. The idea is that of *dwelling*, just as a person dwells at home. The Word of the Lord is the believer's dwelling place. He *continues* and *abides* in God's Word. Very simply, what Jesus was saying is this:

⇒ A person who really begins to believe will "abide" in the Lord's Word. He will continue both to study and to do the Word (2 Tim .2:15).
⇒ A person who does not really believe will not *continue in* the Lord's Word.
⇒ The proof and the evidence that a person "really believes" is that he does "continue" *and abide and dwell* in the Lord's Word.
⇒ The proof and the evidence that a person has made only a false or a superficial profession is that he does not *continue in* the Lord's Word.

> But he who stands firm to the end will be saved. (Mat 24:13)
> Remain in me, and I will remain in you. No branch can bear fruit by itself; it must remain in the vine. Neither can you bear fruit unless you remain in me. "I am the vine; you are the branches. If a man remains in me and I in him, he will bear much fruit; apart from me you can do nothing. If anyone does not remain in me, he is like a branch that is thrown away and

167

withers; such branches are picked up, thrown into the fire and burned. (John 15:4-6)

If you obey my commands, you will remain in my love, just as I have obeyed my Father's commands and remain in his love. (John 15:10)

Therefore, dear friends, since you already know this, be on your guard so that you may not be carried away by the error of lawless men and fall from your secure position. (2 Pet 3:17)

Whoever claims to live in him must walk as Jesus did. (1 John 2:6)

And now, dear children, continue in him, so that when he appears we may be confident and unashamed before him at his coming. (1 John 2:28)

Anyone who runs ahead and does not continue in the teaching of Christ does not have God; whoever continues in the teaching has both the Father and the Son. (2 John 1:9)

(See note, Remaining—Abiding—Jn.6:56 for more discussion.)

2 (8:32) **Salvation, Results**: there are two results of being delivered from sin, two results of salvation and discipleship.

1. The first result is that the true believer will know the truth (see DEEPER STUDY # 1—Jn.8:32. Cp. DEEPER STUDY # 1—Jn.1:9; DEEPER STUDY # 2—14:6 for discussion.)

2. The second result is that the true believer will be made free. (See DEEPER STUDY # 1—Jn.8:32; notes—2 Cor.3:17-18; Eph.2:8, pt.4ᵍ for discussion.)

Thought 1. The truth of Christ is the answer to setting man and his world free, free from all the...

- prejudice and hate
- division and isolation
- hatred and bitterness
- hostility and war
- assault and killing
- crime and injustice
- enslavements and abuses
- emptiness and loneliness
- fear and death
- selfishness and hoarding
- hunger and sickness

DEEPER STUDY # 1

(8:32) **Truth**: moral truth, saving truth, working truth, living truth. It is not simply something to be *known*; it is something to be *done* (Jn.8:31). It is the knowledge and the experience of true reality as opposed to false reality. It is truth in "the inward parts" (cp. Ps.51:6; Eph.5:9). It is diametrically opposed to sham and hypocrisy. It permits no compromise with evil. It even abstains from the appearance of evil (1 Th.5:22). It is a regard for truth in every respect: believing it, reverencing it, speaking it, acting it, hoping in it, and rejoicing in it. Such truthful behavior frees a person from all the bondages and impediments of life. (See DEEPER STUDY # 1—Jn.1:9; DEEPER STUDY # 2—14:6.)

Jesus answered, "My teaching is not my own. It comes from him who sent me. If anyone chooses to do God's will, he will find out whether my teaching comes from God or whether I speak on my own. (John 7:16-17)

To the Jews who had believed him, Jesus said, "If you hold to my teaching, you are really my disciples. Then you will know the truth, and the truth will set you free." (John 8:31-32)

I want to know Christ and the power of his resurrection and the fellowship of sharing in his sufferings, becoming like him in his death, (Phil 3:10)

And we pray this in order that you may live a life worthy of the Lord and may please him in every way: bearing fruit in every good work, growing in the knowledge of God, (Col 1:10)

Let us acknowledge the LORD; let us press on to acknowledge him. As surely as the sun rises, he will appear; he will come to us like the winter rains, like the spring rains that water the earth." (Hosea 6:3)

God's Word is said to be the Truth (Jn.17:17), and Jesus Christ Himself claimed to be the Truth (Jn.14:6). To distinguish between the two, God's Word is sometimes said to be the *Written Truth*, and Jesus Christ is sometimes said to be the *Living Truth*.

1. The truth sets men free from the shadow of doubt and despair. Man no longer has to grasp and grope about to know the truth, whether it be the truth of God or of his own world. Jesus Christ has revealed the truth: the nature, the meaning, and the destiny of all things.

The true light that gives light to every man was coming into the world. The Word became flesh and made his dwelling among us. We have seen his glory, the glory of the One and Only, who came from the Father, full of grace and truth. (John 1:9, 14)

Now the Lord is the Spirit, and where the Spirit of the Lord is, there is freedom. (2 Cor 3:17)

2. The truth sets men free from the bondages of sin. Man no longer has to grasp after the power to overcome; nor does he have to struggle against the weight of guilt. The search for deliverance and for the power to conquer, to overcome, to attain, and to live is now over. It is all found in Jesus Christ. (Cp. Ro.6:1f. See note—Ro.8:28-39.)

Yet to all who received him, to those who believed in his name, he gave the right to become children of God— (John 1:12)

Jesus answered, "I am the way and the truth and the life. No one comes to the Father except through me. (John 14:6)

But I see another law at work in the members of my body, waging war against the law of my mind and making me a prisoner of the law of sin at work within my members. What a wretched man I am! Who will rescue me from this body of death? Thanks be to God—through Jesus Christ our Lord! So then, I myself in my mind am a slave to God's law, but in the sinful nature a slave to the law of sin. (Rom 7:23-25)

The mind of sinful man is death, but the mind controlled by the Spirit is life and peace; For you did not receive a spirit that makes you a slave again to fear, but you received the Spirit of sonship. And by him we cry, "Abba, Father." (Rom 8:6, 15)

3. The truth sets men free from the bondage of death. Man no longer has to be subjected to the fear of death. Jesus Christ—by His death and resurrection—has now conquered death (Heb.2:14-15). In His death and resurrection man now has the most glorious of hopes: he can now live eternally.

"I tell you the truth, whoever hears my word and believes him who sent me has eternal life and will not be condemned; he has crossed over from death to life. I tell you the truth, a time is coming and has now come when the dead will hear the voice of the Son of God and those who hear will live. For as the Father has life in himself, so he has granted the Son to have life in himself. And he has given him authority to judge because he is the Son of Man. "Do not be amazed at this, for a time is coming when all who are in their graves will hear his voice and come out—those who have done good will rise to live, and those who have done evil will rise to be condemned. (John 5:24-29)

Because through Christ Jesus the law of the Spirit of life set me free from the law of sin and death. (Rom 8:2)

Since the children have flesh and blood, he too shared in their humanity so that by his death he might destroy him who holds the power of death—that is, the devil—and free those who all their lives were held in slavery by their fear of death. (Heb 2:14-15)

4. The truth sets men free from the bondage of judgment and hell. The darkness of an unknown future and the apprehension of an impending judgment constantly faces man. At best, man can only hope for annihilation, and he shudders at the thought. At worst, he can expect torture by the gods that be, and he trembles at the possibility. But Jesus Christ has revealed the truth. He Himself has borne the judgment and the punishment of judgment for man.

"For God so loved the world that he gave his one and only Son, that whoever believes in him shall not perish but have eternal life. (John 3:16)

You see, at just the right time, when we were still powerless, Christ died for the ungodly. But God demonstrates his own love for us in this: While we were still sinners, Christ died for us. Since we have now been justified by his blood, how much more shall we be saved from God's wrath through him! (Rom 5:6, 8-9)

He himself bore our sins in his body on the tree, so that we might die to sins and live for righteousness; by his wounds you have been healed. (1 Pet 2:24)

For Christ died for sins once for all, the righteous for the unrighteous, to bring you to God. He was put to death in the body but made alive by the Spirit, (1 Pet 3:18)

5. The truth sets men free to be saved to the uttermost. Existence, love, joy, peace, satisfaction, pleasure, hope—nothing has to be incomplete any longer. No good thing ever again has to be denied man. Jesus Christ, the Truth, is able to save man to the uttermost—completely, perfectly, finally, and eternally. All a person has to do is to come to Christ for salvation, for Christ lives forever to intercede for every man.

Therefore he is able to save completely those who come to God through him, because he always lives to intercede for them. (Heb 7:25)

But the fruit of the Spirit is love, joy, peace, patience, kindness, goodness, faithfulness, gentleness and self-control. Against such things there is no law. (Gal 5:22-23)

For in Christ all the fullness of the Deity lives in bodily form, and you have been given fullness in Christ, who is the head over every power and authority. (Col 2:9-10)

		F. Man's Enslavement by Sin, 8:33-40	descendants. Yet you are ready to kill me, because you have no room for my word.	3	Proof 2: Man opposes & makes no room in his heart for Jesus' Word
1	**Man's denial**		38 I am telling you what I have seen in the Father's presence, and you do what you have heard from your father."	**4**	**Proof 3: Man follows the wrong father, the devil**[DS1]
	a. He claims a godly heritage	33 They answered him, "We are Abraham's descendants and have never been slaves of anyone. How can you say that we shall be set free?"			
	b. He denies that he is enslaved to sin				
2	**Proof 1: Man commits sin**	34 Jesus replied, "I tell you the truth, everyone who sins is a slave to sin.	39 "Abraham is our father," they answered. "If you were Abraham's children," said Jesus, "then you would do the things Abraham did.	**5**	**Proof 4: Man fails to do the works of Abraham**
	a. He is a slave to sin				
	b. He is warned	35 Now a slave has no permanent place in the family, but a son belongs to it forever.			
	1) A slave is not free within a household		40 As it is, you are determined to kill me, a man who has told you the truth that I heard from God. Abraham did not do such things.		a. Abraham did not seek to kill the messengers of truth
	2) The Son can make him free	36 So if the Son sets you free, you will be free indeed. 37 I know you are Abraham's			b. Abraham believed the truth

DIVISION IX

THE REVELATION OF JESUS, THE LIGHT OF LIFE, 8:1-9:41

F. Man's Enslavement by Sin, 8:33-40

(8:33-40) Introduction: man is enslaved by sin. He denies it; nevertheless, he is. Personal experience, greed, lust, selfish behavior, and world history bear clear evidence. Any honest person can clearly see the evidence.

1. Man's denial (v.33).
2. Proof 1: man commits sin (v.34-36).
3. Proof 2: man opposes and makes no room in his heart for Jesus' Word (v.37).
4. Proof 3: man follows the wrong father, the devil (v.38).
5. Proof 4: man fails to do the works of Abraham (v.39-40).

1 (8:33) **Man, State of—Sin, Enslavement to**: man denies he is enslaved. The Jews misunderstood Jesus. They thought He was referring to being conquered and enslaved by a foreign nation. They denied such. They had, of course, been conquered by many nations and were in fact being ruled by the Romans at that very time. What they meant by not ever being enslaved is that they had never surrendered their will to any ruler. They had always given their allegiance to God, not to men, no matter how powerful the men were.

Note two things.

1. Jesus meant something entirely different. Jesus meant that the Jews and all other men were enslaved by sin. They could not help sinning no matter how much they tried not to sin.

2. Man denies being enslaved by sin. He claims a godly heritage and believes it frees him and makes him acceptable to God. The Jews claimed they were *the seed, the descendants* or the children of Abraham, the children of one of the godliest men who ever lived. They felt, therefore, that his godliness and the godliness of those who followed him made their nation and its people very special to God. They felt they were acceptable to God no matter how they lived. They believed that every true Jew was covered by the godliness of their forefathers (see DEEPER STUDY # 1—Jn.4:22).

Most men believe the same thing. They deny being so enslaved by sin that they are unacceptable to God. Men believe that God will accept them, that they have enough *good heritage* to receive God's approval. They feel they have not done enough bad to be enslaved to sin nor to be be rejected by God. Their heritage—their parents, their family, their friends, their good works, something in their lives—is good enough to keep them from being enslaved and doomed.

> **Produce fruit in keeping with repentance. And do not begin to say to yourselves, 'We have Abraham as our father.' For I tell you that out of these stones God can raise up children for Abraham. (Luke 3:8)**
>
> **Then they hurled insults at him and said, "You are this fellow's disciple! We are disciples of Moses!   (John 9:28)**
>
> **If you are convinced that you are a guide for the blind, a light for those who are in the dark, (Rom 2:19)**
>
> **Who can bring what is pure from the impure? No one! (Job 14:4)**
>
> **'I am pure and without sin; I am clean and free from guilt. (Job 33:9)**
>
> **Many a man claims to have unfailing love, but a faithful man who can find? (Prov 20:6)**
>
> **Who can say, "I have kept my heart pure; I am clean and without sin"? (Prov 20:9)**
>
> **All a man's ways seem right to him, but the LORD weighs the heart. (Prov 21:2)**
>
> **those who are pure in their own eyes and yet are not cleansed of their filth; (Prov 30:12)**

2 (8:34-36) **Sin, Enslavement to**: the first proof that man is enslaved by sin is undeniable—man commits sin. "Everyone who sins" (poion) is continuous action. Man continues to commit sin. It is his habit, his practice to sin. He cannot keep from sinning; therefore, he is a slave to sin. The word "slave" (doulos) means slave or bond-slave (see note—Ro.1:1). The bond-slave was purchased and bound to the person who bought him. The idea is that man is *bought* by sin. When a man sins, he is giving himself over to sin. He becomes enslaved to sin; he is a sinner forever: in a *condition*, a *state*, a *being of sin*. Very simply, he is unable to keep from sinning, no matter how hard he tries.

Jesus warned man. A slave is not a permanent member of a family, but the Son is. The slave has no rights and no claims to privileges within the family. He is a slave and can be rejected and cast out of the house anytime, but not the Son. The Son is always the Son. It is He that has all the rights and privileges to the house. However, there is a way the slave can become a member of the house. The Son can free the slave and ask the Father to adopt him, and if the Son makes the slave free, the slave is free indeed.

Note that Jesus claims four significant things.

a. He, Jesus Christ, is the Son of God.

> "For God so loved the world that he gave his one and only Son, that whoever believes in him shall not perish but have eternal life. (John 3:16; cp. v.17-18)
>
> Jesus heard that they had thrown him out, and when he found him, he said, "Do you believe in the Son of Man?" "Who is he, sir?" the man asked. "Tell me so that I may believe in him." Jesus said, "You have now seen him; in fact, he is the one speaking with you." (John 9:35-37)
>
> What about the one whom the Father set apart as his very own and sent into the world? Why then do you accuse me of blasphemy because I said, 'I am God's Son'? (John 10:36)

b. Man is in slavery to sin.

> Jesus replied, "I tell you the truth, everyone who sins is a slave to sin. (John 8:34)
>
> For I see that you are full of bitterness and captive to sin." (Acts 8:23)
>
> For all have sinned and fall short of the glory of God, (Rom 3:23)
>
> Don't you know that when you offer yourselves to someone to obey him as slaves, you are slaves to the one whom you obey—whether you are slaves to sin, which leads to death, or to obedience, which leads to righteousness? (Rom 6:16)
>
> We know that the law is spiritual; but I am unspiritual, sold as a slave to sin. (Rom 7:14)
>
> But I see another law at work in the members of my body, waging war against the law of my mind and making me a prisoner of the law of sin at work within my members. (Rom 7:23)
>
> And that they will come to their senses and escape from the trap of the devil, who has taken them captive to do his will. (2 Tim 2:26)
>
> They promise them freedom, while they themselves are slaves of depravity—for a man is a slave to whatever has mastered him. (2 Pet 2:19)

c. He, Jesus Christ, can free man.

> Then you will know the truth, and the truth will set you free." (John 8:32; cp. Jn.14:6)
>
> You have been set free from sin and

have become slaves to righteousness. (Rom 6:18)

> Because through Christ Jesus the law of the Spirit of life set me free from the law of sin and death. (Rom 8:2)
>
> It is for freedom that Christ has set us free. Stand firm, then, and do not let yourselves be burdened again by a yoke of slavery. (Gal 5:1)
>
> Now the Lord is the Spirit, and where the Spirit of the Lord is, there is freedom. (2 Cor 3:17)

d. Man can be adopted.

> Yet to all who received him, to those who believed in his name, he gave the right to become children of God— (John 1:12)
>
> Because those who are led by the Spirit of God are sons of God. (Rom 8:14)
>
> "Therefore come out from them and be separate, says the Lord. Touch no unclean thing, and I will receive you." "I will be a Father to you, and you will be my sons and daughters, says the Lord Almighty." (2 Cor 6:18)
>
> But when the time had fully come, God sent his Son, born of a woman, born under law, to redeem those under law, that we might receive the full rights of sons. Because you are sons, God sent the Spirit of his Son into our hearts, the Spirit who calls out, "Abba, Father." (Gal 4:4-6)

3 (8:37) **Sin, Enslavement to**: the second proof that man is enslaved by sin is that he opposes and makes no room in his heart for Jesus' Word.

1. Man rejects and opposes Christ. Man rejects the claims of Christ upon his life; he refuses to deny himself and take up the cross as demanded by Christ (see DEEPER STUDY # 1—Lk.9:23). He does not want the claims of Christ to control his life; he wants to do his own thing and to live as he pleases. Therefore, he rejects Christ and goes about fulfilling his own desires, securing or taking whatever he wants. He ridicules and speaks against Christ and those who follow Christ whenever possible. Very simply, man wants little if anything to do with Christ; he wants Christ to have little if any say-so in his life.

2. Man makes no room in his heart for Jesus' Word (see note, pt.2—Jn.8:31 for discussion).

> Thus you nullify the word of God by your tradition that you have handed down. And you do many things like that." (Mark 7:13)
>
> There is a judge for the one who rejects me and does not accept my words; that very word which I spoke will condemn him at the last day. (John 12:48)
>
> He who does not love me will not obey my teaching. These words you hear are not my own; they belong to the Father who sent me. (John 14:24)
>
> If anyone teaches false doctrines and does not agree to the sound instruction of our Lord Jesus Christ and to godly teaching, he is conceited and understands nothing. He has an unhealthy interest in contro-

versies and quarrels about words that result in envy, strife, malicious talk, evil suspicions and constant friction between men of corrupt mind, who have been robbed of the truth and who think that godliness is a means to financial gain. (1 Tim 6:3-5)

You hate my instruction and cast my words behind you. (Psa 50:17)

Therefore, as tongues of fire lick up straw and as dry grass sinks down in the flames, so their roots will decay and their flowers blow away like dust; for they have rejected the law of the LORD Almighty and spurned the word of the Holy One of Israel. (Isa 5:24)

To whom can I speak and give warning? Who will listen to me? Their ears are closed so they cannot hear. The word of the LORD is offensive to them; they find no pleasure in it. (Jer 6:10)

They made their hearts as hard as flint and would not listen to the law or to the words that the LORD Almighty had sent by his Spirit through the earlier prophets. So the LORD Almighty was very angry. (Zec 7:12)

4 (8:38) **Unbelievers—Satan**: the third proof that man is enslaved by sin is that he follows the wrong father, the devil (cp. v.44). There is a strong contrast here between the Father of Christ and the father of man, the devil. (See DEEPER STUDY # 1—Rev.12:9.)

1. What Christ speaks is what He has seen in his Father's presence. What Christ saw came from the very side of the Father. Christ was from the very presence of God, so what He spoke was God's Word. His message was the Word of God Himself. What was His message?
⇒ Man must "believe in Him" (v.31).
⇒ Man must "hold to his teaching [His Word]" (v.31).
⇒ Man is "enslaved by sin" (v.34).
⇒ Man can be freed and adopted as a child of God's by the eternal Son (v.35-36).

2. What man does is what he sees and hears with his father. Christ identifies the father of man as the devil (v.44). Man, walking in sin, is by the very side of the devil (by the side of the devil's place, domain, rule, and reign). So much of what man does is, therefore, of the devil. What are the deeds of the devil that man does? Both man and his father (the devil)...
• lust (cp. 1 Jn.2:15-16; Ro.12:1-2; 2 Cor.6:17-18).
• murder (cp. Mt.5:21-22).
• fail to hold to the truth. (See DEEPER STUDY # 1—Jn.8:32.)
• believe, live, and speak a lie. Man lives and talks about a life that is a lie, that is not permanent and lasting nor sure and secure.

No man is free of these deeds of the devil. Man is enslaved by sin, desperately needing to be set free. (Just think! If men were freed of these devilish deeds, what a different world this would be!)

DEEPER STUDY # 1
(8:38) **Unbelievers**: all men who practice unrighteousness are men who have not been born of God. They are said to be children of Satan (1 Jn.3:8-10).

The field is the world, and the good seed stands for the sons of the kingdom. The weeds are the sons of the evil one, (Mat 13:38)

You belong to your father, the devil, and you want to carry out your father's desire. He was a murderer from the beginning, not holding to the truth, for there is no truth in him. When he lies, he speaks his native language, for he is a liar and the father of lies. (John 8:44)

"You are a child of the devil and an enemy of everything that is right! You are full of all kinds of deceit and trickery. Will you never stop perverting the right ways of the Lord? (Acts 13:10)

In which you used to live when you followed the ways of this world and of the ruler of the kingdom of the air, the spirit who is now at work in those who are disobedient. (Eph 2:2)

5 (8:39-40) **Sin, Enslavement to—Man, Depravity**: the fourth proof that man is enslaved by sin is that he fails to do the works of Abraham. What is said now is crucial.

1. The Jews cried out, " 'Abraham is our Father.' Our father was a good man, a man of great goodness. And our people have done *enough good* through the years for us to claim God as our Father. Our father is certainly God, not someone else."

Note that few men would ever say the devil is their father. To most people such an idea is preposterous, even repulsive. It arouses emotions ranging from mild amusement to anger. There is the feeling that too much good is done upon earth for the devil to be called the father of the world or of man.

2. Jesus replied, "If you were Abraham's children...then you would do the the things Abraham did." Two works in particular are mentioned.
a. Abraham did not attempt to kill the messengers of truth: "Abraham did not do such things." He did not oppose the messengers of the truth but received and accepted the truth whenever a messenger crossed his path. However, many of the people were set on getting rid of Jesus.
b. Abraham believed God and the truth of God (see outlines and DEEPER STUDY # 1—Ro.4:1-25).

The point Jesus was making is this: a man cannot claim the goodness of others for himself. If a man is a child of Abraham's faith, that is, of God...
• he will do the things Abraham did (believe and diligently seek God, continuing in the truth). (See note—Jn.8:31.)
• he will not do the works of the devil (cp. Jn.8:44).

Thought 1. The true child of God is a person who does the things of the Lord.
1) He hears and receives the truth.

The Word became flesh and made his dwelling among us. We have seen his glory, the glory of the One and Only, who came from the Father, full of grace and truth. (John 1:14)

Jesus answered, "I am the way and the truth and the life. No one comes to the Fa-

172

ther except through me. (John 14:6)

"You are a king, then!" said Pilate. Jesus answered, "You are right in saying I am a king. In fact, for this reason I was born, and for this I came into the world, to testify to the truth. Everyone on the side of truth listens to me." (John 18:37)

This is how we know who the children of God are and who the children of the devil are: Anyone who does not do what is right is not a child of God; nor is anyone who does not love his brother. This is the message you heard from the beginning: We should love one another. (1 John 3:10-11)

2) He does not try to kill and eliminate the greatest truth God has given to this earth, the truth of His own Son.

This is how we know who the children of God are and who the children of the devil are: Anyone who does not do what is right is not a child of God; nor is anyone who does not love his brother. This is the message you heard from the beginning: We should love one another. (1 John 3:10-11)

Do not love the world or anything in the world. If anyone loves the world, the love of the Father is not in him. For everything in the world—the cravings of sinful man, the lust of his eyes and the boasting of what he has and does—comes not from the Father but from the world. (1 John 2:15-16)

But they were furious and began to discuss with one another what they might do to Jesus. (Luke 6:11)

"But his subjects hated him and sent a delegation after him to say, 'We don't want this man to be our king.' (Luke 19:14)

The world cannot hate you, but it hates me because I testify that what it does is evil. (John 7:7)

"If the world hates you, keep in mind that it hated me first. (John 15:18)

But this is to fulfill what is written in their Law: 'They hated me without reason.' (John 15:25)

As soon as the chief priests and their officials saw him, they shouted, "Crucify! Crucify!" But Pilate answered, "You take him and crucify him. As for me, I find no basis for a charge against him." (John 19:6)

	G. Man's Depravity—Illegitimate Birth, 8:41-47		3 Proof 2: Man shows by his works that his father is the devil
1 The fact stated a. Man denies b. Man claims God is his Father	41 You are doing the things your own father does." "We are not illegitimate children," they protested. "The only Father we have is God himself."	44 You belong to your father, the devil, and you want to carry out your father's desire. He was a murderer from the beginning, not holding to the truth, for there is no truth in him. When he lies, he speaks his native language, for he is a liar and the father of lies.	a. Satan & man lust[DS1] b. Satan & man murder c. Satan and man do not hold to the truth d. Satan & man lie
2 Proof 1: Man does not love Christ a. Christ came from God b. Christ was sent by God c. Man does not understand the words & claims of Christ	42 Jesus said to them, "If God were your Father, you would love me, for I came from God and now am here. I have not come on my own; but he sent me. 43 Why is my language not clear to you? Because you are unable to hear what I say.	45 Yet because I tell the truth, you do not believe me! 46 Can any of you prove me guilty of sin? If I am telling the truth, why don't you believe me? 47 He who belongs to God hears what God says. The reason you do not hear is that you do not belong to God."	**4 Proof 3: Christ is sinless—He is of God** a. Men still do not believe b. The reason: Man is not of God—man is sinful 1) He does not hear God's words 2) Because he is not of God

DIVISION IX

THE REVELATION OF JESUS, THE LIGHT OF LIFE, 8:1-9:41

G. Man's Depravity—Illegitimate Birth, 8:41-47

(8:41-47) **Introduction**: this passage shatters man's concept of himself. Nevertheless, it is a passage that must be studied very carefully, for it is one of the shocking truths revealed by Christ. Man's destiny hangs upon what He revealed.

Man is a sinner and short of God's glory. Man sins because he is depraved, that is, born illegitimately. Depravity means that a man *is always short* of God's glory, and is *always coming short* of God, and is *always failing* to measure up to God. Very simply, man *is not holy* as God is holy; man *is not perfect* as God is perfect. Why? Because man is born with an illegitimate, sinful, and depraved nature. Man is born with a nature that sins, ages, deteriorates, dies, and decays—a nature that is imperfect and as radically different from God's perfect nature as it can be. (See outline and notes—1 Jn.3:4-9 for more discussion.)

1. The fact stated (v.41).
2. Proof 1: man does not love Christ. (v.42-43).
3. Proof 2: man shows by his works that his father is the devil (v.44).
4. Proof 3: Christ is sinless—He is of God (v.45-47).

1 (8:41) **Man, Depravity—Profession, False**: the fact is stated most emphatically. Man sins by doing the deeds of and following after a father other than God.

⇒ Sin is not of God.
⇒ Evil deeds are not of the Father in heaven.
⇒ Therefore, they must be of another father.

A man who sins and does evil is following another father, an illegitimate father. Sinful man...

• reveals a depraved nature, a nature that cannot keep from sinning no matter how hard it tries. (See notes—Ro.3:9-20; 3:9.)
• reveals a nature of some father who stands diametrically opposed to the Father in heaven.

Note: sin and evil are due to the nature of a spiritual father (the devil). Man sins because he is in the family likeness of that father (by nature). However, man denies the fact. The Pharisees, the strongest religionists who have

ever lived (representing all mankind), knew exactly what Jesus was saying. They knew that Jesus was speaking spiritually and that He was charging them...

• with being sinful and depraved, always coming short
• with following some father other than the Father of heaven

The Jewish religionists (as most men) denied that they had an idolatrous father. In their minds God was their Father and they were children of God, and there was no question about it. They claimed that...

• they believed in and professed the God of the Bible
• they worshipped the true God
• they followed the true God
• they did enough good to be accepted by God
• they had not done enough evil deeds to be rejected by God
• they had done the best they could to please God
• they had enough righteousness to be acceptable to God
• they had enough godly heritage (parents, family, friends, works) to be accepted by God

Thought 1. The tragic fact is this: the vast majority of people make the very same claim, refusing to accept the truth. However, their claim is a false profession. What Christ was doing was trying to get men to see the truth. Men desperately need to turn away from their evil deeds to God, to genuinely believe and diligently seek God (Heb.11:6).

"Not everyone who says to me, 'Lord, Lord,' will enter the kingdom of heaven, but only he who does the will of my Father who is in heaven. (Mat 7:21)

He replied, "Isaiah was right when he prophesied about you hypocrites; as it is written: "'These people honor me with their lips, but their hearts are far from me. (Mark 7:6)

They claim to know God, but by their actions they deny him. They are detestable, disobedient and unfit for doing anything good. (Titus 1:16)

And without faith it is impossible to please God, because anyone who comes to him must believe that he exists and that he rewards those who earnestly seek him. (Heb 11:6)

How great is the love the Father has lavished on us, that we should be called children of God! And that is what we are! The reason the world does not know us is that it did not know him. (1 John 3:1)

2 (8:42-43) **Man, Depravity:** the first proof of man's depravity is that man does not love Jesus. Picture the scene. God sent His Son into the world and man...
- does not recognize Him
- does not recognize His words
- does not recognize His works

If man were of God, that is, of the same spiritual world and dimension as Jesus, he would recognize Jesus and recognize His words and works. It would be impossible not to recognize Him. This is what Jesus was saying. He "came from God," that is, from the spiritual world and dimension of heaven itself. Any man who is of God is bound to recognize Him. Any man who is truly of God will love and welcome Him, not reject and oppose Him. The man who wants nothing to do with Jesus is not of the family of God; he is not a child of God. He is a child of some father other than the Father of Jesus.

Note another fact: no man could possibly be of God...
- who does not understand the speech (teaching) of Christ
- who does not hear the word of Christ (open his heart to it)

A man who has the same Father as Jesus Christ will understand His teaching, and hear His Word and open his heart to *what* Christ teaches. When a man shuts his heart to the teaching of Christ, that man shows that he has a father other than Christ's Father.

Jesus said to them, "If God were your Father, you would love me, for I came from God and now am here. I have not come on my own; but he sent me. (John 8:42)

For I have come down from heaven not to do my will but to do the will of him who sent me. (John 6:38)

If you really knew me, you would know my Father as well. From now on, you do know him and have seen him." Philip said, "Lord, show us the Father and that will be enough for us." Jesus answered: "Don't you know me, Philip, even after I have been among you such a long time? Anyone who has seen me has seen the Father. How can you say, 'Show us the Father'? Don't you believe that I am in the Father, and that the Father is in me? The words I say to you are not just my own. Rather, it is the Father, living in me, who is doing his work. (John 14:7-10)

No, the Father himself loves you be-cause you have loved me and have believed that I came from God. (John 16:27)

Now we can see that you know all things and that you do not even need to have anyone ask you questions. This makes us believe that you came from God." (John 16:30)

Grace to all who love our Lord Jesus Christ with an undying love. (Eph 6:24)

Note the word "unable." It is strong. They *could have understood and heard* His Word, but they *would not*; that is, they refused His Word, for it repelled them. They rejected it, deliberately willed to turn from it.

For this people's heart has become calloused; they hardly hear with their ears, and they have closed their eyes. Otherwise they might see with their eyes, hear with their ears, understand with their hearts and turn, and I would heal them.' (Acts 28:27)

There is no one who understands, no one who seeks God. (Rom 3:11)

Always learning but never able to acknowledge the truth. (2 Tim 3:7)

3 (8:44) **Man, Depravity:** the second proof of man's depravity is that man shows that his father is the devil. It is *man's works* that reveal his true father. Man objects and denies this fact rather strongly, sometimes angrily. Many think the idea is repulsive and horrible, a terrible thing to say. And it is. This is just what Jesus wants man to recognize. The fact has to be faced; it has to be felt so repulsive and horrible that a man will do something about it. It is shocking for some persons to hear that Jesus even said such a thing.

The point is this: man's sinful behavior and evil works prove that his father is not the Father of Jesus. Sinful behavior and evil deeds are not of the Father in heaven; they are of the father in hell. The sins and evil mentioned by Jesus show this.

1. Satan and men lust—They are both controlled by desires (see Deeper Study # 1, Lust—Jn.8:44; Deeper Study # 1—Jas.4:1-3; note—4:2 for discussion).

2. Satan and men murder. Satan is a murderer in three senses.
   a. He was behind the first murder: Cain's killing his brother Abel (Gen.4:8).
   b. He was behind the sin of Adam, which brought death to the whole human race. He is the murderer, the one who caused the death of men.

Therefore, just as sin entered the world through one man, and death through sin, and in this way death came to all men, because all sinned— (Rom 5:12)

   c. He is behind the murder of human life and behind the loss of man's experiencing real life here on earth. The devil destroys life and all abundant living when he can: all love, joy, peace, patience, gentleness, goodness, faith, meekness, discipline.

When anyone hears the message about the kingdom and does not understand it, the evil one comes and snatches away what was sown in his heart. This is the seed sown along the path. (Mat 13:19)

Be self-controlled and alert. Your enemy the devil prowls around like a roaring lion looking for someone to devour. (1 Pet 5:8)

"Does Job fear God for nothing?" Satan replied. "Have you not put a hedge around him and his household and everything he has? You have blessed the work of his hands, so that his flocks and herds are spread throughout the land. But stretch out your hand and strike everything he has, and he will surely curse you to your face." (Job 1:9-11)

Jesus was saying that one thing is certain: God is not the father of murder—the devil is. They who commit murder are children of the devil. But note the real meaning of murder revealed by Jesus (see note 2—Mt.5:22 for discussion). Murder is...

- anger
- bitterness
- enmity
- an uncontrolled spirit
- desiring a person's ruin
- striking out at a person
- slandering, maligning, speaking ill about a person and destroying a person's image (who is created in God's image)
- envying & killing a person's happiness

3. Satan and men hate the truth. Both reject the truth and refuse to "hold to" it, refuse to abide in God's truth (see DEEPER STUDY # 1—Jn.8:32).

You belong to your father, the devil, and you want to carry out your father's desire. He was a murderer from the beginning, not holding to the truth, for there is no truth in him. When he lies, he speaks his native language, for he is a liar and the father of lies. (John 8:44)

He who does what is sinful is of the devil, because the devil has been sinning from the beginning. The reason the Son of God appeared was to destroy the devil's work. (1 John 3:8)

4. Satan and men lie and deceive. It is their nature to lie and to protect and to look after themselves. This is the meaning of the phrase, "he speaks his native language"; that is, he is at ease and comfortable in lying. It is man's nature to lie; he lies out of his own being. This hurts the pride of man, but it is his nature...

- to look after himself even if he has to lie (cheat, steal, manuever, whatever) to get
- to protect himself by misleading, deceiving, and twisting the truth

And even if our gospel is veiled, it is veiled to those who are perishing. The god of this age has blinded the minds of unbelievers, so that they cannot see the light of the gospel of the glory of Christ, who is the image of God. (2 Cor 4:3-4)

For such men are false apostles, deceitful workmen, masquerading as apostles of Christ. And no wonder, for Satan himself masquerades as an angel of light. It is not surprising, then, if his servants masquerade as servants of righteousness. Their end will be what their actions deserve. (2 Cor 11:13-15)

Note: anything that is not true is false—whether a lie, thoughts, ideas, words, or acts. Lying is of the devil and exposes a person to be a child of the devil. A person is certainly not of God if he is lying. His father is not the Father of Jesus.

I do not write to you because you do not know the truth, but because you do know it and because no lie comes from the truth. Who is the liar? It is the man who denies that Jesus is the Christ. Such a man is the antichrist—he denies the Father and the Son. No one who denies the Son has the Father; whoever acknowledges the Son has the Father also. (1 John 2:21-23)

Note also that Jesus is telling man the truth, but man refuses to accept it (v.45). It is tough to accept the truth that one follows and actually behaves as a child of the devil. However, man must accept the truth if he is to change and see his world changed and become a child of God's, the Father of the Lord Jesus Christ.

DEEPER STUDY # 1
(8:44) **Desires—Lusts** (epithumia): a strong desire, a yearning passion for. The word is used in a good sense three different times in Scripture (Lk.22:15; Ph.1:23; 1 Th.2:17). A man is to turn his strong desires toward righteousness and godliness; however, a man has to struggle to turn away from the desire to *please* himself. Man's natural tendency is the desire or lust to satisfy self before others, in particular when survival and comfort are at stake.

1. The very nature of man is lust, the lust of the flesh (sinful nature) and of the mind (Eph.2:2-3). Sinful and evil lust show that men are *by nature*...

- objects of wrath
- disobedient
- followers of the spirit who is the ruler of the kingdom of the air, that is, the devil

In which you used to live when you followed the ways of this world and of the ruler of the kingdom of the air, the spirit who is now at work in those who are disobedient. (Eph 2:2)

2. The very nature of man and of the world is lust and desire—a tendency both *to be* and *to get*.

Do not love the world or anything in the world. If anyone loves the world, the love of the Father is not in him. For everything in the world—the cravings of sinful man, the lust of his eyes and the boasting of what he has and does—comes not from the Father but from the world. The world and its desires pass away, but the man who does the will of God lives forever. (1 John 2:15-17) (1 Jn.2:15-17. Cp. Ro.13:14; Gal.5:16, 24; Col.3:5; 1 Th.4:5; 1 Tim.6:9; 2 Tim. 3:6; 4:3; Tit.2:12; 3:3; 1 Pt.1:14; 2:11; 3:3; 4:2; 2 Pt.2:1, 8, 10, 18; Jude 18; Rev. 18:14.)

What a man discovers is that his cravings are never satisfied; they have to be controlled. There is something within man's innermost being that craves for more and more; and as more and more is taken, the lust does not diminish, it grows. It craves for still more and more. Man's cravings are never satisfied; his only answer is to control them (see note, Lust—Jas.4:2 for a discussion of the Spirit of God's control. Cp. Gal.5:22-23.)

4 (8:45-47) **Jesus Christ, Without Sin**: the third proof of man's depravity is the sinlessness of Jesus. Jesus made the most staggering claim: no man could prove Him to be a sinner. No person could prove a single sin in Him. He was sinless and perfect. He was in the closest imaginable relationship with God, of the very same nature as God: sinless, holy, righteous, pure—perfectly so. Jesus claimed to be the Perfect Man.

God made him who had no sin to be sin for us, so that in him we might become the righteousness of God. (2 Cor 5:21)

For we do not have a high priest who is unable to sympathize with our weaknesses, but we have one who has been tempted in every way, just as we are—yet was without sin. (Heb 4:15)

Such a high priest meets our need—one who is holy, blameless, pure, set apart from sinners, exalted above the heavens. (Heb 7:26)

"He committed no sin, and no deceit was found in his mouth." (1 Pet 2:22)

But you know that he appeared so that he might take away our sins. And in him is no sin. (1 John 3:5)

Note the all important question: Since He was sinless, why do men not believe Him? He was telling the truth. Therefore, men should believe Him. Jesus answered His own question.

⇒ He that is "of God" hears God's Words.
⇒ He that is "not of God" does not hear God's Words. The person who does not belong to God does not hear and believe because he is not a child of God. He is a child of the father of lies, the devil.

For this people's heart has become calloused; they hardly hear with their ears, and they have closed their eyes. Otherwise they might see with their eyes, hear with their ears, understand with their hearts and turn, and I would heal them.' (Mat 13:15)

They will turn their ears away from the truth and turn aside to myths. (2 Tim 4:4)

"But they refused to pay attention; stubbornly they turned their backs and stopped up their ears. (Zec 7:11)

177

	H. Man's Escape from Death, 8:48-59	and so did the prophets. Who do you think you are?"	3 The great authority of Jesus to promise deliverance from death
1 A harsh insult—Jesus is a Samaritan & demon-possessed	48 The Jews answered him, "Aren't we right in saying that you are a Samaritan and demon-possessed?"	54 Jesus replied, "If I glorify myself, my glory means nothing. My Father, whom you claim as your God, is the one who glorifies me.	a. He was honored by God 1) The God often professed by men 2) The God unknown by so many men
a. Jesus' strong denial b. Jesus' purpose: To honor God	49 "I am not possessed by a demon," said Jesus, "but I honor my Father and you dishonor me.	55 Though you do not know him, I know him. If I said I did not, I would be a liar like you, but I do know him and keep his word.	b. He personally knew God, obeyed His Word
c. Jesus' honor is God's concern	50 I am not seeking glory for myself; but there is one who seeks it, and he is the judge.	56 Your father Abraham rejoiced at the thought of seeing my day; he saw it and was glad."	c. He was the One that Abraham hoped for & actually saw 1) The Messiah
2 The great revelation: Man can escape death[DS1] a. The condition: "If...." b. The reaction to Jesus' promise: A charge that He was demon-possessed 1) The charge: All godly men have died	51 I tell you the truth, if anyone keeps my word, he will never see death." 52 At this the Jews exclaimed, "Now we know that you are demon-possessed! Abraham died and so did the prophets, yet you say that if anyone keeps your word, he will never taste death.	57 "You are not yet fifty years old," the Jews said to him, "and you have seen Abraham!" 58 "I tell you the truth,"Jesus answered, "before Abraham was born, I am!" 59 At this, they picked up stones to stone him, but Jesus	2) The Jews misinterpreted Jesus' claim d. He was the great "I Am"[DS2] 1) Before Abraham 2) The reaction against Him: Rejection
2) The question: Who do you claim to be?	53 Are you greater than our Father Abraham? He died,	hid himself, slipping away from the temple grounds.	

DIVISION IX

THE REVELATION OF JESUS, THE LIGHT OF LIFE, 8:1-9:41

H. Man's Escape from Death, 8:48-59

(8:48-59) **Introduction**: this is an astonishing claim—a person does not have to die (v.51). We can all escape death.
1. A harsh insult—Jesus is a Samaritan and demon-possessed (v.48-50).
2. The great revelation: a person can escape death (v.51-53).
3. The great authority of Jesus to promise deliverance from death (v.54-59).

1 (8:48-50) **Jesus Christ, Charges Against—Purpose**: the religionists cast a harsh insult against Jesus. They called Him a Samaritan and accused Him of being demon-possessed.
⇒ Being a Samaritan was a charge that He was full of heresy, not worshipping the true God, but following and building up the false religion of the Samaritans (see DEEPER STUDY # 1—Jn.4:5. The Jews despised the Samaritans.)
⇒ Being demon-possessed was a charge that He was full of an evil spirit, a spirit that was out to destroy man and the true religion of God and its people (see notes—Jn.7:20-24; 7:32; DEEPER STUDY # 4—Mt.12:24).

Jesus answered the charges, but said absolutely nothing about their racial slur. (A racial slur was not worthy of comment by Him.) But He strongly denied their charge that He was demon-possessed. He knew exactly what He was saying and doing. He was not insane. He was perfectly conscious of His actions. Note that Jesus made three claims.
1. Jesus claimed that His very purpose was to honor

God. There was not an evil spirit within Him setting out to destroy man and the worship of God. Contrariwise, His very purpose was *to honor God* and to turn men to God. Note: He called God "My Father."
2. Jesus claimed that man was the one who did evil to God. While Jesus honored God, man (in particular false religionists) tried to dishonor Jesus. In dishonoring Jesus, they were dishonoring God. It was the love of God that had sent Him into the world to offer salvation (v.31-32). The real demon-possession or spirit of evil was seen in those who dishonored Him while He offered God's salvation to men.
3. Jesus did not seek His own glory; contrariwise, He sought to glorify God by leading men to God. However...
• there was One who sought the glory of Jesus, that is, God Himself.
• God will judge those who truly glorified Christ. He will reveal what Christ did to glorify God and what religionists did to dishonor God. One (Christ) shall be proven and accepted, and the other (religionists) disproven and condemned.

2 (8:51-53) **Jesus Christ, Deliverer from Death**: there is the great revelation and promise—a person can escape death. (See DEEPER STUDY # 1, Death—Jn.8:51 for discussion.)
Note the reaction to Jesus' phenomenal claim: man thought Jesus must be under a demon's spell, that he was mad and insane. He was bound to be demon-possessed, for every one knows that man dies. Even the godliest men such as Abraham and the prophets died. Who did Jesus think He was? Did He think He was greater than Abraham and the prophets? Who was He claiming to be?

178

DEEPER STUDY # 1

(8:51) Death—Deliverance—Jesus Christ, Deliverance from Death: this is one of the great promises of Scripture. "I tell you the truth, if anyone keeps my word, he will never see death" (v.51).

1. Note the eye-catching words "I tell you the truth." What is said is of critical importance: "Listen—listen."

2. Note how the sentence really stresses the glorious truth.

⇒ The word "death" is emphatic in the Greek: it begins the sentence. "Death in no wise will he ever see."

⇒ There is a double negative used (ou me): "Death *in no wise*, and *by no means* will he ever see."

3. Note the phrases "see death" (theorese thanaton) and "taste death" (geusetai thanatou, v.52). The meaning is that a genuine follower of Christ will...

• never experience death nor see death
• never know death nor partake of death
• never face the condemnation of death
• never experience the terror, the hurt, the pain, and the suffering of death; never experience the anguish of being separated from God and from the glory, beauty, perfection, and life of heaven

In a flash, quicker than lightning or the blinking of an eye, the follower of Christ passes from this world into the next. He never ceases to experience life and never loses consciousness. One moment he is in this world, the next moment he is in the presence of God Himself.

Note the reason why the believer will never "see death" (v.51) or "taste death" (v.52): it is because Jesus came "by the grace of God [to] taste death for evryone" (Heb.2:9).

4. Note: there is a condition for escaping death: "If anyone keeps my word" (logon, word). A person must keep the Word of Christ to escape death. The word "keeps" (terese) means to watch over, to keep, to obey with diligence. It means to fix and set one's heart upon the Word of Christ and keep it with all diligence. If a man is persistent in obeying Christ, he will never see death. (See note—Jn.8:31 for discussion and verses of Scripture. See DEEPER STUDY # 1, Death—Heb.9:27.)

5. Note the glorious truth of this claim.

Man Does...	*But the Follower of Christ...*
• pass through physical death	• never sees death
• have his body decay	• never tastes death
• face the judgment of God	• lives now and forever

"For God so loved the world that he gave his one and only Son, that whoever believes in him shall not perish but have eternal life. (John 3:16)

Do not work for food that spoils, but for food that endures to eternal life, which the Son of Man will give you. On him God the Father has placed his seal of approval." (John 6:27)

The thief comes only to steal and kill and destroy; I have come that they may have life, and have it to the full. (John 10:10)

My sheep listen to my voice; I know them, and they follow me.I give them eternal life, and they shall never perish; no one can snatch them out of my hand. (John 10:27-28)

And whoever lives and believes in me will never die. Do you believe this?" (John 11:26)

For you granted him authority over all people that he might give eternal life to all those you have given him. Now this is eternal life: that they may know you, the only true God, and Jesus Christ, whom you have sent. (John 17:2-3)

And this is what he promised us—even eternal life. (1 John 2:25)

Keep yourselves in God's love as you wait for the mercy of our Lord Jesus Christ to bring you to eternal life. (Jude 1:21)

3 (8:54-59) **Jesus Christ, Deity—Oneness with God**: there is the great authority of Jesus to make such a glorious promise. He made four unique claims.

1. Jesus claimed that He was honored by God. He was not out to honor Himself. If He sought His own honor, His honor would amount to nothing. When a man is seen honoring and praising himself, it is considered false honor. Self-honor is discounted and considered distasteful and usually turns people away. It certainly does not attract people.

However, there is One who does honor Christ: His Father honors Him.

And a voice from heaven said, "This is my Son, whom I love; with him I am well pleased." (Mat 3:17)

There is another who testifies in my favor, and I know that his testimony about me is valid. (John 5:32)

And the Father who sent me has himself testified concerning me. You have never heard his voice nor seen his form, nor does his word dwell in you, for you do not believe the one he sent. (John 5:37-38)

I am one who testifies for myself; my other witness is the Father, who sent me." (John 8:18)

We accept man's testimony, but God's testimony is greater because it is the testimony of God, which he has given about his Son. Anyone who believes in the Son of God has this testimony in his heart. Anyone who does not believe God has made him out to be a liar, because he has not believed the testimony God has given about his Son. And this is the testimony: God has given us eternal life, and this life is in his Son. He who has the Son has life; he who does not have the Son of God does not have life. (1 John 5:9-12)

Now, note a phenomenal claim. Who is Jesus' Father? He is the very One "you claim as your God" (v.54).

a. He is the God who men so often profess as *their God*.

b. But He is the God who men do not really know. Men may say they know Him, professing...

• God to be the creator and sustainer of all
• to worship and follow Him
• to be looked after and cared for by Him

But such claims are only imaginations, only ideas in man's mind. Jesus said that man does not really know God, not the only true and living God—not really—not personally.

> "Not everyone who says to me, 'Lord, Lord,' will enter the kingdom of heaven, but only he who does the will of my Father who is in heaven. (Mat 7:21)
> He replied, "Isaiah was right when he prophesied about you hypocrites; as it is written: "'These people honor me with their lips, but their hearts are far from me. (Mark 7:6)
> "Why do you call me, 'Lord, Lord,' and do not do what I say? (Luke 6:46)
> They claim to know God, but by their actions they deny him. They are detestable, disobedient and unfit for doing anything good. (Titus 1:16)
> Dear children, let us not love with words or tongue but with actions and in truth. (1 John 3:18)

2. Jesus claimed that He personally knew God and obeyed God's Word. He had a unique and very special knowledge of God. Jesus knew God as no one else had ever known Him.

> "All things have been committed to me by my Father. No one knows the Son except the Father, and no one knows the Father except the Son and those to whom the Son chooses to reveal him. (Mat 11:27)
> But I know him because I am from him and he sent me." (John 7:29)
> But he continued, "You are from below; I am from above. You are of this world; I am not of this world. (John 8:23)
> Though you do not know him, I know him. If I said I did not, I would be a liar like you, but I do know him and keep his word. (John 8:55)
> Just as the Father knows me and I know the Father—and I lay down my life for the sheep. (John 10:15)
> Jesus said to them, "If God were your Father, you would love me, for I came from God and now am here. I have not come on my own; but he sent me. (John 8:42)
> "Righteous Father, though the world does not know you, I know you, and they know that you have sent me. (John 17:25)

Note that Jesus refused to lie. Most men lie when they claim to know God, but He would not lie like they did (v.55). He knew God and He would not lower nor retract His claim although He knew it would mean His death. Note also that Jesus kept God's Word. This meant that He had to tell the truth. He did know God personally, and He must proclaim the glorious Word of God to men. He had to do what God said. He had to keep God's Word and fulfill God's purpose so that men might be saved. (Note that Jesus was claiming to be sinless, to keep God's Word perfectly.)

> But the world must learn that I love the Father and that I do exactly what my Father has commanded me. "Come now; let us leave. (John 14:31)
> For just as through the disobedience of the one man the many were made sinners,

> so also through the obedience of the one man the many will be made righteous. (Rom 5:19)

3. Jesus claimed that He was the One that Abraham hoped for and actually saw. Abraham held a unique position in the Jewish nation, for he was the founder of the nation. He was the man whom God had challenged to be a witness to the other nations of the world—a witness to the only true and living God. Therefore, God had appeared to Abraham and challenged him to leave his home, his friends, his employment, and his country. If Abraham would follow God unquestionably, God made one great promise: Abraham would become the father of a new nation and of a great host of people, and God would cause all nations to be blessed by his seed (offspring) (Gen.13:14-17; 15:1-7; 17:1-8, 15-19; 22:15-18; 26:2-5, 24; 28:13-15; 35:9-12). (See DEEPER STUDY # 1—Jn.4:22.)
Scripture says that Abraham did as God requested. He went out not knowing where he went (Heb.11:8). He completely and unquestionably trusted God and took God at His word. The point is this: Abraham rejoiced to see the Messiah's day, the day when the promised Seed (offspring) was sent into the world.

a. When Abraham was on earth he saw the Messiah's day by faith. He was hopeful and he rejoiced as much as any Old Testament saint.

> All these people were still living by faith when they died. They did not receive the things promised; they only saw them and welcomed them from a distance. And they admitted that they were aliens and strangers on earth. (Heb 11:13)

b. When Jesus was born, Abraham was alive in heaven, living in the very presence of God Himself (see note, pt.3—Mt.22:31-32). He saw the Messiah's coming to earth and rejoiced with all of heaven. Salvation, the vindication of faith, was now to be secured by the Son of God Himself.

Note that the Jews misinterpreted Jesus' words. Men usually do. They saw Jesus as a mere man, a man who lived upon earth only for a few years. How could He possibly see Abraham, a man who had died hundreds and hundreds of years before?

> The god of this age has blinded the minds of unbelievers, so that they cannot see the light of the gospel of the glory of Christ, who is the image of God. (2 Cor 4:4)
> They are darkened in their understanding and separated from the life of God because of the ignorance that is in them due to the hardening of their hearts. (Eph 4:18)

4. Jesus claimed that He was the great "I Am." (See DEEPER STUDY # 1, I Am—Jn.6:20 for discussion.) This was the climactic claim—the claim...

- to be preexistent, always existing, to have been living when Abraham was born (Greek aorist tense, "came into being")
- to be above and beyond time
- to be eternal

The point is striking. Jesus was there when Abraham was born. He is God Himself, the great "I Am" standing upon earth and in a human body. Why? Note the question is not *how*. God can do anything, even stand upon earth in a human body if He wills. Therefore, the question is never *how*, but *why*. Why would God come to earth as a Man? The answer is clearly stated: to bring the message of God to the world, the glorious gospel (Jn.8:31-32).

However, note the reaction of men to God's presence. They rejected and opposed Him and tried to get rid of Him. They wanted nothing to do with Him, lest His claims lay hold of their lives and they be forced to change the way they lived.

> **But they were furious and began to discuss with one another what they might do to Jesus. (Luke 6:11)**

> **"But his subjects hated him and sent a delegation after him to say, 'We don't want this man to be our king.' (Luke 19:14)**

> **The world cannot hate you, but it hates me because I testify that what it does is evil. (John 7:7)**

DEEPER STUDY # 2
(8:58) **Jesus Christ, Deity—"I Am"**: see DEEPER STUDY # 1— Jn.6:20.

	CHAPTER 9	played in his life	2 Jesus came to work the works of God
	I. Man's Eyes Opened (Part 1): The Mission of Jesus,[DS1] **9:1-7**	4 As long as it is day, we must do the work of him who sent me. Night is coming, when no one can work.	
1 Jesus passed by a. He saw a man blind from birth	As he went along, he saw a man blind from birth.	5 While I am in the world, I am the light of the world."	**3 Jesus came to be the Light of the world** **4 Jesus came to give sight to men**
b. He was asked a question about suffering & sin	2 His disciples asked him, "Rabbi, who sinned, this man or his parents, that he was born blind?"	6 Having said this, he spit on the ground, made some mud with the saliva, and put it on the man's eyes.	a. Jesus' act: He made contact
c. He replied that this man's suffering was not due to sin but to show forth the works of God	3 "Neither this man nor his parents sinned," said Jesus," but this happened so that the work of God might be dis-	7 "Go," he told him, "wash in the Pool of Siloam" (this word means Sent). So the man went and washed, and came home seeing.	b. Man's act: He had to obey to receive his sight

DIVISION IX

THE REVELATION OF JESUS, THE LIGHT OF LIFE, 8:1-9:41

I. Man's Eyes Opened (Part I): The Mission of Jesus, 9:1-7

(9:1-7) Introduction: man is spiritually blind, and his eyes need to be opened. The mission of Jesus is to open the eyes of man.
1. Jesus passed by (v.1-3).
2. Jesus came to work the works of God (v.4).
3. Jesus came to be the Light of the world (v.5).
4. Jesus came to give sight to men (v.6-7).

DEEPER STUDY # 1

(9:1-41) Spiritual Sight: this passage is a continuation of the subject *Man's Sinfulness*. Jesus took a man's physical blindness and demonstrated the stages of spiritual insight and sight (Jn.9:8-41). It should be noted that *spiritual insight* has to do with seeing Jesus and Jesus alone. Jesus is the very theme of God's revelation. He alone is the perfect revelation of God, and a man's spiritual eyes can be opened to see God only through Him. Apart from Jesus, no man will ever see God.

Jesus answered, "I am the way and the truth and the life. No one comes to the Father except through me. (John 14:6)

1 (9:1-3) **Suffering**: Jesus passed by (just where is not stated). As He passed by, He saw a man who had been blind since birth. There was something about the man that attracted both Jesus and the disciples.
⇒ Jesus "saw" him, which indicated interest, care, concern, compassion.
⇒ The disciples apparently felt the same interest and concern for the man, for they began to wonder why he had been doomed to suffer so terribly throughout his life.

It was a common belief that a man suffered because of sin, either his own sin or his parents' sin. The disciples were attracted to the man and wondered about him. Was he suffering because of some great sin committed by his parents, or because God had foreseen that the man would be a great sinner before he was born?

The question is often asked: How can a man who is not yet born be punished for sin he has not yet committed? Ap-

parently, Jewish belief was that a person's sin was foreseen; therefore, the person was "born in sins" and thereby punished [cp. v.34]). Note two points.

1. Jesus said that the man's suffering was not due to sin but that he suffered so that the works of God could be demonstrated in his life. Man suffers...

So that God can...
• have an opportunity to work
• show his compassion
• prove His power
• demonstrate that He does care and look after men
• lead unbelievers to trust Him

So that man can...
• give God an opportunity to show what He can do in a life
• learn to trust God more and more
• demonstrate a special strength and endurance
• set forth a dynamic example of God's care and power to a lost world
• better learn and know that he lives in a sinful, corruptible world and desperately needs deliverance

Thought 1. The sufferer has a very special opportunity to show forth the works of God in his life. He can allow the Spirit of God to be demonstrated in a much more powerful way than a healthy person. The sufferer can show that the grace and power of God are sufficient much more than a healthy person can. Very often a person suffers not because of sin but because God desires a unique opportunity to show forth His works. (See outline and notes—Lk.13:1-9. Also see notes—Lk.5:18-20; Jas.5:14-15 for more discussion.)

2. Jesus carried the discussion beyond the man's blindness. The disciples were perplexed over this man's situation, wondering and asking questions about the problem of suffering and sin. How could a man such as this be punished from birth? Jesus picked up the question, moving it to His worldwide mission as the Light of the world (v.5). He dealt with the problem of suffering and sin throughout the whole world. His very mission upon earth was to work the works of God.

2 (9:4) **Jesus Christ, Mission—God, Works of**: Jesus came to work the works of God. Note four points.

1. Note the words "sent me." God sent Jesus. Jesus had come into the world on God's mission. He was *of God*, from God's very presence, from the closest possible relationship with God (see notes—Jn.3:32-34; DEEPER STUDY # 3—3:34 for verses of Scripture).

2. Note that Jesus came to do the works of God. It was God's works that had to be done. Four works are stressed in this passage.

   a. There is the work of seeking man. God seeks man. Jesus took the initiative with this man, reaching out to help him. It was not the man who reached out for help. In fact, the man was blind; he did not even know that help was available. If Jesus had not reached out for him, he would have remained blind and been in darkness forever.

> **For the Son of Man came to seek and to save what was lost." (Luke 19:10)**

   b. There is the work of caring for man. God cares that man is blind.

> **Just as the Son of Man did not come to be served, but to serve, and to give his life as a ransom for many." (Mat 20:28)**
> **Cast all your anxiety on him because he cares for you. (1 Pet 5:7)**

   c. There is the work of loving and having compasion. God loves and has compassion for man in his blindness and darkness.

> **For we do not have a high priest who is unable to sympathize with our weaknesses, but we have one who has been tempted in every way, just as we are—yet was without sin. Let us then approach the throne of grace with confidence, so that we may receive mercy and find grace to help us in our time of need. (Heb 4:15-16)**
> **In all their distress he too was distressed, and the angel of his presence saved them. In his love and mercy he redeemed them; he lifted them up and carried them all the days of old. (Isa 63:9)**

   d. There is the work of delivering from darkness and giving sight.

> **For he has rescued us from the dominion of darkness and brought us into the kingdom of the Son he loves, (Col 1:13)**

3. Note the urgency of the mission. This is stressed by two things.

   a. The word "must" (dei) means compulsion and necessity. There are no questions, no suggestions, no urgings about the matter. The works of God *must* be done.

   b. The time for work is limited. Christ and His followers do not have forever to do the work. It has to be done now or the opportunity will be lost. Only so much time has been given. Whatever is to be done must be done today, while there is still some daylight left. Night is coming, the time when no man can work. Time will end and the opportunity will be gone forever.

> **"My food," said Jesus, "is to do the will of him who sent me and to finish his work. (John 4:34)**
> **What I mean, brothers, is that the time is short. From now on those who have wives should live as if they had none; those who mourn, as if they did not; those who are happy, as if they were not; those who buy something, as if it were not theirs to keep; (1 Cor 7:29-30)**
> **Making the most of every opportunity, because the days are evil. (Eph 5:16)**
> **Be wise in the way you act toward outsiders; make the most of every opportunity. (Col 4:5)**
> **For this reason I remind you to fan into flame the gift of God, which is in you through the laying on of my hands. (2 Tim 1:6)**

4. Note: the better texts read "us" or "we" (emas) instead of "I" (eme, v.4): "It is necessary for us to work" or "We must work the works of God." If this is accurate, then a wonderful truth is stated. Jesus ties us to His mission from the Father. We, too, are in the world to do the works of God. Our very purpose for being on earth is to proclaim and show forth the works of God.

> **Again Jesus said, "Peace be with you! As the Father has sent me, I am sending you." (John 20:21)**
> **For we cannot help speaking about what we have seen and heard." (Acts 4:20)**
> **Yet when I preach the gospel, I cannot boast, for I am compelled to preach. Woe to me if I do not preach the gospel! (1 Cor 9:16)**

3 (9:5) **Jesus Christ, Light**: Jesus came to be the Light of the world (see DEEPER STUDY # 1—Jn.8:12 for discussion). If man wishes to be delivered from darkness, he must come to Christ. Christ is the only One who gives sight to man and His world.

> **In him was life, and that life was the light of men. (John 1:4)**
> **When Jesus spoke again to the people, he said, "I am the light of the world. Whoever follows me will never walk in darkness, but will have the light of life." (John 8:12)**
> **For God, who said, "Let light shine out of darkness," made his light shine in our hearts to give us the light of the knowledge of the glory of God in the face of Christ. (2 Cor 4:6)**
> **For it is light that makes everything visible. This is why it is said: "Wake up, O sleeper, rise from the dead, and Christ will shine on you." (Eph 5:14)**

4 (9:6-7) **Spiritual Sight**: Jesus came to demonstrate the power to give sight. Note that Jesus did not just speak the *word of healing* to the man. His Word alone was the method He often used in healing, but this was not the case with this man. He did much more, and by His act He demonstrated two things to the world:

⇒ He will do everything He can to deliver a man from darkness and give him sight.

⇒ He has the power to deliver man and to give him sight.

The man's faith needed to be aroused and stirred. Jesus used two things to awaken the man's faith.

1. He used a point of contact, the touch of His hands upon the man's eyes. Note that He made some mud with the saliva. People of that day believed saliva had some curing qualities, and perhaps Jesus used spittle because of this. The man's faith would certainly be helped by thinking of its healing qualities. However, Jesus would not want the man thinking that it was saliva that cured him. The man must know beyond question that Jesus was the One who healed him. So at most, the saliva would be used to stir the thoughts of healing in the man's mind.

2. Jesus sent the man to wash in the pool of Siloam. Note the parenthesis "this word means, Sent" (v.7). Jesus was using the pool as a symbol of the Messiah who was sent by God to give sight to the world. The blind man, by obeying Jesus and going to the pool, would receive his sight. His obedience would demonstrate to the blind of the world that they, too, could receive their sight by coming to Jesus and obeying Him.

The man washed and "came home seeing." He received his sight because He did exactly what Jesus said.

Thought 1. Man's eyes can be opened; and he can be delivered from the darkness of sin and shame, death and corruption, hell and destruction by coming to Jesus Christ and by obeying Him.

So keep up your courage, men, for I have faith in God that it will happen just as he told me. (Acts 27:25)

Yet he did not waver through unbelief regarding the promise of God, but was strengthened in his faith and gave glory to God, being fully persuaded that God had power to do what he had promised. This is why "it was credited to him as righteousness." (Rom 4:20-22)

How great is your goodness, which you have stored up for those who fear you, which you bestow in the sight of men on those who take refuge in you. (Psa 31:19)

Commit your way to the LORD; trust in him and he will do this: (Psa 37:5)

Who among you fears the LORD and obeys the word of his servant? Let him who walks in the dark, who has no light, trust in the name of the LORD and rely on his God. (Isa 50:10)

1 Stage 1: Seeing Jesus as a man
  a. The man's neighbors were amazed, & they questioned the man's deliverance

  b. The man testified: A man called Jesus gave me sight

2 Stage 2: Seeing Jesus as a Helper or a Healer

  a. The problem: The Sabbath law was broken

  b. The Pharisees questioned how the man could now see
  c. The man testified: Jesus healed me

3 Stage 3: Seeing Jesus as a prophet
  a. The Pharisees were divided

  b. The Pharisees questioned the man again

  c. The man testified: Jesus is a prophet
4 Stage 4: Seeing Jesus as the Savior
  a. The Pharisees' unbelief
  b. The Pharisees called & questioned the man's parents

J. Man's Eyes Opened (Part II): The Stages of Spiritual Sight, 9:8-41

8 His neighbors and those who had formerly seen him begging asked, "Isn't this the same man who used to sit and beg?"
9 Some claimed that he was. Others said, "No, he only looks like him." But he himself insisted, "I am the man."
10 "How then were your eyes opened?" they demanded.
11 He replied, "The man they call Jesus made some mud and put it on my eyes. He told me to go to Siloam and wash. So I went and washed, and then I could see."
12 "Where is this man?" they asked him. "I don't know," he said.
13 They brought to the Pharisees the man who had been blind.
14 Now the day on which Jesus had made the mud and opened the man's eyes was a Sabbath.
15 Therefore the Pharisees also asked him how he had received his sight. "He put mud on my eyes," the man replied, "and I washed, and now I see."
16 Some of the Pharisees said, "This man is not from God, for he does not keep the Sabbath." But others asked, "How can a sinner do such miraculous signs?" So they were divided.
17 Finally they turned again to the blind man, "What have you to say about him? It was your eyes he opened."
  The man replied, "He is a prophet."
18 The Jews still did not believe that he had been blind and had received his sight until they sent for the man's parents.
19 "Is this your son?" they asked. "Is this the one you say was born blind? How is it that now he can see?"

20 "We know he is our son," the parents answered, "and we know he was born blind.
21 But how he can see now, or who opened his eyes, we don't know. Ask him. He is of age; he will speak for himself."
22 His parents said this because they were afraid of the Jews, for already the Jews had decided that anyone who acknowledged that Jesus was the Christ would be put out of the synagogue.
23 That was why his parents said, "He is of age; ask him."
24 A second time they summoned the man who had been blind. "Give glory to God, " they said. "We know this man is a sinner."
25 He replied, "Whether he is a sinner or not, I don't know. One thing I do know. I was blind but now I see!"
26 Then they asked him, "What did he do to you? How did he open your eyes?"
27 He answered, "I have told you already and you did not listen. Why do you want to hear it again? Do you want to become his disciples, too?"
28 Then they hurled insults at him and said, "You are this fellow's disciple! We are disciples of Moses!
29 We know that God spoke to Moses, but as for this fellow, we don't even know where he comes from."
30 The man answered, "Now that is remarkable! You don't know where he comes from, yet he opened my eyes.
31 We know that God does not listen to sinners. He listens to the godly man who does his will.
32 Nobody has ever heard of opening the eyes of a man born blind.
33 If this man were not from God, he could do nothing."
34 To this they replied, "You were steeped in sin at birth; how dare you lecture us!" And they threw him out.
35 Jesus heard that they had thrown him out, and when he found him, he said, "Do you believe in the Son of Man?"

  c. The parents' testimony
    1) They identified their son

    2) They denied being eye-witnesses

    3) They feared pre-judgment & excommunication: Feared being banished from the synagogue

  d. The Pharisees' demand that Jesus be denied

  e. The man's testimony
    1) I was blind, but now I see (Jesus saved me & gave me sight)

    2) The clear evidence

5 Stage 5: Seeing Jesus as being "from God"
  a. The Pharisees' case
    1) Accused the man of being Jesus' disciple
    2) Questioned the origin of Jesus

  b. The man's testimony
    1) A marvelous thing

    2) God does not hear sinners, but worshippers

    3) My experience: Proves Jesus is "from God"

  c. The Pharisees' denial of the man's experience & proof: They threw the man out

6 Stage 6: Seeing Jesus as the Son of God
  a. Jesus sought the man who had been thrown out

b. Jesus invited him to believe c. The man requested to know the Son of God d. Jesus identified Himself as The Son of God, cp. v.35 e. The man believed **7 Conclusion: The lesson of Jesus' revelation**	36 "Who is he, sir?" the man asked. "Tell me so that I may believe in him." 37 Jesus said, "You have now seen him; in fact, he is the one speaking with you." 38 Then the man said, "Lord, I believe," and he worshiped him. 39 Jesus said, "For judgment I have come into this world,	so that the blind will see and those who see will become blind." 40 Some Pharisees who were with him heard him say this and asked, "What? Are we blind too?" 41 Jesus said, "If you were blind, you would not be guilty of sin; but now that you claim you can see, your guilt remains.	a. His mission: To bring judgment b. The religionists' expectation: To be exempt from judgment

DIVISION IX

THE REVELATION OF JESUS, THE LIGHT OF LIFE, 8:1-9:41

J. Man's Eyes Opened (Part II): The Stages of Spiritual Sight, 9:8-41

(9:8-41) **Introduction**: the blind man had been delivered from darkness and given sight by the compassion of the Lord Jesus. In this passage the delivered man is confronted by his neighbors (v.8-12), by the Pharisees (v.13-34), and by Jesus (v.35-41).

The scene flows rapidly, and the man's growing knowledge of Jesus is easily seen and grasped. The outline should be adequate in carrying one through this passage. Therefore, the footnotes will not discuss each point; but rather concentrate on Jesus as seen by the man, that is, on the six stages of spiritual sight.

1. Stage 1: seeing Jesus as a man (v.8-12).
2. Stage 2: seeing Jesus as a Helper or a Healer (v.13-15).
3. Stage 3: seeing Jesus as a prophet (v.16-17).
4. Stage 4: seeing Jesus as the Savior (v.18-27).
5. Stage 5: seeing Jesus as being "from God" (v.28-34).
6. Stage 6: seeing Jesus as the Son of God (v.35-38).
7. The conclusion: the lesson of Jesus' revelation (v.39-41).

1 (9:8-12) **Spiritual Sight—Salvation—Jesus Christ, Misconceptions of**: the first stage of spiritual sight is *seeing Jesus as a man* (v.11). Note: all the healed man knew was that "a man they call Jesus" had commanded him to do certain things, and he did them and received his sight. Note what happened to the blind man.

⇒ He was confronted by Jesus.
⇒ He was commanded to do some things.
⇒ He obeyed the commands of Jesus.
⇒ He was delivered from darkness and given sight.

The blind man was blessed by Jesus despite an inadequate understanding of Christ. But note the crucial point: his heart was right toward Jesus. It was tender and willing to do what Jesus said.

The first stage in a man's spiritual journey is to *learn about Jesus*. A man must learn about Jesus before he can ever *learn of Jesus*, before he can ever come to know Jesus personally. But once a man has learned *about* Jesus, it is imperative that he move on and come to know Jesus personally. The blind man could have stopped at any stage and failed in his spiritual journey.

> **"Come to me, all you who are weary and burdened, and I will give you rest. Take my yoke upon you and learn from me, for I am gentle and humble in heart, and you will find rest for your souls. (Mat 11:28-29)**

Thought 1. There are many men like the blind man. They know *about Jesus*, but they do not *know Jesus*, not personally. They know His name, but little else. They have little understanding of His...

- teaching and claims
- presence and strength
- love and care
- power and promises

2 (9:13-15) **Spiritual Sight—Salvation—Jesus Christ, Misconceptions of**: the second stage of spiritual sight is seeing Jesus as a Helper or a Healer (v.15). The delivered man was brought before the religionists (by whom we are not told) because the Sabbath law had been broken. This was a serious offense to the Jews (see DEEPER STUDY # 2—Jn.5:15-16).

Note the man's answer to the religionists' question. He said that "He [the man, Jesus] put mud on my eyes...and I washed, and now I see." He still saw Jesus only as a man, but as a man who had done a great thing by helping him and healing him. He saw Jesus as a great *Helper* and a great *Healer*. Note: this is a confession; the man was giving an answer to some questioners. He was confessing Jesus to be the great *Helper* and *Healer*.

Thought 1. Many confess Jesus just as the man confessed Him. They confess that He is a *great man*, a great...

• Teacher	• Preacher
• Moralist	• Helper
• Martyr	• Law Giver
• Healer	• Example

But note the critical point. This concept still comes far short of the truth. The delivered man did not yet know Jesus personally. He had not reached the stage of belief, of true salvation and worship (cp. v.35-38).

> **All spoke well of him and were amazed at the gracious words that came from his lips. "Isn't this Joseph's son?" they asked. (Luke 4:22)**
> **They were amazed at his teaching, because his message had authority. (Luke 4:32)**

What did he mean when he said, 'You will look for me, but you will not find me,' and' Where I am, you cannot come'?" (John 7:36)

3 (9:16-17) **Spiritual Sight—Prophet—Jesus Christ, Misconceptions of**: the third stage of spiritual sight is seeing Jesus as a prophet (v.17). The man really progressed in his view of Jesus at this point. The people saw a prophet as the highest office a man could hold, the most authoritative voice among the people.

A prophet was a man chosen by God...
- to walk close to God.
- to represent God among the people.
- to proclaim the message of God (cp. Amos 3:7).
- to demonstrate the power of God.
- to help people by demonstrating God before them and by guiding and warning and ministering to them.

But again, Jesus was still seen only as a man, a godly man yes, but only a man. Such a concept was still short. The blind man's concept was still inadequate. He had not yet reached the stage of belief and worship (v.35-38).

When Jesus came to the region of Caesarea Philippi, he asked his disciples, "Who do people say the Son of Man is?" They replied, "Some say John the Baptist; others say Elijah; and still others, Jeremiah or one of the prophets." (Mat 16:13-14)
When Jesus entered Jerusalem, the whole city was stirred and asked, "Who is this?" The crowds answered, "This is Jesus, the prophet from Nazareth in Galilee." (Mat 21:10-11)
They looked for a way to arrest him, but they were afraid of the crowd because the people held that he was a prophet. (Mat 21:46)

4 (9:18-27) **Spiritual Sight—Testimony**: the fourth stage of spiritual sight is seeing Jesus as the Savior (v.25). The man now confessed the immortal words, "One thing I do know, I was blind but now I see!" (v.25).

The man underwent the most severe questioning and attack imaginable. He should have been gripped with fear and quaking in his shoes, but instead he was giving one of the strongest confessions possible—his own personal experience with Jesus. He was blind, but now he could see. He saw the hand of God...
- in his own life
- in the touch of Jesus
- in the feelings within his heart
- in the beauty of nature

Note that he was confessing his personal experience: he was blind, but now he could see. He could not answer the theological question: Is Jesus a mere man as all other men, or is He of God? But he could answer one thing: his own personal experience.

The point is this: he had progressed in his view of Jesus. He saw that Jesus may be more than a mere man like other men, but he could not say for sure. Just like a child, he did not know the theological terms nor how to express the nature of Jesus, but he did know one thing: Jesus had delivered and saved him from blindness. Jesus was his Savior and Deliverer from blindness to sight.

For the Son of Man came to seek and to save what was lost." (Luke 19:10)
For God did not send his Son into the world to condemn the world, but to save the world through him. (John 3:17)
Here is a trustworthy saying that deserves full acceptance: Christ Jesus came into the world to save sinners—of whom I am the worst. (1 Tim 1:15)

5 (9:28-34) **Spiritual Sight—Jesus Christ, Deity**: the fifth stage of spiritual sight is seeing Jesus as being "from God" (v.32-33). This was the man's final answer to those who questioned his confession of Jesus. He confessed that Jesus was *from God*." He reasoned that...
- helping and delivering a blind man was God's will
- Jesus delivered him. God heard Jesus' prayer for him and empowered Jesus to heal him
- Jesus was bound to be *from God*"

The man knew that the works of Jesus were proof that He was from God. Therefore, Jesus was not a liar and a deceiver; Jesus was not an evil man. He was bound to be who He claimed to be; He was bound to be "from God." (See note—Jn.7:25-31.)

For I have come down from heaven not to do my will but to do the will of him who sent me. (John 6:38)
Then Jesus, still teaching in the temple courts, cried out, "Yes, you know me, and you know where I am from. I am not here on my own, but he who sent me is true. You do not know him, but I know him because I am from him and he sent me." (John 7:28-29)
Jesus said to them, "If God were your Father, you would love me, for I came from God and now am here. I have not come on my own; but he sent me. (John 8:42)

6 (9:35-38) **Jesus Christ, Deity—Spiritual Sight**: the sixth stage of spiritual sight is seeing Jesus as the Son of God. Note two points.

1. Jesus was the One who did the seeking. He sought the man who had been thrown out.

Thought 1. Anyone can throw a person out—a business, a church, a family, neighbors, friends. But Jesus seeks the person who is thrown out and rejected. He always does, no matter who the person is or what the person has done.

2. The climactic stage of spiritual sight is clearly demonstrated by the man's experience.
   a. It is seeing Jesus as the Son of God (see notes—Jn.1:1-2; 1:34).

Then those who were in the boat worshiped him, saying, "Truly you are the Son of God." (Mat 14:33)
The beginning of the gospel about Jesus Christ, the Son of God. (Mark 1:1)

I have seen and I testify that this is the Son of God." (John 1:34)

"For God so loved the world that he gave his one and only Son, that whoever believes in him shall not perish but have eternal life. For God did not send his Son into the world to condemn the world, but to save the world through him. Whoever believes in him is not condemned, but whoever does not believe stands condemned already because he has not believed in the name of God's one and only Son. (John 3:16-18)

What about the one whom the Father set apart as his very own and sent into the world? Why then do you accuse me of blasphemy because I said, 'I am God's Son'? (John 10:36)

"Yes, Lord," she told him, "I believe that you are the Christ, the Son of God, who was to come into the world." (John 11:27)

How much more severely do you think a man deserves to be punished who has trampled the Son of God under foot, who has treated as an unholy thing the blood of the covenant that sanctified him, and who has insulted the Spirit of grace? (Heb 10:29)

If anyone acknowledges that Jesus is the Son of God, God lives in him and he in God. (1 John 4:15)

b. It is believing Jesus to be the Son of God and worshipping Him (see DEEPER STUDY # 2, Belief—Jn.2:24).

That everyone who believes in him may have eternal life. "For God so loved the world that he gave his one and only Son, that whoever believes in him shall not perish but have eternal life. (John 3:15-16)

"I tell you the truth, whoever hears my word and believes him who sent me has eternal life and will not be condemned; he has crossed over from death to life. (John 5:24)

That if you confess with your mouth, "Jesus is Lord," and believe in your heart that God raised him from the dead, you will be saved. For it is with your heart that you believe and are justified, and it is with your mouth that you confess and are saved. (Rom 10:9-10)

7 (9:39-41) **Conclusion**: the lesson of Jesus' revelation. Note two significant points.

1. Jesus stated that His mission upon earth was to bring judgment. Jesus judges man—all generations of men.

a. He judges the man who knows he is spiritually blind and wants to see. He takes the man who is spiritually blind and gives him sight—if that man really desires to see.

When Jesus spoke again to the people, he said, "I am the light of the world. Whoever follows me will never walk in darkness, but will have the light of life." (John 8:12)

I have come into the world as a light, so that no one who believes in me should stay in darkness. (John 12:46)

For it is light that makes everything visible. This is why it is said: "Wake up, O sleeper, rise from the dead, and Christ will shine on you." (Eph 5:14)

b. He judges the man who claims to have spiritual sight apart from Him. The man who says he sees spiritually and claims to know God apart from Christ is judged to be blind. (Cp. Jn.14:6-9.)

But if your eyes are bad, your whole body will be full of darkness. If then the light within you is darkness, how great is that darkness! (Mat 6:23)

The light shines in the darkness, but the darkness has not understood it. (John 1:5)

This is the verdict: Light has come into the world, but men loved darkness instead of light because their deeds were evil. (John 3:19)

2. The religionists expected exemption from judgment. They were opposing Jesus, so they expected Him to say they were blind, but He shocked them. He said that blindness was an excuse. If they had been blind, they would have been excused; for they would have been acting in ignorance, not knowing what they were doing. (Cp. Ro.5:13.) But they...
- knew the law of God
- knew about spiritual things
- claimed to see
- did not recognize God's Son

They were, therefore, guilty and were judged "blind" and were to be condemned.

But I tell you, it will be more bearable for Tyre and Sidon on the day of judgment than for you. (Mat 11:22)

This is the verdict: Light has come into the world, but men loved darkness instead of light because their deeds were evil. (John 3:19)

For God does not show favoritism. All who sin apart from the law will also perish apart from the law, and all who sin under the law will be judged by the law. (Rom 2:11-12)

         1 The sheep pen **2 The false shepherd** a. Enters the wrong way b. Is a thief & robber: Seizes by false entry & force **3 The true shepherd** a. Enters the appointed door	**CHAPTER 10** **X. THE REVELATION OF JESUS, THE SHEPHERD OF LIFE, 10:1-42** **A. The Shepherd & His Sheep: False vs. True Teachers, 10:1-6** “I tell you the truth, the man who does not enter the sheep pen by the gate, but climbs in by some other way, is a thief and a robber. 2 The man who enters by thegate is the shepherd of his sheep.	3 The watchman opens the gate for him, and the sheep listen to his voice. He calls his own sheep by name and leads them out. 4 When he has brought out all his own, he goes on ahead of them, and his sheep follow him because they know his voice. 5 But they will never follow a stranger; in fact, they will run away from him because they do not recognize a stranger’s voice.” 6 Jesus used this figure of speech, but they did not understand what he was telling them.	b. Is known by the watchman (God) c. Knows sheep by name d. Leads & shepherds the sheep **4 The sheep** a. Know the shepherd’s voice b. Follow the shepherd who goes before them c. Flee from strange voices **5 The parable or figure of speech: Was not understood**

DIVISION X

THE REVELATION OF JESUS, THE SHEPHERD OF LIFE, 10:1-42

A. The Shepherd and His Sheep: False vs. True Teachers, 10:1-6

(10:1-6) **Introduction**: this passage begins the great revelation of Jesus as the Shepherd of Life. Jesus is pictured as the only true Shepherd of the sheep.

1. The sheep pen (v.1).
2. The false shepherd (v.1).
3. The true shepherd (v.2-3).
4. The sheep (v.4-5).
5. The parable not understood (v.6).

1 (10:1) **Sheep pen—Salvation, Position—Security**: the sheep pen. Jesus begins the parable with the solemn “I tell you the truth.” What He had to say was of critical importance.

There is a sheep pen, a place where all the sheep are kept. The sheep pen pictures the place of acceptance by God, or the place of safety and security in God’s presence (see DEEPER STUDY # 3, Kingdom of God—Mt.19:23-24). It is the *position* of salvation, of spiritual sight that comes by believing Jesus to be Son of God (Jn.9:36-38). It is the *position* of being accepted by God because a man approaches God “in the name of His Son, Jesus Christ.” The sheep pen symbolizes the place where the sheep (believers) are kept. The sheep are kept…

- in the church
- in heaven
- in salvation
- in spiritual sight
- in the place of acceptance
- in the Kingdom of God
- in eternal life
- in spiritual deliverance from darkness
  in the position of faith

Now note: the whole parable has to do with a false shepherd and the true shepherd. Both go after the sheep. The true shepherd is Christ and the false shepherds are those who opposed Christ, the world’s religionists—the false teachers—who so blindly stood against His claim to be “the Light of the world” (Jn.8:12; 9:5; cp. 9:40).

2 (10:1) **Shepherds, False—False Teachers**: the false shepherd. Note three points.

1. The sheep pen can be entered. There is a gate into the sheep pen—an entrance, a way to get in—and the gate is the only *acceptable* way to enter.

2. Some shepherds climb into the sheep pen by“some other way” (allachothen). The word *by* is important. It indicates origin. The false shepherd *comes by* and *originates from…*

- some other direction
- some other way
- some other position
- some other source
- some other road

Note also the terms thief (kleptes) and robber (leistes). The very same words were used to describe Judas (a thief) and Barabbas (a robber). It is an awful thing for a person to be put into the same class as Judas and Barabbas, two who were as opposite from Christ as any men could be.

The false shepherd is…

- a thief: a seducer and a deceiver, a crafty and dishonest man, a man who will use any means to get into the sheep pen to steal the sheep.
- a robber: a man who will use violence and cruelty and will destroy and devour if necessary to get into the sheep pen.

God has much to say to false shepherds. (Also see outlines and notes—1 Tim.6:3-5; Tit.1:10-16; 2 Pt.2:1-22; Jude 1:3-16.)

Come, all you beasts of the field, come and devour, all you beasts of the forest! Israel’s watchmen are blind, they all lack knowledge; they are all mute dogs, they cannot bark; they lie around and dream, they love to sleep. They are dogs with mighty appetites; they never have enough. They are shepherds who lack understand-

ing; they all turn to their own way, each seeks his own gain. "Come," each one cries, "let me get wine! Let us drink our fill of beer! And tomorrow will be like today, or even far better." (Isa 56:9-12)

"Woe to the shepherds who are destroying and scattering the sheep of my pasture!" declares the LORD. Therefore this is what the LORD, the God of Israel, says to the shepherds who tend my people: "Because you have scattered my flock and driven them away and have not bestowed care on them, I will bestow punishment on you for the evil you have done," declares the LORD. (Jer 23:1-2;cp. Jer.25:34-38)

"My people have been lost sheep; their shepherds have led them astray and caused them to roam on the mountains. They wandered over mountain and hill and forgot their own resting place. (Jer 50:6)

The word of the LORD came to me: "Son of man, prophesy against the shepherds of Israel; prophesy and say to them: 'This is what the Sovereign LORD says: Woe to the shepherds of Israel who only take care of themselves! Should not shepherds take care of the flock? You eat the curds, clothe yourselves with the wool and slaughter the choice animals, but you do not take care of the flock. You have not strengthened the weak or healed the sick or bound up the injured. You have not brought back the strays or searched for the lost. You have ruled them harshly and brutally. So they were scattered because there was no shepherd, and when they were scattered they became food for all the wild animals. My sheep wandered over all the mountains and on every high hill. They were scattered over the whole earth, and no one searched or looked for them. (Ezek 34:1-6; cp. Ezk.34:7-31)

3 (10:2-3) **Shepherd**: the true shepherd. Note four points.

1. The shepherd who enters the appointed gate is the true shepherd (Jesus Christ). He knows where the gate is and the way into the sheep pen. Therefore, He uses the gate. There is no reason for Him not to use it, no reason for Him to climb in any other way.

⇒ His purpose is not to steal some sheep from the Owner (God) and start a flock of His own. Such a thought is the farthest thing from His mind. His thoughts are focused upon the sheep and the Owner's will.

⇒ His purpose is to be the Shepherd of the Owner (God), to serve Him and to do His will.

Therefore, the Shepherd enters the sheep pen by the gate. The gate was made for Him and the sheep to enter; therefore, He uses it.

2. The Shepherd is known by the "Watchman" (God or the Holy Spirit). This point is critical. The Holy Spirit (as God) is the One who opens the gate into the sheep pen. The One who comes to the gate is known by the Watchman; He is known to be the Shepherd. The Shepherd therefore...

• is not afraid to face the Watchman.
• has been appointed to use the gate
• has the authority and the right to enter

Just as the Father knows me and I know the Father—and I lay down my life for the sheep. (John 10:15)

3. The Shepherd knows the sheep; He knows each one by name. This is said to have been a fact among shepherds and their sheep in Jesus' day. Shepherds actually knew each sheep individually, even in large herds. The fact is certainly true with Christ and His sheep. The words "His own" (sidia) mean He calls His own, not as a whole, not as a herd, but as individuals. The Shepherd, the Lord Jesus Christ, knows each of His sheep by name.

"I am the good shepherd; I know my sheep and my sheep know me— (John 10:14)

But the man who loves God is known by God. (1 Cor 8:3)

Nevertheless, God's solid foundation stands firm, sealed with this inscription: "The Lord knows those who are his," and, "Everyone who confesses the name of the Lord must turn away from wickedness." (2 Tim 2:19)

But now, this is what the LORD says— he who created you, O Jacob, he who formed you, O Israel: "Fear not, for I have redeemed you; I have summoned you by name; you are mine. (Isa 43:1)

4. The Shepherd leads and shepherds the sheep. He loves them as His own; therefore He must lead them to the green pastures and still waters. He must see that they are nourished and protected and given the very best care possible. (See note—Mk.6:34 for more discussion, what happens to sheep without a Shepherd.)

a. He feeds the sheep even if He has to gather them in His arms and carry them to the feasting pasture.

He tends his flock like a shepherd: He gathers the lambs in his arms and carries them close to his heart; he gently leads those that have young. (Isa 40:11)

b. He guides the sheep to the pasture and away from the rough places and precipices.

A psalm of David. The LORD is my shepherd, I shall not be in want. He makes me lie down in green pastures, he leads me beside quiet waters, he restores my soul. He guides me in paths of righteousness for his name's sake. Even though I walk through the valley of the shadow of death, I will fear no evil, for you are with me; your rod and your staff, they comfort me. (Psa 23:1-4)

c. He seeks and saves the sheep who get lost.

"What do you think? If a man owns a hundred sheep, and one of them wanders away, will he not leave the ninety-nine on the hills and go to look for the one that wandered off? (Mat 18:11-12)

I will search for the lost and bring back the strays. I will bind up the injured and strengthen the weak, but the sleek and the strong I will destroy. I will shepherd the flock with justice. (Ezek 34:16)

d. He protects the sheep. He even sacrifices His life for the sheep.

> "I am the good shepherd. The good shepherd lays down his life for the sheep. (John 10:11)
> May the God of peace, who through the blood of the eternal covenant brought back from the dead our Lord Jesus, that great Shepherd of the sheep, (Heb 13:20)

e. He restores the sheep who go astray and returns them to the sheep pen.

> For you were like sheep going astray, but now you have returned to the Shepherd and Overseer of your souls. (1 Pet 2:25)

f. He rewards the sheep for obedience and faithfulness.

> And when the Chief Shepherd appears, you will receive the crown of glory that will never fade away. (1 Pet 5:4)

g. He shall keep the sheep separate from the goats.

> All the nations will be gathered before him, and he will separate the people one from another as a shepherd separates the sheep from the goats. He will put the sheep on his right and the goats on his left. (Mat 25:32-33)

4 (10:4-5) **Sheep—Disciples—Believers**: the sheep are disciples or believers of the Lord. Note three points.

1. The sheep know the Shepherd's voice. They know both His sound and His words.
   ⇒ The sound of His voice is not uncertain and unclear, not weak and frail, not quivering and indecisive. It is clear, strong, sure, and decisive.
   ⇒ The words of His voice are words of care and tenderness, of warning and safety, of truth and security.

Thought 1. Believers trust the voice, the Word of Christ, because they know His voice.

> For the one whom God has sent speaks the words of God, for God gives the Spirit without limit. (John 3:34)
> The Spirit gives life; the flesh counts for nothing. The words I have spoken to you are spirit and they are life. (John 6:63)
> Simon Peter answered him, "Lord, to whom shall we go? You have the words of eternal life. (John 6:68)
> I tell you the truth, if anyone keeps my word, he will never see death." (John 8:51)
> "You are a king, then!" said Pilate. Jesus answered, "You are right in saying I am a king. In fact, for this reason I was born, and for this I came into the world, to testify to the truth. Everyone on the side of truth listens to me." (John 18:37)
> And we also thank God continually because, when you received the word of God, which you heard from us, you accepted it not as the word of men, but as it actually is, the word of God, which is at work in you who believe. (1 Th 2:13)
> Beyond all question, the mystery of godliness is great: He appeared in a body, was vindicated by the Spirit, was seen by angels, was preached among the nations, was believed on in the world, was taken up in glory. (1 Tim 3:16)
> Like newborn babies, crave pure spiritual milk, so that by it you may grow up in your salvation, now that you have tasted that the Lord is good. (1 Pet 2:2-3)
> That which was from the beginning, which we have heard, which we have seen with our eyes, which we have looked at and our hands have touched—this we proclaim concerning the Word of life. The life appeared; we have seen it and testify to it, and we proclaim to you the eternal life, which was with the Father and has appeared to us. We proclaim to you what we have seen and heard, so that you also may have fellowship with us. And our fellowship is with the Father and with his Son, Jesus Christ. (1 John 1:1-3)

2. The sheep follow the Shepherd. Note He goes before them to lead the way. He does not drive them like cattle. He leads in order to pick out the safe and secure way to the pasture. He leads to show the sheep that the road is clear and safe. The sheep know this, so they follow the Shepherd, knowing they are perfectly safe and secure following the path He has laid out before them. (Cp. Jn.14:6.)

a. They follow Him because He saves them and gives them life.

> Just as the Father knows me and I know the Father—and I lay down my life for the sheep. (John 10:15)
> My sheep listen to my voice; I know them, and they follow me. I give them eternal life, and they shall never perish; no one can snatch them out of my hand. (John 10:27-28)
> The LORD their God will save them on that day as the flock of his people. They will sparkle in his land like jewels in a crown. (Zec 9:16)

b. They follow Him because they are the sheep of His pasture.

> Know that the LORD is God. It is he who made us, and we are his ; we are his people, the sheep of his pasture. (Psa 100:3)

c. They follow Him because they wish to give Him praise forever.

> As for me, I will declare this forever; I will sing praise to the God of Jacob. (Psa 75:9)

d. They follow Him because they are sheep in the midst of wolves.

> I know that after I leave, savage wolves will come in among you and will not spare the flock. (Acts 20:29)

e. They follow Him because He assures them and delivers them from fear.

> **"Do not be afraid, little flock, for your Father has been pleased to give you the kingdom. (Luke 12:32)**

f. They follow Him because they have learned that without Him they are scattered and lost.

> **"You will all fall away," Jesus told them, "for it is written: "'I will strike the shepherd, and the sheep will be scattered.' (Mark 14:27 cp. Mt.26:31).)**

g. They follow Him because He takes care of all their wants.

> **A psalm of David. The LORD is my shepherd, I shall not be in want. (Psa 23:1)**

3. The sheep flee from strange voices. Note two things.
   a. They *will never* (ou me) follow a stranger. This is a double negative. They will never, in any case, follow a stranger.
   b. They flee from the strange voice. They do not know a stranger's voice. Its sound and words are different.

Thought 1. The strange voice can be the voice of...
- false religion
- false science
- false psychology
- false philosophy
- humanism
- materialism
- worldiness
- fame

5 (10:6) **Jesus Christ, Rejection—Natural Man**: the parable was not understood. The spiritual truth was beyond the religionists, the false teachers. They could not grasp the truth with their natural minds. They could not see themselves as false shepherds, and they could not see Jesus as the true Shepherd. Natural man rebels against being called *false* and against Christ's being the *only Shepherd* of the sheep.

> **For this people's heart has become calloused; they hardly hear with their ears, and they have closed their eyes. Otherwise they might see with their eyes, hear with their ears, understand with their hearts and turn, and I would heal them.' (Acts 28:27)**
>
> **Always learning but never able to acknowledge the truth. (2 Tim 3:7)**

	B. The Gate of the Sheep, The Only Way to God, 10:7-10	to them. 9 I am the gate; whoever enters through me will be saved. He will come in and go out, and find pasture. 10 The thief comes only to	not listen to them
1 Jesus is the only gate of the sheep	7 Therefore Jesus said again, "I tell you the truth, I am the gate for the sheep.	steal and kill and destroy; I have come that they may	**2 Jesus is the only gate that leads to salvation** a. "In & out": Security b. "Pasture": Provision
a. All others are thieves & robbers b. Proof: The sheep did	8 All who ever came before me were thieves and robbers, but the sheep did not listen	have life, and have it to the full.	**3 Jesus is the only gate that leads to abundant life** a. All others come to take and to steal b. Jesus comes to give life^{DS1}

DIVISION X

THE REVELATION OF JESUS, THE SHEPHERD OF LIFE, 10:1-42

B. The Gate of the Sheep: The Only Way To God, 10:7-10

(10:7-10) **Introduction—Jesus—Gate**: Jesus claims to be the Gate of the sheep. Jesus is probably referring to the gate of a community sheep pen or a community pasture which housed all the flocks of an area. There is, however, another descriptive picture of Jesus as the gate. When the sheep were kept out in the hill country overnight, they were kept in ravines surrounded by several rocky walls. Naturally, the opening into these ravines had no gate at all. The shepherd himself literally became the gate, for during the night he would simply lie across the opening. The sheep could get out only by going over him, and the enemies of the sheep could get in to the sheep only by going through him. Access in or out was only through the shepherd.

1. Jesus is the only gate of the sheep (v.7-8).
2. Jesus is the only gate that leads to salvation (v.9).
3. Jesus is the only gate that leads to abundant life (v.10).

1 (10:7-8) **Salvation—Gate—Mediator**: Jesus is the *only* Gate of the sheep. Note the words "I tell you the truth"; they stress the critical importance of what Jesus was about to say. By "gate" Jesus meant He is the way or entrance into the sheep gate. Jesus Christ is the way...

- into God's presence
- into God's acceptance
- into salvation
- into the true church
- into heaven
- into the Kingdom of God
- into eternal life

Therefore, if a man wishes to enter where God is, he must enter the Gate of Christ. A man enters God's sheep gate only through the Gate of Christ, for Christ is the *only* Gate into God's presence.

> Jesus answered, "I am the way and the truth and the life. No one comes to the Father except through me. (John 14:6)
> For through him we both have access to the Father by one Spirit. (Eph 2:18)
> For there is one God and one mediator between God and men, the man Christ Jesus, (1 Tim 2:5)
> But the ministry Jesus has received is as superior to theirs as the covenant of which he is mediator is superior to the old one, and it is founded on better promises. (Heb 8:6; cp. Heb 12:24)
> For this reason Christ is the mediator of a new covenant, that those who are called may receive the promised eternal inheritance—now that he has died as a ransom to set them free from the sins commit-

> ted under the first covenant. (Heb 9:15)
> For Christ did not enter a man-made sanctuary that was only a copy of the true one; he entered heaven itself, now to appear for us in God's presence. (Heb 9:24)
> If it could, would they not have stopped being offered? For the worshipers would have been cleansed once for all, and would no longer have felt guilty for their sins. (Heb 10:2)
> My dear children, I write this to you so that you will not sin. But if anybody does sin, we have one who speaks to the Father in our defense—Jesus Christ, the Righteous One. (1 John 2:1)

Note: Jesus used the clear claim to deity: "I Am." This gives additional stress to His claim to be the *only Gate* to God. Now note two points.

1. All others who claim to be the gate are thieves and robbers. There are some who claim to be the gate and to have the way to God. They claim to know the right way and to have the newest ideas and the latest truth and knowledge. They claim to have the right teaching, religion, works, maturity, philosophy, psychology, ideas, and novel concepts. They claim to be the gate that opens into God's presence. But Jesus says that they are thieves and robbers. They are out to steal the sheep, both their wool (possessions) and their lives (loyalty). They want both their wool and their lives, for if they have both they have the sheep's *permanent loyalty*. (See note, False Shepherd—Jn.10:1 for more discussion and verses.)

> It is true that some preach Christ out of envy and rivalry, but others out of goodwill. (Phil 1:15)
> "From the least to the greatest, all are greedy for gain; prophets and priests alike, all practice deceit. (Jer 6:13)
> I will place shepherds over them who will tend them, and they will no longer be afraid or terrified, nor will any be missing," declares the LORD. (Jer 23:4)
> But if the watchman sees the sword coming and does not blow the trumpet to warn the people and the sword comes and takes the life of one of them, that man will be taken away because of his sin, but I will hold the watchman accountable for his blood.' (Ezek 33:6)
> Her leaders judge for a bribe, her priests teach for a price, and her prophets tell fortunes for money. Yet they lean upon

the LORD and say, "Is not the LORD among us? No disaster will come upon us." (Micah 3:11)

2. The proof that Jesus is the only Gate and that all others are false gates is the sheep themselves. The sheep do not listen to the voices of false *gates*, not if they are the real sheep of the Shepherd. The real sheep of God know the Shepherd's voice and have the ability to discern it. If they hear the voice of a false shepherd, they know that he and his sheep gate are false. His voice and message are not the voice and message of the true gate, the Son of God Himself.

"I am the good shepherd; I know my sheep and my sheep know me— (John 10:14)

My sheep listen to my voice; I know them, and they follow me. I give them eternal life, and they shall never perish; no one can snatch them out of my hand. (John 10:27-28)

We have not received the spirit of the world but the Spirit who is from God, that we may understand what God has freely given us. The man without the Spirit does not accept the things that come from the Spirit of God, for they are foolishness to him, and he cannot understand them, because they are spiritually discerned. (1 Cor 2:12, 14)

2 (10:9) **Salvation—Pasture—Nourishment**: Jesus is the only gate that leads to salvation. Jesus said that He is the Gate that leads to three great things.

1. Jesus is the only gate that opens to salvation.

Salvation is found in no one else, for there is no other name under heaven given to men by which we must be saved." (Acts 4:12)

No! We believe it is through the grace of our Lord Jesus that we are saved, just as they are." (Acts 15:11)

"For God so loved the world that he gave his one and only Son, that whoever believes in him shall not perish but have eternal life. For God did not send his Son into the world to condemn the world, but to save the world through him. (John 3:16-17)

Since we have now been justified by his blood, how much more shall we be saved from God's wrath through him! (Rom 5:9)

For God did not appoint us to suffer wrath but to receive salvation through our Lord Jesus Christ. (1 Th 5:9)

This is good, and pleases God our Savior, who wants all men to be saved and to come to a knowledge of the truth. For there is one God and one mediator between God and men, the man Christ Jesus, who gave himself as a ransom for all men—the testimony given in its proper time. (1 Tim 2:3-6)

And, once made perfect, he became the source of eternal salvation for all who obey him (Heb 5:9)

So Christ was sacrificed once to take away the sins of many people; and he will

appear a second time, not to bear sin, but to bring salvation to those who are waiting for him. (Heb 9:28)

2. Jesus is the only gate that opens to peace and security. He is the only gate that allows the sheep to *come in and to go out*. This was a common Jewish phrase. If a man could "come in and go out" without difficulty or danger, it meant he was *safe and secure*. Jesus brings to the believer safety and security, peace and tranquility.

But the Counselor, the Holy Spirit, whom the Father will send in my name, will teach you all things and will remind you of everything I have said to you. (John 14:26)

I will remain in the world no longer, but they are still in the world, and I am coming to you. Holy Father, protect them by the power of your name—the name you gave me—so that they may be one as we are one. (John 17:11)

"I have told you these things, so that in me you may have peace. In this world you will have trouble. But take heart! I have overcome the world." (John 16:33)

Being confident of this, that he who began a good work in you will carry it on to completion until the day of Christ Jesus. (Phil 1:6)

But the Lord is faithful, and he will strengthen and protect you from the evil one. (2 Th 3:3)

That is why I am suffering as I am. Yet I am not ashamed, because I know whom I have believed, and am convinced that he is able to guard what I have entrusted to him for that day. (2 Tim 1:12)

The Lord will rescue me from every evil attack and will bring me safely to his heavenly kingdom. To him be glory for ever and ever. Amen. (2 Tim 4:18)

Who through faith are shielded by God's power until the coming of the salvation that is ready to be revealed in the last time. (1 Pet 1:5)

To him who is able to keep you from falling and to present you before his glorious presence without fault and with great joy— (Jude 1:24)

Since you have kept my command to endure patiently, I will also keep you from the hour of trial that is going to come upon the whole world to test those who live on the earth. (Rev 3:10)

I am with you and will watch over you wherever you go, and I will bring you back to this land. I will not leave you until I have done what I have promised you." (Gen 28:15)

The eternal God is your refuge, and underneath are the everlasting arms. He will drive out your enemy before you, saying, 'Destroy him!' (Deu 33:27)

Indeed, he who watches over Israel will neither slumber nor sleep. (Psa 121:4)

So do not fear, for I am with you; do not be dismayed, for I am your God. I will strengthen you and help you; I will uphold you with my righteous right hand. (Isa 41:10)

Even to your old age and gray hairs I am he, I am he who will sustain you. I have made you and I will carry you; I will sustain you and I will rescue you. (Isa 46:4)

In all their distress he too was distressed, and the angel of his presence saved them. In his love and mercy he redeemed them; he lifted them up and carried them all the days of old. (Isa 63:9)

3. Jesus is the only gate that opens to healthy and lasting nourishment. He is the only gate that leads to the true pasture, the pasture that has the living stream flowing through it and the pasture that has the living food in it.

a. His pasture alone can satisfy the soul.

For he satisfies the thirsty and fills the hungry with good things. (Psa 107:9)

The LORD will guide you always; he will satisfy your needs in a sun-scorched land and will strengthen your frame. You will be like a well-watered garden, like a spring whose waters never fail. (Isa 58:11)

b. His pasture alone can restore the soul.

He makes me lie down in green pastures, he leads me beside quiet waters, he restores my soul. He guides me in paths of righteousness for his name's sake. (Psa 23:2-3)

c. His pasture alone can give life and give it forever.

I am the living bread that came down from heaven. If anyone eats of this bread, he will live forever. This bread is my flesh, which I will give for the life of the world." (John 6:51)

d. His pasture alone can feed with knowledge and understanding.

Then I will give you shepherds after my own heart, who will lead you with knowledge and understanding. (Jer 3:15)

3 (10:10) **Jesus Christ, the Gate**: Jesus is the only gate that leads to abundant life. This is a sharp contrast between the thief and Christ.

1. The person who says there is another gate is a thief and a robber. The person steals and kills and destroys the sheep. The thief misleads and deceives the sheep, leading them through a gate that leads to destruction.

There are some who definitely want the wool and life of the sheep (false and liberal religions and false philoso-

phies). They want the sheep to follow them and their position, so they do all they can to secure the sheep's...

- loyalty
- allegience
- possessions
- time
- effort
- energy
- recognition
- praise
- honor

By leading the sheep away from the *restrictiveness* of Christ, the false teacher becomes a thief—a thief in that he steals the soul of the sheep from God, leading it into a sheep pen that will be destroyed. It causes the sheep never to know the true Shepherd.

2. Jesus came not to steal life, but to give abundant life (see DEEPER STUDY # 1—Jn.10:10 for discussion).

DEEPER STUDY # 1
(10:10) **Jesus Christ, Purpose—Life**: life is one of the great words of the Scriptures. The word "life" (zoe) and the verb "to live" or "to have life" (zen) have a depth of meaning. (See DEEPER STUDY # 2—Jn.1:4; DEEPER STUDY # 1—17:2-3.)

1. Life is the energy, the force, the power of being.
2. Life is the opposite of perishing. It is deliverance from condemnation and death. It is the stopping or cessation of deterioration, decay, and corruption (Jn.3:16; 5:24, 29; 10:28).
3. Life is eternal (aionios). It is forever. It is the very life of God Himself (Jn.17:3). However, eternal life does not refer just to duration. Living forever would be a curse for some persons. The idea of eternal life is also quality, a certain kind of life, a life that consistently knows love, joy, peace, power, and responsibility (Jn.10:10).
4. Life is satisfaction (Jn.6:35).
5. Life is security and enjoyment (Jn.10:10).
6. Life is found only in God. God is the source and author of life, and it is God who has appointed Jesus Christ to bring life to man. Jesus Christ gives the very life of God Himself (Jn.5:26; 6:27, 40; 10:28; 17:23).
7. Life has now been revealed. It has been unveiled and is clearly seen in Jesus Christ. Jesus Christ shows man what life is (Jn.1:4-5; 5:26; 1 Jn.1:2).
8. Life only comes to a man by believing in Jesus Christ. A man outside Jesus Christ only exists. He merely has the existence of an animal. Real life is found only in God. This is to be expected and it is logically true, for God is the creator of life. As the creator of life, He alone knows what life really is and what it is supposed to be (Jn.3:36; 5:24; 6:47). This is the reason He sent His Son, the Lord Jesus Christ, into the world: to show men what life is. When a person looks at Jesus Christ, he sees exactly what life is, exactly what it involves (cp. Gal.5:22-23):

⇒ love   ⇒ patience   ⇒ faithfulness
⇒ joy   ⇒ kindness   ⇒ gentleness
⇒ peace   ⇒ goodness   ⇒ self-control

	C. The Good Shepherd: Jesus, the True Savior of the World,ᴰˢ¹ 10:11-21	not of this sheep pen. I must bring them also. They too will listen to my voice, and there shall be one flock and one shepherd.	the pen
1 The meaning of "Good Shepherd"	11 "I am the good shepherd. The good shepherd lays down his life for the sheep.	17 The reason my Father loves me is that I lay down my life—only to take it up again.	**3 The final proof is the sacrificial death & resurrection of Jesus**
a. A sacrificial lifeᴰˢ²	12 The hired hand is not the	18 No one takes it from me,	a. The very reason God
b. Not a hired or em-	shepherd who owns the	but I lay it down of my own	loves Him so much
ployed shepherd	sheep. So when he sees the	accord. I have authority to	b. His death was the su-
1) He sees danger—	wolf coming, he abandons the	lay it down and authority to	preme act of obedience
acts cowardly, flees	sheep and runs away. Then	take it up again. This com-	1) Was voluntary
2) He causes the sheep	the wolf attacks the flock and	mand I received from my	2) Was a command
to be caught—in	scatters it.	Father."	
error	13 The man runs away be-	19 At these words the Jews	**4 The reaction to Jesus'**
3) He lacks genuine	cause he is a hired hand and	were again divided.	**claim**
care	cares nothing for the sheep.	20 Many of them said, "He is	
	14 "I am the good shepherd;	demon-possessed and raving	a. Some reject: Call Jesus
2 The proof that Jesus is the "Good Shepherd"	I know my sheep and my sheep know me—	mad. Why listen to him?"	demon-possessed and mad
a. He knows His sheep	15 just as the Father knows	21 But others said, "These	b. Some question: Per-
b. He knows His Father—	me and I know the Father—	are not the sayings of a man	haps Jesus is who He
the Owner	and I lay down my life for the	possessed by a demon. Can a	claims
c. He will die for His	sheep.	demon open the eyes of the	
sheep	16 I have other sheep that are	blind?"	
d. He works to enlarge			

DIVISION X

THE REVELATION OF JESUS, THE SHEPHERD OF LIFE, 10:1-42

C. The Good Shepherd: Jesus, the True Savior of the World, 10:11-21

(10:11-21) **Introduction**: Jesus Christ claimed to be "the Good Shepherd." He is not a bad or a false shepherd.
1. The meaning of "Good Shepherd" (v.11-13).
2. The proof that Jesus is the "Good Shepherd" (v.14-16).
3. The final proof: the sacrificial death and resurrection of Jesus (v.17-18).
4. The reaction to Jesus' claim (v.19-21).

DEEPER STUDY # 1

(10:11-21) **Jesus, The Shepherd—God, the Shepherd**: God foretold that He would send a Shepherd to save and to take care of His people.

> **See, the Sovereign LORD comes with power, and his arm rules for him. See, his reward is with him, and his recompense accompanies him. He tends his flock like a shepherd: He gathers the lambs in his arms and carries them close to his heart; he gently leads those that have young. (Isa 40:10-11)**

> **I will save my flock, and they will no longer be plundered. I will judge between one sheep and another. I will place over them one shepherd, my servant David, and he will tend them; he will tend them and be their shepherd. (Ezek 34:22-23)**

> **They will no longer defile themselves with their idols and vile images or with any of their offenses, for I will save them from all their sinful backsliding, and I will cleanse them. They will be my people, and I will be their God. "'My servant David will**

> **be king over them, and they will all have one shepherd. They will follow my laws and be careful to keep my decrees. (Ezek 37:23-24)**

> **The LORD their God will save them on that day as the flock of his people. They will sparkle in his land like jewels in a crown. (Zec 9:16)**

Jesus' work as the Shepherd is fourfold.
1. Jesus Christ is the *Good Shepherd*. He is called "good" because He risks and sacrifices His life for the sheep (Jn.10:11, 15; cp. Ps.22).
2. Jesus Christ is the *Great Shepherd*. He is called "great" because He arose from the dead and He perfects the sheep (Heb.13:20-21).
3. Jesus Christ is the *Shepherd and Overseer* of our souls. He is called the "shepherd and overseer" because He welcomes those who wandered off and went astray (1 Pt.2:25).
4. Jesus Christ is the *Chief Shepherd*. He is called "chief" because He is to return to earth with great glory to reward the faithful (1 Pt.5:4).
Note: God also is called a Shepherd in Scripture (Gen.48:15; Ps.23:1; 77:20; 80:1; Is.40:11; Ezk.34:11-31).

1 (10:11-13) **Jesus Christ, the Good Shepherd—Hired Hand—False Teachers—Irresponsible Teachers**: the meaning of "Good Shepherd." There are two reasons why Jesus is called the Good Shepherd.
1. Jesus is called the "Good Shepherd" because He gave and sacrificed His life *for the sheep* (see DEEPER STUDY # 2—Jn.10:11 for discussion).

2. Jesus is called the "Good Shepherd" because He is not a hired or employed shepherd. Jesus is the Shepherd by birth. He was born to be the Shepherd with all the Shepherd's rights. The sheep are His and He is the sheep's. The hired shepherd was just a man passing through who was temporary help. He was a man hired to look after the sheep until the real shepherd came along. He was not the true, permanent shepherd. He was a false, unfaithful, and irresponsible shepherd. His interest was not a calling, but...

- a job and profession
- money and comfort
- acceptance and recognition
- position and prestige
- authority and esteem

The false, unfaithful, and irresponsible shepherd has little if any sense of responsibility for the sheep. He seeks to benefit self, not the sheep.

⇒ He is a shepherd for what he can get out of it, not to serve and care for the sheep.
⇒ His primary interest is not the sheep but job security: wages and benefits, position and prestige, money and comfort.
⇒ He values himself much more than the sheep.
⇒ He seeks His own things and not the things of others (1 Cor.10:24; Ph.2:3-4).
⇒ He has no *natural* care for the state of the sheep (Ph.2:20).
⇒ He has no interest in seeking the lost sheep, lest his life be threatened "in the open country" (cp. Lk.15:4).

Note that Jesus says three significant things about the hired or employed shepherd.

1. The irresponsible shepherd runs away when he sees danger (the wolf). He seeks to save himself and to protect his own security and position even if it means forsaking the sheep and leaving them exposed to the danger.

2. The irresponsible shepherd causes the sheep to be caught in the danger and in the error.

⇒ Some of the sheep are ravaged and eaten by the dangerous wolf. The wolf is any thing or any power that seeks to destroy the sheep, such as worldliness, false teaching, and carnal men.
⇒ The remaining sheep are scattered throughout the wilderness of the world and lost to the Owner (God).

3. The irresponsible shepherd lacks genuine care for the sheep. He is not involved and concerned with the fate and eternal welfare of the sheep. (See note, False Shepherds—Jn.10:1 for verses of Scripture.)

DEEPER STUDY # 2

(10:11) **Jesus Christ, Death**: the word "for" (huper) is a simple word with profound meaning when used with the death of Christ. It proclaims the most wonderful truth known to man. Note this striking truth: it does *not mean* that Christ died only as an example for us, showing us how we should be willing to die for the truth or for some great cause. What it means is that Christ died *in our place, in our stead, in our room, as our substitute*. This meaning is unquestionably clear. (See note—Eph.5:2; DEEPER STUDY # 1—1 Pt.2:21-25 for more discussion.)

1. The idea of sacrifice to the Jewish and pagan mind of that day was the idea of a life given in another's place. It was *a substitutionary sacrifice*.

2. The idea of sacrifice is often in the very context of the words, "Christ gave Himself up for us" (Eph.5:2).

> I am the living bread that came down from heaven. If anyone eats of this bread, he will live forever. This bread is my flesh, which I will give for the life of the world." (John 6:51)
> "I am the good shepherd. The good shepherd lays down his life for the sheep. (John 10:11)
> Just as the Father knows me and I know the Father—and I lay down my life for the sheep. (John 10:15)
> He did not say this on his own, but as high priest that year he prophesied that Jesus would die for the Jewish nation, (John 11:51)
> Greater love has no one than this, that he lay down his life for his friends. (John 15:13)
> For them I sanctify myself, that they too may be truly sanctified. (John 17:19)

(Cp. Ro.8:32; Gal.1:4; 2:20; Eph.5:2; 1 Tim.2:6; Tit.2:14.)

2 (10:14-16) **Jesus Christ, the Good Shepherd**: the proof that Jesus is the "Good Shepherd." There are four proofs.

1. Jesus knows His sheep, and they know Him. There is an intimate knowledge between Jesus and His sheep.

a. He knows them, their lives, their being, their all. He knows them...
- by name, individually and personally
- in all their joy and blessings
- in all their trials and sorrows
- in all their wanderings and stumblings
- in all their need and lack

He keeps His mind upon them, looking after them by His Spirit and caring for them through intercession as well as by companionship. This is proof that He is the "Good Shepherd" of the sheep.

> The watchman opens the gate for him, and the sheep listen to his voice. He calls his own sheep by name and leads them out. (John 10:3)
> "I am the good shepherd; I know my sheep and my sheep know me— (John 10:14)
> But the man who loves God is known by God. (1 Cor 8:3)
> Nevertheless, God's solid foundation stands firm, sealed with this inscription: "The Lord knows those who are his," and, "Everyone who confesses the name of the Lord must turn away from wickedness." (2 Tim 2:19)

b. The sheep know Him, His life, His being, His all. They know Him, believing and trusting...
- His love and care
- His mind and Word
- His companionship and leadership
- His experience and knowledge
- His destiny and pasture (heaven)

The fact that the sheep know Him so well is clear proof that Jesus is the "Good Shepherd" of their lives.

They said to the woman, "We no longer believe just because of what you said; now we have heard for ourselves, and we know that this man really is the Savior of the world." (John 4:42)

When he has brought out all his own, he goes on ahead of them, and his sheep follow him because they know his voice. (John 10:4)

My sheep listen to my voice; I know them, and they follow me. (John 10:27)

Now this is eternal life: that they may know you, the only true God, and Jesus Christ, whom you have sent. (John 17:3)

But whatever was to my profit I now consider loss for the sake of Christ. What is more, I consider everything a loss compared to the surpassing greatness of knowing Christ Jesus my Lord, for whose sake I have lost all things. I consider them rubbish, that I may gain Christ (Phil 3:7-8)

That is why I am suffering as I am. Yet I am not ashamed, because I know whom I have believed, and am convinced that he is able to guard what I have entrusted to him for that day. (2 Tim 1:12)

Dear friends, now we are children of God, and what we will be has not yet been made known. But we know that when he appears, we shall be like him, for we shall see him as he is. (1 John 3:2)

I know that my Redeemer lives, and that in the end he will stand upon the earth. (Job 19:25)

2. Jesus knows the Father, the Owner of the sheep. The question naturally arises, how well does He know Him? One thing is of critical importance. When Jesus claims to know the Father, He does not mean that He knows God in the same sense as other men know Him. Note His exact words:

Just as the Father knows me and I know the Father—and I lay down my life for the sheep. (John 10:15)

How well does God know any man? However well God knows Jesus, that is how well Jesus knows God. That is what Jesus is claiming. God, of course, knows every man perfectly, knows everything there is to know about a person. Therefore, Jesus knows the Father perfectly, just as God knows everything about Him. Jesus and "the Father are one" (v.30). There is a perfect, intimate knowledge and relationship between them.

This is exactly what Jesus was claiming. He was claiming to be *the Good Shepherd,"* the very One sent by God to be the Good Shepherd of the sheep. The proof is that He knows the Father even (as well) as the Father knows Him.

"All things have been committed to me by my Father. No one knows the Son except the Father, and no one knows the Father except the Son and those to whom the Son chooses to reveal him. (Mat 11:27)

But I know him because I am from him and he sent me." (John 7:29)

Though you do not know him, I know him. If I said I did not, I would be a liar like you, but I do know him and keep his word. (John 8:55)

Just as the Father knows me and I know the Father—and I lay down my life for the sheep. (John 10:15)

"Righteous Father, though the world does not know you, I know you, and they know that you have sent me. (John 17:25)

3. Jesus will die for the sheep. He was the "Good Shepherd," not a bad shepherd; therefore, He would face the enemy of the sheep. He would not run away from His calling and purpose. He would stand and fight the enemy as the Good Shepherd was sent to do. Note two striking facts.

   a. Jesus did not say that He would fight and protect the sheep. He said He would die for the sheep—definitely die. He knew that death awaited Him, that His purpose was to die for them.

   b. Jesus dropped the imagery of the shepherd in this statement. He no longer said, "the good shepherd lays down His life" (v.11); He now said "I lay down my life." (See DEEPER STUDY # 2, Jesus Christ, Death—Jn.10:11 for more discussion and verses of Scripture.)

4. Jesus worked to enlarge the fold, "the sheep pen." Note several facts.

   a. The "other sheep" was a reference to world-wide evangelism. It referred to all believers who were not standing there with Him. It included all countries and generations. It foresaw every believer of all time.

For there is no difference between Jew and Gentile—the same Lord is Lord of all and richly blesses all who call on him, (Rom 10:12)

   b. The words "I have other sheep" is a close, intimate term. The closest bond and fellowship imaginable, a Spirit-filled and supernatural relationship were to exist between Christ and these future sheep. (See DEEPER STUDY # 3, Fellowship—Acts 2:42 for discussion.)

   c. The word "must" (dei) means necessity, constraint. Jesus was compelled to reach the other sheep.

"My food," said Jesus, "is to do the will of him who sent me and to finish his work. (John 4:34)

As long as it is day, we must do the work of him who sent me. Night is coming, when no one can work. (John 9:4)

   d. The future sheep were to become sheep of His by "listening to His voice" (see note—Jn.10:4-5 for discussion).

   e. There is to be one flock, not two flocks. Every believer becomes a part of the Good Shepherd's flock. Note: there are not several shepherds and several flocks. There are not even two shepherds and two flocks. There is only one shepherd and one flock, and that is the flock of the Good Shepherd, of the Lord Jesus Christ Himself.

Who wants all men to be saved and to come to a knowledge of the truth. For there is one God and one mediator between God and men, the man Christ Jesus, who gave himself as a ransom for all men—the testimony given in its proper time. (1 Tim 2:4-6)

Now note: The very fact that Jesus enlarges the sheep pen is proof that He is the Good Shepherd. He is the Good Shepherd in that He works and labors for both the Owner and the sheep. He works to keep the sheep healthy so that they will reproduce and increase the flock. An enlarged and healthy flock, of course, means a pleased Owner (the Father).

3 (10:17-18) **Jesus Christ, Death—God, Love for Jesus:** the final proof that Jesus is the "Good Shepherd" is His sacrificial death and resurrection. A shepherd could do no greater "good" than to give his life for his sheep. A shepherd who died for his sheep was beyond question a good shepherd. But there is something else here as well. The owner was pleased, deeply appreciative that the shepherd gave his life for the flock. The owner *counted* the shepherd to be a "good" shepherd.

Jesus made two revealing points.

1. His sacrificial death was the very reason God loves His Son so much. Of course this does not mean that God does not love His Son just because of who He is. God naturally loves His Son just as any man loves his child. But God loves Jesus *even more*, in a much more special way, because Jesus was willing to pay such a price to bring men to God.

Note that Jesus died so that He might arise from the dead.

a. He took the sin of man upon Himself to free man from sin, (that is, to provide righteousness for man, positionally). (See note—Jn.1:51 for more discussion.)

> He himself bore our sins in his body on the tree, so that we might die to sins and live for righteousness; by his wounds you have been healed. (1 Pet 2:24)
> But you know that he appeared so that he might take away our sins. And in him is no sin. (1 John 3:5)

b. He arose from the dead to free man from death (that is, to provide eternal life for man).

> But also for us, to whom God will credit righteousness—for us who believe in him who raised Jesus our Lord from the dead. He was delivered over to death for our sins and was raised to life for our justification. (Rom 4:24-25)
> We were therefore buried with him

> through baptism into death in order that, just as Christ was raised from the dead through the glory of the Father, we too may live a new life. If we have been united with him like this in his death, we will certainly also be united with him in his resurrection. (Rom 6:4-5)

2. His death was the supreme act of obedience. It was voluntary; He willingly died. No man took His life; He sacrificed it Himself. The power to take it was His and His alone.

Note the critical point: this "command" to die was of God. This gives a higher meaning to the death of Jesus than just meeting man's need. It means that Jesus did not just die because of sin but because He wished to glorify and honor God. He wished above all else to show His love and adoration for God.

This is an aspect of Jesus' death that is often overlooked—an aspect that rises far above the mere meeting of our need. For in giving Himself as an "offering to God," Christ was looking beyond our need to the majestic responsibility of glorifying God. This means that His first purpose was the glory of God. He was concerned primarily with doing the will of God, with obeying God. God had been terribly dishonored by the first man, Adam, and by all those who followed after him. Jesus Christ wished to honor God by showing that at least one man thought more of God's glory than of anything else. Jesus wished to show that God's will meant more than any personal desire or ambition which He might have.

He said: "but the world must learn that I love the Father and that I do exactly what my Father has commanded me [to die for man]" (Jn.14:31; cp. Lk.22:42; Jn.5:30). (See DEEPER STUDY # 2, Jesus Christ, Death—Jn.10:11 for verses of Scripture.)

4 (10:19-21) **Jesus Christ, Response to:** the reaction to Jesus' claim was mixed. Some said that Jesus was demon-possessed and mad (cp. Jn.7:20; 8:48, 52). Others said that He was perhaps the Messiah (cp. Jn.7:12, 40-44).

> "I have testimony weightier than that of John. For the very work that the Father has given me to finish, and which I am doing, testifies that the Father has sent me. And the Father who sent me has himself testified concerning me. You have never heard his voice nor seen his form, nor does his word dwell in you, for you do not believe the one he sent. (John 5:36-38)

D. The Great Shepherd's Claims, 10:22-42

1 Jesus was in Jerusalem at the Feast of DedicationDS1
  a. It was winter
  b. He was walking in Solomon's colonnade
  c. The religionists approached & questioned Him

2 Claim 1: He is the MessiahDS2
  a. Religionists did not believe
    1) His clear claim
    2) His works are proof
    3) Reason: The religionists were not of His sheep
  b. His sheep believeDS3
    1) Are receptive
    2) Are known
    3) Do follow, v.27
    4) Are given life
    5) Are kept from perishing
    6) Are secure
    7) Are assured a double security in God Himself

3 Claim 2: He is one with God, that is, He is God Himself
  a. The religionists reacted
  b. Jesus questioned their reaction
  c. The religionists admitted

22 Then came the Feast of Dedication at Jerusalem. It was winter,
23 And Jesus was in the temple area walking in Solomon's Colonnade.
24 The Jews gathered around him, saying, "How long will you keep us in suspense? If you are the Christ, tell us plainly."
25 Jesus answered, "I did tell you, but you do not believe. The miracles I do in my Father's name speak for me,
26 But you do not believe because you are not my sheep.
27 My sheep listen to my voice; I know them, and they follow me.
28 I give them eternal life, and they shall never perish; no one can snatch them out of my hand.
29 My Father, who has given them to me, is greater than all; no one can snatch them out of my Father's hand.
30 I and the Father are one."
31 Again the Jews picked up stones to stone him,
32 But Jesus said to them, "I have shown you many great miracles from the Father. For which of these do you stone me?"
33 "We are not stoning you for any of these," replied the Jews, "but for blasphemy, because you, a mere man, claim to be God."
34 Jesus answered them, "Is it not written in your Law, 'I have said you are gods'?
35 If he called them 'gods,' to whom the word of God came—and the Scripture cannot be broken—
36 What about the one whom the Father set apart as his very own and sent into the world? Why then do you accuse me of blasphemy because I said, 'I am God's Son'?
37 Do not believe me unless I do what my Father does.
38 But if I do it, even though you do not believe me, believe the miracles, that you may know and understand that the Father is in me, and I in the Father."
39 Again they tried to seize him, but he escaped their grasp.
40 Then Jesus went back across the Jordan to the place where John had been baptizing in the early days. Here he stayed
41 And many people came to him. They said, "Though John never performed a miraculous sign, all that John said about this man was true."
42 And in that place many believed in Jesus.

    that His works were good
  d. The religionists understood His claim, but they rejected Him

4 Claim 3: He is the Son of God
  a. Jesus showed man's inconsistency

  b. Jesus' claim
    1) The Father sanctified Him, set Him apart
    2) The Father sent Him
    3) He is the Son of God

5 Claim 4: God is in Him & He is in God—absolutely
  a. His works prove

  b. He was still rejected

6 Conclusion: Jesus retired
  a. Jesus went to the area of John the Baptist

  b. John's crowds began to follow Jesus

  c. Many believed in Jesus

DIVISION X

THE REVELATION OF JESUS, THE SHEPHERD OF LIFE, 10:1-42

D. The Great Shepherd's Claims, 10:22-42

(10:22-42) **Introduction**: Jesus Christ is the *Great* Shepherd—great because of who He is. Note the phenomenal claims He made.

1. Jesus was in Jerusalem at the Feast of Dedication (v.22-24).
2. Claim 1: He is the Messiah (v.25-29).
3. Claim 2: He is one with God, that is, He is God Himself (v.30-33).
4. Claim 3: He is the Son of God (v.34-36).
5. Claim 4: God is in Him and He is in God—absolutely (v.37-39).
6. Conclusion: Jesus retired (v.40-42).

1 (10:22-24) **Jesus Christ, Messiah**: Jesus was in Jerusalem at the Feast of Dedication. (See DEEPER STUDY # 1—Jn.10:22.) He was walking in Solomon's colonnade (see note—Mk.11:27). Note how the Jews surrounded and encircled Him, for they were determined to get a straight an-

swer: "If you are the Christ, tell us plainly." Is Jesus the Messiah or not?

DEEPER STUDY # 1

(10:22) **Feast of Dedication**: this feast was founded to celebrate the freedom of Israel from Syria in 164 B.C. What had happened was terrible. Antiochus Epiphanes, the King of Syria from 175 to 164 B.C., loved Greek society and wanted to turn his part of the world into a model Greek society. William Barclay points out that he ran into trouble when he tried to make the Jews into full-fledged Greeks both in custom and religion. At first he tried peacefully, and some of the Jews adopted Greek ideas; but as history has shown, most Jews were not going to surrender their beliefs. In order to be successful, Antiochus knew that he had to destroy Jewish religion. He attacked Jerusalem, slaughtering 80,000 Jews by the most horrible means imaginable and enslaving another 80,000. He then desecrated the Jewish temple by...

JOHN 10:22-42

- turning the great altar of the burnt offering into an altar to the Greek god, Zeus.
- sacrificing swine flesh upon the altar.
- setting up a trade of prostitution in the temple chambers.

Such abhorrent acts caused some Jews to go underground and to take up the struggle against Antiochus. Judas Maccabaeus and his brothers soon came to the forefront as the leaders of the revolt against Syria. In 165 B.C. they were successful, and one of their first acts was to cleanse, restore, and rededicate the temple. It was for the purpose of celebrating the rededication of the temple to the worship of God that the *Feast of Dedication* was founded.

The feast has also been called the Festival of Lights. Its Jewish name is Hanukkah, and it is still celebrated today. The Festival lasted eight days and was characterized by the burning of lights. Lights were burned in every Jewish home throughout the city and countryside and in every corner of the temple. Every place throughout the land was lit up to celebrate the great day of deliverance. The lights symbolized the light of freedom that had been newly won for the nation. Note: the feast took place in the winter; its festivities were similar to the feast of tabernacles (2 Macc.1:9; 10:6). This is the only time the feast is mentioned in the gospels.

2 (10:25-29) **Jesus Christ, Messiah**: the first claim of Jesus was that He is the Messiah. There is a contrast in these verses (v.24-29), a contrast between the religionists and the Lord's sheep, between not believing and believing.

1. The religionists did not believe (v.25-26).
   a. Jesus had clearly claimed to be the Messiah. (See DEEPER STUDY # 2—Jn.10:25.) Note His words: "I did tell you." He had told them time and again.
   b. Jesus' works proved that He was who He claimed to be. (See notes—Jn.5:19; 5:20; 5:36.)
   c. The religionists did not believe Jesus' claims. Why? *Because* they were not His sheep. Note an important fact. Jesus did not say, "You are not my sheep because you do not believe"; but He said, "You do not believe because you are not my sheep." He was saying they did not believe because they were not His followers. This is the thread of predestination that John stresses throughout His gospel. (See notes—Jn.6:44-46; 6:37 for discussion.) The religionists did not belong to God. They claimed to be His followers, but their claim was only a verbal profession. Their hearts and lives were far from God; therefore, what Jesus claimed, they rejected. They were not the sheep of Jesus; therefore, they rejected His claims and Words.
2. The sheep of Jesus believe. They believe in the Shepherd. (See DEEPER STUDY # 3—Jn.10:27-29 for discussion.)

DEEPER STUDY # 2
(10:25) **Jesus Christ, Claims—Deity**: Jesus was asked, "If you are the Christ, tell us plainly." Just in the last few days the people had heard Him proclaim the truth as forcefully as He could. The problem was not His proclaiming the fact in clear language; the problem was the unbelief of the people. They only pretended not to understand. They understood, but they refused to believe. This is, of course, the problem with most men. In unmistakable terms, Jesus proclaims...

- that His teaching is not His, but God's (see note—Jn.7:16-19).

Jesus answered, "My teaching is not my own. It comes from him who sent me. (John 7:16)

- that He knows God intimately and was sent from God (see notes—Jn.7:25-31; 8:54-59; 10:14-16).

But I know him because I am from him and he sent me." (John 7:29)

- that He is the Source of life and the One who gives the Holy Spirit to men (see note—Jn.7:37-39).

On the last and greatest day of the Feast, Jesus stood and said in a loud voice, "If anyone is thirsty, let him come to me and drink. By this he meant the Spirit, whom those who believed in him were later to receive. Up to that time the Spirit had not been given, since Jesus had not yet been glorified. (John 7:37, 39)

- that He is the Light of the world (see DEEPER STUDY # 1—Jn.8:12; note—Jn.9:5).

When Jesus spoke again to the people, he said, "I am the light of the world. Whoever follows me will never walk in darkness, but will have the light of life." (John 8:12; cp. 9:5)

- that He is the Revelation of God (see note—Jn.8:19).

Then they asked him, "Where is your father?" "You do not know me or my Father," Jesus replied. "If you knew me, you would know my Father also." (John 8:19)

- that He has a different origin from man (see DEEPER STUDY # 2—Jn.8:23).

But he continued, "You are from below; I am from above. You are of this world; I am not of this world. (John 8:23)

- that if a man does not believe in Him, that man shall die in his sins (see note—Jn.8:23-24).

I told you that you would die in your sins; if you do not believe that I am the one I claim to be, you will indeed die in your sins." (John 8:24)

- that He is the Spokesman for God (see note—Jn.8:26).

"I have much to say in judgment of you. But he who sent me is reliable, and what I have heard from him I tell the world." (John 8:26)

- that He is the Son of Man who was to be lifted up on the cross (see note—Jn.8:28).

201

So Jesus said, "When you have lifted up the Son of Man, then you will know that I am the one I claim to be and that I do nothing on my own but speak just what the Father has taught me. (John 8:28)

- that God never left Him alone; that He never sinned; that He never failed to please God (see note—Jn.8:29).

The one who sent me is with me; he has not left me alone, for I always do what pleases him." (John 8:29)

- that He came from God (see note—Jn.8:42-43).

Jesus said to them, "If God were your Father, you would love me, for I came from God and now am here. I have not come on my own; but he sent me. (John 8:42)

- that He is sinless (see note—Jn.8:45-47. Cp. notes—Jn.8:29; 8:54-59.)

Yet because I tell the truth, you do not believe me! Can any of you prove me guilty of sin? If I am telling the truth, why don't you believe me? (John 8:45-46)

- that He is the Savior or Deliverer from death; that a man who keeps His Word shall never see death (see notes—Jn.8:51-53; 8:51).

I tell you the truth, if anyone keeps my word, he will never see death." (John 8:51)

- that He is the great "I Am" (see note—Jn.8:54-59).

"I tell you the truth," Jesus answered, "before Abraham was born, I am!" (John 8:58)

- that He is the Son of God (see note—Jn.9:35-38).

Jesus heard that they had thrown him out, and when he found him, he said, "Do you believe in the Son of Man?" "Who is he, sir?" the man asked. "Tell me so that I may believe in him." Jesus said, "You have now seen him; in fact, he is the one speaking with you." (John 9:35-37)

- that He is the Gate of the sheep (see note—Jn.10:7-10).

Therefore Jesus said again, "I tell you the truth, I am the gate for the sheep. I am the gate; whoever enters through me will be saved. He will come in and go out, and find pasture. (John 10:7, 9)

- that He is the Good Shepherd (see note—Jn.10:11-13; DEEPER STUDY # 2—10:11).

"I am the good shepherd. The good shepherd lays down his life for the sheep. "I am the good shepherd; I know my sheep and my sheep know me— (John 10:11, 14)

DEEPER STUDY # 3

(10:27-29) **Sheep**: the sheep of the Shepherd believe in the Shepherd. Others may not, but the sheep do. This is what Jesus was saying. Note how He used the traits of sheep to describe His followers (believers).

1. Sheep are *receptive* to the voice of the Shepherd. They know His voice and respond to it. When He calls them, they come and do what He says. Note also that they know the voice of false shepherds. (See note—Jn.10:4-5.)

2. Sheep are *known* by the Shepherd, and this knowledge leads them to trust Him explicitly. The Shepherd responds to the sheep and to their faith and trust in Him. He cares for them deeply, leading and looking after them. He even knows them individually, calling them by name (see note—Jn.10:2-3). The fact that He responds to them with such care and attention gives them even greater faith and trust. They trust their Shepherd without question.

3. Sheep *follow* the shepherd. They obey Him, knowing He goes *before* them in order to remove all obstacles and dangers (see notes—Jn.10:4-5).

4. Sheep are *communal*. Because of space, this fact is not given in the outline above. Note the sheep follow in a group. They form a commune or a fellowship of sheep. They are a body who follow the Shepherd. (See DEEPER STUDY # 3, Fellowship—Acts 2:42.)

5. Sheep are given *eternal life*. And note: eternal life includes an abundant life while on this earth, which begins the moment the sheep become a follower of the shepherd (see DEEPER STUDY # 1—Jn.10:10).

6. Sheep are *kept from perishing*. (See DEEPER STUDY # 2, Perishing—Jn.3:16.)

7. Sheep are *secure*. No man (no one, Greek) can snatch them out of the Shepherd's hand. The person who is truly in the Shepherd's hand will not be lost. The Shepherd promises this time and again (cp. Jn.6:37-39). Note exactly what Jesus said. The sheep are saved from someone *trying to pluck* them away, and they are saved no matter how great the *attempt* may be. (They are secure, kept from the evil one, even the devil himself.)

8. Sheep possess a *double security* in the Owner, that is, God Himself. They are secure not only because they are in the hands of the Shepherd but because they belong to the Owner. The Owner is God, and God is greater than all. Therefore being the greatest, no one is now able or ever will be able to pluck the sheep out of God's hand. (Cp. Ro.8:38-39.) (Not even the devil.)

3 (10:30-33) **Jesus Christ, Deity**: the second claim of Jesus was that He is One with God, that is, He is God Himself. But note: Jesus was not claiming to be the same person as God. He was claiming to have the same *nature* of God, to be One with God…

- in nature
- in being
- in substance
- in power
- in essence
- in glory

This is seen in the word "one." It is neuter, not masculine. It means *thing*, not *person*. Jesus is of the very same thing, of the very same substance as God.

There is no question that this is exactly what Jesus was claiming. His claim was perfectly understood by those standing around Him. The Scripture and outline clearly show this. Note the clear accusation: "We are not stoning you for any of these…but for blasphemy, because you, a mere man, claim to be God" (v.33).

In the beginning was the Word, and the Word was with God, and the Word was

God. He was with God in the beginning. (John 1:1-2)

When he looks at me, he sees the one who sent me. (John 12:45)

If you really knew me, you would know my Father as well. From now on, you do know him and have seen him." Philip said, "Lord, show us the Father and that will be enough for us." Jesus answered: "Don't you know me, Philip, even after I have been among you such a long time? Anyone who has seen me has seen the Father. How can you say, 'Show us the Father'? (John 14:7-9)

All that belongs to the Father is mine. That is why I said the Spirit will take from what is mine and make it known to you. (John 16:15)

Theirs are the patriarchs, and from them is traced the human ancestry of Christ, who is God over all, forever praised! Amen. (Rom 9:5)

For in Christ all the fullness of the Deity lives in bodily form, (Col 2:9)

Beyond all question, the mystery of godliness is great: He appeared in a body, was vindicated by the Spirit, was seen by angels, was preached among the nations, was believed on in the world, was taken up in glory. (1 Tim 3:16)

Which God will bring about in his own time—God, the blessed and only Ruler, the King of kings and Lord of lords, who alone is immortal and who lives in unapproachable light, whom no one has seen or can see. To him be honor and might forever. Amen. (1 Tim 6:15-16)

4 (10:34-36) **Jesus Christ, Deity**: the third claim of Jesus was that He is the Son of God. Those who rejected Jesus had stones in their hands, and they were ready to get rid of Him. Note two things.

1. Jesus showed man's inconsistency. He referred them to their history when they called their rulers or judges "gods." Their ancestors had used the word "gods" to mean that their judges were rulers of men—rulers who had been appointed by God to represent God among men (Ex.22:28; Ps.82:6). Jesus simply asked, if some rulers of Israel were called "gods," why was He being accused of blasphemy for claiming to be the Son of God?

2. Jesus made a threefold claim; however, note a critical point. Jesus was not saying, "Rulers were called gods, so I am to be called a 'god' as they were." He was claiming to be distinct from all other men. He claimed that He was...

- the One "whom the Father sanctified [set apart]." (See Deeper Study # 1, Sanctify—1 Pt.1:15-16.)
- the One whom the Father sent into the world. (See Deeper Study # 3—Jn.3:34.)
- the Son of God. (See notes—Jn.1:1-2; 1:34.)

How could they reject Him? Their rulers were mere men, yet they were called "gods." He was much, much more—the very One sanctified, set apart, and sent by God, the very Son of God Himself. How could they accuse Him of blasphemy when they so readily received rulers of the past as "gods" and the rulers were mere men?

"For God so loved the world that he gave his one and only Son, that whoever believes in him shall not perish but have eternal life. (John 3:16; cp. v.17-18)

Jesus heard that they had thrown him out, and when he found him, he said, "Do you believe in the Son of Man?" "Who is he, sir?" the man asked. "Tell me so that I may believe in him." Jesus said, "You have now seen him; in fact, he is the one speaking with you." (John 9:35-37)

Jesus said to her, "I am the resurrection and the life. He who believes in me will live, even though he dies; and whoever lives and believes in me will never die. Do you believe this?" "Yes, Lord," she told him, "I believe that you are the Christ, the Son of God, who was to come into the world." (John 11:25-27)

5 (10:37-39) **Jesus Christ, Deity**: the fourth claim of Jesus was that God is in Him and He is in God. (See note—Jn.14:10.) This is the indwelling presence of each in the other. Jesus is One with the Father, and the Father is One with Him. They are of one Mind and Spirit, one being and nature, one purpose and work.

For in Christ all the fullness of the Deity lives in bodily form, (Col 2:9)

Note a critical point: it is absolutely essential for a person to know and believe this truth. Jesus was pleading with the unbeliever:

But if I do it, even though you do not believe me, believe the miracles, that you may know and understand that the Father is in me, and I in the Father." (John 10:38)

Note that Jesus' works, His miracles, prove the indwelling presence of God in Him and He in God. But they rejected His claim.

I and the Father are one." (John 10:30)

Don't you believe that I am in the Father, and that the Father is in me? The words I say to you are not just my own. Rather, it is the Father, living in me, who is doing his work. (John 14:10)

I will remain in the world no longer, but they are still in the world, and I am coming to you. Holy Father, protect them by the power of your name—the name you gave me—so that they may be one as we are one. (John 17:11)

I have given them the glory that you gave me, that they may be one as we are one: (John 17:22)

6 (10:40-42) **Conclusion**: Jesus retired to the area where John had first baptized, and many of John's followers began to follow Jesus. Note that many believed in Jesus. John's faithfulness in the ministry throughout this area reaped great fruit.

That everyone who believes in him may have eternal life. (John 3:15)

CHAPTER 11

XI. THE REVELATION OF JESUS, THE RESURRECTION AND THE LIFE, 11:1-12:11

A. The Death of Lazarus and Its Purposes, 11:1-16

1 **Lazarus was sick**
  a. His home was Bethany

  b. His sisters were Mary & Martha

  c. His sisters sent the news of Lazarus' sickness to Jesus
2 **Purpose 1: To glorify God & to proclaim that Jesus is the Son of God**

3 **Purpose 2: To show Jesus' great love**
4 **Purpose 3: To show the necessity for waiting upon God in great crises**
5 **Purpose 4: To teach the**

Now a man named Lazarus was sick. He was from Bethany, the village of Mary and her sister Martha. 2 This Mary, whose brother Lazarus now lay sick, was the same one who poured perfume on the Lord and wiped his feet withher hair. 3 So the sisters sent word to Jesus, "Lord, the one you love is sick." 4 When he heard this, Jesus said, "This sickness will not end in death. No, it is for God's glory so that God's Son may be glorified through it." 5 Jesus loved Martha and her sister and Lazarus. 6 Yet when he heard that Lazarus was sick, he stayed where he was two more days. 7 Then he said to his disciples,

"Let us go back to Judea." 8 "But Rabbi," they said, "a short while ago the Jews tried to stone you, and yet you are going back there?" 9 Jesus answered, "Are there not twelve hours of daylight? A man who walks by day will not stumble, for he sees by this world's light. 10 It is when he walks by night that he stumbles, for he has no light." 11 After he had said this, he went on to tell them, "Our friend Lazarus has fallen asleep; but I am going there to wake him up." 12 His disciples replied, "Lord, if he sleeps, he will get better." 13 Jesus had been speaking of his death, but his disciples thought he meant natural sleep. 14 So then he told them plainly, "Lazarus is dead, 15 and for your sake I am glad I was not there, so that you may believe. But let us go to him." 16 Then Thomas (called Didymus) said to the rest of the disciples, "Let us also go, that we may die with him."

need to grasp opportunity
  a. The disciples protested Jesus' return to Jerusalem: Because of the threat to His life
  b. Jesus reply: There is a duty to work—to do what is right, to grasp the opportunity—regardless of the danger

6 **Purpose 5: To show Jesus' power over death**
  a. Jesus called Lazarus "our friend"
  b. Jesus predicted Lazarus would be raised
  c. The disciples misunderstood
  d. Jesus said that death is as "sleep"[DS1]

7 **Purpose 6: To help strengthen the disciples' belief**

8 **Purpose 7: To stir the disciples' courage & loyalty**

DIVISION XI

THE REVELATION OF JESUS, THE RESURRECTION AND THE LIFE, 11:1-12:11

A. The Death of Lazarus and Its Purposes, 11:1-16

(11:1-16) **Introduction**: Jesus Christ is the resurrection and the life. The death of Lazarus gave Jesus the opportunity to reveal Himself as the resurrection and the life. There were seven purposes for Lazarus' death. (Note: each purpose is also applicable to the death of the believer.)

  1. Lazarus was sick (v.1-3).
  2. Purpose 1: to glorify God and to proclaim that Jesus is the Son of God (v.4).
  3. Purpose 2: to show Jesus' great love (v.5).
  4. Purpose 3: to show the necessity for *waiting upon God* in great crises (v.6).
  5. Purpose 4: to teach the need to grasp opportunity (v.7-10).
  6. Purpose 5: to show Jesus' great power over death (v.11-14).
  7. Purpose 6: to help strengthen the disciples' belief (v.15).
  8. Purpose 7: to stir the disciples' courage and loyalty (v.16).

1 (11:1-3) **Jesus Christ, Family of—Martha**: Lazarus was sick. Jesus had said, "foxes have holes, and birds of the air have nests; but the Son of Man has no place to lay his head" (Mt.8:20; Lk.9:58). At this particular time Jesus was being rejected by almost everyone. Apparently He was

an unwelcome guest in most homes. He was walking about preaching and proclaiming that He was One with God, the Son of God Himself (see outline and notes—Jn.10:22-42). Just imagine a man making such a claim. He was thought to be "mad" and demon-possessed (Mk.3:20-21; Lk.4:25). His own family was even having difficulty with Him at this time. They were apparently so embarrassed by His claims and the rumors of His insanity that on one occasion they travelled a great distance to bring Him home lest He be harmed. (See outline and notes—Mt.12:46-50.)

However, there was one family who always opened their home to Jesus when He was in and around Jerusalem—the family of Lazarus, Martha, and Mary, who were brother and sisters. They lived in Bethany, a suburb about two miles outside Jerusalem. Their closeness to Jesus is the reason the sisters felt so free to interrupt His evangelistic tour with the request to help their sick brother. Jesus' great love for this family should be noted throughout this passage.

2 (11:4) **Sickness—Jesus Christ, Glorified**: the first purpose of Lazarus' sickness was to glorify God and to proclaim that Jesus is the Son of God. Lazarus' sickness was not *for* death. He was to die *for* the glory of God and Christ. He was sick, and he was to die so that the works of God could be demonstrated. Lazarus died so that...

God could be glorified…
- By showing His desire for man to have life
- By proving His power to give life
- By showing His approval of Christ by which He proved that He really did love the world enough to send His Son to save the world

Christ could be glorified…
- By having the opportunity to do the work of God
- By demonstrating God's power
- By showing compassion
- By strengthening the faith of believers
- By leading unbelievers to believe

In raising Lazarus from the dead, both Jesus and His Father were glorified as the *Life* of the world. In dealing with the blind man, both were glorified as the *Light* of the world (Jn.9:3, 5). (See note—Jn.9:5 for more discussion.)

> That all may honor the Son just as they honor the Father. He who does not honor the Son does not honor the Father, who sent him. (John 5:23)
> Ascribe to the LORD the glory due his name; worship the LORD in the splendor of his holiness. (Psa 29:2)
> Glorify the LORD with me; let us exalt his name together. (Psa 34:3)
> My mouth is filled with your praise, declaring your splendor all day long. (Psa 71:8)
> They will speak of the glorious splendor of your majesty, and I will meditate on your wonderful works. (Psa 145:5)
> O LORD, you are my God; I will exalt you and praise your name, for in perfect faithfulness you have done marvelous things, things planned long ago. (Isa 25:1)

3 (11:5) **Jesus Christ, Love for Man**: the second purpose of Lazarus' sickness was to show Jesus' great love. Note: each member of the family is mentioned personally. He loved the family, but He also loved each one individually. This is a fact in the Scripture that needs to be stressed, for each one had a need, and each one needed and received the help of Jesus. Lazarus' death gave Him the opportunity to demonstrate His great love not only for the families of the world but for each individual in the world.

> The watchman opens the gate for him, and the sheep listen to his voice. He calls his own sheep by name and leads them out. (John 10:3)
> It was just before the Passover Feast. Jesus knew that the time had come for him to leave this world and go to the Father. Having loved his own who were in the world, he now showed them the full extent of his love. (John 13:1)
> "As the Father has loved me, so have I loved you. Now remain in my love. (John 15:9)
> Who shall separate us from the love of Christ? Shall trouble or hardship or persecution or famine or nakedness or danger or sword? (Rom 8:35)

> I have been crucified with Christ and I no longer live, but Christ lives in me. The life I live in the body, I live by faith in the Son of God, who loved me and gave himself for me. (Gal 2:20)
> This is how we know what love is: Jesus Christ laid down his life for us. And we ought to lay down our lives for our brothers. (1 John 3:16)

4 (11:6) **Trial—Waiting Upon God**: the third purpose of Lazarus' sickness was to show the necessity for *waiting upon God* in great crises. Jesus was not waiting two days so that Lazarus would die and He could perform a great miracle. Jesus knew that Lazarus was either already dead or that Lazarus was going to die on the very day the person brought word of Lazarus' illness. We know this because Lazarus had already been buried four days when Jesus arrived in Bethany (v.17, 39). Jewish burial immediately followed death. The four days would be counted from…
- the day of travel by the messengers in bringing word to Jesus (v.3).
- the two days needed for Jesus to complete His ministry (v.6).
- the day or two needed by Jesus to travel to Bethany (v.17). (Remember huge crowds thronged Jesus, which prevented Him from travelling rapidly. It is possible He completed His ministry in one day and took two days for travel to Bethany.)

The point is this: Martha and Mary were learning to wait upon God throughout the whole experience. In facing severe illness or death, there is no answer but to wait upon God. Jesus knows when to act. He knows the exact moment, the best time…
- for us to bear the trial
- for us to stand
- for us to be helped
- for us to learn the most
- for us to bear testimony of God's power and strength

Whenever that moment arrives, the Lord arises to meet the need of the believer. What the believer must do is what Martha and Mary had to do: learn to *wait upon God*. The Lord will act at the right moment.

> **Thought 1.** We cannot dictate to God when to act nor how to act. Note two examples.
> 1) Note Mary, Jesus' own mother. At the marriage feast she wanted Him to go and secure more wine. He rebuked her for interfering with His work, the work of God. He has His own way and time, the very best way and time for meeting the need (cp. Jn.2:3-4).
> 2) Note Jesus' own brothers. They tried to ridicule Him into going by caravan with them to the feast in Jerusalem. Jesus rebuked them for the same reason He had rebuked Mary. He, the Son of God, knew how to conduct His ministry and when to go about doing it. He knew what was best.

> Guide me in your truth and teach me, for you are God my Savior, and my hope is in you all day long. (Psa 25:5)
> Wait for the LORD; be strong and take heart and wait for the LORD. (Psa 27:14)

Find rest, O my soul, in God alone; my hope comes from him. (Psa 62:5)

As the eyes of slaves look to the hand of their master, as the eyes of a maid look to the hand of her mistress, so our eyes look to the LORD our God, till he shows us his mercy. (Psa 123:2)

Do not say, "I'll pay you back for this wrong!" Wait for the LORD, and he will deliver you. (Prov 20:22)

But those who hope in the LORD will renew their strength. They will soar on wings like eagles; they will run and not grow weary, they will walk and not be faint. (Isa 40:31)

But you must return to your God; maintain love and justice, and wait for your God always. (Hosea 12:6)

5 (11:7-10) **Opportunity—Service**: the fourth purpose of Lazarus' sickness was to teach the need to grasp opportunity. It had been three days since Jesus had received word of Lazarus' illness. Jesus now said it was time to go into Judaea, for Bethany was in the district of Judaea. The disciples protested, for it was the Judaean leaders who had stood so opposed to Jesus and had threatened to kill Him (Jn.10:31). The disciples could not believe their ears. Why would Jesus jeopardize their lives?

Jesus' answer was forceful, and it stands as a great lesson for all of us. There are only twelve hours in a day. Jesus must walk, that is...

- go and do His work while it is day.
- go and do what is right, regardless of the danger.
- go and do what is right lest the day pass and the opportunity be lost. (Cp. Jn.9:4.)

If Jesus had walked in the dark, failing to work and failing to do what He knew to be right, He would have stumbled. He would have shown that there is no light in Him. The idea is, of course, that there is light in Him. He knew the work to be done and the right thing to do, so He must go into Judaea.

Thought 1. A man must do the same as Jesus. A man has only twelve hours of daylight (approximately).

⇒ He must walk, that is, work and do what is right, grasping the opportunity while it is day.
⇒ If he walks in the night, he will stumble. When the night comes, it is too late to walk. Works cannot be done in the night without stumbling about. The opportunity is lost.

"My food," said Jesus, "is to do the will of him who sent me and to finish his work. (John 4:34)

As long as it is day, we must do the work of him who sent me. Night is coming, when no one can work. (John 9:4)

And do this, understanding the present time. The hour has come for you to wake up from your slumber, because our salvation is nearer now than when we first believed. The night is nearly over; the day is almost here. So let us put aside the deeds of darkness and put on the armor of light. (Rom 13:11-12)

Making the most of every opportunity, because the days are evil. (Eph 5:16)

Be wise in the way you act toward outsiders; make the most of every opportunity. (Col 4:5)

Note the term, "the Light of this world." Jesus is "the Light of this world." A person has only twelve hours, only a certain amount of time to see "the Light of the world." Once the night comes, the opportunity is lost. Note also the statement, "for he has no light [in him]." Man has no light within. All he can do is walk...

- as he sees
- as other men see
- as the world sees

The problem with such a walk is that no man or any combination of men can see beyond the physical and material world, and the end of the world is fear—the fear and trembling brought about by bondage and death. (Note the fear of the disciples above, v.8.) The end of the world is not life. Life comes only from Jesus, "the Light of this world" (see DEEPER STUDY # 1—Jn.8:12).

But if your eyes are bad, your whole body will be full of darkness. If then the light within you is darkness, how great is that darkness! (Mat 6:23)

In him was life, and that life was the light of men. (John 1:4)

This is the verdict: Light has come into the world, but men loved darkness instead of light because their deeds were evil. (John 3:19)

When Jesus spoke again to the people, he said, "I am the light of the world. Whoever follows me will never walk in darkness, but will have the light of life." (John 8:12)

Then Jesus told them, "You are going to have the light just a little while longer. Walk while you have the light, before darkness overtakes you. The man who walks in the dark does not know where he is going. (John 12:35)

I have come into the world as a light, so that no one who believes in me should stay in darkness. (John 12:46)

For it is light that makes everything visible. This is why it is said: "Wake up, O sleeper, rise from the dead, and Christ will shine on you." (Eph 5:14)

6 (11:11-14) **Death—Jesus Christ, Power**: the fifth purpose of Lazarus' sickness was to show Jesus' great power over death. Jesus stated very plainly what He was going to do. Lazarus was asleep; therefore, He would go and awaken Lazarus out of his sleep. However, the disciples misunderstood what Jesus was saying. *By sleep,* Jesus meant that Lazarus was dead, but the disciples thought He meant that Lazarus was resting in sleep. Note that Jesus gave His meaning of sleep: "Lazarus is dead." Note four significant things.

1. Jesus called Lazarus "our friend." He was dead, but he was still "our friend." This is a hint that Lazarus is still a friend despite being dead, that he is still living, still alive in another

world. Note the strong feelings Jesus had for this believer, Lazarus.

Thought 1. Jesus' love reaches out for every believer just as much as it did for Lazarus. Jesus calls every believer His friend. And note the words *"our friend."* Every believer is to be the friend of all other believers. There is to be a sweet fellowship between all believers.

2. Jesus predicted that He would raise Lazarus from the dead. He would "wake him up" and resurrect him. This is a picture of the resurrection of believers (cp. v.23-26).

> **Jesus said to her, "I am the resurrection and the life. He who believes in me will live, even though he dies; (John 11:25)**
> **"Do not be amazed at this, for a time is coming when all who are in their graves will hear his voice and come out—those who have done good will rise to live, and those who have done evil will rise to be condemned. (John 5:28-29)**

3. The disciples misunderstood. Many still do. They misunderstand the meaning of death and the resurrection.

4. Jesus said that death is as "sleep" (see DEEPER STUDY # 1—Jn.11:13).

DEEPER STUDY # 1

(11:13) **Sleep—Death**: death is sometimes spoken of as sleep when referring to believers. (See DEEPER STUDY # 1—Lk.8:50 for more discussion. Cp. Mt.27:52; Acts 7:60; 13:36; 1 Cor.15:18, 20, 51; 1 Th.4:13-15; 2 Pt.3:4.)

⇒ Jesus said that Jairus' daughter was asleep (Mt.9:24).
⇒ When Stephen was martyred, he is said to have fallen asleep (Acts 7:60).
⇒ Some of the five hundred witnesses to Jesus' ascension are said to have "fallen asleep" (1 Cor.15:6).
⇒ Believers already in heaven are said to be asleep in Jesus (1 Th.4:13).

Death is called "sleep" in order to picture the idea that the believer is...

• resting in the presence and comfort of God.
• resting from the labor of his service on earth.
• resting and refreshing himself for a greater service for God.

Many within the world picture death as annihilation, as ceasing to exist. Scripture says it is not. Believers continue to exist, resting in the life and comfort of God. The body lays down and, so to speak, sleeps; but not the soul of man.

> **We are confident, I say, and would prefer to be away from the body and at home with the Lord. (2 Cor 5:8; cp. Ph.1:23)**

7 (11:15) **Hope—Resurrection**: the sixth purpose of Lazarus' sickness was to help strengthen the disciples' belief. Jesus said an astonishing thing: He was rejoicing that He was not in Bethany when Lazarus was sick. Why? Jesus joyed over what was to happen. Lazarus was to be raised from the dead, which meant that every thoughtful believer, both then and in succeeding generations, would experience a great leap in faith.

Thought 1. The glorious event of Lazarus' resurrection stirs the heart of sincere seekers, for it pictures the most glorious hope of life possible. Jesus Christ has the power to give life and to raise the dead (Jn.5:24-29; 1 Th.4:13f; 1 Cor.15:1-58). Any follower of Christ who truly experiences the scene of Lazarus' resurrection is bound...

• to take a great leap in faith.
• to have his faith stirred to new heights.
• to see his faith grow progressively.

> **Jesus did many other miraculous signs in the presence of his disciples, which are not recorded in this book. But these are written that you may believe that Jesus is the Christ, the Son of God, and that by believing you may have life in his name. (John 20:30-31)**

8 (11:16) **Courage—Loyalty**: the seventh purpose of Lazarus' sickness was to stir the disciples' courage and loyalty. Note that Thomas took the lead here. He showed great courage and loyalty to Christ, a dynamic example for every believer. He demonstrated...

• a deep love for Christ, a love that was ready to die for Him.
• a willingness to stand and to die with his fellow believers in the Lord's work.
• a knowledge that to die for Christ is better than to live without Him.

> **No, the Father himself loves you because you have loved me and have believed that I came from God. (John 16:27)**
> **Though you have not seen him, you love him; and even though you do not see him now, you believe in him and are filled with an inexpressible and glorious joy, (1 Pet 1:8)**

	B. Jesus and Martha: A Growth in Faith, 11:17-27	22 But I know that even now God will give you whatever you ask." 23 Jesus said to her, "Your brother will rise again." 24 Martha answered, "I know he will rise again in the resurrection at the last day." 25 Jesus said to her, "I am the resurrection and the life. He who believes in me will live, even though he dies; 26 and whoever lives and believes in me will never die. Do you believe this?" 27 "Yes, Lord," she told him, "I believe that you are the Christ, the Son of God, who was to come into the world."	That His power was less than God's power
1 The scene was Bethany, a suburb of Jerusalem— about two miles away	17 On his arrival, Jesus found that Lazarus had already been in the tomb for four days.		**3 Martha's fundamental faith**
a. Lazarus: Had been in the tomb for four days	18 Bethany was less than two miles from Jerusalem,		a. Jesus' declaration
	19 and many Jews had come to Martha and Mary to comfort them in the loss of their brother.		b. Martha's expression of faith
b. Friends: Comforted the family			**4 Martha's declared faith**
			a. Jesus' great claim
c. Martha: Went to meet Jesus	20 When Martha heard that Jesus was coming, she went out to meet him, but Mary stayed at home.		b. Jesus' promise: Believe 1) He who believes & dies shall live
d. Mary: Stayed at home			2) He who lives and believes shall never die; he never perishes
2 Martha's complaining, limited faith	21 "Lord," Martha said to Jesus, "if you had been here, my brother would not have died.		c. Martha's declaration 1) The Christ 2) The Son of God 3) Sent by God
a. Her *complaining* belief b. Her *limited* belief:			

DIVISION XI

THE REVELATION OF JESUS, THE RESURRECTION AND THE LIFE, 11:1-12:11

B. Jesus and Martha: A Growth in Faith, 11:17-27

(11:17-27) **Introduction**: this passage is a dynamic conversation between Jesus and Martha. What happened caused a great growth in Martha's faith. A seeking heart and a study of the conversation will cause any believer's faith to grow significantly.

1. The scene was Bethany, a suburb of Jerusalem about 2 miles away (v.17-20).
2. Martha's complaining, limited faith (v.21-22).
3. Martha's fundamental faith (v.23-24).
4. Martha's declared faith (v.25-27).

1 (11:17-20) **Jesus Christ, Ministry—Compassion**: the scene was Bethany, a suburb of Jerusalem about two miles away. When Jesus arrived, someone told Him that Lazarus had already been buried for four days (see note—Jn.11:6). Jesus did not actually enter the city of Bethany. He apparently stayed on the outskirts of the city. Just why we are not told. Perhaps the multitude following Him was too large to crowd into the city, or perhaps He was simply avoiding those who were so bitterly opposed to Him. There was an enormous number of mourners who had come to comfort the family, and some of these were opposed to Jesus (v.46).

Whatever the reason for remaining on the outskirts of the city, Jesus apparently sent a messenger to tell Martha that He had arrived (cp. v.28). As soon as she heard, she quietly left the house and ran out to meet Him. (Cp. v.28 for what apparently happened with Martha as well as Mary.) Mary, however, remained at home.

Note the striking contrast between Martha and Mary, a contrast that is ever so characteristic. Martha was the woman of action and energy, the one brimming with initiative; therefore, she was the one who went out to meet Jesus. Mary was the contemplative and meditative one; therefore, she remained at home to receive the mourners (cp. Lk.10:38-42).

2 (11:21-22) **Faith**: Martha's complaining, limited faith in Jesus. Martha believed in Jesus. She even believed that Je-

sus could have healed Lazarus and kept him from dying. But Jesus had not come immediately when He was called; therefore, her brother was dead. Why did Jesus not come when He was called? Why did He not heal Lazarus when she and the family loved Jesus so much and had done so much for Him? Why did He let Lazarus die?

The point is this: Martha did believe in Jesus, but her faith was a complaining faith. She did not believe to the point of *resting* in faith. She did not believe with an *unlimited and resting faith*. She was not entrusting the matter completely into the Lord's hands. She was not yet convinced that what had happened was for the best. She trusted Jesus as her Savior, but she questioned what had happened. She complained and even reproached Jesus.

A complaining, questioning faith is a *limited faith*. It is a faith that questions Jesus' Lordship...

- that questions if Jesus has done what is best.
- that questions if Jesus knows what is best.

It says to Jesus, "If you had been here, if you had acted differently, if you had done this or that, then this trial would not have happened." Note that Martha was convicted immediately for having complained and reproached Jesus. She blurted out:

> **But I know that even now God will give you whatever you ask." (v.22)**

But note even here how her *limited faith* showed itself. She did not say, "Lord, I know that you can do anything you will." She said, "God will give you whatever you ask." She was still *limiting* Jesus to some level below God. She was not grasping that Jesus Himself was the Resurrection and the Life. She had a complaining, limited faith in Jesus.

> **He replied, "You of little faith, why are you so afraid?" Then he got up and rebuked the winds and the waves, and it was completely calm. (Mat 8:26)**
> **Immediately Jesus reached out his hand and caught him. "You of little faith,"**

208

he said, "why did you doubt?" And when they climbed into the boat, the wind died down. (Mat 14:31-32)

Aware of their discussion, Jesus asked, "You of little faith, why are you talking among yourselves about having no bread? Do you still not understand? Don't you remember the five loaves for the five thousand, and how many basketfuls you gathered? (Mat 16:8-9)

Don't you believe that I am in the Father, and that the Father is in me? The words I say to you are not just my own. Rather, it is the Father, living in me, who is doing his work. (John 14:10)

3 (11:23-24) **Faith—Resurrection**: Martha's fundamental faith. Jesus made a striking declaration, "Your brother will rise again." He could have said it no clearer. Lazarus was to arise from the dead.

Martha misunderstood. She thought Jesus meant that Lazarus would arise in the resurrection at the last day.

1. Note that Martha had a *fundamental faith*. She believed in the resurrection, one of the fundamentals of the faith. She believed what Jesus had taught, and He had been drilling the resurrection into His followers (cp. Jn.5:28-29; 6:39, 40, 44, 54; 12:48).

2. Martha's fundamental faith experienced disappointment. The promise of a future resurrection and reunion is not always a comfort. Her loved one was gone. There was now no contact and no relationship with him, not on this earth. Everything about her life was now completely changed. Her household was radically different. She believed in the resurrection and believed in all the fundamentals of the faith, but the resurrection was so far in the future that it was of little comfort to her then.

The point is this: a *fundamental faith* is essential. A person must believe in the fundamentals of the faith, but a fundamental faith is short—it is not all there is to faith and to our life in Christ. It is not a living faith, not a faith that lives in the presence of Christ. And what is so desperately needed by man is what was needed by Martha: a living faith, a faith that is alive and vibrant, dynamic and moving, conscious and acting, communicating and fellowshipping. What is needed is the knowledge that Jesus, the very One who stands before us, *is* "the resurrection and the life."

You diligently study the Scriptures because you think that by them you possess eternal life. These are the Scriptures that testify about me, (John 5:39)

"Not everyone who says to me, 'Lord, Lord,' will enter the kingdom of heaven, but only he who does the will of my Father who is in heaven. (Mat 7:21)

He replied, "Isaiah was right when he prophesied about you hypocrites; as it is written: "'These people honor me with their lips, but their hearts are far from me. (Mark 7:6)

Having a form of godliness but denying its power. Have nothing to do with them. (2 Tim 3:5)

4 (11:25-27) **Jesus Christ, Claim—Faith—Heaven—Death**: Martha's declared faith. Note three points.

1. Jesus' great claim: "I Am the resurrection and the life." Here is a critical fact: Jesus did not say that He *gives* the resurrection and life to man, but He *is* the Resurrection and the Life. Jesus, of course, does give the resurrection and life to believers; but His point is not this fact. His point is far more important. Jesus declared that He is the very being and essence, the very power and energy, of life. Therefore, He can...

- give and sustain life as He wills.
- resurrect and restore life as He wills.

This is a phenomenal claim. It means that man—in fact all of life—exists only by the will and power of Jesus. Being the power and energy of life, Jesus is the Source of all life. There is nothing existing apart from His will; therefore, if a dead person wishes to live, only Jesus can give him life. And if a living person does not wish to die, only Jesus can keep him from dying.

In him was life, and that life was the light of men. (John 1:4)

For as the Father has life in himself, so he has granted the Son to have life in himself. (John 5:26)

The thief comes only to steal and kill and destroy; I have come that they may have life, and have it to the full. (John 10:10)

Jesus answered, "I am the way and the truth and the life. No one comes to the Father except through me. (John 14:6)

So that, just as sin reigned in death, so also grace might reign through righteousness to bring eternal life through Jesus Christ our Lord. (Rom 5:21)

But it has now been revealed through the appearing of our Savior, Christ Jesus, who has destroyed death and has brought life and immortality to light through the gospel. (2 Tim 1:10)

He who has the Son has life; he who does not have the Son of God does not have life. (1 John 5:12)

2. Jesus' great promise: believe, and two phenomenal things happen.
- a. "He who believes in me will live, even though he dies [kan a pothanen]." He lives in the other world: in heaven, in the spiritual dimension of being, in the very presence of God Himself. The believer who has passed from this world is not some place...
  - in a semi-conscious state.
  - in a deep sleep, locked up in a compartment someplace.
  - in space moving about and floating around on a fluffy cloud.

The believer is fully alive: he lives in heaven, in the other world, in the very presence of God Himself. Another world exists just as this world exists. It is not a world that lies out in the future; it is a world that exists now—a spiritual world—a spiritual dimension—a world that the Bible calls heaven. It is the spiritual world and dimension where God and Christ and angels and all those who have gone on before now live.

The point is this: when a person who has *believed in Jesus* dies, he goes to live in heaven, in the spiritual world where God and Christ and the heavenly hosts live. *Hallelujah*! is the only word that can express the hope and joy that fills the soul of the true believer.

> **Two men, Moses and Elijah, appeared in glorious splendor, talking with Jesus. They spoke about his departure, which he was about to bring to fulfillment at Jerusalem. (Luke 9:30-31)**
> **Jesus answered him, "I tell you the truth, today you will be with me in paradise." (Luke 23:43)**
> **Whoever serves me must follow me; and where I am, my servant also will be. My Father will honor the one who serves me. (John 12:26)**
> **"Father, I want those you have given me to be with me where I am, and to see my glory, the glory you have given me because you loved me before the creation of the world. (John 17:24)**
> **We are confident, I say, and would prefer to be away from the body and at home with the Lord. (2 Cor 5:8)**
> **I am torn between the two: I desire to depart and be with Christ, which is better by far; (Phil 1:23)**

b. "Whoever lives and believes in me will never die." The idea is that the believer will never taste death, that is, never experience death. Quicker than the believer can blink an eye, he passes from this world into the next world. He is transported and transferred into heaven. The believer never loses a single moment of consciousness. One moment he is conscious and living in this world; the next moment he is conscious and present in the next world. There is only one difference. He is immediately made perfect: transformed, made much more conscious and aware, more knowledgeable and alive than ever before. (See DEEPER STUDY # 1—2 Tim.4:18 for more discussion. Also see DEEPER STUDY # 2—Jn.1:4; DEEPER STUDY # 1—10:10; DEEPER STUDY # 1—17:2-3.)

> **That everyone who believes in him may have eternal life. (John 3:15)**
> **"I tell you the truth, whoever hears my word and believes him who sent me has eternal life and will not be condemned; he has crossed over from death to life. (John 5:24)**
> **I tell you the truth, if anyone keeps my word, he will never see death." (John 8:51)**
> **The one who sows to please his sinful nature, from that nature will reap destruction; the one who sows to please the Spirit, from the Spirit will reap eternal life. (Gal 6:8)**

c. Note a crucial point. Receiving eternal life is conditional: a person must believe. It is "who believes" and "whoever lives and believes" that lives and never dies. It is as Jesus asked Martha: "Do you believe this?" If a person believes Jesus, he never dies; he shall live forever.

3. Martha's great declaration. Martha believed, and she confessed and called Jesus "Lord" (see DEEPER STUDY # 2—Jn.2:24). She declared that she believed three things:

a. That Jesus is the Christ, the Messiah (see note—Jn.1:35-42).

> **The woman said, "I know that Messiah" (called Christ) "is coming. When he comes, he will explain everything to us." Then Jesus declared, "I who speak to you am he." (John 4:25-26)**
> **But I know him because I am from him and he sent me." (John 7:29)**

b. That Jesus is the Son of God (see note—Jn.1:34. Cp. John the Baptist, Jn.1:34; Peter, Mt.16:16; Jesus, Jn.11:41; 26:63f; John the Apostle, Jn.20:31.)

> **"For God so loved the world that he gave his one and only Son, that whoever believes in him shall not perish but have eternal life. (John 3:16)**
> **When he looks at me, he sees the one who sent me. (John 12:45)**

c. That Jesus is the One who was to be sent into the world by God (see DEEPER STUDY # 1-Jn.3:31).

> **The one who sent me is with me; he has not left me alone, for I always do what pleases him." (John 8:29)**
> **Jesus said to them, "If God were your Father, you would love me, for I came from God and now am here. I have not come on my own; but he sent me. (John 8:42)**

Thought 1. Knowing that Jesus is the Resurrection and the Life means three things. It means...

- that Jesus is alive, living right before us in the person of the Holy Spirit. He is both *in us* and *all around us*. Our faith is living and alive and in constant communion and fellowship with Him.
- that our loved one is present with Jesus, no longer imperfect in mind and body, but perfect: more conscious, more aware, more alive than he was on earth. How do we know this? Jesus is alive in heaven, and "to be away from the body [is] to be at home with the Lord" (2 Cor.5:8).
- that Jesus is alive, so the resurrection of our glorified bodies is assured (1 Cor.15:1-58).

	C. Jesus and Mary: The Needs of Man, 11:28-37	32 When Mary reached the place where Jesus was and saw him, she fell at his feet and said, "Lord, if you had been here, my brother would not have died."	**4 Need 4: The confession of faith (even if it is limited & weak)** a. The confession: Lord b. The complaining, limited faith
1 Need 1: The glorious message of Christ a. He is the "Teacher"[DS1] b. The Teacher "is here" c. The Teacher asks "for you"	28 And after she had said this, she went back and called her sister Mary aside. "The Teacher is here," she said, "and is asking for you."	33 When Jesus saw her weeping, and the Jews who had come along with her also weeping, he was deeply moved in spirit and troubled.	**5 Need 5: The understanding, feelings, and compassion of Jesus** a. He was deeply moved 1) Over death 2) Over man's pain
2 Need 2: The right response—arise quickly & come to Christ	29 When Mary heard this, she got up quickly and went to him. 30 Now Jesus had not yet entered the village, but was still at the place where Martha had met him.	34 "Where have you laid him?" he asked. "Come and see, Lord," they replied. 35 Jesus wept.	b. He asks where the dead person is c. He weeps in love: Over death & man's pain
3 Need 3: The reaching out of people to help others	31 When the Jews who had been with Mary in the house, comforting her, noticed how quickly she got up and went out, they followed her, supposing she was going to the tomb to mourn there.	36 Then the Jews said, "See how he loved him!" 37 But some of them said, "Could not he who opened the eyes of the blind man have kept this man from dying?"	**6 Conclusion: The misunderstanding of man—how could Jesus love so much & let this happen?**

DIVISION XI

THE REVELATION OF JESUS, THE RESURRECTION AND THE LIFE, 11:1-12:11

C. Jesus and Mary: The Real Needs of Man, 11:28-37

(11:28-37) **Introduction**: man has great needs. These are seen in the experience of Mary with Jesus.

1. Need 1: the glorious message of Christ (v.28).
2. Need 2: the right response—arise quickly and come to Christ (v.29-30).
3. Need 3: the reaching out of people to help others (v.31).
4. Need 4: the confession of faith (even if it is limited and weak) (v.32).
5. Need 5: the understanding, feelings, and compassion of Jesus (v.33-36).
6. Conclusion: the misunderstanding of man—how could Jesus love so much and let this happen (v.37)?

1 (11:28) **Jesus Christ, Message**: the first need is for the glorious message of Christ. Martha had made a great confession of faith: "Lord, I believe that you are the Christ, the Son of God, who was to come into the world" (Jn.11:27).

The great confession apparently struck some kind of hope within Martha. Just what she was expecting, perhaps even she did not know, but there was a spark of hope. Her Lord, the Son of God Himself, was now with her. Whatever could be done would be done; whatever help was available would be given. Her faith and trust were in Him. Only one thing was missing: her dear sister, Mary. So she hastened to share the glorious news with her. Note that she shared three things.

1. The Teacher (see DEEPER STUDY # 1—Jn.11:28).

2. The Teacher "is here." The answer that we so desperately need is now available. The One who can give us the help we need has now come: the Teacher who can teach us how to meet all of our…

- needs and necessities
- troubles and trials
- sorrow and hurt
- loneliness and emptiness

Just as the Son of Man did not come to be served, but to serve, and to give his life as a ransom for many." (Mat 20:28)

"The Spirit of the Lord is on me, because he has anointed me to preach good news to the poor. He has sent me to proclaim freedom for the prisoners and recovery of sight for the blind, to release the oppressed, to proclaim the year of the Lord's favor." (Luke 4:18-19)

The thief comes only to steal and kill and destroy; I have come that they may have life, and have it to the full. (John 10:10)

Therefore he is able to save completely those who come to God through him, because he always lives to intercede for them. (Heb 7:25)

3. The Master asks "for you." Jesus calls and summons you. He wonders where you are and why you have not come. He wants you now.

"Come to me, all you who are weary and burdened, and I will give you rest. Take my yoke upon you and learn from me, for I am gentle and humble in heart, and you will find rest for your souls. (Mat 11:28-29)

"Come, all you who are thirsty, come to the waters; and you who have no money, come, buy and eat! Come, buy wine and milk without money and without cost. (Isa 55:1)

DEEPER STUDY # 1
(11:28) **Teacher, The** (ho didaskalos): the definite article (the) is important. Jesus is not just another teacher like all

other teachers. He is *the* Teacher, the teaching Master. This means at least two things.

1. Jesus is the Supreme Teacher, the very best teacher who has ever lived. He is known for being the greatest of teachers. No one even comes close to comparing with Him. He stands alone as *the Teacher*.

2. Jesus is the Master, the Lord, the Teacher of all men. In calling Jesus *the* Teacher, there is the idea of His Lordship and deity. Note that He claims deity Himself: "You call me Teacher and Lord: and rightly so, for that is what I am" (Jn.13:13). His being *the Teacher* is tied closely with His being *the Lord*. In fact, logic alone would tell us that *the Lord* would be *the greatest Teacher* among all men.

> "Therefore let all Israel be assured of this: God has made this Jesus, whom you crucified, both Lord and Christ." (Acts 2:36)
>
> God exalted him to his own right hand as Prince and Savior that he might give repentance and forgiveness of sins to Israel. (Acts 5:31)
>
> That if you confess with your mouth, "Jesus is Lord," and believe in your heart that God raised him from the dead, you will be saved. (Rom 10:9)
>
> God, who has called you into fellowship with his Son Jesus Christ our Lord, is faithful. (1 Cor 1:9)
>
> Yet for us there is but one God, the Father, from whom all things came and for whom we live; and there is but one Lord, Jesus Christ, through whom all things came and through whom we live. (1 Cor 8:6)
>
> Therefore I tell you that no one who is speaking by the Spirit of God says, "Jesus be cursed," and no one can say, "Jesus is Lord," except by the Holy Spirit. (1 Cor 12:3)

2 (11:29-30) **Jesus Christ, Response to**: the second need is to make the right response to Christ—the response of arising quickly and running to Him.

1. The message of Christ was enough to stir Mary. It is enough to stir action within the heart of any person who honestly seeks the answer to the riddle and trials of life and death.

2. When Mary heard, she responded quickly. The idea is that she jumped up quickly and ran to meet Jesus. Hope and expectation were stirred in her heart. Note that the message had come to her in a very quiet manner: secretly, in a whisper, without anyone else knowing it (v.28).

Thought 1. No matter how quietly the message is proclaimed, man is to respond by arising quickly and running to meet Jesus.

3. Mary acted on her own and made her own decision.
⇒ She did not consult with friends and neighbors, not even with those who were closest to her. She got up and went to Jesus, leaving both friends and neighbors behind.
⇒ She did not consult with religionists. Religion was important to her. The local religious leaders were even present, visiting and comforting her in her sorrow and sharing the comfort that their religion offered. But it helped her so little. When she heard the message that the Lord *was calling*

for her, she went to Him, saying nothing to the religionists.
⇒ She did not consider appearance or decorum. Think about the situation. The house was full of friends and neighbors. Who was going to greet them, receive their sympathies, express appreciation, and handle their presence? None of that mattered to Mary, not now. The Lord was calling for her. She must respond and go to Him immediately.
⇒ She did not consider the distance. Jesus had not yet entered town, so Mary had to walk a considerable distance to reach Him. She had to make the decision to break away from those back in the house despite what they might think and feel. She had to march forward and travel to Him in order to respond to His call.

> "So I say to you: Ask and it will be given to you; seek and you will find; knock and the door will be opened to you. For everyone who asks receives; he who seeks finds; and to him who knocks, the door will be opened. (Luke 11:9-10)
>
> For he says, "In the time of my favor I heard you, and in the day of salvation I helped you." I tell you, now is the time of God's favor, now is the day of salvation. (2 Cor 6:2)
>
> This day I call heaven and earth as witnesses against you that I have set before you life and death, blessings and curses. Now choose life, so that you and your children may live (Deu 30:19)

3 (11:31) **Ministering**: the third need is for people, friends and neighbors, to reach out to help each other. This is a touching picture. When the neighbors and friends saw Mary leave quickly, they thought she was going to the tomb to mourn over Lazarus. They were with her for one reason: to "comfort" her. Naturally, they followed her, thinking she needed help in bearing up under her loss. Note what happened.

1. They, too, were brought face to face with Jesus. Because they were set on comforting Mary, they were to share in Mary's experience with Christ.

2. They, too, were given the opportunity to trust Christ. In fact, many did believe, "put their faith in Him" (v.45).

Thought 1. The friends and neighbors set a clear example of helping others. The world needs more and more neighbors such as these. Note the result of sincere help. It does not go unnoticed by Christ. Many are brought to Christ when they help those who already know Christ.

> In everything I did, I showed you that by this kind of hard work we must help the weak, remembering the words the Lord Jesus himself said: 'It is more blessed to give than to receive.'" (Acts 20:35)
>
> We who are strong ought to bear with the failings of the weak and not to please ourselves. (Rom 15:1)
>
> Carry each other's burdens, and in this way you will fulfill the law of Christ. (Gal 6:2)
>
> Remember those in prison as if you

were their fellow prisoners, and those who are mistreated as if you yourselves were suffering. (Heb 13:3)

Religion that God our Father accepts as pure and faultless is this: to look after orphans and widows in their distress and to keep oneself from being polluted by the world. (James 1:27)

4 (11:32) **Confession**: the fourth need is the confession of faith, even if the faith is limited and weak. As soon as Mary saw Jesus, she fell at His feet in homage and worship and made a confession of faith in Him.

1. She called Him, "Lord" (see DEEPER STUDY # 1—Jn.11:28; DEEPER STUDY # 1—Ph.2:11).

2. She expresses, however, the same complaining, limited faith that Martha did (see note—Jn.11:21-22 for discussion).

Thought 1. The need of man is to make a genuine confession of faith. Even if one's belief and confession are weak, they will grow as one walks with Jesus day by day.

"Whoever acknowledges me before men, I will also acknowledge him before my Father in heaven. (Mat 10:32)

That if you confess with your mouth, "Jesus is Lord," and believe in your heart that God raised him from the dead, you will be saved. For it is with your heart that you believe and are justified, and it is with your mouth that you confess and are saved. (Rom 10:9-10)

And every tongue confess that Jesus Christ is Lord, to the glory of God the Father. (Phil 2:11)

If anyone acknowledges that Jesus is the Son of God, God lives in him and he in God. (1 John 4:15)

5 (11:33-36) **Jesus Christ, Compassion**: the fifth need is the understanding, feelings, and compassion of Jesus. Note three things.

1. Jesus "was deeply moved [enebrimesato] in spirit." The word "moved" is often interpreted to mean stern reaction, displeasure, or anger (because of its use in other places). Some interpreters feel that Jesus was angry with the friends and neighbors because of their loud wailing and moaning, feeling that they were being hypocritical and insincere in their sorrow. This interpretation is difficult to see.

⇒ Mary was certainly sincere in her sorrow, and Jesus was definitely touched by her need.

⇒ The Jewish friends and neighbors (which were "many," v.19) were sincere in "comforting" her (v.31), and many were open to trusting the Lord (v.45). Jesus was certainly touched by those as well.

In light of the whole scene, it seems best to see Jesus gripped with intense emotion. He was deeply moved...
• by Mary, who was so broken in sorrow.
• by Martha, who was gripped by pain and hurt.
• by those who were really feeling the death of Lazarus and the sorrow of the family.
• by the terrible tragedy of death and the pain it causes.

• by the terrible price He was soon to pay conquering death. (This was certainly glimpsed by Jesus in such a scene as He was now experiencing.)

Jesus is *deeply moved in spirit*: He is moved in understanding and feeling and compassion for all who are hurting and suffering. The word "troubled" (etaraxen heauton) means agitated, moved deeply, disturbed within. Jesus was actually feeling the misery and pain of all. His spirit was disturbed and agitated, deeply moved by the whole scene of sorrow and death.

2. Jesus asked where the dead (person) was. Note that Jesus knew where the grave was, but He asked where it was for two reasons.

⇒ If He had gone straight to the tomb, there was the possibility of some charging Him and Lazarus with being in collusion and tricking the people.

⇒ He needed to distract the people from their deep wailing and arouse their expectation for something unusual about to happen.

Note also that Jesus demonstrated His concern over the dead. He wishes to know where every dead person is, both those who are *spiritually dead* and those who are *physically dead*. He wants to point man's attention to the fact that all men lie in the grave. All must look to Him if they wish to escape death (see DEEPER STUDY # 1—Heb.9:27. Cp. Jn.3:16; 5:24.)

3. "Jesus wept" in love. Why? He wept over death, over man's pain, sorrow, suffering, and fate. Man was never made for sin and death; man was made for righteousness and life. Sin and death...
• deceive and lie
• hurt and maim
• separate and alienate
• misuse and defeat
• destroy and corrupt
• condemn and doom eternally

Who shall separate us from the love of Christ? Shall trouble or hardship or persecution or famine or nakedness or danger or sword? (Rom 8:35)

For we do not have a high priest who is unable to sympathize with our weaknesses, but we have one who has been tempted in every way, just as we are—yet was without sin. (Heb 4:15)

He remembered that they were but flesh, a passing breeze that does not return. (Psa 78:39)

As a father has compassion on his children, so the LORD has compassion on those who fear him; (Psa 103:13)

But from everlasting to everlasting the Lord's love is with those who fear him, and his righteousness with their children's children— (Psa 103:17)

In all their distress he too was distressed, and the angel of his presence saved them. In his love and mercy he redeemed them; he lifted them up and carried them all the days of old. (Isa 63:9)

6 (11:37) **Man, Misunderstanding—Trials—Evil, Problem of**: the misunderstanding of man. The people asked the same question that is so often asked by men of every generation. How could Jesus love so much and let this happen? The problem, of course, is not Jesus. People just do not understand...

- that the nature of the world is decay and corruption, trial and trouble, suffering and pain, death and hell—all because of selfishness and sin.
- that trials and sickness can be an opportunity for God to do a great work (see note—Jn.11:4).

That you may be sons of your Father in heaven. He causes his sun to rise on the evil and the good, and sends rain on the righteous and the unrighteous. (Mat 5:45)

So will it be with the resurrection of the dead. The body that is sown is perishable, it is raised imperishable; it is sown in dis-honor, it is raised in glory; it is sown in weakness, it is raised in power; it is sown a natural body, it is raised a spiritual body. If there is a natural body, there is also a spiritual body. (1 Cor 15:42-44)

I declare to you, brothers, that flesh and blood cannot inherit the kingdom of God, nor does the perishable inherit the imperishable. (1 Cor 15:50)

Through these he has given us his very great and precious promises, so that through them you may participate in the divine nature and escape the corruption in the world caused by evil desires. (2 Pet 1:4)

	D. Jesus and Lazarus: Power Over Death, 11:38-46	42 I knew that you always hear me, but I said this for the benefit of the people standing here, that they may believe that you sent me."	c. Offered thanksgiving d. Expressed perfect confidence e. Bore testimony
1 Jesus confronted the dead a. He was deeply moved	38 Jesus, once more deeply moved, came to the tomb. It was a cave with a stone laid across the entrance.	43 When he had said this, Jesus called in a loud voice, "Lazarus, come out!"	**4 The great shout of power over death** a. Was by Christ alone b. Was personal: By name
b. He was confronted with a believer's objection	39 "Take away the stone," he said. "But, Lord," said Martha, the sister of the dead man, "by this time there is a bad odor, for he has been there four days."	44 The dead man came out, his hands and feet wrapped with strips of linen, and a cloth around his face. Jesus said to them, "Take off the grave clothes and let him go."	c. The result 1) The dead arose 2) The resurrected received Jesus' personal attention*DS2*
2 The great promise of unlimited, resting faith*DS1*	40 Then Jesus said, "Did I not tell you that if you believed, you would see the glory of God?"	45 Therefore many of the Jews who had come to visit Mary, and had seen what Jesus did, put their faith in him.	**5 Conclusion: The reaction to Jesus' great power** a. Some believed, put their faith in Him
3 The great prayer of purpose a. Addressed God as "Father" b. Made a request	41 So they took away the stone. Then Jesus looked up and said, "Father, I thank you that you have heard me.	46 But some of them went to the Pharisees and told them what Jesus had done.	b. Some caused trouble

DIVISION XI

THE REVELATION OF JESUS, THE RESURRECTION AND THE LIFE, 11:1-12:11

D. Jesus and Lazarus: Power Over Death, 11:38-46

(11:38-46) **Introduction**: Jesus Christ confronted death and demonstrated His great power over death. In confronting and conquering the tomb of Lazarus, He demonstrated that the believer's hope is not in vain. The believer will be raised from the dead, resurrected by the great shout of the Lord's power.

1. Jesus confronted the dead (v.38-39).
2. The great promise of unlimited, resting faith (v.40).
3. The great prayer of purpose (v.41-42).
4. The great shout of power over death (v.43-44).
5. Conclusion: the reaction to Jesus' great power (v.45-46).

1 (11:38-39) **Jesus Christ, Compassion—Comfort**: Jesus confronted the dead. Note two striking points.

1. Jesus was deeply moved within Himself. He stood face to face with the grave. Again...

- He saw the pain of Mary and Martha and their dear friends.
- He sensed the terrible dread and bondage that death held over His dear friend Lazarus and over the whole human race.
- He was keenly conscious of His own terrible death that lay only a few days away.

He felt the emotions of both compassion and anger, sympathy and indignation. He was moved from deep within, sensing an intense love for all who suffer and a holy anger and displeasure against death (see note—Jn.11:33-36).

2. Jesus was confronted with an objection *from a believer*. Note two things.

a. An unbeliever might question if Lazarus were truly dead. Note the emphasis upon the fact that Lazarus *was* truly dead.

⇒ Lazarus was in a real tomb, a tomb of the wealthy. Martha's wealth was indicated by her having owned a house large enough to lodge Jesus and His disciples. If by any chance Lazarus had only been mistaken for dead before, he was certainly dead now. It had been four days since he had been placed in an enclosed tomb. Four days without food or water in such circumstances would kill any weak and critically ill person.

⇒ There was Martha's shock at Jesus' request. The body would have started to decompose after four days.

b. It was a believer who objected to Jesus' confronting the situation. There was distrust and uneasiness in Martha's objection. She was not sure that Jesus' action was wise nor for the best. She was uneasy about what Jesus was doing and asking. She did not want the situation disturbed. She was satisfied with things as they were, with Lazarus laid to rest as he was. What she wanted was to be comforted, not disturbed.

Thought 1. Many believers want things left alone, being happy with things as they are. They want only enough of Christ to give them comfort and security and ease. They want little if anything to do with His demands and confrontation with the sin and death of the world (see DEEPER STUDY # 1—Lk.9:23).

> **And he did not do many miracles there because of their lack of faith. (Mat 13:58)**
>
> **Even after Jesus had done all these miraculous signs in their presence, they still would not believe in him. (John 12:37)**
>
> **Granted. But they were broken off because of unbelief, and you stand by faith. Do not be arrogant, but be afraid. (Rom 11:20)**
>
> **See to it, brothers, that none of you has a sinful, unbelieving heart that turns away from the living God. But encourage one**

215

another daily, as long as it is called Today, so that none of you may be hardened by sin's deceitfulness. We have come to share in Christ if we hold firmly till the end the confidence we had at first. (Heb 3:12-14)

Let us, therefore, make every effort to enter that rest, so that no one will fall by following their example of disobedience. (Heb 4:11)

Though you already know all this, I want to remind you that the Lord delivered his people out of Egypt, but later destroyed those who did not believe. (Jude 1:5)

2 (11:40) **Trust—Faith**: the great promise of unlimited, resting faith. Jesus challenged Martha to take an enormous leap of faith. He wanted her to conquer her complaining and to set aside her objections (see note—Jn.11:21-22). He wanted her to trust Him, to quit questioning what He did. He wanted her to trust...

- His judgment and will
- His knowledge and understanding
- His Word and instructions

Very simply, He wanted her to *rest* in Him, to place an unlimited, resting faith in Him. (See DEEPER STUDY # 1—Jn.11:40 for discussion.)

Note what the promise was to Martha (and to all): if she would believe and simply rest in Him, she would "see the glory of God." By glory, Jesus meant His mercy and power, love and care on this earth. However, the promise applies to the next world as well. The person who will step back and let God act as He wills—the person who truly rests in God—will see the glory of God in the next world.

DEEPER STUDY # 1
(11:40) **Faith, Unlimited; Resting**: there is a rest for the believer. It is called *the believer's rest* or *God's rest*. The believer enters *God's rest* by what may be called a *resting faith* or an *unlimited faith*. An unlimited, resting faith is the summit, the highest level or stage of faith. It is the level of faith God desires for every believer. He longs for every child of His to enter the rest of God. A resting (unlimited) faith is a faith that rests in at least four things.

1. A resting faith is a rest of *deliverance and salvation*. It is to rest in God's Word, to know beyond all question...

- that one is truly saved and delivered from sin and shame, death and hell.
- that one is freed from the guilt and nagging of conscience.
- that one has open access into God's presence through prayer.

To whom he said, "This is the resting place, let the weary rest"; and, "This is the place of repose"— but they would not listen. (Isa 28:12)

This is what the Sovereign LORD, the Holy One of Israel, says: "In repentance and rest is your salvation, in quietness and trust is your strength, but you would have none of it. (Isa 30:15)

"Come to me, all you who are weary and burdened, and I will give you rest. (Mat 11:28)

Therefore, since we have been justified through faith, we have peace with God through our Lord Jesus Christ, (Rom 5:1)

Now we who have believed enter that rest, just as God has said, "So I declared on oath in my anger, 'They shall never enter my rest.'" And yet his work has been finished since the creation of the world. (Heb 4:3)

2. A resting faith is a rest of *service and ministry*. It is not inactivity, not a life that does nothing for God and the world. It is a rest that comes from committing one's life to the call and purpose of Jesus Christ, a rest that is...

- filled with purpose, meaning, and significance.
- committed to sharing Christ with a world lost, full of desperate needs.
- surrendered to God's call for personal involvement and service.
- filled with God's Spirit and equipped with His gifts for service.
- pleased with God's call and gifts, with one's lot in life and place of service.
- complete, fulfilled, satisfied, and unashamed in one's life.

Take my yoke upon you and learn from me, for I am gentle and humble in heart, and you will find rest for your souls. (Mat 11:29)

All this is from God, who reconciled us to himself through Christ and gave us the ministry of reconciliation: that God was reconciling the world to himself in Christ, not counting men's sins against them. And he has committed to us the message of reconciliation. We are therefore Christ's ambassadors, as though God were making his appeal through us. We implore you on Christ's behalf: Be reconciled to God. (2 Cor 5:18-20)

Let us, therefore, make every effort to enter that rest, so that no one will fall by following their example of disobedience. (Heb 4:11)

"Submit to God and be at peace with him; in this way prosperity will come to you. (Job 22:21)

3. A resting faith is a rest of *assurance and confidence* in the future. It is a rest of peace about the future. It is...

- the knowledge that all the enslavements and bondages of this life have been conquered in Christ, even death.
- the knowledge and experience of God's daily care through all of life; the knowledge that God will take care no matter what may come or fall.
- the knowledge and very real presence of hope: the hope of eternal life, of heaven, of the *eternal and perfect rest* for the people of God.

Peace I leave with you; my peace I give you. I do not give to you as the world gives. Do not let your hearts be troubled and do not be afraid. (John 14:27)

"I have told you these things, so that in me you may have peace. In this world you will have trouble. But take heart! I have overcome the world." (John 16:33)

Then I heard a voice from heaven say, "Write: Blessed are the dead who die in the Lord from now on." "Yes," says the Spirit, "they will rest from their labor, for their deeds will follow them." (Rev 14:13)

On the day the LORD gives you relief from suffering and turmoil and cruel bondage, (Isa 14:3)

You will keep in perfect peace him whose mind is steadfast, because he trusts in you. (Isa 26:3)

4. A resting faith is a rest of *courage and knowledge*. It is a faith that does not question or complain. It is a faith that truly believes, trusts, and rests in God, that actually...

- takes God at His Word and does exactly what He says.
- knows that God's presence and blessing are upon one's life.
- puts everything into God's hands and launches out as He says.
- knows that what happens is under God's control.
- knows that all things, no matter how terrible, will be worked out for good to those who love God (Ro.8:28).
- experiences God's presence and care day by day.
- knows victory over all: being filled with all confidence, assurance, hope, and peace.

And we know that in all things God works for the good of those who love him, who have been called according to his purpose. (Rom 8:28)

Do not be anxious about anything, but in everything, by prayer and petition, with thanksgiving, present your requests to God. And the peace of God, which transcends all understanding, will guard your hearts and your minds in Christ Jesus. (Phil 4:6-7)

Be at rest once more, O my soul, for the LORD has been good to you. (Psa 116:7)

Great peace have they who love your law, and nothing can make them stumble. (Psa 119:165)

3 (11:41-42) **Prayer, Purpose of; Power of**: the great prayer of purpose. Note the wording of this point: *prayer of purpose*. Every prayer is to be a prayer of purpose. This is Jesus' point. He was praying for a specific purpose, and in so doing He demonstrated the purpose and the power of prayer. When a man truly prays with purpose, he receives the answer to his prayer and witnesses to the power of prayer. Note Jesus' prayer.

1. Jesus addressed God as "Father." Jesus had an intimate and continuous relationship with God: a Father-Son relationship. He knew God as His "Father," and God knew Jesus as His Son (see note—Jn.10:14-16; esp. cp. v.15).

Thought 1. Believers are hereby taught to call upon God as "Father" and to approach God as a child would: intimately and boldly, yet respectfully and reverently.

2. Jesus requested that His Father do something: "You have heard me." What Jesus asked was not stated, but the reader knows from the context that it has to do with...

- the power to conquer death.
- the strengthening of believers standing around and watching Him.
- the stirring of others to believe and trust Him.

3. Jesus offered thanksgiving to the Father, praising the Father for the glorious privilege of prayer and of being heard and having His prayers answered. This is a striking lesson for believers. God is to be praised for prayer, for the open access He allows into His presence and for the glorious fact that He hears and answers us (cp. Jn.16:23-24, 26-27).

4. Jesus expressed a perfect and confident knowledge in God: "You always hear me." There is no hesitancy, doubt, or questioning on Jesus' part. He knew perfectly that God heard His prayers—*always*.

5. Jesus bore testimony through the prayer. He prayed...

- to show the close personal relationship between Himself and God.
- to stir belief that He was the *Sent One* of God (see DEEPER STUDY # 3—Jn.3:34; 4:31-35).

Note that the above points could be stated as the fivefold purposes for prayer.

1. To honor and worship God as "Father."

For you did not receive a spirit that makes you a slave again to fear, but you received the Spirit of sonship. And by him we cry, "Abba, Father." The Spirit himself testifies with our spirit that we are God's children. (Rom 8:15-16)

But when the time had fully come, God sent his Son, born of a woman, born under law, to redeem those under law, that we might receive the full rights of sons. Because you are sons, God sent the Spirit of his Son into our hearts, the Spirit who calls out, "Abba, Father." (Gal 4:4-6)

2. To secure whatever is needed to live righteously and to minister.

If you believe, you will receive whatever you ask for in prayer." (Mat 21:22)

"So I say to you: Ask and it will be given to you; seek and you will find; knock and the door will be opened to you. (Luke 11:9)

You may ask me for anything in my name, and I will do it. (John 14:14)

If you remain in me and my words remain in you, ask whatever you wish, and it will be given you. (John 15:7)

3. To praise and thank God.

So that with one heart and mouth you may glorify the God and Father of our Lord Jesus Christ. (Rom 15:6)

You were bought at a price. Therefore honor God with your body. (1 Cor 6:20)

Ascribe to the LORD the glory due his name; worship the LORD in the splendor of his holiness. (Psa 29:2)

Glorify the LORD with me; let us exalt his name together. (Psa 34:3)

My mouth is filled with your praise, declaring your splendor all day long. (Psa 71:8)

Let them exalt him in the assembly of the people and praise him in the council of the elders. (Psa 107:32)

They will speak of the glorious splendor of your majesty, and I will meditate on your wonderful works. (Psa 145:5)

O LORD, you are my God; I will exalt you and praise your name, for in perfect faithfulness you have done marvelous things, things planned long ago. (Isa 25:1)

4. To prove and demonstrate one's confidence in God.

This is the confidence we have in approaching God: that if we ask anything according to his will, he hears us. And if we know that he hears us—whatever we ask—we know that we have what we asked of him. (1 John 5:14-15)

And receive from him anything we ask, because we obey his commands and do what pleases him. (1 John 3:22)

5. To bear testimony and proclaim that Jesus is the One sent by God.

For I have come down from heaven not to do my will but to do the will of him who sent me. (John 6:38)

Jesus said to them, "If God were your Father, you would love me, for I came from God and now am here. I have not come on my own; but he sent me. (John 8:42)

For I gave them the words you gave me and they accepted them. They knew with certainty that I came from you, and they believed that you sent me. (John 17:8)

Thought 1. Jesus always prayed with purpose; therefore, He always received the answer to His prayer and bore testimony to the power of prayer. So it is with every true believer. When we pray with purpose, God answers our prayer, and by so doing He proclaims...

- that Christ is the Son of the living God.
- that Christ is the One sent into the world to open the door (secure access) into God's presence.
- that Christ is the One who has the power over death.

4 (11:43-44) **Death, Deliverance from**: the great shout of power. Note three significant points. (Note also how the resurrection of Lazarus pictures the coming resurrection of the believer. Cp. 1 Cor.15:12-58.)

1. The power over death comes from Jesus alone. Few prophets have ever raised a dead person except Jesus. Jesus alone has the power to raise the dead. Note that He simply spoke three words, "Lazarus, come out"; but He shouted them out with a loud voice. Why?
   a. A shout matched the enormity of the miracle. It stressed the enormous power required to raise the dead.
   b. A shout stressed that the power within Jesus is the power of God Himself. With just a shout Jesus can...
   - call forth the enormous power of God.
   - call forth the greatest amount of power imaginable, the power to raise a person from the dead.

For as the Father has life in himself, so he has granted the Son to have life in himself. (John 5:26)

Since the children have flesh and blood, he too shared in their humanity so that by his death he might destroy him who holds the power of death—that is, the devil—and free those who all their lives were held in slavery by their fear of death. (Heb 2:14-15)

2. The shout of Jesus is personal. Jesus shouted the name of Lazarus. He did not just shout, "Come out"; He shouted "Lazarus, come out." Jesus knows every believer by name, and He is personally concerned over the death of everyone. The day is coming when He will shout "Come out," and only the ones personally known by Him will respond.

In my Father's house are many rooms; if it were not so, I would have told you. I am going there to prepare a place for you. And if I go and prepare a place for you, I will come back and take you to be with me that you also may be where I am. (John 14:2-3)

The watchman opens the gate for him, and the sheep listen to his voice. He calls his own sheep by name and leads them out. (John 10:3)

"I am the good shepherd; I know my sheep and my sheep know me— (John 10:14)

My sheep listen to my voice; I know them, and they follow me. (John 10:27)

3. The results of the shout of Jesus were twofold.
   a. The person who was dead came forth. The Son of God spoke and called him forth. There was no way he could remain in the grave, no power that could hold him there. He came forth...
   - immediately
   - obediently
   - just as he was
   - perfectly
   - visibly
   - unquestionably

   b. The person who was resurrected received the personal attention of Jesus. Note the attention and the thoughtfulness of Jesus: "Take off the grave clothes and let him go." The wonder of the miracle did not detract Him from continuing to minister and to help wherever He could. It was not enough to share in the wonder of the miracle. Service to God was, and always will be, the call of our Lord Jesus to every man, even in eternity.

"His master replied, 'Well done, good and faithful servant! You have been faithful with a few things; I will put you in charge of many things. Come and share your master's happiness!' (Mat 25:23)

Do you not know that we will judge angels? How much more the things of this life! (1 Cor 6:3)

There will be no more night. They will not need the light of a lamp or the light of the sun, for the Lord God will give them light. And they will reign for ever and ever. (Rev 22:5)

DEEPER STUDY # 2

(11:44) **Grave Clothes**: note there was a cloth wrapped around the face of Lazarus. This is important to note for two reasons.

1. Jesus had a cloth wrapped around His face when He was buried. It was folded either by Him or an angel and laid to the side after His resurrection. The folded cloth was the immediate thing that convinced John of the Lord's resurrection. (See note—Jn.20:7-10.)

2. The cloth showed that the grave clothes of Jesus' day included at least two pieces of clothing: a strip of linen wrapped around His body and a separate cloth or napkin wrapped around the face. The facial cloth is mentioned two times in the New Testament (Jn.11:44; 20:7. Cp. Lk.19:20; Acts 19:12 for two other uses of the same Greek word, soudarioi.)

5 (11:45-46) **Jesus Christ, Response to**: the reaction to Jesus' great power was divided. Some believed and put their faith in Him (see DEEPER STUDY # 2—Jn.2:24). Others were gripped with obstinate unbelief and caused trouble. They refused to accept Jesus as the Son of God despite the most powerful evidence. They ignored the evidence and evaded the issue of His demand for belief. Therefore, they lost their opportunity "to see the glory of God" (v.40).

> **Whoever believes in the Son has eternal life, but whoever rejects the Son will not see life, for God's wrath remains on him." (John 3:36)**

> **I told you that you would die in your sins; if you do not believe that I am the one I claim to be, you will indeed die in your sins." (John 8:24)**

	E. Jesus and the Religious Leaders: Unbelief & Opposition, 11:47-57	52 And not only for that nation but also for the scattered children of God, to bring them together and make them one.	2) He was predicting that Jesus was to die for the world
1 The Sanhedrin met to discuss Jesus[DS1] **2 The causes of unbelief & opposition** a. The fear of losing one's recognition, esteem, & following b. The fear of losing one's position, influence, & authority **3 The conclusion of unbelief & opposition** a. Suggested by the religious leader himself[DS2] b. The conclusion: To sacrifice Jesus for the people c. The mystery of the conclusion 1) He was predicting that Jesus was to die for the Jews	47 Then the chief priests and the Pharisees called a meeting of the Sanhedrin. "What are we accomplishing?" they asked. "Here is this man performing many miraculous signs. 48 If we let him go on like this, everyone will believe in him, and then the Romans will come and take away both our place and our nation." 49 Then one of them, named Caiaphas, who was high priest that year, spoke up, "You know nothing at all! 50 You do not realize that it is better for you that one man die for the people than that the whole nation perish." 51 He did not say this on his own, but as high priest that year he prophesied that Jesus would die for the Jewish nation,	53 So from that day on they plotted to take his life. 54 Therefore Jesus no longer moved about publicly among the Jews. Instead he withdrew to a region near the desert, to a village called Ephraim, where he stayed with his disciples. 55 When it was almost time for the Jewish Passover, many went up from the country to Jerusalem for their ceremonial cleansing before the Passover. 56 They kept looking for Jesus, and as they stood in the temple area they asked one another, "What do you think? Isn't he coming to the Feast at all?" 57 But the chief priests and Pharisees had given orders that if anyone found out where Jesus was, he should report it so that they might arrest him.	d. The decision was made: Reject Jesus—do away with Him **4 The response of Jesus to unbelief & opposition** a. He withdrew from the rejecters b. He concentrated on His disciples **5 The providence of God in moving events despite unbelief & opposition** a. God controlled the time: The Passover b. God stirred the people's interest: Caused them to seek for Jesus c. God controlled man's devilish plots: Kept the people from helping & contributing to the evil

DIVISION XI

THE REVELATION OF JESUS, THE RESURRECTION AND THE LIFE, 11:1-12:11

E. Jesus and the Religious Leaders: Unbelief and Opposition, 11:47-57

(11:47-57) **Introduction**: this passage gives an excellent lesson on unbelief and opposition to Jesus Christ, a lesson that needs to be studied by every man.
1. The Sandedrin's meeting to discuss Jesus (v.47).
2. The causes of unbelief and opposition (v.47-48).
3. The conclusion of unbelief and opposition (v.49-53).
4. The response of Jesus to unbelief and opposition (v.54).
5. The providence of God in moving events despite unbelief and opposition (v.55-57).

1 (11:47) **Jesus Christ, Response to—Religionists**: the Sanhedrin met to discuss Jesus and to decide what to do about Him. This was an official meeting of the nation's leaders, including religious leaders. (See DEEPER STUDY # 1, Sanhedrin—Jn.11:47.) These were the very ones who should have been leading the people to God and giving moral and spiritual direction to the nation. Yet, here they were determining what to do about Jesus. The scene was pathetic and ironic.
1. There was Jesus, the Son of God, standing right before them, having come to reveal God to all men everywhere.
2. There were the "many miraculous signs" which Jesus had done to prove that He was truly the Son of God (v.47).
3. There were the leaders, the very ones...
- who should have been rejoicing and receiving Him.
- who recognized and acknowledged His "many miraculous signs" and His great teaching—so

great that "everyone" was about to follow Him (v.48).
- who were taking the lead in rejecting and opposing Him.

Thought 1. The scene is repeated every time a person deliberately rejects and opposes Christ. A person who hears and sees the works of Christ should...
- rejoice and receive Him.
- recognize and acknowledge His work.
- not reject and oppose Him and His salvation.

DEEPER STUDY # 1
(11:47) **Sanhedrin**: the ruling body, both the governing council and supreme court of the Jews. It had seventy-one members and was presided over by the High Priest. However, it took a quorum of only twenty-three members to pass the laws of the nation. Its membership was made up of Pharisees, Sadducees, Teachers of the law (Scribes or lawyers), and elders who were lay leaders from among the people. The legal power of the Sanhedrin to pass the death sentence was restricted about twenty years before the trial of Jesus. However, they did retain the right of excommunication (cp. Jn.9:22). To secure Jesus' death, they were forced by law to appeal to the Romans for the death sentence.

2 (11:47-48) **Unbelief, Cause of—Fear—Selfishness—Worldliness**: the cause of unbelief and opposition. The basic reason for unbelief and opposition is *selfish fear*. Self-

220

centered fear, the fear of losing something, causes man to reject and oppose others. Three things in particular caused the leaders to fear Jesus.

1. There was the fear of losing their esteem, recognition, and following. If the leaders lost the "people," they would have lost the same as any man who loses his circle of attention (friends, fellow-workers, neighbors, whomever):

- acceptance
- recognition
- loyalty
- following
- prestige
- esteem
- image
- friends

2. There was the fear of losing their place, position, influence, and authority. If they lost their place, they would have again lost what every man loses, his...

- job
- profession
- livelihood
- security
- comfort
- authority
- power
- wealth

3. There was the fear of losing their nation. (See DEEPER STUDY # 1, Religionists—Mt.12:10 for discussion.)

Thought 1. It is a man's selfishness that causes him to cling both to himself and to his possessions. Man wants...

- to control all he is and has.
- to do his own thing as he wills and desires.
- to have no interference in his life and desires, or as little as possible.

But the worries of this life, the deceitfulness of wealth and the desires for other things come in and choke the word, making it unfruitful. (Mark 4:19)

Then he said to them, "Watch out! Be on your guard against all kinds of greed; a man's life does not consist in the abundance of his possessions." (Luke 12:15)

People who want to get rich fall into temptation and a trap and into many foolish and harmful desires that plunge men into ruin and destruction. For the love of money is a root of all kinds of evil. Some people, eager for money, have wandered from the faith and pierced themselves with many griefs. (1 Tim 6:9-10)

But mark this: There will be terrible times in the last days. People will be lovers of themselves, lovers of money, boastful, proud, abusive, disobedient to their parents, ungrateful, unholy, (2 Tim 3:1-2)

If anyone has material possessions and sees his brother in need but has no pity on him, how can the love of God be in him? (1 John 3:17)

Israel was a spreading vine; he brought forth fruit for himself. As his fruit increased, he built more altars; as his land prospered, he adorned his sacred stones. (Hosea 10:1)

"From the least to the greatest, all are greedy for gain; prophets and priests alike, all practice deceit. (Jer 6:13)

And when you were eating and drinking, were you not just feasting for yourselves? (Zec 7:6)

When Jesus comes along demanding that a man change by denying himself and giving all he is and has to meet the desperate needs of a lost and starving world—man rejects and opposes Jesus. Man is unwilling to deny himself, unwilling to live a life that is totally sacrificial (see DEEPER STUDY # 1—Lk.9:23. See notes—Mt.19:21-22; 19:23 for more discussion, in particular dealing with possessions.)

Then he said to them all: "If anyone would come after me, he must deny himself and take up his cross daily and follow me. For whoever wants to save his life will lose it, but whoever loses his life for me will save it. What good is it for a man to gain the whole world, and yet lose or forfeit his very self? (Luke 9:23-25)

Sell your possessions and give to the poor. Provide purses for yourselves that will not wear out, a treasure in heaven that will not be exhausted, where no thief comes near and no moth destroys. For where your treasure is, there your heart will be also. (Luke 12:33-34)

3 (11:49-53) **Unbelief—Jesus Christ, Death—Rejection:** the conclusion of unbelief and opposition. Note four points.

1. The decision to oppose Jesus was made by the High Priest himself, Caiaphas, the highest religious leader in the nation. The very person who should have been leading the others to Jesus was suggesting that everyone reject and oppose Him (see DEEPER STUDY # 2—Jn.11:49 for more discussion).

Thought 1. How tragic it is...

- that religious positions sometimes become political
- that men reject Christ for the things of this world
- that men exchange eternity for a few short years

Israel's watchmen are blind, they all lack knowledge; they are all mute dogs, they cannot bark; they lie around and dream, they love to sleep. They are dogs with mighty appetites; they never have enough. They are shepherds who lack understanding; they all turn to their own way, each seeks his own gain. (Isa 56:10-11)

"Son of man, prophesy against the shepherds of Israel; prophesy and say to them: 'This is what the Sovereign LORD says: Woe to the shepherds of Israel who only take care of themselves! Should not shepherds take care of the flock? You eat the curds, clothe yourselves with the wool and slaughter the choice animals, but you do not take care of the flock. (Ezek 34:2-3)

But there were also false prophets among the people, just as there will be false teachers among you. They will secretly introduce destructive heresies, even denying the sovereign Lord who bought them— bringing swift destruction on themselves. (2 Pet 2:1)

Many deceivers, who do not acknowledge Jesus Christ as coming in the flesh, have gone out into the world. Any such person is the deceiver and the antichrist. (2 John 1:7)

2. The conclusion suggested by the High Priest was that Jesus should be sacrificed for the people. The people were following Jesus in such numbers that the leaders feared two things.

⇒ The Romans might conclude that Jesus was arousing the people to riot. The Romans would, therefore, move in and disperse the people, taking away even what little liberty they had as a conquered nation.

⇒ The Romans might blame them, the present leadership, and remove them from power.

The thought proposed was that it was better for Jesus to die than for the people to perish. Jesus should be sacrificed and killed in order to save the people.

3. The mystery of the conclusion was astounding. Note that the High Priest was being used as a spokesman by God: "He did not say this on his own." He was predicting the death of Jesus Christ. He proclaimed that Jesus should die *for* the people and be sacrificed in order to save the people. Note two facts.

a. The idea of *substitution* was the suggestion: that "Jesus would die *for* the Jewish nation" (v.51).

"I am the good shepherd. The good shepherd lays down his life for the sheep. (John 10:11)

Greater love has no one than this, that he lay down his life for his friends. (John 15:13)

You see, at just the right time, when we were still powerless, Christ died for the ungodly. (Rom 5:6)

For what I received I passed on to you as of first importance : that Christ died for our sins according to the Scriptures, (1 Cor 15:3)

And he died for all, that those who live should no longer live for themselves but for him who died for them and was raised again. (2 Cor 5:15)

Who gave himself for our sins to rescue us from the present evil age, according to the will of our God and Father, (Gal 1:4)

And live a life of love, just as Christ loved us and gave himself up for us as a fragrant offering and sacrifice to God. (Eph 5:2)

Who gave himself for us to redeem us from all wickedness and to purify for himself a people that are his very own, eager to do what is good. (Titus 2:14)

This is how we know what love is: Jesus Christ laid down his life for us. And we ought to lay down our lives for our brothers. (1 John 3:16)

b. Jesus Christ was to die to save both Jew and Gentile, all "the scattered children of God" (cp. Acts 2:5; 10:2; 17:4).

In him we have redemption through his blood, the forgiveness of sins, in accordance with the riches of God's grace to be put into effect when the times will have reached their fulfillment—to bring all things in heaven and on earth together under one head, even Christ. (Eph 1:7, 10)

But now in Christ Jesus you who once were far away have been brought near through the blood of Christ. For he himself is our peace, who has made the two one and has destroyed the barrier, the dividing wall of hostility, (Eph 2:13-14)

4. The decision was made and Jesus was rejected. They wanted nothing to do with Him. Note the words "from that day on." The idea is that from that very moment on, they were set on doing away with Him.

Thought 1. How tragic the decision...
• to reject Christ
• to have nothing to do with Him
• to push Him off to the side, out of the way, as unimportant
• to do away with Him
• to oppose Him

He came to that which was his own, but his own did not receive him. (John 1:11)

There is a judge for the one who rejects me and does not accept my words; that very word which I spoke will condemn him at the last day. (John 12:48)

Whoever believes in the Son has eternal life, but whoever rejects the Son will not see life, for God's wrath remains on him." (John 3:36)

I told you that you would die in your sins; if you do not believe that I am the one I claim to be, you will indeed die in your sins." (John 8:24)

DEEPER STUDY # 2

(11:49) **High Priest—Caiaphas**: the office of High Priest began with Aaron and his sons (Ex.28:1). The office was hereditary and was for life; however, when the Romans conquered Palestine, they made the office political. They chose their own man, a man who would cooperate with the Roman government. Finding such a man was often difficult. For example, between 37 B.C. and 67 A.D. there were at least twenty-eight High Priests. These men were greatly respected and highly honored throughout life. Even when they were removed from power by the Romans, they were still consulted by other Jewish leaders. The ex-High Priest, Annas, is a prime example. He still wielded unusual power (cp. Jn.18:13; Acts 4:6). He and the other men who had served as High Priests or else held the top positions of leadership were also called "chief priests."

The term of office for a High Priest was determined solely by the Romans. The Romans let a High Priest reign as long as he pleased them. The reign of each of the twenty-eight priests averaged only about three years, except for Caiaphas. Caiaphas was High Priest for eighteen years (18 A.D. to 36 A.D.). Apparently he was a master of intrigue and compromise. This throws great light on his fearing an uproar (Mt.26:5) and wishing to wait until the feast was over to arrest Jesus. There was the danger that the people might rally to the support of Jesus if they saw Him arrested. So many believed Him to be a great prophet that a serious uprising was a real possibility. Caiaphas knew the Romans would hold him responsible and remove him from office. He would lose everything he had. The shrewdness of the man is seen in the strategy he laid. They were to arrest Jesus quietly after the masses had left the feast.

4 (11:54) **Unbelief**: the response of Jesus to unbelief and opposition.
1. Jesus withdrew from those who rejected Him. He...
   - went away
   - pleaded no more with them
   - no longer moved about publicly among the Jews
   - gave them up to their own desires (see note—Ro.1:24-32)

The Lord's Spirit does not always strive or contend with men (see note—Jn.7:33-34). Jesus even told His disciples to turn their backs upon rejecters (cp. Mt.10:14; Mk.6:11; Lk.9:5).

> Then the LORD said, "My Spirit will not contend with man forever, for he is mortal ; his days will be a hundred and twenty years." (Gen 6:3)
> Blessed is the man who always fears the LORD, but he who hardens his heart falls into trouble. (Prov 28:14)
> A man who remains stiff-necked after many rebukes will suddenly be destroyed—without remedy. (Prov 29:1)
> Or do you show contempt for the riches of his kindness, tolerance and patience, not realizing that God's kindness leads you toward repentance? But because of your stubbornness and your unrepentant heart, you are storing up wrath against yourself for the day of God's wrath, when his righteous judgment will be revealed. (Rom 2:4-5)
> See to it, brothers, that none of you has a sinful, unbelieving heart that turns away from the living God. But encourage one another daily, as long as it is called Today, so that none of you may be hardened by sin's deceitfulness. We have come to share in Christ if we hold firmly till the end the confidence we had at first. (Heb 3:12-14)

2. Jesus concentrated on and drew closer to His disciples.

> For where two or three come together in my name, there am I with them." (Mat 18:20)
> As they talked and discussed these things with each other, Jesus himself came up and walked along with them; (Luke 24:15)
> They asked each other, "Were not our hearts burning within us while he talked with us on the road and opened the Scriptures to us?" (Luke 24:32)
> When they saw the courage of Peter and John and realized that they were unschooled, ordinary men, they were astonished and they took note that these men had been with Jesus. (Acts 4:13)

> God, who has called you into fellowship with his Son Jesus Christ our Lord, is faithful. (1 Cor 1:9)
> We proclaim to you what we have seen and heard, so that you also may have fellowship with us. And our fellowship is with the Father and with his Son, Jesus Christ. (1 John 1:3)
> Here I am! I stand at the door and knock. If anyone hears my voice and opens the door, I will come in and eat with him, and he with me. (Rev 3:20)

5 (11:55-57) **God, Providence**: the providence of God in moving events despite unbelief and opposition.
1. God controlled the time. It was the Passover season, a significant fact. The Feast symbolized the removal of sins. Note that while the people were celebrating the Passover Feast, the leaders were seeking to commit the most heinous crime: the murder of the very Son of God Himself. (See Deeper Study # 1—Lk.22:7.)
2. God stirred the people's interest. Pilgrims flooded into Jerusalem by the hundreds of thousands during the Passover season. The picture is that of people buzzing about wondering and asking if Jesus would come to the Feast. Note that the people actually "kept looking for" Jesus (v.56). God took even the rejection of evil men and worked it out to cause others to seek His Son.

Thought 1. God takes the rejection and opposition of men and uses it to stir interest in His Son. Throughout history some of the greatest movements and revivals of Christianity have been the result of persecution and attempts to stamp out the name of Christ. A man's rejection is often used by God to stir salvation in others.

> All men will hate you because of me, but he who stands firm to the end will be saved. (Mat 10:22)
> And we know that in all things God works for the good of those who love him, who have been called according to his purpose. (Rom 8:28)
> For we who are alive are always being given over to death for Jesus' sake, so that his life may be revealed in our mortal body. (2 Cor 4:11)
> For our light and momentary troubles are achieving for us an eternal glory that far outweighs them all. (2 Cor 4:17)
> But he said to me, "My grace is sufficient for you, for my power is made perfect in weakness." Therefore I will boast all the more gladly about my weaknesses, so that Christ's power may rest on me. (2 Cor 12:9)
> Now I want you to know, brothers, that what has happened to me has really served to advance the gospel. As a result, it has become clear throughout the whole palace guard and to everyone else that I am in chains for Christ. Because of my chains, most of the brothers in the Lord have been

encouraged to speak the word of God more courageously and fearlessly. (Phil 1:12-14)

For it has been granted to you on behalf of Christ not only to believe on him, but also to suffer for him, (Phil 1:29)

Brothers, as an example of patience in the face of suffering, take the prophets who spoke in the name of the Lord. (James 5:10)

3. God controlled man's devilish plots. He kept the people from cooperating with the leaders and betraying His Son. No man can move against the name of Christ nor against the followers of Christ until God is ready. Although the world is corrupt and evil, God controls the times of His Son and His Son's followers. Not a hair of their head can be touched until God is ready to use the trial and persecution for good.

Do not be afraid of those who kill the body but cannot kill the soul. Rather, be afraid of the One who can destroy both soul and body in hell. Are not two sparrows sold for a penny ? Yet not one of them will fall to the ground apart from the will of your Father. And even the very hairs of your head are all numbered. So don't be afraid; you are worth more than many sparrows. "Whoever acknowledges me before men, I will also acknowledge him before my Father in heaven. But whoever disowns me before men, I will disown him before my Father in heaven. (Mat 10:28-33)

	CHAPTER 12	sold and the money given to the poor? It was worth a year's wages."	a. He followed Jesus, but he criticized believers
	F. Jesus & Reactions to His Revelation, 12:1-11 (Mt.26:6-13; Mk.14:3-9)	6 He did not say this because he cared about the poor but because he was a thief; as keeper of the money bag, he	b. He expressed concern for the ministry, but he had an ulterior motive
1 Jesus dined in a home in Bethany a. The place where Lazarus was raised b. Six days before the Passover c. Martha served d. Lazarus was present	**S**ix days before the Passover, Jesus arrived at Bethany, where Lazarus lived, whom Jesus had raised from the dead. 2 Here a dinner was given in Jesus' honor. Martha served, while Lazarus was among those reclining at the table with him.	used to help himself to what was put into it. 7 "Leave her alone," Jesus replied. "It was intended that she should save this perfume for the day of my burial. 8 You will always have the poor among you, but you will not always have me."	c. He worked for Jesus, but he did not love Jesus
2 The supreme believer a. The repentant love b. A sacrificial & costly love c. A believing love: The Christ, the Anointed	3 Then Mary took about a pint of pure nard, an expensive perfume; she poured it on Jesus' feet and wiped his feet with her hair. And the house was filled with the fragrance of the perfume.	9 Meanwhile a large crowd of Jews found out that Jesus was there and came, not only because of him but also to see Lazarus, whom he had raised from the dead.	**4 The half-sincere seekers** a. Came to see Jesus b. Came to see the spectacular c. Came for socializing
3 The hypocritical, unbelieving disciple	4 But one of his disciples, Judas Iscariot, who was later to betray him, objected, 5 "Why wasn't this perfume	10 So the chief priests made plans to kill Lazarus as well, 11 For on account of him many of the Jews were going over to Jesus and putting their faith in him.	**5 The fearful, self-seeking religionists** a. They plotted to destroy Jesus b. They feared personal loss

DIVISION XI

THE REVELATION OF JESUS, THE RESURRECTION AND THE LIFE, 11:1-12:11

F. Jesus and Reactions to His Revelation, 12:1-11

(12:1-11) **Introduction**: Jesus Christ had just revealed Himself to be the Resurrection and the Life. John gives four reactions to that revelation.

1. Jesus dined in a home in Bethany (v.1-2).
2. The supreme believer (v.3).
3. The hypocritical, unbelieving disciple (v.4-8).
4. The half-sincere seekers (v.9).
5. The fearful, self-seeking religionists (v.10-11).

1 (12:1-2) **Jesus Christ, Ministry—Fellowship**: Jesus dined in a home in Bethany. Both Matthew and Mark record this anointing of Jesus. Note that John says it actually took place six days before the Passover. Matthew arranged his gospel by subjects, so he placed it in the midst of discussing Jesus' death. Note that Matthew and Mark say that Jesus was in the house of Simon the Leper, and John says that Martha served (Mt.26:6; Mk.14:3). Apparently Simon the Leper was the husband of Martha (see DEEPER STUDY # 1— Mt.26:6 for more discussion).

Note that the stress of the Scripture is twofold.

⇒ Jesus was with Lazarus, the young man who was raised from the dead.
⇒ Jesus was facing the Passover. He was only six days away from becoming the Passover Lamb who takes away the sin of the world.

2 (12:3) **Believer**: there was the reaction of the supreme believer. By supreme is meant the supreme quality of life, *love*. The supreme believer is a person like Mary who *loves* the Lord with her whole being, sacrificing all that she is and has. Mary gave herself out of a heart of pure love for the Lord.

1. The supreme believer expresses a repentant love. Mary had criticized and accused Jesus of neglecting her family when He had not come sooner to the aid of her brother Lazarus (cp. Jn.11:32). Here she is seen repenting of her sin. (See outline notes 2, 4—Jn.21:15-17; DEEPER STUDY # 1—Acts 17:29-30.)

> **Blessed are those who mourn, for they will be comforted. (Mat 5:4)**
>
> **Repent of this wickedness and pray to the Lord. Perhaps he will forgive you for having such a thought in your heart. (Acts 8:22)**
>
> **If my people, who are called by my name, will humble themselves and pray and seek my face and turn from their wicked ways, then will I hear from heaven and will forgive their sin and will heal their land. (2 Chr 7:14)**
>
> **Blessed are they who keep his statutes and seek him with all their heart. (Psa 119:2)**
>
> **Let the wicked forsake his way and the evil man his thoughts. Let him turn to the LORD, and he will have mercy on him, and to our God, for he will freely pardon. (Isa 55:7)**
>
> **'Even now,' declares the LORD, 'return to me with all your heart, with fasting and weeping and mourning.' (Joel 2:12)**

2. The supreme believer expresses a sacrificial and costly love. Note the word "expensive." The ointment

(murou) was a perfume or oil. The perfume was worth about a year's wage. Just imagine the scene! A bottle of perfume worth a whole year's wage being poured upon the feet of Jesus. Think of the costly sacrifice being made. Perfume was the most precious thing to Eastern women. Mary was taking her most precious possession and giving it to her Lord.

3. The supreme believer expresses a believing love. She honored her Lord as the Christ, the *Anointed One*. Mary's anointing was an act of love and faith in the Lord Jesus. Very simply put, Mary anointed Jesus to show how deeply she loved Him and believed Him to be the true Messiah, *the anointed One of God* (see notes—Mt.26:6-13; cp. Mt.1:18). He was her Savior, Lord, and King. He had done so much for her and her family that she wanted Him to know how much she appreciated and loved Him.

Something else needs to be noted as well. Mary sensed something within Jesus: a foreboding, a preoccupation of mind, a heaviness of heart, a weight of tremendous pressure. Her heart reached out to Him and wanted to encourage and help Him. Being a young woman in the presence of so many men, she was not allowed to vocally express herself that much. Such a privilege was not allowed women of that day, so she did all that she could. She acted by arising and going after the most precious gift she could think of—a very expensive bottle of perfume. She gave it to Jesus in such a way that He would know that at least one person truly loved Him and believed Him to be the Messiah. Her hope was that such worship and love would boost His spirit. (See note—Mt.26:6-13 for a descriptive picture of what Mary sensed.)

Thought 1. What do we do to show our love and faith to Christ? Imagine how difficult it was for Mary to do what she did in the presence of so many men. She set aside pride and embarrassment in order to demonstrate her love and faith in Jesus. How far are we willing to go in order to show our love and faith?

Thought 2. Note how Mary demonstrated her love and faith.

1) Mary gave the most precious possession she had to the Lord.

> **But store up for yourselves treasures in heaven, where moth and rust do not destroy, and where thieves do not break in and steal. (Mat 6:20)**
> **Sell your possessions and give to the poor. Provide purses for yourselves that will not wear out, a treasure in heaven that will not be exhausted, where no thief comes near and no moth destroys. (Luke 12:33)**
> **In the same way, any of you who does not give up everything he has cannot be my disciple. (Luke 14:33)**
> **What is more, I consider everything a loss compared to the surpassing greatness of knowing Christ Jesus my Lord, for whose sake I have lost all things. I consider them rubbish, that I may gain Christ (Phil 3:8)**
> **In this way they will lay up treasure for themselves as a firm foundation for the coming age, so that they may take hold of the life that is truly life. (1 Tim 6:19)**

2) Mary publicly demonstrated her love and faith in Christ.

> **Love the LORD your God with all your heart and with all your soul and with all your strength. (Deu 6:5)**
> **Love the LORD, all his saints! The LORD preserves the faithful, but the proud he pays back in full. (Psa 31:23)**
> **"Whoever acknowledges me before men, I will also acknowledge him before my Father in heaven. (Mat 10:32)**
> **And anyone who does not take his cross and follow me is not worthy of me. Whoever finds his life will lose it, and whoever loses his life for my sake will find it. (Mat 10:38-39)**
> **Grace to all who love our Lord Jesus Christ with an undying love. (Eph 6:24)**
> **Because I hear about your faith in the Lord Jesus and your love for all the saints. (Phile 1:5)**
> **Though you have not seen him, you love him; and even though you do not see him now, you believe in him and are filled with an inexpressible and glorious joy, (1 Pet 1:8)**
> **Keep yourselves in God's love as you wait for the mercy of our Lord Jesus Christ to bring you to eternal life. (Jude 1:21)**

3 (12:4-8) **Hypocrite—Betrayer—Apostate:** there was the hypocritical, unbelieving disciple. This was Judas. A study of Judas' character in these verses reveals what it is that often causes a disciple to become hypocritical and unbelieving.

1. Judas followed Jesus, but he criticized other believers. He was a professing believer, but when he disagreed with others, he criticized them. He criticized even...
- those who had great devotion and love for the Lord
- those who repented to the point of making great sacrificial gifts

Mark pointed out that Judas was especially strong in his criticism. He says that Judas was indignant, growling, rebuking, scolding (see note—Mk.14:4-5).

Thought 1. Criticism is a sign of hypocrisy, for all stand in need of repentance and devotion, and all need to give more and more. When we come so short ourselves, how can we possibly criticize what we consider to be the mistakes of others?

> **"Why do you look at the speck of sawdust in your brother's eye and pay no attention to the plank in your own eye? (Mat 7:3; cp.v.1-5)**
> **Who are you to judge someone else's servant? To his own master he stands or falls. And he will stand, for the Lord is able to make him stand. (Rom 14:4)**
> **Therefore let us stop passing judgment on one another. Instead, make up your mind not to put any stumbling block or obstacle in your brother's way. (Rom 14:13)**
> **Therefore judge nothing before the appointed time; wait till the Lord comes. He will bring to light what is hidden in darkness and will expose the motives of men's hearts. At that time each will receive his**

praise from God. (1 Cor 4:5)

You want something but don't get it. You kill and covet, but you cannot have what you want. You quarrel and fight. You do not have, because you do not ask God. (James 4:2)

2. Judas expressed concern for the ministry, but he had an ulterior motive. Again, imagine the scene. A bottle of perfume worth a whole year's wage was being poured over the feet of Jesus. Common sense would seem to say, "Sell it. Use the money for the poor, the hungry and the homeless." This is just what Judas did say. He questioned the act, what he considered a waste. After all, if Mary wished to anoint Jesus, she could have used a less expensive perfume.

However, Judas' motive was impure. The words "keeper of the money bag" mean that Judas was the treasurer of the small band of Jesus' disciples (v.6). However, he was a thief; he had been swindling some of the money. A gift of a year's worth of wages would have allowed him the chance to steal quite a sum. Deep within he was angry at the lost chance to enrich himself; he was angry at Mary, but even more he was angry at Jesus for allowing such wastefulness.

Thought 1. How many express concern for the ministry but do so in order to gain from it? Their concern is shown by joining a church and making some contribution, or by showing interest in some venture or need. However, their motive is...

- to be socially acceptable
- to be recognized and honored
- to please some family member
- to gain some credit with God
- to get a tax write-off from the government

"Woe to you, teachers of the law and Pharisees, you hypocrites! You clean the outside of the cup and dish, but inside they are full of greed and self-indulgence. (Mat 23:25)

In the same way, on the outside you appear to people as righteous but on the inside you are full of hypocrisy and wickedness. (Mat 23:28)

For the love of money is a root of all kinds of evil. Some people, eager for money, have wandered from the faith and pierced themselves with many griefs. (1 Tim 6:10)

Your gold and silver are corroded. Their corrosion will testify against you and eat your flesh like fire. You have hoarded wealth in the last days. (James 5:3)

Do not love the world or anything in the world. If anyone loves the world, the love of the Father is not in him. For everything in the world—the cravings of sinful man, the lust of his eyes and the boasting of what he has and does—comes not from the Father but from the world. (1 John 2:15-16)

A fortune made by a lying tongue is a fleeting vapor and a deadly snare. (Prov 21:6)

Whoever loves money never has money enough; whoever loves wealth is never satisfied with his income. This too is meaningless. (Eccl 5:10)

Has this house, which bears my Name, become a den of robbers to you? But I have been watching! declares the LORD. (Jer 7:11)

3. Judas worked for Jesus, but he did not love Jesus. Jesus was strong with Judas: "Leave her alone." The reason for this sharp rebuke was that Judas did not understand, and the reason he did not understand was because he did not love Jesus. Note: just because someone works for Jesus does not mean that he loves Jesus. Note two significant points.

a. Jesus said that Mary's anointing pointed toward His burial, that is, His death. This is exactly what Jesus said: "She did it for my burial." Some commentators think that Mary knew what she was doing, that she understood what Jesus had been saying when He predicted His death. They feel that Mary grasped the fact when others did not. But this is unlikely. The atmosphere surrounding the whole scene was that the Kingdom of God was about to be set up and Israel was about to be freed from Roman domination and set up as the center of God's rule upon earth. However, whether she knew what she was doing or not, Jesus took her act and applied it to His death. He said that her love and faith, the anointing of His body, pointed toward His death. In simple terms, Mary's love and faith and her gift and anointing *were a witness of anticipation*. She was witnessing to the Lord's death by looking ahead to it.

Today the believer's love and faith and his gift and anointing are *a witness of fact*. The believer is to witness to the Lord's death by looking back to it. It is a fact: He did die for the sins of the world.

For what I received I passed on to you as of first importance : that Christ died for our sins according to the Scriptures, that he was buried, that he was raised on the third day according to the Scriptures, (1 Cor 15:3-4)

My dear children, I write this to you so that you will not sin. But if anybody does sin, we have one who speaks to the Father in our defense—Jesus Christ, the Righteous One. He is the atoning sacrifice for our sins, and not only for ours but also for the sins of the whole world. (1 John 2:1-2)

He said to them, "Go into all the world and preach the good news to all creation. (Mark 16:15)

b. Judas lost the opportune time; Mary grasped it. Mary *loved* Jesus and Judas did not. Jesus made a significant point that is often missed: opportunities come and go, and once they are gone, they are gone forever. Mary demonstrated the difference. The poor would always be present for believers to help, but the privilege of ministering to Jesus would not always be available. Therefore, if His disciples were to minister to Him, they had to grasp the opportunity while He was with them.

Thought 1. What a lesson for mankind! The presence of Jesus—a sense of His presence and of His Word—is not always pounding away at the mind and heart of man. Man must grasp the opportunity to show his love and sacrifice for Christ when it presents itself. The opportunity will pass. In fact life, which is an opportunity and a privilege within itself, will pass and pass soon. The servant of the Lord must love and act while it is still day. The night will come when no man can work.

> **And do this, understanding the present time. The hour has come for you to wake up from your slumber, because our salvation is nearer now than when we first believed. The night is nearly over; the day is almost here. So let us put aside the deeds of darkness and put on the armor of light. (Rom 13:11-12)**
> **Making the most of every opportunity, because the days are evil. (Eph 5:16)**
> **Be wise in the way you act toward outsiders; make the most of every opportunity. (Col 4:5)**

4 (12:9) **Jesus Christ, Seeking—Sincerity—Hypocrisy:** there are the half-sincere seekers. A person who is only half-sincere has three clear traits. These are clearly seen in the crowd thronging the dinner which Jesus attended.

1. The crowd came to see Jesus. Jesus was the central figure; He was the Person being proclaimed by some to be the Messiah and being talked about so much by all. Everyone was wondering and questioning and had some desire to see Him and to find out for themselves. At the least, they wanted to find out what was going on and causing so much conversation across the country.

2. The crowd came to see the spectacular, that is, to see Lazarus, the man rumored to have been raised from the dead. They were anxious to see one who had experienced such a phenomenal event and to see if a resurrected man was any different. (See note—Jn.2:23; Lk.4:9-12.)

3. The crowd came to a social occasion, a festive atmosphere. Wherever Jesus was, there was action and things were happening. It was where everyone was gathering. This is clearly seen when man keeps in mind the teeming thousands flooding into the area for the Passover and the atmosphere that surrounds such a convention-like crowd. There was bound to be a worldly, carnival atmosphere despite the religious observances. Half-sincere seekers always add to the carnality of a worldly atmosphere, no matter the focus of an event.

> **Thought 1.** How many sitting in the presence of the Lord and His church are only half-sincere? How many come to church just because it is the thing to do, the place to be, the place where everyone else is? How many seek the spectacular signs only?

> **Then some of the Pharisees and teachers of the law said to him, "Teacher, we want to see a miraculous sign from you." (Mat 12:38)**
> **In the same way, on the outside you appear to people as righteous but on the inside you are full of hypocrisy and wickedness. (Mat 23:28)**
> **He replied, "Isaiah was right when he prophesied about you hypocrites; as it is written: "'These people honor me with their lips, but their hearts are far from me. (Mark 7:6)**

> **Hypocrites! You know how to interpret the appearance of the earth and the sky. How is it that you don't know how to interpret this present time? "Why don't you judge for yourselves what is right? (Luke 12:56-57)**
> **"Unless you people see miraculous signs and wonders," Jesus told him, "you will never believe." (John 4:48)**
> **So they asked him, "What miraculous sign then will you give that we may see it and believe you? What will you do? (John 6:30)**
> **Jews demand miraculous signs and Greeks look for wisdom, but we preach Christ crucified: a stumbling block to Jews and foolishness to Gentiles, (1 Cor 1:22-23)**
> **They claim to know God, but by their actions they deny him. They are detestable, disobedient and unfit for doing anything good. (Titus 1:16)**

5 (12:10-11) **Jesus Christ, Response to—Religionists:** there are the fearful, self-seeking religionists. (See outline above and notes—Jn.11:47-48; 11:49-53 for discussion of this point.) Note two points.

1. The leaders now sought to destroy Lazarus also. They probably thought Lazarus and Jesus were collaborating to deceive the people. Note also the impact the miracle was having. So many people were affected by the miracle that the authorities felt they had to destroy Lazarus in order to prove that Jesus could not raise the dead.

> **As it is, you are determined to kill me, a man who has told you the truth that I heard from God. Abraham did not do such things. You are doing the things your own father does." "We are not illegitimate children," they protested. "The only Father we have is God himself." You belong to your father, the devil, and you want to carry out your father's desire. He was a murderer from the beginning, not holding to the truth, for there is no truth in him. When he lies, he speaks his native language, for he is a liar and the father of lies. Yet because I tell the truth, you do not believe me! (John 8:40-41, 44-45)**

2. "Many" of the Jews, those who had formerly opposed Jesus, were now beginning to believe in Jesus. This is significant. It shows that the impact upon the nation was enormous, affecting even the religious leaders.

> **That everyone who believes in him may have eternal life. (John 3:15)**
> **"I tell you the truth, whoever hears my word and believes him who sent me has eternal life and will not be condemned; he has crossed over from death to life. (John 5:24)**
> **Jesus said to her, "I am the resurrection and the life. He who believes in me will live, even though he dies; (John 11:25)**
> **I have come into the world as a light, so that no one who believes in me should stay in darkness. (John 12:46)**

	XII. THE REVELATION OF JESUS, THE GLORIFIED SON OF MAN, 12:12-50	Daughter of Zion; see, your king is coming, seated on a donkey's colt."	A young colt b. The prophecy: The King comes in peace
	A. Jesus Proclaimed as King: The Triumphal Entry, 12:12-19 (Mt.21:1-11; Mk.11: 1-11; Lk.19:28-40)	16 At first his disciples did not understand all this. Only after Jesus was glorified did they realize that these things had been written about him and that they had done these things to him.	**4 The disciples' reaction** a. The bewilderment: Did not grasp the significance b. Their understanding: Grasped after His resurrection
1 Crowds gathered for the Passover (11:55f)	12 The next day the great crowd that had come for the Feast heard that Jesus was on his way to Jerusalem.	17 Now the crowd that was with him when he called Lazarus from the tomb and raised him from the dead continued to spread the word.	**5 The people's reaction** a. The eye-witnesses to Lazarus' resurrection: They buzzed about
2 The false concept of Christ a. Held by "many" people b. Went out to meet Him c. Took palm branches^DS1 d. Cried Hosanna (save) e. Thought He was a political Messiah	13 They took palm branches and went out to meet him, shouting, "Hosanna!" "Blessed is he who comes in the name of the Lord!" "Blessed is the King of Israel!"	18 Many people, because they had heard that he had given this miraculous sign, went out to meet him.	b. The hearers of the miracle: They sought Him, sought for the sensational
3 The true concept of Christ a. The symbol of peace:	14 Jesus found a young donkey and sat upon it, as it is written, 15 "Do not be afraid, O	19 So the Pharisees said to one another, "See, this is getting us nowhere. Look how the whole world has gone after him!"	**6 The religionists' reaction: Despair & rage**

DIVISION XII

THE REVELATION OF JESUS, THE GLORIFIED SON OF MAN, 12:12-50

A. Jesus Proclaimed as King: The Triumphal Entry, 12:12-19

(12:12-19) **Introduction**: this is the revelation of Jesus as the coming King. It involves both a false concept and the true concept of His coming. It is a picture of how men have seen Jesus down through the centuries.

1. The crowds gathered for the Passover (v.12).
2. The false concept of Christ (v.12-13).
3. The true concept of Christ (v.14-15).
4. The disciples' reaction (v.16).
5. The people's reaction (v.17-18).
6. The religionists' reaction: despair and rage (v.19).

1 (12:12) **Passover**: the crowds gathered for the Passover. Note the words "the great crowd": a great number of pilgrims were swarming into Jerusalem for the Passover. Josephus, the notable Jewish historian of that day, estimated that over two million people were involved in the great Passover Feast. It is known that 256,500 lambs were slain at one Passover and that each lamb represented at least ten worshippers. This, of course, puts the number of people well over two million (William Barclay. *The Gospel of John*, Vol.2, p.134f). Teeming thousands from all over the world were flooding into the city to observe the Passover. The mass of people and the necessary housing and food arrangements to handle such a mass of people can hardly be imagined. An excitable vacation and carnival-like atmosphere was bound to prevail over such a mob of people. Such was the scene as the people gathered for the great Feast.

2 (12:12-13) **Messiah, Misconceptions of—Deliverer—Utopia**: the false concept of Christ. The false concept sees Jesus as an earthly Savior, One who is to bring utopia to earth for the people of God. The false concept sees Jesus...

- as the *Conqueror*: as the One who is to straighten out the problems of this earth by overcoming all the enemies of mankind including evil men, hunger, disease, and poverty.
- as the *Provider*: as the One who is to feed, house, and give health, plenty, and success to man; as the One who is to be sought to bless man in all the good things of life.
- as the *Indulgent, Passive Lord*: as the One who accepts man no matter what man does, just so he is somewhat religious; as the One who allows man to live as he desires, doing his own thing despite the sin and injustices and immorality of his behavior.

The false concept fails to see two things in understanding the Messiahship of Jesus.

⇒ It fails to see the demand of Christ: the demand to serve by reaching out to a world that is lost and reeling in needs so desperate that the thoughtful mind staggers at the reality of it. It fails to see the demand of Christ for self-denial, a denial that demands the giving of all one is and has to meet the needs of the world.

⇒ It fails to see the spiritual concern of Christ: His concern with bringing peace between man and God—with saving man and being mindful that man lives *with God* and not separate from God; His concern with man understanding that God is holy, righteous, and pure; His concern with man's living a life of faith and diligently seeking God; His concern with man's living a holy, righteous, and pure life in order to be acceptable to God.

Note several significant facts in this point—facts that clearly show the false concept of Christ held by so many, both in Jesus' day and down through the centuries.

1. "Many people" were involved in welcoming Jesus in the Triumphal scene. Many held the false concept of Jesus as the earthly King and Savior of man, as the One who was to be sought in order to secure all the good things of this earth.

2. The people "went out" to welcome Jesus. Note that they were not just sitting and waiting for Him to come. When they "heard" about Him, they actually went out to meet Him.

3. The people took palm branches to wave and lay before Him (see DEEPER STUDY # 1—Jn.12:13).

4. The people cried "Hosanna," which means *save now*, or *save, we pray*. Man desires to be free, but note: man desires to be free on this earth so that he can move about and do as he pleases. He thinks little if any about being free from the bondages of this earth. He loves this earth and he wants all of it that he can get: houses, lands, clothes, food, sex, and recreation. Man thinks little about being held in bondage by such things; he thinks little about sin and death. He thinks little of being set free from the power of this earth and its possessions so that he can live eternally. He thinks little of spiritual freedom.

5. The people received Jesus as the political King and Messiah (see note—Jn.1:23).

Thought 1. How much like what happens today. The false concept of Christ that sees Him as the One who gives us *material blessings* is proclaimed, and people rush "out to meet Him." (See note—Eph.1:3.) What men fail to understand is that they must come to Jesus because they love Him, not because they can get something out of Him. They must come because of who He is, not because He blesses them with the possessions of this earth.

> With many other words he warned them; and he pleaded with them, "Save yourselves from this corrupt generation." (Acts 2:40)
>
> Therefore, I urge you, brothers, in view of God's mercy, to offer your bodies as living sacrifices, holy and pleasing to God—this is your spiritual act of worship. Do not conform any longer to the pattern of this world, but be transformed by the renewing of your mind. Then you will be able to test and approve what God's will is—his good, pleasing and perfect will. (Rom 12:1-2)
>
> Those who use the things of the world, as if not engrossed in them. For this world in its present form is passing away. (1 Cor 7:31)
>
> "Therefore come out from them and be separate, says the Lord. Touch no unclean thing, and I will receive you." "I will be a Father to you, and you will be my sons and daughters, says the Lord Almighty." (2 Cor 6:17-18)
>
> May I never boast except in the cross of our Lord Jesus Christ, through which the world has been crucified to me, and I to the world. (Gal 6:14)
>
> Have nothing to do with the fruitless deeds of darkness, but rather expose them. (Eph 5:11)

> In the name of the Lord Jesus Christ, we command you, brothers, to keep away from every brother who is idle and does not live according to the teaching you received from us. (2 Th 3:6)
>
> No one serving as a soldier gets involved in civilian affairs—he wants to please his commanding officer. (2 Tim 2:4)
>
> Do not love the world or anything in the world. If anyone loves the world, the love of the Father is not in him. For everything in the world—the cravings of sinful man, the lust of his eyes and the boasting of what he has and does—comes not from the Father but from the world. (1 John 2:15-16)

DEEPER STUDY # 1

(12:13) **Palm Branches**: these were a symbol of victory and triumph. They were waved triumphantly as a conqueror rode victoriously through the city streets. The point is this: the people were welcoming Jesus as the great Conqueror and mighty Deliverer. But Jesus had come in peace, not as the judge or conqueror of the Romans nor of anyone else—not right then and not right now. Presently He is the Savior of all men; later when He returns, He will come as King.

---

3 (12:14-15) **Messiah, True Concept—Jesus Christ, Purpose—Colt**: the true concept of Christ. This was symbolized clearly in the riding of the young colt or donkey. In ancient days the colt was a noble animal. It was used as a beast of service to carry the burdens of men, but more significantly, it was used by Kings and their emissaries. When they entered a city in peace, they rode a colt to symbolize their peaceful intentions (cp. the judges of Israel and the chieftains throughout the land, Judges 5:10; 10:4). This differed dramatically from a conquering King. When a King entered a city as a conqueror, he rode a stallion.

Jesus was dramatically demonstrating two things for the people: first, that He was unquestionably the promised King, the Savior of the people; and second, that He was not coming as the conquering King. His mission was not to come as a worldly potentate, in pomp and ceremony, not to be the leader of an army to kill, injure and maim; consequently, the people had to change their concept of the Messiah. The Messiah was coming as the Savior of Peace who had been sent to save all men. He was coming to show men that God is the God of love and reconciliation.

1. The colt was a symbol of peace. Jesus came to bring peace, as pointed out in the above discussion.

> Therefore, since we have been justified through faith, we have peace with God through our Lord Jesus Christ, (Rom 5:1)
>
> But now in Christ Jesus you who once were far away have been brought near through the blood of Christ. For he himself is our peace, who has made the two one and has destroyed the barrier, the dividing wall of hostility, (Eph 2:13-14)
>
> And through him to reconcile to himself all things, whether things on earth or things in heaven, by making peace through his blood, shed on the cross. (Col 1:20)

2. The colt symbolized service. It was a noble animal, an animal used in the service of men to carry their burdens.

Jesus came upon the colt symbolizing that He came to serve men and to bear their burdens for them.

> **Just as the Son of Man did not come to be served, but to serve, and to give his life as a ransom for many." (Mat 20:28)**

> **But made himself nothing, taking the very nature of a servant, being made in human likeness. And being found in appearance as a man, he humbled himself and became obedient to death— even death on a cross! (Phil 2:7-8)**

> **Since the children have flesh and blood, he too shared in their humanity so that by his death he might destroy him who holds the power of death—that is, the devil—and free those who all their lives were held in slavery by their fear of death. (Heb 2:14-15)**

> **For this reason he had to be made like his brothers in every way, in order that he might become a merciful and faithful high priest in service to God, and that he might make atonement for the sins of the people. Because he himself suffered when he was tempted, he is able to help those who are being tempted. (Heb 2:17-18)**

> **For we do not have a high priest who is unable to sympathize with our weaknesses, but we have one who has been tempted in every way, just as we are—yet was without sin. Let us then approach the throne of grace with confidence, so that we may receive mercy and find grace to help us in our time of need. (Heb 4:15-16)**

3. The colt symbolized sacredness. This particular colt had never been ridden before, and this fact had a sacred meaning (Mk.11:2). Animals and things used for religious purposes had to be animals and things that had never been used before (Num.19:2; Dt.21:3; 1 Sam.6:7). This detail points to the very sacredness of the event. It pictured for everyone that Jesus was deliberately taking every precaution to proclaim that *He was the sacred hope*, the promised Messiah of the people.

> **For I have come down from heaven not to do my will but to do the will of him who sent me. (John 6:38)**

> **So Jesus said, "When you have lifted up the Son of Man, then you will know that I am the one I claim to be and that I do nothing on my own but speak just what the Father has taught me. The one who sent me is with me; he has not left me alone, for I always do what pleases him." (John 8:28-29)**

> **Jesus said to her, "I am the resurrection and the life. He who believes in me will live, even though he dies; and whoever lives and believes in me will never die. Do you believe this?" "Yes, Lord," she told him, "I believe that you are the Christ, the Son of God, who was to come into the world." (John 11:25-27)**

4 (12:16) **Scripture, Understanding of—Study of**: the disciples' reaction is clearly stated. They simply…

- did not grasp the meaning and significance of what was happening.
- misunderstood Jesus' Messiahship and Kingship.
- thought that Jesus was to be a worldly King and earthly Messiah.

The disciples were as guilty as the people in misunderstanding Scripture. The truth of Scripture—its prediction of these things and how Jesus fulfilled them—was made clear after the resurrection of Jesus. The task of revealing the truth to the heart of man was to be the task of the Holy Spirit (Jn.14:26).

When the Holy Spirit came, He quickened the truth to the disciples' minds, and the disciples saw clearly how Jesus had fulfilled the Scripture in the Triumphal Entry.

Thought 1. Scripture is unfathomable; its depth cannot be measured. There is a world of truth herein, an eternity of insight. The Holy Spirit takes the believer and quickens his mind and heart to grasp the Scripture.

⇒ To the man who seeks after the Word, the Spirit unfolds the Word of God and reveals the glorious truths of God.

⇒ To the man who hungers after the Word, the Spirit fills his soul with the good things of God's Word.

⇒ To the man who thirsts after the Word, the Spirit pours the living waters of the Word into his being.

> **For the Holy Spirit will teach you at that time what you should say." (Luke 12:12)**

> **But the Counselor, the Holy Spirit, whom the Father will send in my name, will teach you all things and will remind you of everything I have said to you. (John 14:26)**

> **This is what we speak, not in words taught us by human wisdom but in words taught by the Spirit, expressing spiritual truths in spiritual words. (1 Cor 2:13)**

> **As for you, the anointing you received from him remains in you, and you do not need anyone to teach you. But as his anointing teaches you about all things and as that anointing is real, not counterfeit— just as it has taught you, remain in him. (1 John 2:27)**

Thought 2. Since Jesus has risen and been glorified, no man has an excuse for not understanding the mission of Jesus. Jesus came as the Prince of Peace and as the Savior of the world. He did not come to fulfill the lustful cravings and worldly ambitions of men. Men are to be saved by Him and to surrender their lives to Him as the Lord of glory who now sits at the right hand of God the Father.

> **And saying, "Repent, for the kingdom of heaven is near." (Mat 3:2)**

> **I tell you, no! But unless you repent, you too will all perish. (Luke 13:3)**

> **Peter replied, "Repent and be baptized, every one of you, in the name of Jesus Christ for the forgiveness of your sins. And you will receive the gift of the Holy Spirit. (Acts 2:38)**

Repent, then, and turn to God, so that your sins may be wiped out, that times of refreshing may come from the Lord, (Acts 3:19)

Repent of this wickedness and pray to the Lord. Perhaps he will forgive you for having such a thought in your heart. (Acts 8:22)

You were bought at a price. Therefore honor God with your body. (1 Cor 6:20)

Thought 3. Believers must depend upon the Holy Spirit to understand Scripture. Scripture *cannot be understood* apart from the Spirit of God. Believers must...

- be the Lord's in the truest sense.
- hunger and thirst after righteousness.
- come to the Word, the Bible.
- seek the Spirit for understanding.
- seek exactly what the Word says (not what men say).
- seek what the Word says to a man's own heart (application).
- be prayerful, open-minded, depending upon the Spirit for illumination (eliminating all preconceived notions).
- study, rightly dividing the Word, letting the Word interpret the Word.
- study, *seeking the approval of God*, not of men.

The man without the Spirit does not accept the things that come from the Spirit of God, for they are foolishness to him, and he cannot understand them, because they are spiritually discerned. (1 Cor 2:14; cp. v.9-15)

You diligently study the Scriptures because you think that by them you possess eternal life. These are the Scriptures that testify about me, (John 5:39)

Like newborn babies, crave pure spiritual milk, so that by it you may grow up in your salvation, now that you have tasted that the Lord is good. (1 Pet 2:2-3)

Do your best to present yourself to God as one approved, a workman who does not need to be ashamed and who correctly handles the word of truth. (2 Tim 2:15)

All Scripture is God-breathed and is useful for teaching, rebuking, correcting and training in righteousness, (2 Tim 3:16)

Let the word of Christ dwell in you richly as you teach and admonish one another with all wisdom, and as you sing psalms, hymns and spiritual songs with gratitude in your hearts to God. (Col 3:16)

Now the Bereans were of more noble character than the Thessalonians, for they received the message with great eagerness and examined the Scriptures every day to see if what Paul said was true. (Acts 17:11)

"Now I commit you to God and to the word of his grace, which can build you up and give you an inheritance among all those who are sanctified. (Acts 20:32)

5 (12:17-18) **Jesus Christ, Reaction to**: the people's reaction. Many of the people were sincere: they "put their faith in Jesus" (Jn.11:45). But many were as so many are in a crowd—simply sightseers, wanting to be where the people were and where the action was. They were after the excitement, the sensational, the spectacular (see DEEPER STUDY # 1—Jn.2:23; note—12:9 for more discussion and application).

Then some of the Pharisees and teachers of the law said to him, "Teacher, we want to see a miraculous sign from you." (Mat 12:38)

In the same way, on the outside you appear to people as righteous but on the inside you are full of hypocrisy and wickedness. (Mat 23:28)

He replied, "Isaiah was right when he prophesied about you hypocrites; as it is written: "'These people honor me with their lips, but their hearts are far from me. (Mark 7:6)

Hypocrites! You know how to interpret the appearance of the earth and the sky. How is it that you don't know how to interpret this present time? "Why don't you judge for yourselves what is right? (Luke 12:56-57)

"Unless you people see miraculous signs and wonders," Jesus told him, "you will never believe." (John 4:48)

So they asked him, "What miraculous sign then will you give that we may see it and believe you? What will you do? (John 6:30)

Jews demand miraculous signs and Greeks look for wisdom, but we preach Christ crucified: a stumbling block to Jews and foolishness to Gentiles, (1 Cor 1:22-23)

They claim to know God, but by their actions they deny him. They are detestable, disobedient and unfit for doing anything good. (Titus 1:16)

6 (12:19) **Jesus Christ, Reaction to**: the religionists' reaction was that of despair and rage. Standing there, they witnessed the whole scene of surging thousands thronging the roadway welcoming Jesus as the Messiah. They became so upset and full of despair that they began to accuse and blame each other for the failure of their plots against Jesus.

Whoever believes in the Son has eternal life, but whoever rejects the Son will not see life, for God's wrath remains on him." (John 3:36)

I told you that you would die in your sins; if you do not believe that I am the one I claim to be, you will indeed die in your sins." (John 8:24)

See to it, brothers, that none of you has a sinful, unbelieving heart that turns away from the living God. (Heb 3:12)

Note the exclamatory truth they proclaimed: "The whole world has gone after Him." John pictured a most dramatic scene: even the enemies of Jesus saw Jesus conquering the world. Practically every pilgrim in the city must have been caught up in the excitement. Teeming thousands upon thousands were lining the roadway between Bethany and Jerusalem crying for their Savior.

Thought 1. What a picture of how the world should be crying for the Lord's deliverance! Men by teeming thousands should be lining the roadways crying for His salvation.

God did this so that men would seek him and perhaps reach out for him and find him, though he is not far from each one of us. (Acts 17:27)

But if from there you seek the LORD your God, you will find him if you look for him with all your heart and with all your soul. (Deu 4:29)

Seek the LORD while he may be found; call on him while he is near. (Isa 55:6)

You will seek me and find me when you seek me with all your heart. (Jer 29:13)

This is what the LORD says to the house of Israel: "Seek me and live; (Amos 5:4)

	B. Jesus Approached as King: The Misunderstood Messiah, 12:20-36	Then a voice came from heaven, "I have glorified it, and will glorify it again."	c. His prayer d. God's audible approval e. The people's confusion
1 Some Greeks, representing the world, sought Jesus (cp.12:19) a. Jesus was accepted as king, 12:12f b. Some Greeks requested to see the king	20 Now there were some Greeks among those who went up to worship at the Feast. 21 They came to Philip, who was from Bethsaida in Galilee, with a request. "Sir," they said, "we would like to see Jesus." 22 Philip went to tell Andrew; Andrew and Philip in turn told Jesus.	29 The crowd that was there and heard it said it had thundered; others said an angel had spoken to him. 30 Jesus said, "This voice was for your benefit, not mine. 31 Now is the time for judgment on this world; now the prince of this world will be driven out.	f. God's purpose: To show His approval of Christ **4 Misunderstanding 3: The world** a. It has to be judged[DS2] b. It is ruled by an alien prince[DS3] c. It is conquered by the cross[DS4]
2 Misunderstanding 1: His glory a. His hour had come[DS1] 1) He had to die first 2) He could then bear fruit or produce many seeds b. Man's hour is come 1) Man must lose his life to bear eternal life 2) Man must serve & follow Jesus to be assured of Jesus' presence & God's honor **3 Misunderstanding 2: His cause** a. His troubled heart b. His great cause	23 Jesus replied, "The hour has come for the Son of Man to be glorified. 24 I tell you the truth, unless a kernel of wheat falls to the ground and dies, it remains only a single seed. But if it dies, it produces many seeds. 25 The man who loves his life will lose it, while the man who hates his life in this world will keep it for eternal life. 26 Whoever serves me must follow me; and where I am, my servant also will be. My Father will honor the one who serves me. 27 "Now my heart is troubled, and what shall I say? 'Father, save me from this hour'? No, it was for this very reason I came to this hour. 28 Father, glorify your name!"	32 But I, when I am lifted up from the earth, will draw all men to myself." 33 He said this to show the kind of death he was going to die. 34 The crowd spoke up, "We have heard from the Law that the Christ will remain forever, so how can you say, 'The Son of Man must be lifted up'? Who is this 'Son of Man'?" 35 Then Jesus told them, "You are going to have the light just a little while longer. Walk while you have the light, before darkness overtakes you. The man who walks in the dark does not know where he is going. 36 Put your trust in the light while you have it, so that you may become sons of light." When he had finished speaking, Jesus left and hid himself from them.	**5 Misunderstanding 4: The Messiah (the Light)** a. The people misunderstood the Messiah b. The claim: He is the Light (the Messiah)—the light is to be extinguished[DS5] c. The need 1) To walk in the light 2) To believe in the light

DIVISION XII

THE REVELATION OF JESUS, THE GLORIFIED SON OF MAN, 12:12-50

B. Jesus Approached as King: The Misunderstood Messiah, 12:20-36

(12:20-36) **Introduction**: man misunderstands the Messiah. There are four misunderstandings in particular.
1. Some Greeks, representing the world, sought Jesus (v.20-22).
2. Misunderstanding 1: His glory (v.23-26).
3. Misunderstanding 2: His cause (v.27-30).
4. Misunderstanding 3: the world (v.31-33).
5. Misunderstanding 4: the Messiah (the Light)—the light is to be extinguished (v.34-36).

(12:20-36) **Another Outline**: The Glory and Power of the Cross.
1. Some Greeks, representing the world, sought Jesus (v.20-22).
2. The cross is the glory of the Messiah (v.23).
3. The cross brings forth fruit or produces many seeds (v.24).
4. The cross demands man's death to self (v.25-26).
   a. Man must lose his life to bear eternal life.

   b. Man must serve and follow Jesus to be assured of Jesus' presence and God's honor.
5. The cross fulfills Jesus' cause (v.27).
6. The cross glorifies God's name (v.28-30).
7. The cross judges the world—the prince of the world (v.31).
8. The cross draws all men (v.32-33).
9. The cross reveals the true Messiah (v.34-36).

(12:20-36) **Another Outline**: there are really seven pictures here. (1) A kernel of wheat (v.24). (2) A life lost (v.25). (3) A servant (v.26). (4) A troubled heart (v. 27-30). (5) A prince driven out (v.31). (6) The cross (v.32-33). (7) A light extinguished (v.34-36).

1 (12:20-22) **Greeks...Would See Jesus**: some Greeks, representing the world, sought Jesus. The scene was as follows. Jesus had just been hailed as the coming King and Messiah by teeming thousands of people: "The whole

234

world has gone after Him" (Jn.12:19). Some Greek pilgrims who had come to attend the Passover Feast wished to see this Jesus who was being proclaimed King. In the author's mind, these Greeks represented the Gentile world, all the God-fearing people of the world who would see Jesus.

2 (12:23-26) **Jesus Christ, Glory of—Jesus Christ, Purpose**: the first misunderstanding is the Messiah's glory. The Greeks had just seen Jesus *glorified* as Messiah by teeming thousands. It was as if the world were going after Him. They wanted to be part of the movement, so they requested an interview with Him. What Jesus did was try to correct the misunderstood idea of the Messiah held by the world. He wanted to prepare both the Greeks and those standing around (the whole world) for His death. He wanted to teach that the way to glory is not through triumph and praise, not through domination and subjection. The way to glory is through death to self and through service to God and man. Jesus did two things.

1. Jesus said that His hour had come: the Son of Man was now to be glorified. His hour, of course, referred to His death (as the next verse clearly states and this whole passage shows. See note—Jn.2:3-5.)

Note that Jesus revealed His death by using the picture of a grain of wheat. As stated, Jesus said that He would now be glorified, but His glory was not to be the glory of an earthly potentate. His glory was to be the glory of the cross. It was to be by death that He was to gain the allegiance of men and be exalted as King.

⇒ God would exalt Him as King because He had done exactly what God wished: He died for the sins of the whole world. (See note—Jn.10:17-18 for important discussion of this fact.)

⇒ Men would become His subjects because He had died for them and given them an eternal inheritance with God the Father.

The picture of the wheat can be simply stated: before the glory—before fruit or seeds can be borne—death is a necessity. Jesus must die before He can be enthroned as King and bear the fruit of subjects and a kingdom. (See note—Jn.13:31-32 for more discussion.)

Thought 1. The glory of Christ is the glory of the cross.

1) It is the cross that stirs God to exalt His dear Son above every name that is named.

> For this very reason, Christ died and returned to life so that he might be the Lord of both the dead and the living. (Rom 14:9)

> And being found in appearance as a man, he humbled himself and became obedient to death— even death on a cross! Therefore God exalted him to the highest place and gave him the name that is above every name, that at the name of Jesus every knee should bow, in heaven and on earth and under the earth, and every tongue confess that Jesus Christ is Lord, to the glory of God the Father. (Phil 2:8-11)

> In whom we have redemption, the forgiveness of sins. And he is the head of the body, the church; he is the beginning and the firstborn from among the dead, so that in everything he might have the supremacy. (Col 1:14, 18)

> But about the Son he says, "Your throne, O God, will last for ever and ever, and righteousness will be the scepter of your kingdom. You have loved righteousness and hated wickedness; therefore God, your God, has set you above your companions by anointing you with the oil of joy." (Heb 1:8-9)

> But we see Jesus, who was made a little lower than the angels, now crowned with glory and honor because he suffered death, so that by the grace of God he might taste death for everyone. (Heb 2:9)

> He himself bore our sins in his body on the tree, so that we might die to sins and live for righteousness; by his wounds you have been healed. For you were like sheep going astray, but now you have returned to the Shepherd and Overseer of your souls. (1 Pet 2:24-25)

> For Christ died for sins once for all, the righteous for the unrighteous, to bring you to God. He was put to death in the body but made alive by the Spirit, who has gone into heaven and is at God's right hand—with angels, authorities and powers in submission to him. (1 Pet 3:18, 22)

> Therefore I will give him a portion among the great, and he will divide the spoils with the strong, because he poured out his life unto death, and was numbered with the transgressors. For he bore the sin of many, and made intercession for the transgressors. (Isa 53:12)

2) It is the cross that stirs men to offer themselves as living sacrifices to God's dear Son (in appreciation and love for saving them).

> The death he died, he died to sin once for all; but the life he lives, he lives to God. In the same way, count yourselves dead to sin but alive to God in Christ Jesus. (Rom 6:10-11)

> If we live, we live to the Lord; and if we die, we die to the Lord. So, whether we live or die, we belong to the Lord. For this very reason, Christ died and returned to life so that he might be the Lord of both the dead and the living. (Rom 14:8-9)

> For Christ's love compels us, because we are convinced that one died for all, and therefore all died. And he died for all, that those who live should no longer live for themselves but for him who died for them and was raised again. (2 Cor 5:14-15)

> You were bought at a price. Therefore honor God with your body. (1 Cor 6:20)

> I have been crucified with Christ and I no longer live, but Christ lives in me. The life I live in the body, I live by faith in the Son of God, who loved me and gave himself for me. (Gal 2:20)

> And live a life of love, just as Christ loved us and gave himself up for us as a fragrant offering and sacrifice to God. (Eph 5:2)

> Who gave himself for us to redeem us from all wickedness and to purify for him-

self a people that are his very own, eager to do what is good. (Titus 2:14)

This is how we know what love is: Jesus Christ laid down his life for us. And we ought to lay down our lives for our brothers. (1 John 3:16)

2. Jesus also said that man's hour had now come. Man must do the same as He did.
   a. Man must lose his life. If he does, he will gain eternal life. What did Jesus mean by this unusual statement? Very simply, the person who *abandons* this life and world, who *sacrifices and gives* all that he is and has for Christ, will save his life. But the person who *keeps* his life and what he has and *seeks* more and more of this life, will lose his life completely and eternally.

The person who "saves his life"...
- who seeks to avoid aging and death and denies Christ—will lose his life eternally.
- who seeks to make his life more and more comfortable and easy and secure (beyond the necessary) and neglects Christ—will lose his life eternally.
- who seeks to gain wealth and power and fame by compromising Christ—will lose his life eternally.
- who seeks the excitement and stimulation of this world and ignores Christ—will lose his life eternally.

As said above, the person who loses his life for Christ and sacrifices all he is and has for Christ saves his life and saves it eternally. The person who keeps his life and what he has for himself will lose his life and lose it eternally. The call of Christ is just what He says—a life of denial that takes up the cross and follows in His steps.

Your wrongdoings have kept these away; your sins have deprived you of good. (Jer 5:25)

What good is it for a man to gain the whole world, yet forfeit his soul? (Mark 8:36)

But the one who hears my words and does not put them into practice is like a man who built a house on the ground without a foundation. The moment the torrent struck that house, it collapsed and its destruction was complete." (Luke 6:49)

Then he said to them all: "If anyone would come after me, he must deny himself and take up his cross daily and follow me. (Luke 9:23)

For if you live according to the sinful nature, you will die; but if by the Spirit you put to death the misdeeds of the body, you will live, (Rom 8:13)

Those who belong to Christ Jesus have crucified the sinful nature with its passions and desires. (Gal 5:24)

   b. Man must serve and follow Jesus. The man who does is assured...
- of Jesus' presence: "Where I am, my servant also will be."
- of the Father's (God's) honor. The Father will honor any person who honors His Son—His only Son whom He loves with His whole Being.

Not so with you. Instead, whoever wants to become great among you must be your servant, and whoever wants to be first must be slave of all. (Mark 10:43-44)

Peter answered him, "We have left everything to follow you! What then will there be for us?" Jesus said to them, "I tell you the truth, at the renewal of all things, when the Son of Man sits on his glorious throne, you who have followed me will also sit on twelve thrones, judging the twelve tribes of Israel. And everyone who has left houses or brothers or sisters or father or mother or children or fields for my sake will receive a hundred times as much and will inherit eternal life. (Mat 19:27-29)

When Jesus spoke again to the people, he said, "I am the light of the world. Whoever follows me will never walk in darkness, but will have the light of life." (John 8:12)

Worship the LORD your God, and his blessing will be on your food and water. I will take away sickness from among you, (Exo 23:25)

He will call upon me, and I will answer him; I will be with him in trouble, I will deliver him and honor him. (Psa 91:15)

DEEPER STUDY # 1

(12:23-24) **Jesus Christ, Hour of**: the phrase "the hour" or "my hour" or "my time" is a constant symbol of Jesus' death. "The hour" or "the time" refers to all the events of the cross and all the trouble and sufferings surrounding the cross. Note two facts.

1. "The hour" is a set, fixed time in the purpose of God.
   ⇒ Jesus said, "The hour has come" (Jn.12:23-24, 27; 13:1; 17:1; Mt.26:18, 45; Mk.14:41).
   ⇒ He had said some time before, "My *time* has not yet come" (Jn.2:4; cp. 7:6, 8, 30; 8:20).

The hour of Jesus was inevitable: a definite period of time, a set of events, a number of experiences that He had to face and go through. As He said, He must die in order to bring forth fruit (v.24).

2. The hour was to have a definite beginning. There was a set time for the trouble to begin (v.27), a set time for Him to begin suffering for the sins of the world. There was a fixed hour when He was to begin suffering the pain and anguish, the agitation and disturbance, the pressure and weight, the strain and stress of having to be separated from God in behalf of man (see notes—Mt.20:18; 27:46-49).

---

3 (12:27-30) **God, Glory of—Jesus Christ, Purpose**: the second misunderstanding is the Messiah's cause or purpose. Note six points.

1. Jesus was experiencing a "troubled" heart. "Troubled" (tetaraktai) means agitated, pressured, heavy, weighed down, strained, stressed, disturbed.

2. The reason His heart was so troubled was that He was about to face the great cause for which He had come into the world. His hour was at hand, staring Him in the face; the terrible sufferings were now beginning (see DEEPER STUDY # 1, Hour—Jn.12:23-24). Note two things.

a. His supreme purpose was to face the hour God had set for Him: He was to die. He had come to die, and to die was the supreme cause of His life.
b. His supreme obedience. Imagine the terrible sufferings of the hour. Should He pray, "Father save me from this hour?" He could not, for He had come to die. He must obey God, and to obey God was the supreme act of His life (see note—Jn.10:17-18).

3. Jesus prayed for the glory of God. He prayed for the Father to glorify His own name. This is significant. It shows a complete *selflessness* on the part of Jesus. It shows that the primary concern of Jesus was to complete His purpose and cause on earth, which was to glorify God by doing exactly what God wanted. How was God glorified? By Jesus' obedience. God was glorified in the same way a superior is honored and respected. His Word was carried out and obeyed.

Note: the verb "*glorify*" is in the Greek aorist tense which points to a single act or event which would glorify God (v.28). The single act concerned the cross. Jesus was asking His Father to glorify His own name through the cross.

a. God would be glorified in the cross by the *supreme act of obedience* on the part of Jesus. It was God's will for Jesus to die for the sins of men. By dying, Jesus would show that God is the supreme Being of the universe. God is the One who is to be honored and respected and obeyed. He would thereby be glorified.

Going a little farther, he fell with his face to the ground and prayed, "My Father, if it is possible, may this cup be taken from me. Yet not as I will, but as you will." (Mat 26:39)

The reason my Father loves me is that I lay down my life—only to take it up again. No one takes it from me, but I lay it down of my own accord. I have authority to lay it down and authority to take it up again. This command I received from my Father." (John 10:17-18)

This man was handed over to you by God's set purpose and foreknowledge; and you, with the help of wicked men, put him to death by nailing him to the cross. (Acts 2:23)

And live a life of love, just as Christ loved us and gave himself up for us as a fragrant offering and sacrifice to God. (Eph 5:2)

Therefore, when Christ came into the world, he said: "Sacrifice and offering you did not desire, but a body you prepared for me; with burnt offerings and sin offerings you were not pleased. Then I said, 'Here I am—it is written about me in the scroll— I have come to do your will, O God.'" And by that will, we have been made holy through the sacrifice of the body of Jesus Christ once for all. (Heb 10:5-7, 10)

b. God would be glorified in the cross by *men's seeing the love of God* in the cross. God gave His only Son to die *for* men that they might not perish but have eternal life. Some men would see and believe this glorious truth; therefore, they would bow down, surrendering their whole beings to God. They would begin to follow and obey His will, honoring and praising Him for all He had done and was doing for them. The name of God would thereby be glorified by the cross. (See note, pt.1—Jn.12:23-26 for verses of Scripture.)

4. God accepted and approved Jesus' prayer. Note that the approval was audible. God actually spoke from heaven, saying that He had glorified His name and that He would glorify it again. Note three things.

a. Jesus prayed according to God's will: "Glorify [honor] your name" (cp. Mt.6:9). Therefore, God answered His prayer.

Thought 1. God will answer any prayer that is according to His will (1 Jn.5:14-15). This stresses the importance of knowing God's will. Studying God's Word is the only way to know the will of God.

b. God accepted Jesus' prayer. This means He accepted Jesus' death in behalf of man. We can rest assured that we are delivered from death if we believe in Jesus (cp. Jn.5:24).
c. God will glorify His name in the future. He will keep His Word and fulfill all His promises. We can rest assured of the promises of God.

5. The people standing around were confused. Some thought the voice was merely thunder; others thought that an angel had spoken to Jesus.
6. Jesus plainly told the people that a voice had spoken. It had spoken for their sakes in order to help them believe that He was the Son of God.

The point is this. By the thousands, people had just welcomed Jesus in the triumphal entry, welcomed Him as their earthly King and Messiah, the One who was to bring heaven and utopia to earth. (See outline and notes—Jn.8:21-24.) Jesus had to correct the misunderstanding of His cause. He had come not to rule as an earthly King for man; He had come to die for man. God's concern was not just for the seventy years of a man's life; God's concern was to save man eternally.

"For God so loved the world that he gave his one and only Son, that whoever believes in him shall not perish but have eternal life. For God did not send his Son into the world to condemn the world, but to save the world through him. (John 3:16-17)

The thief comes only to steal and kill and destroy; I have come that they may have life, and have it to the full. (John 10:10)

Just as the Father knows me and I know the Father—and I lay down my life for the sheep. (John 10:15)

He himself bore our sins in his body on the tree, so that we might die to sins and live for righteousness; by his wounds you have been healed. (1 Pet 2:24)

For Christ died for sins once for all, the righteous for the unrighteous, to bring you to God. He was put to death in the body but made alive by the Spirit, (1 Pet 3:18)

4 (12:31-33) **World, Corruption—Creation**: the third misunderstanding concerns the world. The world is not what it should be. It is not what it was created to be: perfect and permanent. The world was perfect in its distant past: it was created perfectly, just as it should be. However, man misunderstands the world. He ignores and neglects *the fact* that the world…

- is not perfect; is not in its original state or even close to it; is not what it should be; is not in the condition for which it was meant.
- is not permanent as it is; will not always be here; was not always here.
- is to be changed and recreated into a new heavens and earth just as God intended.

Standing there, the people had welcomed Jesus in the triumphal entry, thinking He was going to set up a worldly kingdom upon this *present earth*. They thought in terms of the physical earth, in terms of worldly kingdoms and material wealth and power. Jesus had to correct their misconception. He had to show them that God's concern was not for man and his world to exist for just a brief span of time, but for eternity.

What Jesus said was an alarming revelation. Note the phenomenal claim in the word "now." He said *"Now,"* it is I—my being lifted up, my cross and death—that would cause these things to happen.

1. Jesus said that this world is to be judged (see Deeper Study # 2, World—Jn.12:31).

2. Jesus said that the world is ruled by an alien power (see Deeper Study # 3, Satan—Jn.12:31).

3. Jesus said that both the world and Satan would be conquered by the cross, by His death (see Deeper Study # 4, Cross—Jn.12:32).

DEEPER STUDY # 2
(12:31) World, Judgment of—Nature, Judgment of—Man, Judgment of—Corruption: the world has to be judged…

- judged as being imperfect
- judged as being in some state other than what it should be
- judged as being short of God's glory and of God's will

If the world is ever to be perfected, it has to be judged as imperfect. God has to judge the world as less than what He wills. Once the world is judged as defective and imperfect…

- then it can be condemned and destroyed
- then it can be recreated in a perfect form and state of being

This is exactly what Scripture teaches. Scripture says three things about the world's having to be judged and recreated in order to be perfected.

1. The earth itself and the heavenly bodies above have to be judged. Why? Because they are imperfect; they have the seed of corruption within. The earth and the world are *running down*, wasting away, failing and dying. Eventually, even if the world were allowed to run long enough, the earth could not sustain life. The Bible says the earth…

- has to be judged because it is not perfect.
- has to be made perfect by being recreated and put into a permanent state. (Cp. 2 Pt.2:3-4, 8-13 for discussion.)

2. Nature itself, the animal and vegetation life of the earth, has to be judged. (Note: this fact is closely aligned to point one above. It is separated only in an attempt to simplify the discussion and to help in understanding the teaching of Scripture.) Nature is imperfect; it has the seed of corruption within. Nature is often beautiful in its sunsets, green pastures, and animal life. But nature is also destructive in its storms, earthquakes, fires, and struggle for survival. The beautiful mockingbird sitting in a tree can be singing its song, and in a moment's time turn into a savage by attacking the worm. Nature is not perfect, not what it should be. It is short of God's glory and short of what God wills it to be. God's will is for *a nature* in which the lion lies down with the lamb, a nature in which all things are at peace and without corruption. In its present condition, nature…

- despite its beauty, can be savage
- despite its peace, can be stormy
- despite its producing good, can produce bad
- despite its being right, can be evil
- despite its enticements, can destroy
- despite its nourishment, can starve

The Bible says that nature has to be judged because it is not perfect. It has to be made perfect, that is, recreated and put into a permanent and perfect state.

> The creation waits in eager expectation for the sons of God to be revealed. For the creation was subjected to frustration, not by its own choice, but by the will of the one who subjected it, in hope that the creation itself will be liberated from its bondage to decay and brought into the glorious freedom of the children of God. We know that the whole creation has been groaning as in the pains of childbirth right up to the present time. (Ro.8:19-22).

3. Man (and his world system) has to be judged. Man is imperfect; he has the seed of corruption within. Man lies, steals, cheats, and kills. Man has many good moments—every man, no matter who he is—but he also has many bad moments. Moods, feelings, thoughts, weaknesses of both body and mind—so much causes man to come ever so short. In addition man ages; he wastes away and dies—and nothing can stop the process. Man is short of God's glory; he is not perfect; therefore, he must be judged. He has to be recreated and made into a perfect creature; he has to be given a perfect and permanent body.

> So will it be with the resurrection of the dead. The body that is sown is perishable, it is raised imperishable; it is sown in dishonor, it is raised in glory; it is sown in weakness, it is raised in power; it is sown a natural body, it is raised a spiritual body. If there is a natural body, there is also a spiritual body. (1 Cor 15:42-44)
> And just as we have borne the likeness of the earthly man, so shall we bear the likeness of the man from heaven. I declare to you, brothers, that flesh and blood cannot inherit the kingdom of God, nor does the perishable inherit the imperishable. Listen, I tell you a mystery: We will not all sleep, but we will all be changed—in a flash, in the twinkling of an eye, at the last trumpet. For the trumpet will sound, the

dead will be raised imperishable, and we will be changed. For the perishable must clothe itself with the imperishable, and the mortal with immortality. When the perishable has been clothed with the imperishable, and the mortal with immortality, then the saying that is written will come true: "Death has been swallowed up in victory." (1 Cor 15:49-54)

It is important to note why the seed of corruption is in the world. The world was not corrupted by its own will or act. It was corrupted because of sin (cp. Ro.8:20). The sin of man brought corruption into the world. As soon as man sinned...

- the world was no longer perfect. It was contaminated, polluted, dirtied, corrupted.
- the seed of corruption, of wasting away, deteriorating, decaying and dying was planted in the world.
- the results of sin fell upon the world as well as falling upon man.

The world had been made for man, for man's dwelling place and enjoyment (cp. Gen.1:1-3:24). And God gave man a choice: if man chose perfection, his world would remain perfect just as God had created it; but if man chose sin and evil and death, his world would become imperfect, full of sin and evil and death. Therefore, when man sinned and became corrupted, he plunged the world into corruption. All creation became as man, just as man had chosen.

As stated, the world and its physical dimension of being were made for man; therefore, it was bound to suffer the very same fate as man. God had so ordained it. Therefore, when man is saved and delivered from sin and corruption, his world will also share the deliverance of man. The world will be saved and delivered from sin and corruption. There is to be a glorious day of redemption, a redemption both for man and his world. God will give all believers a redeemed and perfected world in which to live. As God declares, "I am making everything new" (Rev.21:5).

First of all, you must understand that in the last days scoffers will come, scoffing and following their own evil desires. They will say, "Where is this 'coming' he promised? Ever since our fathers died, everything goes on as it has since the beginning of creation." But do not forget this one thing, dear friends: With the Lord a day is like a thousand years, and a thousand years are like a day. The Lord is not slow in keeping his promise, as some understand slowness. He is patient with you, not wanting anyone to perish, but everyone to come to repentance. But the day of the Lord will come like a thief. The heavens will disappear with a roar; the elements will be destroyed by fire, and the earth and everything in it will be laid bare. Since everything will be destroyed in this way, what kind of people ought you to be? You ought to live holy and godly lives as you look forward to the day of God and speed its coming. That day will bring about the destruction of the heavens by fire, and the elements will melt in the heat. But in keeping with his promise we are looking forward to a new heaven and a new earth, the home of righteousness. (2 Pet 3:3-4, 8-13)

DEEPER STUDY # 3

(12:31) **Satan**: Jesus said the world is ruled by an alien prince. The world is not ruled by God; it is ruled by Satan. The Bible says three significant things.

1. Satan is the ruler and the prince, that is, the power of the world in all its evil and corruption (Jn.12:31; 14:30; 16:11; 2 Cor.4:4; Eph.2:2. See DEEPER STUDY # 1—Rev.12:9 for more discussion.)

2. The sin and evil of the world prove the world is ruled by an alien prince. God is not the author of sin. God *does not* tempt men, not with evil (Jas.1:13). God is not the Father of sin and evil, of destruction and devastation. God does not do such things. The father of such corruption is the devil (see DEEPER STUDY # 1—Jn.8:38; note—8:41-47; DEEPER STUDY # 1 and note—8:44 for discussion).

3. Satan is now "driven out" by the cross of Christ. Note the words "driven out" (ekblethesetai exo, future passive of ekballo which means a sure fact *lying in the future*). The words mean to drive out of, to drive from or forth, to drive *clean out* (exo) of a place. Satan in all his power, rule, and reign is driven out by the death of Christ. His power, rule, and reign over lives is now broken.

a. Satan's power *to charge men with sin* is now "driven out." Men now have the power to escape the penalty of sin. Christ took the sins of men upon Himself and paid the penalty for their sin. He died for the sins of the world.

   He himself bore our sins in his body on the tree, so that we might die to sins and live for righteousness; by his wounds you have been healed. (1 Pet 2:24)
   Who will bring any charge against those whom God has chosen? It is God who justifies. (Rom 8:33)

b. Satan's power *to cause death* is now "driven out." Men no longer have to die. Christ died *for man*, became man's substitute in death.

   Since the children have flesh and blood, he too shared in their humanity so that by his death he might destroy him who holds the power of death—that is, the devil—and free those who all their lives were held in slavery by their fear of death. (Heb 2:14-15)

c. Satan's power *to cause men to be separated from God* is now driven out. Men no longer have to go to hell. Christ was separated from God *for man* (see note—Mt.27:46-49). Man can now live forever with God.

   For Christ died for sins once for all, the righteous for the unrighteous, to bring you to God. He was put to death in the body but made alive by the Spirit, (1 Pet 3:18)
   And if the Spirit of him who raised Jesus from the dead is living in you, he who raised Christ from the dead will also give life to your mortal bodies through his Spirit, who lives in you. (Rom 8:11)

d. Satan's power *to enslave men* with the habits of sin and shame is now "driven out." By His death, Christ made it possible for man to be freed from sin. The believer, cleansed by the blood of Christ, becomes a holy temple unto God, a temple fit for the presence and power of God's Spirit. Men can now conquer the enslaving habits of sin by the power of God's Spirit.

> Do you not know that your body is a temple of the Holy Spirit, who is in you, whom you have received from God? You are not your own; you were bought at a price. Therefore honor God with your body. (1 Cor 6:19-20)
> You, dear children, are from God and have overcome them, because the one who is in you is greater than the one who is in the world. (1 John 4:4)

Thought 1. Jesus Christ has destroyed and triumphed over the power of Satan (see DEEPER STUDY # 4, Cross—Jn.12:32 for discussion of how the cross delivers and gives man so much.)

> I will not speak with you much longer, for the prince of this world is coming. He has no hold on me, (John 14:30)
> For he has rescued us from the dominion of darkness and brought us into the kingdom of the Son he loves, in whom we have redemption, the forgiveness of sins. (Col 1:13-14)
> And having disarmed the powers and authorities, he made a public spectacle of them, triumphing over them by the cross. (Col 2:15)
> He who does what is sinful is of the devil, because the devil has been sinning from the beginning. The reason the Son of God appeared was to destroy the devil's work. (1 John 3:8)

DEEPER STUDY # 4

(12:32) **Jesus Christ, Cross**: the words "lifted up" refer to the cross of Christ, to His death upon the cross. Jesus said that once He is "lifted up," He will draw all men to Himself. Note two points.

1. Note why the cross of Christ attracts men. It was the cross...

- that delivered men from sin, death, and hell.
- that made it possible for men to live abundantly and eternally.
- that gave to men the presence and power of God's Spirit to guide and care for them day by day.

2. Note how the cross of Christ gives so much to man. Very simply stated, Jesus died *for man* on the cross. When a man believes that Jesus died *for him*, God takes that man's belief and *counts* it as righteousness. God simply *counts* the man as perfect. The man is not righteous, nowhere close to perfect. The man, God, and everyone else knows he is not perfect. But the man honors God's Son by believing on Him; therefore, God honors the man.

The point to see is that God will do anything for the person who truly honors His Son. God loves His Son so much that He is willing to do anything for anyone who honors Jesus. If a man honors Jesus by believing and following Jesus, God will take that man's faith and...

- count his faith as righteousness.
- deliver him from sin and from death.
- give him both abundant and eternal life (Jn.10:10).

- place the Holy Spirit and His power within the man to help him live day by day (cp. 1 Cor.6:19-20; Ro.8:1-39; Gal.5:22-23).

The point is this: it is the cross of Christ that breaks the power of Satan in the world. It is the cross of Christ that "drives out" Satan: his power, his rule, and his reign. Man, by believing that Christ died for him, can now be counted righteous and delivered from the power of Satan, from the evil power that entices him to sin and that causes him to die and face the judgment of God. Man can now know the power of God, the power that freely forgives him and gives him life forever. Man can now experience the marvelous grace of God. (See DEEPER STUDY # 1, Grace—Tit.2:11-15. See notes, Justification—Ro.4:22; 5:1.)

5 (12:34-36) **Jesus Christ, The Light**: the fourth misunderstanding concerns the Messiah (the Light). Note: the people clearly understood that Jesus was speaking of death, but it was this that confused them. They had just acknowledged Him to be the Messiah, and they had always understood the Messiah was to live forever (cp. Ps.89:36; 110:4; Is.9:7; Dan.7:14). Was He really the Messiah? Could they be mistaken? Was the Son of Man someone else? Jesus answered two things.

1. Jesus claimed to be the Messiah, *the Light of the world* (see DEEPER STUDY # 5—Jn.12:35-36; DEEPER STUDY # 1—8:12). But He stressed a critical point. The Light was to be with them for only a little while longer; the Light was to be extinguished.

2. Jesus pointed out the twofold need of man.

a. Man must walk in the Light *while* he has light. If the Light was to be extinguished, it would not always be present for men to see. And once men lost the Light two things would happen.
⇒ Darkness would overtake and overcome men.
⇒ Men would not know where they were going. They would be groping and stumbling, falling and dooming themselves to an eternity of darkness.

b. Man must believe in the Light. If men believed, something significant would happen. They would become children (huioi, sons) of the Light.
⇒ Believe or "trust" (pisteuete) is continuous action.
⇒ "Become" (genesthe) is a once-for-all act, a personal experience that happens all at once.
A man who truly sees Jesus Christ as the Light of the world believes and trusts and continues to believe and trust. And the very moment his heart leaps toward Christ in belief and trust, he becomes a child of the Light, a child of God Himself. The man sees the Light and begins to walk in the Light, living the kind of life he should.

> In him was life, and that life was the light of men. (John 1:4)
> When Jesus spoke again to the people, he said, "I am the light of the world. Whoever follows me will never walk in darkness, but will have the light of life." (John 8:12)
> For it is light that makes everything visible. This is why it is said: "Wake up, O sleeper, rise from the dead, and Christ will shine on you." (Eph 5:14)

DEEPER STUDY # 5

(12:35-36) **Light—Believers**: light is one of the great words of Scripture. (See Deeper Study # 1—Jn.8:12.)

1. God is light and in Him there is no darkness at all (1 Jn.1:5).

2. Jesus Christ is the Light of the world—the very embodiment of the heavenly light (Jn.8:12; 9:5).

3. The light of the knowledge of God is seen in the face of Jesus Christ (2 Cor.4:6).

4. Jesus Christ "gives light to every man" who comes into the world (Jn.1:9).

5. Believers are said to become "children of light" through belief in the Light, Jesus Christ Himself (Jn.12:36).

6. Believers have been transferred from the dominion of darkness into the Kingdom of Christ, the inheritance of light (Col.1:13).

7. Before they come to Christ, believers are not only in darkness but are an embodiment of darkness. But when they come to Christ, believers are placed in the Light and become an embodiment of the Light itself (Eph.5:8).

8. Believers are the light of the world (Mt.5:14-16).

9. Believers are to set their light on a lampstand—to make their light conspicuous (Mt.5:15).

10. Evil doers shun the light (Jn.3:20f).

11. The creation of light is a picture of the expulsion of spiritual darkness (Gen.1:2f).

1 The unbelievers
a. They act illogically
  1) They reject miraculous signs
  2) They reject revelation
 	
  3) They reject the arm of the Lord
 	
b. The results of unbelief: A just, judicial rejection by God[DS1]
  1) Man is blinded
  2) Man is hardened, deadened
  3) Man is condemned to be lost
  4) Man is condemned to remain unhealed
  5) Man never sees the glory of the Lord
2 The silent believers
a. They fail to confess Jesus
b. They fail, fearing personal loss
	C. Jesus Rejected and Accepted as King, 12:37-50
	
	37 Even after Jesus had done all these miraculous signs in their presence, they still would not believe in him.
	38 This was to fulfill the word of Isaiah the prophet: "Lord, who has believed our message and to whom has the arm of the Lord been revealed?"
	39 For this reason they could not believe, because, as Isaiah says elsewhere:
	40 "He has blinded their eyes and deadened their hearts, so they can neither see with their eyes, nor understand with their hearts, nor turn—and I would heal them."
	41 Isaiah said this because he saw Jesus' glory and spoke about him.
	42 Yet at the same time many even among the leaders believed in him. But because of the Pharisees they would not confess their faith for fear they would be put out of the synagogue;
		43 for they loved praise from men more than praise from God.
		44 Then Jesus cried out, "When a man believes in me, he does not believe in me only, but in the one who sent me.
		45 When he looks at me, he sees the one who sent me.
		46 I have come into the world as a light, so that no one who believes in me should stay in darkness.
		47 "As for the person who hears my words but does not keep them, I do not judge him. For I did not come to judge the world, but to save it.
		48 There is a judge for the one who rejects me and does not accept my words; that very word which I spoke will condemn him at the last day.
		49 For I did not speak of my own accord, but the Father who sent me commanded me what to say and how to say it.
		50 I know that his command leads to eternal life. So whatever I say is just what the Father has told me to say."
			c. They fail, loving the praise of men more than God
			3 The true believer
			a. Believes on God—thru Jesus, the Mediator[DS2]
			b. Sees God—thru Jesus, the Mediator
			c. Is delivered from darkness—thru Jesus, the Light
			
			4 The unbeliever—his judgment
			a. Judged not by Jesus: He came to save, not judge
			
			b. Judged by the words of salvation: The very words he rejected will stand as a witness against him
			  1) Because Jesus' words are God's commandment
			  2) Because God's word is life
			  3) Because the words of Jesus are the truth

DIVISION XII

THE REVELATION OF JESUS, THE GLORIFIED SON OF MAN, 12:12-50

C. Jesus Rejected and Accepted as King, 12:37-50

(12:37-50) **Introduction**: this is a clear picture of Jesus' being rejected and accepted as King.
1. The unbelievers (v.37-41).
2. The silent believers (v.42-43).
3. The true believer (v.44-46).
4. The unbeliever—his judgment (v.47-50).

1 (12:37-41) **Unbelief**: there are the unbelievers who act illogically. Their unbelief makes no sense, for God has done all He can to help man believe, yet man rejects and refuses to believe.

1. Unbelief rejects miracles. Note three significant facts.
  a. Note the words "all these miraculous signs." Jesus was deeply touched by the sufferings of man. He reached out in a moving and loving compassion. He helped and ministered to everyone He could possibly reach—an innumerable number. In fact, Christ performed so many works and miracles that, if they should be written, "the whole world would not have room for the books" (Jn.21:25). Jesus worked...
- miracle after miracle
- compassion after compassion
- help after help
- sign after sign
- healing after healing

Note also that the kind of miraculous sign is emphasized. They were miraculous signs of quality, signs arising from the heart of God Himself. They were signs of compassion and help. They were signs arising from sincere motive of heart, a heart that had been touched by suffering humanity. They were pure signs, strong signs—signs that God's power alone could do.

  b. Note the words "in their presence." Jesus did not do His works out in a desert, that is, far off in a corner in some obscure place out of the sight of people. Jesus did His miraculous signs before the people, where the people could easily see them and where the miraculous signs would demonstrate His deity and help the people to believe.

  c. Note the words, "they still would not believe in him." The Greek tense is continuous: "they were not believing on Him" even while He was ministering and demonstrating such enormous compassion and power. Their hearts were shut, closed to the clear and undeniable evidence that Jesus was truly the Son of God. They were in a *state of unbelief*. Their unbelief was illogical, making no sense whatsoever.

And he did not do many miracles there because of their lack of faith. (Mat 13:58)
Jesus answered, "I did tell you, but

you do not believe. The miracles I do in my Father's name speak for me, (John 10:25)

Do not believe me unless I do what my Father does. But if I do it, even though you do not believe me, believe the miracles, that you may know and understand that the Father is in me, and I in the Father." (John 10:37-38)

Believe me when I say that I am in the Father and the Father is in me; or at least believe on the evidence of the miracles themselves. (John 14:11)

If I had not done among them what no one else did, they would not be guilty of sin. But now they have seen these miracles, and yet they have hated both me and my Father. (John 15:24)

2. Unbelief rejects revelation. Note: this fact is a fulfillment of prophecy (Is.53:1). Isaiah had proclaimed the report or the message of God, yet the people did not believe. They rejected and acted illogically. Their unbelief cut deeply and broke the heart of Isaiah. Filled with compassion and hurt for the people, Isaiah cried out to God, "Who has believed our message?" The cry was the beginning of the greatest prophecy ever made about Jesus.

"Who has believed our message?" The "message" was from God Himself, His message and revelation to the world. The "message" was both the words and deeds of Jesus. All that Jesus did through preaching and teaching revealed the truth; however, the "message" was more than words and deeds. Jesus Himself was the "message," the revelation of God to the world. God gave man...

- more than just words
- more than just ink and paper
- more than just the sounds of a voice

God gave man a Life to live out the words. He gave man a *Person*...

- not only to speak the truth, but to live the truth.
- not only to speak the works, but to do the works.
- not only to preach God's will, but to demonstrate God's will.
- not only to teach men, but to show men how to live.

The Person, of course, was God's own Son, Jesus Christ. Yet despite the fact that God sent His own Son into the world to proclaim His "message" or His revelation, men still do not believe. They reject Jesus Christ, denying the message. They act illogically, making no sense whatsoever.

I tell you the truth, we speak of what we know, and we testify to what we have seen, but still you people do not accept our testimony. (John 3:11)

The Spirit gives life; the flesh counts for nothing. The words I have spoken to you are spirit and they are life. Yet there are some of you who do not believe." For Jesus had known from the beginning which of them did not believe and who would betray him. (John 6:63-64)

When Jesus spoke again to the people, he said, "I am the light of the world. Whoever follows me will never walk in darkness, but will have the light of life." The Pharisees challenged him, "Here you are, appearing as your own witness; your testimony is not valid." Jesus answered, "Even if I testify on my own behalf, my testimony is valid, for I know where I came from and where I am going. But you have no idea where I come from or where I am going. You judge by human standards; I pass judgment on no one. But if I do judge, my decisions are right, because I am not alone. I stand with the Father, who sent me. In your own Law it is written that the testimony of two men is valid. I am one who testifies for myself; my other witness is the Father, who sent me." Then they asked him, "Where is your father?" "You do not know me or my Father," Jesus replied. "If you knew me, you would know my Father also." (John 8:12-19)

3. Unbelief rejects the arm of the Lord. This, too, is a fulfillment of the same prophecy (Is.53:1). The arm of the Lord means the strength of God, His power to save and to deliver and to give life. It can also mean the Savior and Deliverer Himself. The *Arm* that saves and gives life is Jesus Christ. When it comes to God's strength to save and deliver...

- who knows it?
- who has experienced it?
- to whom has it been revealed?
- who has humbled himself so that God could reveal it?
- who has diligently sought enough so that God could reveal it?

Unbelief rejects the arm and salvation of the Lord. Such is illogical, making no sense whatsoever.

"If you are the Christ, " they said, "tell us." Jesus answered, "If I tell you, you will not believe me, (Luke 22:67)

Whoever believes in the Son has eternal life, but whoever rejects the Son will not see life, for God's wrath remains on him." (John 3:36)

Then Jesus declared, "I am the bread of life. He who comes to me will never go hungry, and he who believes in me will never be thirsty. But as I told you, you have seen me and still you do not believe. (John 6:35-36)

I told you that you would die in your sins; if you do not believe that I am the one I claim to be, you will indeed die in your sins." (John 8:24)

For this people's heart has become calloused; they hardly hear with their ears, and they have closed their eyes. Otherwise they might see with their eyes, hear with their ears, understand with their hearts and turn, and I would heal them.' (Acts 28:27)

See to it, brothers, that none of you has a sinful, unbelieving heart that turns away from the living God. (Heb 3:12)

Now note a critical matter about unbelief. Unbelief results in some serious consequences (see DEEPER STUDY # 1—Jn.12:39-41 for discussion).

DEEPER STUDY # 1

(12:39-41) **Unbelief—Judicial Judgment**: this passage says that God blinds and hardens or deadens man. A man cannot reject Jesus Christ and expect matters to stay as they are. No matter how mild a man's rejection is, the matter is serious to God. A man may reject Jesus in thought only, never saying a word or committing a public (visible) sin against Him. But no matter how mild the rejection, God still cannot overlook the rejection of His Son. He loves His Son too much, and His Son has done too much for man. His Son has taken the sin of man upon Himself and borne the punishment for man. His Son died for man. Jesus has done too much for God to by-pass man's unbelief and rejection. When a man has the chance to see and open his heart but chooses not to look and closes his heart, that man suffers the consequences.

Another way to say the same thing is this: when God has loved the world and done so much for man, man cannot deny God's Son and expect to suffer no consequences. The consequences and results of unbelief are clearly spelled out, and they are terrible consequences, an awful fate for a person to suffer.

⇒ God blinds the eyes of the unbeliever.
⇒ God hardens the heart of the unbeliever.
⇒ God condemns the unbeliever to be lost.
⇒ God condemns the unbeliever to be unhealed.
⇒ God never reveals His glory to the unbeliever.

Now for an important question: Does this mean that God causes the unbelief of a man and condemns that man to be lost before he is ever born? No! Scripture shouts a thousand "No's!" A man is not lost...

• apart from his will
• against his will

A man is lost only because he chooses to have nothing to do with God and to be lost. What Scripture teaches is that God has set certain laws in the universe...

• laws both within man and within nature
• laws which go into motion and take effect when man acts

If a man does something, certain things will happen. If a man does something else, then something else will happen. Scripture teaches that unbelief is governed by these laws.

⇒ There is the law of sowing and reaping. If a man sows unbelief, he reaps unbelief.

Do not be deceived: God cannot be mocked. A man reaps what he sows. The one who sows to please his sinful nature, from that nature will reap destruction; the one who sows to please the Spirit, from the Spirit will reap eternal life. (Gal 6:7-8)

⇒ There is the law of measure. If a man measures unbelief, he is measured unbelief. Whatever a man measures, he receives.

For in the same way you judge others, you will be judged, and with the measure you use, it will be measured to you. (Mat 7:2)

⇒ There is the law of seeking. If a man seeks, he finds. The harder he seeks, the more he finds.

"Ask and it will be given to you; seek and you will find; knock and the door will be opened to you. (Mat 7:7)

⇒ There is the law of wilful stubbornness and obstinance. The more stubborn a man becomes, the more he refuses to repent, the more hardened he becomes. In fact, a man can become so stubborn and hardened that he never repents, never even thinks about repenting. Such a man stores up wrath against himself.

But because of your stubbornness and your unrepentant heart, you are storing up wrath against yourself for the day of God's wrath, when his righteous judgment will be revealed. God "will give to each person according to what he has done." (Rom 2:5-6)

⇒ There is the law of being "prepared" for destruction. The more a man refuses to believe, the more he is "prepared" and conditioned for destruction. Note that a man through his unbelief prepares and conditions himself.

What if God, choosing to show his wrath and make his power known, bore with great patience the objects of his wrath prepared for destruction? (Rom 9:22)

⇒ There is the law of God's patience. God is "not wanting anyone to perish, but everyone to come to repentance." Therefore, God allows the world to continue, allowing more and more to be saved. He endures with patience the unbelievers who harden themselves and store up wrath against themselves in order that some might be saved and given the privilege of knowing the riches of His grace (Ro.2:5; cp. Ro.9:22-23).

First of all, you must understand that in the last days scoffers will come, scoffing and following their own evil desires. They will say, "Where is this 'coming' he promised? Ever since our fathers died, everything goes on as it has since the beginning of creation." But do not forget this one thing, dear friends: With the Lord a day is like a thousand years, and a thousand years are like a day. The Lord is not slow in keeping his promise, as some understand slowness. He is patient with you, not wanting anyone to perish, but everyone to come to repentance. (2 Pet 3:3-4, 8, 9)

⇒ There is the law of God's supreme purpose. God's supreme purpose is that His Son "be the firstborn among many brothers" (Ro.8:29). God wants Jesus to have many brothers—brothers who will be conformed to His image and count Him as the Elder Brother: as the first and most honored, as the One who is to be worshipped and served eternally.

And we know that in all things God works for the good of those who love him, who have been called according to his purpose. For those God foreknew he also predestined to be conformed to the likeness of his Son, that he might be the firstborn among many brothers. (Rom 8:28-29)

In order for Christ to gain more and more brothers who will honor Him, God is willing for unbelievers to continue on in their unbelief, ever hardening themselves under the just and judicial laws He has established. Men are allowed to go on in their unbelief, condemning themselves under the just and judicial laws of the universe.

These laws are what men call *the law of conditioning.* Men would simply say that the more a man does anything, the more he conditions himself to do that thing. The more he does it, the more it becomes a habit. (Cp. smoking, eating, or anything else.) This is what the Bible is saying: if a man hardens his mind and heart to the truth, he becomes conditioned more and more against the truth. His openness and sensitivity to Jesus Christ dwindles more and more, and it can dwindle so much that it is gone forever. Therefore, the more a man rejects Christ, the more he decreases his sensitivity and chance of ever accepting Christ.

What Scripture teaches can be summarized under what might be called *the law of judicial blindness and rejection.* This simply means that the person who rejects God's Son chooses to be blind and to harden his heart. Therefore, he is given over to a *just punishment.* He is justly blinded and hardened (conditioned) more and more. A man is led to a judicial blindness and rejection by God through…
- obstinate unbelief
- constant sin
- continued rejection

God's Word plainly says that there are conditioning laws within man and nature, and it is a fact that unbelievers have to live under these laws the same as believers. God cannot play favorites; He cannot snatch unbelievers out from under the just and judicial laws of the universe and force them to believe, taking away their wills. God has to allow all men to live under the same laws and to make the choices of life day by day. Believers have made the choice to follow God's Son. Unbelievers have made the choice not to follow God's Son. There can be no violation of their wills: unbelievers have to be allowed to go on in their unbelief, ever hardening themselves under the just laws of God's will established in the universe. As Jesus Christ clearly said, the words of judgment are already spoken: they are set up as God's law and will within the universe. It is the law and will of God that Jesus Christ proclaimed, and it will be His words that will judge men in the end time (Jn.12:48).

In addition to the above laws, compare the following verses.

Therefore God gave them over in the sinful desires of their hearts to sexual impurity for the degrading of their bodies with one another. Because of this, God gave them over to shameful lusts. Even their women exchanged natural relations for unnatural ones. Furthermore, since they did not think it worthwhile to retain the knowledge of God, he gave them over to a depraved mind, to do what ought not to be done. (Rom 1:24, 26, 28. See outline and notes-- Ro.1:24-32.)

Then the LORD said, "My Spirit will not contend with man forever, for he is mortal ; his days will be a hundred and twenty years." (Gen 6:3)

"But my people would not listen to me; Israel would not submit to me. So I gave them over to their stubborn hearts to follow their own devices. (Psa 81:11-12)

A man who remains stiff-necked after many rebukes will suddenly be destroyed-- without remedy. (Prov 29:1)

I will not accuse forever, nor will I always be angry, for then the spirit of man would grow faint before me-- the breath of man that I have created. (Isa 57:16)

Ephraim is joined to idols; leave him alone! (Hosea 4:17)

(See note—Jn.6:44-46 for a discussion of God's part in *drawing* men to salvation.)

2 (12:42-43) **Believers, Silent—Confession**: there are the silent believers. These were the chief rulers and leaders among the people, and they were many. They believed on Jesus, realizing that He was who He claimed to be—the true Messiah; but they had one serious flaw. They were silent; therefore, they failed in three critical areas.

1. They failed to confess Christ. They *would not* confess Him.

"Whoever acknowledges me before men, I will also acknowledge him before my Father in heaven. But whoever disowns me before men, I will disown him before my Father in heaven. (Mat 10:32-33)

"I tell you, whoever acknowledges me before men, the Son of Man will also acknowledge him before the angels of God. But he who disowns me before men will be disowned before the angels of God. (Luke 12:8-9)

And this is his command: to believe in the name of his Son, Jesus Christ, and to love one another as he commanded us. (1 John 3:23)

2. They failed because they feared loss. They feared they would be excommunicated, put out of the synagogue. They feared they would lose their…
- position
- job
- security
- profession
- livelihood
- authority
- recognition
- esteem
- honor

What good will it be for a man if he gains the whole world, yet forfeits his soul? Or what can a man give in exchange for his soul? (Mat 16:26)

Set your minds on things above, not on earthly things. (Col 3:2)

If we endure, we will also reign with him. If we disown him, he will also disown us; (2 Tim 2:12)

You adulterous people, don't you know that friendship with the world is hatred toward God? Anyone who chooses to be a

friend of the world becomes an enemy of God. (James 4:4)

3. They failed because they loved the praise of men more than the praise of God. They loved what men gave:

- acceptance
- esteem
- favor
- recognition
- prestige
- commendation
- honor
- image
- glory

They would rather be accepted and approved by men than to be accepted and approved by God.

> **How can you believe if you accept praise from one another, yet make no effort to obtain the praise that comes from the only God ? (John 5:44)**
>
> **But no one would say anything publicly about him for fear of the Jews. (John 7:13)**
>
> **Later, Joseph of Arimathea asked Pilate for the body of Jesus. Now Joseph was a disciple of Jesus, but secretly because he feared the Jews. With Pilate's permission, he came and took the body away. (John 19:38)**
>
> **Do not show partiality in judging; hear both small and great alike. Do not be afraid of any man, for judgment belongs to God. Bring me any case too hard for you, and I will hear it. (Deu 1:17)**
>
> **Their tombs will remain their houses forever, their dwellings for endless generations, though they had named lands after themselves. But man, despite his riches, does not endure; he is like the beasts that perish. This is the fate of those who trust in themselves, and of their followers, who approve their sayings. Selah (Psa 49:11-13)**
>
> **"I, even I, am he who comforts you. Who are you that you fear mortal men, the sons of men, who are but grass, (Isa 51:12)**

3 (12:44-46) **Believer—Jesus Christ, Mediator**: there is the true believer. The stress of these verses is Jesus Christ, the Mediator (see DEEPER STUDY # 2—Jn.12:44). It is easier to see the meaning of the verses by switching the clauses as the outline does.

⇒ Through believing in Jesus Christ (the Mediator), a man believes in God.
⇒ Through seeing Jesus Christ (the Mediator), a man sees God.

1. A man believes in God—truly believes in God—only when he believes in Jesus Christ. Christ is the Mediator, the bridge builder between God and man. If a man wishes to approach God, the only living and true God, he can do so only by believing in Christ first. When a man claims to believe in God apart from Christ, he is believing in a god of imagination, a god of his own making. (Cp. Jn.14:6; 1 Tim.2:5.)

Note also that when a man believes in Christ, his faith is placed in God, the Sovereign Majesty who sent Christ to save the world.

> **"I tell you the truth, whoever hears my word and believes him who sent me has eternal life and will not be condemned; he**

has crossed over from death to life. (John 5:24)

> **Then they asked him, "What must we do to do the works God requires?" Jesus answered, "The work of God is this: to believe in the one he has sent." (John 6:28-29)**
>
> **Jesus answered, "I am the way and the truth and the life. No one comes to the Father except through me. (John 14:6)**
>
> **He who does not love me will not obey my teaching. These words you hear are not my own; they belong to the Father who sent me. (John 14:24)**
>
> **For I gave them the words you gave me and they accepted them. They knew with certainty that I came from you, and they believed that you sent me. (John 17:8)**
>
> **That all of them may be one, Father, just as you are in me and I am in you. May they also be in us so that the world may believe that you have sent me. (John 17:21)**
>
> **This is good, and pleases God our Savior, who wants all men to be saved and to come to a knowledge of the truth. For there is one God and one mediator between God and men, the man Christ Jesus, who gave himself as a ransom for all men--the testimony given in its proper time. (1 Tim 2:3-6)**

2. A man sees God only through seeing Jesus Christ. Christ claimed, "Anyone who has seen me has seen the Father" (Jn.14:9). When a person looks at Christ, they see the very nature of God—the very acts and words of God Himself. Christ is the revelation of God who came to earth to reveal God. See DEEPER STUDY # 1,2,3—Jn.14:6.)

> **I and the Father are one." (John 10:30)**
>
> **Do not believe me unless I do what my Father does. But if I do it, even though you do not believe me, believe the miracles, that you may know and understand that the Father is in me, and I in the Father." (John 10:37-38)**
>
> **When he looks at me, he sees the one who sent me. (John 12:45)**
>
> **If you really knew me, you would know my Father as well. From now on, you do know him and have seen him." Philip said, "Lord, show us the Father and that will be enough for us." Jesus answered: "Don't you know me, Philip, even after I have been among you such a long time? Anyone who has seen me has seen the Father. How can you say, 'Show us the Father'? Don't you believe that I am in the Father, and that the Father is in me? The words I say to you are not just my own. Rather, it is the Father, living in me, who is doing his work. (John 14:7-10)**

3. A man is delivered from darkness only through Jesus Christ, the Light. Christ is the Light of the world (see note—Jn.8:12). He came to be the Light of the world in order to bring light and salvation to man. His very purpose on earth was to save and to give light. Christ came as a light into the world so that men would not have to live in a state of darkness. The man who believes on Christ is given

light, the light to see and learn the truth of God and of himself, of the world and of others, of the future and of eternity.

> But if your eyes are bad, your whole body will be full of darkness. If then the light within you is darkness, how great is that darkness! (Mat 6:23)
>
> In him was life, and that life was the light of men. The light shines in the darkness, but the darkness has not understood it. (John 1:4-5)
>
> This is the verdict: Light has come into the world, but men loved darkness instead of light because their deeds were evil. (John 3:19)
>
> When Jesus spoke again to the people, he said, "I am the light of the world. Whoever follows me will never walk in darkness, but will have the light of life." (John 8:12)
>
> Then Jesus told them, "You are going to have the light just a little while longer. Walk while you have the light, before darkness overtakes you. The man who walks in the dark does not know where he is going. (John 12:35)
>
> For it is light that makes everything visible. This is why it is said: "Wake up, O sleeper, rise from the dead, and Christ will shine on you." (Eph 5:14)
>
> The night is nearly over; the day is almost here. So let us put aside the deeds of darkness and put on the armor of light. (Rom 13:12)
>
> If we claim to have fellowship with him yet walk in the darkness, we lie and do not live by the truth. (1 John 1:6)

DEEPER STUDY # 2

(12:44) **Jesus the Mediator**: represents God before men and men before God. In Latin, the word for mediator is *pontifex*. It means bridge builder. (See note—Jn.19:23-24.)

---

4 (12:47-50) **Judgment**: there is the unbeliever, his judgment. Christ said two significant things.

1. The unbeliever is not judged by Christ. Christ came to save the world, not to judge it.

2. The unbeliever is judged by the words of salvation. The very words which man rejects will stand as a witness against him. The unbeliever rejected the words of salvation, so they will be his judge. Note that the unbeliever condemns himself, for the words of salvation have now been brought to earth by Jesus Christ. The full message of salvation is now available. No one is keeping man away from the words; no man is hiding the words from him. All man has to do is accept them and carry them to other men. If man rejects the words of salvation, he condemns and judges himself. Why? Because in the last days, when the man stands before God, the words of salvation will *not be found* in him. The words will be *outside* the unbeliever, standing there to judge him.

There are three reasons why the words of Christ shall judge a man:

⇒ Because they are the very commands of God Himself.

> And this is his command: to believe in the name of his Son, Jesus Christ, and to love one another as he commanded us. (1 John 3:23)

⇒ Because God's commands are life.

> The Spirit gives life; the flesh counts for nothing. The words I have spoken to you are spirit and they are life. (John 6:63)
>
> Simon Peter answered him, "Lord, to whom shall we go? You have the words of eternal life. (John 6:68)
>
> I tell you the truth, if anyone keeps my word, he will never see death." (John 8:51)

⇒ Because the words of Christ are the truth, the very words which the Father told Christ to say.

> For the one whom God has sent speaks the words of God, for God gives the Spirit without limit. (John 3:34)
>
> He who does not love me will not obey my teaching. These words you hear are not my own; they belong to the Father who sent me. (John 14:24)
>
> For I gave them the words you gave me and they accepted them. They knew with certainty that I came from you, and they believed that you sent me. (John 17:8)

	CHAPTER 13 **XIII. THE REVELATION OF JESUS, THE GREAT MINISTER AND HIS LEGACY, 13:1-16:33** **A. The Demonstration of Royal Service, 13:1-17** (Mt.26:20-24; Mk.14: 14-17; Lk.22:14, 21-23)	realize now what I am doing, but later you will understand." 8 "No," said Peter, "you shall never wash my feet." Jesus answered, "Unless I wash you, you have no part with me."	b. Washing has a deeper meaning: Spiritual cleansing
1 In the Upper Room right before the Passover **2 The impetus for royal service** a. Knowing His time, His hour, had come b. Loving His followers to the very end c. Knowing His enemies	It was just before the Passover Feast. Jesus knew that the time had come for him to leave this world and go to the Father. Having loved his own who were in the world, he now showed them the full extent of his love. 2 The evening meal was being served, and the devil had already prompted Judas Iscariot, son of Simon, to betray Jesus.	9 "Then, Lord," Simon Peter replied, "not just my feet but my hands and my head as well!" 10 Jesus answered, "A person who has had a bath needs only to wash his feet; his whole body is clean. And you are clean, though not every one of you." 11 For he knew who was going to betray him, and that was why he said not every one was clean.	c. Washing is requested d. Washing is thorough & permanent e. Washing is not automatic nor by association
3 The extreme demonstration of royal service a. Knowing His mission b. Laying aside His outer clothing c. Washing the disciples' feet[DS1]	3 Jesus knew that the Father had put all things under his power, and that he had come from God and was returning to God; 4 So he got up from the meal, took off his outer clothing, and wrapped a towel around his waist. 5 After that, he poured water into a basin and began to wash his disciples' feet, drying them with the towel that was wrapped around him.	12 When he had finished washing their feet, he put on his clothes and returned to his place. "Do you understand what I have done for you?" he asked them. 13 "You call me 'Teacher' and 'Lord,' and rightly so, for that is what I am. 14 Now that I, your Lord and Teacher, have washed your feet, you also should wash one another's feet.	**5 The meaning of royal service** a. To serve Jesus as Teacher & Lord b. To serve other believers royally, sacrificially, leading them to be washed & cleansed
4 The prerequisite for royal service: Washing & cleansing a. Washing is misunderstood	6 He came to Simon Peter, who said to him, "Lord, are you going to wash my feet?" 7 Jesus replied, "You do not	15 I have set you an example that you should do as I have done for you. 16 I tell you the truth, no servant is greater than his master, nor is a messenger greater than the one who sent him. 17 Now that you know these things, you will be blessed if you do them."	**6 The reasons for royal service** a. Because of Jesus' example b. Because believers are not as great as the Lord c. Because of resulting joy

DIVISION XIII

THE REVELATION OF JESUS, THE GREAT MINISTER AND HIS LEGACY, 13:1-16:33

A. The Demonstration of Royal Service, 13:1-17

(13:1-17) **Introduction**: the disciples had been arguing over who would hold the leading positions in the government Jesus was about to set up (cp. Lk.22:24; Mk.10:35-45, esp. v.41). The discussion was heated. They were caught up in the ambition for position and power and authority. How the heart of Jesus must have been cut! He had so little time left for them to learn that the way to glory is through service and not through position and authority. How could He get the message across forcibly enough so that they would never forget the truth? It was this that led Jesus to wash the disciples' feet and to demonstrate what true royalty is: serving others.

1. In the Upper Room right before the Passover (v.1).
2. The impetus for royal service (v.1-2).
3. The extreme demonstration of royal service (v.3-5).

4. The prerequisite for royal service: washing and cleansing (v.6-11).
5. The meaning of royal service (v.12-14).
6. The reasons for royal service (v.15-17).

1 (13:1) **Upper Room**: this event took place right before the Passover. It took place in the Upper Room where so many significant events took place.

2 (13:1-2) **Ministry—Service**: the impetus for royal service. Three things *drove* Jesus to wash the disciples' feet and to demonstrate the royalty of service and ministry.

1. He knew "His time [hour]" had come (see DEEPER STUDY # 1, Hour—Time—Jn.12:23-24). He was to die and

His time was short. Whatever He hoped to teach His disciples had to be taught now, for there would soon be no more time.

2. He loved His own, that is, His followers upon earth, those for whom He was responsible. *His own* includes *both* the heavenly host and all believers who have gone on to heaven. He is Lord, the Son of the living God to whom all has been given; therefore, His own includes all those in both heaven and earth who are followers of Him. And He loves them all. However, the present point is this: He loves "His own...*in the world.*" Therefore, He was compelled to zero in on them and to do whatever was necessary to help them, no matter the cost. He was compelled by love to wash their feet, no matter the humiliation and the degree of abasement required.

3. He knew His enemy, and He knew the enemy was about to strike and betray Him. He had to act before the enemy struck. The disciples had to be strengthened and fortified, shown and taught immediately. Once the enemy struck, it would be too late.

Thought 1. The same three things should *drive* every believer to serve and to serve now:

1) Knowing the time, the hour, has come, the time is ever so short.

> **"My food," said Jesus, "is to do the will of him who sent me and to finish his work. (John 4:34)**
>
> **As long as it is day, we must do the work of him who sent me. Night is coming, when no one can work. (John 9:4)**
>
> **And do this, understanding the present time. The hour has come for you to wake up from your slumber, because our salvation is nearer now than when we first believed. The night is nearly over; the day is almost here. So let us put aside the deeds of darkness and put on the armor of light. (Rom 13:11-12)**
>
> **What I mean, brothers, is that the time is short. From now on those who have wives should live as if they had none; (1 Cor 7:29)**
>
> **Making the most of every opportunity, because the days are evil. (Eph 5:16)**
>
> **Be wise in the way you act toward outsiders; make the most of every opportunity. (Col 4:5)**
>
> **For this reason I remind you to fan into flame the gift of God, which is in you through the laying on of my hands. (2 Tim 1:6)**

2) Loving "his own," those for whom the believer is responsible.

> **"As the Father has loved me, so have I loved you. Now remain in my love. (John 15:9)**
>
> **Greater love has no one than this, that he lay down his life for his friends. (John 15:13)**
>
> **For Christ's love compels us, because we are convinced that one died for all, and therefore all died. And he died for all, that those who live should no longer live for themselves but for him who died for them and was raised again. (2 Cor 5:14-15)**
>
> **This is how we know what love is: Jesus Christ laid down his life for us. And we ought to lay down our lives for our brothers. (1 John 3:16)**

3) Knowing the enemy, that he is going to strike immediately and with all the force he can.

> **When anyone hears the message about the kingdom and does not understand it, the evil one comes and snatches away what was sown in his heart. This is the seed sown along the path. (Mat 13:19)**
>
> **Finally, be strong in the Lord and in his mighty power. Put on the full armor of God so that you can take your stand against the devil's schemes. (Eph 6:10-11)**
>
> **Submit yourselves, then, to God. Resist the devil, and he will flee from you. (James 4:7)**
>
> **Be self-controlled and alert. Your enemy the devil prowls around like a roaring lion looking for someone to devour. Resist him, standing firm in the faith, because you know that your brothers throughout the world are undergoing the same kind of sufferings. (1 Pet 5:8-9)**

Note: the same facts should drive us to be faithful to our service, laboring all the time, persisting and persevering.

> **Therefore, my dear brothers, stand firm. Let nothing move you. Always give yourselves fully to the work of the Lord, because you know that your labor in the Lord is not in vain. (1 Cor 15:58)**

3 (13:3-5) **Service—Ministry**: the extreme demonstration of royal service. The service was *royal* because it was being performed by Jesus Christ, the Son of God Himself. He and He alone is Lord of lords and King of kings. As mentioned above, both the heavenly host and believers, whether on earth or in heaven, are His. This is the stress of this point: Jesus knew who He was. He knew His glorious Person, yet He humbled and even abased Himself. Note exactly what is said.

Jesus knew that the Father had given all things into His hands: all power and authority and glory and honor—all beings both in heaven and earth—all administration (ministry) and rule—all judgment and responsibility for saving the universe.

⇒ Jesus knew that He had come from God. He knew the exalted position from which He had come and the enormous condescension He had made. He knew the great gulf He had spanned in coming to earth.

⇒ Jesus knew the splendor and brilliance and glory of His Person.

⇒ Jesus knew that He was going to be returning to God to assume His former position of glory, honor, and rule. He knew that He was to take His place at the right hand of God very soon.

But note: He, who was King of kings and Lord of lords, who was God of very God, took off His "outer clothing" aside and began to wash the feet of men. He who was …
- Master became the slave
- the Lord took on the ministry of humiliation
- the Highest took the place of the lowest
- the Sovereign became the subject

Jesus knew who He was, yet He still gave the most extreme demonstration of service possible. He chose the most extreme act possible to demonstrate that there is royalty in service and ministry.

> **Just as the Son of Man did not come to be served, but to serve, and to give his life as a ransom for many." (Mat 20:28)**
> **But you are not to be like that. Instead, the greatest among you should be like the youngest, and the one who rules like the one who serves. For who is greater, the one who is at the table or the one who serves? Is it not the one who is at the table? But I am among you as one who serves. (Luke 22:26-27)**
> **For by the grace given me I say to every one of you: Do not think of yourself more highly than you ought, but rather think of yourself with sober judgment, in accordance with the measure of faith God has given you. (Rom 12:3)**
> **Do nothing out of selfish ambition or vain conceit, but in humility consider others better than yourselves. Each of you should look not only to your own interests, but also to the interests of others. (Phil 2:3-4)**
> **Humble yourselves before the Lord, and he will lift you up. (James 4:10)**
> **Young men, in the same way be submissive to those who are older. All of you, clothe yourselves with humility toward one another, because, "God opposes the proud but gives grace to the humble." (1 Pet 5:5)**

DEEPER STUDY # 1

(13:4-5) **Service—Greatness**: in the hot, dusty country of Palestine, most people wore sandals and their feet became extremely dirty. A water basin sat at the entrance of most Jewish homes. Upon entering a person's home, the poor would wash their own feet, and the rich would have a servant available to wash their feet.

Jesus was assuming the place of a servant or of a slave (doulos) who had no rights whatsoever. (See note—Ro.1:1.) He was demonstrating the route to royal service, demonstrating that…
- the way to royalty is service
- the way to greatness is ministry
- the way to power is humility
- the way to position is serving
- the way to rule is giving

Luke tells us that the disciples were arguing over who was to assume the leading positions in Jesus' government when He took over the kingdom (Lk.22:24; cp. Mk.10:35-45). The disciples were probably so caught up in their thirst for power and authority that they were beyond considering anything rationally. What Jesus did was demonstrate for them the way of true royalty, the walk of a true statesman. There is a royalty to service—a kingly aire to

---

ministry—a real dignity in humbling oneself to meet the needs of others. There is such a thing as royal service.

---

4 (13:6-11) **Cleansed—Washed—Forgiveness—Salvation**: the prerequisite for royal service is that of being washed and cleansed. What happened now was critical for every person who claimed to be a follower and a servant of the Lord. The crucial point is this statement:

> **"No," said Peter, "you shall never wash my feet." Jesus answered, "Unless I wash you, you have no part with me." (John 13:8)**

There is a deeper meaning to what Jesus was doing, a spiritual meaning. A person has to be washed and cleansed by Jesus…
- before he can become a part of Jesus
- before he can serve Jesus

Another way to say the same thing is this: before a person can ever serve Christ, he must be a part of Christ. However, before a person can become a part of Christ, there is a *critical prerequisite*, an absolute essential: a person must be washed and cleansed by Christ.

Now, note what happened.

1. Washing and cleansing are misunderstood. Jesus approached Peter to wash his feet, that is, to clean the dirt and pollution from the lowliest part of his being (his feet). Peter saw Jesus washing him and the others (mankind) and counted it too humiliating a thing for his Lord to do. Therefore, Peter drew his feet back in objection. Never would the Lord of the universe be allowed to do such a thing.

However, Peter saw only the human and physical act of Jesus in serving him and the others (mankind).

> **Thought 1.** Most men misunderstand and object to the cleansing act of Jesus…
> - to the humiliation and condescension of "His time (hour)" (the cross v.1).
> - to the cleansing blood of the Lamb, the Lord Himself.
>
> Most men misunderstand the mission and service…
> - that He came to wash and cleanse men from their sin and death, from condemnation and hell.
> - that He came to cleanse men in His blood that they might be acceptable to God eternally.
> - that He came to cleanse men that they might be fit to serve God, both now and forever.

2. Washing and cleansing have a deeper meaning, a spiritual meaning. (See the earlier part of this point for explanation.) Peter did not understand at first, but he did after Jesus' death and resurrection (cp. 1 Pt.2:24; 3:18).

> **Thought 1.** Today there is no excuse for not understanding what Jesus was doing.
>
> **At one time we too were foolish, disobedient, deceived and enslaved by all kinds of passions and pleasures. We lived in malice and envy, being hated and hating one another. But when the kindness and love of God our Savior appeared, he saved us, not because of righteous things we had**

---

done, but because of his mercy. He saved us through the washing of rebirth and renewal by the Holy Spirit, (Titus 3:3-5)

How much more, then, will the blood of Christ, who through the eternal Spirit offered himself unblemished to God, cleanse our consciences from acts that lead to death, so that we may serve the living God! (Heb 9:14)

But if we walk in the light, as he is in the light, we have fellowship with one another, and the blood of Jesus, his Son, purifies us from all sin. (1 John 1:7)

3. Washing and cleansing are requested. Every man should cry out as Peter did: "Lord, not just my feet but my hands and my head as well." Note that Peter cried for a whole cleansing. He craved to be washed all over, through and through.

Thought 1. There is no such thing as holding back a part of one's body or behavior for oneself, to do as one pleases. There is no such thing as a partial cleansing. The tongue, the eyes, the hands—what one says, looks at, touches—must all be washed and cleansed by Christ, or "you have no part with me."

Who can discern his errors? Forgive my hidden faults. (Psa 19:12)

Wash away all my iniquity and cleanse me from my sin. (Psa 51:2)

Cleanse me with hyssop, and I will be clean; wash me, and I will be whiter than snow. (Psa 51:7)

Help us, O God our Savior, for the glory of your name; deliver us and forgive our sins for your name's sake. (Psa 79:9)

4. Washing and cleansing are thorough and permanent. Peter had just cried for a whole and thorough cleansing. Now note a glorious truth, one of the most glorious truths in all of Scripture.

Jesus answered, "A person who has had a bath needs only to wash his feet; his whole body is clean. And you are clean, though not every one of you." (John 13:10)

Once a man is washed, he is already cleansed. Peter had already been cleansed; therefore, he did not need another bath (experience of being saved and cleansed). But note what was needed: his feet needed to be cleansed. As he walked through the dirt of the world, he needed to ask Jesus to cleanse him from the pollution which he had picked up. He needed a localized cleansing, a cleansing of the body parts that had become dirty.

Since we have these promises, dear friends, let us purify ourselves from everything that contaminates body and spirit, perfecting holiness out of reverence for God. (2 Cor 7:1)

If a man cleanses himself from the latter, he will be an instrument for noble purposes, made holy, useful to the Master and prepared to do any good work. Flee the evil desires of youth, and pursue righteousness, faith, love and peace, along with those who call on the Lord out of a pure heart. (2 Tim 2:21-22)

If we confess our sins, he is faithful and just and will forgive us our sins and purify us from all unrighteousness. (1 John 1:9)

Dear friends, now we are children of God, and what we will be has not yet been made known. But we know that when he appears, we shall be like him, for we shall see him as he is. Everyone who has this hope in him purifies himself, just as he is pure. (1 John 3:2-3)

5. Washing and cleansing are not automatic nor do they come by association. This is clearly seen in Judas. Judas had been with Jesus, working by His side day in and day out. He was a professed follower and servant of the Lord, and so far as could be seen, he had no glaring public sin or corrupt habits. Yet, he never allowed Jesus to wash and cleanse him.

And now what are you waiting for? Get up, be baptized and wash your sins away, calling on his name.' (Acts 22:16)

Your boasting is not good. Don't you know that a little yeast works through the whole batch of dough? Get rid of the old yeast that you may be a new batch without yeast—as you really are. For Christ, our Passover lamb, has been sacrificed. (1 Cor 5:6-7)

And that is what some of you were. But you were washed, you were sanctified, you were justified in the name of the Lord Jesus Christ and by the Spirit of our God. (1 Cor 6:11; cp. v.9-10)

Come near to God and he will come near to you. Wash your hands, you sinners, and purify your hearts, you double-minded. (James 4:8)

Wash and make yourselves clean. Take your evil deeds out of my sight! Stop doing wrong, (Isa 1:16)

O Jerusalem, wash the evil from your heart and be saved. How long will you harbor wicked thoughts? (Jer 4:14)

5 (13:12-14) **Service—Ministry**: the meaning of royal service. Jesus asked the pointed question, "Do you understand what I have done for you?" Then He demanded two things from His followers and servants.

1. The servant of Jesus must *serve Jesus as Teacher and Lord*. Note Jesus' claim: "*I Am*" Teacher and Lord. The servant of the Lord Jesus is not just a follower of Jesus. He is a servant, a slave (doulos) with no rights of his own whatsoever. He is at the beck and call of Jesus. He does not act on his own, nor do his own thing. He does not seek the things of the world: its positions, wealth, power, recognition, honor. He is not existing to *secure* these things; he is existing to serve Jesus and to serve Him alone. (See note, Slave—Ro.1:1.)

"Therefore let all Israel be assured of this: God has made this Jesus, whom you crucified, both Lord and Christ." (Acts 2:36)

Yet for us there is but one God, the Father, from whom all things came and for whom we live; and there is but one Lord,

Jesus Christ, through whom all things came and through whom we live. (1 Cor 8:6)

For this very reason, Christ died and returned to life so that he might be the Lord of both the dead and the living. (Rom 14:9)

God, who has called you into fellowship with his Son Jesus Christ our Lord, is faithful. (1 Cor 1:9)

And he is the head of the body, the church; he is the beginning and the first-born from among the dead, so that in everything he might have the supremacy. (Col 1:18)

Whoever serves me must follow me; and where I am, my servant also will be. My Father will honor the one who serves me. (John 12:26)

Obey them not only to win their favor when their eye is on you, but like slaves of Christ, doing the will of God from your heart. Serve wholeheartedly, as if you were serving the Lord, not men, (Eph 6:6-7)

Whatever you do, work at it with all your heart, as working for the Lord, not for men, since you know that you will receive an inheritance from the Lord as a reward. It is the Lord Christ you are serving. (Col 3:23-24)

2. The servant of Jesus is to serve other believers royally and sacrificially, leading them to walk in open confession and to be washed and cleansed from the dirt of the world.
   a. The servant of Jesus is to serve others just as Jesus did by ministering to the human needs of others in all humility.

And if anyone gives even a cup of cold water to one of these little ones because he is my disciple, I tell you the truth, he will certainly not lose his reward." (Mat 10:42)

Not so with you. Instead, whoever wants to become great among you must be your servant, and whoever wants to be first must be slave of all. (Mark 10:43-44)

"Which of these three do you think was a neighbor to the man who fell into the hands of robbers?" The expert in the law replied, "The one who had mercy on him." Jesus told him, "Go and do likewise." (Luke 10:36-37)

"A new command I give you: Love one another. As I have loved you, so you must love one another. (John 13:34)

You, my brothers, were called to be free. But do not use your freedom to indulge the sinful nature ; rather, serve one another in love. (Gal 5:13)

Carry each other's burdens, and in this way you will fulfill the law of Christ. (Gal 6:2)

Therefore, as we have opportunity, let us do good to all people, especially to those who belong to the family of believers. (Gal 6:10)

b. The servant of Jesus is to minister to the spiritual needs of others by leading them to Christ for washing and cleansing from the dirt of the world.

Just as the Son of Man did not come to be served, but to serve, and to give his life as a ransom for many." (Mat 20:28)

Again Jesus said, "Peace be with you! As the Father has sent me, I am sending you." (John 20:21)

Again Jesus said, "Simon son of John, do you truly love me?" He answered, "Yes, Lord, you know that I love you." Jesus said, "Take care of my sheep." (John 21:16)

"Come now, let us reason together," says the LORD. "Though your sins are like scarlet, they shall be as white as snow; though they are red as crimson, they shall be like wool. (Isa 1:18)

6 (13:15-17) **Service—Ministry**: the reasons for royal service are threefold.

1. A believer is to serve because of Jesus' example. It would be easy to wash Jesus' feet, but to wash each others' feet is where the difficulty lies.
   ⇒ Is there someone's feet I am unwilling to wash? Remember Jesus washed even Judas' feet.

Then Jesus said to his disciples, "If anyone would come after me, he must deny himself and take up his cross and follow me. (Mat 16:24)

May the God who gives endurance and encouragement give you a spirit of unity among yourselves as you follow Christ Jesus, (Rom 15:5)

Be imitators of God, therefore, as dearly loved children and live a life of love, just as Christ loved us and gave himself up for us as a fragrant offering and sacrifice to God. (Eph 5:1-2)

Your attitude should be the same as that of Christ Jesus (Phil 2:5)

Therefore, as God's chosen people, holy and dearly loved, clothe yourselves with compassion, kindness, humility, gentleness and patience. Bear with each other and forgive whatever grievances you may have against one another. Forgive as the Lord forgave you. (Col 3:12-13)

2. A believer is to serve because believers are not as great as the Lord. Note: we are less than Jesus Christ...
   • in person and position
   • in mission and work

(The same saying is found in Mt.10:24; Lk.6:40; Jn.15:20. Cp. also Lk.22:26-27 for a picture of the truth.)

3. A believer is to serve because of resulting joy. The Greek tense is continuous, "Blessed are you if you keep on doing them [these things, serving]." Just knowing the truth is not enough. We must do the truth and keep on doing the truth. When we do, we are filled with joy. (Cp. Jn.15:11.)

Take my yoke upon you and learn from me, for I am gentle and humble in heart, and you will find rest for your souls. (Mat 11:29)

If anyone chooses to do God's will, he will find out whether my teaching comes from God or whether I speak on my own. (John 7:17)

Until now you have not asked for anything in my name. Ask and you will receive, and your joy will be complete. (John 16:24)

"I am coming to you now, but I say these things while I am still in the world, so that they may have the full measure of my joy within them. (John 17:13)

For the kingdom of God is not a matter of eating and drinking, but of righteousness, peace and joy in the Holy Spirit, (Rom 14:17)

Though you have not seen him, you love him; and even though you do not see him now, you believe in him and are filled with an inexpressible and glorious joy, (1 Pet 1:8)

I delight greatly in the LORD; my soul rejoices in my God. For he has clothed me with garments of salvation and arrayed me in a robe of righteousness, as a bridegroom adorns his head like a priest, and as a bride adorns herself with her jewels. (Isa 61:10)

When your words came, I ate them; they were my joy and my heart's delight, for I bear your name, O LORD God Almighty. (Jer 15:16)

B. The Prediction of the Betrayer: A Picture of Apostasy, 13:18-30			
1 There is the heartbreak of betrayal a. Betrayer is not chosen b. Betrayer is of the basest sort: Eats with, yet turns away[DS1] **2 There is the prediction of betrayal** a. To assure that Jesus is the Messiah b. To strengthen the dignity of the Lord's call c. To give assurance of God's indwelling presence **3 There is the last chance given to the betrayer** a. The betrayer's presence exposed b. Jesus' distress c. The disciples' perplexity, nervousness, & self-consciousness	18 "I am not referring to all of you; I know those I have chosen. But this is to fulfill the scripture: 'He who shares my bread has lifted up his heel against me.' 19 "I am telling you now before it happens, so that when it does happen you will believe that I am He. 20 I tell you the truth, whoever accepts anyone I send accepts me; and whoever accepts me accepts the one who sent me." 21 After he had said this, Jesus was troubled in spirit and testified, "I tell you the truth, one of you is going to betray me." 22 His disciples stared at one another, at a loss to know which of them he meant. 23 One of them, the disciple whom Jesus loved, was reclining next to him.	24 Simon Peter motioned to this disciple and said, "Ask him which one he means." 25 Leaning back against Jesus, he asked him, "Lord, who is it?" 26 Jesus answered, "It is the one to whom I will give this piece of bread when I have dipped it in the dish." Then, dipping the piece of bread, he gave it to Judas Iscariot, son of Simon. 27 As soon as Judas took the bread, Satan entered into him. "What you are about to do, do quickly," Jesus told him, 28 But no one at the meal understood why Jesus said this to him. 29 Since Judas had charge of the money, some thought Jesus was telling him to buy what was needed for the Feast, or to give something to the poor. 30 As soon as Judas had taken the bread, he went out. And it was night.	d. Peter's gesture for John to inquire further e. John's inquiry f. Jesus' indirect & merciful identification: The giving of a last chance **4 There is the warning against betrayal** a. The evil possession b. The charge: Act now c. The deceiving of the disciples by the betrayer d. The judgment: Seen in the betrayer being separated immediately

DIVISION XIII

THE REVELATION OF JESUS, THE GREAT MINISTER AND HIS LEGACY, 13:1-16:33

B. The Prediction of the Betrayer: A Picture of Apostasy, 13:18-30

(13:18-30) **Introduction**: this is a clear picture of betrayal and apostasy, of a man who turns away from Christ to the world. It stands as a strong warning to every man who *professes* to follow Christ.

1. There is the heartbreak of betrayal (v.18).
2. There is the prediction of betrayal (v.19-20).
3. There is the last chance given to the betrayer (v.21-26).
4. There is the warning against betrayal (v.27-30).

1 (13:18) **Betrayal—Apostasy**: there is the heartbreak of betrayal. When Judas or any other man betrays the Lord, the Lord's heart is cut to the core, for a soul is being lost. There are two things in particular that cut deeply.

1. The betrayer is not chosen by Christ. He cannot be, for he has rejected Christ; therefore, Christ has to reject him (Mt.10:32-33). Christ did draw Judas; He did move upon Judas' heart to quicken his mind. He did stir Judas to understand that He, Jesus, *was* the Messiah, the very Son of God Himself. But Judas rebelled against the *drawing power* of Christ and rejected the *quickening power* of Christ.

When a man is so drawn and quickened by God's Spirit, he must respond then and there. God says, "My Spirit will not always contend [strive] with man forever" (Gen.6:3). Most persons are aware of a tugging and a pull to decide for God sometime in their lives. However, when the tug and the drawing power are rejected, it soon leaves; and the person ceases to think too much about the matter.

> **Then the LORD said, "My Spirit will not contend with man forever, for he is**

> **mortal ; his days will be a hundred and twenty years." (Gen 6:3)**
> **A man who remains stiff-necked after many rebukes will suddenly be destroyed— without remedy. (Prov 29:1)**

The point is this. When a person betrays Christ and begins to live in sin, he shows that he did not truly respond to *the movement* of God's Spirit within his heart. He exposes his true unregenerate nature: he is not one of the chosen of God. This breaks the heart of Christ, for He wants every man to pay attention to the call of the Spirit, to respond to His offer of eternal salvation. He wants everyone to become a true follower of His. He wants no one to be lost.

> **The Lord is not slow in keeping his promise, as some understand slowness. He is patient with you, not wanting anyone to perish, but everyone to come to repentance. (2 Pet 3:9)**
> **"For many are invited, but few are chosen." (Mat 22:14.** See notes—Jn.6:44-46; DEEPER STUDY #1—12:39-41 for more discussion.)

2. The betrayer is of the basest sort: he eats with Christ, yet his heel is against Christ. Judas actually ate bread with Jesus. Judas was a friend of Jesus, not an enemy. He did not hate Jesus; he cared for Him. He often walked into the house of God with Jesus and had close fellowship with Him. Judas was His follower, a choice disciple, yet Judas lifted up his heel against Jesus. The very wording of the prophecy shows the heartrending tragedy of the situation.

The term "lifted up his heel" is the picture of a horse lifting up his hoof to kick. Judas *kicked* Jesus. He struck Him with the fatal blow...

⇒ of disloyalty: he forsook Christ.
⇒ of contempt: he rejected Christ.
⇒ of betrayal: he spurned the love of Christ, turning his back upon Him.

The whole scene is one of tragedy, a tragedy that is deplorable and heartbreaking One who professed Christ was not a true follower of Christ. He was in fact a betrayer, an enemy, a person who chose and stood for the things of the world (money, recognition, power. See note—Jn.12:4-8.)

> For of this you can be sure: No immoral, impure or greedy person—such a man is an idolater—has any inheritance in the kingdom of Christ and of God. Let no one deceive you with empty words, for because of such things God's wrath comes on those who are disobedient. (Eph 5:5-6)
> For if the message spoken by angels was binding, and every violation and disobedience received its just punishment, how shall we escape if we ignore such a great salvation? This salvation, which was first announced by the Lord, was confirmed to us by those who heard him. (Heb 2:2-3)

DEEPER STUDY # 1
(13:18) **Prophetic Reference**: cp. Ps.41:9.

---

2 (13:19-20) **Betrayal—Apostasy—Minister, Dignity of**: there is the prediction of the betrayal. Christ predicted the betrayal to strengthen and assure the disciples.

1. Christ wanted His disciples to be strong in their belief in Him as the Messiah. Once the prophecy came to pass, they would know He was omniscient (that He knew all things). And only God knows all things. Therefore, they would know that He was exactly who He claimed to be, the Son of God, the One who has the very nature of God Himself. Their faith in Him would be strongly strengthened.

Thought 1. God knows every person's heart. Even a person's inner thoughts are known to God, as well as what a person does. No one can hide what He does from God, not even a thought. God knows if a man is betraying His Son. He even knows if a man is thinking about sinning and turning his back on Jesus. The more a man thinks about sinning, the more likely he is to turn back. His betrayal can be predicted.

> For there is nothing hidden that will not be disclosed, and nothing concealed that will not be known or brought out into the open. (Luke 8:17)
> Yet there are some of you who do not believe." For Jesus had known from the beginning which of them did not believe and who would betray him. (John 6:64)
> "His eyes are on the ways of men; he sees their every step. (Job 34:21)
> For a man's ways are in full view of the LORD, and he examines all his paths. (Prov 5:21)
> My eyes are on all their ways; they are not hidden from me, nor is their sin concealed from my eyes. (Jer 16:17)

> Then the Spirit of the LORD came upon me, and he told me to say: "This is what the LORD says: That is what you are saying, O house of Israel, but I know what is going through your mind. (Ezek 11:5)

Thought 2. The fulfillment of prophecy is strong evidence for both the deity of Christ and the inspiration of the Bible.

> So Jesus said, "When you have lifted up the Son of Man, then you will know that I am the one I claim to be and that I do nothing on my own but speak just what the Father has taught me. The one who sent me is with me; he has not left me alone, for I always do what pleases him." (John 8:28-29)
> I tell you the truth, until heaven and earth disappear, not the smallest letter, not the least stroke of a pen, will by any means disappear from the Law until everything is accomplished. (Mat 5:18)
> But I the LORD will speak what I will, and it shall be fulfilled without delay. For in your days, you rebellious house, I will fulfill whatever I say, declares the Sovereign LORD.'" (Ezek 12:25)

2. Christ wanted His disciples to be assured of the dignity of their call as servants of God. Judas had betrayed the call, and his betrayal had left a bad image in people's minds and reflected a poor image of the ministry. It could affect some people, causing them to question the power of Christ, even causing others to actually withdraw and turn away from the ministry. The betrayal could also cause true disciples to become discouraged, feeling that God's call and ministry did not have the dignity Christ claimed.

> Now we ask you, brothers, to respect those who work hard among you, who are over you in the Lord and who admonish you. Hold them in the highest regard in love because of their work. Live in peace with each other. (1 Th 5:12-13)
> The elders who direct the affairs of the church well are worthy of double honor, especially those whose work is preaching and teaching. (1 Tim 5:17)
> Remember your leaders, who spoke the word of God to you. Consider the outcome of their way of life and imitate their faith. (Heb 13:7)

Christ was clear. The man may be dirty and unclean; he may even be a betrayer, but the call and ministry are not touched. The office of His servant and follower cannot be affected. Nothing can affect the relationship between Him and His true disciple, nor the relationship between the Father and His disciple. People will still continue to be saved. Nothing can change this. People out in the world...

• who receive the Lord's messenger receive the Lord.
• who receive the Lord receive God.

> For, "Everyone who calls on the name of the Lord will be saved." (Rom 10:13)
> Here I am! I stand at the door and knock. If anyone hears my voice and opens the door, I will come in and eat with him, and he with me. (Rev 3:20)

3. Christ wanted His disciples to be assured of God's indwelling presence. Note that Christ put Himself on a par with God. To receive Christ is to receive God, and to receive Christ's indwelling presence is to have God's indwelling presence. What a glorious promise to the believer! His body is the temple of God (cp. 1 Cor.6:19-20. See DEEPER STUDY # 4—Jn.20:22; 2 Cor.4:7 for more discussion.)

> **That all of them may be one, Father, just as you are in me and I am in you. May they also be in us so that the world may believe that you have sent me. (John 17:21; cp. Jn.10:37-38; 14:10).)**
>
> **I in them and you in me. May they be brought to complete unity to let the world know that you sent me and have loved them even as you have loved me. (John 17:23)**
>
> **Do you not know that your body is a temple of the Holy Spirit, who is in you, whom you have received from God? You are not your own; you were bought at a price. Therefore honor God with your body. (1 Cor 6:19-20)**

3 (13:21-26) **Betrayal—Decision—Last Chance**: there is the last chance given to the betrayer. This scene is most descriptive. Jesus exposed Judas, but He did it quietly, and He did it to give Judas a last chance to repent and to turn from his evil.

Note that Jesus was "troubled in spirit" and "testified" (a strong, solemn witness), that he used the solemn attention getter, "I tell you the truth." All this stresses the extreme seriousness of betrayal. Jesus was "troubled in spirit": distressed, moved, disturbed over the desertion of this false believer and servant—this betrayer who was turning back to the sin of the world.

The disciples were perplexed and became nervous and self-conscious over Jesus' exposure of a betrayer. The disciples had no idea; they were totally unaware of a deserter. They looked at one another wondering just who it might be. Note two things.

⇒ Judas was a counterfeit disciple, an exceptional deceiver. In public he was ideal: moral, decent, upright. No one ever suspected him—not at all. It was what Judas did in secret that doomed him, not what he did in public. He was a deserter, a man of the world behind the scenes.

⇒ Note the tenderness of Jesus. He did not reveal the betrayer by name. Jesus was making the man aware that He knew about his desertion, and He was hoping that the man would begin to fear and turn from his evil deed.

The disciples wanted to know who the traitor was. One of the disciples who was leaning next to Jesus, apparently John himself (out of humility he did not give his name), was beckoned by Peter to ask Jesus for the name of the betrayer.

Note Jesus' tenderness and appeal: His love still reached out to Judas.

⇒ Jesus did not name Judas as the traitor, not vocally. He did not want the disciples to know who the betrayer was. Judas still had a chance.

⇒ Jesus drew Judas close by His side. Apparently, He asked Judas to sit by His side. He was close enough that Jesus could reach him and hand the piece of bread to him. Jesus wanted him close so that Judas would be in a position to consider the

seriousness of what he was doing. (Note: if the listener of this point is living in sin, God has him listening. God wants him to consider the seriousness of his sin. God will place the betrayer in a position where he has to consider the seriousness of what he is doing.)

⇒ Jesus gave very special attention to Judas. He gave the piece of bread to Judas. The piece of bread (a morsel of food or meat) was a sign of special attention and affection. This act of affection actually turned suspicion away from Judas, for Jesus seemed to be saying "Judas means something special to me." This act also gave Judas a chance to repent.

⇒ Jesus identified Judas, but only to John. However, John did not fully grasp what was happening. Remember the disciples had no idea that Jesus was about to be murdered. The giving of the piece of bread, because of its sign of affection, also threw suspicion away from Judas.

The whole scene, in all its descriptive drama and tragedy, is a picture of strong appeal—the appeal of the Lord to a man who was about to sell his soul for the goods of the world. It is the picture of a last chance being given to a betrayer.

Thought 1. Note that this is the last chance Judas would ever have to repent. There would be no more opportunities. The Lord was appealing and doing all He could. The decision was the deserter's. He would either turn to Christ or to the world. There would be no more chances.

> **Repent, then, and turn to God, so that your sins may be wiped out, that times of refreshing may come from the Lord, (Acts 3:19)**
>
> **Repent of this wickedness and pray to the Lord. Perhaps he will forgive you for having such a thought in your heart. (Acts 8:22)**

4 (13:27-30) **Betrayal—Apostasy**: there is the warning against betrayal. This whole scene is a warning to every person who claims to be a follower of Christ. Remember, Judas was a disciple, a man who ate with Jesus and was a close friend of Jesus.

1. Evil possessed Judas; Satan entered him. This was a critical moment. Sitting there, Judas stiffened and refused to listen. He hardened his heart and made the decision...

- to give himself over to evil and to do the work of Satan.
- to be filled with the thoughts of wrong and of Satan.
- to act for sin and for Satan.
- to be controlled by evil and controlled by Satan.

Judas made the decision to do as he had planned. He gave himself over to evil: to be possessed by Satan and evil.

Thought 1. The warning is clear. To do sin is to be possessed by sin and by Satan himself.

2. Jesus charged Judas: act now and act quickly. Once a person has made the decision to desert Him, Jesus wants no

dallying around. He wants the traitor and counterfeit disciple out from among His fellowship.

3. The deception of the disciples. Judas had hid his sin well. The other disciples had no idea what was happening.

Thought 1. Being able to hide and keep sin a secret...
- is not a cute trick
- is not a reason for feeling more suave or capable than others
- is not a reason for feeling that one's ego is boosted

Hiding and keeping sin a secret is building one's life upon a false foundation that will result in a collapsed life. The very fact that true disciples are unaware of a person's sin is a warning to the sinner. He is building a life of deception and lies that will crumble every worthwhile relationship he has.

> But everyone who hears these words of mine and does not put them into practice is like a foolish man who built his house on and. The rain came down, the streams rose, and the winds blew and beat against that house, and it fell with a great crash."
(Mat 7:26-27)

> There is a judge for the one who rejects me and does not accept my words; that very word which I spoke will condemn him at the last day. (John 12:48)

> For the wages of sin is death, but the gift of God is eternal life in Christ Jesus our Lord. (Rom 6:23)

> How shall we escape if we ignore such a great salvation? This salvation, which was first announced by the Lord, was confirmed to us by those who heard him. (Heb 2:3)

> Who is the liar? It is the man who denies that Jesus is the Christ. Such a man is the antichrist—he denies the Father and the Son. (1 John 2:22)

> For every living soul belongs to me, the father as well as the son—both alike belong to me. The soul who sins is the one who will die. (Ezek 18:4)

4. The judgment is descriptive. The deserter...
- was separated immediately
- went out into the night and into the darkness (see note—Jn.3:18-20; Deeper Study # 2—8:12)

1 Jesus' death brought a threefold glory	C. The Departure of Jesus From This World (Part 1) 13:31-38 (Mt.26:30-35; Mk.14: 26-31; Lk.22:31-34)	you: Love one another As I have loved you, so you must love one another. 35 By this all men will know that you are my disciples, if you love one another."	To love as Jesus loved
a. The Son of Man's glory: The cross	31 When he was gone, Jesus said, "Now is the Son of Man glorified and God is glorified in him.		c. The mark of a true disciple: Love
b. God's glory: Jesus' obedience	32 If God is glorified in him, God will glorify the Son in himself, and will glorify him at once.	36 Simon Peter asked him, "Lord, where are you going?" Jesus replied, "Where I am going, you cannot follow now, but you will follow later."	3 Jesus' death revealed stumbling loyalty a. Cause 1: Misunderstanding Jesus' death
c. Jesus' glory: The resurrection			
2 Jesus' death demanded a new commandment	33 "My children, I will be with you only a little longer. You will look for me, and just as I told the Jews, so I tell you now: Where I am going, you cannot come.	37 Peter asked, "Lord, why can't I follow you now? I will lay down my life for you." 38 Then Jesus answered, "Will you really lay down your life for me? I tell you the truth, before the rooster crows, you will disown me three times!	b. Cause 2: Carnal commitment
a. The reason: His departure from the earth			
b. The new commandment:	34 "A new command I give		

DIVISION XIII

THE REVELATION OF JESUS, THE GREAT MINISTER AND HIS LEGACY, 13:1-16:33

C. The Departure of Jesus From This World, 13:31-38

(13:31-38) **Introduction**: the death and departure of Jesus from the world was most significant.
1. Jesus' death brought a threefold glory (v.31-32).
2. Jesus' death demanded a new commandment (v.33-35).
3. Jesus' death revealed a stumbling loyalty (v.36-38).

1 (13:31-32) **Jesus Christ, Glory; Death**: Jesus' death brought a threefold glory.
1. There was the Son of Man's glory. The glory of Jesus was the cross. This was true in four senses. (See note—Jn.12:23-26 for more discussion.)
   a. Jesus was now ready to secure an eternal righteousness for man. He was now ready to take the final step as the Son of Man...
   • as the One who was the Servant of all men.
   • as the One who was to secure perfect righteousness by dying as God willed.
   • as the One who was to pay the supreme price in obeying God (to die).
   • as the One who was ready to die in obedience to God's will so that God could save man.

   Jesus became the Perfect and Ideal Man because He was perfectly obedient to God, even in dying. As the Ideal Man, His righteousness and death could stand for every man's righteousness and death. A person just has to believe the fact that Jesus' death covers him. There was glory in being the Son of Man: in being every man's Ideal righteousness and death. The cross glorifies Jesus as the Son of Man. (See notes, Son of Man—Jn.1:51; DEEPER STUDY # 1,2—Justification—Ro.4:22; note—5:1 for more discussion.)

   Just as Moses lifted up the snake in the desert, so the Son of Man must be lifted up,
   That everyone who believes in him may have eternal life. (John 3:14-15)

God made him who had no sin to be sin for us, so that in him we might become the righteousness of God. (2 Cor 5:21)

   b. Jesus was now ready to make the final sacrifice for man, and He was ready to pay the supreme price to bring about the greatest event in all history: the salvation of man. The cross attracts and stirs men to give themselves to Jesus and to honor and praise Him. It is in the cross that men find their salvation; therefore, the cross is the glory of Jesus.
   c. Jesus was now ready to triumph over Satan by breaking Satan's power over death and over the souls of men. (See DEEPER STUDY # 1—Mt.8:28-34; DEEPER STUDY # 2—Jn.12:31 for more discussion.)
   ⇒ Jesus spoiled rulers and authorities, principalities and powers, triumphing over them in the cross.

   When you were dead in your sins and in the uncircumcision of your sinful nature, God made you alive with Christ. He forgave us all our sins, (Col 2:13)

   ⇒ Jesus destroyed the devil's work.

   He who does what is sinful is of the devil, because the devil has been sinning from the beginning. The reason the Son of God appeared was to destroy the devil's work. (1 John 3:8)

   ⇒ Jesus broke the power and fear of Satan over lives and death.

   Since the children have flesh and blood, he too shared in their humanity so that by his death he might destroy him who holds the power of death--that is, the devil--and free those who all their lives

were held in slavery by their fear of death. (Heb 2:15)

There is glory in the triumph and victory over Satan, especially over one so powerful and influential as Satan. The cross is the glory of Christ.

Now is the time for judgment on this world; now the prince of this world will be driven out. But I, when I am lifted up from the earth, will draw all men to myself." (John 12:31-32)

d. Jesus demonstrated what perfect sacrifice and self-denial, courage and strength, love and compassion really are when He died on the cross. There is great glory in every one of these qualities. The cross is the glory of Christ.

2. There is God's glory. The glory of God was the perfect obedience of Jesus.

a. God was glorified by the supreme obedience of Jesus dying on the cross (see note, pt.3—Jn.12:27-30 for discussion). His obedience in dying upon the cross glorifies God.

The reason my Father loves me is that I lay down my life—only to take it up again. No one takes it from me, but I lay it down of my own accord. I have authority to lay it down and authority to take it up again. This command I received from my Father." (John 10:17-18)

And live a life of love, just as Christ loved us and gave himself up for us as a fragrant offering and sacrifice to God. (Eph 5:2)

Although he was a son, he learned obedience from what he suffered (Heb 5:8)

b. God's justice was perfectly satisfied on the cross. His honor was restored by the cross, for the evil done against Him was justly punished upon the cross. The cross glorifies God.

God presented him as a sacrifice of atonement, through faith in his blood. He did this to demonstrate his justice, because in his forbearance he had left the sins committed beforehand unpunished— (Rom 3:25)

He himself bore our sins in his body on the tree, so that we might die to sins and live for righteousness; by his wounds you have been healed. (1 Pet 2:24)

He is the atoning sacrifice for our sins, and not only for ours but also for the sins of the whole world. (1 John 2:2)

c. God's love was perfectly demonstrated on the cross. He gave His *only* Son to pay the supreme price *for* man: to sacrifice His life *for* man. The cross glorifies God.

But God demonstrates his own love for us in this: While we were still sinners, Christ died for us. (Rom 5:8)

3. There is Jesus' glory "in Himself." This glory is the resurrection, ascension, and exaltation. What is meant by "in Himself"? There are two possible answers.

⇒ Jesus was asking to be glorified in God Himself: with God's own Person, with His very special presence and power and glory. This, of course, was done when Christ was set upon the throne of God Himself (Rev.3:21).

⇒ Jesus was asking to be glorified *in His own Person*: to be infused with a manifestation of God's presence and power and glory. This was done in the resurrection, ascension, and exaltation of Christ (Ph.2:8-11).

Note: Jesus said that God would "immediately glorify" Him.

Jesus replied, "The hour has come for the Son of Man to be glorified. I tell you the truth, unless a kernel of wheat falls to the ground and dies, it remains only a single seed. But if it dies, it produces many seeds. (John 12:23-24)

After Jesus said this, he looked toward heaven and prayed: "Father, the time has come. Glorify your Son, that your Son may glorify you. I have brought you glory on earth by completing the work you gave me to do. And now, Father, glorify me in your presence with the glory I had with you before the world began. (John 17:14-5)

2 (13:33-35) **Love—Jesus Christ, Death**: Jesus' death demanded a new commandment. Again, note the reference to Jesus' death.

1. Jesus said that He was departing, that He would be with the disciples for only a little while longer. This was *the reason* Jesus had to give His disciples a new commandment. He was leaving. There were three reasons the new commandment on love was needed by every generation of believers.

a. There are times when believers differ. There is always the danger of becoming critical, judgmental, censorious, and divisive. Remember, the disciples had just been arguing over who should receive the highest positions of authority in Jesus' new government (see note—Lk.22:24-30). They had been struggling against each other and were highly critical and judgmental of each other. They had been deeply divided. The need for a new commandment and a new supernatural love existed then even as it does today.

b. There are times when believers feel a keen need for Jesus' physical presence. Jesus knew this. That is the reason He said that the disciples would seek His presence. True, believers have the Holy Spirit, and He is the all-sufficient Comforter and the abiding Presence of God Himself. But being human, believers need another human presence with them. They need a brother or a sister, a genuine believer who loves them with the supernatural love of Jesus Himself. Jesus knew this, so He commanded believers to love each other. Believers are to meet the needs of each other for companionship and fellowship and for care and concern.

c. There is the need for some supernatural force to hold the disciples together. Jesus' physical presence had been the cohesive force that had held the disciples together when He was on earth. But once He had gone, His followers would need something else to hold them together. They must stay and serve together in one spirit and purpose. But how? The new commandment is the answer.

2. The new commandment is to love *as Christ loved.* Note several points.

a. This is not the old commandment, "Love your neighbor as yourself." It is not a human, neighborly love that is being commanded. This *new commandment* was given to *disciples only.* It is the spiritual love that is to exist between believers as brothers and sisters and as servants of God who minister together.

b. The love being commanded is the love of Jesus Himself which is the love of God Himself, the love that can be shed abroad in our hearts only by the Holy Spirit (cp. Ro.5:5). It is not the normal physical love among human neighbors which is being commanded by God. It is a spiritual love that is wrought only by the Spirit of God.

Note: the distinctiveness of this love is that it is the love of Jesus Himself that dwells in the heart of the believer. Only the Spirit of God can put the love of Jesus there within the heart of the believer. The Holy Spirit can create within the believer the love of Jesus Himself, the very same love which Jesus had while here on earth. The love of Jesus is ...

• the love of *spiritual being*: the love that causes one to hunger after union with God and God's people.
• the love of *spiritual life*: the love that shares the same life with all believers, both abundant and eternal life.
• the love of *spiritual union*: the love that binds and ties believers together in life and purpose.
• the love of *spiritual attachment or fellowship*: the love that shares needs and blessings and joys and sorrows and gifts together.

The Holy Spirit can create within the believer a love that can melt and mold his heart to the hearts of other believers. But note: it is a commandment; therefore, it is conditional. The Holy Spirit *can* create such a love, but believers *have to receive it.* When the love of Jesus dwells in the heart of a believer, several things happen. The believer has a love that *causes* him...

• to bind his life to the lives of other believers.
• to tie his life to the same purpose as other believers.
• to surrender his will and to be of the same mind as other believers.
• to understand and feel with other believers.
• to forgive other believers—always.
• to sacrifice himself for other believers—always.
• to seek the welfare of other believers before his own.
• to deny self completely.

c. The new commandment is the mark of a true disciple. The distinguishing mark of a true believer is not the normal human love of neighbors, not even the love of brothers and sisters or of husband and wife. It is the spiritual and supernatural love of Jesus Himself that dwells within the life of the believer. By this love shall all men know that a person is a *true* disciple of the Lord.

> **My command is this: Love each other as I have loved you. (John 15:12)**
> **Now that you have purified yourselves by obeying the truth so that you have sincere love for your brothers, love one another deeply, from the heart. (1 Pet 1:22)**
> **This is how we know what love is: Jesus Christ laid down his life for us. And we ought to lay down our lives for our brothers. (1 John 3:16)**
> **Dear friends, let us love one another, for love comes from God. Everyone who loves has been born of God and knows God. Whoever does not love does not know God, because God is love. (1 John 4:7-8)**

3 (13:36-38) **Peter, Denial—Cross, Misunderstood**: Jesus' death revealed stumbling and faltering loyalty. Note what Peter did. He paid no attention to the new commandment Jesus had just given. His Lord had just said that He was going away and leaving them, but Jesus had not been clear. He had spoken in dark, secretive terms. It was this that had gripped Peter's heart. He must know what Jesus was talking about: if Jesus were talking about some spiritual truth and using symbolic terms or if He were really going to be leaving them.

Now note what Jesus did. He still used the same language: He was leaving, and where He was going they could not follow, not now. But they would follow Him later.

Peter was delving into things he could not yet understand. Jesus was returning to heaven and going back to the Father from whom He had come. He could not say it any clearer than what He had said. The disciples could not and would not understand until after the resurrection and ascension.

Thought 1. How often our curiosity is aroused by the hints of Scripture about future events, the details of which are kept secret—all because it is not yet time for us to fully understand. Just think! If all were revealed, how could we walk by faith and prove our faith? If we walked by sight (seeing and understanding all), there would be nothing to believe.

Thought 2. Note another fact. Peter got distracted and paid no attention to the greatest commandment Jesus had ever given His followers (Jn.13:34-35). It was the future event of Jesus' return to heaven that aroused his curiosity. It distracted his attention from where it should have been.

Jesus used the occasion to reveal Peter's stumbling and faltering faith. Peter stumbled for two reasons.

1. Peter misunderstood Jesus' death. Jesus was going to die and arise from the dead and then return to the Father. He had drilled this fact into the disciples for some months now, using words as clear and simple as possible (see note—Mt.16:21-28). Yet, they refused to accept His prediction. They thought of God's kingdom in terms of a physical kingdom and government set up upon this earth. They saw the Messiah ruling over all the nations of the earth with Israel as the central capital of the world. They thought in terms of earthly freedom, position, power,

fame, wealth, possessions, comfort, pleasure, and satisfaction. They saw the physical and were blind to the spiritual. They did not see...

- God's concern with eternity and the need for the cross.
- that man had to be created spiritually: created anew with the very same nature as God in order to live with God.
- that the cross was God's way for man to be saved: created anew, forgiven and made clean and acceptable before God. (Cp. 1 Pt.2:24; 3:18.)

Very simply stated, it was the idea of Jesus hanging upon the cross that was going to cause Peter to deny Jesus. Jesus had told Peter about the cross, but Peter had refused to believe it (cp. Mt.12:22; 18:1). The fact that human flesh was so depraved that God would have to crucify His own Son in order to save man was just too much to grasp. (See outline and DEEPER STUDY # 1—Lk.9:23; DEEPER STUDY # 2—Ro.6:3-5; notes—Ro.6:6-7; Gal.2:19-21; 5:24; pt.1, Gal.6:14-17. Cp. Ro.6:2; Col.3:3.)

Thought 1. How many make the same mistake about the cross? Misunderstanding the cross and Jesus as the exalted Lord (as opposed to His being just a great teacher) causes stumbling and faltering faith.

For the message of the cross is foolishness to those who are perishing, but to us who are being saved it is the power of God. (1 Cor 1:18)
But we preach Christ crucified: a stumbling block to Jews and foolishness to Gentiles, (1 Cor 1:23)
And even if our gospel is veiled, it is veiled to those who are perishing. The god of this age has blinded the minds of unbelievers, so that they cannot see the light of the gospel of the glory of Christ, who is the image of God. For we do not preach ourselves, but Jesus Christ as Lord, and ourselves as your servants for Jesus' sake. (2 Cor 4:3-5)

2. Peter's commitment was a carnal, fleshly commitment. It was caused by not knowing himself—his own personal weaknesses or the weaknesses of his human flesh. Peter's self-image was strong. He saw himself as being above *serious* sin and failure. He asserted with all the confidence in the world that he would die for Jesus before denying Him.

Note several things.

a. Peter was a strong believer, one of the strongest.
b. Peter really failed to understand self and the flesh. The one sin that a believer should not commit is to deny Jesus. To die for Jesus rather than to deny Him is the one thing a genuine believer would be expected to do.
c. Peter believed strongly that he (his flesh) was above serious sin (cp. Ro.3:9f; 7:8, 14-18; Gal. 5:19f).
d. Peter failed not once, but three times, and all three failures were on the same night with Jesus right off to his side (Lk.22:61).

The man who thinks he knows something does not yet know as he ought to know. (1 Cor 8:2)
So, if you think you are standing firm, be careful that you don't fall! (1 Cor 10:12)
If anyone thinks he is something when he is nothing, he deceives himself. (Gal 6:3)
Do you see a man wise in his own eyes? There is more hope for a fool than for him. (Prov 26:12)
He who trusts in himself is a fool, but he who walks in wisdom is kept safe. (Prov 28:26)

	CHAPTER 14
	D. Jesus' Death Delivers Troubled Hearts (Part 2) 14:1-3
1 Delivers through trust, belief	"Do not let your hearts be troubled. Trust in God; trust also in me.
2 Delivers through the hope for God's house & its rooms or mansions	2 In my Father's house are many rooms; if it were not so, I would have told you. I am going there to prepare a place for you.
3 Delivers through Jesus' work	
4 Delivers through Jesus' return^DS1	3 And if I go and prepare aplace for you, I will come back and take you to be with me that you also may be where I am.
5 Delivers through an eternal habitation with Jesus	

DIVISION XIII

THE REVELATION OF JESUS, THE GREAT MINISTER AND HIS LEGACY, 13:1-16:33

D. Jesus' Death Delivers Troubled Hearts, 14:1-3

(14:1-3) **Introduction**: Jesus' death delivers troubled hearts. The disciples had reason to be troubled. Several things had just happened that would disturb any body of people.

⇒ *Divisiveness* had set in among them (see note—Lk.22:24-30).
⇒ *Desertion and betrayal* by one of them was now known (Jn.13:18f).
⇒ *Separation from the Lord* had been the topic of discussion (Jn.13:33).
⇒ *Denying Jesus* had just been talked about (Jn.13:38).

The scene needs to be clearly viewed, even felt in order to grasp the impact of what Jesus was about to say.

⇒ The disciples were greatly troubled (tarassestho): disturbed, agitated, perplexed, worried, tossed about, confused, distressed.
⇒ The disciples needed to be settled down and given some sense of peace: to receive some encouragement and some new hope.

(How much like believers! How often we are afflicted with trouble and need the same words of encouragement and hope—the same deliverance!) Jesus said that deliverance from trouble comes through five things.

1. Delivers through trust, belief (v.1).
2. Delivers through the hope for God's house and its rooms or mansions (v.2).
3. Delivers through Jesus' work (v.2).
4. Delivers through Jesus' return (v.3).
5. Delivers through an eternal habitation with Jesus (v.3).

(14:1-3) **Another Outline**: Jesus' Death Delivers Troubled Hearts.

1. His commandment: trust, believe in me (v.1).
2. His assurance: God has a house (v.2).
3. His departure: to prepare (v.2).
4. His great promise: to return (v.3).
5. His great purpose: an eternal reunion (v.3).

1 (14:1) **Belief—Faith—Deliverance**: deliverance from troubled hearts comes through trust, through belief in Jesus Christ as well as in God.

1. "You trust in God, trust also in Me. I Am the revelation of God, the Son of God Himself. Trusting in me, that I am the Son of God, will deliver you from trouble." (See notes—Jn.14:6; 14:27 for discussion.)

2. "Trust in God; trust also in Me. Continuing to trust even while you are in the midst of trouble will carry you through. Trusting in God and His Son will deliver your troubled hearts." (See DEEPER STUDY # 2, Believe—Jn.2:24 for discussion.)

> **That everyone who believes in him may have eternal life. (John 3:15)**
> **Whoever believes in the Son has eternal life, but whoever rejects the Son will not see life, for God's wrath remains on him." (John 3:36)**
> **"I tell you the truth, whoever hears my word and believes him who sent me has eternal life and will not be condemned; he has crossed over from death to life. (John 5:24)**
> **Then they asked him, "What must we do to do the works God requires?" Jesus answered, "The work of God is this: to believe in the one he has sent." (John 6:28-29)**
> **Jesus said to her, "I am the resurrection and the life. He who believes in me will live, even though he dies; (John 11:25)**
> **But these are written that you may believe that Jesus is the Christ, the Son of God, and that by believing you may have life in his name. (John 20:31)**
> **That if you confess with your mouth, "Jesus is Lord," and believe in your heart that God raised him from the dead, you will be saved. For it is with your heart that**

you believe and are justified, and it is with your mouth that you confess and are saved. (Rom 10:9-10)

And this is his command: to believe in the name of his Son, Jesus Christ, and to love one another as he commanded us. (1 John 3:23)

2 (14:2) **Heaven—Hope**: deliverance from troubled hearts comes through the hope for God's house. Note several points.

1. Jesus called God "My Father." He knew His Father just as any son knows his father. He knew the truth: His Father *is*, really does exist and live. (Cp. Heb.11:6.) Note the claim to deity Jesus was making (see note—Jn.1:51).

2. Jesus knew *His Father's house*, the truth and reality of it. God's house is real; it does exist. It is a real world that exists in another dimension of being, the spiritual dimension. It is named heaven, for it is His Father's house. This world—the physical and material world—is the property of God, but it is not His house. This earth is not the eternal and permanent dwelling place of God. Heaven is the spiritual world or dimension of being, the *home* of God where the rooms or mansions for believers exist.

3. The word "rooms" or mansion (monai) means abiding place. It means places, residences, dwellings, areas, spaces for living. What a glorious hope! How much clearer could Jesus be: *a place* for every one of us—a place for every believer to dwell and live. Just as we have dwellings and homes here on earth, so Jesus promises us dwellings and homes (mansions) in heaven.

And note: there is no shortage. There are "many rooms." (In the other gospels, Jesus talks a great deal about believers inheriting huge areas or places, even whole realms and kingdoms, which probably mean the heavenly bodies all throughout the universe that will be recreated in the new heavens and earth; 2 Pt.3:10-13; Rev.21:1. See notes—Mt.19:28; 24:45-47; 25:20-23.)

Note how Jesus stressed the truth and reality of "God's house" and its "rooms": "If it were not so, I would have told you." Jesus did not lie. He told only the truth. Note something else: one thing is essential to inherit these mansions—belief in Christ (v.1).

Now we know that if the earthly tent we live in is destroyed, we have a building from God, an eternal house in heaven, not built by human hands. (2 Cor 5:1)

It teaches us to say "No" to ungodliness and worldly passions, and to live self-controlled, upright and godly lives in this present age, while we wait for the blessed hope—the glorious appearing of our great God and Savior, Jesus Christ, (Titus 2:12-13)

When Christ came as high priest of the good things that are already here, he went through the greater and more perfect tabernacle that is not man-made, that is to say, not a part of this creation. (Heb 9:11)

For he was looking forward to the city with foundations, whose architect and builder is God. (Heb 11:10)

All these people were still living by faith when they died. They did not receive the things promised; they only saw them and welcomed them from a distance. And they admitted that they were aliens and strangers on earth. People who say such things show that they are looking for a country of their own. (Heb 11:13-14)

For here we do not have an enduring city, but we are looking for the city that is to come. (Heb 13:14)

Praise be to the God and Father of our Lord Jesus Christ! In his great mercy he has given us new birth into a living hope through the resurrection of Jesus Christ from the dead, and into an inheritance that can never perish, spoil or fade—kept in heaven for you, (1 Pet 1:3-4)

And he carried me away in the Spirit to a mountain great and high, and showed me the Holy City, Jerusalem, coming down out of heaven from God. (Rev 21:10)

"Blessed are those who wash their robes, that they may have the right to the tree of life and may go through the gates into the city. (Rev 22:14)

3 (14:2) **Jesus Christ, Death; Resurrection—Exaltation**: deliverance from troubled hearts comes through Jesus' work. Picture Jesus seated in the Upper Room surrounded by His disciples. He said, "I am going there to prepare a place for you." Where is He to go?

1. Jesus Christ went to the cross: to prepare redemption for us, even the forgiveness of sins.

Just as the Son of Man did not come to be served, but to serve, and to give his life as a ransom for many." (Mat 20:28)

In him we have redemption through his blood, the forgiveness of sins, in accordance with the riches of God's grace (Eph 1:7)

For there is one God and one mediator between God and men, the man Christ Jesus, who gave himself as a ransom for all men—the testimony given in its proper time. (1 Tim 2:5-6)

For you know that it was not with perishable things such as silver or gold that you were redeemed from the empty way of life handed down to you from your forefathers, But with the precious blood of Christ, a lamb without blemish or defect. (1 Pet 1:18-19)

He himself bore our sins in his body on the tree, so that we might die to sins and live for righteousness; by his wounds you have been healed. (1 Pet 2:24)

For Christ died for sins once for all, the righteous for the unrighteous, to bring you to God. He was put to death in the body but made alive by the Spirit, (1 Pet 3:18)

And they sang a new song: "You are worthy to take the scroll and to open its seals, because you were slain, and with your blood you purchased men for God from every tribe and language and people and nation. (Rev 5:9)

2. Jesus Christ went to be raised from the dead: to prepare the conquest of death and a new life and power for us.

> We were therefore buried with him through baptism into death in order that, just as Christ was raised from the dead through the glory of the Father, we too may live a new life. (Rom 6:4)
>
> By his power God raised the Lord from the dead, and he will raise us also. (1 Cor 6:14)
>
> For to be sure, he was crucified in weakness, yet he lives by God's power. Likewise, we are weak in him, yet by God's power we will live with him to serve you. (2 Cor 13:4)
>
> Having been buried with him in baptism and raised with him through your faith in the power of God, who raised him from the dead. (Col 2:12)
>
> I pray also that the eyes of your heart may be enlightened in order that you may know the hope to which he has called you, the riches of his glorious inheritance in the saints, and his incomparably great power for us who believe. That power is like the working of his mighty strength, (Eph 1:18-19)

3. Jesus Christ went to ascend into heaven and be exalted: to prepare an access into the presence of God and an eternal home for us.

> Through whom we have gained access by faith into this grace in which we now stand. And we rejoice in the hope of the glory of God. (Rom 5:2)
>
> Made us alive with Christ even when we were dead in transgressions—it is by grace you have been saved. And God raised us up with Christ and seated us with him in the heavenly realms in Christ Jesus, (Eph 2:5-6)
>
> Since, then, you have been raised with Christ, set your hearts on things above, where Christ is seated at the right hand of God. (Col 3:1)
>
> Here is a trustworthy saying: If we died with him, we will also live with him; (2 Tim 2:11)

Such a magnificent work in our behalf is bound to deliver us from trouble. But remember that Jesus began by stating a condition: "Trust in *God, trust* also in me."

4 (14:3) **Jesus Christ, Return**: deliverance from troubled hearts comes through Jesus' return. Note why He is to return: to receive us unto Himself. There are two times when Jesus comes for the believer.

1. There is death or the passing of the believer into heaven. Death is a private escort or a private presentation to the Lord (2 Cor.5:8). It is not the triumphant entrance and glorious march of victory which is promised when Jesus returns. (See DEEPER STUDY # 1—Jn.14:3 for more discussion.)

> We are confident, I say, and would prefer to be away from the body and at home with the Lord. (2 Cor 5:8)

2. There is the return of Jesus Himself to gather all His dear followers unto Himself. It is this return of Himself to which He is referring in this passage.

Believers are to be glorified with the Father and Jesus. Such a glorious hope—meditating upon and grasping it—will carry a troubled soul through any trial, even the trial of martyrdom. But note again: believing in God and in His Son Jesus is the only way man can take part in His return. (See outline and notes—1 Th.4:13-5:3. Cp. Jn.5:28-29; Tit.2:12-13; 2 Pt.3:3-4, 8-16 for more discussion.)

> I tell you the truth, a time is coming and has now come when the dead will hear the voice of the Son of God and those who hear will live. (John 5:25)
>
> "Do not be amazed at this, for a time is coming when all who are in their graves will hear his voice and come out—those who have done good will rise to live, and those who have done evil will rise to be condemned. (John 5:28-29)
>
> For the Lord himself will come down from heaven, with a loud command, with the voice of the archangel and with the trumpet call of God, and the dead in Christ will rise first. After that, we who are still alive and are left will be caught up together with them in the clouds to meet the Lord in the air. And so we will be with the Lord forever. (1 Th 4:16-17)
>
> It teaches us to say "No" to ungodliness and worldly passions, and to live self-controlled, upright and godly lives in this present age, while we wait for the blessed hope—the glorious appearing of our great God and Savior, Jesus Christ, (Titus 2:12-13)

DEEPER STUDY # 1

(14:3) **Jesus Christ, Return—Death**: there is a difference in the Bible between the believer's meeting Jesus in death and meeting Jesus in the air at His return.

1. The believer does meet Jesus at death. The believer passes from this world into the next world, into heaven itself; and he passes quickly, *never tasting the pain of death* (see note—Jn.8:51). He passes quicker than the blinking of an eye, never losing a moment's consciousness. One moment he is in this world; the next moment he is in the presence of the Lord. This is the believer's personal presentation to the Lord. It is the very first sight the believer will have of his Lord.

⇒ Stephen, while being stoned to death, anticipated going immediately to be with the Lord (Acts 7:59).

⇒ Stephen even "saw the glory of God, and Jesus standing at the right hand of God" (Acts 7:55).

⇒ Paul actually said: "to be away from the body is to be at home with the Lord" (2 Cor.5:8).

⇒ Paul even said "he had a desire" to depart, and be with Christ, which is better by far" (Ph.1:23).

⇒ Jesus had even promised the thief: "today you will be with me in paradise" (Lk.23:43).

⇒ The believers of Thessalonica who had already died are said to "have fallen asleep in him [Jesus]" (1 Th.4:14). By "asleep" is meant they are resting in the presence of the Lord (see note—Jn.11:13).

> Jesus answered him, "I tell you the truth, today you will be with me in para-

dise." (Luke 23:43)

Whoever serves me must follow me; and where I am, my servant also will be. My Father will honor the one who serves me. (John 12:26)

And if I go and prepare a place for you, I will come back and take you to be with me that you also may be where I am. (John 14:3)

"Father, I want those you have given me to be with me where I am, and to see my glory, the glory you have given me because you loved me before the creation of the world. (John 17:24)

We are confident, I say, and would prefer to be away from the body and at home with the Lord. (2 Cor 5:8)

I am torn between the two: I desire to depart and be with Christ, which is better by far; (Phil 1:23)

After that, we who are still alive and are left will be caught up together with them in the clouds to meet the Lord in the air. And so we will be with the Lord forever. (1 Th 4:17)

The Lord will rescue me from every evil attack and will bring me safely to his heavenly kingdom. To him be glory for ever and ever. Amen. (2 Tim 4:18)

2. The believer, his body, does arise and meet Jesus in the air when He returns. The deceased bodies of believers will arise from wherever and however many places they lie on earth. And the believers who are still living on earth will arise in their bodies to meet the Lord in the air. It will be as quick as the blinking of an eye, and it will happen. All believers, both in heaven and on earth, will arise and receive their glorified bodies—dramatically and instantaneously. Jesus promised that He would come again, and He will. We must never forget: God promised that His Son would come the first time, and He came; so He will come again despite the unbelief of the vast majority of people.

Jesus Christ is coming again to give both Himself and His people a glorious reunion and march of triumph over sin, death, and hell…

- A reunion and march so glorious it explosively exceeds all that a man can think or dream.
- A reunion and march of indescribable perfection and joy, a march when all of the dear followers of Christ shall be gathered together before Him for the very first time. Each shall experience the presence and joy of all the saints, the dear, dear saints who have gone before and who have come after—including Paul, Peter, Augustine, Luther, Calvin, Wesley, Moody and all the other well-known servants of God; the multitudes who have been unknown to men, but are well-known to God—known to be first because they labored in the insignificant spots of the world as God directed and were ever so faithful.

There, before the Lord Jesus Christ, we will all stand for the very first time, every believer who has ever lived.

It will be good for those servants whose master finds them watching when he comes.

I tell you the truth, he will dress himself to serve, will have them recline at the table and will come and wait on them. (Luke 12:37)

And if I go and prepare a place for you, I will come back and take you to be with me that you also may be where I am. (John 14:3)

But our citizenship is in heaven. And we eagerly await a Savior from there, the Lord Jesus Christ, who, by the power that enables him to bring everything under his control, will transform our lowly bodies so that they will be like his glorious body. (Phil 3:20-21)

When Christ, who is your life, appears, then you also will appear with him in glory. (Col 3:4)

May he strengthen your hearts so that you will be blameless and holy in the presence of our God and Father when our Lord Jesus comes with all his holy ones. (1 Th 3:13)

For the Lord himself will come down from heaven, with a loud command, with the voice of the archangel and with the trumpet call of God, and the dead in Christ will rise first. After that, we who are still alive and are left will be caught up together with them in the clouds to meet the Lord in the air. And so we will be with the Lord forever. (1 Th 4:16-17)

And when the Chief Shepherd appears, you will receive the crown of glory that will never fade away. (1 Pet 5:4)

Dear friends, now we are children of God, and what we will be has not yet been made known. But we know that when he appears, we shall be like him, for we shall see him as he is. (1 John 3:2)

5 (14:3) **Eternal Life—Heaven:** deliverance from troubled hearts comes through an eternal habitation with Jesus. Note the very reason Jesus will return to earth: "That you also may be where I am." Where is Jesus? Wherever He is, the very place He is, is exactly where we shall be. We shall be with Him—with our precious Lord forever—with Him who has saved us—with Him who has forgiven our sins despite their awfulness—with Him who has delivered us from the bondage of sin, death, and hell—with Him who has cared for us and guided us day by day—with Him who has shared and given us His presence. Again, we shall be with our wonderful Lord forever and ever. This is the very longing of His heart, the very thing for which He prayed so intensely:

"Father, I want those you have given me to be with me where I am, and to see my glory, the glory you have given me because you loved me before the creation of the world. (John 17:24)

But our citizenship is in heaven. And we eagerly await a Savior from there, the Lord Jesus Christ, who, by the power that enables him to bring everything under his control, will transform our lowly bodies so that they will be like his glorious body. (Phil 3:20-21)

	E. The Way to God Is By Jesus Alone, 14:4-7
1 **Jesus' destination** a. The destination is known b. The way is known, v.4 c. Thomas' contradiction & skepticism	4 You know the way to the place where I am going." 5 Thomas said to him, "Lord, we don't know where you are going, so how can we know the way?"
2 **The way to God is Jesus Himself**[DS1,2,3] 3 **The destination is God** 4 **The only way to God is Jesus** 5 **The only way to God is now revealed—unmistakably**	6 Jesus answered, "I am the way and the truth and the life. No one comes to the Father except through me. 7 If you really knew me, you would know my Father as well. From now on, you do know him and have seen him."

DIVISION XIII

THE REVELATION OF JESUS, THE GREAT MINISTER AND HIS LEGACY, 13:1-16:33

E. The Way to God Is by Jesus Alone, 14:4-7

(14:4-7) Introduction: this subject is a continuation of Jesus' departure from this world. It is outlined separately because it is spurred on by another question, this one by Thomas. (Cp. Jn.13:36 for the first question by Peter.)

This is a critical passage—one of the most critical in all of Scripture. Jesus declared in unmistakable terms how a person gets to God, and He makes it clear: there is no other way to God.

1. Jesus' destination (v.4-5).
2. The way to God is Jesus Himself (v.6).
3. The destination is God (v.6).
4. The only way to God is Jesus (v.6).
5. The only way to God is now revealed—unmistakably (v.7).

1 (14:4-5) **Jesus Christ, Ascension; Exaltation**: Jesus' destination is under discussion. He had shaken the disciples badly, discussing at length the fact that He was leaving them. This is, of course, a prediction of His death and ascension (Jn.13:33, 36; 14:3, 4). Note two points.

1. Jesus told the disciples, "You know the way to the place where I am going." And they did, for He had told them time and time again.

   a. "You know the way": He was going back to the Father from whom He had come.

   Jesus knew that the Father had put all things under his power, and that he had come from God and was returning to God; (John 13:3)

   In my Father's house are many rooms; if it were not so, I would have told you. I am going there to prepare a place for you. (John 14:2)

   "Now I am going to him who sent me, yet none of you asks me, 'Where are you going?' in regard to righteousness, because I am going to the Father, where you can see me no longer; Some of his disciples said to one another, "What does he mean by saying, 'In a little while you will see me no more, and then after a little while you will

see me,' and' Because I am going to the Father'?" (John 16:5, 10, 17)

   b. "The way to get there you know": *through Him*.

   "For God so loved the world that he gave his one and only Son, that whoever believes in him shall not perish but have eternal life. (John 3:16)
   "I tell you the truth, whoever hears my word and believes him who sent me has eternal life and will not be condemned; he has crossed over from death to life. (John 5:24)
   Jesus said to her, "I am the resurrection and the life. He who believes in me will live, even though he dies; and whoever lives and believes in me will never die. Do you believe this?" (John 11:25-26)

2. Thomas contradicted Jesus and spoke with skepticism.
   ⇒ We do not know where you are going.
   ⇒ How can we know the way?

Here sat the disciples, thinking that Jesus was about to lead them to set up the Kingdom of God on earth, freeing Israel and establishing it as the greatest nation on earth. Then all of a sudden He began to talk about going someplace; in addition, He insisted they could not follow Him.

They were, of course, thinking in terms of an earthly and temporal government, of worldly positions and power, of wealth and possessions, of pomp and ceremony. This was their problem. Jesus had told them where He was going in simple and clear terms. He had said frequently that He was...
   • to die and rise again (see notes—Jn.7:33-34; Mt.16:21-28; 17:1-13; 17:22; 17:24-27).
   • to go to the Father (see note—Jn.7:33-34. Cp. Jn.8:14; 13:3; 14:2-3; 16:5, 10, 17.)

However, they refused to accept the fact. The result was inevitable. They were misunderstanding what He was saying and doomed to fail in their allegiance to Him.

Thought 1. Note the contradiction and skepticism of the world even today. The world proclaims: "We do not know where God is, not really. Even if He exists, we can only seek Him the best we can, trying to find out just where He is. Every man must find and discover his own way and hope he has found it."

> Then they asked him, "Where is your father?" "You do not know me or my Father," Jesus replied. "If you knew me, you would know my Father also." (John 8:19)
>
> They will do such things because they have not known the Father or me. (John 16:3)
>
> For as I walked around and looked carefully at your objects of worship, I even found an altar with this inscription: TO AN UNKNOWN GOD. Now what you worship as something unknown I am going to proclaim to you. (Acts 17:23)
>
> For this people's heart has become calloused; they hardly hear with their ears, and they have closed their eyes. Otherwise they might see with their eyes, hear with their ears, understand with their hearts and turn, and I would heal them.' (Acts 28:27)
>
> They are darkened in their understanding and separated from the life of God because of the ignorance that is in them due to the hardening of their hearts. (Eph 4:18)

Thought 2. The man who thinks in worldly terms and lives for the earth (position, power, wealth, honor, possessions) shall never know where Christ has gone nor how to get there. As Christ told Nicodemus, unless he was *born again* he would not "see the kingdom of God" nor "enter the kingdom of God."

> In reply Jesus declared, "I tell you the truth, no one can see the kingdom of God unless he is born again." Jesus answered, "I tell you the truth, no one can enter the kingdom of God unless he is born of water and the Spirit. (John 3:3, 5)
>
> The man without the Spirit does not accept the things that come from the Spirit of God, for they are foolishness to him, and he cannot understand them, because they are spiritually discerned. (1 Cor 2:14)

2 (14:6) **Jesus Christ, Mediator**: the way to God is through Jesus Christ Himself. This is a critical verse, for Jesus said that no man could reach God unless he approached God through Jesus Himself. Note Jesus' claim to deity: "I Am" (see note—Jn.6:20). Jesus made three phenomenal claims.

1. I Am the Way (see DEEPER STUDY # 1, Jesus the Way—Jn.14:6).

2. I Am the Truth (see DEEPER STUDY # 2, Jesus the Truth—Jn.14:6).

3. I Am the Life (see DEEPER STUDY # 3, Jesus the Life—Jn.14:6).

DEEPER STUDY # 1

(14:6) **Jesus the Way**: there is a difference between pointing the way to a particular place and taking someone by the hand to lead him there. The person who guides someone to his destination literally becomes the way himself. Jesus Christ not only points out how to walk through life and how to reach God, He personally shows the person the way. Therefore, He Himself is the Way. Note the repetition of the word "way" (v.4, 5, 6).

> Therefore, brothers, since we have confidence to enter the Most Holy Place by the blood of Jesus, by a new and living way opened for us through the curtain, that is, his body, (Heb 10:19-20)

DEEPER STUDY # 2

(14:6) **Jesus the Truth**: there is a difference between telling someone about the truth and living the truth before them. The one who lives the truth literally becomes the truth.

1. Jesus Christ is the *Embodiment* of truth (Jn.14:6). He is the picture of truth. God not only talks to man about Himself, God shows man what He is like in the person of Jesus Christ. Man can look at Jesus Christ and see a perfect picture of the truth of God.

> I and the Father are one." (John 10:30)
>
> Do not believe me unless I do what my Father does. But if I do it, even though you do not believe me, believe the miracles, that you may know and understand that the Father is in me, and I in the Father." (John 10:37-38)
>
> Don't you believe that I am in the Father, and that the Father is in me? The words I say to you are not just my own. Rather, it is the Father, living in me, who is doing his work. (John 14:10)
>
> I will remain in the world no longer, but they are still in the world, and I am coming to you. Holy Father, protect them by the power of your name—the name you gave me—so that they may be one as we are one. (John 17:11)

2. Jesus Christ is the *Communicator* of truth. He Himself—His Person and His Life—makes things perfectly clear. He reveals the ultimate source and meaning and end of all things. He reveals the truth of man himself and of the world surrounding man. He shows man the right way to the truth, and He enables man to choose the right way to the truth.

> I tell you the truth, we speak of what we know, and we testify to what we have seen, but still you people do not accept our testimony. (John 3:11)
>
> Now John also was baptizing at Aenon near Salim, because there was plenty of water, and people were constantly coming to be baptized. (John 3:23)
>
> For the one whom God has sent speaks the words of God, for God gives the Spirit without limit. (John 3:34)
>
> "I tell you the truth, whoever hears my word and believes him who sent me has eternal life and will not be condemned; he has crossed over from death to life. (John 5:24)

The Spirit gives life; the flesh counts for nothing. The words I have spoken to you are spirit and they are life. (John 6:63)

Simon Peter answered him, "Lord, to whom shall we go? You have the words of eternal life. (John 6:68)

Jesus answered, "Even if I testify on my own behalf, my testimony is valid, for I know where I came from and where I am going. But you have no idea where I come from or where I am going. (John 8:14)

He who does not love me will not obey my teaching. These words you hear are not my own; they belong to the Father who sent me. (John 14:24)

For I gave them the words you gave me and they accepted them. They knew with certainty that I came from you, and they believed that you sent me. (John 17:8)

I have given them your word and the world has hated them, for they are not of the world any more than I am of the world. (John 17:14)

"You are a king, then!" said Pilate. Jesus answered, "You are right in saying I am a king. In fact, for this reason I was born, and for this I came into the world, to testify to the truth. Everyone on the side of truth listens to me." (John 18:37)

And from Jesus Christ, who is the faithful witness, the firstborn from the dead, and the ruler of the kings of the earth. To him who loves us and has freed us from our sins by his blood, (Rev 1:5)

3. Jesus Christ is the *Liberator* of truth (Jn.8:32; 15:3). He sets men free from the great gulf (estrangement) which exists between man and God, between man and his world, and between man and man. He sets man free from the frustrations which he constantly experiences. He frees man from the fears and weaknesses and defects that plague him. Jesus Christ is the only lasting Liberator on earth. (See DEEPER STUDY # 1—Jn.1:9; DEEPER STUDY # 2—8:23.)

Then you will know the truth, and the truth will set you free." (John 8:32)

You are already clean because of the word I have spoken to you. (John 15:3)

DEEPER STUDY # 3
(14:6) **Jesus the Life**: there is a difference between telling someone about life and actually living life. The one who lives is the one who possesses life, and the more perfect one lives, the more life one possesses. Jesus Christ lived perfectly; therefore, He possesses life perfectly. He is the Life: the very embodiment, energy, force, and source of life itself. (See notes—Jn.1:4; 10:10; 17:2-3.)

In him was life, and that life was the light of men. (John 1:4)

The thief comes only to steal and kill and destroy; I have come that they may have life, and have it to the full. (John 10:10)

Jesus said to her, "I am the resurrection and the life. He who believes in me will live, even though he dies; (John 11:25)

So that, just as sin reigned in death, so also grace might reign through righteous-

ness to bring eternal life through Jesus Christ our Lord. (Rom 5:21)

But it has now been revealed through the appearing of our Savior, Christ Jesus, who has destroyed death and has brought life and immortality to light through the gospel. (2 Tim 1:10)

3 (14:6) **Resurrection—Ascension**: the destination is God. Again, Jesus clearly said where He was going. He was going to "the Father." He was not going to remain dead. He was going to arise and ascend to the Father. This was a picture of both the resurrection and ascension of Jesus.

Now note: Jesus had just said He was going to His "Father's house." Now He said that He was going to "the Father" of the house. His destination was not so much the house, as glorious as the house is, but the Father Himself. The house without the Father would not be *home*; it would not be heaven.

This says something of vital importance to the believer. The believer's primary objective is to go to the Father Himself, not to heaven, not to a place. The believer's aim is to live in the *Father's presence* forever.

1. The believer longs to know and ever learn of the Father *personally*…

- to know the Father face to face as his Father: as the One who created him, both physically and spiritually; as the One who loves the world so much that He would give His only Son to save mankind and provide so glorious a salvation.
- to know the Father face to face as the Creator and Sustainer of all things: of all life and all worlds, of all universes and in all dimensions of being.
- to know the Father face to face as the glorious Person who dwells in Light so brilliant and full of splendor that no man can approach Him.
- to know the Father face to face as the Supreme Majesty of the universe: the Supreme Majesty both of this world and of the world to come; the King of kings and Lord of lords who is above all, before all, over all, and forever shall be.

2. The believer longs to honor and worship the Father face to face: to praise the Father for Himself and for the wonderful privilege of life; to join in the praise of the universe which is to be given Him who is worthy of all praise, honor, glory, and worship forever and ever.

3. The believer longs to serve the Father face to face: to serve in perfection, without the blemishes and weaknesses so common in one's life and ministry here on earth.

Thought 1. The destination of Jesus was "the Father" Himself. The believer has the same destination: the believer's destination is "the Father," the One who so willingly and graciously adopted him into the family of God.

For you did not receive a spirit that makes you a slave again to fear, but you received the Spirit of sonship. And by him we cry, "Abba, Father." The Spirit himself testifies with our spirit that we are God's children. Now if we are children, then we are heirs—heirs of God and co-heirs with Christ, if indeed we share in his sufferings in order that we may also share in his glory. (Rom 8:15-17)

But when the time had fully come, God sent his Son, born of a woman, born under law, to redeem those under law, that we might receive the full rights of sons. Because you are sons, God sent the Spirit of his Son into our hearts, the Spirit who calls out, "Abba, Father." So you are no longer a slave, but a son; and since you are a son, God has made you also an heir. (Gal 4:4-7)

It teaches us to say "No" to ungodliness and worldly passions, and to live self-controlled, upright and godly lives in this present age, while we wait for the blessed hope—the glorious appearing of our great God and Savior, Jesus Christ, (Titus 2:12-13)

4 (14:6) **Jesus Christ, Mediator—Salvation:** the only way to God is by Jesus Christ (see outline and notes—Jn.10:7-10 for discussion).

Jesus answered, "I am the way and the truth and the life. No one comes to the Father except through me. (John 14:6)

Salvation is found in no one else, for there is no other name under heaven given to men by which we must be saved." (Acts 4:12)

For there is one God and one mediator between God and men, the man Christ Jesus, who gave himself as a ransom for all men—the testimony given in its proper time. (1 Tim 2:5-6)

But the ministry Jesus has received is as superior to theirs as the covenant of which he is mediator is superior to the old one, and it is founded on better promises. (Heb 8:6)

For this reason Christ is the mediator of a new covenant, that those who are called may receive the promised eternal inheritance—now that he has died as a ransom to set them free from the sins committed under the first covenant. (Heb 9:15)

To Jesus the mediator of a new covenant, and to the sprinkled blood that speaks a better word than the blood of Abel. (Heb 12:24)

My dear children, I write this to you so that you will not sin. But if anybody does sin, we have one who speaks to the Father in our defense—Jesus Christ, the Righteous One. (1 John 2:1)

5 (14:7) **Jesus Christ, Revelation:** the only way to God is now revealed, and it is revealed unmistakably. Jesus Christ Himself is the perfect revelation of God. If a man wishes to see exactly who God is and what God is like, he must look at Jesus Christ. The supreme revelation of Jesus Christ is that God is love (Jn.3:16). And a God of love is bound to reveal the way, the truth, and the life in the most perfect picture possible. A God of love would never leave man in the dark, ever seeking, and never able to find and to know. (See notes—Jn.1:18; 3:13; DEEPER STUDY # 1—3:31 for more discussion. Also see outlines and notes—Jn.1:1-2; 1:14; 1:18.)

1. A God of love is bound (by absolute love) to show man THE WAY to Himself. As love, He would never leave man in the dark, feeling about and stumbling after the Way. Jesus Christ is THE WAY. Jesus Christ is the perfect picture of the Way.

2. A God of love is bound (by absolute love) to show man THE TRUTH about Himself. As love, He would never leave man in the dark, searching and grasping after the Truth. Jesus Christ is THE TRUTH. Jesus Christ is the perfect picture of the Truth.

3. A God of love is bound (by absolute love) to show man THE LIFE of Himself. As love, He would never leave man in the dark, wandering aimlessly about and being hopeless in seeking after the Life. Jesus Christ is THE LIFE. Jesus Christ is the perfect picture of the Life.

When he looks at me, he sees the one who sent me. (John 12:45)

Don't you believe that I am in the Father, and that the Father is in me? The words I say to you are not just my own. Rather, it is the Father, living in me, who is doing his work. (John 14:10)

All that belongs to the Father is mine. That is why I said the Spirit will take from what is mine and make it known to you. (John 16:15)

The Son is the radiance of God's glory and the exact representation of his being, sustaining all things by his powerful word. After he had provided purification for sins, he sat down at the right hand of the Majesty in heaven. (Heb 1:3)

		living in me, who is doing his work.	
	F. The Embodiment of God is Jesus Himself, 14:8-14	11 Believe me when I say that I am in the Father and the Father is in me; or at least believe on the evidence of the miracles themselves.	**4 The clear challenge: Believe the claim of Jesus**[DS1]
1 Philip's request—show us the Father, a dazzling sight	8 Philip said, "Lord, show us the Father and that will be enough for us."	12 I tell you the truth, anyone who do what I have been doing. He will do even greater things than these, because I am going to the Father.	**5 The clear promises: Are conditional—to the person who believes on Jesus** a. The power to do great works[DS2]
2 The revelation: Jesus is the full embodiment of God	9 Jesus answered: "Don't you know me, Philip, even after I have been among you such a long time? Anyone who has seen me has seen the Father. How can you say, 'Show us the Father'?	13 And I will do whatever you ask in my name, so that the Son may bring glory to the Father.	b. The answer to all prayers[DS3]
3 The clear evidence a. God's presence b. Jesus' words c. Jesus' works	10 Don't you believe that I am in the Father, and that the Father is in me? The words I say to you are not just my own. Rather, it is the Father,	14 You may ask me for anything in my name, and I will do it.	

DIVISION XIII

THE REVELATION OF JESUS, THE GREAT MINISTER AND HIS LEGACY, 13:1-16:33

F. The Embodiment of God Is Jesus Himself, 14:8-14

(14:8-14) **Introduction**: this is one of the most astounding claims ever made—Jesus Christ is the very embodiment of God Himself.

1. Philip's request—show us the Father, a dazzling sight (v.8).
2. The revelation: Jesus is the full embodiment of God (v.9).
3. The clear evidence (v.10).
4. The clear challenge: believe the claim of Jesus (v.11).
5. The clear promises: are conditional—to the person who believes in Jesus (v.12-14).

1 (14:8) **Spectacular—Dazzling—Signs**: Philip's request was, "show us the Father"—a dazzling spectacular sight, a visible sight of God, a tangible God. Jesus had been discussing the fact that He was returning to the Father and that the disciples could not go with Him, not now (Jn.13:33-14:7). Philip's request shows how the disciples interpreted His words. They thought Jesus meant that He was going to some mountaintop or some other quiet place to meet God face to face just as great men of God had done in the past, men such as...

- Jacob (Gen.28:12f; 32:24f)
- Moses (Ex.3:1f; 24:9-11; 33:14-23; 34:5-9)
- Joshua (Josh.5:13f)
- Gideon (Judges 6:21f)
- Elijah (1 Kings 19:4f)
- Isaiah (Is.6:1f)
- Ezekiah (Ezk.1:1f; 10:1f)

Philip wanted to go with Jesus to see the Father as well. Why? Note two things.

1. Philip felt that a dramatic experience with God—that seeing God—would calm their troubled hearts and solve their problems...
- of strife and division (see notes—Jn.14:1-3; Lk.22:24-30)
- of betrayal and desertion (Jn.13:18f)
- of denial (Jn.13:38)
- of ignorance and misunderstanding (Jn.1:36; 14:5)

Thought 1. Note the emphasis upon the dramatic experience: upon seeking the spectacular and the dazzling, the physical and visible—some sign that God *is*—that He actually exists. How many ask for the dramatic experience and the spectacular sign? They think that once they have had a dazzling sight of God, then...
- their peace will come
- their problems will be solved
- they will believe
- they will serve God
- they will change
- they will do right

2. Philip was not satisfied with what he saw in Jesus, nor with what He had received in Jesus. Walking by faith was not enough. Philip wanted to see some astounding and spectacular Person who appeared in dazzling form. Jesus, although the Son of God, appeared before Philip as a mere man in bodily form. He was not appearing in the dazzling, glorious Being of a heavenly Person. He was not in a spectacular form or vision as men of old had seen and as men usually think of God, the Supreme Universal Being. Jesus was appearing and communicating and living as a mere human being. Philip wanted more than what Jesus was.

Thought 1. What an indictment against men! Men often say, "Jesus is not enough. More is needed. Jesus was a mere man; He could not be *the Son* of God. Perhaps He was *a son* of God in the sense that He was the best man who ever lived, but no more." Such men walk through life being blind to the great love of God.

"For God so loved the world that he gave his one and only Son, that whoever believes in him shall not perish but have eternal life. (John 3:16)

But God demonstrates his own love for us in this: While we were still sinners, Christ died for us. (Rom 5:8)

The god of this age has blinded the minds of unbelievers, so that they cannot see the light of the gospel of the glory of Christ, who is the image of God. (2 Cor 4:4)

They are darkened in their understanding and separated from the life of God because of the ignorance that is in them due to the hardening of their hearts. (Eph 4:18)

2 (14:9) **Jesus Christ, Revelation**: the revelation was astounding—Jesus was the full embodiment of God. "Anyone who has seen me has seen the Father." When a man sees Jesus, he sees a Person...

- who is the very nature of God
- who is the very character of God
- who is the very substance of God
- who is the very perfection of God
- who is God in all of His perfect Being

Jesus Christ is not the same Person as God the Father, but He has the same perfect nature. Jesus Christ is God the Son. Therefore, the person who has seen Jesus Christ has seen the Father in all the fulness of the Father's nature—that person has seen in Jesus the very embodiment of perfection, the perfect embodiment of Being, both perfect love and perfect righteousness.

When he looks at me, he sees the one who sent me. (John 12:45)

If you really knew me, you would know my Father as well. From now on, you do know him and have seen him." (John 14:7)

All that belongs to the Father is mine. That is why I said the Spirit will take from what is mine and make it known to you. (John 16:15)

For in Christ all the fullness of the Deity lives in bodily form, (Col 2:9)

Beyond all question, the mystery of godliness is great: He appeared in a body, was vindicated by the Spirit, was seen by angels, was preached among the nations, was believed on in the world, was taken up in glory. (1 Tim 3:16)

The Son is the radiance of God's glory and the exact representation of his being, sustaining all things by his powerful word. After he had provided purification for sins, he sat down at the right hand of the Majesty in heaven. (Heb 1:3)

(See notes—Jn.14:6; 14:7. Also see notes—Jn.1:1-2; 1:14; 1:18 for more discussion.)

Thought 1. Note the emphasis is upon God *as Father*. Just as an earthly father, God is not distant and far off. He has not created and wound up the world and left it to run on its own, being unconcerned and uncaring. As Father, God is exactly as Jesus showed us...

- loving and just
- giving and helpful
- full of goodness and truth
- responsible and accountable
- directing and correcting
- forgiving and caring

If you, then, though you are evil, know how to give good gifts to your children, how much more will your Father in heaven give good gifts to those who ask him! (Mat 7:11)

"For God so loved the world that he gave his one and only Son, that whoever believes in him shall not perish but have eternal life. For God did not send his Son into the world to condemn the world, but to save the world through him. (John 3:16-17)

No, the Father himself loves you because you have loved me and have believed that I came from God. (John 16:27)

For you did not receive a spirit that makes you a slave again to fear, but you received the Spirit of sonship. And by him we cry, "Abba, Father." The Spirit himself testifies with our spirit that we are God's children. Now if we are children, then we are heirs—heirs of God and co-heirs with Christ, if indeed we share in his sufferings in order that we may also share in his glory. (Rom 8:15-17)

How great is the love the Father has lavished on us, that we should be called children of God! And that is what we are! The reason the world does not know us is that it did not know him. (1 John 3:1)

3 (14:10) **Jesus Christ, Deity—Words of—Revelation**: the clear evidence that Jesus was the embodiment of God is threefold.

1. God's presence was proof that Jesus was the embodiment of God. God was *in* Jesus, and Jesus was *in* God. This can be called the *mutual Indwelling Presence* of God and Christ, each dwelling in the other. This simply means that each has the nature and being, the Spirit and Mind, of the other. Each has the Presence, the very Being and Spirit, of the other dwelling within Him—*perfectly*.

Note the point Jesus was making. The proof that He was the embodiment of God, that He was the One who came to earth to reveal God, is clear: God's presence is not only with Him; God's presence is in Him. He Himself *is* God. He Himself—His Person, His Being, His nature, His character, His love, His care, His just dealings, all that He is—revealed exactly what God is. Note also that Jesus asked Philip a question: "Dont you believe that I am in the Father, and that the Father is in me?"

I and the Father are one." (John 10:30)

Do not believe me unless I do what my Father does. But if I do it, even though you do not believe me, believe the miracles, that you may know and understand that the Father is in me, and I in the Father." (John 10:37-38)

Don't you believe that I am in the Father, and that the Father is in me? The words I say to you are not just my own. Rather, it is the Father, living in me, who is doing his work. Believe me when I say that I am in the Father and the Father is in me; or at least believe on the evidence of the miracles themselves. (John 14:10-11)

On that day you will realize that I am in my Father, and you are in me, and I am in you. (John 14:20)

I will remain in the world no longer, but they are still in the world, and I am coming to you. Holy Father, protect them by the power of your name—the name you gave me—so that they may be one as we are one. (John 17:11)

That all of them may be one, Father, just as you are in me and I am in you. May they also be in us so that the world may believe that you have sent me. I have given them the glory that you gave me, that they may be one as we are one: (John 17:21-22)

2. Jesus' words were proof that He was the embodiment of God. His words were the very Words of God which God Himself wanted to say to man. When Jesus spoke, it was the Father who was speaking through Him. Look at His words, His teaching, and His doctrine, and know that He was who He claimed to be: the Son of God Himself, the very embodiment of God. (See note—Jn.7:16-19 for more discussion.)

Heaven and earth will pass away, but my words will never pass away. (Mark 13:31)

All spoke well of him and were amazed at the gracious words that came from his lips. "Isn't this Joseph's son?" they asked. (Luke 4:22)

They were amazed at his teaching, because his message had authority. (Luke 4:32)

For the one whom God has sent speaks the words of God, for God gives the Spirit without limit. (John 3:34)

The Spirit gives life; the flesh counts for nothing. The words I have spoken to you are spirit and they are life. (John 6:63)

Simon Peter answered him, "Lord, to whom shall we go? You have the words of eternal life. (John 6:68)

Jesus answered, "My teaching is not my own. It comes from him who sent me. (John 7:16)

"No one ever spoke the way this man does," the guards declared. (John 7:46)

I tell you the truth, if anyone keeps my word, he will never see death." (John 8:51)

There is a judge for the one who rejects me and does not accept my words; that very word which I spoke will condemn him at the last day. (John 12:48)

Jesus replied, "If anyone loves me, he will obey my teaching. My Father will love him, and we will come to him and make our home with him. He who does not love me will not obey my teaching. These words you hear are not my own; they belong to the Father who sent me. (John 14:23-24)

If anyone teaches false doctrines and does not agree to the sound instruction of our Lord Jesus Christ and to godly teaching, he is conceited and understands nothing. He has an unhealthy interest in controversies and quarrels about words that result in envy, strife, malicious talk, evil suspicions (1 Tim 6:3-4)

We know that we have come to know him if we obey his commands. (1 John 2:3)

Anyone who runs ahead and does not continue in the teaching of Christ does not have God; whoever continues in the teaching has both the Father and the Son. (2 John 1:9)

3. Jesus' works were proof that He was the embodiment of God (see notes—Jn.5:19; 5:20; 5:36; DEEPER STUDY # 2—10:25 for discussion).

4 (14:11) **Jesus Christ, Deity—Belief**: the clear challenge is forceful—believe the claim of Jesus. He was the embodiment of God. He was *in* the Father, and the Father was *in* Him—perfectly. Jesus was the One whom God sent into the world to show men who He is and what He is like. Jesus Christ was the revelation of God to man, who came to the world to show man that God is "the Father," the Father who loves and cares, forgives and executes justice. The challenge is to believe Jesus…

- believe in Him as a Person, as the Son of God Himself.
- believe in His claim, that His testimony and witness to Himself is absolutely true.

If a person has difficulty believing His claim, then he should look at His miraculous works: believe Him because of His phenomenal miracles; do whatever is needed to secure the evidence, but believe and accept His claim (see DEEPER STUDY # 2, Believe—Jn.2:24).

"I have testimony weightier than that of John. For the very work that the Father has given me to finish, and which I am doing, testifies that the Father has sent me. (John 5:36)

As long as it is day, we must do the work of him who sent me. Night is coming, when no one can work. (John 9:4)

Jesus answered, "I did tell you, but you do not believe. The miracles I do in my Father's name speak for me, (John 10:25)

But if I do it, even though you do not believe me, believe the miracles, that you may know and understand that the Father is in me, and I in the Father." (John 10:38)

Believe me when I say that I am in the Father and the Father is in me; or at least believe on the evidence of the miracles themselves. (John 14:11)

If I had not done among them what no one else did, they would not be guilty of sin. But now they have seen these miracles, and yet they have hated both me and my Father. (John 15:24)

"Men of Israel, listen to this: Jesus of Nazareth was a man accredited by God to you by miracles, wonders and signs, which God did among you through him, as you yourselves know. (Acts 2:22)

DEEPER STUDY # 1

(14:11) **Jesus Christ, Works**: note the purpose for the Lord's miraculous works—to stir the belief that He is the Son of God (Jn.10:38; 14:11; Acts 2:22).

---

5 (14:12-14) **Belief**: the clear promise to those who believe Jesus. There are two promises to the believer. Note the words "I tell you the truth"—words that call one to rouse up and listen closely. What was being said was of tremendous importance.

1. The first promise is the power to do great works: the power to do the very same works that Jesus did. (See DEEPER STUDY # 2—Jn.14:12 for discussion.)

2. The second promise is the answer to all prayers. (See DEEPER STUDY # 3—Jn.14:13-14 for discussion.)

DEEPER STUDY # 2

(14:12) **Jesus Christ, Works—Believer, Works**: this is a surprising statement. It is a great promise: the believer will do the very same things or works and even greater works than Jesus did. Note three facts.

1. The genuine believer will do the same *kind* of work that Jesus did, work that is characterized...
* by loving and caring
* by ministering and healing
* by proclaiming and teaching
* by witnessing and testifying
* by sharing and discipling
* by helping and performing miracles

The believer will work, doing all he can to demonstrate the love of God in order to lead men to a saving knowledge of His Son, Jesus Christ.

> **Just as the Son of Man did not come to be served, but to serve, and to give his life as a ransom for many." (Mat 20:28)**
>
> **For the Son of Man came to seek and to save what was lost." (Luke 19:10)**
>
> **Again Jesus said, "Peace be with you! As the Father has sent me, I am sending you." (John 20:21)**

2. The genuine believer will work hard for the very same purpose as Jesus did. He will work...
* to show men the love and justice of God.
* to help men in all their need.
* to lead men to believe on the Son of God that they might be saved and delivered from sin, death, and hell.

> **Therefore go and make disciples of all nations, baptizing them in the name of the Father and of the Son and of the Holy Spirit, and teaching them to obey everything I have commanded you. And surely I am with you always, to the very end of the age." (Mat 28:19-20)**
>
> **He said to them, "Go into all the world and preach the good news to all creation. (Mark 16:15)**
>
> **And the things you have heard me say in the presence of many witnesses entrust to reliable men who will also be qualified to teach others. Endure hardship with us like a good soldier of Christ Jesus. (2 Tim 2:2-3)**

3. The genuine believer will do even greater things or works than Jesus did. This means that the true servant of God will *reach more* people and have *broader results* than Jesus did. The whole world would eventually hear, and an impact would be made upon many societies and nations as a whole. But note the crucial point.
⇒ Greater works are possible only through Jesus, only because He has gone to His Father and is sitting at the right hand of the Father. From there—from the throne of power—He equips and enables the believer to do the works. The believer is able to do great works only through the presence and power of Jesus who is with the Father. (See note—Mt.28:19-20.)

> **But you will receive power when the Holy Spirit comes on you; and you will be my witnesses in Jerusalem, and in all Judea and Samaria, and to the ends of the earth." (Acts 1:8)**
>
> **With great power the apostles continued to testify to the resurrection of the Lord Jesus, and much grace was upon them all. (Acts 4:33)**
>
> **Now to him who is able to do immeasurably more than all we ask or imagine, according to his power that is at work within us, (Eph 3:20)**
>
> **Because our gospel came to you not simply with words, but also with power, with the Holy Spirit and with deep conviction. You know how we lived among you for your sake. (1 Th 1:5)**

DEEPER STUDY # 3

(14:13-14) **Prayer—Jesus Christ, Name of**: this is one of the most wonderful promises in all the Bible. God hears the prayers of the dear believer. Note three points.

1. The only prayers heard and answered are those asked "in Jesus' name." What does it mean to pray "in Jesus' name"? It means two things.
a. The believer prays knowing that...
* the only acceptance to God is *in Jesus*. God hears the believer only because Jesus is acceptable to Him and the believer comes in the name of Jesus.
* the only Mediator between God and men is Jesus; therefore, the believer approaches God in the name of Jesus.
* the only Intercessor before God, the only Person asking God to accept man is Jesus.
* the only Person, the only name that is perfect enough to approach God is Jesus; therefore, the believer prays in the name of Jesus.
(See notes—Jn.12:44-46; DEEPER STUDY # 2—12:44; notes—16:23-24; 16:25-27 for more discussion.)
b. The believer seeks to glorify the name of Jesus only. To pray "in His name" means that the believer asks only those things that will...
* honor His name
* praise His name
* bring glory to His name
* lead to His name's being lifted up

It means that the believer will ask nothing that would detract, lower, or lead away from His name.

> **You did not choose me, but I chose you and appointed you to go and bear fruit—fruit that will last. Then the Father will give you whatever you ask in my name. (John 15:16)**
>
> **In that day you will no longer ask me anything. I tell you the truth, my Father will give you whatever you ask in my name.**

Until now you have not asked for anything in my name. Ask and you will receive, and your joy will be complete. (John 16:23-24)

2. Note why Jesus answers the prayers of the believer. His purpose is to glorify God. When Jesus answers prayer, not only is the Father glorified, but so is Jesus. The power and wisdom, love and care shown in answered prayer are of God through the name of Jesus. Therefore, when the believer prays and receives what he asked for...

- his attention is upon both the Father and the Son.
- his praise and thanksgiving are heaped upon both the Father and the Son.
- his loyalty and surrender to both the Father and the Son are deeper and more mature.

Giving thanks to the Father, who has qualified you to share in the inheritance of the saints in the kingdom of light. For he has rescued us from the dominion of darkness and brought us into the kingdom of the Son he loves, in whom we have redemption, the forgiveness of sins. (Col 1:12-14)

Give thanks in all circumstances, for this is God's will for you in Christ Jesus. (1 Th 5:18)

And we, who with unveiled faces all reflect the Lord's glory, are being transformed into his likeness with ever-increasing glory, which comes from the Lord, who is the Spirit. (2 Cor 3:18)

Through Jesus, therefore, let us continually offer to God a sacrifice of praise—the fruit of lips that confess his name. (Heb 13:15)

But you are a chosen people, a royal priesthood, a holy nation, a people belonging to God, that you may declare the praises of him who called you out of darkness into his wonderful light. (1 Pet 2:9)

Ascribe to the LORD the glory due his name; worship the LORD in the splendor of his holiness. (Psa 29:2)

Enter his gates with thanksgiving and his courts with praise; give thanks to him and praise his name. (Psa 100:4)

3. Jesus said that the believer is to pray to Him as well as to God. Jesus said, "You may ask me for anything in my name, and I will do it." Jesus is claiming to be God, to have...

- the wisdom and knowledge,
- the power and ability,
- the love and care,
- the desire and willingness,

...to do anything. A phenomenal claim! Yet it is a reasonable claim for the Son of God.

Don't you believe that I am in the Father, and that the Father is in me? The words I say to you are not just my own. Rather, it is the Father, living in me, who is doing his work. (John 14:10)

If you believe, you will receive whatever you ask for in prayer." (Mat 21:22)

And I will do whatever you ask in my name, so that the Son may bring glory to the Father. You may ask me for anything in my name, and I will do it. (John 14:13-14)

If you remain in me and my words remain in you, ask whatever you wish, and it will be given you. (John 15:7)

This is the confidence we have in approaching God: that if we ask anything according to his will, he hears us. And if we know that he hears us—whatever we ask—we know that we have what we asked of him. (1 John 5:14-15)

	G. The Holy Spirit: Who He Is, 14:15-26	is the one who loves me. He who loves me will be loved by my Father, and I too will love him and show myself to him."	within the believer[DS3] a. The special presence is conditional: Must obey & love Christ b. The special presence is questioned
1 **Fact: If a person loves Jesus, he will keep His commandments**	15 "If you love me, you will obey what I command.	22 Then Judas (not Judas Iscariot) said, "But, Lord, why do you intend to show yourself to us and not to the world?"	
2 **He is the Counselor, the Comforter, the other Helper**[DS1]	16 And I will ask the Father, and he will give you another Counselor to be with you forever—	23 Jesus replied, "If anyone loves me, he will obey my teaching. My Father will love him, and we will come to him and make our home with him.	6 **He is the abiding presence of the Trinity** a. Is conditional: Must love & obey Jesus[DS4] b. Is the love & presence of God & Christ c. Is not given to those who do not love and obey Christ d. Is assured by God Himself
3 **He is the Spirit of truth** a. The world cannot accept Him b. The believer does receive Him & know Him	17 the Spirit of truth. The world cannot accept him, because it neither sees him nor knows him. But you know him, for he lives with you and will be in you.	24 He who does not love me will not obey my teaching. These words you hear are not my own; they belong to the Father who sent me.	
4 **He is the personal presence of Christ** a. A spiritual presence not a physical one b. A living, eternal presence c. A living union between God, Christ, & the believer[DS2]	18 I will not leave you as orphans; I will come to you. 19 Before long, the world will not see me anymore, but you will see me. Because I live, you also will live. 20 On that day you will realize that I am in my Father, and you are in me, and I am in you.	25 "All this I have spoken while still with you. 26 But the Counselor, the Holy Spirit, whom the Father will send in my name, will teach you all things and will remind you of everything I have said to you.	7 **He is the Holy Spirit, the Teacher** a. The facts 1) He is promised 2) He is given by the Father in the name of Jesus b. His purpose 1) To teach the believer 2) To help the bel. remember
5 **He is the very special manifestation of Christ**	21 Whoever has my commands and obeys them, he		

DIVISION XIII

THE REVELATION OF JESUS, THE GREAT MINISTER AND HIS LEGACY, 13:1-16:33

G. The Holy Spirit: Who He Is, 14:15-26

(14:15-26) **Introduction—Holy Spirit, Doctrine of**: there are three great Scriptures that deal with the doctrine of the Holy Spirit at length.
1. The Identity of the Holy Spirit or who He is (Jn.14:15-26).
2. The Work of the Holy Spirit (Jn.16:7-15).
3. The Power of the Holy Spirit (Ro.8:1-17).

Note this significant fact: two of the passages involve a discussion by the Lord Himself. He is in the Upper Room spending the last hours He will ever have with His apostles while on earth. He is covering the major subjects they need to grasp before His death, revealing and filling them with the glorious truths that will help them through the upcoming trials they are to face.

The greatest help the believers are to receive is the very presence of God Himself in the Person of the Holy Spirit. It is this that Jesus now reveals. He reveals the Holy Spirit, His identity, who He is. (See outline and notes—Jn.16:7-15 where Jesus reveals the work of the Holy Spirit. Also see outline and notes—Ro.8:1-17 where the power of the Holy Spirit is revealed.)
1. Fact: if a person loves Jesus, he will keep His commandments (v.15).
2. He is the Counselor, the Comforter, the other Helper (v.16).
3. He is the Spirit of truth (v.17).
4. He is the personal presence of Christ (v.18-20).
5. He is the very special manifestation of Christ within the believer (v.21-22).
6. He is the abiding presence of the Trinity (v.23-24).
7. He is the Holy Spirit, the Teacher (v.25-26).

1 (14:15) **Love—Obedience**: a fact—if a person loves Jesus, he *will* keep the commandments of Jesus. Note two things.

1. Obedience is not optional for believers. Jesus stated a simple fact that must be clearly understood: "If you love me you *will* obey [teresete] what I command." This is the correct translation. Jesus is not giving an *optional commandment*, "If you love me, [then, optional] obey what I command." He is saying that the man who truly loves Him *will* obey His commandments. To the believer, there is no option. He loves Jesus; therefore, he obeys His commands. In this the believer is not claiming perfection, but he is claiming to love Jesus and to believe with all his heart that Jesus is the Son of God. Therefore, he diligently seeks Jesus, and he seeks to please Him in all that he does (cp. Heb.11:6).

2. What it means to love Jesus must be clearly understood.
   a. To love Jesus is not an emotional thing. It involves emotions, but it is not *based* upon emotions. It is not *feelings*: not feeling good today and loving Jesus, and feeling bad tomorrow and not loving Jesus. Loving Jesus is not a fluctuating experience, not an up and down emotion. It is not an *emotional love* that changes with feelings.
   b. To love Jesus is not a rational or mental commitment. Of course it involves the mind, but it is not just deciding that Jesus is the Son of God and adopting His teachings and morality as one's standard in life. It is not just living by His teachings and doing the best a person can. It is not a matter

of the mind alone, not a matter of disciplining one's life to keep the law and its rules and regulations.

c. To love Jesus is a matter of the heart and of the spirit: a matter of man's most vital part, man's innermost being, all that a man is. The heart is the *seat* of man's affection and will (devotion). The heart attaches and focuses our affection and will and devotion to an object or a person. The heart causes a man to will to give himself either to good or bad. To love Jesus means that a man focuses his heart and affections and will (devotion) upon God by giving and receiving the love of God. It means that a man gives his *affection* and *will* (devotion), all he is and has, to Jesus Christ. It means he...

- freely accepts Jesus
- cherishes and attaches himself to Jesus
- sacrificially gives all he is and has to Jesus
- commits all he is and has to serve Jesus and His cause

(See outlines and notes—Mt.22:37-40; Jn.13:33-35; 21:15-17 for more discussion.)

If you obey my commands, you will remain in my love, just as I have obeyed my Father's commands and remain in his love. You are my friends if you do what I command. (John 15:10, 14)

We know that we have come to know him if we obey his commands. (1 John 2:3)

2 (14:16) **Holy Spirit**: the Holy Spirit is the Comforter, the other Helper. Note four points.

1. The Holy Spirit is the Counselor or Comforter (see DEEPER STUDY # 1—Jn.14:16).

2. The acceptance of the Holy Spirit is conditional. Note the conjunction "and." It is the person who *loves* Jesus who is given the Holy Spirit. Note also that the Spirit is given because Jesus prays for us. He is our *Intercessor*, the One who pleads our case. It is not that God is unwilling to give the Holy Spirit. That is not the point. The point is that Jesus Christ is our Mediator—our Intercessor—the One who makes it possible for us to accept or receive the Spirit (cp. 1 Jn.2:1-2). If a person truly loves Jesus, that person is given the Holy Spirit.

3. The source of the Holy Spirit is "the Father." It is the Father who gave the Son, and it is the Father who gives the Holy Spirit. The picture is touching in that God is seen longing ever so deeply...

- to give the Holy Spirit to those who love His *only* Son.
- to do everything He can for the person who loves His Son, and of course the greatest thing God can do is to put His Spirit into a person.

If you then, though you are evil, know how to give good gifts to your children, how much more will your Father in heaven give the Holy Spirit to those who ask him!" (Luke 11:13)

4. The Holy Spirit abides forever with the believer. His presence continues and never ends. The idea is that He never withdraws His presence.

DEEPER STUDY # 1
(14:16) **Comforter—Counselor** (paracletos): one called in, one called to the side of another. The purpose is to help in any way possible. (1) There is the picture of a friend called in to help a person who is troubled or distressed or confused. (2) There is the picture of a commander called in to help a discouraged and dispirited army. (3) There is the picture of a lawyer, an advocate, called in to help a defendant who needs his case pleaded. No one word can adequately translate *paracletos*. The word that probably comes closest is simply *Helper*.

3 (14:17) **Holy Spirit**: the Holy Spirit is the Spirit of Truth. Note three facts.

1. The Holy Spirit is the Spirit of Truth, the very same Truth that Christ is. He is the Embodiment, the Communicator, and the Liberator of truth (see DEEPER STUDY # 2, Jesus the Truth—Jn.14:6).

2. The world *cannot* accept the Holy Spirit. Note the word "cannot." It is impossible for the world to accept the Holy Spirit. Why? Because the world of unbelievers does not "see" or "know" the Holy Spirit. The world lives only for what it can see and know, only for the physical and material, only for what it can touch and feel, taste and consume, think and use.

The point is this: unbelievers reject Jesus. They do not love Him, and they care little if anything about Him. They are not interested in seeing or knowing Jesus. The result is natural:

⇒ They do not see the spiritual world or know it; therefore, they do not see or know the Spirit of that world.
⇒ They are unaware of the spiritual world; therefore, they are unaware of the Spirit of that world.
⇒ They do not know and love Jesus; therefore, they do not "know" the Spirit of Christ.

(Note this contrast between the "Spirit of the world" and the "Spirit of God," 1 Cor.2:12-14.)

The man without the Spirit does not accept the things that come from the Spirit of God, for they are foolishness to him, and he cannot understand them, because they are spiritually discerned. (1 Cor 2:14; cp. v.12-13)

3. The believer does know the Holy Spirit. The believer knows the Spirit both by experience and by His presence.

⇒ The Holy Spirit "*lives with*" the believer: giving assurance, looking after, caring, guiding, and teaching.
⇒ The Holy Spirit is *in* the believer: communing, fellowshipping, sharing, and conforming the believer to the image of Christ.

The Spirit of truth. The world cannot accept him, because it neither sees him nor knows him. But you know him, for he lives with you and will be in you. (John 14:17)

But I tell you the truth: It is for your good that I am going away. Unless I go away, the Counselor will not come to you; but if I go, I will send him to you. (John 16:7)

For the Holy Spirit will teach you at that time what you should say." (Luke 12:12)

You, however, are controlled not by the sinful nature but by the Spirit, if the Spirit of God lives in you. And if anyone does not have the Spirit of Christ, he does not belong to Christ. (Rom 8:9)
because those who are led by the Spirit of God are sons of God. (Rom 8:14)

The Spirit himself testifies with our spirit that we are God's children. (Rom 8:16)

Because you are sons, God sent the Spirit of his Son into our hearts, the Spirit who calls out, "Abba, Father." (Gal 4:6)

Guard the good deposit that was entrusted to you—guard it with the help of the Holy Spirit who lives in us. (2 Tim 1:14)

We have not received the spirit of the world but the Spirit who is from God, that we may understand what God has freely given us. (1 Cor 2:12)

Don't you know that you yourselves are God's temple and that God's Spirit lives in you? (1 Cor 3:16)

Do you not know that your body is a temple of the Holy Spirit, who is in you, whom you have received from God? You are not your own; (1 Cor 6:19)

As for you, the anointing you received from him remains in you, and you do not need anyone to teach you. But as his anointing teaches you about all things and as that anointing is real, not counterfeit—just as it has taught you, remain in him. (1 John 2:27)
Those who obey his commands live in him, and he in them. And this is how we know that he lives in us: We know it by the Spirit he gave us. (1 John 3:24)

We know that we live in him and he in us, because he has given us of his Spirit. (1 John 4:13)

This is the one who came by water and blood—Jesus Christ. He did not come by water only, but by water and blood. And it is the Spirit who testifies, because the Spirit is the truth. (1 John 5:6)

And I will put my Spirit in you and move you to follow my decrees and be careful to keep my laws. (Ezek 36:27)

4 (14:18-20) **Indwelling Presence**: the Holy Spirit is the personal presence of Christ. Note four points.

1. Jesus said, "I will come to you." He meant that He would return after He had gone away, that is, died. He would come back to give believers His personal presence. He would not leave them comfortless (orphanous); the word means to be orphaned, to be without parental help, to be helpless. Jesus would not leave them to struggle through the trials of life alone.

Jesus' presence with His followers began with His resurrection and with the coming of the Holy Spirit. Jesus was saying that He would come to the believer in the person of the Holy Spirit.

2. The world lost its opportunity to see Jesus. He said so. He said that He would be present for only a short time longer, then the world would not see Him "anymore." (The next time the world sees Him, He will be coming in judgment.)

3. The presence of Jesus is a living, eternal presence. He died, but He did not stay dead. He arose and conquered death. He arose to live forever. Now think: if Jesus Christ is living forever and He dwells within the believer, then the believer lives eternally. Christ the Eternal Presence lives *within* the believer; therefore, the believer becomes eternal. He never dies. (See DEEPER STUDY # 1—Jn.8:51.) The believer is made eternal by the eternal presence of Christ *within* him.

In fact, when Jesus says "I live," He means He lives abundantly and eternally: He lives life in all of its full meaning. Therefore, by living *within* the believer, Christ imparts the same kind of life to the believer, a life that is both abundant and eternal. (See DEEPER STUDY # 2—Jn.1:4; DEEPER STUDY # 1—10:10; DEEPER STUDY # 1—17:2-3.)

4. The presence of Christ is a living union, a *mutual indwelling* between God, Christ, and the believer. "On that day" refers to Jesus' resurrection and the coming of the Holy Spirit.

Now note: when Jesus arose from the dead, believers knew something. His claim was true in an absolute sense. Jesus really was "in" God. God is eternal, so by being "in" God, Jesus was bound to live forever; He was bound to arise from the dead.

Something else was known. All that Jesus had said was true. He was placing all believers "*in*" Himself and Himself "*in*" them; or to say it another way, when the Holy Spirit came, believers were placed "in" His Spirit and His Spirit "in" them. (See DEEPER STUDY # 1, Holy Spirit—Acts 2:1-4 for more discussion.)

DEEPER STUDY # 2
(14:20) **Christ in You**: this is the first time the glorious truth of *Christ in you* is revealed to the disciples. The full understanding of the indwelling Christ was given and explained by Paul (see DEEPER STUDY #4—Jn.20:22; notes—1 Cor.3:16; 6:19; Eph.3:6; Col.1:26-27; cp. Jn.14:17-18, 20, 23; Ro.8:9; 1 Cor.2:11-12; 3:16; 6:19; 2 Tim.1:14; 1 Jn.2:27; Ezk. 36:27).

On that day you will realize that I am in my Father, and you are in me, and I am in you. (John 14:20)

I in them and you in me. May they be brought to complete unity to let the world know that you sent me and have loved them even as you have loved me. (John 17:23)

You, however, are controlled not by the sinful nature but by the Spirit, if the Spirit of God lives in you. And if anyone does not have the Spirit of Christ, he does not belong to Christ. (Rom 8:9)

I have been crucified with Christ and I no longer live, but Christ lives in me. The life I live in the body, I live by faith in the Son of God, who loved me and gave himself for me. (Gal 2:20)

So that Christ may dwell in your hearts through faith. And I pray that you, being rooted and established in love, (Eph 3:17)

To them God has chosen to make known among the Gentiles the glorious

> riches of this mystery, which is Christ in
> you, the hope of glory. (Col 1:27)
>
> Those who obey his commands live in
> him, and he in them. And this is how we
> know that he lives in us: We know it by the
> Spirit he gave us. (1 John 3:24)
>
> Here I am! I stand at the door and
> knock. If anyone hears my voice and opens
> the door, I will come in and eat with him,
> and he with me. (Rev 3:20)

5 (14:21-22) **Holy Spirit, Manifestation; Infilling—Revelation**: the Holy Spirit is the very special manifestation of Christ within the believer. Apparently, this refers to very special manifestations of the Lord to the heart of the believer, those very special times when there is a deep consciousness of love between the Lord and His dear follower (see DEEPER STUDY # 3—Jn.14:21). This is bound to be what Christ means, for He has already spoken about His personal presence within the believer (v.18-20). When believers go through terrible trials and experience severe crises, God knows and He loves and cares; so He moves to meet the need of His dear children. He moves within the believer's heart, manifesting His presence and giving a deep sense of His love and care, helping and giving confidence, forgiveness, and assurance—giving whatever the believer needs. The depth of the experience and the intensity and emotion of the *special manifestation* depends upon the need of the believer. God knows and loves His dear child perfectly, so He gives whatever experience and depth of emotion are needed to meet the need of His child. We must always remember that God loves each one of us so much He will do whatever is needed...

- to lift us up
- to strengthen us
- to conform us to the image of His dear Son, the Lord Jesus Christ

Note that the *special manifestations* of the Lord's presence are given only to the believer who does two things.

⇒ The believer who has Jesus' commandments receives the special manifestations of the Holy Spirit. To have His commandments means that the believer has searched and possesses the commandments of Jesus Christ. He has them in his heart, knows them, has made them his own (cp. Ps.119:11).

⇒ The believer who obeys the commandments of Jesus.

The believer who does these two things shows that he *truly* loves the Lord Jesus, and he that loves the Lord Jesus shall be loved of the Father and the Lord will love him as well. In fact, the Lord will *manifest* Himself to the believer who hides His commandments in his heart.

Note an important fact: the special manifestation is questioned. Judas asked the question for the first time, but the special manifestation of Christ's presence has been questioned and doubted by thousands ever since. Judas was thinking like all men think—in terms of a physical manifestation, a visible appearance.

DEEPER STUDY # 3

(14:21) **Manifestation—Shows Himself—Revelation** (phaneroo; emphanizo): when used in the sense of an unveiling or revelation, it suggests that a new thing has come to light; that something never known by man before is made known. Some mystery has now been revealed. It is something that cannot be discovered by man's reason or wisdom. It is a mystery that is hidden from man and beyond his grasp. Here in Jn.14:21-22, it means that Jesus' presence is revealed (brought to light), illuminated, manifested, quickened in the life of the believer. It means that He shows, *manifests,* Himself to His disciples in a very special way. He discloses His person, His nature, His goodness. He illuminates Himself *within* their hearts and lives. He gives a very special consciousness within their souls. (See notes—Jn.14:21-22; DEEPER STUDY # 1—Acts 2:1-4.)

> Whoever believes in me, as the Scripture has said, streams of living water will flow from within him." By this he meant the Spirit, whom those who believed in him were later to receive. Up to that time the Spirit had not been given, since Jesus had not yet been glorified. (John 7:38-39)
>
> Whoever has my commands and obeys them, he is the one who loves me. He who loves me will be loved by my Father, and I too will love him and show myself to him." Then Judas (not Judas Iscariot) said, "But, Lord, why do you intend to show yourself to us and not to the world?" Jesus replied, "If anyone loves me, he will obey my teaching. My Father will love him, and we will come to him and make our home with him. (John 14:21-23)
>
> All of them were filled with the Holy Spirit and began to speak in other tongues as the Spirit enabled them. (Acts 2:4)
>
> After they prayed, the place where they were meeting was shaken. And they were all filled with the Holy Spirit and spoke the word of God boldly. (Acts 4:31)
>
> And the disciples were filled with joy and with the Holy Spirit. (Acts 13:52)
>
> Do not get drunk on wine, which leads to debauchery. Instead, be filled with the Spirit. (Eph 5:18)

6 (14:23-24) **Holy Spirit—Trinity**: the Holy Spirit is the abiding presence of the Trinity. Note the words, "My Father...we will come...and make our home with him [the believer]." Both the Father and Christ come to abide in the believer in the person of the Holy Spirit (v.16-17, 26). All three live or dwell within the believer. Note four simple but profound facts.

1. The abiding presence of the Trinity is conditional: one must obey Christ, that is, love and keep His words.

2. The abiding presence of the Trinity is the *love* and *presence* of God and Christ and the Holy Spirit—all three dwelling within the life of the believer.

3. The abiding presence of the Trinity is not "in" the man who does not love and obey Jesus.

4. The abiding presence of the Trinity is assured by God Himself. Note what Jesus said: His words are the words of the Father who sent Him (see note, pt.2—Jn.14:10).

> I will remain in the world no longer, but they are still in the world, and I am coming to you. Holy Father, protect them by the power of your name—the name you gave me—so that they may be one as we are one. (John 17:11)
>
> I have given them the glory that you gave me, that they may be one as we are one: I in them and you in me. May they be

brought to complete unity to let the world know that you sent me and have loved them even as you have loved me. (John 17:22-23)

DEEPER STUDY # 4

(14:23) **Love—Commandments**: the person who really loves Jesus will want to help Jesus by doing what He asks. Therefore, love and obedience are tied together so tightly that a person cannot love and not obey. A person's love is proven and clearly seen in his obedience. (Cp. 1 Jn.2:9-11; 3:10-17; 4:7-21.)

---

7 (14:25-26) **Holy Spirit**: the Holy Spirit is *the Teacher*. He teaches "all things" which Jesus taught. "All things" means all the things which Jesus taught including the presence of the Counselor or Comforter (Holy Spirit), who is given to help the believer through the trials of life, and the indwelling presence and love of the Father and Son.

However, a crucial point must be heeded. The Counselor or Comforter comes *only from the Father* "in the name" of Jesus.

⇒ In calling God "the Father," a Father-child relationship is stressed. One must become a child of God, that is, of the Father, in order to be given the Father's Counselor or Comforter.

⇒ The words "in the name" of Christ mean that one must approach the Father "in" the name of Christ, that is, recognizing that Jesus alone is acceptable to God (see DEEPER STUDY # 3—Jn.14:13-14 for discussion).

The purpose of the Holy Spirit in the believer's life is twofold.

1. To teach all things: both the words and the life of Christ, both the Truth and the Life, both the Word and how to live the Word, both the theory and the practice, both the principles and the conduct, both the morality and the behavior.

2. To help remember: to help remember all that has been taught in the Word of God, to help especially in the moments of trial when the truth is needed. In a moment of trial the Holy Spirit either infuses the believer with the strength to endure or flashes across his mind the way to escape (cp. 1 Cor.10:13).

For the Holy Spirit will teach you at that time what you should say." (Luke 12:12)

But the Counselor, the Holy Spirit, whom the Father will send in my name, will teach you all things and will remind you of everything I have said to you. (John 14:26)

But when he, the Spirit of truth, comes, he will guide you into all truth. He will not speak on his own; he will speak only what he hears, and he will tell you what is yet to come. (John 16:13)

This is what we speak, not in words taught us by human wisdom but in words taught by the Spirit, expressing spiritual truths in spiritual words. (1 Cor 2:13)

As for you, the anointing you received from him remains in you, and you do not need anyone to teach you. But as his anointing teaches you about all things and as that anointing is real, not counterfeit— just as it has taught you, remain in him. (1 John 2:27)

	H. The Source of Peace, Joy, & Security, 14:27-31	the Father is greater than I.	ascension)
1 The source of peace		29 I have told you now be-	b. The Father's greatness
a. The peace of the world	27 Peace I leave with you;	fore it happens, so that when	c. A confirmed faith
b. The peace of Christ	my peace I give you. I do not	it does happen you will be-	
c. The source: Jesus only	give to you as the world	lieve.	
	gives. Do not let your hearts	30 I will not speak with you	**3 The source of security**
	be troubled and do not be	much longer, for the prince of	a. Jesus' victory over
	afraid.	this world is coming. He has	the prince of the world
2 The source of joy	28 "You heard me say, 'I am	no hold on me,	
(rejoicing, being glad)	going away and I am coming	31 But the world must learn	b. Jesus' obedience to
a. The return of Jesus	back to you.' If you loved	that I love the Father and that	the Father
to the Father (His	me, you would be glad that	I do exactly what my Father	
death, resurrection, &	I am going to the Father, for	has commanded me. "Come now; let us leave.	

DIVISION XIII

THE REVELATION OF JESUS, THE GREAT MINISTER AND HIS LEGACY, 13:1-16:33

H. The Source of Peace, Joy, and Security, 14:27-31

(14:27-31) Introduction: this is a passage which speaks ever so warmly yet forcibly to the needs of men. It covers the source of *peace, joy*, and *security*.

1. The source of peace (v.27).
2. The source of joy (v.28-29).
3. The source of security (v.30-31).

1 (14:27) **Peace**: the source of peace. Peace (eirene) means to bind together, to join, to weave together. It means that a person is bound, woven and joined together with himself and with God and others.

The Hebrew word is *shalom*. It means freedom from trouble and much more. It means experiencing the highest good, enjoying the very best, possessing all the inner good possible. It means wholeness and soundness. It means prosperity in the widest sense, especially prosperity in the spiritual sense of having a soul that blossoms and flourishes.

1. There is the peace of the world. This is a peace of escapism, of avoiding trouble, of refusing to face things, of unreality. It is a peace that is sought through pleasure, satisfaction, contentment, absence of trouble, positive thinking, or denial of problems.

2. There is the peace of Christ and of God. This is, first, a *bosom peace*, a peace deep within. It is a tranquility of mind, a composure, a peace that is calm in the face of bad circumstances and situations. It is more than feelings—even more than attitude and thought.

This is, second, the *peace of conquest* (cp. Jn.16:33). It is the peace independent of conditions and environment; the peace which no sorrow, no danger, no suffering, no experience can take away.

> **"I have told you these things, so that in me you may have peace. In this world you will have trouble. But take heart! I have overcome the world." (John 16:33)**

This is, third, the *peace of assurance* (cp. Ro.8:28). It is the peace of unquestionable confidence; the peace with a sure knowledge that one's life is in the hands of God and that all things will work out for good to those who love God and are called according to His purpose.

> **And we know that in all things God works for the good of those who love him, who have been called according to his purpose. (Rom 8:28)**

This is, fourth, the *peace of intimacy with God* (cp. Ph.4:6-7). It is the peace of the highest good. It is the peace that settles the mind, strengthens the will, and establishes the heart.

3. There is the source of peace. Peace is always born out of reconciliation. Its source is found only in the reconciliation wrought by Jesus Christ. Peace always has to do with personal relationships: a man's relationship to himself, to God, and to his fellow men. A man must be bound, woven, and joined together with himself, with God, and with his fellow man.

> **But now in Christ Jesus you who once were far away have been brought near through the blood of Christ. For he himself is our peace, who has made the two one and has destroyed the barrier, the dividing wall of hostility, (Eph 2:13-14)**
> **And through him to reconcile to himself all things, whether things on earth or things in heaven, by making peace through his blood, shed on the cross. Once you were alienated from God and were enemies in your minds because of your evil behavior. (Col 1:20-21)**

Man secures peace in the following manner.
1. By justification.

> **Therefore, since we have been justified through faith, we have peace with God through our Lord Jesus Christ, (Rom 5:1)**

2. By loving God's Word.

> **Great peace have they who love your law, and nothing can make them stumble. (Psa 119:165)**
> **"I have told you these things, so that in me you may have peace. In this world you will have trouble. But take heart! I have overcome the world." (John 16:33)**

3. By praying about everything.

> **Do not be anxious about anything, but in everything, by prayer and petition, with thanksgiving, present your requests to God. And the peace of God, which transcends all**

understanding, will guard your hearts and your minds in Christ Jesus. (Phil 4:6-7)

4. By being spiritually minded.

The mind of sinful man is death, but the mind controlled by the Spirit is life and peace; (Rom 8:6)

5. By keeping his mind upon God.

You will keep in perfect peace him whose mind is steadfast, because he trusts in you. (Isa 26:3)

Finally, brothers, whatever is true, whatever is noble, whatever is right, whatever is pure, whatever is lovely, whatever is admirable—if anything is excellent or praiseworthy—think about such things. (Phil 4:8)

6. By keeping God's commandments.

If only you had paid attention to my commands, your peace would have been like a river, your righteousness like the waves of the sea. (Isa 48:18)

Whatever you have learned or received or heard from me, or seen in me—put it into practice. And the God of peace will be with you. (Phil 4:9)

The subject of peace is often divided into (1) the peace *with* God, which is wrought through salvation (Ro.5:1; Eph.2:14-17); (2) the peace *of* God, which is the very peace of God Himself and which points to God as the Source of peace (Lk.7:50; Ph.4:6-7); (3) the peace *from* God, which God gives to dwell in the heart of the believer as he walks day by day in the Lord (Ro.1:7; 1 Cor.1:3).

2 (14:28-29) **Joy—Rejoicing**: the source of joy, of rejoicing and being glad. Joy (chara) and rejoicing or being glad (echarete, the same root word as joy) mean an inner gladness and a deep seated pleasure. It is a depth of assurance and confidence that ignites a cheerful heart. It is a cheerful heart that leads to cheerful behavior.

The source of joy is threefold. (See DEEPER STUDY # 1—Jn.15:11 for more discussion.)

1. The return of Jesus to the Father causes believers to joy and rejoice. "I am going away and I am coming back to you" is a reference to His death, resurrection, and ascension.

a. The death or cross of Christ attracts and causes men to joy and rejoice. The cross is the source of their deliverance from sin, death, and hell (see note—Jn.12:32).

But I, when I am lifted up from the earth, will draw all men to myself." (John 12:32)

May I never boast except in the cross of our Lord Jesus Christ, through which the world has been crucified to me, and I to the world. (Gal 6:14)

b. The resurrection and ascension of Christ attracts and causes men to joy and rejoice or be glad. The

resurrection and ascension are the sources of their new life and hope for eternity (see notes, Resurrection—Jn.14:6; 7:33-34; Mk.16:19-20).

Therefore, since we have been justified through faith, we have peace with God through our Lord Jesus Christ, through whom we have gained access by faith into this grace in which we now stand. And we rejoice in the hope of the glory of God. (Rom 5:1-2)

You have made known to me the path of life; you will fill me with joy in your presence, with eternal pleasures at your right hand. (Psa 16:11)

And the ransomed of the LORD will return. They will enter Zion with singing; everlasting joy will crown their heads. Gladness and joy will overtake them, and sorrow and sighing will flee away. (Isa 35:10)

2. The Father's greatness causes believers to joy and rejoice or be glad. The Father demonstrated His great love and power by releasing Jesus …

- from the sinful nature, the flesh: in all its limitations and weaknesses.
- from the world: in all its trials and tensions.
- from the devil: in all his oppressions and attacks.
- from the pressure of men: in all their needful demands and, in some cases, terrible threats and attacks.

The Father took Jesus home, back from where He had come; and He restored Him to His seat of glory, exalting Him above every name that is named (Ph.2:9-11). The believer joys and rejoices in the phenomenal power of the Father's greatness.

Until now you have not asked for anything in my name. Ask and you will receive, and your joy will be complete. (John 16:24)

For the kingdom of God is not a matter of eating and drinking, but of righteousness, peace and joy in the Holy Spirit, (Rom 14:17)

Though you have not seen him, you love him; and even though you do not see him now, you believe in him and are filled with an inexpressible and glorious joy, for you are receiving the goal of your faith, the salvation of your souls. (1 Pet 1:8-9)

Rejoice in the Lord always. I will say it again: Rejoice! (Phil 4:4)

Thought 1. The implication of the Father's power for the believer is phenomenal. The believer will also be released from the sinful nauture, the flesh, the world, the devil, and the pressure of men, just as Jesus was.

I have told you this so that my joy may be in you and that your joy may be complete. (John 15:11)

3. A confirmed faith causes believers to joy and rejoice or be glad. The claims of Jesus have been proven and veri-

fied. Just as He told His disciples, all that He predicted has come to pass.

⇒ He did leave (die).
⇒ He did return (the resurrection).
⇒ He did go to His Father (the ascension).
⇒ He did send the Holy Spirit.

Note: by foretelling these things, Jesus strengthened the faith of believers enormously. (In fact, think about it: He could have chosen no better way to strengthen the faith of believers.)

> I have told you this so that my joy may be in you and that your joy may be complete. (John 15:11)
> "I am coming to you now, but I say these things while I am still in the world, so that they may have the full measure of my joy within them. (John 17:13)
> When your words came, I ate them; they were my joy and my heart's delight, for I bear your name, O LORD God Almighty. (Jer 15:16)

3 (14:30-31) **Security**: the source of security. The believer's security comes from two sources.

1. Security comes from Jesus' victory over Satan. (See DEEPER STUDY # 3—Jn.12:31; DEEPER STUDY # 4—12:32 for discussion.)

a. "Satan is coming": he was using men (Judas and the religionists) to make a last ditch effort to destroy Jesus. But Satan had nothing in Jesus; there was nothing which he could use to attract Jesus to sin. There was no lust, no greed, no selfishness—nothing in Jesus that Satan could use to destroy Him.

> Can any of you prove me guilty of sin? If I am telling the truth, why don't you believe me? (John 8:46)
> God made him who had no sin to be sin for us, so that in him we might become the righteousness of God. (2 Cor 5:21)
> For we do not have a high priest who is unable to sympathize with our weaknesses, but we have one who has been tempted in every way, just as we are—yet was without sin. (Heb 4:15)
> Such a high priest meets our need—one who is holy, blameless, pure, set apart from

sinners, exalted above the heavens. (Heb 7:26)
> But with the precious blood of Christ, a lamb without blemish or defect. (1 Pet 1:19)

b. Jesus was predicting that He would be completely victorious and triumphant over Satan.

> Now is the time for judgment on this world; now the prince of this world will be driven out. (John 12:31)
> I will not speak with you much longer, for the prince of this world is coming. He has no hold on me, (John 14:30)
> And having disarmed the powers and authorities, he made a public spectacle of them, triumphing over them by the cross. (Col 2:15)
> Since the children have flesh and blood, he too shared in their humanity so that by his death he might destroy him who holds the power of death—that is, the devil—and free those who all their lives were held in slavery by their fear of death. (Heb 2:14-15)
> He who does what is sinful is of the devil, because the devil has been sinning from the beginning. The reason the Son of God appeared was to destroy the devil's work. (1 John 3:8)

2. Security comes from Jesus' obedience to the Father. The Father's great commandment was for Jesus to die for the sins of the world. His death was the supreme act of obedience. (See note—Jn.12:27-30.)

> The reason my Father loves me is that I lay down my life—only to take it up again. No one takes it from me, but I lay it down of my own accord. I have authority to lay it down and authority to take it up again. This command I received from my Father." (John 10:17-18)
> "Now my heart is troubled, and what shall I say? 'Father, save me from this hour'? No, it was for this very reason I came to this hour. Father, glorify your name!" Then a voice came from heaven, "I have glorified it, and will glorify it again." (John 12:27-28)
> And live a life of love, just as Christ loved us and gave himself up for us as a fragrant offering and sacrifice to God. (Eph 5:2)

	CHAPTER 15	can you bear fruit unless you remain in me.	Not abiding or remaining, not attached
	I. The Relationship of Jesus to the People of the World,[DS1] **15:1-8**	5 "I am the vine; you are the branches. If a man remains in me and I in him, he will bear much fruit; apart from me you can do nothing.	b. Cannot bear fruit c. Do not understand the nature of bearing fruit in life: Can do nothing apart from Christ
1 Jesus, the Vine; God, the Vinedresser; & man, the branch	**"I** am the true vine, and my Father is the gardener.	6 If anyone does not remain in me, he is like a branch that is thrown away and withers;	d. Are doomed: Gathered, thrown away, burned
2 Unfruitful branches: Are taken away	2 He cuts off every branch in me that bears no fruit, while every branch that does bear	such branches are picked up, thrown into the fire and burned.	
3 Fruitful branches	fruit he prunes so that it will	7 If you remain in me and	**5 Attached branches:**
a. Are pruned	be even more fruitful.	my words remain in you, ask	**Results & promises**
b. The purpose for pruning	3 You are already clean be-	whatever you wish, and it	a. Receive nourishment—
c. How branches are pruned	cause of the word I have spo-	will be given you.	answered prayers
1) By the Word	ken to you.	8 This is to my Father's	b. Glorify God
2) By abiding, remaining[DS2]	4 Remain in me, and I will remain in you. No branch can	glory, that you bear much fruit, showing yourselves to	c. Prove their attachment— discipleship
4 Unattached branches	bear fruit by itself; it must	be my disciples.	
a. Are by themselves:	remain in the vine. Neither		

DIVISION XIII

THE REVELATION OF JESUS, THE GREAT MINISTER AND HIS LEGACY, 13:1-16:33

I. The Relationship of Jesus to the People of the World, 15:1-8

(15:1-8) **Introduction—Jesus Christ, Facing Death**: Jesus was facing the most terrible scene in all human history. The Son of God was about to be murdered at the hands of men. All that He had to face was weighing ever so heavily upon His mind, in particular the reaction of everyone to Him and their fate. He had come to save them all, and few were responding in a genuine way. He was even facing the collapse of His own inner circle. Most tragically, they were falling away.

⇒ One disciple was in the very process of betraying Him (Judas).
⇒ The leader of the disciples was to deny Him three times, even by cursing (Peter).
⇒ The other disciples were to flee and desert Him.

And then, there was the world of men who were rejecting Him: the religionists who strongly professed to know and live for God, and the non-religionists who had no attachment to God and professed none.

He had come to save them all and not one was standing with Him in His most needful hour. As the thought of it all raced through His mind, He recalled the vine of God so often described in the Old Testament (Ps.80:8-16; Is.5:1-7; Jer.2:21; Ezk.15:1-8; 19:10; Hos.10:1). In it He saw a graphic lesson that the disciples needed to learn, the great lesson of "The Vine and the Branches"—the relationship of Jesus to the people of the world.

1. Jesus, the Vine; God, the Vinedresser; and man, the branch (v.1).
2. Unfruitful branches: are taken away (v.2).
3. Fruitful branches (v.2-4).
4. Unattached branches (v.4-6).
5. Attached branches: results and promises (v.7-8).

DEEPER STUDY # 1

(15:1-8) **Fruit-bearing—Abide**: there are four stages of fruit-bearing given: (1) no fruit (v.2), (2) fruit (v.2), (3) more fruit (v.2), and (4) much fruit (vs.5, 8).

What does it mean to say a Christian is to bear fruit? It means to bear converts (Ro.1:13), to bear righteousness (Ro.6:21-23), to bear Christian character or the fruit of the Spirit (see notes—Gal.5:22-23). Note also the conditions for bearing fruit in life: cleansing (v.3) and abiding or remaining in Christ (v.5), and obedience (vs. 10, 12). A true Christian is a person who really does abide in Christ (1 Jn.2:10). John said that to abide or remain in Christ means eight things. (See DEEPER STUDY # 2, Abide—Jn.15:4-6.)

1. A person walks in open confession before God. He walks through life opening up his life to God; he confesses all known sin. He does not walk in sin, and he does not allow any sin to go unconfessed (1 Jn.1:6-10).

2. A person walks and fellowships with Christ. He lives and moves and has his being with Christ. He communes and lives in a consciousness of God's presence, and from God's presence, he learns of God and he draws the strength and authority to live victoriously day by day (1 Jn.2:6; 2:27; cp. Ps.16:11; Pr.3:5-6).

3. A person continues in the church; he has not gone out from the church (1 Jn.2:19).

4. A person possesses confidence, an unashamedness in life, that prepares him for eternity (1 Jn.2:28).

5. A person does not walk in continuous sin (1 Jn.3:6). He experiences constant victory over sin.

6. A person actively surrenders himself to obey God's commandments (1 Jn.3:24).

7. A person experiences the indwelling presence and witness of the Spirit (1 Jn.4:12-13).

8. A person dwells in love and unity and fellowship with all other believers (Jn.17:21-23; 1 Jn.4:16; cp. 1 Jn.4:20).

1 (15:1) **Jesus Christ, The Vine**: Jesus is the Vine; God is the Vinedresser or the Cultivator or the Gardener; and men are branches.

1. Jesus is the *true* Vine. He is the genuine vine, not a false, counterfeit vine. In fact, He is opposed to the coun-

terfeit, the sham, the deceitful, the *pretender*. (See DEEPER STUDY # 1, <u>True</u>—Jn.1:9.)

2. God is the Vinedresser. He is the One who carefully planted the Vine (Christ) and waters and feeds the Vine. He is the One who cares for, looks after, and watches over the Vine and the branches. He is the One who prunes and purges, cleans and protects, the Vine and its branches.

3. Men are branches. And note, they are all judged on the basis of how they relate to the *True* Vine. They are...

- either *unfruitful* (v.2) or *fruitful* branches of the true Vine (v.2-3).
- either *unattached* (v.4-6) or *attached* branches of the true Vine (v.7-8).

2 (15:2) **Profession, False—Believers, Warning to—Fruit Bearing—Judgment of Believers**: there are the unfruitful branches. They are taken away, cut off. Note that these are *attached branches*. They differ from the unattached branches (v.4-6). Jesus said that they are "in me," but they have a problem: they bear no fruit.

1. The unfruitful branches *did become* attached to Christ. They did have some *organic* relationship to Him. There was a time, a point, when they began to bud and sprout. They even grew into branches. They...

- listened to Jesus and the gospel
- opened their ears
- made a profession
- were baptized
- seemed capable of bearing fruit
- appeared to be fruitful branches

2. The branches are unfruitful. They are "in" the Vine, a part of it, but they simply bear no fruit. What does this mean? (See outline and notes, <u>Judas</u>—Jn.13:18-30; <u>The Sower and the Seed</u>—Mt.13:1-9.)

a. Unfruitful branches do not relate enough to Christ; they do not draw enough nourishment from Him...
- to draw life
- to bear fruit
- to continue in the Vine (cp. Mt.24:13; 13:13)

b. Unfruitful branches are *not genuine enough* to bear fruit. Their profession is...
- more *profession* than *possession*
- more *pretending* then *being*
- more *deception* than *truth*
- more *counterfeit* than *real*

c. Unfruitful branches become apostate and deserters—men and women who abandon the faith. (Cp. 1 Jn.2:19.)

> The one who received the seed that fell among the thorns is the man who hears the word, but the worries of this life and the deceitfulness of wealth choke it, making it unfruitful. (Mat 13:22)
>
> Then he told this parable: "A man had a fig tree, planted in his vineyard, and he went to look for fruit on it, but did not find any. (Luke 13:6)
>
> They claim to know God, but by their actions they deny him. They are detestable, disobedient and unfit for doing anything good. (Titus 1:16)
>
> See to it, brothers, that none of you has a sinful, unbelieving heart that turns away from the living God. (Heb 3:12)

> They will be paid back with harm for the harm they have done. Their idea of pleasure is to carouse in broad daylight. They are blots and blemishes, reveling in their pleasures while they feast with you. With eyes full of adultery, they never stop sinning; they seduce the unstable; they are experts in greed—an accursed brood! (2 Pet 2:13-14)

3. God will "cut off" (airei) the unfruitful branches. The word means to take away and to remove. In relation to the vine, the branch is pruned, removed, and taken away. This is a severe warning to every branch "in" the vine, to make sure his profession is genuine enough to bear fruit.

Scripture says at least two things about the judgment of unfruitful branches that sin.

a. The unfruitful branches that sin are cut off and removed from the Vine and destroyed by fire.

> The ax is already at the root of the trees, and every tree that does not produce good fruit will be cut down and thrown into the fire. (Mat 3:10)
>
> They went out from us, but they did not really belong to us. For if they had belonged to us, they would have remained with us; but their going showed that none of them belonged to us. (1 John 2:19)
>
> Therefore consider carefully how you listen. Whoever has will be given more; whoever does not have, even what he thinks he has will be taken from him." (Luke 8:18)
>
> But land that produces thorns and thistles is worthless and is in danger of being cursed. In the end it will be burned. (Heb 6:8)

b. The unfruitful branches that sin are chastened and disciplined by being cut off and removed through death (see note—1 Jn.5:16). The Bible warns professing believers of severe chastening, the chastening of...

- sinful behavior that causes loss of all reward by fire—a loss so great a man is stripped as much as a burned-out building. It is the loss of all except the very salvation of a man (1 Cor. 3:11-15, esp. 15).
- sinful behavior that destroys the flesh so that the Spirit may be saved (1 Cor.5:5).
- sinful behavior that causes death (1 Cor. 11:29-30; 1 Jn.5:16).
- sinful behavior that merits no escape (Heb.2:1-3; 12:25f).
- sinful behavior that prohibits man from ever repenting again (Heb.6:4f).
- sinful behavior that causes man to miss God's rest (Heb.4:1f).
- sinful behavior that prohibits any future sacrifice for sins and merits terrible punishment (Heb.10:26f).

(See DEEPER STUDY # 1—1 Jn.5:16 for more discussion.)

The point must be heeded, for Scripture gives severe warnings to believers, that is, to the branches "in" the Vine. The branches must make sure they are bearing fruit or else face severe judgment. (Again, see DEEPER STUDY # 1— 1 Jn.5:16 for more discussion.)

3 (15:2-4) **Fruit-bearing—Word of God—Believers, Cleansing of**: there are the fruitful branches. Note three points.

1. Fruitful branches are pruned. All bad spots, useless buds, misdirected shoots, and discolored leaves are pruned off. Even fruitful believers have spots, buds, shoots, and leaves that are bad, useless, misdirected, and discolored. Believers have areas and things that must be cleaned away and cleared up, areas of…

- thought
- service
- attitude
- passion
- commitment
- motives
- behavior
- willingness
- relationships

2. The purpose for pruning is *onefold*: to prepare the branch to bear more fruit. The purpose is not to punish, not to hurt and damage the branch. Note two things about fruit-bearing.
   a. The fruit a believer is to bear. (See DEEPER STUDY # 1, Fruit-Bearing—Jn.15:1-8 for discussion.)
   b. The different stages of fruit-bearing. All believers are not 100 percent fruit-bearers. Some bear 60 percent, others only 30 percent. There are degrees of fruit-bearing, of commitment and dedication to Christ (see DEEPER STUDY # 1—Jn.15:1-8; Mt.13:8, 23).

> **Still other seed fell on good soil, where it produced a crop—a hundred, sixty or thirty times what was sown. (Mat 13:8)**
>
> **For the Son of Man is going to come in his Father's glory with his angels, and then he will reward each person according to what he has done. (Mat 16:27)**
>
> **"His master replied, 'Well done, good and faithful servant! You have been faithful with a few things; I will put you in charge of many things. Come and share your master's happiness!' (Mat 25:23)**
>
> **In a large house there are articles not only of gold and silver, but also of wood and clay; some are for noble purposes and some for ignoble. (2 Tim 2:20)**

3. Note how the fruitful branches are pruned (katharoi) or purged and cleansed. There are three ways.
   a. Branches are cleansed by the words which Jesus has given to men, by the Word of the Lord Himself. The Word of God refines men by purging away all the dross and contamination, pollution and dirt that clings to them. When a man comes to the Word of God sincerely, the Word of God shows…
   - what he is doing and what he is not doing.
   - where he fails and how he fails.
   - the sins of commission and of omission.

> **Sanctify them by the truth; your word is truth. (John 17:17)**
>
> **For them I sanctify myself, that they too may be truly sanctified. (John 17:19)**
>
> **Now that you have purified yourselves by obeying the truth so that you have sincere love for your brothers, love one another deeply, from the heart. (1 Pet 1:22)**

> **How can a young man keep his way pure? By living according to your word. (Psa 119:9)**
>
> **I have hidden your word in my heart that I might not sin against you. (Psa 119:11)**

   b. Branches are cleansed by the mirror of the Word of God. When a man looks into the Word of God, he reflects both himself in his shortcomings and Christ in His perfection. The Word of God forces man to measure himself against Christ.

> **Anyone who listens to the word but does not do what it says is like a man who looks at his face in a mirror and, after looking at himself, goes away and immediately forgets what he looks like. (James 1:23-24)**
>
> **All Scripture is God-breathed and is useful for teaching, rebuking, correcting and training in righteousness, (2 Tim 3:16)**

(See DEEPER STUDY # 1—Heb.4:12 for more discussion.)

   c. Branches are cleansed by "remaining [abiding]" in Jesus (see DEEPER STUDY # 2, Abide—Jn.15:4). Note exactly what Jesus said: "Remain in me, and I in you." This can mean at least two things.
   ⇒ It can mean a promise: "Remain [abide] in me and I will remain [abide] in you." The believer is thereby cleansed by his position or by being in Christ (see note, pt.4—Jn.13:6-11).
   ⇒ It can mean a command: "See to it that you remain [abide] in me, and I in you." The believer is cleansed by continuing in Christ and remaining faithful.

DEEPER STUDY # 2

(15:4) **Remain, Abide—Remaining, Abiding**: to remain, abide, dwell, continue, stay, sojourn, rest in or upon. It is being set and fixed and remaining there, continuing on and on in a fixed state, condition, or being. (See DEEPER STUDY # 1, Abide—Jn.15:1-8; 6:56.) It should be noted that the more a branch abides in the vine, that is, the closer the branch abides to the heart of the vine, the more nourishment a branch draws from the vine and the more fruit it bears.

> **Whoever eats my flesh and drinks my blood remains in me, and I in him. (John 6:56)**
>
> **And I will ask the Father, and he will give you another Counselor to be with you forever—the Spirit of truth. The world cannot accept him, because it neither sees him nor knows him. But you know him, for he lives with you and will be in you. (John 14:16-17)**
>
> **If you obey my commands, you will remain in my love, just as I have obeyed my Father's commands and remain in his love. (John 15:10)**
>
> **Whoever claims to live in him must walk as Jesus did. (1 John 2:6)**
>
> **And now, dear children, continue in him, so that when he appears we may be**

> confident and unashamed before him at his coming. (1 John 2:28)
>
> No one who lives in him keeps on sinning. No one who continues to sin has either seen him or known him. (1 John 3:6)
>
> Those who obey his commands live in him, and he in them. And this is how we know that he lives in us: We know it by the Spirit he gave us. (1 John 3:24)
>
> We know that we live in him and he in us, because he has given us of his Spirit. (1 John 4:13)
>
> If anyone acknowledges that Jesus is the Son of God, God lives in him and he in God. And so we know and rely on the love God has for us. God is love. Whoever lives in love lives in God, and God in him. (1 John 4:15-16)
>
> Because of the truth, which lives in us and will be with us forever: (2 John 1:2)
>
> Anyone who runs ahead and does not continue in the teaching of Christ does not have God; whoever continues in the teaching has both the Father and the Son. (2 John 1:9)

4 (15:4-6) **Fruit-bearing—Unbelievers, Life of—Judgment**: there are the unattached branches. Jesus said four things.

1. The unattached branch is "out" and off by itself; it is not abiding, not remaining in the Vine and not attached. Note the words "by itself" (v.4), off by itself. To say that a branch must be attached and must remain (abide) in the vine may sound redundant at first. But the truth is pointed: there is no life and no fruit in life apart from Christ. Just as a branch suspended out in mid-air or lying on the ground without any attachment to the vine is lifeless and meaningless, so a man on the earth without attachment to Christ is lifeless and meaningless.

Those who seek life and meaning someplace other than in Christ are doomed to failure. The unattached and suspended branch is of and by itself—all alone upon this earth—and it is doomed to be by itself.

2. The unattached branch cannot bear fruit, not real and permanent fruit that is *acceptable or pleasing* to God. It cannot bear...

- any good or righteousness that is acceptable to God (Ro.6:21-23).
- character that is acceptable to God (Gal.5:22-23).
- converts to the saving grace of God (Ro.1:13; Tit.2:11-15).

3. The unattached branch does not understand the nature of bearing fruit in life: the fact that he can do nothing—cannot live and produce life—apart from Christ. No one bears fruit apart from Christ...

- no one lives or experiences life. (See DEEPER STUDY # 2—Jn.1:4; DEEPER STUDY # 1—10:10; DEEPER STUDY # 1—17:2-3 for more discussion.)
- a man is helpless to find the meaning, purpose, and significance to life.

4. The unattached branch is doomed. He is cast forth to wither and to be gathered and thrown into the fire and burned.

a. Thrown out (eblethe exo): to be plucked off and cast out, thrown away, discarded, disposed of. The unattached branch chooses to be unattached, so God lets it. It is *given over* and *given up* to be

unattached. God abandons it. It is cast out of the way and left to itself to do as it chooses. (See outline and notes—Ro.1:24-32.)

b. Withers (exeranthe): to be dried up, wrinkled, peeled; to become sapless and bare; to lose energy and strength. The unattached branch experiences everything withering away—its...

- gifts & abilities
- hopes & dreams
- life & body
- confidence & assurance
- family & friends
- purpose & meaning
- fate & destiny

c. Picked up or gathered (sunagousin): the day of judgment arrives. In the Greek text, who it is that gathers is not given. The Greek simply says, "they picked up." This is probably God having His angels gather up all the unattached branches, they who cause "sin and all who do evil" (cp. Mt.13:41).

d. Thrown into the fire and "burned" (kaietai). (See DEEPER STUDY # 2—Mt.5:22; note—8:12; DEEPER STUDY #4—Lk.16:24. Cp. Mt.13:42, 50; Rev.20:15; 21:8.)

> Let both grow together until the harvest. At that time I will tell the harvesters: First collect the weeds and tie them in bundles to be burned; then gather the wheat and bring it into my barn.'" (Mat 13:30)
>
> This is how it will be at the end of the age. The angels will come and separate the wicked from the righteous and throw them into the fiery furnace, where there will be weeping and gnashing of teeth. (Mat 13:49-50)
>
> "Then they will go away to eternal punishment, but the righteous to eternal life." (Mat 25:46)
>
> If anyone's name was not found written in the book of life, he was thrown into the lake of fire. (Rev 20:15)
>
> But for those who are self-seeking and who reject the truth and follow evil, there will be wrath and anger. There will be trouble and distress for every human being who does evil: first for the Jew, then for the Gentile; (Rom 2:8-9)

5 (15:7-8) **Fruit-bearing**: there are the attached branches, and the results and promises made to them. These are the same as the fruitful branches mentioned earlier (v.2-3). Jesus had already covered the pruning or the disciplining of the branches, so here He covers the promises made to them and the results of their abiding or "remaining" in Him. Note that the promises and results are conditional: "If you remain in me...." Note also that the words of Christ must remain or abide in the believer. The thought is that a believer must take the Words of Christ and...

- study and learn them
- have his thoughts and desires controlled by them
- be motivated and controlled by them

> Do your best to present yourself to God as one approved, a workman who does not need to be ashamed and who correctly handles the word of truth. (2 Tim 2:15; cp. Jn.14:15.21 24; 15:10, 14)

The promises and results of remaining (abiding) in Christ are threefold.

1. The attached branch receives nourishment, that is, answered prayers. (See Deeper Study # 3—Jn.14:13-14 for more discussion.)

   a. The branch is attached to the vine. It remains and abides in the vine: dwells and lives and never faces a moment when it is not attached to the vine. So it is with the believer. The believer is attached to Christ: he remains, abides, dwells, lives, and walks in the very presence of Christ, never facing a moment when he is not attached and walking in Christ. A genuine believer walks in constant fellowship and prayer with the Lord. He is always remaining (abiding) and sharing with the Lord.

   b. Similarly, the vine is always nourishing the branch, always sending its life-giving food and drink to the branch. So it is with Christ. Christ is always sharing His life-giving nourishment with the believer, always answering prayer and meeting the needs of the genuine believer.

> **Until now you have not asked for anything in my name. Ask and you will receive, and your joy will be complete. (John 16:24)**
>
> **If you believe, you will receive whatever you ask for in prayer." (Mat 21:22)**
>
> **This is the confidence we have in approaching God: that if we ask anything according to his will, he hears us. And if we know that he hears us—whatever we ask—we know that we have what we asked of him. (1 John 5:14-15)**

2. The attached branch glorifies God by bearing much fruit. Remember what the fruit is. It is...

- righteousness

> **But now that you have been set free from sin and have become slaves to God, the benefit you reap leads to holiness, and the result is eternal life. (Rom 6:22)**
>
> **Filled with the fruit of righteousness that comes through Jesus Christ—to the glory and praise of God. (Phil 1:11)**
>
> **And we pray this in order that you may live a life worthy of the Lord and may please him in every way: bearing fruit in every good work, growing in the knowledge of God, (Col 1:10)**

- godly character

> **But the fruit of the Spirit is love, joy, peace, patience, kindness, goodness, faithfulness, gentleness and self-control. Against such things there is no law. (Gal 5:22-23)**

- converts

> **I do not want you to be unaware, brothers, that I planned many times to come to you (but have been prevented from doing so until now) in order that I might have a harvest among you, just as I have had among the other Gentiles. (Rom 1:13)**

When men see fruit in the life of a believer, they are forced...
- to turn their mind to God
- to acknowledge that only God's power could do such
- to desire God to save them
- to begin asking God for help
- to accept God or to close their mind and reject God

God is glorified by the fruit born in the life of a believer, glorified by *some men* beginning to think about God and calling upon Him.

3. The attached branch proves he is a disciple by bearing fruit. There are ways to tell if a person really is attached to Christ:
- ⇒ Does he bear fruit?
- ⇒ Does he live righteously or do shameful things (Ro.6:21-23)?
- ⇒ Does he bear "love, joy, peace, patience, kindness, goodness, faithfulness, gentleness, self-control" (Gal.5:22-23)?
- ⇒ Does he lead the lost to Christ (Ro.1:13)?

> **"A new command I give you: Love one another. As I have loved you, so you must love one another. By this all men will know that you are my disciples, if you love one another." (John 13:34-35)**

	J. The Relationship of Jesus to Believers, 15:9-11

1 He has loved believers
2 He has one great charge for believers: Continue—abide in His love
  a. Abiding is conditional
  b. Abiding has a standard—the obedience of Jesus
3 He has one great purpose for believers: The completion of their joy*DS1*
	9 "As the Father has loved me, so have I loved you. Now remain in my love.
	10 If you obey my commands, you will remain in my love, just as I have obeyed my Father's commands and remain in his love.
	11 I have told you this so that my joy may be in you and that your joy may be complete.

DIVISION XIII

THE REVELATION OF JESUS, THE GREAT MINISTER AND HIS LEGACY, 13:1-16:33

J. The Relationship of Jesus to Believers, 15:9-11

(15:9-11) **Introduction**: Jesus has a very special relationship with believers, a relationship that delivers them from an existence that is barren, empty, lonely, unmeaningful, and sad.

1. He has loved believers (v.9).
2. He has one great charge for believers: continue—abide in His love (v.9-10).
3. He has one great purpose for believers: the completion of their joy (v.11).

1 (15:9) *Jesus Christ, Love of—God, Love for Christ*: Christ has loved believers. He has loved us with a very special love. Two profound points are being discussed here.

⇒ The Father's love for His Son, Jesus Christ.
⇒ Christ's love for believers.

1. There are three significant reasons why the Father loves Christ.
  a. Christ is His Son, His *only* Son. God loves Christ because of a *natural love*. God naturally loves His Son just as most fathers naturally love their children.

> **To the praise of his glorious grace, which he has freely given us in the One he loves. In him we have redemption through his blood, the forgiveness of sins, in accordance with the riches of God's grace (Eph 1:6-7)**
> **"For God so loved the world that he gave his one and only Son, that whoever believes in him shall not perish but have eternal life. (John 3:16)**
> **For he has rescued us from the dominion of darkness and brought us into the kingdom of the Son he loves, (Col 1:13)**
> **So Christ also did not take upon himself the glory of becoming a high priest. But God said to him, "You are my Son; today I have become your Father." (Heb 5:5)**

  b. God loves Christ with an *obedient* love. God is perfect, which means He is perfect love. There-

fore, being perfect love, God is bound to love His Son. But this means much more than an ordinary love. Christ Himself is Perfect—the Perfect Son of God. Therefore, God loves Christ with a very special love. Imagine how much a parent would love a perfect child, a child who was always obedient: never being disrespectful, rebellious, haughty, selfish; and never causing hurt, pain, or doubt. Most parents love their children, but it is special love based on the perfect obedience of Christ.

> **But the world must learn that I love the Father and that I do exactly what my Father has commanded me. "Come now; let us leave. (John 14:31)**
> **And so the Jews said to the man who had been healed, "It is the Sabbath; the law forbids you to carry your mat." (John 5:10)**
> **Then I said, 'Here I am—it is written about me in the scroll— I have come to do your will, O God.'" (Heb 10:7)**

  c. God loves Christ with a *supreme* love. Christ paid the *supreme* price of obedience. He died and sacrificed Himself in obedience to God's will. Therefore, God's love for His Son is very, very special in that it is a supreme love. (See notes—Jn.10:17-18; 12:27-30 for discussion.)

> **The reason my Father loves me is that I lay down my life—only to take it up again. No one takes it from me, but I lay it down of my own accord. I have authority to lay it down and authority to take it up again. This command I received from my Father." (John 10:17-18)**
> **But the world must learn that I love the Father and that I do exactly what my Father has commanded me. "Come now; let us leave. (John 14:31)**
> **And live a life of love, just as Christ loved us and gave himself up for us as a**

fragrant offering and sacrifice to God. (Eph 5:2)

2. Christ said that He loves believers with the same *kind* of love, the very *same* love that God has for Him.

a. Christ loves us with a natural love.

⇒ Christ loves us because we are God's children.

But when the time had fully come, God sent his Son, born of a woman, born under law, to redeem those under law, that we might receive the full rights of sons. Because you are sons, God sent the Spirit of his Son into our hearts, the Spirit who calls out, "Abba, Father." (Gal 4:4-6)

For you did not receive a spirit that makes you a slave again to fear, but you received the Spirit of sonship. And by him we cry, "Abba, Father." The Spirit himself testifies with our spirit that we are God's children. Now if we are children, then we are heirs—heirs of God and co-heirs with Christ, if indeed we share in his sufferings in order that we may also share in his glory. (Rom 8:15-17)

And, "It will happen that in the very place where it was said to them, 'You are not my people,' they will be called 'sons of the living God.'" (Rom 9:26)

How great is the love the Father has lavished on us, that we should be called children of God! And that is what we are! The reason the world does not know us is that it did not know him. Dear friends, now we are children of God, and what we will be has not yet been made known. But we know that when he appears, we shall be like him, for we shall see him as he is. (1 John 3:1-2)

⇒ Christ loves us because we are brothers of His.

For those God foreknew he also predestined to be conformed to the likeness of his Son, that he might be the firstborn among many brothers. (Rom 8:29)

For whoever does the will of my Father in heaven is my brother and sister and mother." (Mat 12:50)

Both the one who makes men holy and those who are made holy are of the same family. So Jesus is not ashamed to call them brothers. (Heb 2:11)

⇒ Christ loves us because we are the household and family of God.

Consequently, you are no longer foreigners and aliens, but fellow citizens with God's people and members of God's household. (Eph 2:19)

"Therefore come out from them and be separate, says the Lord. Touch no unclean thing, and I will receive you." "I will be a Father to you, and you will be my sons and daughters, says the Lord Almighty." (2 Cor 6:17-18)

b. Christ loves us with an obedient love.

⇒ He loves us because we believe God.

"I tell you the truth, whoever hears my word and believes him who sent me has eternal life and will not be condemned; he has crossed over from death to life. (John 5:24)

⇒ He loves us because we earnestly seek God.

And without faith it is impossible to please God, because anyone who comes to him must believe that he exists and that he rewards those who earnestly seek him. (Heb 11:6)

⇒ He loves us because we obey His commands.

Whoever has my commands and obeys them, he is the one who loves me. He who loves me will be loved by my Father, and I too will love him and show myself to him." (John 14:21)

If you obey my commands, you will remain in my love, just as I have obeyed my Father's commands and remain in his love. You are my friends if you do what I command. (John 15:10, 14)

c. Christ loves us with a supreme love. He loves us because we pay the *supreme* price of obedience: we deny self, take up our cross, and die daily in order to follow Him (see DEEPER STUDY # 1—Lk.9:23 for discussion).

Then he said to them all: "If anyone would come after me, he must deny himself and take up his cross daily and follow me. (Luke 9:23)

This is how we know what love is: Jesus Christ laid down his life for us. And we ought to lay down our lives for our brothers. (1 John 3:16)

2 (15:9-10) **Jesus Christ, Love of—Believers, Duty**: Christ has one great charge for believers—to continue or to remain in His love.

1. "Continuing," "abiding," or "remaining" is conditional. A believer can...

- break fellowship with Christ.
- cease to keep his thoughts upon Christ.
- walk out of the love of Christ.
- get away from the love of Christ.
- turn back to the world and to his old worldly friends (cp. 2 Cor.6:17-18).
- give himself back over to the lusts of the sinful man, the lust of his eyes, and the boasting of what he has and does (1 Jn.2:15-16).

Jesus said that it is up to the believer to continue in His love. How? By doing what any person does when he wants someone to love him. The person draws near to the person he loves: he does good and tries to please the person. So it is with the believer. The believer continues in the love of Christ by drawing near and doing good and seeking to please Him—very simply by obeying His commandments. (Cp. Jn.14:21; 15:10, 14.)

Now note a critical point. Christ always loves; His love is *always* there. But it is up to *man* to walk *in* that love. A man can never know and experience the Lord's love unless he walks *in* it.

> **Whoever has my commands and obeys them, he is the one who loves me. He who loves me will be loved by my Father, and I too will love him and show myself to him." (John 14:21)**
>
> **If you obey my commands, you will remain in my love, just as I have obeyed my Father's commands and remain in his love. You are my friends if you do what I command. (John 15:10, 14)**
>
> **So then, just as you received Christ Jesus as Lord, continue to live in him, (Col 2:6)**
>
> **Whoever claims to live in him must walk as Jesus did. (1 John 2:6)**

2. Abiding or remaining in the love of Christ has a standard, a supreme example: it is Christ Himself. He was perfectly obedient to God; therefore, He continued in the Father's love. We are to look at His obedience as our prime example. (Again, see note—Jn.10:17-18.)

Note another critical point. A believer must do something if He is going to follow Jesus' example and keep Jesus' commandments. The believer must study and learn and remain (abide) in the Word of God, in the commandments and life of Christ. A person cannot keep a commandment unless he knows the commandment.

> **Remain in me, and I will remain in you. No branch can bear fruit by itself; it must remain in the vine. Neither can you bear fruit unless you remain in me. "I am the vine; you are the branches. If a man remains in me and I in him, he will bear much fruit; apart from me you can do nothing. (John 15:4-5)**
>
> **Now the Bereans were of more noble character than the Thessalonians, for they received the message with great eagerness and examined the Scriptures every day to see if what Paul said was true. (Acts 17:11)**
>
> **Do your best to present yourself to God as one approved, a workman who does not need to be ashamed and who correctly handles the word of truth. (2 Tim 2:15)**
>
> **Like newborn babies, crave pure spiritual milk, so that by it you may grow up in your salvation, now that you have tasted that the Lord is good. (1 Pet 2:2-3)**
>
> **And now, dear children, continue in him, so that when he appears we may be confident and unashamed before him at his coming. (1 John 2:28)**
>
> **No one who lives in him keeps on sinning. No one who continues to sin has either seen him or known him. (1 John 3:6)**
>
> **Anyone who runs ahead and does not continue in the teaching of Christ does not have God; whoever continues in the teaching has both the Father and the Son. (2 John 1:9)**

3 **(15:11) Joy—Believers, Purpose**: Christ has one great purpose for believers—the completion of their joy. Note three points.

1. The joy of Christ: "My joy." His joy and glory was doing the will of God and looking ahead to the joy and glory of eternity with His Father and His followers. (See notes—Jn.12:23-26; 14:28-29.)

> **Let us fix our eyes on Jesus, the author and perfecter of our faith, who for the joy set before him endured the cross, scorning its shame, and sat down at the right hand of the throne of God. (Heb 12:2)**

2. The joy of believers is the joy of Christ Himself reigning within their hearts. (See DEEPER STUDY # 1, Joy—Jn.15:11.)

> **Through whom we have gained access by faith into this grace in which we now stand. And we rejoice in the hope of the glory of God. (Rom 5:2)**
>
> **For you know that it was not with perishable things such as silver or gold that you were redeemed from the empty way of life handed down to you from your forefathers, (1 Pet 1:18)**

3. The joy of believers is fulfilled as believers study His Word, the promises and commandments which He made. (See notes—Jn.14:28-29; DEEPER STUDY # 1—15:11 for discussion.)

> **I have told you this so that my joy may be in you and that your joy may be complete. (John 15:11)**
>
> **"I am coming to you now, but I say these things while I am still in the world, so that they may have the full measure of my joy within them. (John 17:13)**
>
> **Like newborn babies, crave pure spiritual milk, so that by it you may grow up in your salvation, now that you have tasted that the Lord is good. (1 Pet 2:2-3)**
>
> **When your words came, I ate them; they were my joy and my heart's delight, for I bear your name, O LORD God Almighty. (Jer 15:16)**

DEEPER STUDY # 1

(15:11) **Joy** (chara): an inner gladness; a deep-seated pleasure. It is a depth of assurance and confidence that ignites a cheerful heart. It is a cheerful heart that leads to cheerful behavior.

Several things need to be said about the believer's joy.

1. Joy is divine. It is possessed and given only by God. Its roots are not in earthly or material things or cheap triumphs. It is the joy of the Holy Spirit, a joy based in the Lord. It is His very own joy (Jn.15:11; Acts 13:52; Ro.14:17; Gal.5:22; 1 Th.1:6).

2. Joy does not depend on circumstances or happiness. Happiness depends upon happenings, but the joy that God implants in the believer's heart overrides all, even the most troublesome matters of life and death (Ps.5:11; 2 Cor.6:10; 7:4).

3. Joy springs from faith (Ro.15:13; Ph.1:25; 2 Tim. 1:4; cp. Mt.2:10).

4. Joy of future reward makes and keeps one faithful (Mt.25:21, 23; Acts 20:24; Heb.12:2).

The source of the believer's joy is severalfold.

1. The fellowship of the Father and His Son brings joy (1 Jn.1:3-4; Ps.16:11).
2. Victory over sin, death, and hell brings joy (Jn.14:28; 16:20-22; Is.12:3; 61:10).
3. Repentance brings joy (Lk.15:7, 10).
4. The hope of glory brings joy (Ro.14:17; Heb.12:2; 1 Pt.4:13).

5. The Lord's Word, the revelations, commandments, and promises which He made bring joy (Jn.15:11).
6. The commandments of Christ and the will of God bring joy. Obeying and doing a good job stirs joy within the believer's heart (Jn.15:11, 32; 17:13; Acts 13:52; Jer.15:16).
7. Prayer brings joy (Jn.16:24).
8. The presence and fellowship of believers bring joy (1 Jn.1:3-4).
9. Converts bring joy (Lk.15:5; Ph.4:1; 1 Th.2:19-20; Ps.126:5).
10. Hearing that others walk in the truth brings joy (3 Jn.1:4).
11. Giving brings joy (2 Cor.8:2; Heb.10:34).

	K. The Relationship of Believers to Believers, 15:12-17	not know his master's business. Instead, I have called you friends, for everything that I learned from my Father I have made known to you.	tion: The words of the Father made known by Christ
1 The supreme command of believers: Love one another	12 My command is this: Love each other as I have loved you.	16 You did not choose me, but I chose you and appointed you to go and bear fruit—fruit that will last. Then the Father will give you whatever you ask in my name.	4 The supreme purpose of believers: Chosen & appointed to go a. To go forth b. To bear fruit c. To receive of God
2 The supreme standard of believers: The love of Jesus	13 Greater love has no one than this, that he lay down his life for his friends.		
3 The supreme bond of believers: Friends of Jesus a. Is conditional:"If" b. Is based upon revela-	14 You are my friends if you do what I command. 15 I no longer call you servants, because a servant does	17 This is my command: Love each other.	5 Conclusion: The supreme command repeated

DIVISION XIII

THE REVELATION OF JESUS, THE GREAT MINISTER AND HIS LEGACY, 13:1-16:33

K. The Relationship of Believers to Believers, 15:12-17

(15:12-17) **Introduction**: how believers relate to other believers is of critical importance. Division will destroy a body of people quicker than any other single thing. Division can...

- destroy the body of Christ
- destroy a fellowship of believers
- destroy the witness of believers
- destroy a human soul seeking God

Too many are known more for their grumbling, griping, complaining, murmuring, and divisiveness than for anything else. Nothing cuts the heart of Jesus more than such self-centered and divisive behavior.

The relationship of believers to each other is of critical importance.

1. The supreme command of believers: love one another (v.12).
2. The supreme standard of believers: the love of Jesus (v.12-13).
3. The supreme bond of believers: "friends" of Jesus (v.14-15).
4. The supreme purpose of believers: chosen and appointed to go (v.16).
5. Conclusion: the supreme command repeated (v.17).

1 (15:12) **Love**: the *supreme command* of believers is to love one another. They are to love one another just as Jesus has loved them. Note: Jesus is clear about what He means. He loved man so much that He paid the ultimate price. He died and sacrificed His life for man. (See notes—Jn.13:33-35 for discussion.)

> "A new command I give you: Love one another. As I have loved you, so you must love one another. By this all men will know that you are my disciples, if you love one another." (John 13:34-35)
> My command is this: Love each other as I have loved you. (John 15:12)
> Love must be sincere. Hate what is evil; cling to what is good. (Rom 12:9)
> Now that you have purified yourselves by obeying the truth so that you have sincere love for your brothers, love one another deeply, from the heart. (1 Pet 1:22)

> And this is his command: to believe in the name of his Son, Jesus Christ, and to love one another as he commanded us. (1 John 3:23)

2 (15:12-13) **Love**: the *supreme standard* of believers is the love of Jesus Christ Himself. He paid the ultimate and supreme price of love. He died and sacrificed Himself for His friends. (See notes—Jn.10:17-18; 12:27-30; 13:31-32.)

> It was just before the Passover Feast. Jesus knew that the time had come for him to leave this world and go to the Father. Having loved his own who were in the world, he now showed them the full extent of his love. (John 13:1)
> Who shall separate us from the love of Christ? Shall trouble or hardship or persecution or famine or nakedness or danger or sword? (Rom 8:35)
> For Christ's love compels us, because we are convinced that one died for all, and therefore all died. (2 Cor 5:14)
> I have been crucified with Christ and I no longer live, but Christ lives in me. The life I live in the body, I live by faith in the Son of God, who loved me and gave himself for me. (Gal 2:20)
> And live a life of love, just as Christ loved us and gave himself up for us as a fragrant offering and sacrifice to God. (Eph 5:2)
> This is how we know what love is: Jesus Christ laid down his life for us. And we ought to lay down our lives for our brothers. (1 John 3:16)

3 (15:14-15) **Believers, Nature—Fellowship—Word of God**: the *supreme bond* of believers is the bond of "friends." Believers form a bond of "friends," a spiritual bond founded by Christ Himself. But note two things.

1. Being a "friend" of Jesus is conditional. A person has to *know* and *do* His commandments in order to be a friend of His. The implication is clear: there is no way to be His friend apart from *knowing what He says*. It is His Word

that tells men about Him. Therefore, a person has to diligently seek to learn His Word and to do what He says in order to know Him and to become His friend. The point is clear: friends relate and commune with each other, *share* and *respond* to the word of each other, rejoicing when the word or conversation is that of joy, and helping when the word or request is that of need.

"No one can serve two masters. Either he will hate the one and love the other, or he will be devoted to the one and despise the other. You cannot serve both God and Money. (Mat 6:24)

For whoever does the will of my Father in heaven is my brother and sister and mother." (Mat 12:50)

If anyone chooses to do God's will, he will find out whether my teaching comes from God or whether I speak on my own. (John 7:17)

Whoever has my commands and obeys them, he is the one who loves me. He who loves me will be loved by my Father, and I too will love him and show myself to him." (John 14:21)

Jesus replied, "If anyone loves me, he will obey my teaching. My Father will love him, and we will come to him and make our home with him. He who does not love me will not obey my teaching. These words you hear are not my own; they belong to the Father who sent me. (John 14:23-24)

If you obey my commands, you will remain in my love, just as I have obeyed my Father's commands and remain in his love. (John 15:10)

Do your best to present yourself to God as one approved, a workman who does not need to be ashamed and who correctly handles the word of truth. (2 Tim 2:15)

We know that we have come to know him if we obey his commands. (1 John 2:3)

The world and its desires pass away, but the man who does the will of God lives forever. (1 John 2:17)

See that what you have heard from the beginning remains in you. If it does, you also will remain in the Son and in the Father. (1 John 2:24)

2. The bond of "friends" is based upon revelation, that is, upon Jesus Christ Himself. Jesus Christ revealed and made known exactly what God told Him. It is *the Word of God* that gives birth and structure to the bond of "friends." The friends of Christ are built upon and centered around *the Word of God* (see notes—Jn.14:10; 7:16-19; DEEPER STUDY # 2—Acts 2:42 for discussion).

"I have much to say in judgment of you. But he who sent me is reliable, and what I have heard from him I tell the world." So Jesus said, "When you have lifted up the Son of Man, then you will know that I am the one I claim to be and that I do nothing on my own but speak just what the Father has taught me. (John 8:26, 28)

For I did not speak of my own accord, but the Father who sent me commanded me what to say and how to say it. I know that his command leads to eternal life. So whatever I say is just what the Father has told me to say." (John 12:49-50)

Don't you believe that I am in the Father, and that the Father is in me? The words I say to you are not just my own. Rather, it is the Father, living in me, who is doing his work. Believe me when I say that I am in the Father and the Father is in me; or at least believe on the evidence of the miracles themselves. I tell you the truth, anyone who has faith in me will do what I have been doing. He will do even greater things than these, because I am going to the Father. And I will do whatever you ask in my name, so that the Son may bring glory to the Father. You may ask me for anything in my name, and I will do it. (John 14:10-14)

Jesus replied, "If anyone loves me, he will obey my teaching. My Father will love him, and we will come to him and make our home with him. He who does not love me will not obey my teaching. These words you hear are not my own; they belong to the Father who sent me. (John 14:23-24)

For I gave them the words you gave me and they accepted them. They knew with certainty that I came from you, and they believed that you sent me. (John 17:8)

However, as it is written: "No eye has seen, no ear has heard, no mind has conceived what God has prepared for those who love him"—but God has revealed it to us by his Spirit. The Spirit searches all things, even the deep things of God. (1 Cor 2:9-10)

And he made known to us the mystery of his will according to his good pleasure, which he purposed in Christ, to be put into effect when the times will have reached their fulfillment—to bring all things in heaven and on earth together under one head, even Christ. (Eph 1:9-10)

The mystery that has been kept hidden for ages and generations, but is now disclosed to the saints. To them God has chosen to make known among the Gentiles the glorious riches of this mystery, which is Christ in you, the hope of glory. (Col 1:26-27)

Both the one who makes men holy and those who are made holy are of the same family. So Jesus is not ashamed to call them brothers. (Heb 2:11)

4 (15:16) **Believers, Purpose**: the *supreme purpose* of believers is to go and bear fruit. Believers are the chosen and appointed of Christ, and they have been given the very same purpose of Christ Himself: to go into all the world and bear fruit among men. This is one of the great verses of Scripture. Note two points.

1. Believers are chosen and appointed by Jesus. We do not choose Him nor do we appoint and send ourselves out to serve Him.
   ⇒ It is God who approaches and draws us (see notes—Jn.6:44-46. Also see note—Jn.6:37.)
   ⇒ It is God who appoints us to live for Him and to serve Him.

> But the Lord said to Ananias, "Go! This man is my chosen instrument to carry my name before the Gentiles and their kings and before the people of Israel. (Acts 9:15)

> Keep watch over yourselves and all the flock of which the Holy Spirit has made you overseers. Be shepherds of the church of God, which he bought with his own blood. (Acts 20:28)

> There came a man who was sent from God; his name was John. (John 1:6)

> But God chose the foolish things of the world to shame the wise; God chose the weak things of the world to shame the strong. He chose the lowly things of this world and the despised things—and the things that are not—to nullify the things that are, so that no one may boast before him. (1 Cor 1:27-29)

> And in the church God has appointed first of all apostles, second prophets, third teachers, then workers of miracles, also those having gifts of healing, those able to help others, those with gifts of administration, and those speaking in different kinds of tongues. (1 Cor 12:28)

> I thank Christ Jesus our Lord, who has given me strength, that he considered me faithful, appointing me to his service. (1 Tim 1:12)

2. Believers are chosen and appointed for three very specific purposes.
   a. To go forth as ambassadors for Christ, proclaiming the glorious message of the great God and our Savior Jesus Christ. Believers are not called to be an exclusive club of retirees who have it made and who can go about doing what they want, knowing they are eternally secure. Believers are the ambassadors of Christ in the world. Once they have been saved, their duty—their sole reason for being *appointed* and *left* in this world—is to deliver the message of their King.

> That God was reconciling the world to himself in Christ, not counting men's sins against them. And he has committed to us the message of reconciliation. We are therefore Christ's ambassadors, as though God were making his appeal through us. We implore you on Christ's behalf: Be reconciled to God. (2 Cor 5:19-20)

> Therefore go and make disciples of all nations, baptizing them in the name of the Father and of the Son and of the Holy Spirit, and teaching them to obey everything I have commanded you. And surely I am with you always, to the very end of the age." (Mat 28:19-20)

> He said to them, "Go into all the world and preach the good news to all creation. (Mark 16:15)

> Again Jesus said, "Peace be with you! As the Father has sent me, I am sending you." (John 20:21)

> But you will receive power when the Holy Spirit comes on you; and you will be my witnesses in Jerusalem, and in all Judea and Samaria, and to the ends of the earth." (Acts 1:8)

   b. To bear fruit (see DEEPER STUDY # 1, Fruit-bearing— Jn.15:1-8 for discussion).

> Produce fruit in keeping with repentance. (Mat 3:8)

> I tell you the truth, unless a kernel of wheat falls to the ground and dies, it remains only a single seed. But if it dies, it produces many seeds. (John 12:24)

> He cuts off every branch in me that bears no fruit, while every branch that does bear fruit he prunes so that it will be even more fruitful. (John 15:2)

> "I am the vine; you are the branches. If a man remains in me and I in him, he will bear much fruit; apart from me you can do nothing. (John 15:5)

> But now that you have been set free from sin and have become slaves to God, the benefit you reap leads to holiness, and the result is eternal life. (Rom 6:22; cp. v.20-21)

> So, my brothers, you also died to the law through the body of Christ, that you might belong to another, to him who was raised from the dead, in order that we might bear fruit to God. (Rom 7:4)

> But the fruit of the Spirit is love, joy, peace, patience, kindness, goodness, faithfulness, gentleness and self-control. Against such things there is no law. (Gal 5:22-23)

> (For the fruit of the light consists in all goodness, righteousness and truth) (Eph 5:9)

> Filled with the fruit of righteousness that comes through Jesus Christ—to the glory and praise of God. (Phil 1:11. cp. v.9-10)

> And we pray this in order that you may live a life worthy of the Lord and may please him in every way: bearing fruit in every good work, growing in the knowledge of God, (Col 1:10)

   c. To receive the things of God (see DEEPER STUDY # 3— Jn.14:13-14; note—15:7-8 for discussion).

> If you believe, you will receive whatever you ask for in prayer." (Mat 21:22)

> "So I say to you: Ask and it will be given to you; seek and you will find; knock and the door will be opened to you. For everyone who asks receives; he who seeks finds; and to him who knocks, the door will be opened. (Luke 11:9-10)

And I will do whatever you ask in my name, so that the Son may bring glory to the Father. You may ask me for anything in my name, and I will do it. (John 14:13-14)

If you remain in me and my words remain in you, ask whatever you wish, and it will be given you. This is to my Father's glory, that you bear much fruit, showing yourselves to be my disciples. (John 15:7-8)

We have not received the spirit of the world but the Spirit who is from God, that we may understand what God has freely given us. (1 Cor 2:12)

And receive from him anything we ask, because we obey his commands and do what pleases him. (1 John 3:22)

This is the confidence we have in approaching God: that if we ask anything according to his will, he hears us. And if we know that he hears us—whatever we ask— we know that we have what we asked of him. (1 John 5:14-15)

5 (15:17) **Love**: the conclusion is forceful. The *supreme command* is repeated: love each other.

And this is his command: to believe in the name of his Son, Jesus Christ, and to love one another as he commanded us. (1 John 3:23)

If it is encouraging, let him encourage; if it is contributing to the needs of others, let him give generously; if it is leadership, let him govern diligently; if it is showing mercy, let him do it cheerfully. Love must be sincere. Hate what is evil; cling to what is good. Be devoted to one another in brotherly love. Honor one another above yourselves. (Rom 12:8-10)

	L. The Relationship of Believers to the World: Persecution (Part I), 15:18-27	22 If I had not come and spoken to them, they would not be guilty of sin. Now, however, they have no excuse for their sin.	d. Because the world is convicted of sin 1) The Lord's message convicts
1 The chilling reality: The world will hate	18 "If the world hates you, keep in mind that it hated me first.	23 He who hates me hates my Father as well.	
2 The unjustified reasons for the world's hatred a. Because believers are a new creation	19 If you belonged to the world, it would love you as its own. As it is, you do not belong to the world, but I have chosen you out of the world. That is why the world hates you.	24 If I had not done among them what no one else did, they would not be guilty of sin. But now they have seen these miracles, and yet they have hated both me and my Father.	2) The Lord's life & works convict
b. Because believers are identified with Christ	20 Remember the words I spoke to you: 'No servant is greater than his master.' If they persecuted me, they will persecute you also. If they obeyed my teaching, they will obey yours also.	25 But this is to fulfill what is written in their Law: 'They hated me without reason.'	3 The terrible guilt of the world: They are without reason 4 The promise of victory over the world
c. Because the world does not really know God	21 They will treat you this way because of my name, for they do not know the One who sent me.	26 "When the Counselor comes, whom I will send to you from the Father, the Spirit of truth who goes out from the Father, he will testify about me. 27 And you also must testify for you have been with me from the beginning."	a. Victory through the Holy Spirit: He is the Counselor or Comforter—the Truth—the Witness b. Victory through one's own witness & fellowship with Christ

DIVISION XIII

THE REVELATION OF JESUS, THE GREAT MINISTER AND HIS LEGACY, 13:1-16:33

L. The Relationship of Believers to the World (Part I): Persecution, 15:18-27

(15:18-27) **Introduction**: the relationship of true believers to the world is a bleak picture. The world hates true believers. The world and its people shun, isolate, talk about, ridicule, mock, bypass, overlook, consider strange, and joke about genuine believers. The persecution often goes even farther, involving abuse and murder within the workplace and community, depending on the society and the laws under which the believer lives. Jesus wanted the believer to be informed and to know what his relationship with the world is.

1. The chilling reality: the world will hate (v.18).
2. The unjustified reasons for the world's hatred (v.19-24).
3. The terrible guilt of the world: they are without reason (v.25).
4. The promise of victory over the world (v.26-27).

1 (15:18) **World—Persecution**: the chilling reality, the world will hate the believer. Note three things.

1. The meaning of the word "if" in this verse should be translated *since*. "Since the world hates you": there is no question about the world's hating the believer. It *will* hate him.

> "Blessed are you when people insult you, persecute you and falsely say all kinds of evil against you because of me. (Mat 5:11)
> All men will hate you because of me, but he who stands firm to the end will be saved. (Mat 10:22)
> For it has been granted to you on behalf of Christ not only to believe on him, but also to suffer for him, (Phil 1:29)

> In fact, everyone who wants to live a godly life in Christ Jesus will be persecuted, (2 Tim 3:12)

2. The "world" refers to the unbeliever: the unredeemed, the lost, those who have never trusted Jesus Christ as Lord and Savior. The "world" stands for every person whose thoughts and lives are centered upon...

- the lust of the flesh, the cravings of the sinful man (food, clothes, money, immorality. Cp. Gal.5:16-21.)
- the lust of his eyes (evil and immoral thoughts, coveting, seeing and desiring people and things).
- the pride of life, boasting of what he has or does (position, boasting, honor, fame, highmindedness, self-centeredness. Cp. 2 Tim.3:1-5.)

> Do not love the world or anything in the world. If anyone loves the world, the love of the Father is not in him. For everything in the world—the cravings of sinful man, the lust of his eyes and the boasting of what he has and does—comes not from the Father but from the world. (1 John 2:15-16)

3. The believer is to "know" something. The world hated Christ *first*.

a. The believer is not to think some strange thing is happening to him; he is not to become discouraged.

> If anyone speaks, he should do it as one speaking the very words of God. If anyone serves, he should do it with the strength God provides, so that in all things God may

be praised through Jesus Christ. To him be the glory and the power for ever and ever. Amen. Dear friends, do not be surprised at the painful trial you are suffering, as though something strange were happening to you. (1 Pet 4:11-12)

Do not be surprised, my brothers, if the world hates you. (1 John 3:13)

b. The believer is to take heart, for Christ was victorious over the hatred. He was triumphant even over the bitterness of death. He arose and ascended to the Father.

Consider him who endured such opposition from sinful men, so that you will not grow weary and lose heart. (Heb 12:3)

In bringing many sons to glory, it was fitting that God, for whom and through whom everything exists, should make the author of their salvation perfect through suffering. (Heb 2:10)

For Christ died for sins once for all, the righteous for the unrighteous, to bring you to God. He was put to death in the body but made alive by the Spirit, (1 Pet 3:18)

But he was pierced for our transgressions, he was crushed for our iniquities; the punishment that brought us peace was upon him, and by his wounds we are healed. (Isa 53:5)

2 (15:19-24) **Persecution, Reasons**: the unjustified reasons for the world's hatred. There are four reasons given.

1. The world hates believers because they are not of the world: they are a new creation. They are *called out* from the world. Believers are *in* the world, but they are not *of* the world. They are separated from the world, from its…

- spirit
- thoughts
- conversation
- pleasures
- friends
- comfort
- religions
- prejudices
- hoarding
- carnality
- passions
- covetousness

Because of their separation, the world does not love believers; it rejects and hates them.

They are not of the world, even as I am not of it. (John 17:16)

Therefore, if anyone is in Christ, he is a new creation; the old has gone, the new has come! (2 Cor 5:17)

"Therefore come out from them and be separate, says the Lord. Touch no unclean thing, and I will receive you." "I will be a Father to you, and you will be my sons and daughters, says the Lord Almighty." (2 Cor 6:17-18)

In the name of the Lord Jesus Christ, we command you, brothers, to keep away from every brother who is idle and does not live according to the teaching you received from us. (2 Th 3:6)

2. The world hates believers because they are identified with Christ. The servant is not above persecution: no servant is above his Lord. The Lord suffered persecution; therefore, the believer will suffer persecution. It is to be expected.

Thought 1. It is an impossibility for a true disciple to be above his Master or for a servant to be above his Lord. If our Master and Lord suffered persecution, so will we. Why? He is our Master and Lord; that is, we are His. What He stands for is what we stand for. Whatever there was about Him that caused men to persecute Him, the same is *in us*. They will persecute us for *the same thing* and for *the same reason*. The genuine believer sacrifices himself, *all he is and has* to the Lord. He strives to conform his life to the Lord's; therefore, persecution is inevitable for the true believer.

Therefore, I urge you, brothers, in view of God's mercy, to offer your bodies as living sacrifices, holy and pleasing to God—this is your spiritual act of worship. Do not conform any longer to the pattern of this world, but be transformed by the renewing of your mind. Then you will be able to test and approve what God's will is—his good, pleasing and perfect will. (Rom 12:1-2)

I have given them your word and the world has hated them, for they are not of the world any more than I am of the world. (John 17:14)

Persecuted, but not abandoned; struck down, but not destroyed. We always carry around in our body the death of Jesus, so that the life of Jesus may also be revealed in our body. For we who are alive are always being given over to death for Jesus' sake, so that his life may be revealed in our mortal body. (2 Cor 4:9-11)

3. The world hates believers because it does not really know God. The world is deceived in its concept and belief of God. The world conceives God to be the One who fulfills their earthly desires and lusts (Jn.6:2, 26). Man's idea of God is that of a *Supreme Grandfather* who protects and provides and gives no matter what a person's behavior is, just so the behavior is not too far out. The world believes that God (the Supreme Grandfather) will accept and work all things out in the final analysis. However, the true believer teaches against this, proclaiming that God is both loving and just. God does love us, but He demands righteousness of us. The world, of course, rebels against this concept of God.

They will put you out of the synagogue; in fact, a time is coming when anyone who kills you will think he is offering a service to God. They will do such things because they have not known the Father or me. (John 16:2-3)

For as I walked around and looked carefully at your objects of worship, I even found an altar with this inscription: TO AN UNKNOWN GOD. Now what you worship as something unknown I am going to proclaim to you. (Acts 17:23)

They are darkened in their understanding and separated from the life of God because of the ignorance that is in them due to the hardening of their hearts. (Eph 4:18)

They are the kind who worm their way into homes and gain control over weak-willed women, who are loaded down with sins and are swayed by all kinds of evil desires, always learning but never able to acknowledge the truth. (2 Tim 3:6-7)

But whoever hates his brother is in the darkness and walks around in the darkness; he does not know where he is going, because the darkness has blinded him. (1 John 2:11)

4. The world hates believers because it is convicted of sin. Jesus said that two things convict the world.
   a. His message convicts the world of sin: it strips away the world's *excuse of sin*. He preaches and teaches righteousness; therefore, His message exposes the sins of people.

Nor does his word dwell in you, for you do not believe the one he sent. (John 5:38)

But I know you. I know that you do not have the love of God in your hearts. (John 5:42)

How can you believe if you accept praise from one another, yet make no effort to obtain the praise that comes from the only God ? (John 5:44)

If you believed Moses, you would believe me, for he wrote about me. But since you do not believe what he wrote, how are you going to believe what I say?" (John 5:46-47)

Once more Jesus said to them, "I am going away, and you will look for me, and you will die in your sin. Where I go, you cannot come." (John 8:21)

But he continued, "You are from below; I am from above. You are of this world; I am not of this world. I told you that you would die in your sins; if you do not believe that I am the one I claim to be, you will indeed die in your sins." (John 8:23-24)

Jesus replied, "I tell you the truth, everyone who sins is a slave to sin. (John 8:34)

You belong to your father, the devil, and you want to carry out your father's desire. He was a murderer from the beginning, not holding to the truth, for there is no truth in him. When he lies, he speaks his native language, for he is a liar and the father of lies. Yet because I tell the truth, you do not believe me! (John 8:44-45)

He who belongs to God hears what God says. The reason you do not hear is that you do not belong to God." (John 8:47)

   b. His life and works convict the world of sin. (See notes—Jn.5:19; 5:20; 5:36; DEEPER STUDY # 2—10:25 for discussion.) Note the words, "they would not be guilty of sin." This does not mean that men would not be guilty of sin if Jesus had not come.

What it means is that since He has come, men have seen exactly who God is. God has been revealed to men; therefore, they stand guilty of the most terrible sin of all: rejecting God and His Son. If He had not come, they would not be guilty of *this sin*.

Note the claim of Jesus to be the revelation of God—to be equal with Him. To hate Him is to hate the Father also.

Then they asked him, "Where is your father?" "You do not know me or my Father," Jesus replied. "If you knew me, you would know my Father also." (John 8:19)

So Jesus said, "When you have lifted up the Son of Man, then you will know that I am the one I claim to be and that I do nothing on my own but speak just what the Father has taught me. The one who sent me is with me; he has not left me alone, for I always do what pleases him." (John 8:28-29)

Jesus said to them, "If God were your Father, you would love me, for I came from God and now am here. I have not come on my own; but he sent me. (John 8:42)

I tell you the truth, if anyone keeps my word, he will never see death." (John 8:51)

Though you do not know him, I know him. If I said I did not, I would be a liar like you, but I do know him and keep his word. (John 8:55)

Jesus answered, "I did tell you, but you do not believe. The miracles I do in my Father's name speak for me, (John 10:25)

Do not believe me unless I do what my Father does. But if I do it, even though you do not believe me, believe the miracles, that you may know and understand that the Father is in me, and I in the Father." (John 10:37-38)

Believe me when I say that I am in the Father and the Father is in me; or at least believe on the evidence of the miracles themselves. (John 14:11)

If I had not done among them what no one else did, they would not be guilty of sin. But now they have seen these miracles, and yet they have hated both me and my Father. (John 15:24)

3 (15:25) **World, Without Excuse:** the terrible guilt of the world. The world is without excuse. (Cp. Ps.35:19.) There is no sense for its hatred of Jesus. The world's hatred is a paradox; it is not understandable. Think about it. The world hates and opposes the One person…
- who lived and spoke for righteousness more than anyone else ever has.
- who cared and ministered more than anyone else ever has.
- who worked for true love and justice and the salvation of the world more than anyone else ever has.

(How deceived is the world and its humanity! To rush onward in madness for nothing but to return to dust and ashes. To seek life for only some seventy years [if that long].)

The world's hatred for Jesus Christ reveals that the true nature of the world is *evil*. The world is without excuse.

> **If I had not come and spoken to them, they would not be guilty of sin. Now, however, they have no excuse for their sin. (John 15:22)**
>
> **For since the creation of the world God's invisible qualities—his eternal power and divine nature—have been clearly seen, being understood from what has been made, so that men are without excuse. (Rom 1:20)**
>
> **They repay me evil for good and leave my soul forlorn. (Psa 35:12)**
>
> **They repay me evil for good, and hatred for my friendship. (Psa 109:5)**

4 (15:26-27) **World, Victory Over—Holy Spirit**: the promise of victory over the world. Victory comes from two sources.

1. There is victory through the Holy Spirit.
   a. He is the believer's Counselor, his Comforter through persecution (see DEEPER STUDY # 1—Jn.14:16).
   b. He is the believer's Spirit of Truth through persecution. The truth will prevail through all persecution. (See note—Jn.14:17.)
   c. He will testify to the world, convicting them even while they are hating Christ. Note: the Holy Spirit is sent "from the Father" and "goes out from the Father" (para tou patros ekporeuetai), that is, "from the side of the Father." He is said to be a *distinct Person* from the Father and Son; He is said to be a *divine Person*, coming "from the very side of the Father."

> **But when they arrest you, do not worry about what to say or how to say it. At that time you will be given what to say, (Mat 10:19)**
>
> **"When you are brought before synagogues, rulers and authorities, do not worry about how you will defend yourselves or what you will say, for the Holy Spirit will teach you at that time what you should say." (Luke 12:11-12)**
>
> **For I will give you words and wisdom that none of your adversaries will be able to resist or contradict. (Luke 21:15)**
>
> **This is what we speak, not in words taught us by human wisdom but in words taught by the Spirit, expressing spiritual truths in spiritual words. (1 Cor 2:13)**

2. There is victory through the believer's own witness and fellowship with Christ. The believer walks and fellowships with Christ from the very beginning of his conversion. He sees and hears with the eyes and ears of his heart, and he learns of Christ. Therefore, he declares the glorious message of Christ so that this world, even its persecutors, may have fellowship with believers and with the Father and His Son (1 Jn.1:3).

Note another fact: the believer bears witness because he really knows Christ. It is practically impossible to know the true Messiah, the Savior of the world—to know that no man has to die—and not proclaim the message. A genuine believer is a person of conviction, a person who cannot keep quiet if he knows and experiences the truth himself.

> **We proclaim to you what we have seen and heard, so that you also may have fellowship with us. And our fellowship is with the Father and with his Son, Jesus Christ. (1 John 1:3)**
>
> **And the things you have heard me say in the presence of many witnesses entrust to reliable men who will also be qualified to teach others. (2 Tim 2:2)**
>
> **When they saw the courage of Peter and John and realized that they were unschooled, ordinary men, they were astonished and they took note that these men had been with Jesus. (Acts 4:13)**
>
> **"You are my witnesses," declares the LORD, "and my servant whom I have chosen, so that you may know and believe me and understand that I am he. Before me no god was formed, nor will there be one after me. (Isa 43:10)**

		3 They will do such things because they have not known the Father or me.
		4 I have told you this, so that when the time comes you will remember that I warned you. I did not tell you this at first because I was with you.
		5 "Now I am going to him who sent me, yet none of you asks me, 'Where are you going?'
		6 Because I have said these things, you are filled with grief.
			3 **The reason for the perse-cution: The religionists do not know God nor His Son**
			4 **The preparation for persecution**
			  a. The believer must ex-pect persecution & not be caught off guard
			  b. The believer must know that God *is* & that Jesus reigns
			  c. The believer must keep his mind on his destiny
			  d. The believer must call upon the Holy Spirit

1 **Jesus warned that religionists would persecute believers**
2 **The persecution: Wor-ship will be forbidden**
  a. Will be put out of worship & killed
  b. To be done by religionsts
	CHAPTER 16
	
	M. The Relationship of Be-lievers to Religionists: Persecution (Part II), 16:1-6
	
	"**A**ll this I have told you so that you will not go astray.
	2 They will put you out of the synagogue; in fact, a time is coming when anyone who kills you will think he is offering a service to God		

DIVISION XIII

THE REVELATION OF JESUS, THE GREAT MINISTER AND HIS LEGACY, 13:1-16:33

M. The Relationship of Believers to Religionists (Part II): Persecution, 16:1-6

(16:1-6) **Introduction—Jesus Christ, Mediator**: believers live in a world of religion and religionists. The world even looks upon believers as religionists, but they are not. Be-lievers are ambassadors of the living Lord, ambassadors who have been left on earth to deliver the message of eter-nal hope and life to a hopeless and dying world. In this fact alone the believer faces a tremendous problem. There is only One God and He has only One Son, whom He loves beyond anything man could ever dream. To demonstrate that love, God has set His Son up as the only way to ap-proach Him. All men must approach God *in the name* of His Son. The world feels this is narrow—much, much too narrow. Therefore, the world rejects God's Son and sets up its own ways to approach God. The end result is a world full of religions and religious approaches to God. (See out-line and notes—Jn.10:7-10 for more discussion.)

This passage deals with the relationship between believ-ers and the religionists of the world.

1. Jesus warned that religionists would persecute believ-ers (v.1).
2. The persecution: worship will be forbidden (v.2).
3. The reason for the persecution: the religionists do not know God or His Son (v.3).
4. The preparation for persecution (v.4-6).

1 (16:1) **Persecution, Response To**: Jesus warned the be-liever that religionists would persecute His followers. Jesus warned the believer because He wants to prevent the be-liever from slipping away. The word "astray" (skan-dalisthete) means to stumble and to trip. Persecution by re-ligionists can be a stumbling block to the believer. The be-liever can find himself being...

- questioned
- ridiculed
- passed over
- rejected
- mocked
- attacked
- criticized
- isolated and cut off
- tortured

The believer can stumble and fall over persecution. Per-secution can...

- cause a believer to question his beliefs.
- cause a believer to weaken and return to the way of false religion.

- silence a believer and his witness.
- cause a believer to deny Jesus.

Therefore let us stop passing judgment on one another. Instead, make up your mind not to put any stumbling block or ob-stacle in your brother's way. (Rom 14:13)

2 (16:2) **Persecution, Kinds; By Whom**: the persecution is to be severe, and it is to be religious in nature. Believers will be forbidden to worship. As an example, Jesus men-tioned the ultimate persecution: the believer will be put out of the church and killed. Note three points.

1. The persecution is religious; it is carried out by those who think they really know God and are doing exactly what God wants. They think they are purifying the church and cleansing it of false teaching, a teaching that is narrow, a teaching that is prejudiced against other religions and be-liefs and other ways to God.

Thought 1. False religionists do not see how there can be only one way to God. They conclude that Christ is wrong, that He is not the only Way, the only Truth, the only Life. They conclude...
- that the way to God is by being good and do-ing good, the best one can.
- that the particular religion does not really matter. What is important is that religion *in-spires* one to be good and caring and to be a better person.

2. False religionists have always rejected and abused true believers and prophets. And they have often been dog-ged in their opposition and abuse. Nothing can be any more harsh and tragic than religious persecution. Religious per-secution involves such things as...
- having one's faith, position, and ministry ques-tioned.
- being accused, abused, talked about, and plotted against.
- being denied rights.
- being silenced, not allowed to worship or serve.
- being removed from service.
- being tried and imprisoned, tortured and killed.

(Cp. Saul of Tarsus, Acts 8:1-3; cp. Acts 26:9; Gal.1:13.)

Brothers, as an example of patience in the face of suffering, take the prophets who spoke in the name of the Lord. (James 5:10)

3. Persecution within the church often happens. On this earth, God's house is full of people who have not really committed their lives to God. They do not know Him personally—not in a real intimate way. Therefore, the believer who truly takes a stand for God and His righteousness is sometimes opposed and persecuted by those within the church. The persecutors do not understand God nor His righteousness; therefore, they can become two faced: slandering, reviling, and insulting the believer behind his back. They can also scold, mock, and attack the believer face to face. They can go so far as to try to destroy a believer's reputation and life, depending on the society in which they live. It is a terrible tragedy when persecution takes place in the walls of God's house.

"Blessed are you when people insult you, persecute you and falsely say all kinds of evil against you because of me. Rejoice and be glad, because great is your reward in heaven, for in the same way they persecuted the prophets who were before you. (Mat 5:11-12)

"Be on your guard against men; they will hand you over to the local councils and flog you in their synagogues. (Mat 10:17)

"Then you will be handed over to be persecuted and put to death, and you will be hated by all nations because of me. At that time many will turn away from the faith and will betray and hate each other, (Mat 24:9-10)

Who are you to judge someone else's servant? To his own master he stands or falls. And he will stand, for the Lord is able to make him stand. (Rom 14:4)

"But before all this, they will lay hands on you and persecute you. They will deliver you to synagogues and prisons, and you will be brought before kings and governors, and all on account of my name. (Luke 21:12)

In fact, everyone who wants to live a godly life in Christ Jesus will be persecuted, while evil men and impostors will go from bad to worse, deceiving and being deceived. (2 Tim 3:12-13)

3 (16:3) **Persecution, Reasons:** the reason for persecution by religionists. Jesus gives one reason that underlies all other reasons for persecution. False religionists do not know God nor His Son, Jesus Christ. This is a staggering statement made by Jesus, for religionists *think* they know God. But Jesus says they do not, not really. They have their own idea of God, but it is only...

- their idea
- their image
- their imagination
- their idol
- their reasoning
- their devices

Religionists are deceived in their concept of God and in their understanding of Christ. They reject Christ, rejecting His claim to be the Son of God and the One who has existed *by the side* of God throughout all eternity. They look upon Christ only as a man: a good man, yes, but only a man. Therefore, they reject Him as the revelation and picture of God. The problem is that they want no God; they want no Lord that demands total self-denial and allegiance—no God other than themselves and their own imaginations. They want the right and freedom to seek their own desires instead of the demands of some supreme Lord. (See DEEPER STUDY # 2—Jn.5:15-16; notes—7:32; 11:47-57 for more discussion.)

They will treat you this way because of my name, for they do not know the One who sent me. (John 15:21)

They will do such things because they have not known the Father or me. (John 16:3)

But whoever lives by the truth comes into the light, so that it may be seen plainly that what he has done has been done through God." (John 3:21)

The people of Jerusalem and their rulers did not recognize Jesus, yet in condemning him they fulfilled the words of the prophets that are read every Sabbath. (Acts 13:27)

Since they did not know the righteousness that comes from God and sought to establish their own, they did not submit to God's righteousness. (Rom 10:3)

They are darkened in their understanding and separated from the life of God because of the ignorance that is in them due to the hardening of their hearts. (Eph 4:18)

Always learning but never able to acknowledge the truth. (2 Tim 3:7)

No one who lives in him keeps on sinning. No one who continues to sin has either seen him or known him. (1 John 3:6)

4 (16:4-6) **Persecution, Overcoming:** the preparation for persecution is fourfold.
1. The believer must expect persecution. He must remember that Jesus foretold that he would be persecuted. Remembering keeps the believer from being caught off guard and stumbling. The believer is to *prepare* for persecution by *thinking through* what he will do when he is...

- ridiculed
- attacked
- criticized
- slandered
- opposed
- tortured
- questioned
- imprisoned
- abused

The point is this: being forewarned, the true believer knows persecution is coming. Therefore, he is to prepare himself.

Remember the words I spoke to you: 'No servant is greater than his master.' If they persecuted me, they will persecute you also. If they obeyed my teaching, they will obey yours also. (John 15:20)

I have told you this, so that when the time comes you will remember that I warned you. I did not tell you this at first because I was with you. (John 16:4)

2. The believer must know that God *is* (exists) and that Jesus reigns. Jesus had told the disciples that they would face trouble and persecution in the world. Now, as He prepared to leave this world, He was revealing more to them and giving them a fuller revelation. (Cp. Jn.15:26-27; 16:7f as well as the whole teaching of Jn.15:18-27; 16:1-6.)

    a. Believers must know that God *is* (exists): that their Lord has definitely gone to the Father who sent Him.

> And without faith it is impossible to please God, because anyone who comes to him must believe that he exists and that he rewards those who earnestly seek him. (Heb 11:6)
> "You heard me say, 'I am going away and I am coming back to you.' If you loved me, you would be glad that I am going to the Father, for the Father is greater than I. (John 14:28)
> "Now I am going to him who sent me, yet none of you asks me, 'Where are you going?' (John 16:5)
> In regard to righteousness, because I am going to the Father, where you can see me no longer; (John 16:10)
> I came from the Father and entered the world; now I am leaving the world and going back to the Father." (John 16:28)
> I will remain in the world no longer, but they are still in the world, and I am coming to you. Holy Father, protect them by the power of your name—the name you gave me—so that they may be one as we are one. (John 17:11)

    b. Believers must know that their Lord truly reigns.

> In a loud voice they sang: "Worthy is the Lamb, who was slain, to receive power and wealth and wisdom and strength and honor and glory and praise!" (Rev 5:12)
> Which he exerted in Christ when he raised him from the dead and seated him at his right hand in the heavenly realms, (Eph 1:20)
> Therefore God exalted him to the highest place and gave him the name that is above every name, (Phil 2:9)
> But we see Jesus, who was made a little lower than the angels, now crowned with glory and honor because he suffered death, so that by the grace of God he might taste death for everyone. (Heb 2:9)
> "He committed no sin, and no deceit was found in his mouth." (1 Pet 2:22)

Knowing these two great facts will help believers of all generations in preparing for persecution.

3. The believer must keep his mind focused on his destiny. Jesus has gone to the Father who sent Him. He has returned to heaven; therefore, the Father and heaven are the believer's destiny. If persecutors kill the believer, he gains; he does not lose. He gains something far better than this life, the presence of God Himself. (See note, Resurrection—Jn.14:6. See note—Lk.21:18-19. Cp. Ph.1:23.)

    Note: the believer is not to wallow around in self-pity and sorrow, moaning over being persecuted. His mind and thoughts are to be on God and heaven.

> Whoever serves me must follow me; and where I am, my servant also will be. My Father will honor the one who serves me. (John 12:26)
> And if I go and prepare a place for you, I will come back and take you to be with me that you also may be where I am. (John 14:3)
> "Father, I want those you have given me to be with me where I am, and to see my glory, the glory you have given me because you loved me before the creation of the world. (John 17:24)
> We are confident, I say, and would prefer to be away from the body and at home with the Lord. (2 Cor 5:8)
> I am torn between the two: I desire to depart and be with Christ, which is better by far; (Phil 1:23)
> You will keep in perfect peace him whose mind is steadfast, because he trusts in you. Trust in the LORD forever, for the LORD, the LORD, is the Rock eternal. (Isa 26:3-4)
> Peace I leave with you; my peace I give you. I do not give to you as the world gives. Do not let your hearts be troubled and do not be afraid. (John 14:27)
> "I have told you these things, so that in me you may have peace. In this world you will have trouble. But take heart! I have overcome the world." (John 16:33)

4. Believers must call upon the Helper, the Holy Spirit. This point is covered in the next few verses and outline. The Holy Spirit is given by God to be the constant companion of the believer, to help and comfort the believer through the persecution. (See outline and notes—Jn.16:7-15.)

> And I will ask the Father, and he will give you another Counselor to be with you forever—the Spirit of truth. The world cannot accept him, because it neither sees him nor knows him. But you know him, for he lives with you and will be in you. (John 14:16-17)
> But the Counselor, the Holy Spirit, whom the Father will send in my name, will teach you all things and will remind you of everything I have said to you. (John 14:26)
> But I tell you the truth: It is for your good that I am going away. Unless I go away, the Counselor will not come to you; but if I go, I will send him to you. (John 16:7)

	N. The Work of the Holy Spirit, 16:7-15	because the prince of this world now stands condemned.	3) Of judgment: Because Jesus condemned Satan^{DS1}

1 He helps believers
a. His help: for the believer's good
b. His name: The Counselor, Comforter, the Helper
2 He convicts & convinces the world
a. He convicts: Of sin, righteousness, and judgment
b. He convinces
  1) Of sin: Because they believe not on Jesus
  2) Of righteousness: Because Jesus' righteousness is proven—He is ascended as Lord
	7 But I tell you the truth: It is for your good that I am going away. Unless I go away, the Counselor will not come to you; but if I go, I will send him to you.
	8 When he comes, he will convict the world of guilt in regard to sin and righteousness and judgment:
	9 In regard to sin, because men do not believe in me;
	10 In regard to righteousness, because I am going to the Father, where you can see me no longer;
	11 And in regard to judgment,
		12 "I have much more to say to you, more than you can now bear.
		13 But when he, the Spirit of truth, comes, he will guide you into all truth. He will not speak on his own; he will speak only what he hears, and he will tell you what is yet to come.
		14 He will bring glory to me by taking from what is mine and making it known to you.
		15 All that belongs to theFather is mine. That is why I said the Spirit will take from what is mine and make it known to you.
			3 He guides believers
			a. Through speaking the truth
			b. Through leading into all truth
			c. Through showing things to come
			4 He glorifies Jesus: He shows the things of Jesus to believers

DIVISION XIII

THE REVELATION OF JESUS, THE GREAT MINISTER AND HIS LEGACY, 13:1-16:33

N. The Work of the Holy Spirit, 16:7-15

(16:7-15) **Introduction**: the clearest revelation of the Holy Spirit is given by our Lord Himself. He had already revealed who the Person of the Holy Spirit is (Jn.14:15-26). Now, He reveals the work of the Holy Spirit.

1. The Holy Spirit helps believers (v.7).
2. The Holy Spirit convicts and convinces the world (v.8-11).
3. The Holy Spirit guides believers (v.12-13).
4. The Holy Spirit glorifies Jesus: He shows the things of Jesus to believers (v.14-15).

1 (16:7) **Holy Spirit**: the Holy Spirit comforts and helps believers. Jesus said a surprising thing: "It is for your good that I am going away." It was for the believer's good (profit, advantage) that Jesus would leave the world. Note the additional weight and emphasis Jesus gave to the fact: "I tell you the truth." It may be difficult for a person to see and understand, for it seems that we would be much better off if Jesus were here physically and bodily. Some people even cry out for His presence, for some sight, some vision, some dream of Him. But Jesus said that it was best that He leave and not be physically present. Why? There is one supreme reason: if He had not left, the Holy Spirit would not have come. The believer is *better off* with the presence of the Holy Spirit than he is with the presence of Jesus.

Now note. How can such a statement be made? How can the believer be better off with the Holy Spirit than with the physical, bodily presence of Jesus?

1. Since Jesus departed, we now have *a glorified and exalted Lord*. We have a Lord who rules and reigns and controls all: who is able to fulfill all His promises and meet our desperate need for life—life that is both abundant and eternal.

> **And his incomparably great power for us who believe. That power is like the working of his mighty strength, which he exerted in Christ when he raised him from the dead and seated him at his right hand in the heavenly realms, (Eph 1:19-20)**

2. Since Jesus departed, we now have an *Intercessor* before the very throne of God. We have a Person who is able to sympathize with our weaknesses—all because He was tempted in every way just as we are.

> **Therefore, since we have a great high priest who has gone through the heavens, Jesus the Son of God, let us hold firmly to the faith we profess. For we do not have a high priest who is unable to sympathize with our weaknesses, but we have one who has been tempted in every way, just as we are—yet was without sin. Let us then approach the throne of grace with confidence, so that we may receive mercy and find grace to help us in our time of need. (Heb 4:14-16)**

3. Since Jesus departed, we now have the *presence of the Holy Spirit* with us at all times. Jesus in His human body could be only in one place at a time; but the Holy Spirit, who is Spirit, is able to be with all believers at the same time no matter where they are.

> **And I will ask the Father, and he will give you another Counselor to be with you forever— (John 14:16)**

4. Since Jesus departed, we now have *a real gospel* to proclaim, the gospel of the risen and exalted Lord who is able to give eternal life to every person who calls upon Him.

> **But what does it say? "The word is near you; it is in your mouth and in your heart," that is, the word of faith we are proclaiming: That if you confess with your mouth, "Jesus is Lord," and believe in your heart that God raised him from the dead, you will be saved. For it is with your**

heart that you believe and are justified, and it is with your mouth that you confess and are saved. for, "Everyone who calls on the name of the Lord will be saved." (Rom 10:8-10, 13)

5. Since Jesus departed, we now have the *worldwide work of the Holy Spirit*, His work of...
- convicting and convincing the world (Jn.16:8-11).
- helping and guiding believers (Jn.16:12-13).
- glorifying Christ (Jn.16:14-15).

Note the Holy Spirit is called the Comforter. (See note—Jn.14:16.)

2 (16:8-11) **Holy Spirit**: the Holy Spirit convicts and convinces the world. The word "convict" (elegxei) means both *to reprove* and *to convince* a person.
⇒ Convict means to prick a person's heart until he senses and knows he is guilty. He has done wrong or failed to do right.
⇒ Convince means to hammer and drive at a person's heart until he knows the fact is true.

The Holy Spirit convicts and convinces the world of three things: sin, righteousness, and judgment.
1. There is the *conviction of sin*.
   a. The Holy Spirit *convicts* the world of its sin, that man is sinful. The Holy Spirit convicts a man that he...
   - misses the mark, that is, falls short of the glory of God.

      For all have sinned and fall short of the glory of God, (Rom 3:23)

   - transgresses, that is, wanders off the right path.

      As for you, you were dead in your transgressions and sins, (Eph 2:1)

   - violates and breaks the law of God.

      For if the message spoken by angels was binding, and every violation and disobedience received its just punishment, how shall we escape if we ignore such a great salvation? This salvation, which was first announced by the Lord, was confirmed to us by those who heard him. (Heb 2:2-3)

   b. The Holy Spirit *convinces* the world that a man's unbelief is wrong. The Holy Spirit convinces the world that Jesus really did die for sin. The Holy Spirit takes a man who does not believe on Jesus and convinces him that Jesus is the Savior—that his sins are really forgiven when he *believes* on Jesus.

      I told you that you would die in your sins; if you do not believe that I am the one I claim to be, you will indeed die in your sins." (John 8:24)
      My dear children, I write this to you so that you will not sin. But if anybody does

sin, we have one who speaks to the Father in our defense—Jesus Christ, the Righteous One. He is the atoning sacrifice for our sins, and not only for ours but also for the sins of the whole world. (1 John 2:1-2)

2. There is the *conviction of righteousness*.
   a. The Holy Spirit *convicts* the world of its lack of righteousness, that a man has no righteousness whatsoever that is acceptable to God. The Holy Spirit convicts a man that his righteousness...
   - is self-righteousness only
   - is human righteousness only
   - is the righteousness of works that are only human and therefore have an end
   - is the righteousness of human goodness and therefore passes away when he dies
   - is inadequate, insufficient, and unacceptable to God

      Clearly no one is justified before God by the law, because, "The righteous will live by faith." (Gal 3:11; cp. Gal.2:16)
      All of us have become like one who is unclean, and all our righteous acts are like filthy rags; we all shrivel up like a leaf, and like the wind our sins sweep us away. No one calls on your name or strives to lay hold of you; for you have hidden your face from us and made us waste away because of our sins. (Isa 64:6-7; cp. v.9-12)

   b. The Holy Spirit *convinces* the world that Jesus' righteousness is acceptable to God. The Holy Spirit convinces a man...
   - that Jesus really was received up into heaven by the Father *because* He was righteous.
   - that Jesus has secured righteousness for every man.
   - that man can approach God through the righteousness of Jesus.
   - that Jesus is the Ideal and Perfect Man, the very Son of Man Himself. (See note—Jn.1:51.)

      God made him who had no sin to be sin for us, so that in him we might become the righteousness of God. (2 Cor 5:21)
      But also for us, to whom God will credit righteousness—for us who believe in him who raised Jesus our Lord from the dead. He was delivered over to death for our sins and was raised to life for our justification. (Rom 4:24-25)

3. There is the *conviction of judgment*.
   a. The Holy Spirit *convicts* the world that judgment is coming, that a man is to face the personal judgment of God. The Holy Spirit convicts a man...
   - that he is both responsible and accountable to God and man.
   - that there is to be a real day of judgment sometime out in the future.
   - that he is to stand face to face with God and be judged.

- that he is to be judged for sin and lack of righteousness, for what he has done and not done.

> So then, each of us will give an account of himself to God. (Rom 14:12)
> Just as man is destined to die once, and after that to face judgment, (Heb 9:27)

b. The Holy Spirit *convinces* the world that Jesus has borne the judgment of sin and death for man. The Holy Spirit convinces a man...
- that Jesus died bearing the penalty and judgment of sin for him.

> He himself bore our sins in his body on the tree, so that we might die to sins and live for righteousness; by his wounds you have been healed. (1 Pet 2:24)
> For Christ died for sins once for all, the righteous for the unrighteous, to bring you to God. He was put to death in the body but made alive by the Spirit, (1 Pet 3:18)

- that Jesus, by His death, destroyed the power of Satan over sin and death.

> Now is the time for judgment on this world; now the prince of this world will be driven out. (John 12:31)
> Since the children have flesh and blood, he too shared in their humanity so that by his death he might destroy him who holds the power of death—that is, the devil—and free those who all their lives were held in slavery by their fear of death. (Heb 2:14-15)

- that man can be freed from sin and death, that he can be forgiven for his sin and given eternal life through the death of Jesus.

> "For God so loved the world that he gave his one and only Son, that whoever believes in him shall not perish but have eternal life. (John 3:16)
> In him we have redemption through his blood, the forgiveness of sins, in accordance with the riches of God's grace (Eph 1:7)

(See DEEPER STUDY # 2,3—Jn.12:31; notes—12:31-33; 14:30-31 for more discussion.)

DEEPER STUDY # 1

(16:11) **Satan**: this passage concerns the judgment of Satan. The judgment of Satan was executed by Christ upon the cross. It was upon the cross that Jesus Christ judged and condemned the devil in all his authority and power. How? There were two ways.

1. Satan is judged and condemned by the obedience of Christ upon the cross. God is perfectly pleased with Christ, for Christ did exactly what God wanted: *He obeyed God perfectly*. Therefore, God is bound to be perfectly pleased.

The point is this: what God wanted most of all was for Christ to die *for man*. Christ Himself said, "I do exactly what my father commanded me" (Jn.14:31). The ultimate commandment that would show perfect obedience was for Him...
- to die for man's sin
- to receive the judgment of (physical and spiritual) death for man's sin
- to suffer separation from God for man

It was upon the cross that Christ obeyed God in the supreme, ultimate, and absolute sense. It was because he died—because He obeyed God perfectly—that God...
- has highly exalted Him (cp. Ph.2:9-11).
- has given Him a name that is above every name.
- has destined that every knee will bow before Him, of things *in heaven*, and things *on earth*, and things *under the earth*.
- has destined that every tongue will confess that Jesus Christ is Lord.
- has judged the world and appointed that it will be recreated and made into a new heavens and earth (2 Pt.3:10-13).
- has thrown out Satan and enthroned Christ, giving Him the loyalty of man and the kingdoms of the whole world (Jn.12:31-32).
- has assured the return of Christ and His rule and reign (Tit.2:12-13).
- has promised that Christ will rule and reign over a new heavens and earth, over all throughout the universe (2 Pt.3:4-5, 8-13).

2. Satan is judged and condemned by the belief of men in the cross, in the death of Christ (see DEEPER STUDY # 4, Cross—Jn.12:32 for discussion).

The cross judged and condemned Satan in all his authority and power. The judgment can be summed up in three areas.

1. The cross judges and breaks the power of Satan over the world (Jn.12:31). Satan is the ruler, the prince, the power of the world. This is taught by the Bible (Jn.12:31; 14:30; 16:11; 2 Cor.4:4; Eph.2:2). The one example of his dominion familiar to most is the temptation of Christ. Satan offered the kingdoms of the world to Christ if Christ would worship him (Lk.4:6). He possessed the kingdoms to offer. But Christ refused to yield to the temptation. Instead He chose to obey God, to secure the authority over the kingdoms of the world by way of the cross. In this particular passage, Christ proclaimed the coming triumph of the cross. The cross broke forever the power of the devil over the kingdoms of the world, and it assures the return of Christ to rule and reign throughout the universe forever.

> For he has rescued us from the dominion of darkness and brought us into the kingdom of the Son he loves, (Col 1:13)
> And having disarmed the powers and authorities, he made a public spectacle of them, triumphing over them by the cross. (Col 2:15)
> Then the end will come, when he hands over the kingdom to God the Father after he has destroyed all dominion, authority and power. For he must reign until he has put all his enemies under his feet. (1 Cor 15:24-25)

And being found in appearance as a man, he humbled himself and became obedient to death— even death on a cross! Therefore God exalted him to the highest place and gave him the name that is above every name, that at the name of Jesus every knee should bow, in heaven and on earth and under the earth, and every tongue confess that Jesus Christ is Lord, to the glory of God the Father. (Phil 2:8-11; cp. Rev.21:1f)

2. The cross judges and breaks the authority and power of Satan over death (Jn.12:31). Satan holds the power of death. It is his selfish and sinful influence that has brought corruption, decay, and death to the earth. But Christ has broken the devil's grip over death forever. The cross delivers man from the fear and bondage of death and assures Christ the authority over life and death.

Since the children have flesh and blood, he too shared in their humanity so that by his death he might destroy him who holds the power of death—that is, the devil—and free those who all their lives were held in slavery by their fear of death. (Heb 2:14-15)

For he must reign until he has put all his enemies under his feet. The last enemy to be destroyed is death. "Where, O death, is your victory? Where, O death, is your sting?" The sting of death is sin, and the power of sin is the law. But thanks be to God! He gives us the victory through our Lord Jesus Christ. (1 Cor 15:25-26, 55-57)

3. The cross judges and breaks the authority and power of Satan to corrupt men through worldliness and sin (Jn.12:32). Satan uses the world—its pleasures and desire for power and wealth and fame—to attract and enslave men, and enslavement inevitably leads to destruction. But the cross brings power to a man, spiritual power...
- to break his habits and bondages
- to keep him from damaging and destroying his body and spirit

The cross and its power to deliver and to give life have become the focal attraction of time and eternity. The cross liberates and frees man forever.

I will not speak with you much longer, for the prince of this world is coming. He has no hold on me, (John 14:30)

No temptation has seized you except what is common to man. And God is faithful; he will not let you be tempted beyond what you can bear. But when you are tempted, he will also provide a way out so that you can stand up under it. (1 Cor 10:13)

He who does what is sinful is of the devil, because the devil has been sinning from the beginning. The reason the Son of God appeared was to destroy the devil's work. (1 John 3:8)

You, dear children, are from God and have overcome them, because the one who is in you is greater than the one who is in the world. (1 John 4:4)

3 (16:12-13) **Holy Spirit**: the Holy Spirit guides believers through three things.

1. The Holy Spirit guides by speaking the truth. Christ said that He had many things to say to the apostles, but they were not able to "bear" (handle, grasp) them, not yet. He would share them later through the Holy Spirit. Christ tells the Spirit what to say and how to guide believers. Christ, of course, is the One who knows the weaknesses and the needs of men. He knows by personal experience (Heb.4:15-16). Therefore, He is the One who is appointed by God to instruct the Spirit in His *guiding* ministry. This should cause our hearts to leap with great joy and confidence, for the Lord know exactly what we face—knows by experience.

"For as many as are led by the Spirit of God, they are the sons of God" (Ro.8:14).

For this God is our God for ever and ever; he will be our guide even to the end. (Psa 48:14)

You guide me with your counsel, and afterward you will take me into glory. (Psa 73:24)

Whether you turn to the right or to the left, your ears will hear a voice behind you, saying, "This is the way; walk in it." (Isa 30:21)

I will lead the blind by ways they have not known, along unfamiliar paths I will guide them; I will turn the darkness into light before them and make the rough places smooth. These are the things I will do; I will not forsake them. (Isa 42:16)

This is what the LORD says— your Redeemer, the Holy One of Israel: "I am the LORD your God, who teaches you what is best for you, who directs you in the way you should go. (Isa 48:17)

2. The Holy Spirit guides by leading into all the truth. The Holy Spirit is called "the Spirit of Truth." He speaks only the truth and guides into "all the truth." The truth, of course, is Jesus Christ Himself. The Spirit leads the believer to Christ, the Truth, and teaches him "all the truth" about Christ. (See DEEPER STUDY # 2—Jn.14:6; note—15:26-27 for more discussion.)

"When the Counselor comes, whom I will send to you from the Father, the Spirit of truth who goes out from the Father, he will testify about me. (John 15:26)

We are from God, and whoever knows God listens to us; but whoever is not from God does not listen to us. This is how we recognize the Spirit of truth and the spirit of falsehood. (1 John 4:6)

3. The Holy Spirit guides by showing (announcing, declaring) things to come. After Jesus arose, the Holy Spirit was the One who led the apostles to write the New Testament and to foresee the things revealed in its pages. Since that day, the Holy Spirit is the One who takes the things revealed in the Word and shows (declares, announces) them to the heart of the believer.

However, as it is written: "No eye has seen, no ear has heard, no mind has conceived what God has prepared for those who love him"—but God has revealed it to us by his Spirit. The Spirit searches all things, even the deep things of God. (1 Cor 2:9-10)

We have not received the spirit of the world but the Spirit who is from God, that we may understand what God has freely given us. (1 Cor 2:12)

Thought 1. Note two critical facts.
1) The believer must be dependent upon the Holy Spirit's leadership in learning the truth.
2) The believer's growth is progressive, coming only from the Holy Spirit's opening up the Word to him.

This is what we speak, not in words taught us by human wisdom but in words taught by the Spirit, expressing spiritual truths in spiritual words. (1 Cor 2:13)

As for you, the anointing you received from him remains in you, and you do not need anyone to teach you. But as his anointing teaches you about all things and as that anointing is real, not counterfeit—just as it has taught you, remain in him. (1 John 2:27)

4 (16:14-15) **Holy Spirit—Trinity**: the Holy Spirit glorifies Christ and *only* Christ. Note that the Spirit "makes Christ known" and shows (declares) it to believers. This means that He reveals and declares…
- only what Christ is
- only what Christ did
- only what Christ said

The Holy Spirit was sent *in Jesus' name* to proclaim Jesus alone. He, the Spirit of Truth, leads believers to Christ, who alone is the Truth. He did not come to proclaim a movement and message of His own but to proclaim the movement and message of Christ.

But the Counselor, the Holy Spirit, whom the Father will send in my name, will teach you all things and will remind you of everything I have said to you. (John 14:26)

Note the phenomenal claim of Jesus. All that the Father has is His. He is the Son of God, the Son of the Father. (See note—Jn.1:34 for more discussion.) Note another fact: Christ is declaring that there is *perfect unity* in the Godhead. All things of the Father…
- are the things of the Son, of Jesus Christ Himself
- are the things shown and declared by the Holy Spirit

I and the Father are one." (John 10:30)

Do not believe me unless I do what my Father does. But if I do it, even though you do not believe me, believe the miracles, that you may know and understand that the Father is in me, and I in the Father." (John 10:37-38)

Don't you believe that I am in the Father, and that the Father is in me? The words I say to you are not just my own. Rather, it is the Father, living in me, who is doing his work. (John 14:10)

I have given them the glory that you gave me, that they may be one as we are one: (John 17:22)

	O. The Resurrection and Its Effects Foretold, 16:16-33	24 Until now you have not asked for anything in my name. Ask and you will receive, and your joy will be complete.	b. The institution of prayer "in Jesus' name"
1 The resurrection perplexes people a. The death & resurrection of Jesus predicted b. The resurrection was perplexing 1) The disciples' perplexity	16 "In a little while you will see me no more, and then after a little while you will see me." 17 Some of his disciples said to one another, "What does he mean by saying, 'In a little while you will see me no more, and then after a little while you will see me,' and' Because I am going to the Father'?" 18 They kept asking, "What does he mean by 'a little while'? We don't understand what he is saying."	25 "Though I have been speaking figuratively, a time is coming when I will no longer use this kind of language but will tell you plainly about my Father. 26 In that day you will ask in my name. I am not saying that I will ask the Father on your behalf. 27 No, the Father himself loves you because you have loved me and have believed that I came from God.	**4 The resurrection reveals all about the Father** a. The resurrection shows & declares the Father clearly b. The resurrection shows that the approach to God is "in Jesus' name" c. The resurrection shows that the Father Himself loves the believer
2) Jesus knew the disciples' perplexity & wished to help	19 Jesus saw that they wanted to ask him about this, so he said to them, "Are you asking one another what I meant when I said, 'In a little while you will see me no more, and then after a little while you will see me'?	28 I came from the Father and entered the world; now I am leaving the world and going back to the Father." 29 Then Jesus' disciples said, "Now you are speaking clearly and without figures of speech.	**5 The resurrection validates the Messiahship of Jesus** **6 The resurrection exposes weak faith**

2 The resurrection brings joy—irrepressible joy
a. There was grief at first: His death
b. There was then joy: His resurrection
c. There was a good illustration: A woman's labor
 	
d. There was irrepressible joy
  1) Because of resurrection
  2) Because no man could take the joy away
3 The resurrection gives open access into God's presence
a. The glorious promise
	20 I tell you the truth, you will weep and mourn while the world rejoices. You will grieve, but your grief will turn to joy.
	21 A woman giving birth to a child has pain because her time has come; but when her baby is born she forgets the anguish because of her joy that a child is born into the world.
	22 So with you: Now is your time of grief, but I will see you again and you will rejoice, and no one will take away your joy.
	23 In that day you will no longer ask me anything. I tell you the truth, my Father will give you whatever you ask in my name.
		30 Now we can see that you know all things and that you do not even need to have anyone ask you questions. This makes us believe that you came from God."
		31 "You believe at last!" Jesus answered.
		32 "But a time is coming, and has come, when you will be scattered, each to his own home. You will leave me all alone. Yet I am not alone, for my Father is with me.
		33 "I have told you these things, so that in me you may have peace. In this world you will have trouble. But take heart! I have overcome the world."
			a. The disciples declared their faith
			
			b. Jesus questioned their weak profession
			c. The cross tested & exposed their profession
			
			7 The resurrection makes available true peace
			a. The world's peace: Trouble
			b. The peace of Jesus: Triumphant

DIVISION XIII

THE REVELATION OF JESUS, THE GREAT MINISTER AND HIS LEGACY, 13:1-16:33

O. The Resurrection and Its Effects Foretold, 16:16-33

(16:16-33) **Introduction**: this is one of the great passages on the resurrection of Jesus Christ, and it is one of the most glorious passages in all of Scripture. It is one of those passages that lays out more than man could ever imagine. Jesus revealed and proclaimed the resurrection and its effects upon the world.

1. The resurrection perplexes people (v.16-19).
2. The resurrection brings joy—irrepressible joy (v.20-22).
3. The resurrection gives open access into God's presence (v.23-24).

4. The resurrection reveals all about the Father (v.25-27).
5. The resurrection validates Jesus' Messiahship (v.28).
6. The resurrection exposes weak faith (v.29-32).
7. The resurrection makes available true peace (v.33).

1 (16:16-19) **Jesus Christ, Resurrection**: the resurrection of Jesus Christ perplexes people. Jesus predicted His death and resurrection.

⇒ His death: "In a little while, <u>you will see me no more</u>."

308

⇒ His resurrection: "And then after a little while you will see me."

The prediction puzzled the disciples, and they began to ask among themselves what Jesus meant (v.18). Jesus knew that they were puzzled and asked them about their perplexity, wishing to help them (v.19).

Note Jesus' claim: "I am going to the Father" (see note, <u>Resurrection</u>—Jn.14:6 for discussion).

Thought 1. The resurrection does puzzle and perplex people; it always has and always will. People are puzzled by both the resurrection of Jesus and the coming resurrection of all men at the end of the world.

1) Some outrightly deny the resurrection, saying such is beyond human experience and could not possibly happen (an atheistic position).

2) Some say the resurrection may be, but it also may not be. Man has never known anything like it other than what Christians and a few others say about Jesus. But that happened so long ago that it cannot be scientifically proven; therefore, there is no way to know if it is true (an agnostic position).

3) Some say that the resurrection can be and that Jesus probably did arise but that it is a meaningless puzzle for *today*: "I will worry about its meaning tomorrow. I have no time to get involved and wrapped up in what it means, not now. Perhaps I will need to sit down and find out its meaning later, but right now other things are pressing and more important."

> **Since they did not know the righteousness that comes from God and sought to establish their own, they did not submit to God's righteousness. (Rom 10:3)**

> **They are darkened in their understanding and separated from the life of God because of the ignorance that is in them due to the hardening of their hearts. (Eph 4:18)**

> **Therefore, prepare your minds for action; be self-controlled; set your hope fully on the grace to be given you when Jesus Christ is revealed. As obedient children, do not conform to the evil desires you had when you lived in ignorance. But just as he who called you is holy, so be holy in all you do; (1 Pet 1:13-15)**

2 (16:20-22) **Jesus Christ, Resurrection**: the resurrection brings irrepressible joy. Note four points.

1. Jesus said there was to be grief at first. He would be going away and leaving the disciples by sacrificing Himself for the world. They would "weep" and "mourn" and experience deep grief. Their hopes would seem to be dashed upon the rocks of man's ultimate enemy: death.

> **My God. My soul is downcast within me; therefore I will remember you from the land of the Jordan, the heights of Hermon—from Mount Mizar. (Psa 42:6)**

> **I sink in the miry depths, where there is no foothold. I have come into the deep waters; the floods engulf me. (Psa 69:2)**

> **But as for me, my feet had almost slipped; I had nearly lost my foothold. (Psa 73:2)**

> **When I tried to understand all this, it was oppressive to me (Psa 73:16)**

> **But Zion said, "The LORD has forsaken me, the Lord has forgotten me." (Isa 49:14)**

Note: Jesus said the world would rejoice at His death. Why? Because death would prove that He was not the Son of God; it would prove that He was only a self-proclaimed savior who was now dead. Death would prove Him false. And being dead, His demands would not be binding; they would be meaningless. Men would not have to do what He said: deny themselves and give all they were and had to Him. They would not have to go and give all they had to meet the desperate needs of a lost world.

> **"But his subjects hated him and sent a delegation after him to say, 'We don't want this man to be our king.' (Luke 19:14)**

> **The man who loves his life will lose it, while the man who hates his life in this world will keep it for eternal life. (John 12:25)**

2. After grief there was to be irrepressible joy. Jesus said that He would arise, and His resurrection would cause His followers to burst forth with joy.

His resurrection meant that death was conquered. Men no longer had to die, no longer had to be condemned for sin. They could be delivered from sin and death by following Jesus (see DEEPER STUDY # 2—Jn.12:31; DEEPER STUDY # 4—12:32; DEEPER STUDY # 1—16:11 for discussion).

Thought 1. This joy is the answer to the weeping and mourning over death. The great source of joy is the glorious news of the resurrection, the absolute knowledge and certainty that Jesus Christ is risen.

3. Jesus gave a good illustration of the violent contrast between the sorrow over death and the joy of the resurrection. The illustration describes a woman's pain in giving birth. She suffers so much that she literally groans and grasps in desperation for the new life to begin. Once the child is born, the sorrow and pain are all forgotten for a new life has emerged.

4. The resurrection brings irrepressible joy just as a newborn baby brings joy to a woman in pain. Two things cause the joy.

a. The resurrection and presence of Jesus Himself brings great joy. Just think: Jesus is not dead. His body has not decayed in a grave: He has arisen. He emerged from the grave and ascended to the Father. There is victory over the grave, triumph over death. Man can now live forever. No truth could fill a man with any more joy and rejoicing than *really knowing* that death has been conquered in the resurrection of Jesus Christ.

> **For Christ died for sins once for all, the righteous for the unrighteous, to bring you to God. He was put to death in the body but made alive by the Spirit, (1 Pet 3:18)**

b. The believer's joy of *really knowing* the resurrection of Jesus Christ cannot be taken away by any man. The fact is there: Jesus did die for man's sins and arise again to give man a new life—a life that is both abundant and eternal. The believer knows it. His joy is permanent, deep-seated, and unmovable. When the trials and grief of earth come upon him, he still...

- knows the joy of the Lord's presence and care

> **And I will ask the Father, and he will give you another Counselor to be with you forever—the Spirit of truth. The world cannot accept him, because it neither sees him nor knows him. But you know him, for he lives with you and will be in you. I will not leave you as orphans; I will come to you. (John 14:16-18)**
>
> **But I tell you the truth: It is for your good that I am going away. Unless I go away, the Counselor will not come to you; but if I go, I will send him to you. (John 16:7)**

- knows that Christ will escort Him into the Father's presence eternally

> **And if I go and prepare a place for you, I will come back and take you to be with me that you also may be where I am. (John 14:3)**
>
> **We are confident, I say, and would prefer to be away from the body and at home with the Lord. (2 Cor 5:8)**
>
> **I am torn between the two: I desire to depart and be with Christ, which is better by far; (Phil 1:23)**
>
> **The Lord will rescue me from every evil attack and will bring me safely to his heavenly kingdom. To him be glory for ever and ever. Amen. (2 Tim 4:18)**

- knows that he will be a child of the new heavens and earth to be created for the Father's family

> **The Spirit himself testifies with our spirit that we are God's children. Now if we are children, then we are heirs—heirs of God and co-heirs with Christ, if indeed we share in his sufferings in order that we may also share in his glory. (Rom 8:16-17)**
>
> **But in keeping with his promise we are looking forward to a new heaven and a new earth, the home of righteousness. (2 Pet 3:13)**
>
> **Then I saw a new heaven and a new earth, for the first heaven and the first earth had passed away, and there was no longer any sea. (Rev 21:1)**

3 (16:23-24) **Jesus Christ, Resurrection:** the resurrection gives open access into God's presence. Note two facts.

1. The glorious promise: an *open door* into God's presence. Jesus said "in that day," after His resurrection, there will be no need to ask Him anything. (This does not mean, of course, that we cannot ask Him, only that we do not have to ask Him.) The believer can walk right into the Father's presence. There is an *open door* into His presence. Whatever the believer asks the Father in Jesus' name, He will give it to the believer. This is the most glorious of promises, that we can approach God as our Father just as a child approaches his earthly father.

2. The institution of prayer—of our approach to God, of our communion with Him—*in Jesus' name.* This is the crucial point. Our approach to the Father, our prayer, must be *in Jesus' name.* (See DEEPER STUDY # 3—Jn.14:13-14.) Before Jesus, men had always asked God for things directly, but no more. The resurrection instituted a new and living way into God's presence. Men must now approach God through Jesus Christ...

- believing that the righteousness of Jesus covers them
- asking God to accept their faith *in* Jesus as righteousness
- thanking God for Jesus, His great love and sacrifice for them

> **God made him who had no sin to be sin for us, so that in him we might become the righteousness of God. (2 Cor 5:21)**
>
> **And I will do whatever you ask in my name, so that the Son may bring glory to the Father. (John 14:13)**
>
> **You did not choose me, but I chose you and appointed you to go and bear fruit—fruit that will last. Then the Father will give you whatever you ask in my name. (John 15:16)**
>
> **Therefore, brothers, since we have confidence to enter the Most Holy Place by the blood of Jesus, by a new and living way opened for us through the curtain, that is, his body, and since we have a great priest over the house of God, let us draw near to God with a sincere heart in full assurance of faith, having our hearts sprinkled to cleanse us from a guilty conscience and having our bodies washed with pure water. (Heb 10:19-22)**

Note two tremendous promises to the man who asks *in Jesus' name.*

⇒ He will receive what he asks.

> **If you remain in me and my words remain in you, ask whatever you wish, and it will be given you. (John 15:7)**

⇒ His joy is full and complete (see DEEPER STUDY # 1—Jn.15:11 for discussion).

> **I have told you this so that my joy may be in you and that your joy may be complete. (John 15:11)**
>
> **For the kingdom of God is not a matter of eating and drinking, but of righteousness, peace and joy in the Holy Spirit, (Rom 14:17)**
>
> **Though you have not seen him, you love him; and even though you do not see him now, you believe in him and are filled with an inexpressible and glorious joy, (1 Pet 1:8)**

4 (16:25-27) **Jesus Christ, Resurrection**: the resurrection reveals all about the Father. Note three points.

1. Jesus said that the resurrection would show (declare) the Father plainly. It shows and declares God's nature...

- of *compassion*: of caring for the welfare of those gripped by sin and death.
- of *salvation*: of delivering men from the fear and bondage of sin and death.
- of *power*: of omnipotence, of being able to plan and carry out the plan of salvation by overruling all and by raising the dead.
- of *life*: possessing life itself and being able to infuse life into the dead.
- of *justice*: not allowing One who was sinless and perfect to be held by death.
- of *Omniscience*: knowing all, knowing the terrible injustice done to the innocent Son of God and knowing how to solve and work the whole scene out for the good of salvation.

> **Praise be to the God and Father of our Lord Jesus Christ! In his great mercy he has given us new birth into a living hope through the resurrection of Jesus Christ from the dead, and into an inheritance that can never perish, spoil or fade—kept in heaven for you. (1 Pet 1:3-4)**

2. It shows that the approach to God—prayer—is in the name of Jesus. (See DEEPER STUDY # 3—Jn.14:13-14 for discussion. Also see note, pt.2—Jn.16:23-24 of this outline.)

3. It shows that the Father Himself loves the believer. Jesus said that He would not have to beg the Father to receive and hear the believer. He does not have to intercede or take the believer to God. The believer does not need an Intercessor to be received by the Father. The Father Himself loves the believer. However, there is a crucial point to note. The Father *loves* the believer for a reason: the believer...

- loves Jesus (see notes—Jn.14:15; 14:23).
- believes that Jesus "came from God" (see DEEPER STUDY # 1—Jn.3:31; DEEPER STUDY # 3—3:34; notes—7:16-19; 7:25-31).

Thought 1. It is because of Jesus that the Father receives and hears the believer. Note how this picture of God as Father differs radically from the normal picture...

- that God is angry and has to be begged by Jesus to receive and hear us.
- that God is far off someplace out in space—almost too far to be reached.
- that maybe God is and maybe He is not, but one needs to go ahead and pray just in case.

> **"For God so loved the world that he gave his one and only Son, that whoever believes in him shall not perish but have eternal life. (John 3:16)**
> **But God demonstrates his own love for us in this: While we were still sinners, Christ died for us. (Rom 5:8)**
> **But because of his great love for us, God, who is rich in mercy, made us alive with Christ even when we were dead in transgressions—it is by grace you have been saved. (Eph 2:4-5)**

> **How great is the love the Father has lavished on us, that we should be called children of God! And that is what we are! The reason the world does not know us is that it did not know him. (1 John 3:1)**

5 (16:28) **Jesus Christ, Resurrection**: the resurrection validates and proves Jesus' claim to be the Messiah. In one brief statement Jesus gave the whole plan of salvation.

1. "I came from the Father and entered the world" (see DEEPER STUDY # 3—Jn.3:34; notes—7:16-19; 7:25-31).

> **But I know him because I am from him and he sent me." (John 7:29)**
> **Jesus said to them, "If God were your Father, you would love me, for I came from God and now am here. I have not come on my own; but he sent me. (John 8:42)**
> **What about the one whom the Father set apart as his very own and sent into the world? Why then do you accuse me of blasphemy because I said, 'I am God's Son'? (John 10:36)**
> **That all of them may be one, Father, just as you are in me and I am in you. May they also be in us so that the world may believe that you have sent me. (John 17:21)**

2. "I am leaving this world and going back to the Father" (see note, Resurrection—Jn.14:6).

> **"You heard me say, 'I am going away and I am coming back to you.' If you loved me, you would be glad that I am going to the Father, for the Father is greater than I. (John 14:28)**
> **"In a little while you will see me no more, and then after a little while you will see me." (John 16:16)**
> **I will remain in the world no longer, but they are still in the world, and I am coming to you. Holy Father, protect them by the power of your name—the name you gave me—so that they may be one as we are one. (John 17:11)**

Note Jesus' phenomenal claim. He came from "the Father" and is returning to "the Father."

> **And who through the Spirit of holiness was declared with power to be the Son of God by his resurrection from the dead: Jesus Christ our Lord. (Rom 1:4)**

6 (16:29-32) **Jesus Christ, Resurrection**: the resurrection exposes weak faith. Something Jesus said struck the disciples' hearts. Just what it was is not really known. It may have been His promise to show them the Father (explain all that He was saying) or the fact that the Father loves them. Whatever it was, it caused the disciples to make a great declaration of faith:

⇒ "You know all things."
⇒ "You came from God."

Thought 1. Note that this confession is the *Incarnation*, God Himself in the person of His Son coming to earth. It is a critical confession that must be made by every man.

> **This is how you can recognize the Spirit of God: Every spirit that acknowledges that Jesus Christ has come in the flesh is from God, but every spirit that does not acknowledge Jesus is not from God. This is the spirit of the antichrist, which you have heard is coming and even now is already in the world. (1 John 4:2-3)**

Jesus questioned their belief and predicted their desertion. Note several clear facts about Jesus, facts that are a great encouragement to the believer.

1. Jesus was never alone, even when men did not stand with Him. The Father was with Him through every situation no matter how terrible. Even when He did not have the support of men, He had God and His support.

> **I and the Father are one." (John 10:30)**
> **But if I do it, even though you do not believe me, believe the miracles, that you may know and understand that the Father is in me, and I in the Father." (John 10:38)**
> **Don't you believe that I am in the Father, and that the Father is in me? The words I say to you are not just my own. Rather, it is the Father, living in me, who is doing his work. (John 14:10)**

2. Jesus was forgiving. He forgave every one of the men, even for deserting Him. He did not hold their sin and failure against them. (How His arms reach out for every deserter, to forgive and to receive back!)

> **He was delivered over to death for our sins and was raised to life for our justification. (Rom 4:25)**
> **That if you confess with your mouth, "Jesus is Lord," and believe in your heart that God raised him from the dead, you will be saved. For it is with your heart that you believe and are justified, and it is with your mouth that you confess and are saved. (Rom 10:9-10)**

3. Jesus knew all. Even when He chose these men, He knew they would fail and desert Him, yet He went ahead and chose them. He knew they were trustworthy and would eventually prove faithful.

> **You did not choose me, but I chose you and appointed you to go and bear fruit—fruit that will last. Then the Father will give you whatever you ask in my name. (John 15:16)**

> **I thank Christ Jesus our Lord, who has given me strength, that he considered me faithful, appointing me to his service. (1 Tim 1:12)**

7 (16:33) **Jesus Christ, Resurrection**: the resurrection makes available true peace, triumphant peace (see note, Peace—Jn.14:27 for discussion). The world can give only trials and trouble. No matter who the person is, the trials and troubles come. Such is the way of the world, and no man can avoid it. Therefore, whatever peace comes to this world is transient, passing ever so quickly.

The peace of Jesus Christ—the peace that is *in Him*—is lasting. It is an *overcoming* peace, a peace that overcomes the trials and troubles of the world, no matter what they are, even the terrible trials of sin and death. But note, the *overcoming peace...*
- is only *in Jesus*
- is only *in His Word*, in the things which He spoke

Note: the peace of God comes only through the resurrection of Jesus Christ, only through His conquest and victory over sin and death.

> **But God raised him from the dead, freeing him from the agony of death, because it was impossible for death to keep its hold on him. (Acts 2:24)**
> **For what I received I passed on to you as of first importance : that Christ died for our sins according to the Scriptures, that he was buried, that he was raised on the third day according to the Scriptures, (1 Cor 15:3-4; cp. v.5-58)**
> **And his incomparably great power for us who believe. That power is like the working of his mighty strength, which he exerted in Christ when he raised him from the dead and seated him at his right hand in the heavenly realms, (Eph 1:19-20)**
> **Brothers, we do not want you to be ignorant about those who fall asleep, or to grieve like the rest of men, who have no hope. We believe that Jesus died and rose again and so we believe that God will bring with Jesus those who have fallen asleep in him. (1 Th 4:13-14)**
> **Praise be to the God and Father of our Lord Jesus Christ! In his great mercy he has given us new birth into a living hope through the resurrection of Jesus Christ from the dead, and into an inheritance that can never perish, spoil or fade—kept in heaven for you, (1 Pet 1:3-4)**

	CHAPTER 17	true God, and Jesus Christ, whom you have sent.
		4 I have brought you glory on earth by completing the work you gave me to do.
		5 And now, Father, glorify me in your presence with the glory I had with you before the world began.
		6 "I have revealed you to those whom you gave me out of the world. They were yours; you gave them to me and they have obeyed your word.
		7 Now they know that everything you have given me comes from you.
		8 For I gave them the words you gave me and they accepted them. They knew with certainty that I came from you, and they believed that you sent me.
			c. Reason: Christ completed God's work
			3 Request 2: Restore your Son to His former glory—to His preexistent exaltation
			a. Because He has revealed the Father's name
			b. Because men now know that He is the Son of God, the revelation of God Himself
			  1) They now accept His Words
			  2) They now know His origin
			  3) They now believe He is sent of God, that He is the Son of God Himself

	XIV. THE REVELATION OF JESUS, THE GREAT INTERCESSOR, 17:1-26		
	A. Jesus Prayed for Himself, 17:1-8		

1 Jesus' time had come, that is, His death
2 Request 1: Glorify your Son—that He may glorify the Father
a. How: By giving Him authority over all people
b. Purpose: That He may give eternal life[DS1]
  1) Eternal life is knowing God
  2) Eternal life is knowing Christ
	After Jesus said this, he looked toward heaven and prayed: "Father, the time has come. Glorify your Son, that your Son may glorify you.
	2 For you granted him authority over all people that he might give eternal life to all those you have given him
	3 Now this is eternal life: that they may know you, the only		

DIVISION XIV

THE REVELATION OF JESUS, THE GREAT INTERCESSOR, 17:1-26

A. Jesus Prayed for Himself, 17:1-8

(17:1-8) **Introduction**: this passage begins the High Priestly Prayer of Jesus (Jn.17:1-26). In this great chapter Jesus is revealed to be *the great Intercessor*. He reached the summit of prayer: He prayed for Himself (v.1-8), for His immediate disciples (v.9-19), and for future believers (v.20-26). He asked only two things for Himself.

1. Jesus' time had come, that is, His death (v.1).
2. Request 1: glorify your Son—that He may glorify the Father (v.1-4).
3. Request 2: restore your Son to His former glory—to His preexistent exaltation (v.5-8).

(17:1-8) **Another Outline**: The Hour Has Come.

1. The time of glory (v.1).
2. The time of power (v.2).
3. The time of eternal life (v.2-3).
4. The time of a finished work (v.4).
5. The time of restored glory (v.5).
6. The time of revelation (v.6).
7. The time of a mission accomplished, or the time of belief (v.7-8).

1 (17:1) **Jesus Christ, Hour of**: Jesus' time had come. "His time" refers to His death (see notes—Jn.2:3-5; 12:23-24). Note that Jesus looked toward heaven and called God "Father." He was claiming to know God intimately, to be the very Son of God. Note also that Jesus made only two requests for Himself (v.1, 5).

2 (17:1-4) **Jesus Christ, Glory of**: the first thing Jesus asked was, "Father...glorify your Son." But quickly note why: "That your Son may glorify you." The whole purpose for God's sending Jesus to earth was to give eternal life to men's; so in asking the two questions, "How is God glori-

fied?" and "How is Jesus glorified?" the answer is simply: "by men's receiving eternal life." Both God's glory and Jesus' glory are found in the completion of the great work of salvation. There is...

- the glory of righteousness which Jesus secured by a perfect life.
- the glory of the cross itself.
- the glory of Jesus' resurrection which vindicates beyond question His Messiahship.
- the glory of Christ's ascension and exaltation.

All is summed up in the glory of man's salvation, in man's receiving eternal life. (See notes, Jesus Christ, Glory of—Jn.12:23-26; God, Glory of—Jn.12:27-30 for discussion. Also see DEEPER STUDY # 4, Hallowed Be—Mt.6:9; DEEPER STUDY # 6, God, Will of—Mt.6:10 for more discussion.)

Now note three things about Jesus' request to be glorified.

1. How is Jesus glorified? By God's giving Him the power and authority over all people (see note—Jn.13:31-32 for discussion. Also see note—Jn.12:23-26 for more discussion. These are important notes in seeing this point.)

"I tell you the truth, whoever hears my word and believes him who sent me has eternal life and will not be condemned; he has crossed over from death to life. I tell you the truth, a time is coming and has now come when the dead will hear the voice of the Son of God and those who hear will live. For as the Father has life in himself, so he has granted the Son to have life in himself. And he has given him authority to judge because he is the Son of Man. (John 5:24-27)

2. The reason Jesus was exalted to be the Sovereign Majesty of the universe is onefold, and it is the most wonderful news in all the universe. Jesus was glorified so that He could give eternal life to men (cp. Jn.3:35-36; 10:28).

a. He gives eternal life. (See DEEPER STUDY # 2—Jn.1:4; DEEPER STUDY # 1—10:10; DEEPER STUDY # 1—17:2-3.)

b. God gives Jesus the persons who are to receive eternal life. Note: a man must be moved upon by the drawing power of God (Holy Spirit) in order to receive eternal life (see notes—Jn.6:44-46).

"No one can come to me unless the Father who sent me draws him, and I will raise him up at the last day. (John 6:44)

3. The reason Jesus was now ready to be glorified is simply stated: He had completed the work God had given Him to do. In doing the work God had given Him to do, He had glorified God on earth.

Thought 1. The only way a person can glorify God on earth is to do what God says. If a man is interested in glorifying God, he will obey God. (See note, God, Glory of—Jn.12:27-30 for more discussion.)

And this is his command: to believe in the name of his Son, Jesus Christ, and to love one another as he commanded us. (1 John 3:23)

"Not everyone who says to me, 'Lord, Lord,' will enter the kingdom of heaven, but only he who does the will of my Father who is in heaven. (Mat 7:21)

This is to my Father's glory, that you bear much fruit, showing yourselves to be my disciples. (John 15:8)

DEEPER STUDY # 1

(17:2-3) **Eternal Life** (ainios): life, real life. It is the very life of God Himself. It is the very energy, force, being, essence, principle, and power of life. It has more to do with quality and with what life really is than with duration. To live forever in the present world is not necessarily a good thing. The world and man's body need changing. That changed life is found only in eternal life. The only being who can be said to be eternal is God. Therefore, life—supreme life—is found only in God. To possess eternal life is to know God. Once a person knows God and Jesus Christ whom He has sent, that person has eternal life—he shall live forever. But more essential, the person has the supreme quality of life, the very life of God Himself. (See DEEPER STUDY # 2—Jn.1:4; DEEPER STUDY # 1—10:10.)

Just as Moses lifted up the snake in the desert, so the Son of Man must be lifted up, that everyone who believes in him may have eternal life. (John 3:14-15)
Whoever believes in the Son has eternal life, but whoever rejects the Son will not see life, for God's wrath remains on him." (John 3:36)

"I tell you the truth, whoever hears my word and believes him who sent me has eternal life and will not be condemned; he has crossed over from death to life. (John 5:24)

For my Father's will is that everyone who looks to the Son and believes in him shall have eternal life, and I will raise him up at the last day." (John 6:40)

Jesus said to her, "I am the resurrection and the life. He who believes in me will live, even though he dies; and whoever lives and believes in me will never die. Do you believe this?" "Yes, Lord," she told him, "I believe that you are the Christ, the Son of God, who was to come into the world." And after she had said this, she went back and called her sister Mary aside. "The Teacher is here," she said, "and is asking for you." (John 11:25-28)

The man who loves his life will lose it, while the man who hates his life in this world will keep it for eternal life. (John 12:25)

So that, just as sin reigned in death, so also grace might reign through righteousness to bring eternal life through Jesus Christ our Lord. (Rom 5:21)

The one who sows to please his sinful nature, from that nature will reap destruction; the one who sows to please the Spirit, from the Spirit will reap eternal life. (Gal 6:8)

But it has now been revealed through the appearing of our Savior, Christ Jesus, who has destroyed death and has brought life and immortality to light through the gospel. (2 Tim 1:10)

We know that we have passed from death to life, because we love our brothers. Anyone who does not love remains in death. (1 John 3:14)

And this is the testimony: God has given us eternal life, and this life is in his Son. He who has the Son has life; he who does not have the Son of God does not have life. (1 John 5:11-12)

3 (17:5-8) **Jesus Christ, Glory of; Exaltation**: the second thing Jesus asked for Himself was to be restored to His former glory, to His preexistent exaltation (see notes—Jn.1:1-2; 13:31-32, pt.3 for discussion). Note what this says.

⇒ Jesus *lived* in a preexistent, eternal state and glory with God.

"I tell you the truth," Jesus answered, "before Abraham was born, I am!" (John 8:58)

I came from the Father and entered the world; now I am leaving the world and going back to the Father." (John 16:28)

The Son is the radiance of God's glory and the exact representation of his being, sustaining all things by his powerful word. After he had provided purification for sins, he sat down at the right hand of the Majesty in heaven. (Heb 1:3)

But about the Son he says, "Your throne, O God, will last for ever and ever, and righteousness will be the scepter of your kingdom. (Heb 1:8)

⇒ Jesus set His glory aside when he came to earth as Man (see note—Ph.2:7).

For you know the grace of our Lord Jesus Christ, that though he was rich, yet for your sakes he became poor, so that you through his poverty might become rich. (2 Cor 8:9)

But made himself nothing, taking the very nature of a servant, being made in human likeness. (Phil 2:7)

⇒ Jesus knew that He would return to the Father and be restored to His former glory.

Jesus said, "I am with you for only a short time, and then I go to the one who sent me. (John 7:33)

"You heard me say, 'I am going away and I am coming back to you.' If you loved me, you would be glad that I am going to the Father, for the Father is greater than I. (John 14:28)

I will remain in the world no longer, but they are still in the world, and I am coming to you. Holy Father, protect them by the power of your name—the name you gave me—so that they may be one as we are one. (John 17:11)

For this very reason, Christ died and returned to life so that he might be the Lord of both the dead and the living. (Rom 14:9)

And being found in appearance as a man, he humbled himself and became obedient to death— even death on a cross! Therefore God exalted him to the highest place and gave him the name that is above every name, that at the name of Jesus every knee should bow, in heaven and on earth and under the earth, and every tongue confess that Jesus Christ is Lord, to the glory of God the Father. (Phil 2:8-11)

There are two reasons why Jesus asked to be restored to His former glory.

1. Jesus had revealed God's name. By "name" is meant the whole character and nature of God—all that God is. This is a phenomenal claim, for Jesus was claiming to be the very revelation of God, the One who reveals God to men (see outline and notes—Jn.14:6; 14:8-11). Note several points.

   a. Jesus revealed God (the full revelation of God) to the people whom God had given Him. He shared the message of God, but He did not scatter the seed among the unthankful and unreceptive. He had even told His followers not to waste time on the unreceptive.

   And if any place will not welcome you or listen to you, shake the dust off your feet when you leave, as a testimony against them." (Mark 6:11)

   b. It was God who gave Jesus the believers who were to be shown and taught all about Himself. God is Sovereign, so He led both Jesus and the disciples together. God stirred and led these men, the first believers, out of the world to follow Jesus and to receive and to be shown the revelation of God. They learned of God—of His Person and nature,

of His love and salvation—because God drew them to His dear Son (see note—Jn.6:44-46).

"No one can come to me unless the Father who sent me draws him, and I will raise him up at the last day. It is written in the Prophets: 'They will all be taught by God.' Everyone who listens to the Father and learns from him comes to me. (John 6:44-45)

My Father, who has given them to me, is greater than all ; no one can snatch them out of my Father's hand. (John 10:29)

   c. The first believers belonged to God. They were His because He drew them to His Son by His Sovereignty and power and by His foreknowledge. He knew that they would believe on Jesus.

   For those God foreknew he also predestined to be conformed to the likeness of his Son, that he might be the firstborn among many brothers. (Rom 8:29)

   d. These men kept God's Word. They obeyed and did exactly what Jesus commanded. (See note— Jn.15:9-10.)

   Jesus replied, "If anyone loves me, he will obey my teaching. My Father will love him, and we will come to him and make our home with him. (John 14:23)

   If you obey my commands, you will remain in my love, just as I have obeyed my Father's commands and remain in his love. (John 15:10)

2. The men now knew that Jesus was the Son of God, the very revelation of God Himself. They knew "everything" *which He had were given by God* (v.7). They knew that He was the very embodiment and revelation of God. (Note: Jesus was looking ahead beyond the resurrection in saying this. It would be the resurrection that would confirm all He had been revealing to them.)

   a. They had now accepted His words as the very words of God (see notes—Jn.7:16-19; 14:10; 12:47-50).

   The Spirit gives life; the flesh counts for nothing. The words I have spoken to you are spirit and they are life. (John 6:63)

   Simon Peter answered him, "Lord, to whom shall we go? You have the words of eternal life. (John 6:68)

   Jesus answered, "My teaching is not my own. It comes from him who sent me. If anyone chooses to do God's will, he will find out whether my teaching comes from God or whether I speak on my own. (John 7:16-17)

   I tell you the truth, if anyone keeps my word, he will never see death." (John 8:51)

   There is a judge for the one who rejects me and does not accept my words; that very word which I spoke will condemn him at the last day. (John 12:48)

   He who does not love me will not obey my teaching. These words you hear are not

my own; they belong to the Father who sent me. (John 14:24)

We know that we have come to know him if we obey his commands. (1 John 2:3)

b. They now knew His origin: He had come *from God* (see DEEPER STUDY # 1—Jn.3:31; DEEPER STUDY # 3—3:34; notes—7:16-19; 7:25-31).

No one has ever gone into heaven except the one who came from heaven—the Son of Man. (John 3:13)

For the bread of God is he who comes down from heaven and gives life to the world." For I have come down from heaven not to do my will but to do the will of him who sent me. (John 6:33, 38)

But he continued, "You are from below; I am from above. You are of this world; I am not of this world. (John 8:23)

Jesus said to them, "If God were your Father, you would love me, for I came from God and now am here. I have not come on my own; but he sent me. (John 8:42)

Now we can see that you know all things and that you do not even need to have anyone ask you questions. This makes us believe that you came from God." (John 16:30)

c. They now believed that God *had* sent Him, that He had come to earth as the Ambassador of God to proclaim and reveal the salvation of God. (See note—Jn.3:32-34; DEEPER STUDY # 3—3:34.)

For I have come down from heaven not to do my will but to do the will of him who sent me. (John 6:38)

But I know him because I am from him and he sent me." (John 7:29)

That all of them may be one, Father, just as you are in me and I am in you. May they also be in us so that the world may believe that you have sent me. (John 17:21)

1 Jesus prayed for His disciples
a. Because they had been entrusted to Him
b. Because they belonged to both Jesus & God[DS1]
c. Because glory came to Jesus through them
d. Because Jesus was leaving the world

2 Request 1: That God would keep them & keep them together as one[DS2]
a. Because they were in the world

b. Because He had kept them & had lost none[DS3]

B. Jesus Prayed for His Disciples, 17:9-19

9 I pray for them. I am not praying for the world, but for those you have given me, for they are yours.
10 All I have is yours, and all you have is mine. And glory has come to me through them.
11 I will remain in the world no longer, but they are still in the world, and I am coming to you. Holy Father, protect them by the power of your name—the name you gave me—so that they may be one as we are one.
12 While I was with them, I protected them and kept them safe by that name you gave me. None has been lost except the one doomed to destruction so that Scripture would be fulfilled.
13 "I am coming to you now, but I say these things while I am still in the world, so that they may have the full measure of my joy within them.
14 I have given them your word and the world has hated them, for they are not of the world any more than I am of the world.
15 My prayer is not that you take them out of the world but that you protect them from the evil one.
16 They are not of the world, even as I am not of it.
17 Sanctify them by the truth; your word is truth.
18 As you sent me into the world, I have sent them into the world.
19 For them I sanctify myself, that they too may be truly sanctified.

3 Request 2: That they might have His joy in all its fullness

4 Request 3: That God would keep them from the evil one or Satan
a. Because world hated them
  1) Because of the Word
  2) Because they are not of the world
b. Because they were needed in the world
c. Because they were now of the same nature as Jesus

5 Request 4: That God would sanctify them[DS4]
a. Because they were sent into the world

b. Because sanctification is the way of salvation

DIVISION XIV

THE REVELATION OF JESUS, THE GREAT INTERCESSOR, 17:1-26

B. Jesus Prayed for His Disciples, 17:9-19

(17:9-19) **Introduction**: Jesus prayed for His disciples. What He prayed was striking and full of meaning for believers of every generation.
  1. Jesus prayed for His disciples (v.9-11).
  2. Request 1: that God would keep them and keep them together as one (v.11-12).
  3. Request 2: that they might have His joy in all its fullness (v.13).
  4. Request 3: that God would keep them from the evil one or Satan (v.14-16).
  5. Request 4: that God would sanctify them (v.17-19).

1 (17:9-11) **Jesus Christ, Ministry—God, Faithfulness of**: Jesus prayed for His disciples. He was not praying for the world, not now. He specifically said so. Why?
  ⇒ It was not because He and the Father do not love the world. They do; they love the world deeply (Jn.3:16). The world was the very reason Jesus had come to earth: to save the world and keep it from perishing.
  ⇒ It was not because the world did not need prayer. It did, and He prayed for the forgiveness and conversion of men in the world (Lk.23:34).
There are four reasons why Jesus was praying only for His disciples. Note that the reasons are part of His prayer.
  1. Jesus' disciples had been given to Him *by His Father* (v.9). They belonged to His Father, but they had been *entrusted into His hands*. He was responsible for them and their welfare. Therefore, He had to pray for them, that His Father would give them special strength in the coming days.

For he chose us in him before the creation of the world to be holy and blameless in his sight. In love (Eph 1:4)

Who have been chosen according to the foreknowledge of God the Father, through the sanctifying work of the Spirit, for obedience to Jesus Christ and sprinkling by his blood: Grace and peace be yours in abundance. (1 Pet 1:2)

  2. Jesus' disciples belonged to both Him and the Father (v.10). Note exactly how Jesus worded this: "All I have is yours, and all you have is mine." All the disciples were God's; they belonged to God. But all the disciples of God also belonged to Jesus. This is the mutual possession of all believers by both Jesus and God. They are both deeply concerned over the welfare of believers. God is as concerned over believers as Jesus is; therefore, Jesus can count on God's hearing and answering His prayer.

My Father, who has given them to me, is greater than all ; no one can snatch them out of my Father's hand. (John 10:29)
I in them and you in me. May they be brought to complete unity to let the world know that you sent me and have loved them even as you have loved me. (John 17:23)
For those God foreknew he also predestined to be conformed to the likeness of his Son, that he might be the firstborn among many brothers. (Rom 8:29)

  3. Jesus' disciples glorified Jesus; their lives brought glory to Him (v.10). They lived for Him by obeying His Word and working for Him and showing loyalty and allegiance. They lifted Him up to the world and proclaimed Him to be the Savior of the world and the Lord of the universe. He was thereby glorified, honored, and praised;

therefore, He prayed for them—that they might become strong in their lives and witness for Him.

> We pray this so that the name of our Lord Jesus may be glorified in you, and you in him, according to the grace of our God and the Lord Jesus Christ. (2 Th 1:12)
> But you are a chosen people, a royal priesthood, a holy nation, a people belonging to God, that you may declare the praises of him who called you out of darkness into his wonderful light. (1 Pet 2:9)

4. Jesus was leaving the world and returning to heaven and the Father (v.11). The whole mission of preaching the gospel to the world rested upon the shoulders of His disciples. They were the ones who were to go out into the world as His ambassadors to proclaim His Word. As they went, they needed to be strengthened and equipped by God to stand against some terrible forces. His followers were the ones who needed special prayer. His whole mission of reaching the world for God depended upon their endurance and faithfulness. In these last hours before He returned to heaven, He had to pray for them with power and intensity, asking great things of God.

> Therefore go and make disciples of all nations, baptizing them in the name of the Father and of the Son and of the Holy Spirit, and teaching them to obey everything I have commanded you. And surely I am with you always, to the very end of the age." (Mat 28:19-20)
> Again Jesus said, "Peace be with you! As the Father has sent me, I am sending you." (John 20:21)

DEEPER STUDY # 1
(17:10) **Jesus—Deity**: "all I have is yours, and all you have is mine"—a phenomenal claim. A man can say that all he is and has belongs to God, but no man can say that all God is and has belongs to him. In Jesus' very prayer He was claiming deity—oneness with God. (See note—Jn.14:10; cp. Jn.10:30.)

> I and the Father are one." (John 10:30)
> Do not believe me unless I do what my Father does. But if I do it, even though you do not believe me, believe the miracles, that you may know and understand that the Father is in me, and I in the Father." (John 10:37-38)
> Don't you believe that I am in the Father, and that the Father is in me? The words I say to you are not just my own. Rather, it is the Father, living in me, who is doing his work. (John 14:10)
> I will remain in the world no longer, but they are still in the world, and I am coming to you. Holy Father, protect them by the power of your name—the name you gave me—so that they may be one as we are one. (John 17:11)
> I have given them the glory that you gave me, that they may be one as we are one: (John 17:22)

2 (17:11-12) **Unity**: first, Jesus prayed that God would keep His disciples—keep them together as one. Jesus was praying for the disciples to be kept from the *divisiveness* of the world, not that they would be kept from evil. He dealt with the evil of the world later (v.14-15). Note two points.
1. The disciples were in an extremely divisive world (see DEEPER STUDY # 2, Unity—Jn.17:11 for discussion).
2. Jesus kept the disciples while He was in the world. He lost none except Judas, and Judas' betrayal was to fulfill Scripture. (See outline and notes—Jn.13:1-30 for discussion of Judas.) Jesus was faithful *to God's name*, faithful in revealing God and lifting up His name to the disciples. Now He was leaving the world, so God had to take over. It was now up to God to keep them, and He would. God would keep the disciples as well as Christ did, for God was both faithful and able.

DEEPER STUDY # 2
(17:11) **Unity—Believers, Walk**: believers are to be one just as Jesus and the Father are one. The unity between believers is to be as strong as the unity between Jesus and His Father. This is a phenomenal truth, a truth that consumed the Lord's thoughts. It was the very theme of Jesus' prayer (v.11, 21, 22, 23). Believers must be one. Note two points.
1. Believers are in an extremely divisive world, a world full of...

- prejudice
- competition
- lust
- selfishness
- egotism
- hurt
- angry spirits
- possessiveness
- pride
- self-praise
- hate
- war

The list is unlimited, for divisiveness comes from the depraved nature of man, the nature that Christ came to change and to convert to love. The divisive world was a threat to the early disciples. Being in the world, they could have been influenced and led astray in the ways of divisiveness. Jesus had to pray for them, for God to keep them together as one.

Note Jesus' request. It is an eye-opener, an astounding request: "That they may be one, as we are one." Believers are to be as unified as God and Christ are. What does this mean? It means that we are to have the *same kind* of unity that Jesus and the Father have. We are to be one in *nature, character, and purpose*.
a. Believers are to be one in nature. The believer is a person who...
- has been "born again" (see DEEPER STUDY # 1—Jn.3:1-15. Cp. Jn.1:13; Tit.3:5; 1 Jn.2:29; 4:7.)

> For you have been born again, not of perishable seed, but of imperishable, through the living and enduring word of God. (1 Pet 1:23)
> Everyone who believes that Jesus is the Christ is born of God, and everyone who loves the father loves his child as well. (1 John 5:1)

- has been made into a "new creation," become a "new self" or "new man" (cp. Gal.6:15; Eph.4:24; Col.3:10).

318

Therefore, if anyone is in Christ, he is a new creation; the old has gone, the new has come! (2 Cor 5:17)

• has become a partaker of the "divine nature."

Through these he has given us his very great and precious promises, so that through Them you may participate in the divine nature and escape the corruption in the world caused by evil desires. (2 Pet 1:4)

However, the nature of believers includes more than just a personal rebirth of one's spirit. When a man becomes a believer, his new nature makes him a member of God's...

• new body of people

And in this one body to reconcile both of them to God through the cross, by which he put to death their hostility. (Eph 2:16)

• new nation

Consequently, you are no longer foreigners and aliens, but fellow citizens with God's people and members of God's household, (Eph 2:19)

• new temple

In him the whole building is joined together and rises to become a holy temple in the Lord. (Eph 2:21)

• new family

Consequently, you are no longer foreigners and aliens, but fellow citizens with God's people and members of God's household, (Eph 2:19)

• new fellowship or church

And in him you too are being built together to become a dwelling in which God lives by his Spirit. (Eph 2:22)

• new building

Built on the foundation of the apostles and prophets, with Christ Jesus himself as the chief cornerstone. In him the whole building is joined together and rises to become a holy temple in the Lord. And in him you too are being built together to become a dwelling in which God lives by his Spirit. (Eph 2:20-22)

• new race (see note—Eph.4:17-19)

So I tell you this, and insist on it in the Lord, that you must no longer live as the Gentiles do, in the futility of their thinking. (Eph 4:17 Note: the word *other* is not in the Greek. The believer is a new creation, a new race distinct from the Gentiles. He is no longer to walk as the Gentiles walk.)

This, of course, means that a believer is to live and walk in unity with other believers. He is not to allow the divisive spirit of the world to infiltrate his life: grumbling, griping, complaining, criticizing, envying, gossiping, opposing, bypassing, overlooking, ignoring, isolating. (See notes—Eph.2:11-22; pt.4, 2:14-15; 1 Cor.3:16 for more discussion.)

b. Believers are to be one in character. They are...

• to be godly and holy, denying the works of the flesh (sinful nature) and living pure lives even as Jesus and His Father are one in their holy Being and Life (cp. "Holy Father," v.11).

It teaches us to say "No" to ungodliness and worldly passions, and to live self-controlled, upright and godly lives in this present age, while we wait for the blessed hope—the glorious appearing of our great God and Savior, Jesus Christ, (Titus 2:12-13)

But just as he who called you is holy, so be holy in all you do; for it is written: "Be holy, because I am holy." (1 Pet 1:15-16)

For this very reason, make every effort to add to your faith goodness; and to goodness, knowledge; and to knowledge, self-control; and to self-control, perseverance; and to perseverance, godliness; and to godliness, brotherly kindness; and to brotherly kindness, love. (2 Pet 1:5-7)

If this is so, then the Lord knows how to rescue godly men from trials and to hold the unrighteous for the day of judgment, while continuing their punishment. (2 Pet 2:9)

The acts of the sinful nature are obvious: sexual immorality, impurity and debauchery; idolatry and witchcraft; hatred, discord, jealousy, fits of rage, selfish ambition, dissensions, factions and envy; drunkenness, orgies, and the like. I warn you, as I did before, that those who live like this will not inherit the kingdom of God. (Gal 5:19-21)

• to bear the fruit of the Spirit.

But the fruit of the Spirit is love, joy, peace, patience, kindness, goodness, faithfulness, gentleness and self-control. Against such things there is no law. (Gal 5:22-23)

c. Believers are to be one in purpose. They are to surrender and give all they are and have to minister and proclaim the message of salvation to a lost and dying world, a world reeling in desperate need. Believers are to give all for the salvation of the world just as Jesus and the Father gave all for the salvation of the world.

(See note, Church, Unity—Eph.4:4-6 for more discussion of the unity upon which believers are built. Also see note—Lk.8:21 for more discussion.)

We are therefore Christ's ambassadors, as though God were making his appeal through us. We implore you on Christ's behalf: Be reconciled to God. (2 Cor 5:20)

> Again Jesus said, "Peace be with you!
> As the Father has sent me, I am sending
> you." (John 20:21)
> Just as the Son of Man did not come to
> be served, but to serve, and to give his life
> as a ransom for many." (Mat 20:28)

DEEPER STUDY # 3

(17:11-12) **Security—Assurance**: the *keeping power* of
God does not mean that God delivers believers from the
trials of this world, but He delivers them through the trials.
It means that He gives a victorious life. The believer is
guaranteed a victorious life if he will just follow Christ.
There are two reasons for this guaranteed security. First,
God is bound to answer the prayer of His Son; and second,
God the Father has given all Christian believers to Christ.
This fact is said six times in this chapter alone (Jn.17:2, 6,
9, 11, 12, 24). God will allow absolutely nothing to sepa-
rate Christian believers from His Son.

> And this is the will of him who sent me,
> that I shall lose none of all that he has given
> me, but raise them up at the last day. (John
> 6:39)
> My sheep listen to my voice; I know
> them, and they follow me. I give them
> eternal life, and they shall never perish; no
> one can snatch them out of my hand. My
> Father, who has given them to me, is
> greater than all ; no one can snatch them
> out of my Father's hand. (John 10:27-29)
> Who shall separate us from the love of
> Christ? Shall trouble or hardship or perse-
> cution or famine or nakedness or danger or
> sword? (Rom 8:35)
> Being confident of this, that he who be-
> gan a good work in you will carry it on to
> completion until the day of Christ Jesus.
> (Phil 1:6)
> But the Lord is faithful, and he will
> strengthen and protect you from the evil
> one. (2 Th 3:3)
> That is why I am suffering as I am. Yet
> I am not ashamed, because I know whom I
> have believed, and am convinced that he is
> able to guard what I have entrusted to him
> for that day. (2 Tim 1:12)
> Who through faith are shielded by
> God's power until the coming of the salva-
> tion that is ready to be revealed in the last
> time. (1 Pet 1:5)
> To him who is able to keep you from
> falling and to present you before his glori-
> ous presence without fault and with great
> joy— (Jude 1:24)
> Since you have kept my command to
> endure patiently, I will also keep you from
> the hour of trial that is going to come upon
> the whole world to test those who live on
> the earth. (Rev 3:10)

3 (17:13) **Joy**: second, Jesus prayed that the disciples
would have His joy in all its full measure. (See note 3 and
DEEPER STUDY # 1, Joy—Jn.15:11; note—14:28-29 for discussion.)

4 (17:14-16) **Persecution—World, Against Believers**:
third, Jesus prayed that God would keep the disciples from
the world and from the evil one or Satan. Both the world
and Satan are evil and stand opposed to all that Jesus and
His disciples proclaimed.

⇒ The world and Satan stand against the love of
God. Why? Because God's love is not the
grandfatherly love of indulgence. God's love is
the true love of obedience, an obedience that
gives all one *is* and *has* to meet the needs of a
desperate world lost in sin and death. True love
loves so much that it gives everything and does
all it can to help any who are in desperate need.
Most men in the world are unwilling to give
anything other than a mere token, and even then
recognition is desired for what little is given.

⇒ The world and Satan stand against the holiness
and justice of God. Why? Because it means that
both must stand before God some day to give an
account of their lives and deeds, sins and dirt,
pollution and evil.

⇒ The world and Satan stand against Jesus. Why?
Because Jesus was the One who claimed to be
the Son of God, and if He is truly the Son of
God, then total allegiance is due Him. And neither the world nor Satan are willing to serve
anyone other than self.

There were three primary reasons why God needed to
protect the disciples from the world and the devil.

1. The world and the devil hated the disciples of Jesus.
Note why.

a. The disciples of Christ have the Word of God. It
is God's Word that reveals...

• God's love, a sacrificial love that gives all it
has, is different from the love the world
wants. (See DEEPER STUDY # 1, Love—Mt.5:44;
notes—22:37-38; 22:39 for discussion.)

• God's holiness and justice and man's depravity, a fact that man rejects and refuses to face.

• Christ, the Son of God Himself, who demands
total allegiance and commitment to become
ministers and servants of God.

b. The disciples were not of the world, even as Jesus
was not of the world.

⇒ Jesus came from God, "out of heaven" (see
DEEPER STUDY # 1—Jn.3:31).

⇒ The disciples and other believers were born
again by the Spirit of God and given the very
nature of God. The world and the devil want
absolutely nothing to do with a selfless and
sacrificial nature, a righteous and godly nature
that gives all one is and has to meet the needs
of the diseased and starving and lost masses of
the world. (See DEEPER STUDY # 1—Jn.3:1-15.
Cp. Jn.1:13; 2 Cor.5:17; Tit.3:5; 1 Pt.1:23;
2 Pt.1:4; 1 Jn.5:1; 2:29; 4:7.)

> "A new command I give you: Love one
> another. As I have loved you, so you must
> love one another. By this all men will know
> that you are my disciples, if you love one
> another." (John 13:34-35)
> But God demonstrates his own love for
> us in this: While we were still sinners,
> Christ died for us. (Rom 5:8)

This is how we know what love is: Jesus Christ laid down his life for us. And we ought to lay down our lives for our brothers. (1 John 3:16)

2. The disciples were needed in the world. The need was not for them to be taken out of the world; the need was for them to be kept from the evil one or from Satan (cp. Eph.6:10-18). The disciples were called to be ambassadors and messengers of God in the world. God's mission to save the world depended upon their loyalty and faithfulness. They had to be kept and protected and covered with the armor of God.

Finally, be strong in the Lord and in his mighty power. Put on the full armor of God so that you can take your stand against the devil's schemes. (Eph 6:10-11)
Be self-controlled and alert. Your enemy the devil prowls around like a roaring lion looking for someone to devour. (1 Pet 5:8)

3. The disciples were now of the same nature as Jesus. This is the same truth stated in v.14. The truth is so glorious, it has to be reemphasized. Note that it is also the main reason the world and the devil attack the believer (see outline and notes—Jn.15:19-24 for more discussion).

Therefore, I urge you, brothers, in view of God's mercy, to offer your bodies as living sacrifices, holy and pleasing to God—this is your spiritual act of worship. Do not conform any longer to the pattern of this world, but be transformed by the renewing of your mind. Then you will be able to test and approve what God's will is—his good, pleasing and perfect will. (Rom 12:1-2)

5 (17:17-19) **Sanctification**: fourth, Jesus prayed that God would sanctify the disciples. Note the two things said about the disciple or believer.
⇒ He is to be sanctified (see DEEPER STUDY # 4—Sanctification—Jn.17:17).
⇒ He is to be sanctified through God's truth, and God's truth is said to be God's Word. God's Word would refer to both the *living Word*, the full revelation of God in Jesus Christ Himself (see DEEPER STUDY # 1—Jn.14:16) and to the spoken or *written Word* (see notes—Jn.7:16-19; 14:10; 2 Tim.3:16; note 3 and DEEPER STUDY # 1,2—2 Pt.1:19-21).
The disciples needed to be set apart to God *through His truth* for two reasons.
1. They were being sent into the world just as Jesus had been sent into the world. Jesus had come into the world to bring men back to God through reconciliation. The disciples had to be *set apart* to this same task.

Again Jesus said, "Peace be with you! As the Father has sent me, I am sending you." (John 20:21)
Just as the Son of Man did not come to be served, but to serve, and to give his life as a ransom for many." (Mat 20:28)
Therefore go and make disciples of all nations, baptizing them in the name of the Father and of the Son and of the Holy Spirit, and teaching them to obey every-thing I have commanded you. And surely I am with you always, to the very end of the age." (Mat 28:19-20)
He said to them, "Go into all the world and preach the good news to all creation. (Mark 16:15)
But you will receive power when the Holy Spirit comes on you; and you will be my witnesses in Jerusalem, and in all Judea and Samaria, and to the ends of the earth." (Acts 1:8)
That God was reconciling the world to himself in Christ, not counting men's sins against them. And he has committed to us the message of reconciliation. We are therefore Christ's ambassadors, as though God were making his appeal through us. We implore you on Christ's behalf: Be reconciled to God. (2 Cor 5:19-20)
But in your hearts set apart Christ as Lord. Always be prepared to give an answer to everyone who asks you to give the reason for the hope that you have. But do this with gentleness and respect, (1 Pet 3:15)

2. Sanctification is the way of salvation chosen to reach the world. Jesus had set Himself apart to please God, and He pleased God to the ultimate degree. No matter the cost, the glory of God was to be done. Perfect obedience to God was the chosen way of salvation. Being set apart to serve and worship God is what salvation is all about. This is the reason Jesus prayed for His disciples to be sanctified. (See DEEPER STUDY # 1, Sanctification—1 Pt.1:15-16 for more discussion.)

Thought 1. Believers are sanctified through the truth, that is, through God's Word. It is through the study and practice of God's Word that believers are set apart unto God. As a believer studies God's Word, he sees more and more how he is to live. As he sees, he sets himself apart to live the way God tells him to live. The Word of God holds new instructions for the believer every day. The Word of God shows the believer how to be more and more conformed to the image of Christ every day. But note the crucial point: the believer must come to the truth, to the Word of God *every day* if he wishes to be *set apart* unto God for that day.

DEEPER STUDY # 4
(17:17) **Sanctify—Sanctification**: the word "sanctify" means to be set apart, to be separated (cp. 1 Pt.1:15-16). There are three stages of sanctification.
1. There is initial or positional sanctification. When a person believes in Jesus Christ, he is immediately set apart for God permanently, once-for-all (Heb.3:1; cp. Heb.10:10).
2. There is progressive sanctification. The true believer makes a determined and disciplined effort to allow the Spirit of God to set him apart day by day. The Spirit of God takes him and conforms him to the image of Christ more and more. This growth takes place as long as the believer walks upon this earth (cp. Jn.17:17; 2 Cor.3:18; Eph.5:25-26; 1 Th.5:23-24).
3. There is eternal sanctification. The day is coming when the believer will be perfectly set apart unto God and His service—without any sin or failure whatsoever. That day will be the great and glorious day of the believer's eternal redemption (Eph.5:27; 1 Jn.3:2).

	C. Jesus Prayed for Future Believers, 17:20-26	world know that you sent me and have loved them even as you have loved me.	b. Reason: To convince the world 1) God sent Christ 2) God loves believers
1 Jesus prayed for all future believers	20 "My prayer is not for them alone. I pray also for those who will believe in me through their message,	24 "Father, I want those you have given me to be with me where I am, and to see my glory, the glory you have given me because you loved me before the creation of the world.	**4 Request 3: That believers may be with Him in glory** a. The reason: To see His glory b. The assurance: God's love
2 Request 1: That believers may be one a. The standard: As God & Christ are one b. The purpose: That the world may believe c. The source: God's glory*DS1*	21 That all of them may be one, Father, just as you are in me and I am in you. May they also be in us so that the world may believe that you have sent me. 22 I have given them the glory that you gave me, that they may be one as we are one:	25 "Righteous Father, though the world does not know you, I know you, and they know that you have sent me. 26 I have made you known to them, and will continue to make you known in order that the love you have for me may be in them and that I myself may be in them."	**5 Conclusion: A testimony** a. Of the world: Has not known God b. Of Jesus: Knew God c. Of believers: Have known that God sent Jesus d. Jesus' faithfulness 1) He declared God 2) His purpose: That men might know God's love
3 Request 2: That believers be perfected in unity*DS2* a. Source: Jesus within	23 I in them and you in me. May they be brought to complete unity to let the		

DIVISION XIV

THE REVELATION OF JESUS, THE GREAT INTERCESSOR, 17:1-26

C. Jesus Prayed for Future Believers, 17:20-26

(17:20-26) **Introduction**: Jesus prayed for future believers, for all those who would believe in Him from that moment to the end of the world. What He prayed is very precious to believers, but it is also an indictment against believers of every generation (see DEEPER STUDY # 1—Jn.17:23).

1. Jesus prayed for all future believers—for all who would believe the Word (v.20).
2. Request 1: that believers may be one (v.21-22).
3. Request 2: that believers may be perfected in unity (v.23).
4. Request 3: that believers may be with Him in glory (v.24).
5. Conclusion: a testimony (v.25-26).

1 (17:20) **Salvation, Essentials—Jesus Christ, Prayer Life**: Jesus prayed for future believers, for all those who would believe the message of the early disciples. This is most precious. Jesus prayed for us—for you and for me—for all of us who believe today. Just think for a moment. Who is the weakest believer on earth today? Who is the strongest? Of course only God knows, but think of the preciousness of the fact: Jesus prayed for every one of us...

- for the weakest as well as for the strongest.
- for the diseased as well as for the healthy.
- for the orphan as well as for the children of the family.
- for the widow and widower as well as for the couple.
- for the prisoner as well as for the free.
- for the believer in the darkest jungle as well as for the believer in the limelight.

There is no thought any more precious than the thought that Jesus prayed for us all—every one of us who believe today.

Note: this verse gives the three essentials for men to become believers.

1. There is the messenger of God, the disciple of Christ, the person who proclaims the Word so that men can *believe in* the name of Jesus. There has to be a messenger to carry and proclaim the message.

> **How, then, can they call on the one they have not believed in? And how can they believe in the one of whom they have not heard? And how can they hear without someone preaching to them? (Rom 10:14)**
>
> **We are therefore Christ's ambassadors, as though God were making his appeal through us. We implore you on Christ's behalf: Be reconciled to God. God made him who had no sin to be sin for us, so that in him we might become the righteousness of God. (2 Cor 5:20-21)**

2. There is God's Word. The messenger is *God's* messenger, *His* ambassador. Therefore, the Word he takes to the world is God's Word. Note the references to God's Word in this chapter alone.

> **"I have revealed you to those whom you gave me out of the world. They were yours; you gave them to me and they have obeyed your word. (John 17:6)**
>
> **I have brought you glory on earth by completing the work you gave me to do. (John 17:4)**
>
> **Sanctify them by the truth; your word is truth. (John 17:17)**

3. There is belief. We must believe the Word. We are the Lord's disciples today because we believe the Word (see DEEPER STUDY # 2—Jn.2:24).

"I tell you the truth, whoever hears
my word and believes him who sent me
has eternal life and will not be condemned; he has crossed over from death
to life. (John 5:24)

The Spirit gives life; the flesh counts
for nothing. The words I have spoken to
you are spirit and they are life. (John
6:63)

I tell you the truth, if anyone keeps
my word, he will never see death." (John
8:51)

2 (17:21-22) **Unity**: first, Jesus requested that we may
be one. This is critical, the imperative that absolutely
must exist between believers. It is the central theme of
Jesus' prayer (v.11, 21, 22, 23). Believers *must be one*.
Note exactly what Jesus said.

1. The standard for unity is the *oneness* between Jesus and His Father. Believers are to be one just as the
Father and Jesus are one. The very *same kind* of unity
they have is to be the unity existing between us. (See
DEEPER STUDY # 2, Unity—Jn.17:11 for discussion and
verses of Scripture.)

2. The purpose for unity is that the world may *believe*
that the Father sent Jesus.

⇒ God sent Jesus (see notes—Jn.3:32-34; DEEPER
STUDY # 3—3:34).

But I know him because I am from
him and he sent me." (John 7:29)
Jesus said to them, "If God were
your Father, you would love me, for I
came from God and now am here. I have
not come on my own; but he sent me.
(John 8:42; cp. Jn.6:38; 10:36)

⇒ Jesus came that men might have life and have
it to the full, have it more abundantly.

The thief comes only to steal and kill
and destroy; I have come that they may
have life, and have it to the full. (John
10:10)
"I tell you the truth, whoever hears
my word and believes him who sent me
has eternal life and will not be condemned; he has crossed over from death
to life. (John 5:24)

⇒ A divided witness confuses the issue and cannot stand, just as a divided house and kingdom
cannot stand (cp. Mt.12:25). There are not
many messages nor many ways to God. There
is only one message and one way.

"For God so loved the world that he
gave his one and only Son, that whoever
believes in him shall not perish but have
eternal life. (John 3:16; cp. Ro.5:8; 1 Pt.
2:24; 3:18)
Jesus answered, "I am the way and the
truth and the life. No one comes to the Father except through me. (John 14:6; cp.

1 Tim. 2:5; Heb. 8:6; 9:5, 24; 12:24; 1 Jn.
2:1)

Another approach to what Jesus is saying is this. Believers must *be one*: be unified, of one spirit and mind in
proclaiming the central message of the gospel.

⇒ There is only one central message: that God
sent Jesus "out of" heaven into the world.
⇒ There is only one request of men: to believe
that God did send Jesus into the world.
⇒ There is only one mission: that men be one
(unified) in proclaiming the message of the
glorious gospel.

Thought 1. A terrible tragedy! There are many
voices proclaiming so many different messages,
messages of...
• works
• ritual and ceremony
• denominationalism
• rules and regulations
• morality
• false prophets
• humanism
• brotherhood
• secularism

3. The source of unity is God's glory, the very glory
which Jesus Himself possessed. (See DEEPER STUDY # 1—
Jn.17:22 for discussion.) It is the glory of God given to
believers that unites believers and makes them one with
Jesus and His Father and one with each other. When believers *experience* the glory of God, they become one in
being, character, and purpose. Their lives are given to
each other to help one another...
• to be the new creature God has made them.
• to live as new creatures should, holy and
righteous and pure.
• to proclaim the glorious message that God
has sent His Son into the world.

DEEPER STUDY # 1
(17:22) **Glory—Unity**: this is a significant verse dealing
with the glory of the believer. Note the points made by
Christ.
⇒ God gave glory to His Son Jesus Christ.
⇒ Jesus has given the very *same* glory to believers
(see note—2 Th.2:14).
⇒ It is the glory of God that brings unity to believers, that causes them to surround God and live
and work together to please Him.

So in Christ we who are many form
one body, and each member belongs to
all the others. (Rom 12:5)
Because there is one loaf, we, who
are many, are one body, for we all partake of the one loaf. (1 Cor 10:17)
There is neither Jew nor Greek,
slave nor free, male nor female, for you
are all one in Christ Jesus. (Gal 3:28)
until we all reach unity in the faith
and in the knowledge of the Son of God
and become mature, attaining to the
whole measure of the fullness of Christ.
(Eph 4:13)

What is the glory of God that He gave to Christ and that Christ in turn gives to believers?

The glory of Christ is...
The glory of righteousness which
He secured by living a perfect life.
(See note—Jn.13:31-32.)

The glory of the cross (see notes—
Jn.12:23-26; 12:27-30).

The glory of the resurrection
which wrought victory over death
and hell. (See note—Jn.13:31-32.)

The glory of the ascension and
exaltation.(See note—Jn.17:5-8.)

The glory of the believer is...
The glory of righteousness which Christ
gives to the believer by faith. (See notes—
Jn.1:51; 13:31-32; DEEPER STUDY # 1,2—Ro.4:22.)

The glory of the cross which gives to
the believer both forgiveness of sins and
the privilege of serving God Himself: the
privilege of sacrificing all he is and has
to God in order to reach a lost and desperate
world. (See notes—Jn.12:23-26; DEEPER STUDY # 1—
Lk.9:23. Cp. 1 Pt.2:24.)

The glory of the resurrection which gives
the believer a new life in Christ.
(Cp. Ro.6:4-5; 2 Cor.5:17.)

The glory of living eternally in the presence of
God and of being exalted to serve Him by ruling
and reigning with His Son, Jesus Christ, forever.
(Cp. Jn.14:2-3; Ro.8:16-17; Tit.2:12-13; 3:7.)

3 (17:23) **Unity—Love—Believers, Indictment Against—Mission—Evangelism:** second, Jesus requested that believers be *perfected* in unity, perfected as one body, that they "be brought to complete unity." This stresses beyond question the absolute necessity that believers live in unity. The world has not been reached for Christ—millions have been lost—because believers have not been unified enough to penetrate the world with the gospel. This is the terrible indictment against believers. The problem is certainly not God. He is willing and He is loving and powerful enough to use believers to reach the whole world. The problem is unquestionably believers, and as Jesus made pointedly clear in this verse, the problem is our love for one another.

The concern of Jesus is that we be *perfected* in one. (See DEEPER STUDY # 2, Perfect—Jn.17:23.) Note two things.

1. The believer's source of unity is the Indwelling Presence of Christ within his life. Note that God is *in* Christ; therefore, the presence of Christ *in the believer* means that God dwells "in" the believer. The believer actually partakes of the divine nature of God (2 Pt.1:4. See note, Indwelling Presence—Jn.10:37-39; 14:10; 14:18-20; 14:23-24.)

On that day you will realize that I am in my Father, and you are in me, and I am in you. (John 14:20)
Jesus replied, "If anyone loves me, he will obey my teaching. My Father will love him, and we will come to him and make our home with him. (John 14:23)
I in them and you in me. May they be brought to complete unity to let the world know that you sent me and have loved them even as you have loved me. (John 17:23)
I have been crucified with Christ and I no longer live, but Christ lives in me. The life I live in the body, I live by faith in the Son of God, who loved me and gave himself for me. (Gal 2:20)

so that Christ may dwell in your hearts through faith. And I pray that you, being rooted and established in love, (Eph 3:17)
To them God has chosen to make known among the Gentiles the glorious riches of this mystery, which is Christ in you, the hope of glory. (Col 1:27)
Those who obey his commands live in him, and he in them. And this is how we know that he lives in us: We know it by the Spirit he gave us. (1 John 3:24)
Here I am! I stand at the door and knock. If anyone hears my voice and opens the door, I will come in and eat with him, and he with me. (Rev 3:20)

2. The purpose for a perfected unity is that the world may *know* that God sent Jesus into the world to save it. Now note a significant point: there is a difference each time Jesus prays for unity in this chapter. And each difference or point proclaims a strong message to the believer.

There is...
• the *unity of God's name*, of calling upon God's name to keep believers from a divided world and its divisive influence (v.11).
• the *unity of God's protective power*, of calling upon God's power to deliver believers from the evil of the world and the devil (v.15).
• the *unity of witness*, that the world may believe that God sent Christ (see notes—Jn.3:32-34; DEEPER STUDY # 1—3:34). They will believe through a unified witness (v.21).
• the *unity of love*, that the world may know that God sent Christ. They will know through a unified love (v.23).

There is a world of difference between a unity of witness and a unity of love. The world may come to believe the gospel by a unified witness for Christ, but the only way the world can ever know the gospel is by a *unified love* among believers. Note two things.

a. What the world needs more than anything else is love, a great demonstration of love from a massive multitude of people. (Cp. 1 Cor.13:4-7 for the behavior and acts of love, and think about the enormous impact we could make upon the world if we really were unified in love.)

b. The love needed among believers is a different love from the *so-called love* of the world. The love needed is a sacrificial love that will give all it *is and has* to minister to a world that is reeling under the weight of starving, diseased, and dying masses of people. (See notes, Love— Jn.13:33-35; 21:15-17.)

> This is how we know what love is: Jesus Christ laid down his life for us. And we ought to lay down our lives for our brothers. (1 John 3:16)
>
> "A new command I give you: Love one another. As I have loved you, so you must love one another. By this all men will know that you are my disciples, if you love one another." (John 13:34-35)
>
> But God demonstrates his own love for us in this: While we were still sinners, Christ died for us. (Rom 5:8)

DEEPER STUDY # 2

(17:23) **Perfect—Perfected** (telelos): the idea of perfection is perfection of purpose. It has to do with an end, an aim, a goal, a purpose. It means fit, mature, fully grown at a particular stage of growth. For example, a fully grown child is a perfect child; he has reached the height of childhood, achieved the purpose of childhood. The word "perfect" does not mean perfection of character, that is, being without sin. It is fitness, maturity for task and purpose. It is full development, maturity of godliness. (See note—Eph.4:12-16; cp. Ph.3:12; 1 Jn.1:8, 10.)

The Bible reveals three stages of perfection.

1. Saving perfection. Christ's death has guaranteed forever the perfection and redemption of those set apart for God (Heb.10:14).

2. Progressive or maturing perfection. God reveals anything that is contrary to His purpose, and the believer is expected to clean it up (Ph.3:13-15, esp. 15). The believer's "perfect holiness" (2 Cor.7:1) is now trying to "attain [his] goal" (Gal.3:3). As a member of the church the believer is experiencing "the preparing of God's people" (Eph.4:12; Col.4:12; Heb.13:21; Jas.1:4; 1 Jn. 4:17-18).

3. Redemptive or resurrected perfection. The believer's purpose and aim is to "attain to the resurrection from the dead....[to be] perfect" (Ph.3:11-12).

The Lord's point is that the mature believer will do good and show kindness to all men, both good and bad men. He is mature in heart when he shows love to his enemies as well as to his friends. The love of God and of Christ are the believer's example of perfected love (see notes—Jn.13:33-35; 21:15-17).

---

4 (17:24) **Glory**: third, Jesus requested that believers may be with Him in glory. (See notes—Jn.17:5-8; 14:1-3; Resurrection—Jn.14:6 for discussion.)

> In my Father's house are many rooms; if it were not so, I would have told you. I am going there to prepare a place for you. And if I go and prepare a place for you, I will come back and take you to be with me that you also may be where I am. (John 14:2-3)
>
> Now we know that if the earthly tent we live in is destroyed, we have a building from God, an eternal house in heaven, not built by human hands. Meanwhile we groan, longing to be clothed with our heavenly dwelling, (2 Cor 5:1-2)
>
> The faith and love that spring from the hope that is stored up for you in heaven and that you have already heard about in the word of truth, the gospel (Col 1:5)
>
> After this I looked and there before me was a great multitude that no one could count, from every nation, tribe, people and language, standing before the throne and in front of the Lamb. They were wearing white robes and were holding palm branches in their hands. (Rev 7:9)
>
> "Blessed are those who wash their robes, that they may have the right to the tree of life and may go through the gates into the city. (Rev 22:14)

---

5 (17:25-26) **Testimony**: the conclusion of Jesus' prayer is a striking testimony.

1. There is the testimony of the world. The world has not known God. Jesus was the revelation of God; therefore, all who saw Jesus saw God. Yet the world rejected Him, refusing to know Him (see note, pt.3—Jn.15:19-24 for discussion).

> Since they did not know the righteousness that comes from God and sought to establish their own, they did not submit to God's righteousness. (Rom 10:3)
>
> They are darkened in their understanding and separated from the life of God because of the ignorance that is in them due to the hardening of their hearts. (Eph 4:18)
>
> I thought, "These are only the poor; they are foolish, for they do not know the way of the LORD, the requirements of their God. (Jer 5:4)
>
> But they do not know the thoughts of the LORD; they do not understand his plan, he who gathers them like sheaves to the threshing floor. (Micah 4:12)

2. There was the testimony of Jesus. He knew God. He was eternal and had always existed with God. He was the Son of God Himself. (See note—Jn.17:5-8 for discussion.)

> "All things have been committed to me by my Father. No one knows the Son except the Father, and no one knows the Father except the Son and those to whom the Son chooses to reveal him. (Mat 11:27)

But I know him because I am from him and he sent me." (John 7:29)

Though you do not know him, I know him. If I said I did not, I would be a liar like you, but I do know him and keep his word. (John 8:55)

Just as the Father knows me and I know the Father—and I lay down my life for the sheep. (John 10:15)

"Righteous Father, though the world does not know you, I know you, and they know that you have sent me. (John 17:25)

3. There is the testimony of believers down through the centuries. Believers know that God sent Christ. (See note, pt.2-3—Jn.17:5-8.)

But I know him because I am from him and he sent me." (John 7:29)

Jesus said to them, "If God were your Father, you would love me, for I came from God and now am here. I have not come on my own; but he sent me. (John 8:42)

What about the one whom the Father set apart as his very own and sent into the world? Why then do you accuse me of blasphemy because I said, 'I am God's Son'? (John 10:36)

That all of them may be one, Father, just as you are in me and I am in you. May they also be in us so that the world may believe that you have sent me. (John 17:21)

4. There is the testimony of the faithfulness of Jesus.
   ⇒ He declared and revealed God (see notes—Jn.14:6).
   ⇒ His purpose was that men might *know* the love of God and *have* the love of God dwelling "in" them. (See notes—Jn.17:23.)

"For God so loved the world that he gave his one and only Son, that whoever believes in him shall not perish but have eternal life. (John 3:16)

But God demonstrates his own love for us in this: While we were still sinners, Christ died for us. (Rom 5:8)

And this is his command: to believe in the name of his Son, Jesus Christ, and to love one another as he commanded us. (1 John 3:23)

CHAPTER 18

XV. THE REVELATION OF JESUS, THE SUFFERING SAVIOR, 18:1-19:42

A. The Arrest: Absolute Surrender, 18:1-11
(Mt.26:36-56; Mk.14: 32-52; Lk.22:39-53)

1 A devotion to God a. Left, went forth to prepare Himself spiritually b. Left, went forth to prepare the scene for God's will 1)Jesus Went to a place known by Judas 2) Judas came forth with a large force to arrest Him^DS1 **2 A willing determination**	When he had finished praying, Jesus left with his disciples and crossed the Kidron Valley. On the other side there was an olive grove, and he and his disciples went into it. 2 Now Judas, who betrayed him, knew the place, because Jesus had often met there with his disciples. 3 So Judas came to the grove, guiding a detachment of soldiers and some officials from the chief priests and Pharisees. They were carrying torches, lanterns and weapons. 4 Jesus, knowing all that was	going to happen to him went out and asked them, "Who is it you want?" 5 "Jesus of Nazareth," they replied. "I am he," Jesus said. (And Judas the traitor was standing there with them.) 6 When Jesus said, "I am he," they drew back and fell to the ground. 7 Again he asked them, "Who is it you want?" And they said, "Jesus of Nazareth." 8 "I told you that I am he," Jesus answered. "If you are looking for me, then let these men go." 9 This happened so that the words he had spoken would be fulfilled: "I have not lost one of those you gave me." 10 Then Simon Peter, who had a sword, drew it and struck the high priest's servant, cutting off his right ear. (The servant's name was Malchus.) 11 Jesus commanded Peter, "Put your sword away! Shall I not drink the cup the Father has given me?"	a. He went forth voluntarily b. A courageous confession & claim c. A miraculous blast of revelation: "I Am" **3 A protective or vicarious commitment** a. He gave Himself for His disciples b. His reason: To fulfill His Word **4 An unswerving obedience** a. Peter's loyal, but carnal zeal b. Jesus' iron determination to obey God's will: To drink the cup^DS2

DIVISION XV

THE REVELATION OF JESUS, THE SUFFERING SAVIOR, 18:1-19:42

A. The Arrest: Absolute Surrender, 18:1-11

(18:1-11) **Introduction**: Jesus Christ gives us an excellent picture of absolute surrender.
1. A devotion to God (v.1-3).
2. A willing determination (v.4-6).
3. A protective or vicarious commitment (v.7-9).
4. An unswerving obedience (v.10-11).

(18:1-11) **Another Outline**: Absolute Surrender—Jesus Left, Went Forth.
1. Jesus went forth—devotionally (v.1-3).
2. Jesus went forth—willingly—confessing who He was (v.4-6).
3. Jesus went forth—vicariously (v.7-9).
4. Jesus went forth purposefully—to die—to drink the cup (v.10-11).

1 (18:1-3) **Devotion**: there is the picture of devotion to God. Note the words "left" and "went out" (exelthen, v.1; exelthon, v.4). The idea being conveyed is *purpose*. Jesus left, went forth deliberately, for a specific purpose, knowing exactly what He was doing.
1. Jesus "left" to prepare Himself spiritually. He was facing *the hour* to which God had called Him, the time of His death (see note, Time—Jn.2:3-5; DEEPER STUDY # 1—12:23-24). He knew that God's will was for Him to die for the sins of the world. He knew the awful separation from God that sin causes; therefore, He knew that He was to be cut off from God's presence, that God would have to for-

sake and turn His back upon Him because of sin. He was feeling the awful pressure of God's coming judgment upon sin which was to be exercised upon Him. In the flesh, He wanted to flee; He wanted another way to be chosen to save man (Mt.26:39, 42, 44). Yet He...
- was committed to God
- was totally *devoted* to His Father
- *must* do God's will

But to do God's will, He had to have God's help. He had to pray and seek God's face. He desperately needed God to meet His need in some special way. It was for this reason that He headed for the garden. He was seeking to be alone with His Father, to have His Father strengthen Him for the terrible ordeal and judgment of the cross.

The point tears at the heart of the believer, for Jesus knew He was to bear the sins of the world upon the cross, and the pressure was almost unbearable. Jesus could have fled; He could have turned away and insisted that the cup pass from Him. But He did not. He was totally devoted to God, so He left, went forth deliberately—for the purpose of praying and seeking strength from God, for the strength to fulfill God's will. (See outline and notes—Mt.26:36-46 for discussion of the experience in the Garden of Gethsemane. John does not cover the actual agony Jesus experienced while in prayer. His purpose is simply to show the total devotion of Jesus to God's will. The other gospels cover the Lord's unbelievable agony.)

2. Jesus left, went forth to prepare the scene so that God's will would be done. He went to the Garden of Gethsemane probably to the very spot where He had often prayed and spent the night when in Jerusalem (cp. Lk.22:39). He did not have to go there. He could have chosen some other direction to go, some other place to seek God. But He went to the place Judas knew. He was totally devoted to God, so He left, went forth to set the scene for God's will to be fulfilled.

Note the large force that came forth to arrest Jesus (see DEEPER STUDY # 1—Jn.18:3).

Thought 1. Jesus is the believer's dynamic example. The believer must be devoted and totally committed to doing God's will. The believer should be *going forth* all the time...

- to prepare himself spiritually
- to prepare the scene for God's will
- to do God's will

After he had dismissed them, he went up on a mountainside by himself to pray. When evening came, he was there alone, (Mat 14:23)

Very early in the morning, while it was still dark, Jesus got up, left the house and went off to a solitary place, where he prayed. (Mark 1:35)

In the same way, the Spirit helps us in our weakness. We do not know what we ought to pray for, but the Spirit himself intercedes for us with groans that words cannot express. (Rom 8:26)

Evening, morning and noon I cry out in distress, and he hears my voice. (Psa 55:17)

But as for me, it is good to be near God. I have made the Sovereign LORD my refuge; I will tell of all your deeds. (Psa 73:28)

He will call upon me, and I will answer him; I will be with him in trouble, I will deliver him and honor him. (Psa 91:15)

You will keep in perfect peace him whose mind is steadfast, because he trusts in you. Trust in the LORD forever, for the LORD, the LORD, is the Rock eternal. (Isa 26:3-4)

'Call to me and I will answer you and tell you great and unsearchable things you do not know.' (Jer 33:3)

DEEPER STUDY # 1

(18:3) **Detachment** (speira): this was a *cohort* of soldiers. A cohort was a tenth part of a Roman legion. It usually had 600 soldiers. On a rare occasion, the word *cohort* was used for a detachment of 200 soldiers. Note the authorities also had their temple police join the force. It was a large armed force of several hundred who came out to arrest Jesus. The rumor had been that the Messiah, the promised Jewish King, had come. Apparently, the Romans felt they had to make sure there would be no uprisings when they arrested Jesus. Note an interesting fact: they brought lanterns and torches. Passover was held during the days of full moon, so there would have been plenty of natural light. Why then, were lanterns and torches needed? They were probably expecting Jesus to flee and hide in the bushes and trees and dark spots of the garden.

---

2 (18:4-6) **Purpose—Determination—Jesus Christ, Deity**: there is the picture of willing determination. Note several significant points.

1. Jesus *went forth* voluntarily. Note the words "knowing all that was going to happen to him." He knew all the suffering and the pain of the judgment of God that was to fall upon Him. But He still went forth to meet the world that was rejecting Him and that was coming to arrest and kill Him. The point is this: He was willing and determined to die for the sins of men. He was voluntarily choosing to die for men. (See note, pt.2—Jn.10:17-18 for more discussion. Also see DEEPER STUDY # 2—Mt.26:37-38.)

2. Jesus made a courageous confession and claim. Note: He did not flee from the world and its persecution.

⇒ He made a courageous confession: I AM. He did not flee into the bushes or caves of the garden, fearing the persecutors. He knew God's will, and He was determined to carry out God's will.

⇒ He made a courageous claim: I AM. This is the claim of deity. Imagine the scene. The soldiers had come out to arrest a peasant. They expected Him to flee and hide for His life. But there He was, a solitary man standing face to face with them, courageously proclaiming "I Am" (see DEEPER STUDY # 1—Jn.6:20).

Thought 1. What a dynamic example for believers! When the will of God is known, it is to be done courageously, no matter the opposition or threat.

Therefore, my dear brothers, stand firm. Let nothing move you. Always give yourselves fully to the work of the Lord, because you know that your labor in the Lord is not in vain. (1 Cor 15:58)

Be on your guard; stand firm in the faith; be men of courage; be strong. (1 Cor 16:13)

Finally, be strong in the Lord and in his mighty power. (Eph 6:10)

You then, my son, be strong in the grace that is in Christ Jesus. (2 Tim 2:1)

For it is God's will that by doing good you should silence the ignorant talk of foolish men. (1 Pet 2:15)

Therefore, since Christ suffered in his body, arm yourselves also with the same attitude, because he who has suffered in his body is done with sin. As a result, he does not live the rest of his earthly life for evil human desires, but rather for the will of God. (1 Pet 4:1-2)

Be strong and courageous. Do not be afraid or terrified because of them, for the LORD your God goes with you; he will never leave you nor forsake you." (Deu 31:6)

Thought 2. Jesus' claim "I AM" is definitely the word of deity. It must have struck Judas. We never know what effect a courageous confession has upon a soul. Our task is to confess and proclaim Christ before a lost and hostile world.

In the sight of God, who gives life to everything, and of Christ Jesus, who while

testifying before Pontius Pilate made the good confession, I charge you to keep this command without spot or blame until the appearing of our Lord Jesus Christ, (1 Tim 6:13-14)

All these people were still living by faith when they died. They did not receive the things promised; they only saw them and welcomed them from a distance. And they admitted that they were aliens and strangers on earth. (Heb 11:13)

This is how you can recognize the Spirit of God: Every spirit that acknowledges that Jesus Christ has come in the flesh is from God, but every spirit that does not acknowledge Jesus is not from God. This is the spirit of the antichrist, which you have heard is coming and even now is already in the world. (1 John 4:2-3)

If anyone acknowledges that Jesus is the Son of God, God lives in him and he in God. (1 John 4:15)

3. There was a miraculous blast of revelation in the words "I AM." As far as we know, there was no burst of majestic light that broke forth from Jesus. There was only the phenomenal statement, "I AM." This is the great claim of God. When Jesus made the claim, something happened. Apparently God miraculously struck the arresting party with the claim, although they did not understand. They were struck with the claim's…
- authority
- power
- presence, embodied in Jesus as He stood there

Remember that Jesus is the "I AM," the Son of God Himself. The very nature of God was embodied in Him. When He made the claim, especially in the face of such an eventful situation, there was bound to be a blast of revelation.

Thought 1. This is critical. Men must heed the claim of Jesus Christ: the blast of revelation that He is the great "I AM." They must heed the claim while there is time. The arresting party, standing there facing Christ, still had time to confess Him. As long as a man is alive, he still has time (2 Cor.6:2).

Whoever believes in him is not condemned, but whoever does not believe stands condemned already because he has not believed in the name of God's one and only Son. (John 3:18)

I told you that you would die in your sins; if you do not believe that I am the one I claim to be, you will indeed die in your sins." (John 8:24)

For he says, "In the time of my favor I heard you, and in the day of salvation I helped you." I tell you, now is the time of God's favor, now is the day of salvation. (2 Cor 6:2)

See to it, brothers, that none of you has a sinful, unbelieving heart that turns away from the living God. But encourage one another daily, as long as it is called Today, so that none of you may be hardened by sin's deceitfulness. We have come to share

in Christ if we hold firmly till the end the confidence we had at first. (Heb 3:12-14)

A man who remains stiff-necked after many rebukes will suddenly be destroyed—without remedy. (Prov 29:1)

"The harvest is past, the summer has ended, and we are not saved." (Jer 8:20)

3 (18:7-9) **Jesus Christ, Death**: there is the picture of protective or vicarious commitment. The disciples were in danger, but Jesus took the lead in saving them by offering Himself in their place. His protective love and vicarious suffering for man is clearly pictured.
⇒ He stepped forward in their place, to save them from suffering and death (see DEEPER STUDY # 2—Jn.10:11).
⇒ He offered to bear death alone. There was no need for them to die. (Cp. Ro.5:8; 1 Pt.3:18.)

Note that Jesus' act fulfilled Scripture. He was not to lose anyone whom God had given Him (Ps.41:9; 109:4-13; see notes—Jn.17:1-4, pt.2; 17:9-11, pt.1 for discussion).

Thought 1. Note three significant points.
1) Note the glorious security of the believer. Jesus will lose no one whom the Father has given Him. Every person should ask God to take his life and to give it to Christ.

I give them eternal life, and they shall never perish; no one can snatch them out of my hand. My Father, who has given them to me, is greater than all ; no one can snatch them out of my Father's hand. (John 10:28-29)

2) Note the protection Christ has provided for man. He has died vicariously for man, but every man must accept His death as his own in order to be saved.

"For God so loved the world that he gave his one and only Son, that whoever believes in him shall not perish but have eternal life. (John 3:16)

But God demonstrates his own love for us in this: While we were still sinners, Christ died for us. (Rom 5:8)

3) Note the protective, vicarious commitment believers are to have to the world. They are to give them- selves—all they are and have—to meet the needs of a desperate world which reels in pain, sin, and death (see DEEPER STUDY # 1—Lk.9:23).

Then he said to them all: "If anyone would come after me, he must deny himself and take up his cross daily and follow me. (Luke 9:23)

4 (18:10-11) **Jesus Christ, Obedience**: there is the picture of Jesus' unswerving obedience. Peter thought the Messiah's time had come, that Jesus Christ was now ready to free Israel and establish the throne of David as the dominant nation in the world (see notes—Mt.1:1; DEEPER STUDY # 2—1:18; DEEPER STUDY # 2—3:11; notes—11:1-6; 11:2-3; DEEPER STUDY # 1—11:5; DEEPER STUDY # 2—11:6; DEEPER STUDY # 1—12:16; notes—22:42; Lk.7:21-23). Peter drew his sword and struck, slashing off the ear of Malchus (note that Peter *had* a sword).

The picture painted by Peter's behavior is carnal commitment, the kind of commitment that acts and struggles in the flesh. Peter took his stand for Jesus *in the flesh*; therefore, he failed. Eventually, he deserted Jesus. Acting in the flesh will always result in failing and deserting Jesus.

> Those who live according to the sinful nature have their minds set on what that nature desires; but those who live in accordance with the Spirit have their minds set on what the Spirit desires. The mind of sinful man is death, but the mind controlled by the Spirit is life and peace; (Rom 8:5-6)
>
> For if you live according to the sinful nature, you will die; but if by the Spirit you put to death the misdeeds of the body, you will live, (Rom 8:13)

Peter misunderstood the Lord's Word. First, Peter thought Jesus was to establish an earthly kingdom. He thought in terms of the physical and material world. Therefore, he failed to grasp the spiritual and eternal kingdom (dimension of being) proclaimed by Jesus. Second, Peter never accepted the Lord's Word. Jesus had predicted His death and forewarned the apostles, giving them extensive training for months (see notes—Mt.16:13-20; 16:21-28; 17:1-13; 17:22; 17:24-27). However, Peter refused to give up his preconceived ideas and accept what Jesus was saying. Therefore, he did not see the eternal world of the Spirit nor the eternal salvation which Jesus was securing.

Note Jesus' iron determination to obey God's will (see DEEPER STUDY # 2—Jn.18:11 for discussion).

> Going a little farther, he fell with his face to the ground and prayed, "My Father, if it is possible, may this cup be taken from me. Yet not as I will, but as you will." (Mat 26:39)
>
> Rise! Let us go! Here comes my betrayer!" (Mark 14:42)
>
> The reason my Father loves me is that I lay down my life—only to take it up again. No one takes it from me, but I lay it down of my own accord. I have authority to lay it down and authority to take it up again. This command I received from my Father." (John 10:17-18)
>
> But the world must learn that I love the Father and that I do exactly what my Father has commanded me. "Come now; let us leave. (John 14:31)

DEEPER STUDY # 2

(18:11) **Cup:** Jesus Christ was determined not to fear nor shrink from death. This is clearly seen in Jn.10:17-18. Death for a cause is not such a great price to pay. Many men have so died—fearlessly and willingly—some perhaps more cruelly than Jesus Himself. What was happening to Christ was not the experience of shrinking from betrayal, beatings, humiliation, and death (all increased by foreknowledge). As stated, some men have faced such circumstances courageously, even *inviting* martyrdom for a cause. The Lord knew He was to die from the very beginning, and He had been preparing His disciples for His death (see note—Mt.16:13-20). It was not just human or physical suffering from which Jesus was shrinking. Such an explanation is totally inadequate in explaining Gethsemane. The great cup or trial Jesus was facing was separation from God (see note and DEEPER STUDY # 2—Mt.26:37-38). He was to be the sacrificial "Lamb of God" who takes away the sins of the world (Jn.1:29). He is to bear the judgment of God for the sins of the world (see note—Mt.27:46-49; cp. Is.53:10). Jesus Himself had already spoken of the "cup" when referring to His sacrificial death (see DEEPER STUDY # 2—Mt.20:22-23; note—Mk.14:41-42; DEEPER STUDY # 2—14:36; note—Jn.18:11).

Scripture speaks of the cup in several ways.

1. The cup is called "the cup of the Lord's wrath" (Is.51:17).

2. The cup is associated with suffering and God's wrath (cp. Is.51:17; Lk.22:42).

3. The cup is also associated with salvation. Because Jesus drank the cup of suffering and wrath for us, we can "lift up the cup of salvation and call upon the name of the Lord" (Ps.116:13). He bears the judgment of God for the sins of the world (Is.53:10).

	B. The Jews and Peter: The Cowardly Denial, 18:12-27 (Mt.26:69-75; Mk.14: 53-72; Lk.22:54-62)	warming himself.	**3 The world's unjust denial**
1 Jesus was arrested, taken & bound	12 Then the detachment of soldiers with its commander and the Jewish officials arrested Jesus. They bound him	19 Meanwhile, the high priest questioned Jesus about his disciples and his teaching.	a. Jesus was asked to incriminate Himself[DS1] 1) To prove His teaching, v.19 2) To incriminate His followers, v.19
a. He was brought to Annas	13 And brought him first to Annas, who was the father-in-law of Caiaphas, the high priest that year.	20 "I have spoken openly to the world," Jesus replied. "I always taught in synagogues or at the temple, where all the Jews come together. I said nothing in secret.	b. Jesus replied forcefully 1) His testimony was public knowledge 2) The world knew His testimony
b. His time to die was rapidly approaching	14 Caiaphas was the one who had advised the Jews that it would be good if one man died for the people.	21 Why question me? Ask those who heard me. Surely they know what I said."	c. Jesus was reacted against & mistreated
2 Peter's unnecessary denial: The denial of association	15 Simon Peter and another disciple were following Jesus. Because this disciple was known to the high priest, he went with Jesus into the high priest's courtyard,	22 When Jesus said this, one of the officials nearby struck him in the face. "Is this the way you answer the high priest?" he demanded.	d. Jesus incriminated the world
a. Peter followed Jesus b. Another disciple also followed Jesus 1) He knew the officials of the palace 2) He arranged for Peter to enter	16 But Peter had to wait outside at the door. The other disciple, who was known to the high priest, came back, spoke to the girl on duty there and brought Peter in.	23 "If I said something wrong," Jesus replied, "testify as to what is wrong. But if I spoke the truth, why did you strike me?" 24 Then Annas sent him, still bound, to Caiaphas the high priest.	e. Jesus was shifted about by the world **4 Peter's cowardly denial: The denial of separation** a. Standing with the crowd, v.18 b. Denying unequivocally
c. Peter was innocently questioned by the door-keeper d. Peter denied being associated with Jesus e. Peter made a carnal attempt to be known as one of the crowd	17 "You are not one of his disciples, are you?" the girl at the door asked Peter. He replied, "I am not." 18 It was cold, and the servants and officials stood around a fire they had made to keep warm. Peter also was standing with them,	25 As Simon Peter stood warming himself, he was asked, "You are not one of his disciples, are you?" He denied it, saying, "I am not." 26 One of the high priest's servants, a relative of the man whose ear Peter had cut off, challenged him, "Didn't I see you with him in the olive grove?" 27 Again Peter denied it, and at that moment a rooster began to crow.	**5 Peter's shattering denial: The denial of discipleship** **6 Conclusion: Jesus' Word was fulfilled**

DIVISION XV

THE REVELATION OF JESUS, THE SUFFERING SAVIOR, 18:1-19:42

B. The Jews and Peter: The Cowardly Denial, 18:12-27

(18:12-27) **Introduction**: this passage is a descriptive picture of cowardly denial—the cowardly denial of both the world and a close disciple of the Lord's. It graphically shows what the Lord faces day by day in too many lives.

1. Jesus was arrested, taken and bound (v.12-14).
2. Peter's unnecessary denial: the denial of association (v.15-18).
3. The world's unjust denial (v.19-24).
4. Peter's cowardly denial: the denial of separation (v.25).
5. Peter's shattering denial: the denial of discipleship (v.26).
6. Conclusion: Jesus' Word was fulfilled (v.27).

(18:12-27) **Another Outline**: Cowardliness
1. Cowardliness is unnecessary (v.15-18).
2. Cowardliness is unjust (v.19-24).
3. Cowardliness is worldly (v.25).
4. Cowardliness is habitual (v.26-27).

5. Cowardliness is running back and forth (v.18:28-19:15).

1 (18:12-14) **Jesus Christ, Arrested**: Jesus was arrested, taken and bound. There are two significant points here.

1. Jesus was led away to Annas. Annas had been the High Priest, but he was not now serving. His son-in-law Caiaphas was the present High Priest. (See note—Jn.11:49 for more discussion.) However, as noted by John, Annas still wielded great influence. The trial before Annas was an informal trial, and the sinister plot was being carried out under the shadow and secrecy of darkness.

2. The significant point is this: Jesus' time to die was now beginning. It had even been predicted by the world itself, the corrupt leader of the religionists (see note—Jn.11:49-53 for discussion. Also see DEEPER STUDY # 1, Hour—Jn.12:23-24.)

2 (18:15-18) **Denial**: there was Peter's unnecessary denial, the denial of association or pretension. Peter and some other disciple followed Jesus up to the gate of the High Priest. The other disciple was probably John, for the account reads like an eyewitness account (see DEEPER STUDY # 1—Jn.1:39; note—Mk.14:54). It was this disciple who knew the High Priest personally. John's father, a very successful businessman, apparently provided fish for the palace. John was therefore well-known to the palace employees. Note that he was allowed entrance into the palace and arranged for Peter to enter the palace (v.16. See DEEPER STUDY # 6—Mk.3:17.)

Note three points about Peter's unnecessary denial.

1. Peter was innocently questioned by the door-keeper. She knew John, that John was one of Jesus' disciples. Since Peter was associated with John, she assumed he was also a disciple of Jesus. She was either just carrying on conversation or else asking Peter for some identification. There seems to be no threat or danger to Peter whatsoever.

2. Peter denied any association with Jesus and gave an unequivocal denial: "I am not." The point is this: Peter was a close friend of John, for John had made a very special request for Peter to be admitted into the palace. The gate-keeper was bound to think such a close associate of John's was also associated with John's Master (Teacher). Peter very simply failed his Lord by denying any association with Him and pretending not to know Him.

3. Peter made an attempt to be known as one of the crowd. He joined the crowd, standing around with them and joining in their conversation and activities.

Thought 1. Too many deny being associated with Christ. People see us in church or associating with other believers—innocently see us—thinking nothing about it. But when and if asked, we deny any association with Christ.

Thought 2. Too many pretend not to know Christ when out in the world…
- at their employment
- at their school
- at their social functions
- among their neighbors
- among their friends
- among strangers

Thought 3. Too many try to fade into the crowd, trying to hide their faith by joining in with the crowd. Standing with and trying to blend in with the crowd will always cause a believer to deny his Lord.

> **But whoever disowns me before men, I will disown him before my Father in heaven. (Mat 10:33)**
> **A false witness will not go unpunished, and he who pours out lies will not go free. (Prov 19:5)**
> **But in your hearts set apart Christ as Lord. Always be prepared to give an answer to everyone who asks you to give the reason for the hope that you have. But do this with gentleness and respect, (1 Pet 3:15)**

3 (18:19-24) **Jesus Christ, Rejected**: there was the world's unjust denial. There are five graphic scenes here.

1. Jesus was asked to incriminate Himself. He was asked about His disciples and asked to prove His doctrine and His claims. How much like the world. The world will ask about Jesus' teaching, but their purpose is…
- not to learn His teaching
- not to allow Him to prove His claims
- not to justify His claims
- not to secure direction and wisdom from Him

The world asks about His teaching to disprove it and to incriminate Him and His followers (see DEEPER STUDY # 1—Jn.18:19). The world wants nothing to do with Him as the Son of God, for then the world would have to repent and subject itself to Him and His demands. Men have to surrender all they are and have to Him if they acknowledge Him to be Lord (see DEEPER STUDY # 1—Lk.9:23).

> **The Spirit gives life; the flesh counts for nothing. The words I have spoken to you are spirit and they are life. (John 6:63)**
> **There is a judge for the one who rejects me and does not accept my words; that very word which I spoke will condemn him at the last day. (John 12:48)**
> **He who does not love me will not obey my teaching. These words you hear are not my own; they belong to the Father who sent me. (John 14:24)**
> **Let the wicked forsake his way and the evil man his thoughts. Let him turn to the LORD, and he will have mercy on him, and to our God, for he will freely pardon. (Isa 55:7)**
> **The eunuch was reading this passage of Scripture: "He was led like a sheep to the slaughter, and as a lamb before the shearer is silent, so he did not open his mouth. (Acts 8:32)**

2. Jesus' reply was forceful: His teaching and claim had been declared publicly. He had done nothing in secret. His doctrine was not a message of duplicity. He did not have one message for the public and another message which He followed in secret. He had openly and clearly proclaimed the truth, and the world knew exactly what He had taught and claimed.

Thought 1. The problem with the world is twofold.
1) The world refuses to believe Jesus' claim to be the Son of God.

> **For I have come down from heaven not to do my will but to do the will of him who sent me. (John 6:38)**
> **But I know him because I am from him and he sent me." (John 7:29)**
> **Jesus said to them, "If God were your Father, you would love me, for I came from God and now am here. I have not come on my own; but he sent me. (John 8:42)**
> **What about the one whom the Father set apart as his very own and sent into the world? Why then do you accuse me of blasphemy because I said, 'I am God's Son'? (John 10:36)**

2) The world seeks for some secret, symbolic meaning and teaching in the Word of Christ.

Jesus said to them, "If God were your Father, you would love me, for I came from God and now am here. I have not come on my own; but he sent me. Why is my language not clear to you? Because you are unable to hear what I say. (John 8:42-43)

He who belongs to God hears what God says. The reason you do not hear is that you do not belong to God." (John 8:47)

Since they did not know the righteousness that comes from God and sought to establish their own, they did not submit to God's righteousness. (Rom 10:3)

They are darkened in their understanding and separated from the life of God because of the ignorance that is in them due to the hardening of their hearts. (Eph 4:18)

They will turn their ears away from the truth and turn aside to myths. (2 Tim 4:4)

And if anyone takes words away from this book of prophecy, God will take away from him his share in the tree of life and in the holy city, which are described in this book. (Rev 22:19)

To whom can I speak and give warning? Who will listen to me? Their ears are closed so they cannot hear. The word of the LORD is offensive to them; they find no pleasure in it. (Jer 6:10)

But they do not know the thoughts of the LORD; they do not understand his plan, he who gathers them like sheaves to the threshing floor. (Micah 4:12)

Do not add to what I command you and do not subtract from it, but keep the commands of the LORD your God that I give you. (Deu 4:2)

See that you do all I command you; do not add to it or take away from it. (Deu 12:32)

"Every word of God is flawless; he is a shield to those who take refuge in him. Do not add to his words, or he will rebuke you and prove you a liar. (Prov 30:5-6)

3. Jesus was reacted against and mistreated: He was slapped in the face. This is a picture of how the world mistreats Jesus. Throughout His whole ministry, Jesus had insisted time and again that He was the Revelation of God, the Son of God Himself. (Quickly refer back to the overall outline or glance quickly over chapters 5-6, 8-12 for a feeling of how forceful and rapidly Jesus was proclaiming His deity.) Yet, the world shut its ears and reacted. It wanted nothing to disturb it, not even its religion. It wanted no rebuttal and no other answer given to the High Priest of its religion.

Thought 1. The world's religion allows man to continue in his own way and do pretty much as he wishes and still feel acceptable to God. Just think for a moment! How few religions—how few churches—how few priests and ministers—proclaim the true teaching of the *Lord* Jesus. So few are willing to sacrifice their lives for the world and all they are and have in order to reach a lost, starving, and diseased world.

Then he said to them all: "If anyone would come after me, he must deny himself and take up his cross daily and follow me. (Luke 9:23 See notes—Mt.19:21-22; 19:23-26 for more discussion.)

Therefore, I urge you, brothers, in view of God's mercy, to offer your bodies as living sacrifices, holy and pleasing to God—this is your spiritual act of worship. Do not conform any longer to the pattern of this world, but be transformed by the renewing of your mind. Then you will be able to test and approve what God's will is—his good, pleasing and perfect will. (Rom 12:1-2)

"Therefore come out from them and be separate, says the Lord. Touch no unclean thing, and I will receive you." "I will be a Father to you, and you will be my sons and daughters, says the Lord Almighty." (2 Cor 6:17-18)

Do not love the world or anything in the world. If anyone loves the world, the love of the Father is not in him. For everything in the world—the cravings of sinful man, the lust of his eyes and the boasting of what he has and does—comes not from the Father but from the world. (1 John 2:15-16)

4. Jesus incriminated the world. The world could not charge Jesus with evil. He was sinless, completely without fault. He had not lied; He had always told the truth. He was the *perfect Son of God* who had came to earth to proclaim the teaching of God perfectly.

Can any of you prove me guilty of sin? If I am telling the truth, why don't you believe me? (Jn.8:46; cp. 2 Cor.5:21; Heb. 4:15; 7:26; 1 Pt.1:19; 2:22)

However, the world stands incriminated, for the world has always rejected and mistreated the Perfect Man, the Son of God Himself. In its rejection, the world exposes itself as evil, and its most terrible evil is the rejection of the Perfect Man. (Note something: rejection of Jesus is unpardonable. The man who rejects Jesus will not be saved. A person must believe and accept the doctrine of the Lord Jesus Christ to be saved.)

We are therefore Christ's ambassadors, as though God were making his appeal through us. We implore you on Christ's behalf: Be reconciled to God. God made him who had no sin to be sin for us, so that in him we might become the righteousness of God. (2 Cor 5:20-21)

For you know that it was not with perishable things such as silver or gold that you were redeemed from the empty way of life handed down to you from your forefathers, but with the precious blood of Christ, a lamb without blemish or defect. (1 Pet 1:18-19)

5. Jesus was shifted about by the world. This is a picture of men seeking help from others to disprove Jesus. Jesus (His life, teaching, claims) was cast back and forth by the hands of men who were seeking evidence to prove that He was not the Son of God.

Then we will no longer be infants, tossed back and forth by the waves, and blown here and there by every wind of teaching and by the cunning and craftiness of men in their deceitful scheming. (Eph 4:14)

They mounted up to the heavens and went down to the depths; in their peril their courage melted away. They reeled and staggered like drunken men; they were at their wits' end. (Psa 107:26-27)

DEEPER STUDY # 1

(18:19) **Jesus' Jewish Trial**: demanding that Jesus incriminate Himself was against the law of Jewish justice. Under Jewish law, a defendant was not required to admit any guilt; therefore, the Jewish trial of Jesus was a mockery of justice. Several facts show this.

1. They had hastily assembled the court *at night*, but it was illegal to try cases at night. All criminals had to be tried in the day.

2. They were meeting in Annas' palace (home), not in the official court. This, too, was illegal. All cases had to be tried in court.

3. Jesus was being tried during the Passover week, but no cases were supposed to be tried during that week.

4. The leaders had not met to try Jesus, but to secretly devise charges and to condemn Him to death.

---

4 (18:25) **Peter—Denial**: there was Peter's cowardly denial, the denial of separation. Peter had joined the crowd, attempting to become one of them. When asked about Jesus, he denied his separation from the world saying, "I am not" a disciple of His. I am one of you, just another man standing around and taking part in the significant events of the world (2 Cor.6:17-18).

Thought 1. Too many believers fear, and because they fear, they lose their testimony for Christ and the opportunity to witness and win others to Christ. Too many fear...

- embarrassment
- ridicule
- abuse
- loss of position
- worldly friends
- worldly neighbors
- business management
- loss of promotion

If anyone is ashamed of me and my words in this adulterous and sinful generation, the Son of Man will be ashamed of him when he comes in his Father's glory with the holy angels." (Mark 8:38)

So do not be ashamed to testify about our Lord, or ashamed of me his prisoner. But join with me in suffering for the gospel, by the power of God, (2 Tim 1:8)

Be strong and courageous. Do not be afraid or terrified because of them, for the LORD your God goes with you; he will never leave you nor forsake you." (Deu 31:6)

5 (18:26) **Peter—Denial**: there was Peter's shattering denial, the denial of discipleship. This was the most serious denial of all: "Didn't I see you with him in the olive grove?" Peter denied Jesus for two very basic reasons.

1. Peter *feared* man. When a quick response *was* called for, he *was not* strong and mature enough to stand for Jesus. He feared what the *crowd* might do to him: ridicule, abuse, arrest, and kill him. He feared that the crowd would do to him just what they were doing to Jesus.

2. Peter faltered, stumbled, and failed to die to self. He lacked love enough to deny himself for the sake of others. Jesus died on the cross for the sake of the men who stood at the foot of the cross railing and cursing Him. He willingly died for men that they might live. That is how much He loved. At that point in his life, Peter did not know such self-denying love. He did not know the love that denied and surrendered itself for the sake of others.

Thought 1. This is a strong warning to every believer.
⇒ Peter was a strong disciple.
⇒ Peter knew and had trusted Jesus as the Messiah, the Son of God.
⇒ Peter had a strong profession of loyalty to Jesus.
⇒ Peter had just partaken of the Lord's Supper; in fact, he had just been privileged to partake of the very first Supper.
⇒ Peter had left all to follow Jesus.
⇒ Peter had been taught about God, by Jesus Himself.
⇒ Peter had even been forewarned that the flesh was weak and that he would fail.

Thought 2. Every denial (in fact, every neglect) of Jesus downgrades the Lord. Denial and neglect ignore just who Jesus is, the Son of God in all His power and majesty and dominion. Denial shows that we fear men more than we fear and reverence God. Neglect of Jesus shows how little we fear and reverence Him. The Biblical exhortation always needs to be kept in mind: "The Lord will judge His people. It is a dreadful thing to fall into the hands of the living God" (Heb.10:30-31).

Thought 3. A crowd of unbelievers can put pressure upon any of us. Peter was where he did not belong. He was hanging around in the midst of a worldly crowd. He belonged in one of three places: by the side of Christ; alone with God, seeking answers and understanding; or with the other apostles, rallying them in prayer for understanding and direction.

Do not set foot on the path of the wicked or walk in the way of evil men. (Prov 4:14)

Therefore, dear friends, since you already know this, be on your guard so that you may not be carried away by the error of lawless men and fall from your secure position. (2 Pet 3:17)

They claim to know God, but by their actions they deny him. They are detestable, disobedient and unfit for doing anything good. (Titus 1:16)

If we endure, we will also reign with him. If we disown him, he will also disown us; (2 Tim 2:12)

Without being frightened in any way by those who oppose you. This is a sign to them that they will be destroyed, but that you will be saved—and that by God. (Phil 1:28)

With many other words he warned them; and he pleaded with them, "Save yourselves from this corrupt generation." (Acts 2:40)

6 (18:27) **Jesus Christ, Predictions of**: the conclusion is that Jesus' word was fulfilled, and forgiveness was extended to Peter. This is implied in the rooster's crowing a third time, just as Jesus had predicted (Jn.13:38. See note—Mk.14:72 for discussion.)

C. The Trial Before Pilate: Indecisive Compromise, 18:28-19:15

(Mt.27:11-25; Mk.15:1-15 Lk.23:1-5, 13-25)

1 Jesus was led into the palace or judgment hall

a. It was early in the morning
b. The Jews did not enter
c. Pilate moved back & forth[DS1]

2 Movement 1: To Jesus' accusers—to hear their charges

a. The insolent charge: A criminal—a trial is not necessary (hatred & pride)
b. Pilate refused the case (evading responsibility)
c. The evidence of predetermined guilt: "Execute" (closed hearts)[DS2]
  1) The Jews stoned
  2) The Romans crucified

3 Movement 2: To Jesus—to hear His defense

a. Pilate's scornful question
b. Jesus' challenge to Pilate: A person is responsible for His own verdict
c. Pilate's reaction: Contempt for the Jews

d. Jesus' explanation: His Kingdom is not of this world

e. Pilate's baffled statement
f. Jesus' claim: He is King—to be King was the purpose for His birth[DS3]
g. Jesus' subtle appeal

h. Pilate's sincere question (truth)

4 Movement 3: Back to the people—to declare Jesus' innocence

28 Then the Jews led Jesus from Caiaphas to the palace of the Roman governor. By now it was early morning, and to avoid ceremonial uncleanness the Jews did not enter the palace; they wanted to be able to eat the Passover. 29 So Pilate came out to them and asked, "What charges are you bringing against this man?" 30 "If he were not a criminal," they replied, "we would not have handed him over to you." 31 Pilate said, "Take him yourselves and judge him by your own law." "But we have no right to execute anyone," the Jews objected. 32 This happened so that the words Jesus had spoken indicating the kind of death he was going to die would be fulfilled. 33 Pilate then went back inside the palace, summoned Jesus and asked him, "Are you the king of the Jews?" 34 "Is that your own idea," Jesus asked, "or did others talk to you about me?" 35 "Am I a Jew?" Pilate replied. "It was your people and your chief priests who handed you over to me. What is it you have done?" 36 Jesus said, "My kingdom is not of this world. If it were, my servants would fight to prevent my arrest by the Jews. But now my kingdom is from another place." 37 "You are a king then!" said Pilate. Jesus answered, "You are right in saying I am a king. In fact, for this reason I was born, and for this I came into the world, to testify to the truth. Everyone on the side of truth listens to me." 38 "What is truth?" Pilate asked. With this he went out again to the Jews and said, "I find no basis for a charge against him. 39 But it is your custom for me to release to you one prisoner at the time of the

Passover. Do you want me to release 'the king of the Jews'?" 40 They shouted back, "No, not him! Give us Barabbas!" Now Barabbas had taken part in a rebellion.

CHAPTER 19

Then Pilate took Jesus and had him flogged. 2 The soldiers twisted together a crown of thorns and put it on his head. They clothed him in a purple robe 3 And went up to him again and again, saying, "Hail, king of the Jews!" And they struck him in the face. 4 Once more Pilate came out and said to the Jews, "Look, I am bringing him out to you to let you know that I find no basis for a charge against him." 5 When Jesus came out wearing the crown of thorns and the purple robe, Pilate said to them, "Here is the man!" 6 As soon as the chief priests and their officials saw him, they shouted, "Crucify! Crucify!" But Pilate answered, "You take him and crucify him. As for me, I find no basis for a charge against him." 7 The Jews insisted, "We have a law, and according to that law he must die, because he claimed to be the Son of God." 8 When Pilate heard this, he was even more afraid, 9 And he went back inside the palace. "Where do you come from?" he asked Jesus, but Jesus gave him no answer. 10 "Do you refuse to speak to me?" Pilate said. "Don't you realize I have power either to free you or to crucify you?" 11 Jesus answered, "You would have no power over me if it were not given to you from above. Therefore the one who handed me over to you is guilty of a greater sin." 12 From then on, Pilate tried to set Jesus free, but the Jews kept shouting, "If you let this man go, you are no friend of Caesar. Anyone who claims to be a king opposes Caesar." 13 When Pilate heard this, he

a. Pilate's first attempt to release Jesus: He offers a *substitute*
b. The mob's choice (a man of the world)

5 Movement 4: Back to Jesus—to flog Him

a. Savage, cruel flogging (persecution)[DS4]
b. Crude mockery & scoffing (abused His name & person)
c. Sham obedience (hypocrisy)

6 Movement 5: Back again to the people—to offer a compromise

a. Pilate's second attempt to release Jesus by compromise: Sought the crowd's pity by presenting Jesus beaten & battered by flogging

b. The mob's hatred (harsh, loud, hysterical shouting)
c. Pilate's impossible dare: Angry, sarcastic contempt for the mob[DS5]
d. The Jew's truthful charge[DS6]

7 Movement 6: Back again to Jesus—to investigate the possibility of a supernatural being

a. Pilate's superstitious question: Jesus' origin

b. Pilate's terrifying, frantic cry: Life is in the hands of earthly authority

c. Jesus' revelation: There is a superior, higher authority

d. Jesus' charge of guilt

8 Movement 7: Back again to the people—to release Jesus

a. Pilate's successive attempts to release Jesus
b. Pilate blackmailed: Jesus or Caesar

9 Movement 8: To the

Judgment Seat before all—to give the verdict of crucifixion	brought Jesus out and sat down on the judge's seat at a place known as the Stone Pavement (which in Aramaic is Gabbatha).	king," Pilate said to the Jews. 15 But they shouted, "Take him away! Take him away! Crucify him!" "Shall I crucify your king?" Pilate	b. The Jew's frenzied madness
a. Pilate's choice: Fear of Caesar greater than his fear of Jesus	14 It was the day of Preparation of Passover Week, about the sixth hour. "Here is your	asked. "We have no king but Caesar," the chief priests answered.	c. Pilate's bitter question d. The Jew's fatal choice

DIVISION XV

THE REVELATION OF JESUS, THE SUFFERING SAVIOR, 18:1-19:42

C. The Trial Before Pilate: Indecisive Compromise, 18:28-19:15

(18:28-19:15) **Introduction**: the Roman trial of Jesus is a dramatic picture of indecisive compromise. The scene flows along with Pilate *moving* back and forth to Jesus and to His accusers or the people. The outline is adequate in carrying one through the passage. Therefore, the footnotes will not discuss each point. Notes and application are added where needed. (See outline and DEEPER STUDY # 1—Mt.27:11-25; DEEPER STUDY # 1—Mk.15:1-15; note—Lk.23:1-25 for more detailed discussion.)

1. Jesus led into the judgment hall (v.28).
2. Movement 1: to Jesus' accusers—to hear their charges (v.29-32).
3. Movement 2: to Jesus—to hear His defense (v.33-38).
4. Movement 3: back to the people—to declare Jesus' innocence (v.38-40).
5. Movement 4: back to Jesus—to flog Jesus (Ch.19, v.1-3).
6. Movement 5: back again to the people—to offer a compromise (v.4-7).
7. Movement 6: back again to Jesus—to investigate the possibility of a supernatural being (v.8-11).
8. Movement 7: back again to the people—to release Jesus (v.12).
9. Movement 8: to the Judgment Seat before all—to give the verdict of crucifixion (v.13-15).

1 (18:28) **Jesus Christ, Trials of**: Jesus was led into the palace or hall of judgment. It was early morning. Note the Jews did not enter, for the hall was a Gentile palace or judgment hall and it was the Sabbath of the Passover season. To enter the judgment hall would have polluted and contaminated them ceremonially. They would have been disallowed from participating in the Passover. It was a trifling, superficial concern in light of the trial for a man's life, especially the life of God's own Son.

Thought 1. Too often men (religionists) attack others, arguing over their religion and church and its plans, over ceremonies, rituals, rules, regulations, and practices. They forget the *meat* of the truth: love, joy, peace, care, understanding, and ministry (cp. Jn.13:33-34).

DEEPER STUDY # 1

(18:28) **Pilate**: the procurator of Judaea. He was directly responsible to the Emperor for the administrative and financial management of the country. A man had to work himself up through the political and military ranks to become a procurator. Pilate was therefore an able man, experienced in the affairs of politics and government as well as the military. He held office for ten years, which shows that he was deeply trusted by the Roman government. However, the Jews despised Pilate, and Pilate despised the Jews; in particular he despised their intense practice of religion. When Pilate became procurator of Judaea, he did two things that aroused the people's bitter hatred against him forever. First, on his state visits to Jerusalem, he rode into the city with the Roman standard, an eagle sitting atop a pole. All previous governors had removed the standard because of the Jews' opposition to idols. Second, Pilate launched the construction of a new water supply for Jerusalem. To finance the project, he took the money out of the temple treasury. The Jews never forgot or forgave this act. They bitterly opposed Pilate all through his reign, and he treated them with equal contempt (see DEEPER STUDY # 1—Mk.15:1-15). On several occasions, Jewish leaders threatened to exercise their right to report Pilate to the emperor. This, of course, disturbed Pilate immensely and caused him to become even more bitter toward the Jews.

2 (18:29-32) **Jesus Christ, Trial—Charges Against**: the first movement of Pilate was to Jesus' accusers—to hear their charges.

1. The insolent charge. The religionists were full of hatred and pride. They rejected and hated Jesus, and they set themselves up as His judges. They assumed the right to judge, feeling their verdict and judgment should not be questioned.

Thought 1. Men may reject and hate Christ; they may judge Christ not worthy to be the Lord of their lives. They may try to get rid of Christ by pushing Him away and having nothing to do with Him. But they cannot change the fact: Christ still came to love and save men, and in the final analysis, men will be judged by Christ.

"**For God so loved the world that he gave his one and only Son, that whoever believes in him shall not perish but have eternal life. (John 3:16)**
I told you that you would die in your sins; if you do not believe that I am the one I claim to be, you will indeed die in your sins." (John 8:24)
There is a judge for the one who rejects me and does not accept my words; that very word which I spoke will condemn him at the last day. (John 12:48)
See to it, brothers, that none of you has a sinful, unbelieving heart that turns away from the living God. (Heb 3:12)

336

2. Pilate tried to evade his responsibility.

Thought 1. We are often called upon to take a stand for Christ. It is our duty. Yet how many of us fear ridicule, abuse, and rejection and end up evading our responsibility?

3. The hearts of the religionists were closed; this was their problem. They were mentioning death even before the trial.

Thought 1. Religionists reject Jesus because they do not want to hear Him; they do not want anything to do with the demands He puts upon their lives. The only Lord they want is the *lord of self*.

> For this people's heart has become calloused; they hardly hear with their ears, and they have closed their eyes. Otherwise they might see with their eyes, hear with their ears, understand with their hearts and turn, and I would heal them.' (Acts 28:27)
> You adulterous people, don't you know that friendship with the world is hatred toward God? Anyone who chooses to be a friend of the world becomes an enemy of God. (James 4:4)

DEEPER STUDY # 2

(18:31-32) **Jesus Christ, Death**: the Jews had to force the Romans to crucify Jesus, for the Jews were not allowed to execute a criminal on the Sabbath or on feast days. From God's perspective, it had been prophesied that the Christ was to be crucified, and crucifixion was the method of execution used by the Romans. Therefore, events had to be providentially shifted so there could be a Roman execution by crucifixion (cp. Jn.3:14; 8:28; 12:32; Lk.9:22-23).

---

3 (18:33-38) **Decision**: the second movement of Pilate was to Jesus in order to hear His defense. Note two points.

1. Jesus' challenge to Pilate (v.34). Jesus challenged Pilate to think through the issue himself. In judging Jesus, a person is responsible for his own verdict.

Thought 1. A person is personally responsible for his verdict about Jesus. Everyone *now* has to make a choice, for Jesus claims to be the Son of God, the only Savior of the world. We have to give our verdict: He either *is* or *is not* the King of the Jews.

> He came to that which was his own, but his own did not receive him. Yet to all who received him, to those who believed in his name, he gave the right to become children of God— (John 1:11-12)

Thought 2. People usually choose to follow the man of power and fame and wealth over the man of love and morality and peace. Just take a moment and think how true this is. The immoral emphasis of films and the violent emphasis of the news alone are prime examples. Is there any wonder man has never known a world of love and peace and true justice? The problem is the human heart, the problem which Jesus alone can solve.

> I have come in my Father's name, and you do not accept me; but if someone else comes in his own name, you will accept

him. How can you believe if you accept praise from one another, yet make no effort to obtain the praise that comes from the only God ? (John 5:43-44)
> But the things that come out of the mouth come from the heart, and these make a man 'unclean.' For out of the heart come evil thoughts, murder, adultery, sexual immorality, theft, false testimony, slander. (Mat 15:18-19)
> The good man brings good things out of the good stored up in his heart, and the evil man brings evil things out of the evil stored up in his heart. For out of the overflow of his heart his mouth speaks. (Luke 6:45)
> But the seed on good soil stands for those with a noble and good heart, who hear the word, retain it, and by persevering produce a crop. (Luke 8:15)
> For it is with your heart that you believe and are justified, and it is with your mouth that you confess and are saved. (Rom 10:10)
> Above all else, guard your heart, for it is the wellspring of life. (Prov 4:23)

2. Jesus' kingdom is not of this world, not of the physical dimension of being. It is of heaven, of the spiritual dimension of being (see DEEPER STUDY # 3—Mt.19:23-24; note—Jn.11:25-27, pt.2).

> Jesus said, "My kingdom is not of this world. If it were, my servants would fight to prevent my arrest by the Jews. But now my kingdom is from another place." (John 18:36)
> For the kingdom of God is not a matter of eating and drinking, but of righteousness, peace and joy in the Holy Spirit, (Rom 14:17)
> But about the Son he says, "Your throne, O God, will last for ever and ever, and righteousness will be the scepter of your kingdom. (Heb 1:8)
> But in keeping with his promise we are looking forward to a new heaven and a new earth, the home of righteousness. So then, dear friends, since you are looking forward to this, make every effort to be found spotless, blameless and at peace with him. (2 Pet 3:13-14)
> The seventh angel sounded his trumpet, and there were loud voices in heaven, which said: "The kingdom of the world has become the kingdom of our Lord and of his Christ, and he will reign for ever and ever." (Rev 11:15)

DEEPER STUDY # 3

(18:37) **Jesus Christ, Claims**: there are several claims here.

1. His birth was a means to an end—to be King (Mt.2:2; Jn.1:49; 1 Cor.15:25).
2. He did preexist—He came out of heaven from the very presence of God (see DEEPER STUDY # 1—Jn.1:1-5; note—1:1-2).
3. He was the truth—absolute reality.
4. He revealed the truth (Jn.14:9-11).
5. He was heard by those of the truth (Jn.8:45-47).

4 (18:38-40) **Jesus Christ, Death**: Pilate's third movement was back to the people. He wished to clear Jesus' name and to declare His innocence. Pilate hoped to satisfy the Jews' cry for blood by substituting a real criminal and revolutionary for Jesus, but the Jewish leaders were determined to murder Jesus. Therefore, they chose a man of worldly power and fame over the Man of peace, the Son of God Himself.

Thought 1. Man chooses the path of power and fame, wealth and possessions. He rejects the path of peace if it means the sacrifice of self and possessions. Therefore, man never knows peace—not personal peace or world peace. The only way to peace is to surrender to the Prince of Peace.

"There is no peace," says the LORD, "for the wicked." (Isa 48:22)

The way of peace they do not know; there is no justice in their paths. They have turned them into crooked roads; no one who walks in them will know peace. (Isa 59:8)

Suddenly a great company of the heavenly host appeared with the angel, praising God and saying, "Glory to God in the highest, and on earth peace to men on whom his favor rests." (Luke 2:13-14)

Therefore, since we have been justified through faith, we have peace with God through our Lord Jesus Christ, (Rom 5:1)

For he himself is our peace, who has made the two one and has destroyed the barrier, the dividing wall of hostility, (Eph 2:14)

And through him to reconcile to himself all things, whether things on earth or things in heaven, by making peace through his blood, shed on the cross. (Col 1:20)

Thought 2. Note how the people (the world) rejected Pilate's offer of a substitute for Jesus. God twisted the world's choice and made His Son the *substitute* for every man, even for those who were rejecting Him in this horrible scene.

But God demonstrates his own love for us in this: While we were still sinners, Christ died for us. (Rom 5:8)

For Christ died for sins once for all, the righteous for the unrighteous, to bring you to God. He was put to death in the body but made alive by the Spirit, (1 Pet 3:18)

5 (19:1-3) **Persecution**: Pilate's fourth movement was back to Jesus. He had Jesus flogged. Note how the world treated Jesus. The very same treatment is heaped upon Jesus by men of every generation.

1. Men persecute and attack, crudely mock and scoff at His name, His person, and His Word. They curse, abuse, ridicule, imprison, kill, and heap mistreatment upon His followers.

"Blessed are you when people insult you, persecute you and falsely say all kinds of evil against you because of me. (Mat 5:11)

"Be on your guard against men; they will hand you over to the local councils and flog you in their synagogues. (Mat 10:17)

Remember the words I spoke to you: 'No servant is greater than his master.' If they persecuted me, they will persecute you also. If they obeyed my teaching, they will obey yours also. (John 15:20)

They will put you out of the synagogue; in fact, a time is coming when anyone who kills you will think he is offering a service to God. (John 16:2)

2. Men live hypocritical lives, professing to know and follow Him; but when out in the world, they live as the world.

He replied, "Isaiah was right when he prophesied about you hypocrites; as it is written: "'These people honor me with their lips, but their hearts are far from me. (Mark 7:6)

They claim to know God, but by their actions they deny him. They are detestable, disobedient and unfit for doing anything good. (Titus 1:16)

DEEPER STUDY # 4

(19:1) **Flogging**: Jesus was stripped and beaten with a whip. This was a savage, excruciating punishment. The whip was made of leather straps with two small balls attached to the end of each strap. The balls were made of rough lead or sharp bones or spikes so that they would cut deeply into the flesh. Jesus' hands were tied to a post above His head, and He was flogged. It was the Roman custom for the prisoner to be lashed by the presiding centurion until He was near death (Jewish trials allowed only forty lashes.) The criminal's back was, or course, nothing more than an unrecognizable mass of torn flesh.

---

6 (19:4-7) **Compromise—Decision**: Pilate's fifth movement was back again to the people. He offered a compromise. Pilate was hoping the crowd would pity Jesus when they saw Him so beaten, battered, and bloodied. He hoped the flogging would serve as a compromise and satisfy them.

Thought 1. Compromise is not the way with Jesus. Pilate needed to declare Him innocent, for He was innocent. He was not guilty of any wrongdoing. Every man needs to declare Jesus innocent, for He was completely free of sin. He was the Son of Man Himself who stands before the world as its Savior (see note—Jn.1:51).

Note the truthful charge of the Jews: "He claimed to be the Son of God" (v.7). Jesus did claim to be the Son of God (see note—Jn.1:34).

"He who is not with me is against me, and he who does not gather with me, scatters. (Luke 11:23)

That all may honor the Son just as they honor the Father. He who does not honor the Son does not honor the Father, who sent him. (John 5:23)

This day I call heaven and earth as witnesses against you that I have set before you life and death, blessings and curses. Now choose life, so that you and your children may live (Deu 30:19)

DEEPER STUDY # 5
(19:6) **Jews—Capital Punishment**: the Jews were not allowed the right of capital punishment by their Roman conquerors.

DEEPER STUDY # 6
(19:7) **Capital Punishment**: cp. Lev.24:16 for the law concerning capital punishment.

---

7 (19:8-11) **Sorcery**: Pilate's sixth movement was back again to Jesus. He investigated the possibility of a supernatural being. Note several things.

1. Pilate feared. History tells us that Pilate was an extremely superstitious man. When he heard that Jesus claimed to be the Son of God, he thought Jesus was claiming to be the son of *a god*. The picture in his mind was that of a half-god and half-man, a god-like being that filled the popular literature and beliefs of that day. The possibility of his condemning a god struck fear in Pilate.

> **Thought 1.** Men must not fear (reverence) the astrological charts and fortune signs and evil powers of this world. What men must fear is Him who can destroy both body and soul in hell (Mt.10:28). There is only one Truth and that is Jesus Christ Himself.

> Let no one be found among you who sacrifices his son or daughter in the fire, who practices divination or sorcery, interprets omens, engages in witchcraft, or casts spells, or who is a medium or spiritist or who consults the dead. Anyone who does these things is detestable to the LORD, and because of these detestable practices the LORD your God will drive out those nations before you. (Deu 18:10-12)
> They sacrificed their sons and daughters in the fire. They practiced divination and sorcery and sold themselves to do evil in the eyes of the LORD, provoking him to anger. So the LORD was very angry with Israel and removed them from his presence. Only the tribe of Judah was left, (2 Ki 17:17-18)
> Both of these will overtake you in a moment, on a single day: loss of children and widowhood. They will come upon you in full measure, in spite of your many sorceries and all your potent spells. (Isa 47:9)
> So do not listen to your prophets, your diviners, your interpreters of dreams, your mediums or your sorcerers who tell you, 'You will not serve the king of Babylon.' (Jer 27:9)
> The idols speak deceit, diviners see visions that lie; they tell dreams that are false, they give comfort in vain. Therefore the people wander like sheep oppressed for lack of a shepherd. (Zec 10:2)
> "So I will come near to you for judgment. I will be quick to testify against sorcerers, adulterers and perjurers, against

those who defraud laborers of their wages, who oppress the widows and the fatherless, and deprive aliens of justice, but do not fear me," says the LORD Almighty. (Mal 3:5)
> Now for some time a man named Simon had practiced sorcery in the city and amazed all the people of Samaria. He boasted that he was someone great, and all the people, both high and low, gave him their attention and exclaimed, "This man is the divine power known as the Great Power." They followed him because he had amazed them for a long time with his magic. (Acts 8:9-11)
> But Elymas the sorcerer (for that is what his name means) opposed them and tried to turn the proconsul from the faith. Then Saul, who was also called Paul, filled with the Holy Spirit, looked straight at Elymas and said, "You are a child of the devil and an enemy of everything that is right! You are full of all kinds of deceit and trickery. Will you never stop perverting the right ways of the Lord? (Acts 13:8-10)
> But the cowardly, the unbelieving, the vile, the murderers, the sexually immoral, those who practice magic arts, the idolaters and all liars—their place will be in the fiery lake of burning sulfur. This is the second death." (Rev 21:8)

2. Power is not in the hands of earthly authorities. It is in the hands of God (v.10-11).

> Everyone must submit himself to the governing authorities, for there is no authority except that which God has established. The authorities that exist have been established by God. (Rom 13:1)

8 (19:12) **Decision**: Pilate's seventh movement was back again to the people. He wished to release Jesus. Note that Pilate had to make a decision, choosing either Jesus or Caesar (the world). When the Jews cried out "You are no friend of Caesar" Pilate faced a serious problem. They were threatening to send a report to Caesar (see DEEPER STUDY # 1—Jn.18:28). He was now forced to choose, and he did. Tragically, he chose the world and its way.

> **Thought 1.** Everyone is now forced to choose. Jesus Christ is unquestionably the Son of God; therefore, we choose either Him or this world.

> Whoever believes in him is not condemned, but whoever does not believe stands condemned already because he has not believed in the name of God's one and only Son. (John 3:18)
> I told you that you would die in your sins; if you do not believe that I am the one I claim to be, you will indeed die in your sins." (John 8:24)

9 (19:13-15) **Decision**: Pilate's eighth movement was to the judgment seat before all. He gave the verdict of crucifixion.

1. Pilate's fatal choice. He feared Caesar more than he feared God. Note that he proclaimed the truth, but in ignorance and mockery: "Here is your King." Pilate feared...

- losing the people's favor.
- causing problems for himself.
- losing his position and security (see DEEPER STUDY # 1—Jn.18:28).

> Do not show partiality in judging; hear both small and great alike. Do not be afraid of any man, for judgment belongs to God. Bring me any case too hard for you, and I will hear it. (Deu 1:17)
>
> Fear of man will prove to be a snare, but whoever trusts in the LORD is kept safe. (Prov 29:25)
>
> "I, even I, am he who comforts you. Who are you that you fear mortal men, the sons of men, who are but grass, (Isa 51:12)
>
> "I tell you, my friends, do not be afraid of those who kill the body and after that can do no more. But I will show you whom you should fear: Fear him who, after the killing of the body, has power to throw you into hell. Yes, I tell you, fear him. (Luke 12:4-5)

2. The Jews' fatal choice. They, too, chose the world, the way of Caesar. This was a shocking choice, for God had supposedly been the God of the Jews for centuries. He was said to be the sovereign Lord of their nation (Judg.8:23; 1 Sam.8:7; 12:12). But now, at this very moment, they were rejecting and repudiating God as their sovereign Lord. They were choosing Caesar and the way of the world—the world's...

- security
- position
- power
- acceptance
- livelihood
- honor
- selfishness
- friendship
- religion

> "But his subjects hated him and sent a delegation after him to say, 'We don't want this man to be our king.' (Luke 19:14)
>
> He came to that which was his own, but his own did not receive him. (John 1:11)
>
> There is a judge for the one who rejects me and does not accept my words; that very word which I spoke will condemn him at the last day. (John 12:48)
>
> Do not love the world or anything in the world. If anyone loves the world, the love of the Father is not in him. For everything in the world—the cravings of sinful man, the lust of his eyes and the boasting of what he has and does—comes not from the Father but from the world. (1 John 2:15-16)

D. The Crucifixion: The Major Events of the Cross, 19:16-37
(Mt.27:26-56; Mk.15:16-41; Lk.23:26-49)

1 Event 1: Jesus bearing His cross—willingly went forth
a. Pilate delivered Jesus
b. They led Him
c. He went forth, bore the cross
d. He was the majestic victor, not the victim

2 Event 2: Jesus being crucified between two sinners—the preeminent sacrifice

3 Event 3: The title on the cross
a. Pilate made an ironic announcement, cp.Jn.18:36; 3:5
b. The people were indifferent to the title

c. The religionists objected to the title

d. Pilate sarcastically insisted the title stand

4 Event 4: The soldiers gambling for His clothes
a. The insensitive men: Jesus' mother was standing by, yet not given His clothes
b. The seamless garment: Was the same as the High Priest's garment—the Mediator
c. The fulfillment of Scripture

d. An "eye-witness" verification: John saw the event

5 Event 5: Jesus' great love for His mother
a. There were women at the cross

16 Finally Pilate handed him over to them to be crucified. So the soldiers took charge of Jesus.
17 Carrying his own cross, he went out to the place of the Skull (which in Aramaic is called Golgotha).
18 Here they crucified him, and with him two others—one on each side and Jesus in the middle.
19 Pilate had a notice prepared and fastened to the cross. It read: JESUS OF NAZARETH, THE KING OF THE JEWS.
20 Many of the Jews read this sign, for the place where Jesus was crucified was near the city, and the sign was written in Aramaic, Latin and Greek.
21 The chief priests of the Jews protested to Pilate, "Do not write 'The King of the Jews,' but that this man claimed to be king of the Jews."
22 Pilate answered, "What I have written, I have written."
23 When the soldiers crucified Jesus, they took his clothes, dividing them into four shares, one for each of them, with the undergarment remaining. This garment was seamless, woven in one piece from top to bottom.
24 "Let's not tear it," they said to one another. "Let's decide by lot who will get it." This happened that the scripture might be fulfilled which said, "They divided my garments among them and cast lots for my clothing." So this is what the soldiers did.
25 Near the cross of Jesus stood his mother, his mother's sister, Mary the wife of Clopas, and Mary

Magdalene.
26 When Jesus saw his mother there, and the disciple whom he loved standing nearby, he said to his mother, "Dear woman, here is your son,"
27 and to the disciple, "Here is your mother." From that time on, this disciple took her into his home.
28 Later, knowing that all was now completed, and so that the Scripture would be fulfilled, Jesus said, "I am thirsty."
29 A jar of wine vinegar was there, so they soaked a sponge in it, put the sponge on a stalk of the hyssop plant, and lifted it to Jesus' lips.
30 When he had received the drink, Jesus said, "It is finished." With that, he bowed his head and gave up his spirit.
31 Now it was the day of Preparation, and the next day was to be a special Sabbath. Because the Jews did not want the bodies left on the crosses during the Sabbath, they asked Pilate to have the legs broken and the bodies taken down.
32 The soldiers therefore came and broke the legs of the first man who had been crucified with Jesus, and then those of the other.
33 But when they came to Jesus and found that he was already dead, they did not break his legs.
34 Instead, one of the soldiers pierced Jesus' side with a spear, bringing a sudden flow of blood and water.
35 The man who saw it has given testimony, and his testimony is true. He knows that he tells the truth, and he testifies so that you also may believe.
36 These things happened so that the scripture would be fulfilled: "Not one of his bones will be broken,"
37 And, as another scripture says, "They will look on the one they have pierced."

b. Jesus "saw His mother"

c. Jesus demonstrated responsibility: Discharged His duty even in death

6 Event 6: Jesus' agonizing thirst & His deliberate effort to fulfill Scripture
a. Knew His purpose was achieved
b. Was exhausted, He thirsted
c. Was given hyssop: An act recalling the Passover

7 Event 7: Jesus' great shout of victory—salvation & reconciliation

8 Event 8: The spear being thrust into His side
a. A religious request: Concern for trifles, cp. 18:28

b. A brutal custom: Smashing the victim's legs to cause an earlier death

c. A strange fact: Jesus was already dead

d. A proof of death: Blood & water

e. An insistence upon the accuracy of the account
1) Purpose 1: To stir belief
2) Purpose 2: To fulfill Scripture

DIVISION XV

THE REVELATION OF JESUS, THE SUFFERING SAVIOR, 18:1-19:42

D. The Crucifixion: The Major Events at the Cross, 19:16-37

(19:16-37) **Introduction**: the most significant event in history is the crucifixion of Jesus Christ. We are saved by His death; because He died, we live. However, there is a condition. We must believe, and it is the necessity for belief that John stressed. He was an eyewitness of the crucifixion, and he closed his account of the crucifixion by saying "the man who saw it has given testimony, and his testimony is true...that you also may believe" (Jn.19:35).

1. Event 1: Jesus' bearing His cross—willingly "went out" (v.16-17).
2. Event 2: Jesus' being crucified between two sinners—the preeminent sacrifice (v.18).
3. Event 3: Pilate's writing the title on the cross (v.19-22).
4. Event 4: the soldiers' gambling for His clothes (v.23-24).
5. Event 5: Jesus' great love for His mother (v.25-27).
6. Event 6: Jesus' agonizing thirst and His deliberate effort to fulfill Scripture (v.28-29)
7. Event 7: Jesus' great shout of victory: salvation and reconciliation (v.30).
8. Event 8: the spear's being thrust into His side (v.31-37).

(19:16-37) **Another Outline**: The Crucifixion—the Picture of Jesus Symbolized.

1. Picture 1: Jesus—the Victor (v.16-17).
2. Picture 2: Jesus—the Preeminent Sacrifice (v.18).
3. Picture 3: Jesus—the Proclaimed King (v.19-22).
4. Picture 4: Jesus—the High Priest, the Mediator (v.23-24).
5. Picture 5: Jesus—the Responsible Son of Man (v.25-27).
6. Picture 6: Jesus—the Passover Lamb (v.28-29).
7. Picture 7: Jesus—the Triumphant Messiah (v.30).
8. Picture 8: Jesus—the Lord of the Sacraments, of the Church (v.31-37).

1 (19:16-17) **Bearing the Cross**: the first event of the cross was that of Jesus' bearing His cross. He *willingly* "went forth." Note:

⇒ Pilate delivered Him.
⇒ The soldiers took and led Him.
⇒ It was Jesus, however, who *bore* the cross and *went forth*.

Jesus Christ was the *majestic victor*, not the victim. He was bearing the cross and going forth for a specific purpose—to save man. (See notes—Jn.10:17-18, pt.2; 12:27-30.)

> **Just as Moses lifted up the snake in the desert, so the Son of Man must be lifted up, that everyone who believes in him may have eternal life. (John 3:14-15)**
> **"I am the good shepherd. The good shepherd lays down his life for the sheep. (John 10:11)**
> **Just as the Father knows me and I know the Father—and I lay down my life for the sheep. (John 10:15)**

2 (19:18) **Crucifixion Between Thieves**: the second event of the cross was Jesus' being crucified between two sinners, two unjust thieves. This is a picture of two things.

1. It is a picture of the preeminence of His sacrifice. He was surrounded by a world of unjust men, yet He was dying for them.

> **He himself bore our sins in his body on the tree, so that we might die to sins and live for righteousness; by his wounds you have been healed. (1 Pet 2:24)**
> **For Christ died for sins once for all, the righteous for the unrighteous, to bring you to God. He was put to death in the body but made alive by the Spirit, (1 Pet 3:18)**

2. It is a picture of preeminent guilt. Jesus Christ was being counted as the King of Sinners.

> **We all, like sheep, have gone astray, each of us has turned to his own way; and the LORD has laid on him the iniquity of us all. (Isa 53:6)**
> **God made him who had no sin to be sin for us, so that in him we might become the righteousness of God. (2 Cor 5:21)**

3 (19:19-22) **Title on Cross**: the third event of the cross was the title on the cross. Note three simple facts.

1. The people read the title but were indifferent to it. It had no effect upon them. There was no mass movement of sorrow and repentance, no final acceptance of Him.
2. The religionists objected to the title. However, they did not ask that it be removed. They asked that the wording be changed to read "'This man claimed to be the King of the Jews.'" Their unbelief was foul and obstinate.
3. Jesus claimed to be "the King of the Jews," the promised Messiah.
4. The title "King of the Jews" was written in the three great languages of the world. This providentially symbolized His rightful rule as King of the universe.

> **And being found in appearance as a man, he humbled himself and became obedient to death— even death on a cross! Therefore God exalted him to the highest place and gave him the name that is above every name, that at the name of Jesus every knee should bow, in heaven and on earth and under the earth, and every tongue confess that Jesus Christ is Lord, to the glory of God the Father. (Phil 2:8-11)**
> **To keep this command without spot or blame until the appearing of our Lord Jesus Christ, which God will bring about in his own time—God, the blessed and only Ruler, the King of kings and Lord of lords, who alone is immortal and who lives in unapproachable light, whom no one has seen or can see. To him be honor and might forever. Amen. (1 Tim 6:14-16)**

4 (19:23-24) **Coat—Gambling for Clothes**: the fourth event of the cross was the soldiers' gambling for His clothes. Note several points.

1. The insensitive, worldly-minded men were void of compassion. Jesus' mother Mary was standing by the cross, yet the soldiers showed no compassion whatsoever in sharing His belongings with her. (Cp. Ps.22:28.)

What good is it for a man to gain the whole world, yet forfeit his soul? (Mark 8:36)

2. The seamless coat or outer garment was one piece of cloth, woven from the top to the bottom. The garment or robe was identical to the robe of the High Priest. It symbolized Christ, the *Mediator*, the Pontifex, which in Latin means the bridge builder between God and man. (See note—Jn.12:44; cp. Ps.22:18.)

3. The event fulfilled Scripture (Ps.22:18). God was in charge of the cross, for it was the fulfillment of His purpose, of His great plan of salvation for man.

For there is one God and one mediator between God and men, the man Christ Jesus, who gave himself as a ransom for all men—the testimony given in its proper time. (1 Tim 2:5-6)

For this reason Christ is the mediator of a new covenant, that those who are called may receive the promised eternal inheritance—now that he has died as a ransom to set them free from the sins committed under the first covenant. (Heb 9:15)

For Christ did not enter a man-made sanctuary that was only a copy of the true one; he entered heaven itself, now to appear for us in God's presence. (Heb 9:24)

5 (19:25-27) **Caring for His Mother**: the fifth event of the cross was Jesus' great love for His mother. There are two touching scenes here.

1. The women at the cross. They were there at great risk. Jesus was...
- a revolutionary in the eyes of Rome
- a heretic in the eyes of the religionists

Any supporter of Jesus who stood at the cross ran the risk of ridicule and arrest. Nevertheless, the women stood there. Why? They loved Him. There is no other explanation: they simply loved Him. He had done so much for them that they were willing to stand by Him no matter the cost.

For Christ's love compels us, because we are convinced that one died for all, and therefore all died. And he died for all, that those who live should no longer live for themselves but for him who died for them and was raised again. (2 Cor 5:14-15)

Let us, then, go to him outside the camp, bearing the disgrace he bore. (Heb 13:13)

Then he said to them all: "If anyone would come after me, he must deny himself and take up his cross daily and follow me. (Luke 9:23)

2. Jesus' *care* of His mother. His thoughts were on others, not on Himself. Every fiber of His being existed for others, not for Himself. Even in death, His mind and being were set on taking care of others.
- ⇒ He was touched with the feelings of Mary's hurt and pain. In the last moments of His life upon earth, He made arrangements for her care.

⇒ He is touched with the feeling of our hurt and pain, so he takes care of us.

For we do not have a high priest who is unable to sympathize with our weaknesses, but we have one who has been tempted in every way, just as we are--yet was without sin. Let us then approach the throne of grace with confidence, so that we may receive mercy and find grace to help us in our time of need. (Heb 4:15-16)

6 (19:28-29) **Thirst**: the sixth event of the cross was Jesus' agonizing thirst and deliberate effort to fulfill Scripture.

Jesus said "I am thirsty." It had been hours since He had had a drink of water. But note: the stress of Jesus' words was not that He was physically thirsty. He was not complaining of thirst, not even asking for a drink. The stress was upon His fulfilling Scripture (Ps.69:21)...
- to show that Jesus *was truly* the Promised Messiah, the One who fulfilled Scripture.
- to show that Jesus' mind was *set on* fulfilling the Scriptures of the promised Messiah.
- to show that Jesus had come as the Promised Messiah to do the will of God, dying as the sacrifice for man. He refused to do God's will unthoughtfully, with deadened senses and a semi-conscious mind. He had work to do in sacrificing His life for man: He was to taste death for all men, and He would taste it in full consciousness, being as mentally alert as possible.

But we see Jesus, who was made a little lower than the angels, now crowned with glory and honor because he suffered death, so that by the grace of God he might taste death for everyone. (Heb 2:9)

With burnt offerings and sin offerings you were not pleased. Then I said, 'Here I am—it is written about me in the scroll— I have come to do your will, O God.'" And by that will, we have been made holy through the sacrifice of the body of Jesus Christ once for all. (Heb 10:6-7, 10)

This man was handed over to you by God's set purpose and foreknowledge; and you, with the help of wicked men, put him to death by nailing him to the cross. (Acts 2:23)

7 (19:30) **Jesus Christ, Death**: the seventh event of the cross was Jesus' great shout of victory. Salvation and reconciliation were now possible for man. Note two points.

1. Jesus cried, "It is finished." The Greek word (tetelestai) is the shout of victorious purpose. Jesus had completed His work, His mission, and His task. He was not crying the cry of a defeated martyr. He was crying the cry of a victorious conqueror.

2. Jesus gave up His spirit. It must always be remembered that Jesus *willingly* died. He willingly came to this moment of yielding and giving up His spirit unto death. Both Paul and Peter cover the Lord's work during the three days immediately following His death until the resurrection.

a. Paul says that on the cross this happened:

And having disarmed the powers and authorities, he made a public spectacle of them, triumphing over them by the cross. (Col 2:15. Cp. Eph.6:12)

b. Peter says that on the cross and after death this happened:

For Christ died for sins once for all, the righteous for the unrighteous, to bring you to God. He was put to death in the body but made alive by the Spirit, through whom also he went and preached to the spirits in prison who disobeyed long ago when God waited patiently in the days of Noah while the ark was being built. In it only a few people, eight in all, were saved through water, (1 Pet 3:18-20. See note— 1 Pt.3:18-22; Deeper Study # 1—3:19-20)

c. Paul says that after death this happened:

This is why it says: "When he ascended on high, he led captives in his train and gave gifts to men."(What does "he ascended" mean except that he also descended to the lower, earthly regions? He who descended is the very one who ascended higher than all the heavens, in order to fill the whole universe.) (Eph 4:8-10. See note—Eph.4:8-10)

8 (19:31-37) **The Spear**: the eighth event of the cross was that of the spear's being thrust into Jesus' side.

1. The religionists' concern for trifles was somewhat shocking. Note how religious ceremony and ritual consumed the mind of the religionists and actually became more important than the suffering of a man. But not so with Christ: He was hanging there because He was concerned for man. He felt for the suffering of man, so He had given His life for man.

For surely it is not angels he helps, but Abraham's descendants. For this reason he had to be made like his brothers in every way, in order that he might become a merciful and faithful high priest in service to God, and that he might make atonement for the sins of the people. Because he himself suffered when he was tempted, he is able to help those who are being tempted. (Heb 2:16-18)

2. Christ died prematurely, much sooner than a man was supposed to die from crucifixion. One of the reasons Rome chose crucifixion as the State's method of execution was its slow, lingering death. By law the criminal was to hang upon the cross until he died from thirst, hunger, and exposure. Sometimes a man lingered for days under the heat of the broiling sun or the cold of the winter nights. Such suffering struck fear into the hearts of the captured populace and restrained severe crime. Because Jesus died so quickly, He probably died from the pressure of a broken heart and of being separated from God in behalf of mankind (1 Pt.2:24; 3:18). Apparently His heart burst, and the blood mingled with the water-fluid of the pericardium surrounding the heart. The spear pierced the pericardium causing the blood and water to flow. Perhaps John stressed this incident because he saw the symbol of the two ordinances pictured: baptism and the Lord's Supper.

a. The water symbolized baptism, the washing of regeneration which Jesus was to bring.

But when the kindness and love of God our Savior appeared, he saved us, not because of righteous things we had done, but because of his mercy. He saved us through the washing of rebirth and renewal by the Holy Spirit, (Titus 3:4-5)

b. The blood symbolized the Lord's Supper, the partaking of the blood of Christ which cleanses men of their sins.

But if we walk in the light, as he is in the light, we have fellowship with one another, and the blood of Jesus, his Son, purifies us from all sin. (1 John 1:7)

3. John insisted upon the accuracy of his account. He said, "I saw it and gave testimony; my testimony is true." Note: He also said that God knew he was telling the truth. Why was this stressed? John told us: he stressed his truthfulness that "you also might believe" (see Deeper Study # 2— Jn.2:24).

Note another point. John said we are without excuse if we fail to believe. Why? Because the crucifixion and its events were a fulfillment of Scripture. (Cp. Ex.12:46; Num.9:12. Ps.34:20 predicts that not a bone of His body would be broken. Cp. Zech.12:10 which predicts the spear. Also cp. Is.53 which predicts so much of the crucifixion.)

But these are written that you may believe that Jesus is the Christ, the Son of God, and that by believing you may have life in his name. (John 20:31)

	E. The Burial: The Conquest of Fear, 19:38-42 (Mt.27:57-66; Mk.15:42-47; Lk.23:50-56)	night. Nicodemus brought a mixture of myrrh and aloes, about seventy-five pounds. 40 Taking Jesus' body, the two of them wrapped it, with the spices, in strips of linen. This was in accordance with Jewish burial customs. 41 At the place where Jesus was crucified, there was a garden, and in the garden a new tomb, in which no one had ever been laid. 42 Because it was the Jewish day of Preparation and since the tomb was nearby, they laid Jesus there.	a. He had come at night b. He was now changed by Jesus' death: Helped in the burial
1 Jesus' death conquered fear in a secret disciple: Joseph of Arimathea a. He had feared the Jews b. He was now changed by Jesus' death: He boldly requested the body **2 Jesus' death conquered fear in a cowardly disciple: Nicodemus**	38 Later, Joseph of Arimathea asked Pilate for the body of Jesus. Now Joseph was a disciple of Jesus, but secretly because he feared the Jews. With Pilate's permission, he came and took the body away. 39 He was accompanied by Nicodemus, the man who earlier had visited Jesus at		**3 Jesus' death stirred open commitment** a. Openly took the body b. Openly cared for the body c. Openly gave the best 1) A new tomb, never before used 2) The tomb was close to Calvary d. Openly buried Jesus—just before the Sabbath[DS1]

DIVISION XV

THE REVELATION OF JESUS, THE SUFFERING SAVIOR, 18:1-19:42

E. The Burial: The Conquest of Fear, 19:38-42

(19:38-42) **Introduction**: Jesus' death conquers fear for the genuine believer.
1. Jesus' death conquered fear in a secret disciple: Joseph of Arimathea (v.38).
2. Jesus' death conquered fear in a cowardly disciple: Nicodemus (v.39).
3. Jesus' death stirred open and unashamed commitment (v.40-42).

1 (19:38) **Joseph of Arimathea—Jesus Christ, Death—Confession**: Jesus' death conquered fear in a secret disciple, Joseph of Arimathaea. A revealing picture of Joseph is given in Scripture.

1. He was a counsellor, a senator, a member of the Sanhedrin, which was the ruling body of Israel. He was apparently…
   - highly educated
   - highly esteemed
   - well liked
   - very responsible
   - capable of leadership

2. He was a "good and just" man. He was a man…
   - of good quality
   - of high morals
   - of feelings
   - of compassion
   - of justice
   - of decision
   - of truth
   - of law

3. He was a man looking for the Messiah and the Kingdom of God (see notes—Lk.2:25-27; DEEPER STUDY # 3—Mt.19:23-24).

4. He was, however, a man who feared to stand up for Jesus. John said he was "a disciple of Jesus, but secretly because he feared the Jews" (Jn.19:38). Joseph probably had met Jesus and arranged meetings with Him when the Lord had visited Jerusalem, but he feared making a public profession. His position and prestige were at stake. His peers, the other rulers, opposed Jesus. He believed in Jesus, but out of fear he kept his discipleship a secret. Note: when the vote was taken to put Jesus to death, Joseph did abstain from voting, but he did not stand up for Christ. He did not participate; he simply remained silent.

Thought 1. How many are as Joseph was?
⇒ They are good people and just people.
⇒ They are believers.

⇒ But they fear what their friends and fellow workers will say. They fear the loss of position, prestige, promotion, acceptance, popularity, friends, job, income, livelihood.

If anyone is ashamed of me and my words, the Son of Man will be ashamed of him when he comes in his glory and in the glory of the Father and of the holy angels. (Luke 9:26)

"I tell you, my friends, do not be afraid of those who kill the body and after that can do no more. But I will show you whom you should fear: Fear him who, after the killing of the body, has power to throw you into hell. Yes, I tell you, fear him. (Luke 12:4-5)

For God did not give us a spirit of timidity, but a spirit of power, of love and of self-discipline. (2 Tim 1:7)

Fear of man will prove to be a snare, but whoever trusts in the LORD is kept safe. (Prov 29:25)

"I, even I, am he who comforts you. Who are you that you fear mortal men, the sons of men, who are but grass, (Isa 51:12)

5. He was a man changed by the death of Jesus. This is seen in two facts.
   a. Joseph actually "asked Pilate for the body of Jesus." This was a tremendous act of courage. The Romans either dumped the bodies of crucified criminals in the trash heaps or left the bodies hanging upon the cross for the vultures and animals to consume. The latter served as an example of criminal punishment to the public. Joseph also braved the threat of Pilate's reaction. Pilate was fed up with the *Jesus matter*. Jesus had proven to be very bothersome to him. He could have reacted severely against Joseph.
   b. Joseph risked the disfavor and discipline of the Sanhedrin. They were the ruling body who had instigated and condemned Jesus, and Joseph was a member of the council. There was no question, he

345

would face some harsh reaction from some of his fellow Sanhedrin members and from some of his closest friends.

The thing that turned Joseph from being a secret disciple to a bold disciple seems to be the phenomenal events surrounding the cross (the behavior and words of Jesus, the darkness, the earthquake, the torn veil). When Joseph witnessed all this, his mind connected the claims of Jesus with the Old Testament prophecies of the Messiah. Apparently Joseph saw the prophecies fulfilled in Jesus; therefore, he stepped forward braving all risks and taking his stand for Jesus. A remarkable courage stirred by the death of Jesus!

Thought 1. Every secret believer needs to study the cross of Christ. Really seeing the cross will turn any secret believer into a bold witness for Christ.

Thought 2. Joseph courageously asked to take care of the physical body of Christ. Today, the body of Christ is the church. We are to boldly step forward and take care of the church. There are times within the church when special needs demand that men be courageous and step forward to show care. In those times a fresh look at the cross will be helpful and can be used of God to stir us.

For I resolved to know nothing while I was with you except Jesus Christ and him crucified. (1 Cor 2:2)

Because we know that the one who raised the Lord Jesus from the dead will also raise us with Jesus and present us with you in his presence. All this is for your benefit, so that the grace that is reaching more and more people may cause thanksgiving to overflow to the glory of God. (2 Cor 4:14-15)

And he died for all, that those who live should no longer live for themselves but for him who died for them and was raised again. (2 Cor 5:15)

6. He was a man who cared deeply for Jesus. The words and acts of these two verses express care and tenderness and love and affection as well as courage and boldness. Joseph...
- took the body down from the cross.
- wrapped the body in linen.
- laid the body in a tomb in which no one had ever been laid.
- acted quickly, before the Sabbath began. Jesus died at 3 p.m. Friday afternoon (cp. Mk.15:33-34, 37). Friday was the day of preparation for the Sabbath. Work was forbidden on the Sabbath, so if anything was to be done with Jesus' body, it had to be done immediately. Only three hours remained for work. (See note—Mk.15:42 for more discussion.)

This act alone would leave no doubt about the effect of the cross upon Joseph. The cross changed his life. He was no longer a secret believer; he now demonstrated a public stand for Jesus.

Thought 1. Position, power, wealth, fame—none of these make us bold for Christ. Only true affection for Christ will make us bold, and only as we see the cross of Christ will affection for Christ be aroused.

Thought 2. Christ identified with men perfectly.
⇒ He lived as a man, but perfectly.
⇒ He died as a man, but perfectly (as the Ideal Man).
⇒ He was buried as a man, but perfectly.

He was assigned a grave with the wicked, and with the rich in his death, though he had done no violence, nor was any deceit in his mouth. (Isa 53:9)

For this reason he had to be made like his brothers in every way, in order that he might become a merciful and faithful high priest in service to God, and that he might make atonement for the sins of the people. (Heb 2:17)

Thought 3. God's own Son possessed nothing when He was on earth. Note two things.
⇒ Christ is the Savior of the poorest. He was born in a stable, and throughout His life He had no place of His own to lay His head (Mt.8:20; Lk.9:58). Even His tomb was a borrowed tomb.
⇒ The rich, nonetheless, can serve Him just as Joseph of Arimathaea did.

Jesus replied, "Foxes have holes and birds of the air have nests, but the Son of Man has no place to lay his head." (Luke 9:58)

Sell your possessions and give to the poor. Provide purses for yourselves that will not wear out, a treasure in heaven that will not be exhausted, where no thief comes near and no moth destroys. (Luke 12:33)

In everything I did, I showed you that by this kind of hard work we must help the weak, remembering the words the Lord Jesus himself said: 'It is more blessed to give than to receive.'" (Acts 20:35)

For you know the grace of our Lord Jesus Christ, that though he was rich, yet for your sakes he became poor, so that you through his poverty might become rich. (2 Cor 8:9)

This is how we know what love is: Jesus Christ laid down his life for us. And we ought to lay down our lives for our brothers. (1 John 3:16)

2 (19:39) **Nicodemus—Testimony—Jesus Christ, Death:** Jesus' death conquered fear in a cowardly disciple, Nicodemus. (See note—Jn.3:1-2 for discussion of Nicodemus.) Nicodemus was the leader who came to Jesus by night. He was probably the *Master Teacher*, the leading teacher of all Israel. Holding such a high position in the nation, he feared the leaders of Israel who opposed Jesus. The same fear that was in Joseph was in him: his position, authority, livelihood, and security were at stake; so he kept quiet, refusing to openly confess and take a stand for Jesus.

However, the cross apparently changed Nicodemus just as it had changed Joseph. Being the *Master Teacher* of Israel, Nicodemus, above everyone else, knew the prophetic Scriptures. Apparently, the events of the cross stirred him to begin making connections between the prophecies and Jesus' death. He had already been making connections between the prophecies and the words and works of Jesus. He did not fully understand, but the thoughts that were connecting Jesus and the prophecies would not leave his mind. At some point Nicodemus, although not understanding, knew that Jesus was the Messiah. He, Nicodemus, had failed the Lord when He was alive. He would not fail Him in His death. Perhaps not understanding the movement of his own heart toward Jesus, he boldly and courageously stepped forward to proclaim that He now believed and wanted all to know it. He walked into the stores that sold spices and bought huge amounts, the poundage fit for a king. The spices weighed about seventy pounds, an amount that only royalty could afford and use. Nicodemus wished to give the honor to his Lord which he should have given when his Lord was alive. He had been a proud man, but now he was a broken man. He had been a worldly man, a man who had chosen the world over the Lord, but no more. Broken in heart over his Lord's death, he would now step forth in faith and love to do what he could.

Thought 1. By purchasing the spices for the Lord's body and helping in the burial of Jesus, Nicodemus took his stand for Christ. From that point on, everyone knew he cared for and loved Jesus. What a living example of courage for us as we move about the business establishments of the world.

> But they kept quiet because on the way they had argued about who was the greatest. Sitting down, Jesus called the Twelve and said, "If anyone wants to be first, he must be the very last, and the servant of all." He took a little child and had him stand among them. Taking him in his arms, he said to them, "Whoever welcomes one of these little children in my name welcomes me; and whoever welcomes me does not welcome me but the one who sent me." (Mark 9:34-37)

3 (19:40-42) **Decision—Commitment**: Jesus' death stirred open and unashamed commitment. Both Joseph and Nicodemus had hesitated in trusting Jesus Christ as their Savior. Out of fear they had acted cowardly, keeping their thoughts about Jesus to themselves. But now they showed a courage and a boldness unmatched by all others. They alone demonstrated an open, unashamed commitment to Jesus, and they did it when the apostles themselves deserted Jesus.

1. They openly took the body of Jesus from the cross. In doing so, they risked the disfavor of the Sanhedrin who had instigated and condemned Jesus. Both Joseph and Nicodemus were opposing their fellow members of the council. There was no question that they would face some harsh reaction from some of their fellow Sanhedrin members and from some of their closest friends.

2. They openly cared for Jesus' body. They wound it in strips of linen with the spices.

3. They openly gave Jesus the best. They gave Him a tomb never before used. Apparently it was in a cemetary on Mount Calvary, the mountain where Jesus was crucified. The tomb had been bought by Joseph for his own use (Mt.27:60). This act alone would leave no question about the two men's taking their stand for Jesus.

4. They openly buried Jesus just before the Sabbath. This eliminated them from taking part in the great Passover Feast, and this was never done, even for the most serious reasons. Joseph and Nicodemus, by handling Jesus' body, were considered defiled for seven days for having come in contact with a corpse. Once defiled, Jewish law forbade a person from taking part in Jewish ceremonies.

Simply stated, Joseph and Nicodemus, who had been secret disciples, now stepped forward making an unashamed commitment to Jesus. Everyone would know that they stepped forward and took care of Jesus' body. Joseph even gave his own tomb to Jesus. They were risking their positions, esteem, wealth, and even their lives by making such a pronounced commitment to the affairs of Jesus.

Note the strength of their commitment: no one from Jesus' family or from among His own disciples had stepped forward to claim the Lord's body—but these two men did.

Thought 1. The courage demonstrated by Joseph and Nicodemus is desperately needed by all.

1) The courage to make an unashamed commitment to Christ.
2) The courage to risk all for Christ, even if it does cost us our position, esteem, wealth, and life.
3) The courage to unashamedly care for the body of Christ, His church and its affairs.
4) The courage to be an unashamed witness for Christ, no matter the cost.

> "Whoever acknowledges me before men, I will also acknowledge him before my Father in heaven. But whoever disowns me before men, I will disown him before my Father in heaven. (Mat 10:32-33)
> "I tell you, whoever acknowledges me before men, the Son of Man will also acknowledge him before the angels of God. (Luke 12:8)
> That if you confess with your mouth, "Jesus is Lord," and believe in your heart that God raised him from the dead, you will be saved. For it is with your heart that you believe and are justified, and it is with your mouth that you confess and are saved. (Rom 10:9-10)
> If we endure, we will also reign with him. If we disown him, he will also disown us; (2 Tim 2:12)
> No one who denies the Son has the Father; whoever acknowledges the Son has the Father also. (1 John 2:23)
> If anyone acknowledges that Jesus is the Son of God, God lives in him and he in God. (1 John 4:15)

DEEPER STUDY # 1

(19:42) **Sabbath—Jesus Christ, Burial**: the need for haste was threefold.

1. The Sabbath or Saturday, the day of worship for Jews, began at 6 p.m. (Jewish days began at 6 p.m. and ran until 6 p.m. the next night, that is, from sundown to sundown.) Strict Jewish law said that once the Sabbath began, no work could be done including the burial of the dead.

2. Jesus died at 3 p.m. in the afternoon (cp. Mk.15:33-34, 37). Therefore He died on Friday, the day of preparation for the Sabbath. If anything was to be done with Jesus' body, it had to be done immediately and quickly. Only three hours remained for work.

3. The Romans either dumped the bodies of crucified criminals in the trash heaps or left the bodies hanging upon the cross for the vultures and animals to consume. The latter served as an example of criminal punishment to the public. If Jesus' body were not removed quickly, within these three hours, the fate of His body was set. The Romans would not care what happened to Him, and no Jew could remove Him until the Sabbath was over.

	CHAPTER 20 **XVI. THE REVELATION OF JESUS, THE RISEN LORD, 20:1-21:23** **A. Event 1: The Great Discovery—The Empty Tomb, 20:1-10**	4 Both were running, but the other disciple outran Peter and reached the tomb first. 5 He bent over and looked in at the strips of linen lying there but did not go in. 6 Then Simon Peter, who was behind him, arrived and went into the tomb. He saw the strips of linen lying there,	a. They ran to the tomb b. John glanced in: Saw the strips of linen c. Peter entered: Saw the strips of linen

1 Mary's unquestioning discovery: The unsealed tomb^{DS1}
a. She visited early
b. She saw the stone rolled back
c. She ran to Peter
d. She revealed an unquestioning love: "They have taken the Lord"
	Early on the first day of the week, while it was still dark, Mary Magdalene went to the tomb and saw that the stone had been removed from the entrance.
	2 So she came running to Simon Peter and the other disciple, the one Jesus loved, and said, "They have taken the Lord out of the tomb, and we don't know where they have put him!"
		7 As well as the burial cloth that had been around Jesus' head. The cloth was folded up by itself, separate from the linen.
		8 Finally the other disciple, who had reached the tomb first, also went inside. He saw and believed.
		9 (They still did not understand from Scripture that Jesus had to rise from the dead.)
			3 John's thoughtful discovery: The undisturbed strips of linen
			a. The strips of linen
			  1) They were lying "undisturbed"
			  2) The head wrapping was still folded
			b. The immediate belief
			  1) He saw & believed
			  2) He finally understood the Scripture

2 Peter & John's shocking discovery: The strips of linen	3 So Peter and the other disciple started for the tomb.	10 Then the disciples went back to their homes,	

DIVISION XVI

THE REVELATION OF JESUS, THE RISEN LORD, 20:1-21:23

A. Event 1: The Great Discovery—The Empty Tomb, 20:1-10

(20:1-10) **Introduction—Resurrection, Evidence of**: in studying John's account, it must be remembered that John was writing an historical account. He was not interested in giving insurmountable evidence for the resurrection. His interest was twofold: (1) to give the evidence that led him to immediately understand and believe, and (2) to give enough evidence to lead anyone to immediate belief—if a person is willing to believe. He was interested in giving enough evidence to make anyone's faith viable and respectable. Now having said this, John's record of Jesus' resurrection is a strong historical account of the event. To an honest, objective, and good heart, the evidence is convincing (Lk.8:15).

1. The fact that morality is the point of John's gospel eliminates any possibility of his fabricating a lie, especially a lie of such immoral proportions.

2. The description of so many little details, details that are so human, says that the phenomenal event is an event that actually took place. Such human-like details could never be built around an event whose main point was a fable. For instance, Peter and John's running and John's outrunning Peter; Mary's human response of frantic bewilderment; the young author's fearing and hesitating to enter a tomb; the author's believing without physical fact and admitting that his belief was not based upon an understanding of Scripture. There are, of course, many other examples that point to the event actually taking place.

3. The head wrapping is strong evidence for the resurrection. Only the head piece is actually said to be still folded up by itself. The other pieces are assumed to be still folded up because of the phrase "separate from the linen." Although the phrase substantially supports the assumption, it is only an assumption. The point is this: if John or any other author were fabricating a case for such a phenomenal

event as the resurrection, He would state explicitly that the body wrappings along with the head wrappings were still folded up—building evidence upon evidence.

4. The changed lives of the Lord's disciples are indisputable evidence. It is psychological evidence. From seemingly *irreversible despondency* and from *being hunted down* like insurrectionist dogs, they became new creatures of enthusiasm and motivation. They were propelled by a dynamic power and bold courage. Within thirty days they were seen proclaiming a risen Christ from the very spot where their lives were being threatened. They were preaching to the very people who were seeking to arrest and execute them. Only one thing could cause them to adopt this strategy: the Lord had indeed risen, and He had implanted within them a dynamic new power never before experienced by man.

In discussing evidences, we must remember that God *through inspiration* has not formulated the Scripture to prove anything. God proclaims in Scripture that He *is* (exists), that He is love, and that He has shown His love supremely by sending His own Son to save a lost and dying world. What God wants from us is love and belief, love for the Lord Jesus and belief in the supreme power of a loving God. This is just the point of the resurrection account. We are to believe because we love even as Mary and John loved. (See note 2—Mt.28:1; Jn.20:7-10; cp. Heb.11:6; 1 Jn.3:23.)

1. Mary's unquestioning discovery: the unsealed tomb (v.1-2).
2. Peter and John's shocking discovery: the strips of linen (v.3-6).
3. John's thoughtful discovery: the undisturbed strips of linen (v.7-10).

1 (20:1-2) **Mary Magdalene**: Mary's unquestioning discovery, the unsealed tomb. Note four facts.

1. Mary visited the tomb early when it was still dark. Matthew actually says it was "the end of the sabbath," meaning between 3-6 a.m. (Mt.28:1). This reveals three significant facts.

a. Jesus arose before dawn, before the sun arose on Sunday morning. This was significant to the early Christian believers, so significant that they broke away from the common division of the week which began with the Sabbath or Saturday. They began to count their days beginning with Sunday, the day of the resurrection of their Lord (cp. Acts 20:7; 1 Cor.16:2).

b. Jesus arose on the first day of the week, on Sunday morning. This means that He had been in the grave for three days just as He had said (Mt.12:40; 16:21; 17:23; 20:19; Mk.9:31; 10:34; Lk.9:22; 18:33; 24:7, 46). His arising from the dead was a triumph, a conquest over death. Death reigns no more. Its rule has been broken (1 Cor.15:55-56; 2 Cor.1:9-10; 2 Tim.1:10; Heb.2:9, 14-15).

c. Again, Jesus arose on the first day of the week, Sunday morning. He was in the grave on the Sabbath, unable to observe the laws governing the great season of the Passover and the Sabbath. He was dead to the law and its observances. This is symbolic of the *identification* believers gain in Christ. *In Christ's death* believers become dead to the law (see note—Ro.7:4; Mt.5:17-18).

2. Mary saw the stone rolled back from the tomb (see DEEPER STUDY # 1—Jn.20:1 for discussion).

Thought 1. This is strong evidence for the resurrection. The stone was not rolled back for the benefit of Christ, but for the witnesses to the resurrection. When Christ arose, He was in His resurrection body, the spiritual body of the spiritual dimension which has no physical bounds. He did not need the stone rolled back to leave the tomb, for material substance has no bearing on spiritual substance. However, the witnesses needed to enter the tomb to see the truth (see outline and notes—Jn.10:1-10).

3. Mary ran to Peter. This is important, for it shows that Peter was still the accepted leader. What a man of courageous stature and moral strength! Surely his cowardice had been broadcast and well-rumored, yet he repented and picked himself up to resume his task.

4. Mary revealed an unquestioning love: "They have taken the Lord out of the tomb!" Mary is a supreme example of one who loves and believes, although she did not understand. She was one of the last to leave Jesus at the cross (cp. Mk.15:40, 47); one of the first to attend the tomb; and one who still called Him "Lord." Her belief was a belief of love—not a belief based upon intellect or understanding. She knew what Jesus had done for her, and she loved Him for it. Jesus was her Lord, dead or alive (cp. Jn.20:13f).

> "As the Father has loved me, so have I loved you. Now remain in my love. (John 15:9)
>
> Then Jesus told him, "Because you have seen me, you have believed; blessed are those who have not seen and yet have believed." (John 20:29)

> Grace to all who love our Lord Jesus Christ with an undying love. (Eph 6:24)
>
> Though you have not seen him, you love him; and even though you do not see him now, you believe in him and are filled with an inexpressible and glorious joy, (1 Pet 1:8)
>
> Keep yourselves in God's love as you wait for the mercy of our Lord Jesus Christ to bring you to eternal life. (Jude 1:21)
>
> Love the LORD your God with all your heart and with all your soul and with all your strength. (Deu 6:5)

DEEPER STUDY # 1

(20:1) **Tomb**: In Jesus' day tombs were closed by rolling a huge cartwheel-like stone in front of the entrance. They were almost impossible to remove. A deep slanting groove was hewn out of the rock at the base of the entrance for the circular stone to rest in. The stone usually weighed several tons. Such precautions were essential because there were so many tombs ransacked in those days of poverty.

The tomb was further secured by being sealed. When it was necessary to seal a tomb, the huge stone was cemented to the entrance walls or else some type of rope or binding was wrapped around the entrance stone and fastened to both sides of the tomb. Then the binding was cemented with a hardening clay or wax-like substance. In the case of some burials, usually political figures, the seal of the Emperor was also attached to the walls of the entrance. This was to strike fear of Roman retaliation against any intruder. (Cp. Mt.27:66.)

In the case of Jesus' tomb, further precautions were taken by placing a patrol to guard against any foul play. This guard consisted of a *large number* of men (Mt.28:4, 11f).

2 (20:3-6) **Jesus Christ, Resurrection of**: Peter and John's shocking discovery. They discovered the empty tomb *and the strips of linen*. They "ran" to the tomb. John outran Peter. When John arrived at the tomb, he just glanced in and noticed the strips of linen. Peter actually entered the tomb. He, too, noticed the strips of linen. They both knew the significance. If the body had been removed by the authorities or stolen by someone, the strips of linen would have been taken with the body or left in a disheveled mess, thrown someplace on the floor. From the description and the impact of the event upon the two disciples, neither one discussed his thoughts with the other, not while standing there at that time.

Thought 1. Note a critical point. If a man wishes to discover the empty tomb, he must get up and *go forth* to look at it. He must investigate, and then he will see. Getting up and *going forth* is the only way a man can ever discover the risen Lord. Resting in the comforts and lethargy of this world will never help a man find Jesus.

> You diligently study the Scriptures because you think that by them you possess eternal life. These are the Scriptures that testify about me, (John 5:39)
>
> Now the Bereans were of more noble character than the Thessalonians, for they received the message with great eagerness and examined the Scriptures every day to see if what Paul said was true. (Acts 17:11)

For he vigorously refuted the Jews in public debate, proving from the Scriptures that Jesus was the Christ. (Acts 18:28)

The gospel he promised beforehand through his prophets in the Holy Scriptures regarding his Son, who as to his human nature was a descendant of David, and who through the Spirit of holiness was declared with power to be the Son of God by his resurrection from the dead: Jesus Christ our Lord. (Rom 1:2-4)

And do this, understanding the present time. The hour has come for you to wake up from your slumber, because our salvation is nearer now than when we first believed. The night is nearly over; the day is almost here. So let us put aside the deeds of darkness and put on the armor of light. (Rom 13:11-12)

For what I received I passed on to you as of first importance : that Christ died for our sins according to the Scriptures, that he was buried, that he was raised on the third day according to the Scriptures, (1 Cor 15:3-4)

We want each of you to show this same diligence to the very end, in order to make your hope sure. We do not want you to become lazy, but to imitate those who through faith and patience inherit what has been promised. (Heb 6:11-12)

Therefore, dear friends, since you already know this, be on your guard so that you may not be carried away by the error of lawless men and fall from your secure position. (2 Pet 3:17)

Whatever your hand finds to do, do it with all your might, for in the grave, where you are going, there is neither working nor planning nor knowledge nor wisdom. (Eccl 9:10)

3 20:7-10) **Resurrection—John—Strips of linen**: John's thoughtful discovery. He discovered the undisturbed strips of linen. Note two significant points.

1. Note the strips of linen. Standing outside while Peter was inside the tomb, John's mind was apparently whirling, pondering, wondering, and thinking. Then suddenly it dawned upon him: the strips of linen were lying undisturbed. The Greek word "wrapped together" (entetuligmenon) is the verb which is used for actually the winding linens around a body for burial. The Greek word is saying that the linens were still folded up, wrapped just like they would be wrapped around a body—as if the body had just evaporated. They were not dishevelled or disarranged. This says at least four things.

　a. It would be impossible to extract a body from its wrappings and leave them in such good order.

　b. The wrappings would have been taken with the body if the body had been removed.

　c. The wrappings would have been dishevelled and disarranged and scattered if thieves had ransacked the tomb.

　d. The wrappings (under any circumstances that might be conceived in removing the body) could never be placed in the exact spot on the rock slab where the body lay. Yet, this is just how they were lying according to the Greek text. It was this that led John to an immediate belief.

2. Note John's immediate belief. John did not believe because of insurmountable evidence but because he loved Jesus. Seeing the strips of linen penetrated John's mind, and he remembered Jesus' prophecy that He would arise. John realized what had happened and he believed.

This is the point of this account of the strips of linen and of the way the account is recorded. This is also the point of the resurrection account. A loving God wants love—a heart full of love. He wants a person to simply believe that God *is* (exists) and that God is a rewarder of them that love Him (Heb.11:6).

And without faith it is impossible to please God, because anyone who comes to him must believe that he exists and that he rewards those who earnestly seek him. (Heb 11:6)

"For God so loved the world that he gave his one and only Son, that whoever believes in him shall not perish but have eternal life. For God did not send his Son into the world to condemn the world, but to save the world through him. (John 3:16-17)

This is how we know what love is: Jesus Christ laid down his life for us. And we ought to lay down our lives for our brothers. (1 John 3:16)

And so we know and rely on the love God has for us. God is love. Whoever lives in love lives in God, and God in him. (1 John 4:16)

We love because he first loved us. (1 John 4:19)

	B. Event 2: The Great Re-cognition—Jesus Appears to Mary, 20:11-18 (Mt.28:1-15; Mk.16:1-11;Lk.24:1-49)	15 "Woman," he said, "why are you crying? Who is it you are looking for?" Thinking he was the gardener, she said, "Sir, if you have carried him away, tell me where you have put him, and I will get him."	b. A startling question: Why weep? Who is it you are seeking? c. A false identity 1) Because of her tears 2) Because she faced in the wrong direction—into the grave d. The great recognition
1 Mary returned to the tomb a. Weeping convulsively b. Stooping, she looked in 2 The first startling sight: Two angels[DS1] a. The question of the angels b. Mary's loving devotion & confession: "My Lord" 3 The second startling sight: Jesus Himself a. Mary's sense of another person—turned to see	11 But Mary stood outside the tomb crying. As she wept, she bent over to look into the tomb 12 And saw two angels in white, seated where Jesus' body had been, one at the head and the other at the foot. 13 They asked her, "Woman, why are you crying?" "They have taken my Lord away," she said, "and I don't know where they have put him." 14 At this, she turned around and saw Jesus standing there, but she did not realize that it was Jesus.	16 Jesus said to her, "Mary." She turned toward him and cried out in Aramaic, "Rabboni!" (which means Teacher). 17 Jesus said, "Do not hold on to me, for I have not yet returned to the Father. Go instead to my brothers and tell them, 'I am returning to my Father and your Father, to my God and your God.'" 18 Mary Magdalene wentto the disciples with the news: "I have seen the Lord!" And she told them that he had said these things to her.	4 The third startling sight: The new commission a. Stop clinging to me—selfishly b. Go—tell your great discovery

DIVISION XVI

THE REVELATION OF JESUS, THE RISEN LORD, 20:1-21:23

B. Event 2: The Great Recognition—Jesus Appears to Mary, 20:11-18

(20:11-18) **Introduction**: this is one of the most precious events in history. It was our Lord's first appearance after His resurrection; it was an appearance to a woman who had been saved from the depths of human depravity. It was the appearance to Mary Magdalene, one who loved Jesus with the deepest of loves because of what He had done for her.

1. Mary returned to the tomb (v.11).
2. The first startling sight: two angels (v.12-13).
3. The second startling sight: Jesus Himself (v.14-16).
4. The third startling sight: the new commission (v.17-18).

1 (20:11) **Jesus Christ, Resurrection—Mary Magdalene**: Mary returned to the tomb. Just when is not known, but she probably followed immediately behind Peter and John as they ran to the tomb. When they left, she remained behind. She was weeping convulsively. Seeing Peter and John enter the tomb gave her courage to finally stoop down and look in. What Mary began to experience would revolutionize her life. She could not ask for more.

Thought 1. Two things can revolutionize a man's life.
1) Lingering at the empty tomb of Jesus. Too many rush by His tomb, never thinking, never giving any thought to its meaning.
2) Seeking the truth of the empty tomb, what it means to life and to the world in all its corruption and need.

2 (20:12-13) **Jesus Christ, Resurrection—Angels**: Mary's first startling sight—she saw two angels. Note two points. (See DEEPER STUDY # 1, Angels—Heb.1:4-14.)
1. The two angels were sitting right where Jesus' body had been lying. Angels are messengers of God; they are the ministering spirits of God, servants sent from heaven to carry out His will. On this particular occasion, they were

sent to add to the spectacular significance of the resurrection and to comfort Mary in her grief. They had been sent to her in particular, for they had not been in the tomb when Peter and John looked in. They were clothed in white. Matthew added...

- like "lightning" (visible, quick, startling, striking, frightening, brilliant)
- like "snow" (white, pure, glistening)

The fact that they were dressed in white apparently symbolizes the holiness and purity of God from whose presence they had come.

> **Exalt the LORD our God and worship at his holy mountain, for the LORD our God is holy. (Psa 99:9)**
> **And they were calling to one another: "Holy, holy, holy is the LORD Almighty; the whole earth is full of his glory." (Isa 6:3)**
> **Your eyes are too pure to look on evil; you cannot tolerate wrong. Why then do you tolerate the treacherous? Why are you silent while the wicked swallow up those more righteous than themselves? (Hab 1:13)**
> **Since we have these promises, dear friends, let us purify ourselves from everything that contaminates body and spirit, perfecting holiness out of reverence for God. (2 Cor 7:1)**
> **Make every effort to live in peace with all men and to be holy; without holiness no one will see the Lord. (Heb 12:14)**
> **for it is written: "Be holy, because I am holy." (1 Pet 1:16)**
> **Since everything will be destroyed in this way, what kind of people ought you to be? You ought to live holy and godly lives (2 Pet 3:11)**

2. Mary's loving devotion and confession should touch the heart and life of every believer. (See note, Mary Magdalene, pt.4—Jn.20:1-2 for discussion.)

No, the Father himself loves you because you have loved me and have believed that I came from God. (John 16:27)
Grace to all who love our Lord Jesus Christ with an undying love. (Eph 6:24)
Though you have not seen him, you love him; and even though you do not see him now, you believe in him and are filled with an inexpressible and glorious joy, (1 Pet 1:8)
Keep yourselves in God's love as you wait for the mercy of our Lord Jesus Christ to bring you to eternal life. (Jude 1:21)
Love the LORD your God with all your heart and with all your soul and with all your strength. (Deu 6:5)
"Whoever acknowledges me before men, I will also acknowledge him before my Father in heaven. (Mat 10:32)
If anyone acknowledges that Jesus is the Son of God, God lives in him and he in God. (1 John 4:15)

DEEPER STUDY # 1
(20:12) **Jesus Christ, Resurrection—Strips of Linen**: the two angels were sitting, one where the head of Jesus had lain and the other where his feet had lain. Now note a question. How did Mary know where the feet and head had lain? There were two possible ways.
1. She was possibly one of the women who had followed Joseph of Arimathaea and Nicodemus when they buried Jesus (Lk.23:55).
2. She could see the strips of linen lying still folded up just as they had been when they were wrapped around Jesus (see note—Jn.20:7-10).

3 (20:14-16) **Jesus Christ, Resurrection**: the second startling sight. Mary saw Jesus Himself. Note four significant events.
1. There was a startling sense. While Mary was still speaking to the angels, she sensed another presence behind her. She immediately turned around and saw Jesus standing there, but she did not know that it was Jesus.
2. There was a startling question: "Why are you crying? Who is it you are looking for?" Now note: a graveyard is where one weeps and seeks for a grave.
The point is this: Mary was seeking a dead Savior, a Savior who was as all other men are, frail and powerless to do anything about life and death, eternity and heaven. Her whole being was focused upon a grave where her dead Savior was lying. Mary was living as the world lives, as a "foreigner[s] to the covenants of the promise, without hope, and without God in the world" (Eph.2:12).

Brothers, we do not want you to be ignorant about those who fall asleep, or to grieve like the rest of men, who have no hope. (1 Th 4:13)
my God. My soul is downcast within me; therefore I will remember you from the land of the Jordan, the heights of Hermon—from Mount Mizar. (Psa 42:6)

I sink in the miry depths, where there is no foothold. I have come into the deep waters; the floods engulf me. (Psa 69:2)
When I tried to understand all this, it was oppressive to me (Psa 73:16)
As you do not know the path of the wind, or how the body is formed in a mother's womb, so you cannot understand the work of God, the Maker of all things. (Eccl 11:5)

3. There was the false identity. Mary thought the man was the gardener and that perhaps he had removed the body for some reason. Note why she had not yet recognized Jesus.
⇒ Mary's eyes were full of tears and her head was bowed low in the normal shyness that arises in such scenes.
⇒ Mary was facing in the wrong direction—into the grave. She had turned back around to face where the body had been lying (v.14, cp. v.16).

Thought 1. There is a message here for everyone. We need to fix our eyes upon Jesus in confronting death. Too often, we see the dead and become so wrapped up in grief that we forget the risen Lord and the great hope He gives us (Jn.3:16; 5:24; 14:2-3). There is no question about Jesus' emphasis here. This is the message He was wishing to convey to Mary. There was no need for such convulsive weeping. Weep and grieve, yes, but there is a limit. Mary could have and should have seen Him sooner.

He will swallow up death forever. The Sovereign LORD will wipe away the tears from all faces; he will remove the disgrace of his people from all the earth. The LORD has spoken. (Isa 25:8)
"I tell you the truth, whoever hears my word and believes him who sent me has eternal life and will not be condemned; he has crossed over from death to life. (John 5:24)
When the perishable has been clothed with the imperishable, and the mortal with immortality, then the saying that is written will come true: "Death has been swallowed up in victory." (1 Cor 15:54)
but it has now been revealed through the appearing of our Savior, Christ Jesus, who has destroyed death and has brought life and immortality to light through the gospel. (2 Tim 1:10)
He will wipe every tear from their eyes. There will be no more death or mourning or crying or pain, for the old order of things has passed away." (Rev 21:4)

4. There was the great recognition. This was one of those dramatic moments that exceeds the ability of words to express. Only two words were spoken:
⇒ "Mary"
⇒ "Rabboni"
Note three points.
a. Mary recognized Jesus not by sight, but by His voice and the word spoken by Him. So it is with us today: we know the Lord by His Word and His Spirit.

"You are a king, then!" said Pilate. Jesus answered, "You are right in saying I am a king. In fact, for this reason I was born, and for this I came into the world, to testify to the truth. Everyone on the side of truth listens to me." (John 18:37;cp. Jn.17:17)

Here I am! I stand at the door and knock. If anyone hears my voice and opens the door, I will come in and eat with him, and he with me. (Rev 3:20)

But he who unites himself with the Lord is one with him in spirit. (1 Cor 6:17)

set his seal of ownership on us, and put his Spirit in our hearts as a deposit, guaranteeing what is to come. (2 Cor 1:22; cp. 2 Cor 5:5)

For through him we both have access to the Father by one Spirit. (Eph 2:18; cp.Eph1:13-14)

We know that we live in him and he in us, because he has given us of his Spirit. (1 John 4:13)

b. Jesus called Mary by name; she was one of His sheep. He knows His sheep by name and His sheep know the sound of His voice (His Word).

When he has brought out all his own, he goes on ahead of them, and his sheep follow him because they know his voice. (John 10:4)

"I am the good shepherd; I know my sheep and my sheep know me— (John 10:14)

I have other sheep that are not of this sheep pen. I must bring them also. They too will listen to my voice, and there shall be one flock and one shepherd. (John 10:16)

My sheep listen to my voice; I know them, and they follow me. (John 10:27)

Here I am! I stand at the door and knock. If anyone hears my voice and opens the door, I will come in and eat with him, and he with me. (Rev 3:20)

c. Mary called Jesus "Rabboni," *My Teacher*, not "Rabbi" (Master). Rabboni (Rabbou-nei), My Teacher, was a title of more respect and honor than just Rabbi. She was acknowledging Him to be her supreme Teacher, the One who was due all her honor and respect, loyalty and allegiance. She was acknowledging that He was her Teacher and she was His humble follower (disciple).

"Therefore let all Israel be assured of this: God has made this Jesus, whom you crucified, both Lord and Christ." (Acts 2:36)

God exalted him to his own right hand as Prince and Savior that he might give repentance and forgiveness of sins to Israel. (Acts 5:31)

God, who has called you into fellowship with his Son Jesus Christ our Lord, is faithful. (1 Cor 1:9)

Yet for us there is but one God, the Father, from whom all things came and for whom we live; and there is but one Lord, Jesus Christ, through whom all things came and through whom we live. (1 Cor 8:6)

4 (20:17-18) **Commission—Witnessing**: the third startling sight was Mary's new commission. Apparently Mary was so full of joy and excitement that she just reached out to embrace Jesus. Immediately Jesus fired the command: "Do not hold on to me" (me mou haptou).

The words are present action, *stop clinging to me*. Mary's great love seemingly had one flaw. She wanted to revel in her love for the Lord and in the fellowship that that love brought her. She was reaching out to clutch and to cling to His body (physically), but in doing so, she was missing the point: His cross and resurrection had created a totally new relationship. He was no longer just her Rabboni, her Teacher. He was her Lord and God (cp. Jn.20:28). He was soon to ascend back to the Father, so she must not waste time clutching and clinging. She must run and tell her great discovery. The Teacher was now her Lord and God, for He had created a new spiritual relationship with men.

So from now on we regard no one from a worldly point of view. Though we once regarded Christ in this way, we do so no longer. Therefore, if anyone is in Christ, he is a new creation; the old has gone, the new has come! (2 Cor 5:16-17)

That God was reconciling the world to himself in Christ, not counting men's sins against them. And he has committed to us the message of reconciliation. We are therefore Christ's ambassadors, as though God were making his appeal through us. We implore you on Christ's behalf: Be reconciled to God. God made him who had no sin to be sin for us, so that in him we might become the righteousness of God. (2 Cor 5:19-21)

	C. Event 3: The Great Charter of the Church—Jesus Appears to the Disciples, 20:19-23 (Mk.16:14; Lk.24:36-49)	showed them his hands and side. The disciples were overjoyed when they saw the Lord. 21 Again Jesus said, "Peace be with you! As the Father has sent me, I am sending you."	**b. His wounds: Evidence** **c. His effect: Unbelievable joy & gladness when they saw Him**[DS2,3]
1 The disciples were hiding in fear a. Was the same day: At night b. Discussed reports[DS1] c. Jesus appeared suddenly **2 Subject 1: The risen Lord— His presence was very real** a. His message: Peace	19 On the evening of that first day of the week, when the disciples were together, with the doors locked for fear of the Jews, Jesus came and stood among them and said, "Peace be with you!" 20 After he said this, he	22 And with that he breathed on them and said, "Receive the Holy Spirit. 23 If you forgive anyone his sins, they are forgiven; if you do not forgive them, they are not forgiven."	**3 Subject 2: The great commission** **4 Subject 3: The Holy Spirit** a. The endument or giving of the Spirit[DS4] b. The authority[DS5]

DIVISION XVI

THE REVELATION OF JESUS, THE RISEN LORD, 20:1-21:23

C. Event 3: The Great Charter of the Church—Jesus Appears to the Disciples, 20:19-23

(20:19-23) Introduction: this was the first appearance of Jesus to His disciples as a group after His resurrection. What would He say and talk about? What would be the topic of conversation and the subjects covered? Whatever He chose to say would be of critical importance. It is this that John focuses upon: the subjects and the topics discussed when Jesus first appeared to the disciples.

1. The disciples were hiding in fear (v.19).
2. Subject 1: the risen Lord—His presence was very real (v.19-20).
3. Subject 2: the great commission (v.21).
4. Subject 3: the Holy Spirit (v.22-23).

1 (20:19) **Disciples, Fear of—Jesus Christ, Resurrection**: the disciples were hiding for fear of the Jews. They were behind locked doors, probably in the upper room of the same house where Jesus had met with them just a few days earlier. They were scared and fearful of the authorities who had vented so much wrath and vengeance upon their Lord. There was the imminent danger they could be arrested and imprisoned or executed as revolutionaries just as Jesus had been.

Note that it was Sunday, the very day that Jesus had arisen, and it was nighttime. Luke tells us there were numerous reports that Jesus had been raised from the dead. (See DEEPER STUDY # 1—Jn.20:19.)

Remember: the doors were locked. Suddenly, unexpectedly, Jesus stood before them—right in their midst. He immediately began to discuss the three subjects of the outline.

DEEPER STUDY # 1

(20:19) **Jesus' Resurrection—Reports**: the reports would be about the empty tomb and strips of linen discovered by Peter and John (Jn.20:6f), the appearances to Mary Magdalene (Jn.20:14f), Peter (1 Cor.15:4), the women (Mt.28:1; Mk.16:1f), and the two walking to Emmaus (Lk.24:1).

---

2 (20:19-20) **Jesus Christ, Resurrection**: the first subject was the risen Lord Himself. His presence was very real. His sudden appearance shook and frightened the disciples. They thought they were seeing a vision or a spirit (Lk.24:36-37). The first thing Jesus did was prove that it

was really He. He did this by doing two things. (Also see DEEPER STUDY # 1—Jn.21:1 for more discussion.)

1. He used the simple day-to-day greeting that was common among Jews, "Peace be with you." Using the greeting so familiar to the disciples would help to put them at ease. The fact that He spoke just as He had always spoken would give them some indication that it was really He and not just a vision or a spirit.

> **But now in Christ Jesus you who once were far away have been brought near through the blood of Christ. For he himself is our peace, who has made the two one and has destroyed the barrier, the dividing wall of hostility, (Eph 2:13-14)**
> **Peace I leave with you; my peace I give you. I do not give to you as the world gives. Do not let your hearts be troubled and do not be afraid. (John 14:27)**
> **"I have told you these things, so that in me you may have peace. In this world you will have trouble. But take heart! I have overcome the world." (John 16:33)**

2. He showed them His wounds. This must have been a dramatic and touching moment, a moment that just exploded the minds of the disciples. Jesus probably moved around to each of them, allowing each one to see the wounds. This convinced the disciples. They knew for sure…

- that they were not seeing a vision or a spirit.
- that this was His body, the body of their wonderful Lord, the very same Jesus whom they had known before His crucifixion.

> **That which was from the beginning, which we have heard, which we have seen with our eyes, which we have looked at and our hands have touched—this we proclaim concerning the Word of life. The life appeared; we have seen it and testify to it, and we proclaim to you the eternal life, which was with the Father and has appeared to us. (1 John 1:1-2)**
> **I declare to you, brothers, that flesh and blood cannot inherit the kingdom of**

God, nor does the perishable inherit the imperishable. (1 Cor 15:50)

3. The effect upon the disciples was unbelievable joy and amazement (cp. Lk.24:41). Their spirits and attitudes were charged with joy and were transformed from the lowest point of dejection to the highest point of triumphant conviction. They now knew what Jesus meant, that He was truly...

- the Way to God
- the Truth of God
- the Life of God

In Him was life—His words were *literally* true. He had meant exactly what He had said. They had just spiritualized His words, twisted them to mean what they had wanted. But now they knew.

⇒ When He had said that He was going to die, He meant He was going to die.

⇒ When He had said that He was going to arise, He meant He was going to arise.

And here He was standing before them, revealing the most glorious truth in all the universe. Man could now conquer sin and death and live forever. He had actually come "that they may have life, and have it to the full[est]" (Jn.10:10. Cp. Jn.10:38.) They now saw and understood (see DEEPER STUDY # 2, *See*—Jn.20:20).

DEEPER STUDY # 2

(20:20) **See** (eido): means more than mere sight. It is seeing with understanding. It is the very same word used of John when he *saw and believed* (cp. Jn.20:8).

DEEPER STUDY # 3

(20:20) **Prophecies**: the disciples finally understood that Jesus had meant exactly what He was saying. When He had said that He was going to die and arise from the dead, they had spiritualized His words. But Jesus had meant exactly what He was saying: He was to literally die and arise from the dead and, by such, He was to usher in the Kingdom of God. Of course, this was far more meaningful than the earthly kingdom they had desired. It was the most glorious news in all the world, for man could now live beyond a few short years in an earthly kingdom; man could live in the very presence of God forever. Sin, death, and hell were now conquered.

Jesus constantly shared His death and resurrection. This fact is often overlooked. The predictions in just the Gospel of John are given here.

1. The prophecies concerning His death alone.

"I am the good shepherd. The good shepherd lays down his life for the sheep just as the Father knows me and I know the Father—and I lay down my life for the sheep. (John 10:11, 15)

"Now my heart is troubled, and what shall I say? 'Father, save me from this hour'? No, it was for this very reason I came to this hour. Now is the time for judgment on this world; now the prince of this world will be driven out. But I, when I am lifted up from the earth, will draw all men to myself." He said this to show the kind of death he was going to die. (John 12:27, 31-33)

"My children, I will be with you only a little longer. You will look for me, and just

as I told the Jews, so I tell you now: Where I am going, you cannot come. Simon Peter asked him, "Lord, where are you going?" Jesus replied, "Where I am going, you cannot follow now, but you will follow later." (John 13:33, 36)

My command is this: Love each other as I have loved you. Greater love has no one than this, that he lay down his life for his friends. You are my friends if you do what I command. (John 15:12-14)

"Now I am going to him who sent me, yet none of you asks me, 'Where are you going?' Because I have said these things, you are filled with grief. But I tell you the truth: It is for your good that I am going away. Unless I go away, the Counselor will not come to you; but if I go, I will send him to you. (John 16:5-7)

I came from the Father and entered the world; now I am leaving the world and going back to the Father." (John 16:28)

I will remain in the world no longer, but they are still in the world, and I am coming to you. Holy Father, protect them by the power of your name—the name you gave me—so that they may be one as we are one. "I am coming to you now, but I say these things while I am still in the world, so that they may have the full measure of my joy within them. (John 17:11, 13)

2. The prophecies concerning the resurrection alone.

What if you see the Son of Man ascend to where he was before! (John 6:62)

Jesus answered, "Even if I testify on my own behalf, my testimony is valid, for I know where I came from and where I am going. But you have no idea where I come from or where I am going. (John 8:14)

Jesus said to her, "I am the resurrection and the life. He who believes in me will live, even though he dies; and whoever lives and believes in me will never die. Do you believe this?" (John 11:25-26)

3. The prophecies concerning both His death and resurrection.

Jesus said, "I am with you for only a short time, and then I go to the one who sent me. You will look for me, but you will not find me; and where I am, you cannot come." The Jews said to one another, "Where does this man intend to go that we cannot find him? Will he go where our people live scattered among the Greeks, and teach the Greeks? What did he mean when he said, 'You will look for me, but you will not find me,' and' Where I am, you cannot come'?" (John 7:33-36)

On the last and greatest day of the Feast, Jesus stood and said in a loud voice, "If anyone is thirsty, let him come to me and drink. Whoever believes in me, as the Scripture has said, streams of living water will flow from within him." By this he meant the Spirit, whom those who believed

in him were later to receive. Up to that time the Spirit had not been given, since Jesus had not yet been glorified. (John 7:37-39)

Once more Jesus said to them, "I am going away, and you will look for me, and you will die in your sin. Where I go, you cannot come." This made the Jews ask, "Will he kill himself? Is that why he says, 'Where I go, you cannot come'?" But he continued, "You are from below; I am from above. You are of this world; I am not of this world. I told you that you would die in your sins; if you do not believe that I am the one I claim to be, you will indeed die in your sins." "Who are you?" they asked. "Just what I have been claiming all along," Jesus replied. "I have much to say in judgment of you. But he who sent me is reliable, and what I have heard from him I tell the world." They did not understand that he was telling them about his Father. So Jesus said, "When you have lifted up the Son of Man, then you will know that I am the one I claim to be and that I do nothing on my own but speak just what the Father has taught me. The one who sent me is with me; he has not left me alone, for I always do what pleases him." (John 8:21-29)

The reason my Father loves me is that I lay down my life—only to take it up again. No one takes it from me, but I lay it down of my own accord. I have authority to lay it down and authority to take it up again. This command I received from my Father." (John 10:17-18)

Jesus replied, "The hour has come for the Son of Man to be glorified. I tell you the truth, unless a kernel of wheat falls to the ground and dies, it remains only a single seed. But if it dies, it produces many seeds. (John 12:23-24)

When he was gone, Jesus said, "Now is the Son of Man glorified and God is glorified in him. If God is glorified in him, God will glorify the Son in himself, and will glorify him at once. (John 13:31-32)

In my Father's house are many rooms; if it were not so, I would have told you. I am going there to prepare a place for you. And if I go and prepare a place for you, I will come back and take you to be with me that you also may be where I am. (John 14:2-3)

Before long, the world will not see me anymore, but you will see me. Because I live, you also will live. On that day you will realize that I am in my Father, and you are in me, and I am in you. (John 14:19-20)

"You heard me say, 'I am going away and I am coming back to you.' If you loved me, you would be glad that I am going to the Father, for the Father is greater than I. I have told you now before it happens, so that when it does happen you will believe. I will not speak with you much longer, for the prince of this world is coming. He has no hold on me, (John 14:28-30)

"In a little while you will see me no more, and then after a little while you will see me." Some of his disciples said to one another, "What does he mean by saying, 'In a little while you will see me no more, and then after a little while you will see me,' and' Because I am going to the Father'?" They kept asking, "What does he mean by 'a little while'? We don't understand what he is saying." Jesus saw that they wanted to ask him about this, so he said to them, "Are you asking one another what I meant when I said, 'In a little while you will see me no more, and then after a little while you will see me'? I tell you the truth, you will weep and mourn while the world rejoices. You will grieve, but your grief will turn to joy. A woman giving birth to a child has pain because her time has come; but when her baby is born she forgets the anguish because of her joy that a child is born into the world. So with you: Now is your time of grief, but I will see you again and you will rejoice, and no one will take away your joy. (John 16:16-22)

3 (20:21) **Commission—Witnessing**: the second subject was the great commission. Note two critical points.

1. There is one great qualification for being commissioned: receiving, possessing, and knowing the peace of Christ (see note—Jn.14:27). Unless a person has been reconciled to God *by Christ*, unless he has really made peace with God, he cannot represent God before the world.

2. There is the great link between the mission of Christ and the disciple. The disciple is sent on the very *same* mission as Christ.

⇒ God sent Christ on a specific mission.
⇒ Christ sends His disciple on the very same mission.

What is the mission?

For God did not send his Son into the world to condemn the world, but to save the world through him. (John 3:17)

The thief comes only to steal and kill and destroy; I have come that they may have life, and have it to the full. (John 10:10)

"As for the person who hears my words but does not keep them, I do not judge him. For I did not come to judge the world, but to save it. (John 12:47)

"You are a king, then!" said Pilate. Jesus answered, "You are right in saying I am a king. In fact, for this reason I was born, and for this I came into the world, to testify to the truth. Everyone on the side of truth listens to me." (John 18:37)

The disciple is sent forth to proclaim and bear witness to the salvation of God. The disciple is the prophet and witness of the living Lord.

⇒ Christ is the Way; the disciple *points* the Way.
⇒ Christ is the Truth; the disciple *proclaims* the Truth.
⇒ Christ is the Life; the disciple *shares* the Life.

3. The great words "sent" (apestalken) and "send" (pempo) are different in the Greek. The Father's sending Christ is *apostello*, which means first of all, *a setting apart and sending forth with delegated authority*. There are only four chapters in John where Christ does not claim to have been sent. Christ's sending the believer is *pempo*, which never means delegated authority. It always means to *dispatch under authority*.

God sent Christ and delegated all authority to Him. Christ delegates no authority to the believer. He dispatches messengers.

> We are therefore Christ's ambassadors, as though God were making his appeal through us. We implore you on Christ's behalf: Be reconciled to God. God made him who had no sin to be sin for us, so that in him we might become the righteousness of God. (2 Cor 5:20-21)

> You did not choose me, but I chose you and appointed you to go and bear fruit—fruit that will last. Then the Father will give you whatever you ask in my name. (John 15:16)

> There came a man who was sent from God; his name was John. (John 1:6)

4 (20:22-23) **Holy Spirit**: the third subject was the Holy Spirit. Christ had just commissioned His disciples. He now gave them the power to carry out His orders.

1. There was the enduement or giving of the Spirit (see Deeper Study # 4, Holy Spirit—Jn.20:22).

2. There was the authority (see Deeper Study # 5—Jn.20:23).

DEEPER STUDY # 4

(20:22) **Holy Spirit, Coming**: Jesus' breathing on the disciples was a prophetic sign of the Spirit's coming and a spiritual quickening for the disciples. It was both a symbolic and a spiritual preparation. Jesus was showing His followers that the Spirit's very special presence and power was to indwell both believers and the church as the temple of God. The Spirit, of course, was not to come until Christ's ascension. (See notes—Jn.14:28-29; 16:7; Deeper Study # 1—Acts 2:1-4; Deeper Study # 2—8:14-17; note—10:44-48.)

Note several things.

1. Christ breathed on each individual. He was symbolizing that the Holy Spirit was to indwell, live in, each believer in a very special way.

> And I will ask the Father, and he will give you another Counselor to be with you forever—the Spirit of truth. The world cannot accept him, because it neither sees him nor knows him. But you know him, for he lives with you and will be in you. I will not leave you as orphans; I will come to you. (John 14:16-18)

> Whoever has my commands and obeys them, he is the one who loves me. He who loves me will be loved by my Father, and I too will love him and show myself to him." (John 14:21)

> But you will receive power when the Holy Spirit comes on you; and you will be my witnesses in Jerusalem, and in all Judea

and Samaria, and to the ends of the earth." (Acts 1:8)

> For you did not receive a spirit that makes you a slave again to fear, but you received the Spirit of sonship. And by him we cry, "Abba, Father." The Spirit himself testifies with our spirit that we are God's children. Now if we are children, then we are heirs—heirs of God and co-heirs with Christ, if indeed we share in his sufferings in order that we may also share in his glory. (Rom 8:15-17)

> We have not received the spirit of the world but the Spirit who is from God, that we may understand what God has freely given us. (1 Cor 2:12)

> Do you not know that your body is a temple of the Holy Spirit, who is in you, whom you have received from God? You are not your own; you were bought at a price. Therefore honor God with your body. (1 Cor 6:19-20)

> Now to him who is able to do immeasurably more than all we ask or imagine, according to his power that is at work within us, (Eph 3:20)

2. Christ breathed on the whole group—"on them [all]." He was symbolizing that the Holy Spirit was to indwell the corporate body, the church as a whole in a very special way. This broader picture is further emphasized by Luke when he says there were others present with the apostles on this occasion (Lk.24:33, 49). (See Deeper Study # 2—Jn.14:20; notes—1 Cor.3:16; 6:19; Eph.3:6; Col.1:26-27.)

> Don't you know that you yourselves are God's temple and that God's Spirit lives in you? (1 Cor 3:16)

> All of them were filled with the Holy Spirit and began to speak in other tongues as the Spirit enabled them. (Acts 2:4)

DEEPER STUDY # 5

(20:23) **Forgiving Sins—Ministers, Authority**: this is a disputed passage. There are two things we can know for sure about its meaning.

⇒ No man can forgive another man's sins.
⇒ Believers *can proclaim* that a man's sins are forgiven *if he receives Christ* (Jn.1:12). Believers can also proclaim that a man's sins are not forgiven if he does not receive Christ.

There is only one Mediator between God and man, the Man Christ Jesus (1 Tim.2:5-6). No other man has ever been worthy to give His life as a ransom for others. No other ransom has ever been acceptable to God. Christ Jesus alone is worthy and acceptable to die as a ransom for someone else. He alone is the Perfect Man. Therefore...

• only Christ can forgive and judge sins.

> Moreover, the Father judges no one, but has entrusted all judgment to the Son, (John 5:22)

> And he has given him authority to judge because he is the Son of Man. (John 5:27)

There is a judge for the one who rejects me and does not accept my words; that very word which I spoke will condemn him at the last day. (John 12:48)

When he comes, he will convict the world of guilt in regard to sin and righteousness and judgment: (John 16:8)

- only representatives of Christ (believers) can say that a man is forgiven by Christ or not forgiven by Christ.

I will give you the keys of the kingdom of heaven; whatever you bind on earth will be bound in heaven, and whatever you loose on earth will be loosed in heaven." (Mat 16:19)

"I tell you the truth, whatever you bind on earth will be bound in heaven, and whatever you loose on earth will be loosed in heaven. (Mat 18:18)

If you forgive anyone his sins, they are forgiven; if you do not forgive them, they are not forgiven." (John 20:23)

	D. Event 4: The Great Conviction—Thomas' Confession, 20:24-29	were in the house again, and Thomas was with them. Though the doors were locked, Jesus came and stood among them and said, "Peace be with you!"	doubt for eight days

1 Thomas' frustrated, reactionary spirit
a. The disciples testified; Thomas argued
b. The reason: Guilt—he had forsaken & withdrawn from them
2 Thomas' false picture of Jesus
a. He was just an earthly deliverer
b. He was now dead
c. Result: Persistent
	24 Now Thomas (called Didymus), one of the Twelve, was not with the disciples when Jesus came.
	25 So the other disciples told him, "We have seen the Lord!" But he said to them, "Unless I see the nail marks in his hands and put my finger where the nails were, and put my hand into his side, I will not believe it."
	26 A week later his disciples
		27 Then he said to Thomas, "Put your finger here; seemy hands. Reach out your hand and put it into my side. Stop doubting and believe."
		28 Thomas said to him, "My Lord and my God!"
		29 Then Jesus told him, "Because you have seen me, you have believed; blessed are those who have not seen and yet have believed."
			3 Thomas' critical confrontation & confession: Jesus appeared & challenged & convicted him
			a. The confrontation
			  1) Jesus was aware of Thomas' demands
			  2) Jesus warned & called for belief
			b. The strong confession
			4 Thomas' great lesson for all men

DIVISION XVI

THE REVELATION OF JESUS, THE RISEN LORD, 20:1-21:23

D. Event 4: The Great Conviction—Thomas' Confession, 20:24-29

(20:24-29) **Introduction**: this is an excellent study on conviction and confession. It is the great conviction and confession of Thomas.

1. Thomas' frustrated reactionary spirit (v.24-25).
2. Thomas' false picture of Jesus (v.25-26).
3. Thomas' critical confrontation and confession—Jesus appeared and challenged and convicted him (v.26-28).
4. Thomas' great lesson for all men (v.29).

(20:24-29) **Another Outline**: Conviction—its signs, results, or reactions.

1. A frustrated reactionary spirit (v.24).
2. A false picture of Jesus (v.25).
3. A persistent doubt (v.26).
4. A critical confrontation (v.27).
5. A strong confession (v.28).
6. A great lesson for the church (v.29).

1 (20:24-25) **Unbelief, Cause of—Thomas**: Thomas' frustrated, reactionary spirit. Thomas had not been with the disciples when Jesus first appeared to them. Like so many today, he staunchly refused to believe that Jesus had actually risen from the dead. The disciples *testified* and *bore witness* to the glorious truth. The Greek means they "kept on telling him," but Thomas became stiffnecked and obstinate in his unbelief. He even argued against their testimony, and he argued with deep intensity. He was deeply aggravated and frustrated, feeling great disappointment and guilt. The depth of his aggravation and guilt is seen in his repulsive shout, "Unless I see...put my finger...[and] put my hand into his side, I will not believe it" (Jn.20:25).

What was it that frustrated Thomas so much and caused him to sense such intense guilt and react the way he did? Evidently...

- Thomas *had forsaken* the Lord, and that was enough to frustrate any man's spirit.
- Thomas had also *withdrawn* from the disciples; consequently he was *not present* when the Lord first appeared (Jn.20:24). He missed another opportunity to be identified with Christ.

Of course, this caused Thomas to become aggravated with guilt all over again. He became critical of the body of believers. It was his own fault, but as human nature so often reacts, he blamed others through his aggravated spirit. He argued against their experience with the resurrected Lord. Having taken all he could bear, in utter frustration he shouted out, "Unless I see...put my finger...[and] put my hand into his side, I will not believe it" (Jn.20:25). It was eight days more before the Lord ever appeared to Thomas (Jn.20:26). What a loss he experienced!

Thought 1. Persistent doubt always delays the blessings.

Thought 2. Guilt, frustration, disappointment, and exclusion often result in a...

- haughty spirit
- reaction
- denial of facts
- fierce outburst

> Whenever our hearts condemn us. For God is greater than our hearts, and he knows everything. (1 John 3:20)
> He said to his disciples, "Why are you so afraid? Do you still have no faith?" (Mark 4:40)
> He said to them, "How foolish you are, and how slow of heart to believe all that the prophets have spoken! (Luke 24:25)
> But my righteous one will live by faith. And if he shrinks back, I will not be pleased with him." (Heb 10:38)
> Yet I hold this against you: You have forsaken your first love. (Rev 2:4)
> The faithless will be fully repaid for their ways, and the good man rewarded for his. (Prov 14:14)

2 (20:25-26) **Jesus Christ, Misconceptions**: Thomas' false picture of Jesus. Thomas had always thought in terms of an earthly Messiah or Savior who would make things better upon this earth and in this life. He had become a follower of Jesus thinking that an earthly kingdom was to be set up and that he was to be a leader in that kingdom. He saw Jesus as the promised Messiah who was to be the

Son of David, that is, to come from David's roots. (See DEEPER STUDY # 2—Jn.1:20; note—1:23; DEEPER STUDY # 4—1:49.) He refused to see beyond the human and physical things of this world. Therefore, he could see Jesus only as the man who was nailed to the cross and had a spear thrust into His side and was now dead. (See notes—Jn.13:1-17; Lk.22:24-30 for more discussion.)

Thought 1. False pictures of Jesus lead to unbelief. Jesus is more than...

- a great teacher.
- a great prophet.
- a great man.
- a great founder of a religion.

He is even more than the greatest man who ever lived. All such beliefs—no matter how highly they esteem Jesus—are false beliefs, for they see Jesus only as a man. They see Him as one of the greatest men who ever lived, but they still see Him only as a man.

Thought 2. Men prefer to see Jesus only as a man because it brings Him down to their level. It makes Him less than Lord. They believe it means...

- that man is not totally depraved, not wicked through and through; that man is not so bad that Jesus had to sacrifice His life for them.
- that man can do what Jesus did, the best he can, and God will accept him.
- that man does not have to follow Jesus in every little detail and teaching. Why? Because as man, they believe that Jesus was not absolutely perfect. He was wrong in some things. Where? Each person has to decide the best he can where Jesus was right and wrong. Then that person must do the best he can to follow Jesus where Jesus was right. Men believe it is doing the best they can that God accepts. (Note how this allows each man to *form* God in his own mind and after his own likeness. Man can make God as he wishes God to be. Man can do what he wishes and then say that it was allowed by God.)

When Jesus came to the region of Caesarea Philippi, he asked his disciples, "Who do people say the Son of Man is?" They replied, "Some say John the Baptist; others say Elijah; and still others, Jeremiah or one of the prophets." (Mat 16:13-14)

Isn't this the carpenter? Isn't this Mary's son and the brother of James, Joseph, Judas and Simon? Aren't his sisters here with us?" And they took offense at him. (Mark 6:3)

For although they knew God, they neither glorified him as God nor gave thanks to him, but their thinking became futile and their foolish hearts were darkened. Although they claimed to be wise, they became fools and exchanged the glory of the immortal God for images made to look like mortal man and birds and animals and reptiles. (Rom 1:21-23)

They exchanged the truth of God for a lie, and worshiped and served created things rather than the Creator—who is forever praised. Amen. (Rom 1:25)

3 (20:26-28) **Confession**: Thomas' critical confrontation and conviction. Jesus appeared and challenged and convicted Thomas.

1. Note the confrontation. The doors were again shut and locked (see note—Jn.20:19). Suddenly, unexpectedly, without notice, Jesus stood in the midst of the disciples. Again He eased their shock by giving the normal greeting: "Peace be with you." But then note what He did: He turned immediately to confront Thomas.

   a. Jesus revealed that He knew all about Thomas' unbelief and demands. He used the very same words that Thomas had demanded: "Put your finger here; see my hands. Reach out your hand and put it into my side. Stop doubting and believe" (v.27).

Thought 1. Jesus knows every man's heart: his despair, doubts, fears, hope, love. He knows where and when to strike at a man's heart. However, note a crucial factor: Thomas was where Jesus could reach him. He was in the presence of believers listening to their testimony. He had not shut them out despite his questions.

He did not need man's testimony about man, for he knew what was in a man. (John 2:25)

And again, "The Lord knows that the thoughts of the wise are futile." (1 Cor 3:20)

"Do not keep talking so proudly or let your mouth speak such arrogance, for the LORD is a God who knows, and by him deeds are weighed. (1 Sam 2:3)

"I the LORD search the heart and examine the mind, to reward a man according to his conduct, according to what his deeds deserve." (Jer 17:10)

He reveals deep and hidden things; he knows what lies in darkness, and light dwells with him. (Dan 2:22)

   b. Jesus warned and called for belief. Thomas had been walking down a dangerous road. The disciples had testified to him time and again, but he had refused time and again to accept their testimony.

   ⇒ "Stop doubting" (me ginou apistos): stop becoming an unbeliever. You are running the risk of *becoming faithless* and unbelieving, beyond the point of believing. You have carried your unbelief too far. It is now time to stop the foolishness. The others have been repeatedly testifying the truth to you. Stop the stiffnecked, obstinate unbelief. You are in danger.

Whoever believes in him is not condemned, but whoever does not believe stands condemned already because he has not believed in the name of God's one and only Son. (John 3:18)

Whoever believes in the Son has eternal life, but whoever rejects the Son will not see life, for God's wrath remains on him." (John 3:36)

I told you that you would die in your sins; if you do not believe that I am the one

I claim to be, you will indeed die in your sins." (John 8:24)

How shall we escape if we ignore such a great salvation? This salvation, which was first announced by the Lord, was confirmed to us by those who heard him. (Heb 2:3)

See to it, brothers, that none of you has a sinful, unbelieving heart that turns away from the living God. (Heb 3:12)

Though you already know all this, I want to remind you that the Lord delivered his people out of Egypt, but later destroyed those who did not believe. (Jude 1:5)

⇒ Believe (see DEEPER STUDY # 2—Jn.2:24).

That everyone who believes in him may have eternal life. (John 3:15)

"I tell you the truth, whoever hears my word and believes him who sent me has eternal life and will not be condemned; he has crossed over from death to life. (John 5:24)

Jesus said to her, "I am the resurrection and the life. He who believes in me will live, even though he dies; (John 11:25)

I have come into the world as a light, so that no one who believes in me should stay in darkness. (John 12:46)

But these are written that you may believe that Jesus is the Christ, the Son of God, and that by believing you may have life in his name. (John 20:31)

That if you confess with your mouth, "Jesus is Lord," and believe in your heart that God raised him from the dead, you will be saved. (Rom 10:9)

Thought 1. To doubt is to be Christless, "separate from Christ...without hope and without God in the world" (Eph.2:12).

2. The strong confession. This is one of the great confessions in Scripture. Most likely dropping to his knees, Thomas exclaimed, "My Lord and My God!" He now knew five great things.
   a. That Jesus is truly the risen Lord. All that Jesus had said was true (see DEEPER STUDY # 3—Jn.20:20).

"Therefore let all Israel be assured of this: God has made this Jesus, whom you crucified, both Lord and Christ." (Acts 2:36)

God exalted him to his own right hand as Prince and Savior that he might give repentance and forgiveness of sins to Israel. (Acts 5:31)

and who through the Spirit of holiness was declared with power to be the Son of God by his resurrection from the dead: Jesus Christ our Lord. (Rom 1:4)

That if you confess with your mouth, "Jesus is Lord," and believe in your heart that God raised him from the dead, you will be saved. (Rom 10:9)

God, who has called you into fellowship with his Son Jesus Christ our Lord, is faithful. (1 Cor 1:9)

Yet for us there is but one God, the Father, from whom all things came and for whom we live; and there is but one Lord, Jesus Christ, through whom all things came and through whom we live. (1 Cor 8:6)

b. That Jesus is both Lord and God, the Sovereign majesty of the universe (see note—Jn.1:1-2).

For in Christ all the fullness of the Deity lives in bodily form, and you have been given fullness in Christ, who is the head over every power and authority. (Col 2:9-10)

Beyond all question, the mystery of godliness is great: He appeared in a body, was vindicated by the Spirit, was seen by angels, was preached among the nations, was believed on in the world, was taken up in glory. (1 Tim 3:16)

The Son is the radiance of God's glory and the exact representation of his being, sustaining all things by his powerful word. After he had provided purification for sins, he sat down at the right hand of the Majesty in heaven. (Heb 1:3)

c. That Jesus is the One who has come to truly reveal God, that He is the Mediator between God and man (see note—Jn.14:6; DEEPER STUDY # 1—3:31; DEEPER STUDY # 3—3:34; cp. 1 Tim.2:15).

Jesus answered, "I am the way and the truth and the life. No one comes to the Father except through me. (John 14:6)

For there is one God and one mediator between God and men, the man Christ Jesus, (1 Tim 2:5)

But the ministry Jesus has received is as superior to theirs as the covenant of which he is mediator is superior to the old one, and it is founded on better promises. (Heb 8:6)

For this reason Christ is the mediator of a new covenant, that those who are called may receive the promised eternal inheritance—now that he has died as a ransom to set them free from the sins committed under the first covenant. (Heb 9:15)

For Christ did not enter a man-made sanctuary that was only a copy of the true one; he entered heaven itself, now to appear for us in God's presence. (Heb 9:24)

My dear children, I write this to you so that you will not sin. But if anybody does sin, we have one who speaks to the Father in our defense—Jesus Christ, the Righteous One. (1 John 2:1)

d. That Jesus accepts no half-way commitments. Jesus expected to be his Lord and his God: "My Lord and My God." Therefore, he must personally bow and worship Jesus as his Lord and his God.

Therefore God exalted him to the highest place and gave him the name that is above every name, that at the name of Jesus every knee should bow, in heaven and on earth and under the earth, and every tongue confess that Jesus Christ is Lord, to the glory of God the Father. (Phil 2:9-11)

For this very reason, Christ died and returned to life so that he might be the Lord of both the dead and the living. (Rom 14:9)

And he is the head of the body, the church; he is the beginning and the first-born from among the dead, so that in everything he might have the supremacy. (Col 1:18)

In a loud voice they sang: "Worthy is the Lamb, who was slain, to receive power and wealth and wisdom and strength and honor and glory and praise!" (Rev 5:12)

e. That Jesus expected an open and public confession of Him as Lord and God (Mt.10:32; Lk.12:8).

"Whoever acknowledges me before men, I will also acknowledge him before my Father in heaven. (Mat 10:32)

"I tell you, whoever acknowledges me before men, the Son of Man will also acknowledge him before the angels of God. (Luke 12:8)

No one who denies the Son has the Father; whoever acknowledges the Son has the Father also. (1 John 2:23)

If anyone acknowledges that Jesus is the Son of God, God lives in him and he in God. (1 John 4:15)

4 (20:29) **Belief**: Thomas' great lesson for all men. What is the lesson?

⇒ To believe without having to see evidences and proof.

Then Jesus told him, "Because you have seen me, you have believed; blessed are those who have not seen and yet have believed." (John 20:29)

⇒ To believe because of tenderness and warmth.

But because of his great love for us, God, who is rich in mercy, made us alive with Christ even when we were dead in transgressions—it is by grace you have been saved. For it is by grace you have been saved, through faith—and this not from yourselves, it is the gift of God—not by works, so that no one can boast. (Eph 2:4-5, 8-9)

⇒ To believe because of love and care and because of the need and nature of the human heart.

"For God so loved the world that he gave his one and only Son, that whoever believes in him shall not perish but have eternal life. (John 3:16)

But God demonstrates his own love for us in this: While we were still sinners, Christ died for us. (Rom 5:8)

For all have sinned and fall short of the glory of God, (Rom 3:23)

⇒ To believe because of the need for morality and godly character.

But the fruit of the Spirit is love, joy, peace, patience, kindness, goodness, faithfulness, gentleness and self-control. Against such things there is no law. (Gal 5:22-23; cp. v.19-21)

⇒ To believe because godly witnesses say so.

Again Jesus said, "Peace be with you! As the Father has sent me, I am sending you." (John 20:21)

He said to them, "Go into all the world and preach the good news to all creation. (Mark 16:15)

⇒ To believe because of the inner witness of the heart.

Since they show that the requirements of the law are written on their hearts, their consciences also bearing witness, and their thoughts now accusing, now even defending them.) (Rom 2:15)

⇒ To believe because of the outer witness of nature.

For since the creation of the world God's invisible qualities—his eternal power and divine nature—have been clearly seen, being understood from what has been made, so that men are without excuse. (Rom 1:20)

(See DEEPER STUDY # 1—Jn.2:23; DEEPER STUDY # 1,2,3—Mt.4:1-11 for more discussion.)

Note that Thomas ceased being obstinate and rebellious when he saw Jesus and after Jesus had rebuked him. Thomas had been at fault; he had been doubting, and his unbelief was inexcusable. The men who had proclaimed the truth to him were not liars. Neither could they all have been deceived. Thomas had just refused to believe because he did not want to believe. He had acted intellectually superior and had been about to lose his soul.

The point is this: the person who believes without seeing demonstrates...

• a strength of character
• a tenderness and warmth of heart
• a sensitivity to the witness of the Holy Spirit
• an awareness to the order and beauty of all the world

Therefore, that person will be blessed with a very special joy, an inexpressable and glorious joy.

Though you have not seen him, you love him; and even though you do not see him now, you believe in him and are filled with an inexpressible and glorious joy, (1 Pet 1:8)

Thought 1. When a man truly sees what Jesus has done for Him, or when a man is rebuked by the Spirit of Christ, he must cease his unbelief. He must turn to Christ, for the Lord's Spirit will not always strive and contend with men.

Then the LORD said, "My Spirit will not contend with man forever, for he is mortal; his days will be a hundred and twenty years." (Gen 6:3)

Blessed is the man who always fears the LORD, but he who hardens his heart falls into trouble. (Prov 28:14)

A man who remains stiff-necked after many rebukes will suddenly be destroyed—without remedy. (Prov 29:1)

	E. Event 5: The Great Purpose of the Signs (Wonderful Works) of Jesus, 20:30-31
1 The great fact: Jesus did many signs a. In the disciples' presence b. Not recorded by John **2 The great purpose: To select a few signs that would lead to belief** a. Jesus is the Messiah b. Jesus is the Son of God **3 The great result: Life**	30 Jesus did many other miraculous signs in the presence of his disciples, which are not recorded in this book. 31 But these are written that you may believe that Jesus is the Christ, the Son of God, and that by believing you may have life in his name.

DIVISION XVI

THE REVELATION OF JESUS, THE RISEN LORD, 20:1-21:23

E. Event 5: The Great Purpose of the Signs (Wonderful Works) of Jesus, 20:30-31

(20:30-31) **Introduction**: note two significant facts as an introduction to this passage. First, it is quite clear that the gospel writers did not include all that Jesus did in their gospels. In fact, they recorded very few of the signs. Contrary to what is usually thought, Jesus was apparently ministering and meeting the needs of multitudes every day—from sunrise until sundown.

Second, note the use of the word "signs." In talking about Jesus' life, the word "signs" is chosen by John. All that Jesus was and did were signs—signs demonstrating that He was the Messiah, the Son of God. In these two verses, John gives the great purpose of the signs.

1. The great fact: Jesus did many signs or wonderful works (v.30).
2. The great purpose of John in his Gospel: to select a few signs that would lead to belief (v.31).
3. The great result: life (v.31).

1 (20:30) **Jesus Christ, Works—Ministry—Gospels, Writing of**: the great fact, Jesus did many other signs that are not recorded in this gospel by John. He did many wonderful things. He was busy every day, actively involved either in worshipping God alone or in teaching and ministering to people. For about three years, Jesus was constantly demonstrating that He was the Messiah, the Son of God. He gave all the evidence in the world:

⇒ acts of love and purity
⇒ acts of righteousness and justice
⇒ works of mercy and compassion
⇒ works of miracles and power
⇒ works of godliness and sovereignty
⇒ words of truth and salvation
⇒ words of peace and faith
⇒ words of hope and joy
⇒ words of morality and discipline
⇒ words of commitment and self-denial

The point is that Jesus' life—His character and behavior, His preaching and teaching, His miracles and power—proves that He is the Messiah, the Son of God. No man could do the things He did unless He were the Son of God. Who He was and what He did prove it.

Note that Jesus did not do the signs in secret, that is, out in a desert or off in a corner of the world. He did them out in the open, publicly. John said He did the signs in the presence of His disciples. They witnessed the signs, for Jesus saw to it that there was adequate witness and testimony. Note what John says in his epistle:

> **That which was from the beginning, which we have heard, which we have seen with our eyes, which we have looked at and our hands have touched—this we proclaim concerning the Word of life. The life appeared; we have seen it and testify to it, and we proclaim to you the eternal life, which was with the Father and has appeared to us. We proclaim to you what we have seen and heard, so that you also may have fellowship with us. And our fellowship is with the Father and with his Son, Jesus Christ. We write this to make our joy complete. (1 John 1:1-4)**
> **It is sown a natural body, it is raised a spiritual body. If there is a natural body, there is also a spiritual body. (1 Cor 15:44)**
> **I declare to you, brothers, that flesh and blood cannot inherit the kingdom of God, nor does the perishable inherit the imperishable. (1 Cor 15:50)**
> **"For when David had served God's purpose in his own generation, he fell asleep; he was buried with his fathers and his body decayed. (Acts 13:36)**
> **But the one whom God raised from the dead did not see decay. (Acts 13:37)**
> **So will it be with the resurrection of the dead. The body that is sown is perishable, it is raised imperishable; (1 Cor 15:42)**
> **Now we know that if the earthly tent we live in is destroyed, we have a building from God, an eternal house in heaven, not built by human hands. (2 Cor 5:1)**
> **Meanwhile we groan, longing to be clothed with our heavenly dwelling, (2 Cor 5:2)**

Note one other fact: John says that he has been highly selective in the signs he has chosen to record in his gospel. There were "*many*" signs which Jesus gave; so many in fact, "I suppose that even the whole world itself would not have room for the books that would be written" (Jn.21:25). John selected only a *few* signs to record. He had a specific purpose in mind, so he chose a few signs that would help meet that purpose.

2 (20:31) **Gospel of John, Purpose**: the great purpose of John was to select a few signs that would lead men to believe. (See DEEPER STUDY # 2, Believe—Jn.2:24 for discussion.) Every point in John's purpose is already footnoted and covered in John's gospel. Referring to these notes will give the discussion of this passage.

1. Jesus is the Messiah (see DEEPER STUDY # 2—Jn.1:20; note—1:23; DEEPER STUDY # 4—1:49; notes—3:27-28; 12:12-19; 13:36-38; 20:25-28 for discussion).

2. Jesus is the Son of God (see DEEPER STUDY # 1—Jn.1:1-5; notes—1:1-2; 1:30-31; 1:34 for discussion).

3 (20:31) **Life**: the great result is life through Jesus' name (see DEEPER STUDY # 2—Jn.1:4; DEEPER STUDY # 1—10:10; DEEPER STUDY # 1—17:2-3 for discussion).

CHAPTER 21

F. Event 6: The Great Reality of Jesus' Resurrection Body, 21:1-14

1 **Jesus appeared again**[DS1]
a. Afterward—after these things: Proofs of the resurrection, 20:1-31
b. To seven disciples who were together: Hiding for fear of the authorities

c. Peter went fishing: To meet the need for food
d. A needed lesson: Self-sufficiency is inadequate—must know & depend upon the risen Lord
2 **Jesus stood on the shore—bodily**
a. An immediate presence
b. A bodily presence
3 **Jesus possessed supernatural knowledge**

a. He acted on His supernatural knowledge

Afterward Jesus appeared again to his disciples, by the Sea of Tiberias. It happened this way:
2 Simon Peter, Thomas (called Didymus), Nathanael from Cana in Galilee, the sons of Zebedee, and two other disciples were together.
3 "I'm going out to fish," Simon Peter told them, and they said, "We'll go with you." So they went out and got into the boat, but that night they caught nothing.
4 Early in the morning, Jesus stood on the shore, but the disciples did not realize that it was Jesus.
5 He called out to them, "Friends, haven't you any fish?" "No," they answered.
6 He said, "Throw your net on the right side of the boat and you will find some." When they did, they were unable to haul the net in because of the large number of fish.
7 Then the disciple whom

Jesus loved said to Peter, "It is the Lord!" As soon as Simon Peter heard him say, "It is the Lord," he wrapped his outer garment around him (for he had taken it off) and jumped into the water.
8 The other disciples followed in the boat, towing the net full of fish, for they were not far from shore, about a hundred yards.
9 When they landed, they saw a fire of burning coals there with fish on it, and some bread.
10 Jesus said to them, "Bring some of the fish you have just caught."
11 Simon Peter climbed aboard and dragged the net ashore. It was full of large fish, 153, but even with so many the net was not torn.
12 Jesus said to them, "Come and have breakfast." None of the disciples dared ask him, "Who are you?" They knew it was the Lord.
13 Jesus came, took the bread and gave it to them, and did the same with the fish.
14 This was now the third time Jesus appeared to his disciples after he was raised from the dead.

b. He was identified: "The Lord"
c. Peter accepted John's word as proof & He responded

d. The other disciples responded and followed

4 **Jesus showed the reality of the surroundings**
a. The land & fire
b. The fish & bread
5 **Jesus showed that He could see, speak, hear, & feel**
a. He instructed the disciples
b. Peter obeyed
c. The catch of fish was counted

6 **Jesus showed that His body was real**
a. He invited them to eat
b. He was the Lord

c. He Himself ate

7 **Conclusion: Jesus' resurrection was affirmed**

DIVISION XVI

THE REVELATION OF JESUS, THE RISEN LORD, 20:1-21:23

F. Event 6: The Great Reality of Jesus' Resurrection Body, 21:1-14

(21:1-14) Introduction: Jesus proved the great reality of His resurrection body. He showed that He really did arise from the dead. Death had been conquered and men could now live forever.

1. Jesus showed Himself (v.1-3).
2. Jesus stood on the shore—bodily (v.4).
3. Jesus possessed supernatural knowledge (v.5-8).
4. Jesus showed the reality of the surroundings (v.9).
5. Jesus showed that He could see, speak, hear, and feel (v.10-11).
6. Jesus showed that His body was real (v.12-13).
7. Conclusion: Jesus' resurrection was affirmed (v.14).

1 (21:1-3) **Jesus Christ, Resurrection**: Jesus showed Himself (see DEEPER STUDY # 1—Jn.21:1). Note four things.

1. The word "afterward" refers to the proof of Jesus' resurrection already recorded (Jn.20:1-31).
2. Seven disciples were together. They were apparently in some home continuing to hide for fear of the authorities (see note—Jn.20:19).
3. Peter went fishing to meet the need for food. Note that the others decided to join him and that they went under

the cover of darkness and off on some lonely strand of beach (v.3, 9-14). In the sovereignty of God, the small band of men needed to learn a glorious lesson, so God was setting the stage for them to receive the lesson.

4. They caught nothing, and it was in this that they were to learn the much needed lesson: self-sufficiency is inadequate. They could no longer do anything on their own. They must know the risen Lord, and they must depend upon the risen Lord. They could not provide for themselves in their own strength; they must know that the Lord is really risen, and they must learn to depend upon Him.

Jesus used this experience of catching nothing to teach the disciples that He had truly risen. It was He in the resurrected body. He was truly the Risen Lord, and it was He upon whom they must depend from now on.

DEEPER STUDY # 1

(21:1) Body, Resurrected—Jesus Christ, Resurrection; Shows Himself: "Jesus Christ appeared again." The purpose of His appearances was to prove that Jesus was not a spirit, vision, phantom, hallucination, or any other figment of man's imagination.

He was the risen Lord—bodily. He was not someone else. His body was none other than the body of Jesus, the Carpenter from Nazareth. He had been raised from the dead—physically raised. His body was real. It differed, yes; but it was His body—perfected, no longer subject to the limitations and frailties of the physical universe and its laws. It was His body which was now transformed into a spiritual body by the power of God's Word (cp. Ro.1:3-4).

How did the Lord's body differ since His resurrection? Some idea can be gleaned by looking both at His resurrection body and at the glorified body promised to the believer.

1. The resurrected body of the Lord was His body, but it was radically changed. It had all the appearance of His physical body, yet it was not bound by the physical world and its material substance.

a. It looked like the same material body, the same "flesh and bones," not some other body. It was a body that bore the marks of the nails in His hands and feet (Jn.20:20, 27). It was a body that appeared and looked like a body and that occupied space.

b. It was a body that could travel and appear any place at will or by thought, a body unhampered by space, time, or physical substance. When He appeared, it was suddenly, even behind locked doors (Lk.24:36; Jn.20:19).

c. It was a body that differed enough from the earthly body that it was not clearly recognized, not at first, not until it was closely observed.
⇒ Mary Magdalene thought He was the gardener (Jn.20:15).
⇒ The two disciples walking toward Emmaus thought He was a traveller (Lk.24:31).
⇒ The disciples who were fishing did not recognize Him standing on the seashore (Jn.21:4).

However, after close observation, the Lord was recognized in all these instances. This probably indicates that our heavenly bodies will look like our earthly bodies, differing only in that they are perfected.

2. The resurrected and glorified body that is promised to the believer gives some additional insight into the kind of body Jesus now has. One of the most wonderful promises ever made to man is given in the words:
⇒ "Who, by the power that enables him to bring everything under his control, will transform our lowly bodies so that they will be like his glorious body" (Ph.3:21; cp. Mt.13:43; Ro.8:17; Col.3:4; Rev.22:5).
⇒ We will be "conformed to the likeness of His Son" (Ro.8:29. Cp. 1 Cor.15:49; 2 Cor.3:18.)
⇒ "We shall be like Him; for we shall see Him as He is" (1 Jn.3:2).

The body of the believer is to undergo a radical change just as the Lord's body was radically changed. Several changes are promised the believer.

a. The believer will receive a spiritual body.

it is sown a natural body, it is raised a spiritual body. If there is a natural body, there is also a spiritual body. (1 Cor 15:44)

Note that the *spiritual body* (*soma*) is still a body just like the *earthly body* (soma). The spiritual body still retains the qualities of the earthly body. The difference lies in its nature: it will no

longer be a natural (soulish) body; it will be spiritual. What does this mean? In essence, the body will be perfected and glorified: no longer subject to aging, deterioration, death, decay, pain, tears, sorrow, or crying (Rev.14:4).
⇒ "The body that is sown is perishable [corruptible], it is raised imperishable [incorruptible]."
⇒ "It is sown in dishonor; it is raised in glory."
⇒ "It is sown in weakness; it is raised in power."
⇒ "It is sown a natural body; it is raised a spiritual body."
Note the strong, emphatic declaration: "There is a natural body, and there is a spiritual body" (1 Cor. 15:42-44).

b. The believer will receive a body that is *not flesh and blood.* Flesh and blood are corruptible, they age, deteriorate, die, and decay.

I declare to you, brothers, that flesh and blood cannot inherit the kingdom of God, nor does the perishable inherit the imperishable. (1 Cor 15:50)
"For when David had served God's purpose in his own generation, he fell asleep; he was buried with his fathers and his body decayed. But the one whom God raised from the dead did not see decay. (Acts 13:36-37)
All go to the same place; all come from dust, and to dust all return. (Eccl 3:20)
So will it be with the resurrection of the dead. The body that is sown is perishable, it is raised imperishable; (1 Cor 15:42)
Now we know that if the earthly tent we live in is destroyed, we have a building from God, an eternal house in heaven, not built by human hands. Meanwhile we groan, longing to be clothed with our heavenly dwelling, (2 Cor 5:1-2)

c. The believer will receive a body that will be radically changed.

in a flash, in the twinkling of an eye, at the last trumpet. For the trumpet will sound, the dead will be raised imperishable, and we will be changed. For the perishable must clothe itself with the imperishable, and the mortal with immortality. (1 Cor 15:52-53)

d. The believer will be given a body that will not need reproduction for continuing the (redeemed) human race.

At the resurrection people will neither marry nor be given in marriage; they will be like the angels in heaven. (Mat 22:30)

2 (21:4) **Jesus Christ, Resurrection**: Jesus stood on the shore—bodily.

1. His presence was immediate, sudden, unexpected.
2. His presence was bodily, that is, His body stood there. It was morning, and the disciples saw a person just as they would see any other person standing on the seashore. There was no thought of a vision, hallucination, or spirit. They saw a person on the seashore and thought

nothing strange about it. Note: they did not know it was Jesus, not at first sight.

3 (21:5-8) **Jesus Christ, Knowledge of**: Jesus possessed supernatural knowledge. Jesus knew where the fish were. Remember the disciples had been commercial fishermen before their call to serve the Lord. Jesus was teaching that He, the risen Lord, was the same Lord who took care of them before the crucifixion; therefore, He would take care of them now. But there was one significant difference that they must learn. The resurrection increased His care and added much more to their salvation. He, the risen Lord, was the sovereign majesty of the universe who could use His sovereign knowledge to provide all things for His dear children (cp. Mt.6:25-34).

Now note: John knew immediately that it was the Lord. However, it was the miracle of knowing where the fish were, the Lord's supernatural sovereign knowledge, that told John.

> Now we can see that you know all things and that you do not even need to have anyone ask you questions. This makes us believe that you came from God." (John 16:30)

The response was exactly what it should have been. Peter clothed himself and jumped into the lake and swam to shore. The other disciples followed in the boat.

Thought 1. When men hear that Jesus is really alive—that He is the Sovereign Majesty of the universe—they should do just what these men did: rush to Him as quickly as possible.

> But God raised him from the dead, freeing him from the agony of death, because it was impossible for death to keep its hold on him. (Acts 2:24)
> He was delivered over to death for our sins and was raised to life for our justification. (Rom 4:25)
> That if you confess with your mouth, "Jesus is Lord," and believe in your heart that God raised him from the dead, you will be saved. (Rom 10:9)
> We believe that Jesus died and rose again and so we believe that God will bring with Jesus those who have fallen asleep in him. (1 Th 4:14)
> Praise be to the God and Father of our Lord Jesus Christ! In his great mercy he has given us new birth into a living hope through the resurrection of Jesus Christ from the dead, and into an inheritance that can never perish, spoil or fade—kept in heaven for you, (1 Pet 1:3-4)
> For Christ died for sins once for all, the righteous for the unrighteous, to bring you to God. He was put to death in the body but made alive by the Spirit, (1 Pet 3:18)

Thought 2. Every genuine believer experiences the supernatural care of the risen Lord. The believer knows the sovereign knowledge and care of the Lord in his own life (Mt.6:25-34).

4 (21:9) **Jesus Christ, Resurrection**: Jesus showed the reality of the surroundings. Note the land and fire, the fish and bread. He was showing that He was the same Jesus who had always been with them. He was not a figment of their imagination, not a vision, not even a spirit. He was in a body just like the body they had always known.

> But Jesus immediately said to them: "Take courage! It is I. Don't be afraid." (Mat 14:27)

5 (21:10-11) **Jesus Christ, Resurrection**: Jesus showed that He could see, speak, hear, and feel. He instructed the disciples to gather in the fish, instructing them just as He always had. They obeyed, even to the point of counting the fish. Jesus was heaping proof upon proof, giving the disciples indisputable evidence of His resurrection.

> That which was from the beginning, which we have heard, which we have seen with our eyes, which we have looked at and our hands have touched—this we proclaim concerning the Word of life. The life appeared; we have seen it and testify to it, and we proclaim to you the eternal life, which was with the Father and has appeared to us. We proclaim to you what we have seen and heard, so that you also may have fellowship with us. And our fellowship is with the Father and with his Son, Jesus Christ. (1 John 1:1-3)

6 (21:12-13) **Jesus Christ, Resurrection**: Jesus showed that His body was real. He invited them to eat and He ate with them, just as He always had. Again, the point is that they must *know* it was Jesus. The risen Lord was the same Jesus who had walked and lived with them, the only difference was that He had risen from the dead in a perfected and glorified body.

Note: the disciples knew beyond question that it was the Lord. Humanly, it was not supposed to be; a dead man arising from the grave was impossible. The physical and material world knew nothing but corruption and decay, sin and death. But seated there eating with them was Jesus. He had risen from the dead and come back to life again. They knew that death was now conquered and that man could now live forever (Jn.20:31).

They knew just what Jesus wanted them to know. They knew the great reality of His resurrection body and the great reality of His sovereign majesty and care for them in conquering death.

> "For God so loved the world that he gave his one and only Son, that whoever believes in him shall not perish but have eternal life. (John 3:16)
> "I tell you the truth, whoever hears my word and believes him who sent me has eternal life and will not be condemned; he has crossed over from death to life. (John 5:24)
> Jesus said to her, "I am the resurrection and the life. He who believes in me will live, even though he dies; and whoever lives and believes in me will never die. Do you believe this?" (John 11:25-26)

But it has now been revealed through the appearing of our Savior, Christ Jesus, who has destroyed death and has brought life and immortality to light through the gospel. (2 Tim 1:10)

Since the children have flesh and blood, he too shared in their humanity so that

by his death he might destroy him who holds the power of death—that is, the devil—and free those who all their lives were held in slavery by their fear of death. (Heb 2:14-15)

He will wipe every tear from their eyes. There will be no more death or mourning or crying or pain, for the old order of things has passed away." (Rev 21:4)

7 (21:14) **Jesus Christ, Resurrection**: Jesus' resurrection was affirmed by John. Remember why John was writing.

But these are written that you may believe that Jesus is the Christ, the Son of God, and that by believing you may have life in his name. (John 20:31)

For we cannot help speaking about what we have seen and heard." (Acts 4:20)

We are witnesses of these things, and so is the Holy Spirit, whom God has given to those who obey him." (Acts 5:32)

It is written: "I believed; therefore I have spoken." With that same spirit of faith we also believe and therefore speak, (2 Cor 4:13)

		G. Event 7: The Great Question of a Disciple's Love and Devotion, 21:15-17	son of John, do you truly love me?" He answered, "Yes, Lord, you know that I love you." Jesus said, "Take care of my sheep."	love—love me enough to feed my people? a. God's love (agapao) b. Peter's love (phileo) c. Feed my sheep
1	**After the meal, Jesus focused on Peter**	15 When they had finished eating, Jesus said to Simon Peter, "Simon son of John, do you truly love me more than these?" "Yes, Lord," he said, "you know that I love you." Jesus said, "Feed my lambs."	17 The third time he said to him, "Simon son of John, do you love me?" Peter was hurt because Jesus asked him the third time, "Do you love me?" He said, "Lord, you know all things; you know that I love you." Jesus said, "Feed my sheep.	4 **Do you love me as a loyal brother—love me with agape love or phileo love?** a. Lord's love (phileo) b. Peter's love (phileo) c. Feed my sheep
2	**Do you love me more than these?** a. Pointed to disciples b. Pointed to fishing equipment c. Feed my lambs			
3	**Do you love me with God's**	16 Again Jesus said, "Simon,		

DIVISION XVI

THE REVELATION OF JESUS, THE RISEN LORD, 20:1-21:23

G. Event 7: The Great Question of a Disciple's Love and Devotion, 21:15-17

(21:15-17) **Introduction**: this is a critical passage for the church and its ministers. It has one great lesson: love is the one basic essential for ministry. Without love, ministry counts for nothing in God's eyes. This passage concerns three questions asked by our Lord.

1. After the meal, Jesus focused on Peter (v.15).
2. Do you love me more than these (v.15)?
3. Do you love me with God's love (v.16)?
4. Do you love me as a loyal brother (v.17)?

(Note: this passage is best studied as a whole, comparing each question with the other two questions. Because of this, all three points are studied together and not by separate points. It is also helpful to see notes, Love—Jn.13:33-35; 14:15.)

1 (21:15) **Ministry**: the meal was finished. Jesus and the disciples were sitting around talking and sharing together after the meal. Remember four things.

⇒ Jesus had already met Peter all alone in a private session to discuss Peter's denial and to make sure he was fully restored (cp. 1 Cor.15:4-5).
⇒ Peter's leadership needed to be reinforced publicly among all the disciples. They all knew about Peter's denial.
⇒ Jesus had to make sure Peter would never deny Him nor fall back from his mission again.
⇒ Jesus needed to teach the disciples the one basic essential for ministry. None of them, not even a charismatic leader such as Peter, could ever minister and bear godly fruit unless he *loved* the flock of God. A man may be the most gifted person in the world, but he is nothing and can do nothing of value *in God's eyes* unless he first loves (cp. 1 Cor.13:1-3). Abilities, talents, gifts, commitments, good deeds, and works just do not qualify a man before God nor make a man acceptable to God. The one great thing—in fact the only thing—that makes a man acceptable and that qualifies him to serve God is *love*.

These are the reasons for what Jesus now did. He turned to focus upon Peter. Note: He called Peter by his full name, Simon Peter, and reminded him that he was the son of Jonas (cp. Jn.1:42). This did two things.

⇒ It attracted everyone's attention, stressing that what was to follow was important—more important than usual.
⇒ It reminded Peter where he had come from. He was of humble beginnings, from a lowly father. All that Peter had become and would become was of God. Peter was *nothing apart from Christ* and *nothing apart from the mission he was about to receive*.

Thought 1. A man must know that he is nothing apart from Christ. How many persons would have more in life—more purpose, more meaning, more significance—if they would only surrender to Christ? How many have actually been called by Christ and rejected His call; therefore, they have missed out on their purpose in life and on making their contribution to society and to the world?

2 (21:15) **Love—Commitment**: there is a difference between the three questions Jesus asked of Peter. Question one asked Peter who he loved the most, the Lord Himself or "these." Just what is meant by "these" is not clear. Jesus could have been pointing to the disciples sitting around. If so, He meant, do you love me more than you love these men or your family? Or, Jesus could have been pointing to the fish, the nets, and the boat. If so, He was asking, do you love me more than your profession and career (cp. Jn.21:3)? Perhaps Scripture is unclear at this point in order to make "these" apply to anything and everything in our lives.

Question two asked Peter if he loved with God's love. This is seen in the Greek word for love. Jesus used one word, but Peter used another. Jesus used the word *agape*, the highest form of love, the love of God Himself. But Peter did not reply, "Yes, Lord, I *agape* you." He said, "Yes, Lord, I *phileo* you." That is, I love you just like a brother; I love you with a brotherly love." *Phileo* means brotherly love, the love between two brothers.

Question three probed the genuineness and loyalty of Peter's love. Here Jesus descended to the human level of love. He used *phileo*. He simply asked Peter, "Peter, do you really love, *phileo* me—even as a brother?" And questioning the loyalty of his love grieved Peter. But Jesus assured Peter that his love would one day reach the ultimate height (Jn.21:18). Peter would be called upon to demonstrate *agape* love, the sacrificial love of God. Peter would be called upon to die for Christ, to give his life for preaching the love of God to those who do not care for it and who react violently against it.

Jesus was preparing His disciples for a new kind of love that was yet to come. Up to the time of Christ's death and ascension, the greatest love known to man was *phileo love*, the willingness of a man to die for a friend. But in Christ, God was showing the world a new kind of love—*agape love*. *Agape love* is a love so new that a new meaning had to be given to the Greek word "*agape*." *Agape* became the love that was willing to give and die even for an enemy. The early Christian leaders recognized this new dimension of love, so they lifted the meaning of *agape love* up to God's love for the world. *Agape love* is the highest level of love possible; it is the love of God: "God [who] so loved the world that He gave his one and only Son, that whoever believes in him shall not perish, but have eternal life" (Jn.3:16).

Agape love is Christ's dying…
- for people who have no power (Ro.5:6).
- for the ungodly (Ro.5:6).
- for sinners (Ro.5:8).
- for the enemies of God (Ro.5:10).

Peter and the disciples did not yet understand this. They could not because the Holy Spirit had not yet been given, and *agape love* is shed abroad in the heart only by the Holy Spirit (Ro.5:5). It is a fruit of the Holy Spirit (Gal.5:22).

3 (21:16) **Ministry—Church**: three times Peter was commissioned to feed and tend the flock of God. If Peter really loved the Lord, then he was commissioned to be a shepherd of the flock of God. Note three things.

1. Scripture identifies the lambs and sheep as the flock of God, that is, as the church of God. Jesus was talking about feeding His church, His disciples within the church.

> Keep watch over yourselves and all the flock of which the Holy Spirit has made you overseers. Be shepherds of the church of God, which he bought with his own blood. (Acts 20:28)

Note: in this verse (Acts 20:28) the charge is to guard oneself as well as the flock of God. This is similar to what Jesus was saying to Peter: if you love me, guard youself and be faithful; feed my lambs and sheep, my church.

2. The flock of God is made up of both lambs (arnia, v.15) and sheep (probatia, v.16-17).
⇒ Lambs: children, young converts, the handicapped or special cases, believers who need special attention.
⇒ Sheep: mature believers, believers who have walked and grown in the Lord for a long time. (See note, pt.5—Mt.25:31-33 for more discussion.)

3. The ministry to the flock or church is twofold.
a. The first ministry is to feed (boske, v.15, 17).
⇒ To give food, teaching both the milk and meat of the Word.

> Like newborn babies, crave pure spiritual milk, so that by it you may grow up in your salvation, now that you have tasted that the Lord is good. (1 Pet 2:2-3)
> In fact, though by this time you ought to be teachers, you need someone to teach you the elementary truths of God's word

all over again. You need milk, not solid food! Anyone who lives on milk, being still an infant, is not acquainted with the teaching about righteousness. But solid food is for the mature, who by constant use have trained themselves to distinguish good from evil. (Heb 5:12-14)

⇒ To guide into the study of the Word—preaching oneself approved to God.

> Do your best to present yourself to God as one approved, a workman who does not need to be ashamed and who correctly handles the word of truth. (2 Tim 2:15)

Note that the word used for feeding (boske) is the word used for both the lambs (v.15) and the sheep (v.17). Both the lambs and sheep are to be fed on the same Word and fed in the same way.

> When your words came, I ate them; they were my joy and my heart's delight, for I bear your name, O LORD God Almighty. (Jer 15:16)
> I have not departed from the commands of his lips; I have treasured the words of his mouth more than my daily bread. (Job 23:12)
> He humbled you, causing you to hunger and then feeding you with manna, which neither you nor your fathers had known, to teach you that man does not live on bread alone but on every word that comes from the mouth of the LORD. (Deu 8:3; cp.Mt.4:4)
> How sweet are your words to my taste, sweeter than honey to my mouth! (Psa 119:103)

b. The second ministry is to shepherd (poimaine, v.16). Shepherding involves all the works of the ministry.

> Be shepherds of God's flock that is under your care, serving as overseers—not because you must, but because you are willing, as God wants you to be; not greedy for money, but eager to serve; not lording it over those entrusted to you, but being examples to the flock. (1 Pet 5:2-3)

(See note—Jn.10:2-3 for the work of a shepherd. See note—Mk.6:34.)

4 (21:17) **Love**: Jesus asked Peter if he loved Him with *agape* love or *phileo* love. The difference between *agape love* and *phileo love* is as follows.

Phileo love is the love of tender affection, of warm and deep feelings within the heart. It is the deep and precious love of those near and dear to one's heart. It is brotherly love, a love between family members, a love that would die for its brother.

Agape love is the love of the mind, of the reason, and of the will. It is a love that is born of choice; one simply chooses to love regardless of feelings. A person may insult, injure, or humiliate; but *agape love* chooses to seek only the highest good for that person. It is sacrificial love, a love that is willing to die even for its enemies.

Agape love means…

- sacrificial giving
- free acceptance (one freely accepts without any expectation of return)
- cherished attachment
- unselfish devotion
- personal commitment
- genuine concern
- strong loyalty
- precious tenderness

Agape love was so new and so unusual that it can be said that after Christ a new word for love had to be created. Jesus' primary interest with Peter was, of course, that he possess *agape love*: the love that comes from reason and will, that controls the corruptible lusts and wandering thoughts of life, that puts a willingness within a man to serve and to die for all men—even for a person's enemies. Even the enemies of God must hear the gospel and have an opportunity for salvation. However, the fact that Jesus also used *phileo love* with Peter shows that God wants the love of man's warm instinctive feelings as well.

Agape love means at least eight things.

1. *Agape love* is not only a love of emotions. It is a matter of the mind as well as of the heart, of the will as well as of the emotions.

> **"For God so loved the world that he gave his one and only Son, that whoever believes in him shall not perish but have eternal life. (John 3:16)**
> **You see, at just the right time, when we were still powerless, Christ died for the ungodly. Very rarely will anyone die for a righteous man, though for a good man someone might possibly dare to die. But God demonstrates his own love for us in this: While we were still sinners, Christ died for us. (Rom 5:6-8)**
> **This is how God showed his love among us: He sent his one and only Son into the world that we might live through him. This is love: not that we loved God, but that he loved us and sent his Son as an atoning sacrifice for our sins. (1 John 4:9-10)**

2. *Agape love* is God's love—His very nature. It is the love that God extended toward us, in that while we were still sinners, Christ died for us.

> **But God demonstrates his own love for us in this: While we were still sinners, Christ died for us. For if, when we were God's enemies, we were reconciled to him through the death of his Son, how much more, having been reconciled, shall we be saved through his life! (Rom 5:8, 10)**
> **Dear friends, let us love one another, for love comes from God. Everyone who loves has been born of God and knows God. Whoever does not love does not know God, because God is love. This is how God showed his love among us: He sent his one and only Son into the world that we might live through him. This is love: not that we loved God, but that he loved us and sent his Son as an atoning sacrifice for our sins.**

> **And so we know and rely on the love God has for us. God is love. Whoever lives in love lives in God, and God in him. (1 John 4:7-10, 16)**

3. *Agape love* is a seed that can be planted in the heart only by Christ. It is a fruit of the Spirit of God.

> **And hope does not disappoint us, because God has poured out his love into our hearts by the Holy Spirit, whom he has given us. (Rom 5:5)**
> **But the fruit of the Spirit is love, joy, peace, patience, kindness, goodness, faithfulness, (Gal 5:22)**

4. *Agape love* is the great love that God holds for His own dear Son.

> **If you obey my commands, you will remain in my love, just as I have obeyed my Father's commands and remain in his love. (John 15:10)**
> **I have made you known to them, and will continue to make you known in order that the love you have for me may be in them and that I myself may be in them." (John 17:26)**

5. *Agape love* was perfectly expressed when God gave up His own Son to die for man.

> **For Christ's love compels us, because we are convinced that one died for all, and therefore all died. (2 Cor 5:14)**
> **But because of his great love for us, God, who is rich in mercy, (Eph 2:4)**
> **And to know this love that surpasses knowledge—that you may be filled to the measure of all the fullness of God. (Eph 3:19)**
> **And live a life of love, just as Christ loved us and gave himself up for us as a fragrant offering and sacrifice to God. (Eph 5:2)**

6. *Agape love* is the love which holds believers together. For three years Jesus Himself had held the apostles together. Now that He was about to leave them, what was going to keep them together and keep them at the task? One thing: the new commandment—*agape love*. *Agape love* is the love believers are to have for one another.

> **"My children, I will be with you only a little longer. You will look for me, and just as I told the Jews, so I tell you now: Where I am going, you cannot come. "A new command I give you: Love one another. As I have loved you, so you must love one another. By this all men will know that you are my disciples, if you love one another." (John 13:33-35)**
> **If anyone has material possessions and sees his brother in need but has no pity on him, how can the love of God be in him? Dear children, let us not love with words or tongue but with actions and in truth. (1 John 3:17-18)**

7. *Agape love* is the love which believers are to have for all men.

> Do everything in love. (1 Cor 16:14)
> May the Lord make your love increase and overflow for each other and for everyone else, just as ours does for you. (1 Th 3:12)
> And to godliness, brotherly kindness; and to brotherly kindness, love. (2 Pet 1:7)

a. Agape love seeks the welfare of all.

> Each of us should please his neighbor for his good, to build him up. (Rom 15:2)

b. Agape love works no ill to its neighbor.

> Let no debt remain outstanding, except the continuing debt to love one another, for he who loves his fellowman has fulfilled the law. The commandments, "Do not commit adultery," "Do not murder," "Do not steal," "Do not covet," and whatever other commandment there may be, are summed up in this one rule: "Love your neighbor as yourself." Love does no harm to its neighbor. Therefore love is the fulfillment of the law. (Rom 13:8-10)

c. Agape love seeks opportunities to do good to all men, especially to those of the household of faith.

> Therefore, as we have opportunity, let us do good to all people, especially to those who belong to the family of believers. (Gal 6:10)
> Therefore, as God's chosen people, holy and dearly loved, clothe yourselves with compassion, kindness, humility, gentleness and patience. Bear with each other and forgive whatever grievances you may have against one another. Forgive as the Lord forgave you. And over all these virtues put on love, which binds them all together in perfect unity. (Col 3:12-14; cp. 1 Cor.13:1f)

8. *Agape love* is proven by obedience to Christ. Doing as one wishes instead of doing as God wills shows that one does not have agape love.

> "If you love me, you will obey what I command. Whoever has my commands and obeys them, he is the one who loves me. He who loves me will be loved by my Father, and I too will love him and show myself to him." Jesus replied, "If anyone loves me, he will obey my teaching. My Father will love him, and we will come to him and make our home with him. (John 14:15, 21, 23)
> If you obey my commands, you will remain in my love, just as I have obeyed my Father's commands and remain in his love. (John 15:10)
> But if anyone obeys his word, God's love is truly made complete in him. This is how we know we are in him: (1 John 2:5)
> This is love for God: to obey his commands. And his commands are not burdensome, (1 John 5:3)
> And this is love: that we walk in obedience to his commands. As you have heard from the beginning, his command is that you walk in love. (2 John 1:6)

	H. Event 8: The Great Call to Total Commitment, 21:18-25	asked, "Lord, what about him?"	John's task
1 Total commitment demands following the leadership of another (the Holy Spirit) a. When young: Peter walked and did as he willed b. When old: Another would carry Peter where he would not go	18 I tell you the truth, when you were younger you dressed yourself and went where you wanted; but when you are old you will stretch out your hands, and someone else will dress you and lead you where you do not want to go."	22 Jesus answered, "If I want him to remain alive until I return, what is that to you? You must follow me." 23 Because of this, the rumor spread among the brothers that this disciple would not die. But Jesus did not say that he would not die; he only said, "If I want him to remain	b. Jesus rebuked Peter c. Jesus challenged & called Peter again d. John corrected the rumor
2 Total commitment demands the cross—death to self: "Follow me" **3 Total commitment demands undivided attention to one's own task**	19 Jesus said this to indicate the kind of death by which Peter would glorify God. Then he said to him, "Follow me!" 20 Peter turned and saw that the disciple whom Jesus loved was following them. (This was the one who had leaned back against Jesus at the supper and had said, "Lord, who is going to betray you?")	alive until I return, what is that to you?" 24 This is the disciple who testifies to these things and who wrote them down. We know that his testimony is true. 25 Jesus did many other things as well. If every one of them were written down, I suppose that even the whole world would not have room for the books that would be	**4 Total commitment demands bearing witness to Jesus Christ** a. John bore witness[DS1] b. John's witness was true c. John's witness includes only a few of the things that Jesus did[DS2]
a. Peter questioned	21 When Peter saw him, he	written.	

DIVISION XVI

THE REVELATION OF JESUS, THE RISEN LORD, 20:1-21:23

H. Event 8: The Great Call to Total Commitment, 21:18-25

(21:18-25) **Introduction**: this is the final passage of John's gospel. It is the great call to total commitment.

1. Total commitment demands following the leadership of another (the Holy Spirit) (v.18).
2. Total commitment demands the cross—death to self: "Follow me" (v.19).
3. Total commitment demands undivided attention to one's own task (v.20-23).
4. Total commitment demands bearing witness to Jesus Christ (v.24-25).

1 (21:18) **Commitment—Dedication**: total commitment requires following the leadership of another (the Holy Spirit). Who is meant by "another"? In this context it can mean either those who were to carry Peter to death, the Romans; or the Holy Spirit, who was to carry Peter through a life of suffering and martyrdom for the cause of Christ. Jesus seemed to be referring to the whole of Peter's life, ranging from his earlier years when he did what he wished over to his older years when he would be doing what God wished. Because of this, it seems best to interpret "another" as the Holy Spirit.

Jesus was challenging Peter to serve Him, to "feed my sheep" (v.15-17). He was calling Peter to total commitment, and total commitment requires following the leadership of the Holy Spirit. Note two points.

1. When Peter was young he girded himself, dressed and walked where he willed. Before he knew Christ, he...

- ran his life as he willed
- did what he wanted
- went where he wished
- talked as he willed
- chose the pleasures he desired
- chose the profession he wanted

When he was younger, before he ever came to know Christ, Peter was able to live and do what he wanted when he wanted. But no more. Peter could no longer live as he wished. Jesus Christ, his Savior and Lord, was now to control his life.

2. When Peter was old and mature, the Holy Spirit would dress him and carry him places he would not choose or will to go. This, of course, refers to the suffering and martyrdom Peter was to undergo for the sake of Christ.

Since Peter was accepting the call of Christ to *feed His sheep*, Peter would have to...

- live his life as the Spirit willed.
- do what the Spirit wanted.
- choose the profession the Spirit willed.
- go where the Spirit wished.

Note: Jesus was saying that Peter was to be led "where he did not want to go."

⇒ He was to live a life of suffering (cp. his imprisonments, Acts 4:3; 5:18; 12:4).
⇒ He was to die the death of a martyr. His death was to be for the cause of Christ and the glory of God.

Remember that Peter had a wife (see DEEPER STUDY # 1—Mt.8:14). At the time of this event, Peter was to live some forty years or more, so he was probably a newlywed. Tradition says that Peter's wife served with him in the ministry for many years. A touching picture is given by Clement of Alexandria who says that she was martyred with Peter:

"On seeing his wife led to death, Peter rejoiced on account of her call and her conveyance home, and called very encouragingly and comfortingly, addressing her by name, 'Remember thou the Lord'"

There is strong evidence that Peter was crucified in Rome. Tradition says he felt so unworthy to die in the same manner as His Lord that he begged to be crucified upside down.

Thought 1. The call of Christ is to *total commitment*, not just to commitment. Total commitment demands that we follow the leadership of the Holy Spirit.
1) We can no longer dress and walk as we will.
2) We are to dress and walk as the Holy Spirit wills. (See notes, Holy Spirit—Jn.14:15-26; 16:7-15 for more discussion.)

Thought 2. The call of Christ involves persecution. The true believer lives a sacrificial and godly life, bearing a strong testimony and a strong witness. Such a life is rejected and opposed by most in the world.

In fact, everyone who wants to live a godly life in Christ Jesus will be persecuted, (2 Tim 3:12)

Without being frightened in any way by those who oppose you. This is a sign to them that they will be destroyed, but that you will be saved—and that by God. (Phil 1:28)

Dear friends, do not be surprised at the painful trial you are suffering, as though something strange were happening to you. But rejoice that you participate in the sufferings of Christ, so that you may be overjoyed when his glory is revealed. If you are insulted because of the name of Christ, you are blessed, for the Spirit of glory and of God rests on you. (1 Pet 4:12-14)

To this you were called, because Christ suffered for you, leaving you an example, that you should follow in his steps. (1 Pet 2:21)

The world persecutes the person who lives godly; it persecutes him at work, at play, at home—wherever and whenever it pleases. The world...
- reproaches
- ridicules
- mocks
- by-passes
- shuns
- ignores
- attacks
- curses
- abuses
- martyrs
- murders

Christ was calling Peter to such a life, telling him that the Holy Spirit would carry him to places he would not choose. Christ tells us the same thing. Total commitment requires following the leadership of the Holy Spirit, and all who follow the Holy Spirit shall suffer persecution.

Thought 3. We shall die, everyone of us. How we die should concern us...
- whether we die in self: having lived in comfort, ease, plenty, pleasure, wealth, extravagance, pride, unbelief.
- whether we die for Christ: having lived a godly life, bearing testimony, witnessing, helping, giving, ministering and meeting the desperate needs of a world reeling in sin and death.

Just as man is destined to die once, and after that to face judgment, (Heb 9:27)

For we must all appear before the judgment seat of Christ, that each one may receive what is due him for the things done while in the body, whether good or bad. (2 Cor 5:10)

2 (21:19) **Commitment**: total commitment requires the cross, death to self. One must *follow* Christ (see DEEPER STUDY # 1—Lk.9:23 for discussion).

Then he said to them all: "If anyone would come after me, he must deny himself and take up his cross daily and follow me. (Luke 9:23)

"If anyone comes to me and does not hate his father and mother, his wife and children, his brothers and sisters—yes, even his own life—he cannot be my disciple. (Luke 14:26)

In the same way, any of you who does not give up everything he has cannot be my disciple. (Luke 14:33)

When Jesus spoke again to the people, he said, "I am the light of the world. Whoever follows me will never walk in darkness, but will have the light of life." (John 8:12)

Whoever serves me must follow me; and where I am, my servant also will be. My Father will honor the one who serves me. (John 12:26)

3 (21:20-23) **Commitment**: total commitment requires undivided attention to one's own task. Peter asked Jesus what John would be doing in his ministry. Peter and John were very close. John was younger than Peter, probably still a teenager. Apparently, Peter had taken a very close liking to John and had taken him into his care even before Christ had come along (cp. John, Introduction—Author). Peter's interest in John's task and future was therefore natural. Note three things.

1. Jesus rebuked Peter. He told Peter that John's task was not his concern. His own task was to be his concern. Peter was not to look at another man's call and ministry and...
- be distracted
- wish he had that ministry
- desire another ministry
- compare their calls and ministries
- copy or conform to that ministry
- meddle

Nobody should seek his own good, but the good of others. (1 Cor 10:24)

Do not cause anyone to stumble, whether Jews, Greeks or the church of God—even as I try to please everybody in every way. For I am not seeking my own good but the good of many, so that they may be saved. (1 Cor 10:32-33)

Do nothing out of selfish ambition or vain conceit, but in humility consider others better than yourselves. Each of you should look not only to your own interests, but also to the interests of others. (Phil 2:3-4)

2. Jesus challenged and called Peter again: "Follow me" (v.22).

375

⇒ Concentrate on your own call and task.
⇒ Focus your attention, will, energy, and efforts upon your own call and task.
⇒ Realize that God knows where you can best serve and that He calls you to that task.

Keep watch over yourselves and all the flock of which the Holy Spirit has made you overseers. Be shepherds of the church of God, which he bought with his own blood. (Acts 20:28)

Be shepherds of God's flock that is under your care, serving as overseers—not because you must, but because you are willing, as God wants you to be; not greedy for money, but eager to serve; (1 Pet 5:2)

To the weak I became weak, to win the weak. I have become all things to all men so that by all possible means I might save some. I do all this for the sake of the gospel, that I may share in its blessings. (1 Cor 9:22-23)

I thank Christ Jesus our Lord, who has given me strength, that he considered me faithful, appointing me to his service. (1 Tim 1:12)

Then I will give you shepherds after my own heart, who will lead you with knowledge and understanding. (Jer 3:15)

I will place shepherds over them who will tend them, and they will no longer be afraid or terrified, nor will any be missing," declares the LORD. (Jer 23:4)

"Son of man, I have made you a watchman for the house of Israel; so hear the word I speak and give them warning from me. (Ezek 3:17)

3. John corrected a rumor, an error spreading throughout the church. Some had taken the words of Jesus and misconstrued them, saying that Jesus meant that John would never die. Some were saying that John would survive until Jesus' return to earth. John very simply said this was not what Jesus was saying.

Thought 1. Note how easily the Lord's words are misunderstood unless they are taken at face value, exactly as He spoke them.

Do your best to present yourself to God as one approved, a workman who does not need to be ashamed and who correctly handles the word of truth. (2 Tim 2:15)

4 (21:24-25) Commitment: total commitment demands bearing witness to Jesus Christ and fulfilling one's task on earth, just as John bore witness and fulfilled his task. John bore witness: the Gospel of John is his testimony to the world. And note: John emphasized that his testimony was true; he had not lied.

But these are written that you may believe that Jesus is the Christ, the Son of God, and that by believing you may have life in his name. (John 20:31)

Thought 1. The primary task of every believer is to bear witness to the truth: Jesus is the Christ, the Son of God who has come to give life to man—both abundant and eternal life.

The thief comes only to steal and kill and destroy; I have come that they may have life, and have it to the full. (John 10:10)

But you will receive power when the Holy Spirit comes on you; and you will be my witnesses in Jerusalem, and in all Judea and Samaria, and to the ends of the earth." (Acts 1:8)

And the things you have heard me say in the presence of many witnesses entrust to reliable men who will also be qualified to teach others. (2 Tim 2:2)

But in your hearts set apart Christ as Lord. Always be prepared to give an answer to everyone who asks you to give the reason for the hope that you have. But do this with gentleness and respect, (1 Pet 3:15)

DEEPER STUDY # 1
(21:24) Jesus Christ, Death; Resurrection—World, Hope of—Man: the great witness of John (and of the other gospel writers) is:

"For God so loved the world that he gave his one and only Son, that whoever believes in him shall not perish but have eternal life. (John 3:16)

Very simply stated, the great witness is the glorious news of the death and resurrection of Jesus Christ. The death and resurrection of Jesus Christ changes the fate of world history and the whole attitude of man. If the death and resurrection of Christ had never taken place…

• then of all creatures, man would be the most miserable and hopeless.
• then the life of Jesus Christ would have been the most tragic and despairing event in all history.

Why? Because the most merciful and compassionate, the most giving and helpful human being in all the world was treated and killed in the most savage way. However, the death and resurrection of Jesus Christ did happen, and because it did, it has changed the whole perspective and truth of world history. Because of the death and resurrection of Jesus Christ, life and history have become purposeful. Since Christ has died and risen from the dead, men look at the cross and get a sense, a feeling…

• that the punishment for sin has been paid (atonement).
• that sin can now be forgiven (forgiveness).
• that a perfect life has been sacrificed for man (propitiation).
• that man can now be reconciled and made one with God (reconciliation).
• that man can now be reconciled to man, both personally and worldwide (peace, unity, community, fellowship).
• that man can now be declared righteous (justification).
• that man can be made into a *new creation* before God (regeneration).
• that man can be redeemed (redemption).
• that man can be set apart unto God (sanctification).

DEEPER STUDY # 2
(21:25) See note, Jesus Christ, Works—Jn.20:30 for discussion.

THE
OUTLINE & SUBJECT INDEX

REMEMBER: When you look up a subject and turn to the Scripture reference, you have not only the Scripture, you have *an outline and a discussion* (commentary) of the Scripture and subject.

This is one of the *GREAT VALUES* of **The Preacher's Outline & Sermon Bible**®. Once you have all the volumes, you will have not only what all other Bible indexes give you, that is, a list of all the subjects and their Scripture references, *BUT* you will also have…

- An outline of *every* Scripture and subject in the Bible.
- A discussion (commentary) on every Scripture and subject.
- Every subject supported by other Scriptures or cross references.

DISCOVER THE GREAT VALUE for yourself. Quickly glance below to the very first subject of the Index of John. It is:

> **ABIDE - ABIDING**
> Condition for salvation. Belief & **a.** 8:31

Turn to the reference. Glance at the Scripture and outline of the Scripture, then read the commentary. You will immediately see the *GREAT VALUE* of the *INDEX* of **The Preacher's Outline & Sermon Bible**®.

OUTLINE AND SUBJECT INDEX

ABIDE - ABIDING
Condition for salvation. Belief & **a.** 8:31
Duty.
    To **a.** in Christ. 15:1-8
    To let the Word **a.** or dwell in us. 5:38
Proves. A person's obedience. 15:10
Results of **a.**
    Answered prayer. 15:7
    Comfort & help. 14:15-26
    Deliverance from judgment. 15:6
    Discipline and correction. 15:2-3
    Fruit. 15:5-8
Source of **a.**
    Christ. 15:1-8
    Christ's love. 15:9-11
    Holy Spirit. 14:16-17
Verses. List of. 8:31; 15:4

ABRAHAM
Call of. 4:22; 8:54-59
Place in Jewish history.
    Discussed. 4:22; 8:54-59
    Father of the Jews. 4:22; 8:33, 53
Seed of. Christ. 1:23
Testimony of.
    Hoped for the Messiah. 8:56
    Rejoiced to see Jesus' day. 8:54-59
Work of. Believing. Man fails to follow his belief. 8:39-40

ABUNDANCE - ABUNDANT (See **LIFE; SALVATION; SPIRITUAL FOOD; SPIRITUAL SATISFACTION**)

ACCESS
Source. Is through Christ. 14:6

ADAM
Seed of. Christ. Misunderstood by Jews. 1:23

ADOPTED - ADOPTION
How one is **a.** By the work of Christ. 8:34-36

ADULTERY - ADULTERERS
Duty of the **a.** To seek forgiveness. 8:1-11
Duty of the church.
    To converse with. 4:1-42
    To forgive. 8:1-11
Is committed. In a party-like atmosphere. 8:3-6

ADVERSARY (See **SATAN**)

ADVOCATE (See **JESUS CHRIST**, Deity; Mediator; **MEDIATOR**)

AGNOSTIC
Duty. To be open to the truth. 4:25

AMBASSADORS
Chosen. By Christ to go forth. 15:16

AMBITION - AMBITIOUS
Evil **a.** causes.
    Self-seeking. 11:47-48; 12:10-11; 12:42-43
    The fear of losing followers. 12:10-11; 12:42-43
    The fear of losing position. 11:47-48; 12:42-43

ANDREW, THE APOSTLE
Brings a little boy to Jesus. 6:1-15
Discovers Jesus. The Messiah, the Christ. 1:35-42
Discussed. 6:8-9
Witnesses to his brother, Peter. 1:35-42

ANGELS
Appearances. In the New Testament. To Mary Magdalene at resurrection. 20:11; 12-13
Function toward Christ. Ascend & descend upon. 1:50-51

ANGER
Of Jesus. Over abuse of temple. 2:13-17

ANIMAL (See **SACRIFICE, ANIMAL**)

ANNAS
High priest. Discussed. 18:12-14
Tried Jesus—unofficially. 18:12-27

ANOINT - ANOINTING
Kinds. Day to day courtesy. 12:1-11
Of believers. Foretold. 7:37-39
Of Christ.
    By a thankful person - Mary. 12:1-11
    By the Spirit. 1:32-34

APOSTASY (See **DENIAL**)
Discussed. 13:18-30
Examples. Judas. A picture of **a.** 13:18-30
Traits of. 12:4-8

APOSTLE - APOSTLES (See **DISCIPLE**)
Call of.
    Andrew & Peter. 1:35-42
    Nathanael. 1:46-49
    Philip. 1:43-45

APPEARANCE, OUTWARD
Duty. To judge accurately, not by **a.** 7:24

APPOINT - APPOINTED
Purpose. To bear fruit. Threefold. 15:16
Source. By Christ. 15:16

ARIMATHEA, JOSEPH OF
Buries Jesus. The conquest of fear. 19:38-42

ASSURANCE
Comes by.
    Being born again. Gives absolute **a.** 3:3
    Being washed. 13:6-11
    Coming to Christ. 6:37; 12:44-46
    Five things. 6:37-40
    God working all things out for good. 11:55-57
    God's keeping power. 10:27-29; 17:11-12
    God's predestination. 6:37; 6:39; 6:44-46
    Hearing Jesus' Word. 5:24; 10:27-29; 11:44-46
    Jesus' prayer. 17:9-26
    Three things. 6:40
Discussed. 6:37-40; 10:27-29; 17:9-19
Needed.
    Facing the world. 17:9-19
    Receiving eternal life. 5:24; 10:27-29
    Salvation. 10:7-10
    Securing abundant life. 10:7-10
Verses. List of. 6:39; 10:9

ASTROLOGY
Error of. Causes men to seek fate in stars, magic. 5:2-4

INDEX

INDEX

CHOSEN
By whom. Christ. 13:18
Out of the world. 15:18-19
Purpose. To go; bear fruit; receive things. 15:16

CHRISTIAN (See **BELIEVER**)

CHRISTIANITY
Accused of.
Being a bloody religion; the worship of a "grotesque god." 6:61
Fruit of. Bearing fruit. 15:1-8
Life - Walk - Behavior.
Contrasted with the world's life. 8:1-11

CHURCH
Authority of. Discussed. 20:23
Cleansed - cleansing. By Christ. Supremacy over. 2:12-22
Described.
As flock of God. 21:15-17
As spiritual bond of friends. 15:14-15
Body of Christ. Becomes new temple. 2:18-21
Ministry to. To feed & shepherd. 21:15-17
Mission. (See **COMMISSION**)
Charter of. 20:19-23
Christ needs the c. & the c. needs Christ. 20:21
Nature.
Not a house of merchandise. 2:12-22
Problems. (See **CARNAL**; 2 Corinthians Outline)
Being made a house of merchandise. 2:12-22
Revelling in fellowship and not witnessing. 20:17-18
Supremacy over. By Christ. 2:12-22
Unity of. Discussed. 17:11

CITIZENSHIP (See **GOVERNMENT**)

CLEANSE - CLEANSING
Discussed. 13:6-11
How to be cleansed. By the Word. 17:17

CLEOPHAS
Husband of Mary. 19:25

CLOTHING (See **GARMENT**)

COAT (See **GARMENT**)

COEXISTENT
Of Christ with God. Meaning. 1:1-2

COHORT
Meaning. A regiment of Roman soldiers. 18:3

COLT
Discussed. 12:14-15

COMFORTER, THE (See **HOLY SPIRIT**)

COMMANDMENT - COMMANDMENTS (See **OBEDIENCE**)
Are demanded by J. death. 13:31-35
Jesus' c.
Is a new c. 13:34-35
Is onefold. 13:34-35; 15:12-17
Obeying the c.
Is essential to abide in Christ & God. 15:10, 14-17
Proves one's love. 14:15, 21, 24; 15:10, 14
The new c. - love. 13:31-35

COMMISSION (See **MISSION**)
Described.
As being sent. 20:21
As being sent from the side, the heart of God. 1:6
As proclaiming the resurrection. 20:17-18
Given by.
Christ. 20:21
God. 1:6
Given to. Mary Magdalene. 20:17-18
Great c. 20:19-23
Great charter of church. 20:19-23
Meaning. 1:6
Urgency of. 9:4

COMMIT - COMMITMENT (See **DEDICATION**)
Essential. Love is one basic e. 21:15; 21:15-17
Meaning. 2:23-24

COMMUNION (See **DEVOTION**)

COMPASSION
Of Jesus.
Groans over man's desperate plight. 11:33-36; 11:38-40
Reaches out to man. 5:5-9
Verses. List of. 11:33-36

COMPROMISE
Discussed. 18:28-19:15
Illust. By Pilate. 18:28-19:15

CONDEMN - CONDEMNATION (See **JUDGMENT**, Condemnation)
Caused by. Unbelief. 3:18-21
Deliverance from. Discussed. 3:16-21
Discussed. 3:18-21
Who escapes c. 3:21

CONFESS - CONFESSION
Duty. To c. publicly. 1:49; 19:38-42
Of Christ.
Offends some. 6:59-71
Why some do not c. 6:59-71
Of Thomas. Great conviction & c. 20:24-29
Source - stirred by.
Conviction. 1:49
Death of Jesus. 19:38-42
Resurrection of Jesus. 20:12-13

CONFIDENCE (See **ASSURANCE - SECURITY**)

CONTENTMENT (See **JOY**)

CONVERSION - CONVERTED
How a person is c. By a stirred heart. What happens. 8:31

CONVICTION - CONVICTS
Of Holy Spirit. Meaning. 16:8-11
Of sin. Necessary for salvation. 4:15-18
Signs of. Results, reactions. 20:24-29
Work of. The Holy Spirit. 16:8-11

CORRUPTION
Seed of. In world. 12:31
Physical vs. spiritual dimension. 8:23
Verses. List of. 1:14

COUNSELOR (See **HOLY SPIRIT**)

COURAGE - COURAGEOUS
Failure in c. (See **DENY - DENIAL**) 12:42-43

COVET - COVETOUSNESS (See **GREED**)
Result. Deception, hypocrisy. Verses. List of. 12:4-8

CREATION
Creator of. Christ. 1:1-5; 1:3
Of man.
Discussed. 4:23
In the image & likeness of God. 4:23
Purposes of c. 4:23-24

CRITICIZE - CRITICISM
C. the sacrifice of believers. 12:4-8
Man's c. spirit. 8:3-6
Object of c. Believers & their sacrifice. 12:4-8
Source of. Sinners. Spirit of judging others. 8:3-6

CROSS - SELF-DENIAL
Duty. To sacrifice oneself for Christ. 12:23-26
Misunderstood. By Peter & the disciples. 13:36-38
Verses. List of. 12:23-26

CRUCIFIXION
Described. A lingering death. 19:34

CUP
Meaning. Symbol of Christ's suffering. 18:11

DARKNESS
Discussed. 8:12
Deliverance of. How to get out of. 8:12
Meaning. 8:12
Nature. Loved by unbelievers. Reasons. 3:18-20
Results. Causes fear. 6:17-19
Verses. List of. 3:18-20; 11:7-10
Weakness of.
Cannot overcome light. 1:5
What d. does not do. Three things. 1:5

DAVID
Choosing of. 4:22
Seed of. Messiah.
Promises & fulfillment. 1:45; 1:49
Seen as seed of David by Jews. 1:23

DEATH - DYING
Attitude toward.
Fear of d. 6:17-19
To be a. of hope, not despair. 20:14-16
Caused by.
Nature. 8:23
Sin. Penalty of. 8:21-22
Unbelief. 8:21-22; 8:24
Deliverance from.
By Christ's death. 3:14-15; 3:16-17
By Christ's great power. 11:1-16; 11:41-46
Power over. Discussed. 11:38-46
Through Jesus' return. 14:1-3
Described.
As personal presentation to the Lord. 14:3
As sleep. 11:13

Will not see life. 3:36
Wrath of God. 3:36
Source.
Death of Christ. 3:14-15
Promised by Christ. 3:16-17; 4:14;
5:24-29; 6:35, 40, 51, 58; 10:28;
11:25-27; 12:25, 50; 17:3; 20:31
Verses. List of. 8:51; 11:25-27; 17:2-3

EVANGELISM - EVANGELIZE
Why e. Fields are ripe for harvest. 4:35

EVIL SPIRITS
Work of. To possess evil men. 13:27-30

EXALT - EXALTATION (See **JESUS CHRIST**, Exaltation of)
Duty. To e. Christ & not self. 3:29-30

EXPECTATION (See **HOPE**)

EXPOSURE - EXPOSED
Of sin. Known by God. 1:47-48; 2:24-25;
5:42; 13:19-20

FAITH
Duty. To persevere in f. 4:48-49
Evidence of - Proofs of.
Discussed. 4:43-45
Twofold. 4:43-45
Growth in. Martha's growth in f. 11:17-27
Meaning.
Commit. 2:24
Obedience. 3:36; 4:50; 4:51-53; 5:5-9;
9:6-7
Stages - Kinds.
Beginning f. What happens. 8:31
Complaining, limited f. 11:21-22
Confirmed f. 4:53
Declared f. 11:25-27
Discussed. 4:46-54
Silent f. 12:42-43
Fundamental f. 11:23-24
Pessimistic; questioning; unswerving f.
6:1-15
Resting, unlimited f. 6:10-13; 11:21-
22; 11:40
Three k. 11:17-27
Unlimited, resting f. Meaning. 11:21-
22; 11:40
Weak f. Discussed. 6:7; 6:8-9
Vs. works.
Discussed. 6:28-29
F. apart from works. 4:50

FAITHLESSNESS
Jesus' death reveals weak f. 13:36-38

FALSE PROFESSION (See **PROFESSION, FALSE**)

FALSE TEACHERS (See **TEACHERS, FALSE**)

FAMILY
Duty. To witness to f. 4:53-54
Of Christ. (See **JESUS CHRIST**, Family)

FAVORITISM (See **PARTIALITY, PREJUDICE**)

FEAR, HUMAN
Causes of. 6:16-21
Darkness. Being in the dark; spiritual
blindness. 6:17-19

Men. F. men more than f. God. Reason. 19:13-15
Men. Seeking to harm. 9:22; 20:19
Persecution. 20:19
Deliverance - Overcome by.
Christ's presence. 6:19-21
Discussed. 6:16-21
Results.
Causes silence—a failure to testify.
9:22
Causes unbelief. Three fears. 11:47-48

FEAST - FEASTS
Of Dedication. Discussed. 10:22
Of Tabernacles. Discussed. 7:37

FEEDING OF FIVE THOUSAND
Discussed. 6:1-15

FELLOWSHIP (See **BROTHERHOOD - UNITY**)
Basis - Source.
Abiding in Christ. 15:1-8
Christ. Jesus concentrates upon. 11:54
Danger - Problems.
Revelling in f. and not witnessing.
20:17-18
Withdrawing. What causes. 20:24-25
Described. A spiritual bond of friends.
15:14-15
Discussed. 6:56
Duty. To f. & be sociable. 2:1-2

FIG TREE
Discussed. 1:48

FLESH
Control of. By Christ. Christ counteracts.
1:14
Discussed. 1:14
Meaning. 1:14
Stirs a fleshy, carnal commitment.
13:36-38
Works - Shortcomings of.
Becomes focus of man. Attempts to
dress up. 6:63
Profits nothing. 6:63

FLOG - FLOGGING
Discussed. 19:1

FOOD, SPIRITUAL (See **HUNGER, SPIRITUAL; SPIRITUAL FOOD**)

FOLLOW
Duty. To f. Jesus, seeking salvation &
truth. 1:35-37
Meaning. 1:43

FORGIVENESS, SPIRITUAL
Essential - Necessity. Before service.
13:6-11
Source.
Believers given authority to remit &
retain sins. 20:23
God. Man's dark sinfullness & God's
great f. 8:1-11
Symbolized. In cleansing. 2:6-9

FREEDOM (See **LIBERTY**)

FRIENDS - FRIENDSHIP (See **BROTHERHOOD**)

FRUIT-BEARING (See **BELIEVER; DEDICATION**)
Discussed. 15:1-8
Facts. No f. apart from the vine. 15:4
Meaning. What f. is. Three things. 15:1-8
Purpose.
Of believers. Are chosen for f. 15:16
Of world. Relationship of Jesus to the
people of the world. 15:1-8

FULLNESS OF TIME
World prepared by forerunner. Three
ways. 1:23

FULLNESS, SPIRITUAL (See **HUNGER, SPIRITUAL; SATISFACTION**)
Of life. Discussed. 1:16-17
Source - Provision of.
Discussed. 6:30-36
Jesus Christ. 1:16-17; 10:9
Verses. List of. 6:34-35; 6:55; 10:9

GALILEE
Discussed. 4:43

GARMENT
Of Jesus.
Gambled for. 19:24
Without seams. 19:23

GATE
Title of Christ. G. of sheep. 10:7-10

GENTLENESS (See **HUMILITY**)

GIVE - GIVING
Duty.
To g. what one has. Verses. List of.
6:10-13

GLORY (See **JESUS CHRIST**, Glory of;
GOD, Glory of)
How to secure g. Death to self & service.
12:23-26
Of believer.
Chart of g. of Christ & of believer.
17:22
Discussed. 17:22
Of Christ. Discussed. 1:14; 12:23-26;
17:1
Of God. Supreme purpose of Jesus'
death. 12:27-30; 17:4
Shekinah. Discussed. 1:14

GOD
And Christ.
Beloved Son. Verses. List of. 5:20
Dearest thing to God's heart. 3:16;
3:35-36; 5:20
Mutual Indwelling with C. 5:17-30;
8:15-16; 14:10
Revealed all His works through. 5:20
Intimate knowledge. 5:17-30; 10:14-16
One with Christ. 5:17-30; 8:15-16;
10:14-16; 14:10
Verses. List of. 5:19; 8:54-59
Existence of. Seen in Christ. 1:18; 14:9-11
Holy. Verses. List of. 20:12-13
How to know - Way to God.
Discussed. 1:18; 7:16-19
Ignorance about. Verses. List of. 4:22;
7:25-31; 8:19
Men question. 14:4-5
Only one gate, Christ Himself. 10:7-8
Image of. Man created in i. of God. 4:23

Knowledge - Omniscience.
  Knows all about men. 1:47-48; 2:24-25
  Mutual **k.** between God & Christ.
    10:14-16
Love of.
  A past, proven fact. 3:16
  Cost of. What it cost God to **l.** man.
    3:16
  Gave dearest thing to His heart, Own
    Son. 3:16
  God's great **l.** 3:16-17
  Of religious & non-religious. 3:16
  Shown in most perfect way possible.
    3:16
Name - Titles.
  "My Father." Father of Christ. 1:34;
    10:25, 29-30
  Savior. 4:42
Nature.
  God is True. 3:33
  Has never been seen by man. 1:18;
    5:37-38; 8:19
  Invisible. 1:18; 5:37-38; 8:19
  Not distant & far off. 14:9
  Spirit. 4:23-24; 4:24
Profession of. (See **PROFESSION,**
  FALSE)
Providence - Sovereignty.
  God overrules unbelief & uses it for
    good. Verses. List of. 11:55-57
Purpose. Plan for the ages. 4:22
Revealed - revelation of. Not by man, but
  by Christ. 1:18; 3:13; 3:31
Source of. Life. 5:26
Unseen. Never seen by man. Verses. List
  of. 5:37-38; 8:19
Will of.
  Christ came to do the **w.** of God. 6:38;
    6:39; 6:40
  For believers. To be assured, secured.
    Never lost. 6:39; 6:40
  For Christ. To have many followers.
    6:39
  To save men. 4:31-35
Works of.
  Discussed. 9:4
  Draws man. 6:37-39; 6:44-46
  Revealed in Christ. 5:20
  To save men. 4:31-35

GODS, FALSE (See **IDOLATRY**)
Source. Created by man's imaginations,
  ideas. 8:54-59

GOSPEL
Duty. To be open to **g.** 4:24
Message of. Threefold. 11:28
Of John. Purpose. 20:30-31
Resistance. Response to. 6:44
Response to **g.** Hardened to. Danger of.
  4:25
Writing of. Include only a few of Jesus'
  miracles. 20:30-31

GOSSIP
Prevented. By watching one's behavior
  around opposite sex. 4:27

GOVERNMENT
Official. Comes to Jesus for help. 4:46-47

GRACE
Meaning. 1:14; 1:16-17
Source. Discussed. 1:16-17

GRATITUDE (See **THANKFUL**)

GREATNESS
Condition for. How one achieves. 13:4
Demonstrated. By Jesus. Royal service.
  13:1-17

GREED
Result. Deception, hypocrisy. Verses.
  List of. 12:4-8

GREEKS
Seek & approach Jesus. Four misunderstandings. 12:20-36

GRIEF - GRIEVE - GRIEVED
Caused by. Death. To be conquered.
  20:14-16
Nature of. Often self-centered. 16:5

GROWTH (See **SPIRITUAL FOOD;**
SPIRITUAL GROWTH)

GRUMBLING
Against Christ & His claims. 6:41-43

GUIDANCE
By whom. Holy Spirit. 16:12-13
Promised. Discussed. 16:12-13

GUILE - GUILELESSNESS (See **NOTH-**
ING FALSE)

GUILT
Causes. Unbelief. 20:24-25

HAPPY - HAPPINESS (See **FULLNESS,**
SPIRITUAL; JOY)

HARD - HARDNESS OF HEART
Danger of. 4:25
Reject Christ. 5:40-41

HARVEST
Of souls. Ripe for reaping. 4:35

HEALS - HEALING
Blind man. 9:1-7
Impotent man. 5:1-16
Nobleman's son. 4:46-54
Raises the dead. Lazarus. 11:41-46

HEART
Duty. To be open to truth. 4:25
Troubled **h.** Deliverance from. Fivefold.
  14:1-3

HEAVEN
Believers.
  Are not to make **h.** their object, but
    God. 14:6
  Are to be transported into immedi-
    ately. Never lose consciousness.
    11:25-27
Characteristics - Nature.
  Cannot be penetrated by man. 3:31
  Is real world, spiritual **w.** & dimen-
    sion. 11:25-27
Described. As God's house. 14:1-3
Search for. Man's futile **s.** for Messiah -
  utopia - heaven. 8:21-24

HERESY (See **TEACHERS, FALSE**)

HERITAGE
Weakness of. Does not make one acceptable to God. 8:33

HIGH PRIEST - CHIEF PRIESTS
Discussed. 7:32; 11:49

HISTORY
Christ & **h.**
  Changed by death of Christ. 21:24
  Supreme fact of **h.** - the Incarnation.
    1:10
God & **h.**
  God's plan for ages. 4:22
  Salvation came through the Jews. 4:22

HOLD FAST (See **ENDURANCE; PER-**
SEVERANCE)

HOLY - HOLINESS
Duty. To be holy. Verses. List of. 20:12-
  13
Symbolized. By white dress of angels.
  20:12-13

HOLY SPIRIT
And Christ.
  Came upon as a dove. 1:32
  Came upon without measure. 1:32-33;
    3:34; 5:32
  Given by Christ. Breathed on disci-
    ples. 20:22
  Identified the Messiah for John. 1:30-34
  Why His presence is better than hav-
    ing Christ with us. 16:7
Came upon - received by. Disciples.
  20:22
Deity of. Discussed. 15:26-27; 16:16
Duty.
  Must follow. 21:18-19
  Must receive. Is conditional. 14:16
Discussed. 14:15-26; 16:7-15
Lives with the believer. Verses. List of.
  14:17
Fact. Will not always contend with man.
  7:33-34; 11:54
Infilling. (See **HOLY SPIRIT**, Work of)
  14:21-22
  Verses. List of. 14:21
Names - Titles.
  Abiding Presence of Trinity. 14:23-25
  Christ in the believer. 14:20
  Counselor, Comforter. 14:16; 14:26;
    15:26-27; 16:7
  Living Water. Meaning. 7:37-39
  Spirit of Truth. 15:26-27; 16:13
  Who He is. 14:15-26
Sins against.
  Rejected. Does not always contend
    with man. 7:33-34
  Why the world cannot receive. 14:17
Source of. Christ. 7:37-39
Work of.
  Abundant life. 7:38-39
  Comfort, help. 14:16
  Convicts & convinces. Meaning.
    16:8-11
  Convicts of sin, righteousness, judg-
    ment. 16:8-11
  Difference between Old & New Tes-
    tament. 7:39
  Discussed. 16:7-15
  Gives rivers of living water. 7:37-39
  Gives special experiences, manifesta-
    tions. 14:21-22; 14:21
  Gives victory over world. 15:26-27
  Glorifies Jesus. 16:14-15
  Guides believers. 16:12-13
  Infills. 14:21-22
  Quickens. 6:63

Quickens the gospel to the hearts of men. 6:44-46
Regenerates. 3:5-6 cp. v.3-6
Reveals new truth. 3:5-6
Teaches & helps remember. 14:26
With believers & with world. 16:7-15
Witnesses to Christ. 5:32; 15:26-27

HOME (See **FAMILY**)

HONESTY
Ex. of Nathanael. Did not deceive, bait, or mislead. 1:47

HONOR
Discussed. 4:44
Duty. To **h.** Christ. 4:44
Fact.
God **h.** any man who **h.** His Son. 12:23-26
Prophet without **h.** in own country. 4:44
Some refuse to **h.** 4:44
Of Christ.
By God. 8:54-59
Discussed. 4:44
Evidence of faith. 4:44
Should be. 4:44; 5:22-23
Verses. List of. 3:29-30
Of self.
Discounted, ignored, distasteful. 8:54-59
Results in rejecting Christ. 5:44
Seeking **h.** for self. Verses. List of. 5:44

HOPE
Believer's **h.** The resurrection. 6:37-40, 44
Duty. To persevere in **h.** seeking God's help. 4:46-47

HOPELESS - HOPELESSNESS
Results. Hardness, emptiness, prejudice. 1:46

HOSANNA
Meaning. 12:12-13

HOUR, THE
Meaning. Jesus' death. 12:23-24
Of man's acclaim, not Jesus' **a.** 7:6-9

HOUSE OF GOD, THE (See **CHURCH; TEMPLE**)

HUMILITY
Duty.
Not to push oneself forward. 1:20-22
To exalt Christ & not self. 3:29-30
To seek the help of Christ in **h.** 4:46-47
Example. Jesus washing feet. Royal service. 13:1-17
To serve as a slave. 1:8; 1:27; 13:3-5

HUNGER, SPIRITUAL
Answer to.
Met by man's great **h.** 6:22-29
Verses. List of. 6:34-35; 6:55
Duty. To seek an answer & do something about one's **h.** 1:43-44
Satisfied by believing, not by works. 6:28-29

HYPOCRISY - HYPOCRITE
Discussed. Counterfeit disciples. 6:59-71
Traits of. Deception. Verses. List of. 12:4-8

I AM
Basic name of deity. Meaning. 6:20

IDOLS - IDOLATRY (See **GODS, FALSE**)

IGNORANCE - IGNORANT
About Christ.
Men **i.** that Christ is the only approach to God. 4:22
Verses. List of. 4:22
About God.
Men do not know God. 7:25-31; 8:19
Men **i.** in their worship of God. 4:22
Men question God's existence. 14:4-5
Verses. List of. 4:22; 7:25-31; 8:19

IMAGE OF GOD
Man created in **i.** of God. 4:23

IMAGINATIONS, EVIL
Creates false gods. 8:54-59
Prevented. By guarding self around opposite sex. 4:27

INCARNATION
Cost of. What it **c.** God to give His Son. 3:16
Discussed. 1:14-18
How. By the Word of God. Not by some grotesque method. 1:10; 6:61
Jesus Christ came out of heaven. 8:23
Proof.
Fourfold. 1:14-18
Of God's love. 3:17

INDIFFERENCE (See **HARDNESS; UNBELIEF**)

INDWELLING PRESENCE
Abiding. (See **ABIDE**) 15:1-8
Mutual **i.** between Christ & the believer. 6:56
Verses. List of. 6:56; 17:23
Mutual **i.** between God & Christ. 5:17-30; 8:15-16; 10:14-16; 10:37-39; 14:10; 17:10
Mutual **i.** between God, Christ, & the believer. 10:14-16; 14:18-20; 14:23-24
Of Christ in you. 14:18-20; 14:21; 14:23-24
Verses. List of. 14:20
Of the Holy Spirit. Discussed. 14:15-26; 16:7-15; 20:22-23
Verses. List of. 14:17

INHERITANCE
What the **i.** is. Sharing equally with Christ. 16:14-15

INIQUITY - INIQUITIES (See **SIN**)

INITIATIVE
Essential.
To grasp opportunity. 11:7-10
To work while day before night comes. 11:7-10

INSIGHT (See **SPIRITUAL SIGHT; UNDERSTANDING**)

INTERCESSION (See **PRAYER**)

INVITATION
Source.
Extended by Jesus. He takes the initiative. 1:39-40
God must draw man. 6:44

ISRAEL (See **JEWS**)
Capital punishment not allowed. 19:7
Chosen by God. Reasons. 4:22
Purpose. Why God chose. Fourfold **p.** 4:22
Religionists of Israel. (See **RELIGIONISTS**)

JACOB
Ladder of. Meaning. 1:51

JAMES, THE BROTHER OF JESUS
Confesses deity of Jesus. 1:14
Does not believe in Jesus, not at first. 7:3-5

JESUS CHRIST (See **INCARNATION**)
Accepted. (See **JESUS CHRIST**, Responses to)
Accused - Accusations against.
An insurrectionist. 2:19
A Samaritan. 8:48-50
Of bearing false witness. 8:13
Of being demon-possessed. 7:20-31; 8:48-50
Of opposing religion & **r.** leaders. 7:20-24
And God. (See **GOD**, And Christ)
And the Holy Spirit. (See **HOLY SPIRIT**, And Jesus Christ)
Anointed.
By the Holy Spirit. Full measure of the **S.** 1:32-33; 3:34
By women. Supreme believer. 12:1-11
Approved by God. Audible voice. 12:27-30
Arrested.
Absolute surrender. 18:1-11
Who **a.** 11:55-57
Ascension.
Preciousness of. To **be with** & to **know** the Father. 14:6
Predicted. 7:33-34; 14:4-5; 14:6; 20:17
To make way for the Spirit's coming. 16:7
Authority.
All judgment committed to. 5:22
Five witnesses to. 5:31-39
Jesus' astounding **a.**: Equality with God. 5:17-30
Over life, all of life. 5:1-47
Baptism - baptized. Discussed. 1:29-34
Betrayed. Predicted. 6:70-71; 13:18-30
Birth. (See **JESUS CHRIST**, Origin)
Divine. **b.** From & "out of" heaven. 8:23
Blood of.
Precious. 1:29-30
Repulsive to some. 6:61
Burial. In garden on Mt. Calvary. 19:40-42
Claims. (See **JESUS CHRIST**, Deity; Nature of)
Bread of Life. 6:35; 6:52-53; 6:53
Came from God. 8:42
Deity. List of fifteen or more **c.** 10:25
Verses. List of. 10:30-35

INDEX

INDEX

THE
OUTLINE & SUBJECT INDEX

Seeking man. (See **SEEK - SEEKING,** Christ **S.** Man)

Sent by God. 3:32-34; 3:34; 4:31-35; 8:42

Shepherd.
Contrast with false **s.** 10:16
Great claims of. 10:22-42
Is the gate of the sheep. 10:7-10
Of life. 10:1-42
Spokesman for God. 14:10

Teaching. Is God's **t.** 7:16-17

Temple of **J.** body. Becomes **t.** of men. 2:18-21

Trials, Legal.
Before Caiphas, High Priest. 18:19-24
Before Gentiles. 18:28-19:15
Before Pilate. Indecisive compromise. 18:28-19:15
Three charges against. 2:18; 18:19

Trials - tribulations. (See **CONDE-SCENSION; HUMILIATION; DEATH,** Sufferings; Related Subjects)
One-parent family. Joseph died early. 2:1-2

Triumphal Entry. Proclaimed as King, Messiah. 12:12-19

Will of. Distinct, separate from God. 6:38

Witness of God, The. (See **DEITY**)

Witness to.
By Andrew. The Messiah. 1:35-42
By Christ. Threefold. 1:50-51
By John the apostle.
Five **w.** to. 5:31-39
The Light of men. 1:9-13
The Word. 1:1-5
The Word became flesh. 1:14-18
By John the Baptist.
God became flesh. 1:15
Special **w.** to. 1:6-8
By Nathanael. Son of God, King of Israel. 1:46-49
By Philip. One prophesied. 1:43-45

Words of.
Of God. 14:10; 7:16-19
Prove deity. 14:10; 14:11; 15:15
Rejected. 5:47; 8:37

Work of - Ministry. (See **JESUS CHRIST,** Mission)
Bears witness to deity. 5:19; 5:20; 5:36; 10:25; 14:10
Concerned with every need. 6:1-71
Judgment committed to. Reasons. 5:22
Verses. List of. 5:22-23
Proves deity. 5:36; 14:10; 14:11; 20:30-31
Reveals union with God. 5:20
To be light of world. Discussed. 1:9
To bring peace, joy, security. 14:27-31
To bring satisfaction. 6:30-36
To cleanse God's temple. 2:12-16
To defeat Satan. 12:31; 12:32; 14:30; 16:11; 16:8-11
To give life. 5:21
To judge the world. 5:22
To make secure. 10:9
To open the eyes of man. 9:1-7
To quench man's thirst. 4:15
To resurrect & give life. 11:25-26
To serve and teach. 13:1-17
Was of God. Are God's works. 5:19; 5:20
Verses. List of. 5:20

Worship of. To be a day of universal **w.** 7:6-9

JEWS
Capital punishment not allowed. 19:7
Discussed. 5:10
Errors - Mistakes of.
Claim heritage to be children of Abraham. 8:33
Misinterpreted God's promises. 4:22
Purposes of. Reasons chosen by God. 4:22
Rejected Jesus Christ. (See **JESUS CHRIST,** Responses to; **RELIGIONISTS,** Opposed Christ)
Persecuted Jesus. 5:16; 7:13-15, 19
Sought to kill Jesus. 5:16, 17-18; 7:13, 19; 8:40, 59; 10:31-33, 39
Why Jesus came to earth as a **J.** 4:22

JOHN THE APOSTLE
Discovers empty tomb. Notices strips of linen & believes. 20:7-10
Task of. Completed. 21:24-25
Witness to Christ.
The Word. 1:1-5
Word became flesh. 1:14-18

JOHN THE BAPTIST
A priest, but not a religionist. 1:19
Cousin to Jesus Christ. 1:1:30-31
Forerunner. Why **f.** necessary. 1:23
Life of. Priest, but a different kind of **p.** 1:19
Messenger of God. 1:19-27
Witness to Christ.
God became flesh. 1:15
Lamb of God - Son of God. 1:29-34
Special **w.** to. 1:6-8

JOSEPH OF ARIMATHEA
Buries Jesus. Conquest of fear. 19:38

JOY
Discussed. 14:28-29; 15:11
Meaning. 14:28-29; 15:11
Source. 14:28-29
Access to God. 16:23-27
Jesus' purpose. 15:11
Resurrection of Jesus. 16:20-22
Salvation. Meeting Christ face to face. 1:45

JUDAS ISCARIOT
Betrayed Christ. Predicted. 13:18-30
Traits of.
A thief. Stole money. 12:4-8
Sinful **t.** Threefold. 12:4-8
Was treasurer of disciples. 12:4-8

JUDGE - JUDGING OTHERS (See **CENSORING; CRITICISM**)
Man's condemnatory, judgmental spirit. 8:3-6
Sins of.
Censoring, condemning. 8:3-6
J. by appearance. 7:24
Who can judge. 8:7-9

JUDGMENT
Committed to Christ. 5:22; 5:27
Verses. List of. 5:22-23; 5:28-30
Conviction of. 16:8-11
Described.
Thrown away & burned. 15:4-6
Condemnation. Jesus reveals **c.** 3:18-21
Separation, exclusion, shut out. 7:33-34; 8:21-22

How God judges.
Allows life to perish, corrupt. 3:16
By Christ. 5:22-23
Judges in justice. 12:39-41
Judicial judgment of God. 12:39-41
Of believers.
Already paid in cross of Christ. 12:31-32
Of unbelievers - lost.
To be **j.** by words of Christ. Reason. 12:47-50
Who is to be **j.**
The believer. (See **JUDGMENT,** Of Believers)
The unbeliever. (See **JUDGMENT,** Of Unbelievers)

JUDICIAL BLINDNESS & REJECTION
Law of. Discussed. 12:39-41

JUSTIFIED - JUSTIFICATION
How man is **j.** By cross. Discussed. 12:32

KEPT - KEEPING POWER OF GOD (See **ASSURANCE - PREDESTINATION - SECURITY**)

KIND - KINDNESS (See **CARE - CARING; MINISTERING**)

KINGDOM OF GOD
Misunderstood. Earthly **k.** vs. spiritual. 13:36-38

KNOW - KNOWING - KNOWLEDGE
Christ. (See **INDWELLING PRESENCE**)
Intimate knowledge between **C.** & believers. 10:14-16; 11:5
Intimate knowledge between **C.** & God. 8:55; 10:14-16
God. Intimate knowledge between **G.** & Christ. 10:14-16
How to **k.** God. 7:16-19; 8:31-32
Of what.
New birth. Complete assurance, **k.** 3:9-11
Of Christ. Believers know **C.** by His Word or voice & Spirit. 20:14-16

LABOR - LABORERS (See **BELIEVERS; DISCIPLES; MINISTERS**)
Discussed. Subject of **l.** For God. 4:31-42

LAMB OF GOD
Discussed. 1:29-30

LAW
Kinds. Conditioning **l.** Are eight laws of **c.** 12:39-41
Purpose. To govern behavior & unbelief. 12:39-41
Requires two witnesses to support one's testimony. 8:17-18

LAZARUS, THE BROTHER OF MARY & MARTHA
And Jesus. Power over death. 11:38-46
Death of. Purposes of. 11:1-16

LEVITES
Discussed. 1:19

LIBERATOR
Jesus the **l.** 8:34-36; 14:6

INDEX

MURMURING (See **GRUMBLING**)

NAME
Changed. Peter's **n.** changed by Christ. 1:42

NATHANAEL
Discussed. 1:46-49
Led to the Lord. 1:46-49
Witnesses to Christ: the Son of God, the King of Israel. 1:46-49

NATION (See **GOVERNMENT**)

NATURE
Discussed. Good & evil in the world. 12:31
Judgment of. Reasons. Imperfect, corruptible. 12:31
Laws governing. Eight **l.** 12:39-41

NAZARETH
Discussed. 1:46
Hometown of Christ. Rejected Him. Broke His heart. 4:44

NEEDS - NECESSITIES
Of men - Of life.
Described as hunger. Listed. 6:32
Five great **n.** 11:28-37
For Light of the world. 8:12
Met - Provided. By God. Verses. List of. 6:10-13
No **n.** that Jesus does not want to meet. 6:1-15; 10:9-10
Severe, desperate **n.** of life. 4:46-47
To prepare for the Lord. 1:23
Response to. Four **r.** 6:1-15
Social vs. spiritual **n.** 2:3-5

NEEDY, THE
Picture of. Described. Verses. Listed. 5:2-4

NEW BIRTH
A confrontation with Jesus Christ. 4:30
Discussed. 3:1-15
How to secure. Facing the truth of sin. 4:16-18
Result. Changes a person's life radically. Jn 4:30
Source. Not of man, but of God. 1:12-13

NEW CREATION
Of the world God's plan for the ages. 4:22

NEW MAN (See **NEW BIRTH**)
Result. changes a person radically. 4:30
Source.
A confrontation with Jesus Christ. 4:30
Quickening power of the Holy Spirit. Verses. List of. 6:44-46

NICODEMUS
Buries Jesus. Fear conquered by Jesus' death. 19:39
Discussed. 3:1-2
Speaks up for Christ in the Sanhedrin. 7:42

NOBLEMAN (See **ROYAL OFFICIAL**)

NOTHING FALSE (See **DECEPTION**)
Meaning. 1:47

OBEY - OBEDIENCE
Duty. Not an option if one is a believer. 14:15; 14:23; 15:14-15
Verses. List of. 15:14-15
Meaning. Faith means **o.** 3:36; 4:50; 4:51-53; 5:5-9; 9:6-7
Verses. List of. 4:50
Proves.
One's faith. 4:50
Profession, love for Christ. 14:15, 21, 23-24
Source - Stirred by. Love. 14:15; 14:21; 14:23

OBSTINATE - OBSTINACY (See **HEART**, Hard)

OFFEND - OFFENDING
What **o.** men about Christ.
Claims of Christ. 6:61
Cross, blood of Christ. 6:61
Four things **o.** 6:59-71
Lordship of Christ. 6:62

OMNIPOTENCE (See **JESUS CHRIST**, Power)

OMNISCIENCE (See **JESUS CHRIST**, Knowledge)

OPPORTUNITY
Duty. To be grasped. Timing important. 2:3-5; 11:7-10

OPPOSE - OPPOSITION
To Christ. (See **JESUS CHRIST**, Opposed)
His reply to those who **o.** 7:32-36
Reasons. He is a threat to doing as one wishes. 7:32

OPTIMISM
Faith of. But questions. 6:8-9

ORDAINED - ORDINATION (See **APPOINT - APPOINTED**)
Purpose. To bear fruit. Threefold. 15:16
Source. By Christ. 15:16

ORIGIN
Of Christ (See **JESUS CHRIST**, Nature & Origin)
Of man. (See **SIN**, Nature & Origin)
Of sin. (See **SIN**, Nature & Origin)

OUTWARD APPEARANCE (See **APPEARANCE, OUTWARD**)
Duty. To judge accurately, not by outward appearance. 7:24

PALM BRANCHES
Discussed. 12:13

PARABLE
Vine and branches. Jesus and people. 15:1-8

PARDON (See **FORGIVENESS**)

PARENTS (See **FAMILY**)

PARTIALITY (See **FAVORITISM; PREJUDICE**)

PASSIONS (See **LUST**)

PASSOVER
Atmosphere. 12:12
Attendance. Two to three million. 12:12

PASTORS (See **MINISTERS**)

PATIENCE (See **ENDURANCE; PERSEVERANCE**)
Duty - Essential. To wait upon God. 11:6
Reasons. God knows the exact time, the best time to act. 11:6

PEACE
Discussed. 14:27
Meaning. 14:27
Source. 14:27
Resurrection. Brings triumphant **p.** 16:33

PENALTY
Of sin. Is Death. 8:21-22

PENITENCE (See **CONFESSION; FORGIVENESS; REPENTANCE**)

PERFECT - PERFECTED - PERFECTION
Meaning. 17:23

PERISH - PERISHING
Deliverance from. By death of Christ. 3:14-15
Meaning. 3:16

PERSECUTION - PERSECUTORS
Answer to mockery, ridicule, sarcasm, unbelief. Given by Jesus. 7:6-9
How to overcome in **p.** 16:4-6
Answer given by Jesus. 7:6-9
Kinds - Types of.
Hatred. 17:14-16
Mockery. 7:6-9
Purpose. God uses for a greater witness. Verses. List of. 11:55-57
Reasons for. Discussed. 15:19-24; 17:14-16
Response to. 16:1
By Jesus. 11:54
Warning of. True believers shall suffer. 21:81-19
Who is going to **p.**
Religionists. Discussed. 16:1-6
World. Discussed. 15:18-27
Who is to be **p.** Believers. 4:44

PERSEVERANCE - PERSISTENCE (See **ENDURANCE; PATIENCE; STEADFASTNESS**)
Duty.
To **p.** in faith. Essential. 4:48-49
To **p.** in hope, for God's help. 4:46-47
Example of. Government official. Stages of faith. 4:44-54
Verses. List of. 8:31

PESSIMISM
Discussed. 6:7
Of faith. Discussed. 6:7

PETER
Character - Life.
Cuts off the ear of an officer. 18:10-11
Great confession of. Jesus is Messiah. 6:66-69
Love is questioned by Jesus. 21:15-17
Named changed by Christ. 1:42

Conversion - Call. Led to Lord. By brother Andrew. 1:41-42
Denial of Christ.
    Caused by two things. 13:36-38
    Foretold. Stumbling, faltering loyalty. 13:36-38
    Three **d.** Peter & the Jews. 18:12-27

PHARISEES (See **RELIGIONISTS**)
Error - Fault of.
    Condemnatory, critical spirit. 8:3-6, 33, 39, 41, 48
    Put tradition before men. 9:13-34
    Stumbling blocks to others. 12:42-43
Vs. Jesus.
    Argue over who Jesus is. 7:45-53; 8:13, 25
    Seek to arrest Jesus. 7:32
    Seek to kill Jesus. 8:40, 59; 11:53
    Seek to trap Jesus. 8:3-9

PHILIP THE APOSTLE
Conversion. Led to Lord by Christ. 1:43-45
Witness of Christ. Is the One prophesied. 1:43-45

PHYSICAL DIMENSION (See **CORRUPTION**)
Is corruptible, wasting away. (See **CORRUPTION**; **MAN**, Nature)
Only dimension seen & known by man. 8:14; 8:15-16; 8:23; 8:42-43; 11:7-10
Vs. spiritual dimension. 8:14; 8:15-16; 8:23; 8:42-43; 11:7-10

PHYSICAL FOOD
Vs. spiritual **f.** (See **SPIRITUAL FOOD**) 4:31-35

PILATE
Discussed. 18:28
Superstitious. 19:8-11
Trial of Jesus. Indecisive compromise. 18:28-19:15

PITY (See **COMPASSION**)

PLEASURE (See **WORLDLY - WORLDLINESS**)

POWER
Meaning. 2:23
Results. Led some to believe. 2:23

PRAY - PRAYER - PRAYING
Answers - Answered.
    Very reason God chooses us is to **a.** our prayer. 18:6-8
    Why Jesus **a.** prayer. 14:13-14
Described. Access into God's presence. 16:23-24
How to **p.**
    In name of Jesus. Meaning. 14:13-14
    The prayer of great purpose. 11:41-42
Of Jesus. (See **JESUS CHRIST**, Prayer Life)
Purpose. To bear fruit. 15:16
Results - Assurance.
    Answers to. Why Jesus **a.** prayer. 14:13-14
    Very reason God chooses us. To **a.** our **p.** 15:16

Source.
    Love of God. Do not have to beg God to hear. 16:25-27
    Resurrection of Christ. 16:23-24
When. At meals. 6:11

PREACHING
Described. As voice crying, "Prepare." 1:23
Duty. To exalt Christ & not self. 3:29-30

PREDESTINATION
Described. As those whom God gives to Christ. 6:37; 6:39; 6:44-46
Determined by. Eight laws. 12:39-41
Discussed. 6:37; 6:39; 6:44-46
Purpose.
    That Christ will have many brothers & sisters. 6:39
    To give security to the believer. 6:37; 6:39
Who. The chosen people of God. 15:12-17

PREEMINENCE (See **JESUS CHRIST**, Deity)

PREEXISTENCE
Of Christ. (See **JESUS CHRIST**, Deity; Preexistence)
    Meaning. 1:1-2

PREJUDICE (See **BARRIERS; DISCRIMINATION; DIVISION**)
Broken down - Abolished. By witnessing. 4:1-42
Disregards two things. 1:46
Example of.
    Disciples toward Samaritans. 4:27
    Nathanael. 1:46
Overcome. By following Jesus' example. 4:27

PRESSURE
Cause of. Deliverance from. 4:16-18

PRESTIGE
Fearing the loss of. 11:47-48

PRIDE
Results.
    Seeking approval & honor of men. 5:44
    Verses. List of. 5:44; 8:33

PRIEST (See **HIGH PRIEST**)

PROBLEMS
Caused by. Trials & storms of life. 6:17-19
Deliverance from. 14:1-3
Verses. List of. 6:17-19

PROFESSION
Kinds. Three **p.** 6:66-71

PROFESSION, FALSE - PROFESSION ONLY
Error - Misconception.
    Claim to know God, but do not really know. 8:41; 8:54-59
    Discussed. 2:23; 2:24
Evidence of. Not continuing. 8:31
Described. As betrayal, apostasy, counterfeit. 13:18-19
Kinds. Materialistic **p.** 6:14-15
Some claim to be the light to men. 1:9

PROMISE - PROMISES
Of answers to prayer. (See **PRAYER**, Answers)
    Purpose. To glorify God. 14:13-14
    Very reason Christ chose us. 15:16
Of deliverance from death. Believe & never die. 5:24-25; 11:25-27
Of salvation. Believe & never die. 11:25-27
To laborers. Will do great works & greater than Christ. 14:12

PROPHECY
Curiosity in. Causes distraction from duty. 13:36-38
Facts about. Not evidence of salvation. 11:51
P. about Christ.
    List of & their fulfillments. 1:45
    List of **p.** on death & resurrection in Gospel of John. 20:20
Rejected - Unbelief in. Leads to rejection of Christ. 5:45-46

PROPHET
Honor of. Without **h.** in own country. 4:44
View of. People thought **p.** was highest call. 9:16-17

PROVIDENCE (See **GOD**)

PROVISION, DIVINE
Source. God. Verses. List of. 6:10-13

PUNISHMENT (See **JUDGMENT**)

PURE - PURITY
Of heart. Seeking. 3:22-26

PURPOSE
Of man. Why God created **m.** 4:23-24; 4:23

QUESTIONS
About Christ.
    Are illogical & inconsistent. 12:37-41
    Cause. Unbelief. 7:20-24; 7:25-31

QUICKEN - QUICKENING
Meaning. Seeing & understanding the gospel as never before. 6:44-46
Source. Holy Spirit. Words of Christ. 6:63-64

RABBONI
Meaning. 20:14-16

RACIAL SLUR (See **PREJUDICE**)
Not worthy of comment, attention. 8:48-50

REAL
Jesus, the Real. 1:9

REAP - REAPING (See **WITNESSING**)

REBELLION (See **UNBELIEF**)

RECEPTIVE - RECEPTIVITY (See **JESUS CHRIST**, Response to)
Duty. To be **r.** to Christ. 4:45

RECOMPENSE (See **RETALIATION; REVENGE**)

INDEX

Must follow Christ. 8:12-13
Must know God. 7:16-19
Cost of. (See **JESUS CHRIST**, Death;
Sacrifice)
To God. 3:16
Deliverance.
Answer to man's great hunger. 6:22-29
From condemnation. 3:18-21
From darkness; light of life. 8:12-13
From death. 5:24-25; 8:48-59; 8:51
From fear. 6:20-21
From perishing. 3:14-15; 3:16
From what. Trouble. Fivefold deliver-
ance. 14:1-3
God's eternal plan. 4:22
Man's eyes opened. 9:1-7
Provides for human need. 6:1-15
Stages of spiritual sight. 9:8-41
Described.
As bread of life. 6:30-36; 6:47-51
As living water. 4:10-14
As new birth. 3:1-15
Discussed. 1:12-13; 14:1-3
Duty. To remember **s.** & not forget expe-
rience. 5:13-14
Errors - Misconceptions.
Believe **s.** by heritage, godly parents,
forefathers. 8:33
Man rebels against being disregarded
as the source of **s.** 6:63-64
Spectacular, dramatic experience de-
livers. 14:8
Plan of. God's eternal **p.** 4:22
Rejection of. Is illogical. 12:37-41
Results.
Delivered from death & given life.
5:24-25
Delivered from perishing & given
eternal life. 3:14-15; 3:16
Discussed. 6:52-58
Eyes are opened. 9:1-7
Given assurance. 6:37-40
Given joy. 1:45
Will know the truth & be set free.
8:32
Source.
Bread of life. 6:30-36
Christ. 3:17
Christ alone is the Way to God.
14:4-7
Christ alone. World feels is narrow
view of **s.** 16:1-6
Christ, the Light of the world. 8:12-
13
Eagerness of Christ to save. 1:38-39
Death of Christ. 3:14-15
Gate to. Only gate into God's presence
is Christ Himself. Verses. List of.
10:7-8; 10:9
God.
Men rebel against. 6:65
God's love. 3:16-17
Initiative comes from Christ. 1:43-44
Mediator of. (See **JESUS CHRIST**,
Mediator)
Of spiritual satisfaction. 6:30-36
Salvation is from the Jews. 4:22
Stages of. 9:8-41
Universal. Jesus came to give life to all
men. 6:33
Who is saved.
The person who believes. 3:16
Who receives. 6:59-71

SAMARIA
Discussed. 4:4

SAMARITANS
Discussed. 4:4

SANCTIFICATION
Meaning. 17:17
Of believers. How & why. 17:17-19

SANHEDRIN
Discussed. 11:47

SARCASM
Example of. Brothers of Jesus against
Him. 7:3-5

SATAN
Defeated - Destroyed.
Cast out by the cross. 12:31-33;
12:31; 14:30-31
Condemned, judged by the cross.
16:11
Had nothing in Christ. 14:30-31
Power broken by Christ. 12:31
Described.
As father of man. 8:38
As father of unbelievers. 8:41-47
Discussed. 8:38; 8:44-45
Existence - Nature of.
Does not act against his **n.** 8:44
Names - Titles.
Evil One. 17:15
Prince of this world. 12:31; 14:30
The father of man. 8:44 cp. v.42-44
The father of sin. 8:44 cp. v.42-44
Power of. Broken, judged by the cross.
16:11 Work - Strategy of.
Rules world. 12:31
Threefold. 8:38
To possess evil men. 13:27-30

SATISFACTION (See **FULLNESS,
SPIRITUAL**)
Involves fifteen things. 6:55
Source. Jesus Christ. Verses. List of.
10:9
Verses. List of. 6:34-35; 6:55

SAVIOR
Meaning. Discussed. 4:42
Title.
Of Christ. 4:42
Of God. 4:42

SCOURGE - SCOURGING (See **FLOG**)
Discussed. 19:1

SCRIBES (See **TEACHERS OF THE
LAW**)

SCRIPTURES (See **WORD OF GOD**)
How to study and understand. Discussed.
12:16
Interpretation of. Understood only by the
Holy Spirit. 12:16
Prophecies of. (See **PROPHECY**)
Christ. **P.** of Christ & their fulfillment.
1:45
Work of - Effect. To bear witness to
Christ. 5:39

SEAL
Believers are to set their **s.** to Christ.
3:33
God set His **s.**, witness to Christ. 6:27
Meaning. 3:33

SECURITY
Discussed. 6:37-40; 10:9; 10:27-29
Source.
Being washed & cleansed perma-
nently. 13:6-11
God's keeping power. 17:11-12;
17:14-16
The prayer of Jesus. 17:9-19
Twofold. 14:30-31
Verses. List of. 6:39; 10:9

SEE - SEEING (See **SPIRITUAL SIGHT
- UNDERSTANDING**)

SEEK - SEEKING
Christ **s.** men. Goes to any limit. 1:43-44
Extends invitation; takes the initiative.
1:38-39
Men **s.** Christ.
Half-sincere. Traits of. 12:9
Reason men seek **C.** 12:9
Searches for utopia, earthly messiah.
6:26-29; 8:21-24
Some Greeks **s.** Four misunderstand-
ings. 12:20-36
Men **s.** God. Prepares heart for receiving
Christ. 4:45

SELF-CONFIDENCE (See **SELF-
SUFFICIENCY; SELF-
RIGHTEOUSNESS**)

SELF-EXISTENCE
Meaning. Of Christ. (See **JESUS
CHRIST**, Nature, Eternal) 1:1-2

SELF-RIGHTEOUSNESS
Attitude - Spirit of.
Man's critical, **s. r.** spirit. 8:3-6
Thinking one is good enough to be ac-
ceptable to God. 8:33
Verses. List of. 8:33

SELF-SATISFACTION
Attitude - Spirit of. Does not want situation to be disturbed. 11:38-40

SELF-SEEKING
Cause. Fearing loss of position, esteem,
livelihood, friends, etc. 11:47-48;
12:10-11
Discussed. 11:47-48

SELF-SUFFICIENCY
Results. Leads to unbelief. 5:44
Verses. List of. 8:33

SELFISHNESS
Results.
Causes man to reject & oppose Christ.
11:47-48
Causes unbelief. 11:47-48
Verses. List of. 11:47-48

SENSATIONALISM - SPECTACULAR
(See **SIGNS**)
Seeking.
Crowds sought Jesus for **s.** 12:9
Is requested. 14:8
Reasons. 14:8
Weakness of - Problem with. Appeals to
sensations of men. 2:23

SENSUALITY (See **LUST**)

INDEX

SENT
　Meaning. Commissioned from God.   1:6

SERPENT (See **SNAKE**)

SERVE - SERVICE (See **MINISTRY - MINISTERING**)
　Conditions - Prerequisite for s. Being washed & cleansed.   13:6-11
　How to s. Demonstration of royal s. Washing disciples' feet.   13:1-17
　Subject of. Labor for God.   4:31-42

SHAME (See **GUILT**)

SHEEP
　And their Shepherd.   10:1-6
　Discussed.   10:4-5
　Only one gate into sheep pen. Christ Himself.   10:7-8
　Traits - Characteristics of. Discussed.   10:4-5; 10:27-29

SHEEPFOLD (See **SHEEP PEN**)

SHEEP PEN
　Discussed.   10:1

SHEKINAH GLORY
　Discussed.   1:14

SHEPHERD
　False. Discussed.   10:1; 10:11-13
　False vs. true s.   10:1-6; 10:11-18
　Title of. Christ, The Good Shepherd. Four descriptions.   10:11-21
　Traits - Characteristics of. Discussed.   10:2-3; 10:14-16

SHOWS HIMSELF (See **MANIFESTATION; REVELATION**)
　Meaning.   14:21

SIGNS
　Desire for.
　　Dramatic.   14:8
　　Spectacular. Reasons.   12:9; 14:8
　Discussed. Four Greek words.   2:23
　Purpose. To prove **J.** is the Messiah, the Son of God.   2:23; 6:36; 10:37-38; 14:11; 20:30-31
　Verses. List of.   12:9
　Weakness - Problem with. Not necessary for faith.   4:46-54

SIN
　Acts - Behavior of.
　　Denial. Caused by two things.   13:36-38
　　Immorality. At a party-like atmosphere.   8:3-6
　And suffering. Does not cause suffering.   9:1-3
　Common to. Devil & man.   8:44-45
　Conviction of. Necessary for salvation.   4:16-18; 16:8-11
　Deliverance from. (See **DELIVERANCE; SALVATION**)
　　Conditions. Belief & continuing.   8:31-32
　　Man's s. and God's great forgiveness.   8:1-11
　　Must be faced & renounced.   4:16-18
　　Necessary for salvation.   4:16-18; 16:8-11
　　Power to proclaim forgiveness for.   20:23

Exposed.   2:24-25
　Known by God.   1:47-48; 2:24-25; 5:42; 13:19-20
　Verses. List of.   5:42; 13:19-20
Origin. Satan.   8:44
Results - Penalty.
　Death.   8:21-24
　Dissatisfaction.   4:15
　Emptiness.   4:15
　Enslaves.   8:33-40; 8:34-36
　Known by God. Knows all about s. of men.   4:16-18
　Proves depravity.   8:34-36; 8:41-47
Secret s. (See **SIN**, Exposed)
Work of. Darkness.   8:3-6

SLANDER (See **JESUS CHRIST**, Accusations Against)

SLEEP
　Symbol - Type. Of death. Meaning.   11:13

SNAKE
　Symbolized - Type of. Jesus' death. Lifted up by Moses.   3:14-15

SOCIAL CONCERNS
　Of mankind. Vs. spiritual c.   2:3-5

SOCIAL LIFE
　Duty. To fellowship & be sociable.   2:1-2

SON OF MAN (See **JESUS CHRIST**, Claims, Son of Man)
　Discussed.   1:51

SORCERY (See **SUPERSTITION**)
　Error of.
　　Men fear and respect supenatural forces other than God.   19:8-11
　　Men seek destiny in superstition.   5:2-4
　Verses. List of.   19:8-11

SORROW (See **GRIEF**)
　Danger of. Often becomes self-centered; wallowing around in s.   16:5-6

SOUL - SOULS
　And spirit. Meaning.   4:23; 4:23-24
　Fact. **S.** are ripe for harvest.   4:35

SOUL-WINNING (See **WITNESSING**)

SOVEREIGNTY (See **GOD; JESUS CHRIST**)

SOWING (See **WITNESSING**)
　Law of. Whatever s. shall reap.   12:39-41

SPECTACULAR (See **SENSATIONALISM**)

SPIRIT
　Essential - Duty. Must worship God in s.   4:23-24; 4:23
　God is s.   4:23-24
　Meaning.   4:23-24; 4:23
　Of man. Meaning.   4:23-24; 4:23

SPIRITUAL BLINDNESS
　Delivered by Christ.   9:1-7

SPIRITUAL CONCERN
　Vs. social concern.   2:3-5

SPIRITUAL FOOD (See **SPIRITUAL SATISFACTION**)
　Assured - Promised. To believer.   6:37
　Discussed.   6:1-71
　Results of partaking, eating. Discussed.   6:52-58
　　Does at least four things.   6:35
　　Gives life. Various ways.   6:33
　Source.
　　Believing on Christ.   6:34-35
　　How one secures spiritual **f.**   6:41-51
　Verses. List of.   6:34-35; 6:55
　Vs. physical food.   4:31-35

SPIRITUAL GROWTH - MATURITY
　Concern.
　　Must be spiritul not physical.   4:31-35
　　Must do will & work of God.   4:31-35
　Source - How one **g.**
　　Feasting on God day by day.   6:54
　　Of spiritual satisfaction.   6:30-36
　　Steps to satisfaction.   6:30-36

SPIRITUAL HUNGER (See **HUNGER SPIRITUAL; SPIRITUAL FOOD**)

SPIRITUAL REBIRTH (See **NEW BIRTH; NEW CREATION; NEW MAN**)

SPIRITUAL SATISFACTION
　Assured - Promised. To believer.   6:37
　Source.
　　Christ, the living water.   4:13; 7:37-39
　　How one secures spiritual s.   6:41-51
　　Steps to satisfaction.   6:30-36

SPIRITUAL SIGHT - SPIRITUAL UNDERSTANDING (See **UNDERSTANDING**)
　Focus is Christ & **C.** alone.   9:1-41
　Meaning.   20:20
　Promised. To those who abide in Christ.   1:38-39
　Stages of.   9:8-41

SPIRITUAL THIRST (See **HUNGER & THIRST; SPIRITUAL FOOD**)

SPIRITUAL WORLD - DIMENSION (See **NEW BIRTH**)
　Origin. Of Christ. Vs. man's origin.   8:42-43
　Reality - Truth of. Unknown to man. Must be revealed.   3:13; 3:31; 8:14; 8:15-16; 8:19; 8:23; 8:42-43; 11:7-10
　Vs. physical world, dimension.   8:14; 8:15-16; 8:23

STARS (See **SORCERY; SUPERSTITION**)
　Men seek destiny in.   5:2-4

STEWARDSHIP (See **GIVE - GIVING**)

STORM
　Calming of. Deliverance from fear.   6:16-21

STRESS
　Cause of sin.   4:16-18

STRIFE (See **DIVISION**)

STUDY (See **DEVOTION; MEDITATION; WORD OF GOD**)

INDEX

VISION
Need for. To see fields of souls ready for harvest. 4:35

VOICE
Of Christ. Known by believers. 20:14-16

WAITING UPON GOD
Duty - Essential. In great crises. 11:5

WALKING ON THE WATER
By Jesus. 6:19-21

WANT (See **NEEDS - NECESSITIES**)

WASHED - WASHING
Discussed. 13:6-11
Spiritual **w**. Essential before service. 13:6-11

WATER
Living **w**.
 Discussed. 4:1-14
 Is Christ or the Holy Spirit. Discussed. 4:1-14; 7:37-39
 Verses. List of. 4:13-14
Source. Of new birth. Meaning. 3:5
Symbol - Type.
 Of Christ. 4:1-14; 7:37-39
 Of Holy Spirit. 7:37-39
Turned into wine. 2:1-11
What **w**. does. 7:37

WAY, THE
Identified. As Jesus Christ. Verses. List of. 14:6

WEAKNESS (See **POWER**)

WEARY
Cause of. Deliverance from. 4:16-18
Verses. List of. 5:2-4

WEDDING
Ceremony.
 Honored by Christ. 2:1-2
 Jewish **w**. Discussed. 2:1-2

WHIP (See **FLOG**)
Of cords. Meaning. 2:15

WILL (See **FREE WILL**)
Of Christ.
 Distinct, separate from God. 6:38
 Supreme subjection to God. 10:11; 10:17-18; 12:27-30; 14:30-31; 15:9; 16:11
Of man. (See **PREDESTINATION**)
 Deliberately **w**. to reject Christ. Reason. 5:40-41; 5:42
 Vs. predestination. Discussed. 12:39-41

WITNESS - WITNESSING (See **JESUS CHRIST**, Witness to; **COMMISSION; MISSION**)
Challenge - Need.
 How silence fails. 12:42-43
 Impossible not to **w**. if truly saved. 15:26-27
 To see fields of souls ripe for harvest. 4:35
Commissioned - Commanded.
 Great **C**. 20:19-23
 To go as Jesus went. 20:21
 To **w**. to death & resurrection of Christ. 21:24

Dangers - Problems confronting **w**.
 How silence fails. 12:42-43
 Of a man to self. Is suspicious. 5:31
 Revelling in fellowship - not **w**. 20:17-18
Duty.
 To **w**. after conversion. 4:28-29
 To **w**. to home & family. 4:53-54
 To **w**. to neighbors & city. 4:28-29
 To **w**. to one's brother. 1:35-42
 To **w**. to one's close friend. 1:43-45
 To **w**. to the world. 17:17-19
How to go - Method. Proclaiming Jesus to be Messiah. 4:31-42
Purpose. Called, chosen to **w**. 15:16
Results.
 Strong belief seals the fact that God is true. 3:33
 To be greatly rewarded. 4:36-38
Who **w**. - Bears testimony. Five **w**. to the deity of Christ. 5:31-39

WOMAN CAUGHT IN ADULTERY
Man's dark sinfullness & God's great forgiveness. 8:1-11

WORD, CHRIST AS THE
Discussed. 1:1-5
Became flesh. The Incarnation. 1:14

WORD OF GOD
Described as.
 Spirit & life. 6:63
 The truth. 17:17
 The words of Christ. 14:24
 The words of God. 14:24
Duty.
 Must allow **w**. to abide within. 5:38
 Must depend upon Holy Spirit to understand. Verses. List of. 12:16
 Must hear to be saved. 10:4-5
Gives a knowledge of Christ. 20:14-16
Meaning. Is truth. 17:17-19
Nature of. Truth. 17:17
Rejected - Unbelief in.
 Leads to **u**. in Christ. 5:45-46; 5:47; 8:37
 Seek for symbolic, mystical meaning. Verses. List of. 18:19-24
 Verses. List of. 5:45-46; 8:37
Response to.
 Man makes no room in his heart for. 8:37
 Who hears. 8:47
What the **w**. does.
 Cleanses. 15:3
 Is assurance & security to believer. 6:37
 Verses. List of. 10:4-5
 Sanctifies. 17:17

WORKS
Duty.
 To do good works. 3:21
 To do greater **w**. than Jesus. 14:12
Need. To do the **w**. of God - believe on Christ. 6:29
Purpose. To lead men to believe. 2:9-11; 2:23
Results.
 Led some to believe. Were signs. 2:23-25
 Proves that one follows God. 3:21
Vs. faith.
 Discussed. 6:28-29
 Faith apart from **w**. 4:50

Obedience and love tied together. 14:23

WORLD
Blessed. By God. Ways **b**. 1:9; 1:10-11
Created - Creation. Blessed by God. How. 1:10-11
Deliverance from.
 By Holy Spirit. Convicts of sin. 16:8-11
 Victory over. 15:18-27
Described. As home of Christ. 1:10:11
History. (See **HISTORY**)
 God's plan for the ages. 4:22
Meaning. 15:18
Nature of.
 Corrupt. (See **CORRUPTION**) 12:31
 Good & evil. 12:21
 Ruled over by Satan. 12:31
Relationship to believers. Persecutes & hates. 15:18-27; 15:19-24; 17:14-16
Rejection. Of Christ. Difficult to understand. 1:10-11
State of - Problems with.
 Corruptible, passes away. 6:26-27
 Divisiveness. 17:11
 Focused on materialsim. 6:30-31
 Guilty before God. Without excuse. 15:25
 Ignorant of God. 15:19-24
 Love of. Men fear losing **w**. more than God. 19:13-15
 Misunderstanding. Origin & state. 12:31-33
Vs. Christ.
 Denial of **C**. 18:19-24
 Judged. By cross of Christ. Discussed. 12:31-33; 12:31
 Rejection of Christ. Difficult to understand. 1:10-11
 Was prepared by God for **C**. coming. 1:23
Vs. spiritual **w**. (See **SPIRITUAL WORLD**)

WORLDLY - WORLDLINESS (See **WORLD**)
Deliverance from.
 By Holy Spirit. Convicts of sin. 16:8-11
 Time for sin to be pointed out. 7:6-9
Problem of.
 Does not satisfy or feed the heart. 6:26-27
 Opposes Christ. Reason. A threat to desires. 7:32

WORSHIP
Discussed. 4:19-24
Duty.
 To seek God. Prepares heart for receiving Christ. 4:45
 To **w**. God after He has blessed. 5:13-14
 To **w**. in spirit & truth. 4:23-24
Evaluated by God. God knows man's heart. 1:46-49
How to **w**. Through Christ alone. 4:22
Nature. Is of the Jews. 4:22
Of Jesus Christ. To be a day of universal worship. 7:6-9

WRATH
Meaning. 3:36

396

PURPOSE STATEMENT

LEADERSHIP MINISTRIES WORLDWIDE

exists to equip ministers, teachers, and laymen in their
understanding, preaching, and teaching of God's Word
by publishing and distributing worldwide
The Preacher's Outline & Sermon Bible®
and related *Outline* Bible materials,
to reach & disciple men, women, boys, and girls for Jesus Christ.

•MISSION STATEMENT•

1. To make the Bible so understandable - its truth so clear and plain - that men and women everywhere, whether teacher or student, preacher or hearer, can grasp its Message and receive Jesus Christ as Savior; and...
2. To place the Bible in the hands of all who will preach and teach God's Holy Word, verse by verse, precept by precept, regardless of the individual's ability to purchase it.

The *Outline* Bible materials have been given to LMW for printing and especially distribution worldwide at/below cost, by those who remain anonymous. One fact, however, is as true today as it was in the time of Christ:

• The Gospel is free, but the cost of taking it is not •

LMW depends on the generous gifts of Believers with a heart for Him and a love and burden for the lost. They help pay for the printing, translating, and placing *Outline* Bible materials in the hands and hearts of those worldwide who will present God's message with clarity, authority and understanding beyond their own.

LMW was incorporated in the state of Tennessee in July 1992 and received IRS 501(c) 3 non-profit status in March 1994. LMW is an international, nondenominational mission organization. All proceeds from USA sales, along with donations from donor partners, go 100% into under-writing our translation and distribution projects of *Outline* Bible materials to preachers, church & lay leaders, and Bible students around the world.

9/98

© 1998. Leadership Ministries Worldwide

Box 21310 - Chattanooga, TN 37424 • (423) 855-2181 • FAX (423) 855-8616
• E-Mail - outlinebible@compuserve.com — www.outlinebible.org •

Equipping God's Servants Worldwide

1. **PAYMENT PLANS.** Convenient and affordable ways to get/use your FullSet with easy payments.

2. **NEW TESTAMENT.** In 14 volumes. Deluxe version 3-ring binders. Also: SoftBound Set, 3 volume set, and NIV edition. All on 1 CD-ROM disc.

3. **OLD TESTAMENT.** In process; 1 volume releases about every 6-8 months, in sequence.

4. **THE MINISTERS HANDBOOK.** Acclaimed as a "must-have" for every minister or Christian worker. Outlines more than 400 verses into topics like Power, Victory, Encouragement, Security, Restoration, etc. Discount for quantities.

5. **THE TEACHER'S OUTLINE & STUDY BIBLE™.** Verse-by-verse study & teaching; 45 minute lesson or session. Ideal for study, small groups, classes, even home schooling. Each book also offers a STUDENT JOURNAL for study members.

6. **OUTLINE BIBLE CD-ROM.** Includes all current volumes and books; Preacher, Teacher, and Minister Handbook. 1 disc. WORDsearch STEP format. Also 50+ Bible study tools unlockable on same disc. **FREE Downloads - www.outlinebible.org**

7. THE OUTLINE. Quarterly newsletter to all users and owners of *POSB*. Complimentary.

8. **LMW AGENT PLAN.** An exciting way any user sells *OUTLINE* materials & earns a second income.

9. **DISTRIBUTION.** Our ultimate mission is to provide *POSB* volumes & materials to preachers, pastors, national church leaders around the world. This is especially for those unable to purchase at U.S. price. USA sales gain goes 100% to provide volumes at affordable prices within the local economy.

10. **TRANSLATIONS.** Korean, Russian, & Spanish are shipping first volumes — Others in-process: Hindi, Tamil, Telugu, Chinese, French, German, Finnish.

11. **FUNDING PARTNERS.** To cover the cost of all the translations, plus print, publish, and distribute around the world is a multi million dollar project.

    Church-to-Church Partners send *Outline* Bible books to their missionaries, overseas church leaders, Bible Institues and seminaries...at special prices.

12. **REFERRALS.** Literally thousands (perhaps even you!) first heard of *POSB* from a friend. Now Referral Credit pays $16.00 for each new person who orders from a customer's Referral.

13. **CURRICULUM & COPYRIGHT.** Permission may be given to copy specific portions of *POSB* for special group situations. Write/FAX for details.

9/98

For Information about any of the above, kindly FAX, E-Mail, Call, or Write

Please PRAY 1 Minute/Day for LMW!

PO Box 21310, Chattanooga, TN 37424 • (423) 855-2181 • FAX (423) 855-8616
• E-Mail - outlinebible@compuserve.com — www.outlinebible.org •